Memory and Law

OXFORD SERIES IN NEUROSCIENCE, LAW, AND PHILOSOPHY

SERIES EDITORS

Lynn Nadel, Frederick Schauer, and Walter P. Sinnott-Armstrong

Conscious Will and Responsibility
Edited by Walter P. Sinnott-Armstrong and Lynn Nadel

Memory and Law
Edited by Lynn Nadel and Walter P. Sinnott-Armstrong

Memory and Law

EDITED BY
LYNN NADEL
WALTER P. SINNOTT-ARMSTRONG

OXFORD
UNIVERSITY PRESS

Oxford University Press, Inc., publishes works that further
Oxford University's objective of excellence
in research, scholarship, and education.

Oxford   New York
Auckland   Cape Town   Dar es Salaam   Hong Kong   Karachi
Kuala Lumpur   Madrid   Melbourne   Mexico City   Nairobi
New Delhi   Shanghai   Taipei   Toronto

With offices in
Argentina   Austria   Brazil   Chile   Czech Republic   France   Greece
Guatemala   Hungary   Italy   Japan   Poland   Portugal   Singapore
South Korea   Switzerland   Thailand   Turkey   Ukraine   Vietnam

Copyright © 2012 Oxford University Press

Published by Oxford University Press, Inc.
198 Madison Avenue, New York, New York 10016
www.oup.com

Oxford is a registered trademark of Oxford University Press

All rights reserved. No part of this publication may be reproduced,
stored in a retrieval system, or transmitted, in any form or by any means,
electronic, mechanical, photocopying, recording, or otherwise,
without the prior permission of Oxford University Press.

Library of Congress Cataloging-in-Publication Data
Memory and law/edited by Lynn Nadel and Walter P. Sinnott-Armstrong.
p. cm.
Includes bibliographical references and index.
ISBN 978-0-19-992075-4 (hardback: alk. paper)   1. Memory.   2. Science and law.
I. Nadel, Lynn.   II. Sinnott-Armstrong, Walter, 1955-
BF371.M44816 2012
153.1'202434—dc23
2011046812

9 8 7 6 5 4 3 2 1
Printed in USA
on acid-free paper

PREFACE

The law depends upon memory in diverse ways. Victims of crime, witnesses to crimes, and participants in various stages of the legal process—from judges and juries to prosecutors and defense attorneys as well as police, probation officers, and prison guards—all rely on their memories of what happened. The legal system has frequently assumed that memory is a reliable tool, but this assumption is questioned by the scientific study of memory function, both by cognitive scientists and by neural scientists. Recent research has taught us about the varieties of memory, the malleability of memory, and the ways in which memories can be altered by subsequent experiences. This fascinating work has numerous important implications for the law.

To explore these issues, we decided that a workshop and book focused on memory and law would be a timely addition to the literature. Our primary goal in organizing the workshop on which this book is based was to create a document that would be of use to those in the legal profession. We also hope that this book will prove useful to students, both of the law and of memory.

We are grateful to the sponsors of the workshop, which included the MacArthur Law and Neuroscience Project and several programs at the University of Arizona—the Colleges of Science and Social and Behavioral Sciences, the Philosophy Department, the Law & Society Program, the School of Public Administration and Policy, and the office of the Vice President for Research. Without the support of these varied entities we would not have been able to hold the workshop, which took place in Tucson in January 2010.

Catherine Carlin at Oxford University Press encouraged this project, and we are grateful to her, and to Joan Bossert and Jennifer Milton, at OUP, who have taken charge of seeing this book through to completion. We are pleased that this book will join others in our series of volumes in Neuroscience, Law, and Philosophy.

Lynn Nadel
Walter P. Sinnott-Armstrong

CONTENTS

Contributors ix

PART ONE   General Issues about Memory

Introduction: Memory in the Legal Context 3
    Lynn Nadel and Walter P. Sinnott-Armstrong

1. Emotion's Impact on Memory 7
    Elizabeth A. Phelps

PART TWO   Memory in Eyewitnesses

2. Inconsistencies between Law and the Limits of Human Cognition: The Case of Eyewitness Identification 29
    Deborah Davis and Elizabeth F. Loftus

3. Lineup Procedures in Eyewitness Identification 59
    Scott D. Gronlund, Charles A. Goodsell, and Shannon M. Andersen

4. The Curious Complexity between Confidence and Accuracy in Reports from Memory 84
    Henry L. Roediger III, John H. Wixted, and K. Andrew DeSoto

5. Evaluating Confidence in Our Memories: Results and Implications from Neuroimaging and Eye Movement Monitoring Studies of Metamemory 119
    Elizabeth F. Chua

6. Evidentiary Independence: How Evidence Collected Early in an Investigation Influences the Collection and Interpretation of Additional Evidence 142
    Lisa E. Hasel

PART THREE Memory in Jurors

7. Memory and Jury Deliberation: The Benefits and Costs of Collective Remembering — 161
   William Hirst, Alin Coman, and Charles B. Stone

8. Realizing the Potential of Instructions to Disregard — 185
   Linda J. Demaine

9. The Memory of Jurors: Enhancing Trial Performance — 213
   Anders Sandberg, Walter P. Sinnott-Armstrong, and Julian Savulescu

PART FOUR Neuroimaging Memories

10. Neuroimaging of True, False, and Imaginary Memories: Findings and Implications — 233
    Daniel L. Schacter, Jon Chamberlain, Brendan Gaesser, and Kathy D. Gerlach

11. Detection of Concealed Stored Memories with Psychophysiological and Neuroimaging Methods — 263
    J. Peter Rosenfeld, Gershon Ben-Shakhar, and Giorgio Ganis

PART FIVE Legislative Issues

12. Criminalizing Cognitive Enhancement at the Blackjack Table — 307
    Adam J. Kolber

13. Monetizing Memory Science: Neuroscience and the Future of PTSD Litigation — 325
    Francis X. Shen

PART SIX CODA

14. Ten Things the Law and Others Should Know about Human Memory — 359
    Martin A. Conway

Name Index — 373
Subject Index — 387

CONTRIBUTORS

Shannon M. Andersen
Department of Psychology
University of Oklahoma
Norman, OK, USA

Gershon Ben-Shakhar
Department of Psychology
The Hebrew University of Jerusalem
Jerusalem, Israel

Jon Chamberlain
Department of Psychology
Harvard University
Cambridge, MA, USA

Elizabeth F. Chua
Department of Psychology
Brooklyn College of the City University of New York
Brooklyn, NY, USA

Alin Coman
School of Information Sciences
University of Pittsburgh
Pittsburgh, PA, USA

Martin A. Conway
Department of Psychology
City University
London, U.K

Deborah Davis
Department of Psychology
University of Nevada
Reno, NV, USA

Linda J. Demaine
College of Law
Arizona State University
Tempe, AZ, USA

K. Andrew DeSoto
Department of Psychology
Washington University at St. Louis
St. Louis, MO, USA

Brendan Gaesser
Department of Psychology
Harvard University
Cambridge, MA, USA

Giorgio Ganis
School of Psychology
Plymouth University
Plymouth, UK
and
Martinos Center for Biomedical Imaging
Charlestown, MA, USA

Kathy D. Gerlach
Department of Psychology
Harvard University
Cambridge, MA, USA

Charles A. Goodsell
Department of Psychology
Canisius College
Buffalo, NY, USA

Scott D. Gronlund
Department of Psychology
University of Oklahoma
Norman, OK, USA

Lisa E. Hasel
Department of Sociology and
  Criminology & Law
University of Florida
Gainesville, FL, USA

William Hirst
Department of Psychology
New School for Social Research
New York, NY, USA

Adam J. Kolber
Department of Law
Brooklyn Law School
Brooklyn, NY, USA
and
New York University School of Law
New York, NY, USA

Elizabeth F. Loftus
Psychology & Social Behavior
Criminology, Law & Society
Cognitive Sciences
School of Law
University of California,
  Irvine, CA, USA

Lynn Nadel
Department of Psychology and
  Program in Cognitive Science
School of Mind, Brain, and Behavior
College of Science
University of Arizona
Tucson, AZ, USA

Elizabeth A. Phelps
Lab Director
Department of Psychology
New York University
New York, NY, USA

Henry L. Roediger III
Department of Psychology
Washington University at St. Louis
St. Louis, MO, USA

J. Peter Rosenfeld
Institute for Neuroscience
Department of Psychology
Northwestern University
Evanston, IL, USA

Anders Sandberg
Future of Humanity Institute
Department of Philosophy
University of Oxford
Oxford, UK

Julian Savulescu
Oxford Centre for Neuroethics
University of Oxford
Oxford, UK

Daniel L. Schacter
Department of Psychology
Harvard University
Cambridge, MA, USA

Francis X. Shen
Associate Professor,
University of Minnesota Law School

Walter P. Sinnott-Armstrong
Kenan Institute for Ethics
Department of Philosophy
Duke University
Durham, NC, USA

Charles B. Stone
Department of Psychology
Catholic University of Louvain
Louvain-la-Neuve, Belgium

John H. Wixted
Department of Psychology
University of California at San Diego
La Jolla, CA, USA

PART ONE

General Issues about Memory

Introduction

Memory in the Legal Context

LYNN NADEL AND WALTER P. SINNOTT-ARMSTRONG

The legal system depends upon memory function in a number of critical ways, including (1) the memories of victims, who are often called upon to relate crucial details of what happened to them; (2) the memories of individuals who witness crimes or other critical events and are asked to identify people (in some cases, potential perpetrators) who played critical roles in these events or to recall important details of the events and the settings in which they occurred; (3) the memories of investigators, lawyers, and judges engaged in the legal process, who must recall what has been said by whom before and during the trial, as well as the procedural rules, laws, and precedents that govern the courtroom; and (4) the memories of jurors, who must render a decision based to some extent on how well they remember what transpired in the courtroom and in the jury deliberation phase. How well memory works, how accurate it is, how it is affected by various aspects of the criminal justice system—all these are important issues. But there are others as well: Can we tell when someone is reporting an accurate memory? Can we distinguish a true memory from a false one? Can memories be selectively enhanced or erased? Are memories altered by emotion, by stress, by drugs?

The workshop that led to this book addressed many of these questions, and the chapters that follow spell out what the experts think about all of them and more. Our task in this Introduction (as it was in a brief talk at the outset of the workshop) is merely to set the stage for these deeper explorations by spelling out some basic facts about memory as understood from a psychological and neurobiological perspective. In order for the law to accomplish its goal of determining the truth, and rendering justice, its protagonists must start from a foundation of scientific knowledge about memory. One thing can be said at the outset: Our intuitive understandings of how memory works and doesn't work, which surely shaped our legal systems in the past, are far from the whole truth of the matter.

An obvious example concerns one of the most basic assumptions about memory—that it is a faithful record of what happened in the past. The idea that memory is indeed a reproduction of the past is deeply embedded in popular thinking and in the legal system. However, it is quite clear that this is not the case. Over 80 years ago, the British psychologist Frederick Bartlett (1932) insisted that memory was a "constructive" rather than a reproductive process, and recent research has confirmed his insight. But what does this notion of *reconstruction* actually mean? What seems most plausible, given current understanding of the cognitive and neurobiological mechanisms underlying memory, is that a given memory, say of an episode that occurred yesterday or last week (month, year), is composed of many parts, and that these parts are not stored together in one place, but rather distributed across multiple representational systems in the brain. Thus, the memory for a meal LN ate recently in Barcelona (it was a pretty memorable meal) consists in how the restaurant appeared visually, the sounds of the music in the background, the smells from the fish display, the conversations LN had, the various liquids consumed and their short-term consequences, the taste of the octopus, and so on. Each of these aspects of the memory is represented in its own part of the brain. Recalling this memory in all of its detailed glory requires an act of construction whereby the bits and pieces are pulled together again and knit into a coherent narrative. We know that the hippocampus, among other temporal lobe structures, is crucially involved in pulling all these details together and that this remains the case even for quite old memories.

A direct consequence of this view is that there is no necessary relation between the accuracy of a recalled memory and the amount of detail it contains. A rather sketchy memory can be completely accurate as far as it goes. And it is not the case that the more details one provides, the more accurate a memory is likely to be. We now know that the construction of a memory narrative can involve fleshing it out with details that were not actually part of the event but that make sense given similar experiences in the past.

This last point shows that another notion about memory—that memory for autobiographical episodes is kept strictly separate from what Tulving called *semantic* memory—must be wrong. Our semantic knowledge is used to enrich autobiographical recall, and we typically cannot distinguish the real from the imagined, given that the imagined is highly plausible.

THE MULTIPLEXITY OF MEMORY

Another fact that has not been incorporated into the public understanding of memory is the now-accepted notion that there are multiple kinds of memory. Autobiographical memory is just one type; others include semantic memory (noted above), emotional memory, and procedural memory. This multiplexity is not just of academic interest. The fact that there are multiple types of memory raises the likelihood, now confirmed, that these different kinds of memory depend to a large extent upon different underlying brain circuits. This, in turn, has a number of implications that are important in the legal context. The brain systems underlying the different forms of memory (1) have distinct developmental trajectories; (2) are differentially sensitive to such things as emotion, stress, drugs, and so on; and (3) are subject to differential learning and forgetting rates. Each of these factors introduces wrinkles into memory that are generally not reflected in legal understandings of memory.

THE INSTABILITY OF MEMORY

Yet another feature of memory worth noting here is the fact that memories, once created, are not fixed entities. The public conception, of course, is that memories are permanent imprints that might fade but are otherwise stable. We now know that this is not the case; apparently, stable memories can be altered when they are reactivated. That is, memory is fundamentally malleable. This obviously has major implications, some of which are discussed in various chapters in this volume. The most important implication is that when memories are replayed, as when either a victim or a witness is being questioned by investigators, or giving testimony in the courtroom, or even discussing events with others, this process of reactivating and replaying a memory inalterably changes it going forward.

The foregoing discussion shows clearly that memory is not quite what the legal system has assumed. The ways in which this is true, and the various implications that follow, are the subject matter of the various chapters in this book.

The book starts with two chapters exploring general aspects of memory, starting with a chapter introducing issues central to memory in the legal context (Nadel & Sinnott-Armstrong), and followed by a discussion of how memory is affected by emotion (Phelps). We then move to a set of chapters concerned with memory in eyewitnesses. The first considers how accurate eyewitness identification can be (Davis & Loftus). The next reviews the effect of various procedures on eyewitness identifications (Gronlund, Goodsell, & Andersen). The next two chapters discuss the relations between memory confidence and accuracy, one exploring this issue from a purely cognitive perspective

(Roediger, Wixted, & DeSoto), the other taking neuroscientific considerations into account (Chua). The final chapter in this section explores how evidence gathered early in a legal process can influence what happens next (Hasel).

We then move to three chapters concerned with memory in jurors, beginning with a chapter exploring what happens when jurors start to share their memories (Hirst, Coman, & Stone). This is followed by a chapter exploring the impact on jurors of various kinds of instructions to ignore evidence that was introduced improperly into the courtroom (Demaine). And finally, there is a chapter exploring the issue of memory enhancement in the context of the jury setting (Sandberg, Sinnott-Armstrong, & Savulescu).

Two chapters focused on brain mechanisms follow. The first explores how it might be possible, using neuroimaging methods, to distinguish between true, false, and imaginary memories (Schacter, Chamberlain, Gaesser, & Gerlach), while the second looks at the possibility of detecting concealed memories using brain measures (Rosenfeld, Ben-Shakhar, & Ganis).

The next two chapters consider legislative issues, beginning with a look at the blackjack table (Kolber) and following with a chapter considers how neuroscientific analyses of memory function might impact legal decisions about compensation for crimes (Shen).

Finally, the last chapter provides an overall summary of issues relating to memory and law from the perspective of another culture, albeit one quite closely related to ours (Conway). This survey of issues serves as a fitting overview of many of the issues raised throughout the volume. It is our hope that this collection of chapters from experts in the field will provide a useful tool for many involved in the legal system by detailing what science has told us to date about how memory works, and what implications this might have for the various steps between a crime and how it is dealt with by all those engaged in the legal process.

REFERENCES

Bartlett, F.C. (1932). *Remembering.* Cambridge University Press.

1

Emotion's Impact on Memory

ELIZABETH A. PHELPS

Life events that become relevant to the legal system often involve traumatic, shocking, and emotional situations. For instance, if one is the victim of a crime, the experience of the criminal act would likely elicit a strong emotional reaction. As a consequence, the later recounting of the legally relevant event may differ from the recollection of a more mundane life event. Although most people are aware that their memories of emotional events possess unique qualities, such as a heightened sense of vividness, scientific knowledge of how emotion impacts later memory is not routinely considered when assessing the quality of memory in legal contexts. As the larger psychological literature on human memory and the work presented in this volume illustrate, memories can be quite malleable for reasons that are likely adaptive in everyday life. In the legal context, however, the importance of accuracy of memory is heightened. For this reason, understanding how and when memories are likely to be accurate, and when they are not, is of critical importance.

In this chapter, I review psychological and neuroscience research illustrating how the emotional quality of events might alter later memory for those events. I start by reviewing the literature supporting one of the more surprising but robust findings of emotion's impact on memory—that our highly vivid and detailed memories for emotional events may not be as accurate as they seem. This is followed by a description of research exploring how emotion impacts the different stages of memory formation. Based on this research, I then speculate as to why emotion's impact on mnemonic processes results in stronger confidence in these memories in light of poor memory for some details. Finally, I highlight some potential future research directions and implications for the legal system.

EMOTION ENHANCES CONFIDENCE IN MEMORY ACCURACY MORE THAN ACCURACY

One of the most frequently cited qualities of memories of highly emotional events is their perceived vividness and detail, which is often assumed to reflect memory accuracy. The common statement "I would never forget something like that!" highlights the subjective judgment that a shocking and unusual event results in a uniquely strong memory. Building on this common belief, in 1977 Roger Brown and James Kulik investigated the qualities of memories for public and traumatic events that had occurred in the previous decade (e.g., the assassinations of John F. Kennedy, Martin Luther King, and Malcolm X), as well personal shocking events. They found that, unlike memories of more mundane events, these emotional, surprising, and consequential events resulted in detailed memories for the ongoing circumstances when participants learned of the events, as well as other idiosyncratic details that varied across participants (e.g., color of clothes, weather). They proposed that these memories possessed some of the qualities of a photograph in the minds of the participants and coined the term *flashbulb memory* to describe their unique characteristics. Importantly, they assumed that these detailed memories were accurate and suggested that they result from distinct neural mechanisms that enact something akin to a "print now" command when shocking and consequential events occur (Brown & Kulik, 1977).

Although this initial investigation of memories for shocking and consequential events correctly captured their subjective qualities, subsequent research has demonstrated that the details of flashbulb memories are not as accurate as they may seem. Since 1977, a number of studies have examined the consistency over time of memories of shocking and consequential public events, such as the explosion of the space shuttle *Challenger* (Neisser & Harsch, 1992a, 1992b), the Loma Prieta earthquake (Neisser et al., 1996), the death of Princess Diana (Kvavilashvili, Mirani, Schlagman, & Kornbrot, 2003), and the 9/11 terrorist attacks (Hirst et al., 2009), among others. By comparing the details of flashbulb memories recounted soon after the event and again a year later (e.g., Neisser & Harsch, 1992) and, in some cases, 3 years later (e.g., Schmolk, Buffalo, & Squire, 2000), this body of research has consistently found that memories for the details of these events change over time. Interestingly, in spite of these inconsistencies, participants routinely described their memories as detailed and vivid, and they are highly confident about their accuracy.

For example, in a study examining memory for the terrorists attacks of 9/11, participants from around the country, including New York City, were asked to recount the details of learning about the attacks in the last 2 weeks of September 2001, again in August 2002, and once again in August 2004

(Hirst et al., 2009). Replicating previous results, it was found that the some of the memories for details of the ongoing circumstances when learning about the attack (e.g., who informed you, what you were doing, what your reaction was, what you did afterward) changed from the initial recollection. Specifically, memories for these personal details differed about 37% of the time after 1 year and 43% of the time after 3 years. However, when participants were asked to rate how confident they were about the accuracy of these memory details on a scale of 1 (not at all) to 5 (extremely), their ratings were consistently above 4, with an average of 4.41 after 1 year and 4.25 after 3 three years. Interestingly, participants who were in New York City at the time of the attack showed slightly worse consistency in their memories for details of the ongoing circumstances than non–New York City participants, accompanied by slightly greater confidence in the accuracy of these memories. Although different studies of flashbulb memories report somewhat varying rates of inconsistency over time, one commonality is the dissociation between inconsistent recollections of these details and confidence in the accuracy of these recollections.

The substantial literature on flashbulb memories indicates that memories for some details of shocking and consequential events may not be as accurate as we think they are. However, this research does not indicate whether these memory details are more accurate than details of memories of mundane everyday events. To address this question, Jennifer Talarico and David Rubin (2003) asked participants to recount the circumstances of learning about the 9/11 terrorist attacks on September 12, 2001. Importantly, they also asked participants to recount another, everyday event (e.g., a sporting event or party) that occurred in the prior days. They then asked participants to return either 1 week, 6 weeks, or 32 weeks later, at which time they were asked to recount the events again and rate how much they believed in their memories' accuracy and the vividness of their recollections. When the consistency of memory details over time was compared, no difference was found in recollections of 9/11 compared to everyday events. Details for both types of memories were less consistent over time, indicating forgetting to an equal degree. However, ratings of belief in memory accuracy and vividness of the recollection remained consistently high over time for the 9/11 memories but declined over time for memories of everyday events. These results provide strong support for the conclusion that what makes flashbulb memories special is not the accuracy of details of the memory, but rather our subjective recollective experience and judgments of confidence in the accuracy of the memory.

The investigations of memories for shocking and traumatic public events have highlighted one consequence of emotion's impact on memory that has potentially important legal implications. However, in order to understand the mechanisms underlying the interaction of emotion and memory, we need to be able to investigate similar effects for stimuli presented in the laboratory. Of course, for ethical reasons, any laboratory study of emotion will result in a relatively weak emotion manipulation in comparison to shocking, consequential personal or public events. Nevertheless, findings from initial laboratory studies of emotion's impact on later memory are largely consistent with findings emerging from studies of flashbulb memories. For example, Ochsner (2000) presented participants with pictures of scenes depicting emotionally charged events or neutral events. Two weeks later, these participants were shown the previously presented scenes along with new scenes and were asked to indicate whether the previous scenes were presented before. If so, they were further asked to rate their subjective judgment of recollection as one of "remembering" the contextual details of initially encountering the scene or simply "knowing" that the picture was familiar. Although the accuracy of scene recognition was relatively good for all the scenes, it was slightly higher for the emotional ones, in particular the negative scenes. The primary effect of emotion on later memory was reflected in judgments of remembering. Participants were more likely to indicate that the retrieval of emotional scenes resulted in a rich recollective experience with contextual details in comparison to neutral scenes.

This enhanced subjective sense of remembering for emotional scenes presented in the laboratory mirrors the enhanced vividness and confidence observed for flashbulb memories. However, the measure of memory accuracy differs. In Ochsner's (2000) laboratory study, participants simply indicated whether they had any memory of the scene. In contrast, studies of flashbulb memories examine details of the ongoing circumstances when the event occurred instead of a simple indication of the event's occurrence. Previous studies examining memories for details of emotional and neutral events have found that emotion can enhance or impair detail memory, depending on the type of detail. Specifically, it has been suggested that details that are more central (Christianson & Loftus, 1991) or intrinsic (Mather, 2007) to the emotional components of the event, or represent the gist of the event (Adolphs, Tranel, & Buchanan, 2005), may be remembered better in comparison to similar details of neutral events, while details considered more peripheral are remembered worse (e.g., Heuer & Reisberg, 1992).

In order to examine the relation between subjective judgments of memory confidence and vividness with accuracy for memory details in a laboratory paradigm, Rimmele, Davachi, Petrov, Dougal, and Phelps (2011) presented emotional and neutral scenes and manipulated the inclusion of specific details. At later test, participants were shown the original scenes again, but this time without the manipulated detail, along with new scenes, and were asked to indicate whether each scene was presented before. If so, they were further asked to indicate their confidence in the accuracy of this judgment and whether they remembered the contextual details of their initial encounter with the scene or simply knew that it seemed familiar. Finally, participants were asked to indicate the detail that was originally presented with the scenes, which was either the color of a frame around the scene or an object embedded in the corner of the scene. Consistent with previous studies, Rimmele et al. (2011) found that relative to neutral scenes, participants were more likely to accurately indicate that the emotional scenes had been previously presented, were more confident in their memories of emotional scenes, and had a more vivid recollective experience as indicated by more remember judgments. However, their memories of the specific details were actually somewhat worse for the emotional scenes relative to the neutral scenes. Furthermore, when comparing the accuracy of detail memory for both emotional and neutral scenes that were recollected with equally high levels of confidence and vividness, the detail memory of the emotional scenes was significantly less accurate. Using this simple laboratory paradigm, Rimmele et al. observed the same dissociation reported in studies of flashbulb memories—that is, increased confidence in memory accuracy together with relatively poor memory for some details.

HOW EMOTION ALTERS MEMORY

In order to understand precisely how emotion impacts later memory for an event, it is useful to explore emotion's influence on the different stages of memory formation. There are three distinct stages of memory that can be altered by the emotional significance of an event. The first stage, *encoding*, entails the processing that occurs when an event is first encountered. If emotion alters how we perceive, attend to, or initially reflect on an event, this will impact the ability to remember the event later. The second stage of memory is *storage*. Although there is no conscious awareness of this stage, extensive neurobiological research has shown that memory storage is not an all-or-none process (e.g., see McGaugh, 2000). Instead, it takes time to complete the synaptic changes that form the neural signature of the memory. This process by which memories become increasingly stable over time is called *consolidation*. It has been proposed that emotion can influence this time-dependent consolidation process. The final stage of memory is *retrieval*, in which one attempts to mentally identify a past event. Of course, retrieval is the result of the previous stages, but it also has unique qualities. Retrieval can occur either through conscious recollection (the focus of this chapter) or it can be demonstrated through actions or other bodily responses. As mentioned above, conscious or explicit retrieval of a past event is not an all-or-none process, but rather varies in quality and is accompanied by a host of subjective judgments about the memory.

One of the primary ways emotion alters memory encoding is through influencing attention and perception, thus changing what information comes into memory. Emotion has two distinct but related effects on attention and perception. Emotion enhances attention and perception for some central aspects of the emotional event, and it impairs attention to other, nonemotional components of the event. To understand precisely how this occurs, it is useful to investigate both the psychological and neural mechanisms underlying these effects.

The enhancement of attention by emotion has been demonstrated across a range of paradigms. For example, in a classic task examining the temporal limitations of attention, called the *attentional blink task*, participants are shown a series of stimuli, such as words, presented in rapid succession, often 1 every 100 milliseconds or so (e.g., Raymond, Shapiro, & Arnell, 1992). If, after the presentation of approximately 15 stimuli, participants are asked to report the words presented, they are usually unable to do so and indicate that the words seemed to fly by. However, if two of the words are distinguished by a perceptual feature, such as being printed in a different color ink, and participants are asked to report these two words, they are usually successful. The different perceptual feature allows the participant to focus their attention on the highlighted words and select them for further processing while ignoring the irrelevant words. However, participants' success at this task is diminished if the two words are close together in the visual stream. If one of the target words comes soon after the other target word, the participants often miss the second word. It appears that attending to and encoding the first target word creates a mental refractory period during which it is difficult to notice and encode the second target word. In other words, the first target word causes attention to "blink" due to a temporal limitation of our attentional capacity (Raymond et al., 1992). Studies investigating the influence of emotion on attention have used this task and shown that when the second target word is emotional and arousing, it is more likely to be identified during the blink period than a neutral word (Anderson, 2005). In other words, when attention is limited, emotional stimuli are more likely to be perceived.

Investigations of the brain systems mediating emotion's facilitation of attention and perception highlight a role for the amygdala, a brain region known to be important across a range of emotion tasks as well as in emotion's impact on attention and memory (see Figure 1.1). Patients with damage to the amygdala fail to demonstrate the normal facilitation of the attentional blink for emotional stimuli (Anderson & Phelps, 2001). The amygdala is a small almond-shaped structure in the medial temporal lobe that signals the presence of emotional and relevant stimuli in the environment and has widespread connections with other brain regions that mediate a range of cognitive functions (see Phelps, 2006, for

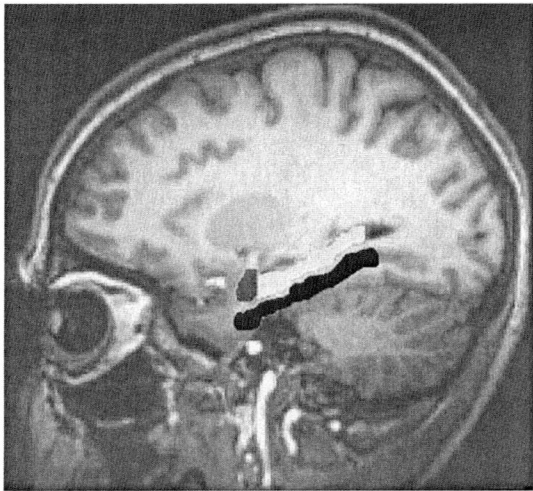

Figure 1.1 Medial temporal lobe structures involved in the interaction of emotion and memory: amygdala (gray), hippocampus (white), parahippocampus (black).

a review). It is proposed that the amygdala's connectivity with the visual cortex may underlie the enhanced perception for emotional stimuli. Specifically, it is thought that the amygdala detects the presence of an emotional event early in stimulus processing and then influences the visual cortex to enhance further perceptual processing (Vuilleumier, Richardson, Armony, Driver, & Dolan, 2004). Consistent with this interpretation, it has been demonstrated that the detection of even very simple perceptual features known to rely on early visual cortical regions, such as subtle changes in contrast, is enhanced for stimuli cued by emotion (Phelps, Ling, & Carrasco, 2006). In other words, emotion might actually improve how well one can see some features of a stimulus, diminishing the requirement for attentional resources in order to identify it.

Although emotion may enhance attention and perception for some central aspects of an event, it also impairs the ability to attend to other details. This impairment in attention with emotion is hypothesized to be due to a *narrowing of attention* around the central emotional details of an event, allowing enhanced processing of these details but diminishing the processing of more peripheral, nonemotional details (Easterbrook, 1959). For example, as described earlier, in the attentional blink task when the first target word is neutral and the second target word is emotional and arousing, the second word is more likely to be detected than a neutral word in the same position. However, if the order is reversed, a different pattern emerges. If the first target word is emotional and arousing and the second target word is neutral, the second target word is less likely to be identified than if it was preceded by a neutral word (Most, Chun,

Widders, & Zald, 2005). In other words, attending to and encoding an emotional and arousing word impairs the ability to detect a second, neutral target word. In this case, the emotional stimulus captures attention, making it hard to disengage and more difficult to process other, nonemotional stimuli. Similar effects have been observed in studies examining the ability to respond to different details presented simultaneously in visual space (e.g., Fox, Russo, Bowles, & Dutton, 2001). For example, when viewing a scene, heightened processing of the details of the scene that are the most emotionally charged may result in impaired processing of other, nonemotional details. In everyday life, this effect can be seen in drivers who slow down to view an accident on the other side of the road. The shocking and emotional qualities of the accident capture their attention, making it hard to look away. The result is less attentional focus on driving and slowed traffic. Interestingly, investigations of the neural mechanisms mediating the capture of attention by emotion have suggested that brain regions that enable us to shift our attention among regions and details in visual space (i.e., the interparietal cortex) are less active in the presence of emotional stimuli (Portois & Vuilleumier, 2006), making it harder to disengage from emotional events in order to focus on other stimuli or details.

The impact of emotion on attention and perception helps ensure that the key aspects of emotional events are preferentially processed quickly and thoroughly, perhaps to facilitate fast action if needed (Davis & Whalen, 2001). The result is that different information comes into memory for emotional and neutral events. Relative to neutral events, a few details of emotional events will be processed and perceived better, while at the same time, the processing of other details will suffer. After this first stage is complete, whatever information of the original event was encoded begins the storage phase or consolidation. Through this storage process, some of the encoded information is retained and becomes part of long-term memory, and other information is not fully stored and is forgotten. Both psychological and neuroscience research have demonstrated that emotion influences memory storage so that events that elicit emotional reactions, which are more likely to be important and consequential, are also more likely to be retained.

In an early demonstration of this effect, Lewis Kleinsmith and Stephen Kaplan (1963) paired digits with words that varied in how much they elicited a physiological arousal response, an indication of an emotional reaction. They then waited 2 minutes, 20 minutes, 45 minutes, 1 day, or 1 week, at which time they presented the words again and asked participants to recall the digit paired with each word. Although at the early time intervals (2 and 20 minutes) the digits paired with low-arousal words were recalled slightly more often, at the longer intervals the digits paired with high-arousal words were recalled significantly more frequently. Memory of the digits paired with low-arousal words declined significantly over time, consistent with gradual forgetting, whereas there was enhanced retention for digits paired with high-arousal words.

Research in rats and humans has shown that the reduced forgetting observed for emotional events is due to emotion's modulation of memory consolidation. The ability to consciously recollect past events critically depends on the hippocampus, a region of the brain in the medial temporal that sits adjacent to the amygdala (see Figure 1.1). Physiological arousal produces neurohormonal changes that signal the amygdala to enhance consolidation mechanisms in the hippocampus leading to less forgetting over time (see McGaugh, 2000, for a review). If the amygdala is damaged, memories can still be stored, but there is no retention benefit for emotional stimuli (e.g., Labar & Phelps, 1998), indicating that the amygdala's primary role is to modulate hippocampal consolidation with arousal. By manipulating arousal or its neurohormonal effects immediately after memory encoding, James McGaugh and colleagues have been able to demonstrate conclusively that the enhanced retention for arousing events results from altering memory consolidation, as opposed to influencing aspects of memory encoding. In fact, McGaugh (2000) speculates that one reason to have a slow memory storage process like consolidation is to allow the consequences of an event, such as the emotional reaction that follows an event, an opportunity to influence later memory. In this way, emotional events that may be more likely to provide important insights for future survival are more likely to be retained.

The final stage of memory is the retrieval of past events, which is obviously linked to the previous two stages. As outlined in the previous section of this chapter, the quality of memory retrieval can vary greatly, from having a vague sense that something seems familiar to having the experience of almost reliving the original event in all of its depth and detail. Emotional events may be more likely to result in a rich recollective experience, but more mundane events can also have these qualities. One of the functions of having varying degrees of recollective experience at retrieval is to provide a subjective indication of whether our memories are reliable or not. Given that emotion may selectively increase the subjective sense of remembering, without necessarily enhancing memory accuracy for all the details of an event, understanding how this occurs might provide important insights when attempting to extrapolate this basic research to the use of memory in a legal context.

One clue can be derived from examining the brain systems mediating subjective judgments of recollection for emotional and neutral events. In order to investigate this, Sharot, Delgado, and Phelps (2004) presented participants with emotional and neutral scenes. An hour later, participants were placed in a magnetic resonance imaging (MRI) scanner, were shown the original scenes along with new scenes, and were asked to indicate if each scene was presented earlier. If they indicated that the scene was old, they were further asked if they remembered the details of the encoding context or simply knew that the scene was familiar. Replicating Ochsner's (2000) behavioral results, participants' recognition was somewhat higher for the emotional negative scenes than for the neutral scenes, but for those scenes correctly identified as old, participants were much more likely to judge the emotional scenes as remembered as opposed to simply known. Sharot, Delgado and Phelps (2004) then compared brain activity patterns separately for emotional and neutral scenes judged as retrieved with a rich recollective experience or not. For neutral scenes, the posterior parahippocampus region of the brain showed greater activity for scenes judged to be remembered versus simply familiar or known (see also Eldridge, Knowlton, Furmanski, Bookheimer, & Engel, 2000). The posterior parahippocampus sits beneath the hippocampus in the medial temporal lobe and is part of the brain circuitry involved in memory formation (see Figure 1.1). Specifically, the posterior parahippocampus is known to play a role in the memory for contextual details of a visual scene (Kohler, Crane, & Milner, 2002). When participants were instructed on this memory task, they were told to indicate that they remembered a scene if its retrieval was accompanied by contextual details of the encoding context. Given these instructions, it is perhaps not surprising that the posterior parahippocampus, which codes contextual details, shows greater activation when the retrieval of a memory includes these details. However, what is surprising is that this same brain region does not differentiate emotional scenes that are judged to be richly recollected versus simply familiar. When the same comparison between scenes rated as remembered versus known was conducted for emotional scenes, the region that emerged was the amygdala, which showed greater activation for remembered emotional scenes. These results suggest that even though the participants were making the same subjective mnemonic judgment for the emotional and neutral scenes, different brain systems were mediating this judgment.

Examining what is known about the role of the amygdala in the different stages of memory formation may provide some insight into what types of information lead to the subjective judgment of a rich recollective experience for emotional events. As outlined above, at encoding the amygdala serves to heighten perception and attention for emotionally salient details, but this comes at the cost of poor attention and diminished processing of other contextual details. At this first stage of memory, the amygdala is tuning what comes in so that a few important details are focused on. However, even though fewer details may be richly encoded for emotional scenes, during the storage process the amygdala plays a role in ensuring that these details are adequately consolidated and are not forgotten over time. The result is that emotion may lead to very strong memories for a few important details but relatively poor memories for other, less critical details. At memory retrieval, it is possible that the rich recollective experience that participants report for emotional scenes is the result of the unusually strong memories for a few critical details. This strength of memory for these few details may result in an unusually strong sense of vividness at recollection, resulting in the mistaken assumption that memories for many additional details are also accurate.

Based on laboratory studies examining the behavioral and neural mechanisms of emotion's influence on memory, we can begin to understand how emotion might impact memory for life events that have legal relevance. However, it is important to demonstrate that more shocking and consequential events retrieved after longer retention intervals share these same properties. To examine this issue, Sharot, Martorella, Delgado, and Phelps (2007) conducted a follow-up study investigating involvement of these brain regions when participants who were in New York City during the terrorist attacks of 9/11 retrieved autobiographical memories from that day. In order to have a baseline with which to compare brain activity linked to the retrieval of memories of 9/11, participants were also asked to retrieve autobiographical memories from other events occurring in the summer of 2001. This study was conducted 3 years after the terrorist attacks, so the other autobiographical events retrieved were memorable and important life events (e.g., a birthday party, moving to New York City), but in general, they were not shocking or traumatic. After retrieving the autobiographical memories from 9/11 and the summer of 2001, participants were asked to rate the subjective qualities of each memory, including its vividness, the sense of reliving the experience when remembering, and confidence in accuracy. Participants who were closer to the attack—and were more likely to have seen it, heard it, and smelled it—rated the recollective experience of retrieving the 9/11 memories as more vivid and detailed than memories for the other life events. These participants showed increased amygdala activity accompanied by less activation of the parahippocampus when retrieving their autobiographical 9/11 memories. This pattern of brain activation mirrors that observed in the laboratory study examining the recollective experience of emotional and neutral scenes (Sharot et al., 2004). These findings provide further support for the assumption that laboratory studies of emotion and memory are tapping into psychological mechanisms that are relevant in understanding memory for real-life shocking and traumatic events, including those with legal implications.

WHY EMOTION ENHANCES CONFIDENCE IN MEMORY MORE THAN ACCURACY

On the surface, it may seem puzzling that our memories for highly emotional events are recollected with a strong sense of vividness and confidence when the accuracy of some memory details is poor. In order to understand why this might occur, it is helpful to consider the functional role that memory vividness and confidence might have served throughout evolution and in everyday life. The general function of memory is to be able to benefit from our past experience to enable more adaptive choices and behaviors in the future. By knowing which situations were beneficial or harmful in the past, we can use this information to project different potential futures and select actions that will be more adaptive moving forward (Schacter, Addis, & Buckner, 2008). In this framework, memory confidence and vividness can be used to gauge how reliably a memory reflects the details of a past event, presumably to aid in deciding whether one should act on the basis of that memory, or alternatively, spend additional time and effort gathering more information before choosing how to proceed.

Consistent with this proposed functional role for subjective judgments of remembering, memory vividness has been found to be a somewhat reliable indicator of memory accuracy for details of neutral events (see Roediger, Wixted, & DeSoto, this volume, for a more detailed discussion of this topic). For example, a study by Perfect, Mayes, Downes, and Van Eijk (1996) examined the relationship between judgments of remembering or knowing previously presented neutral words and accuracy in recollecting a range of contextual encoding details. It was found that regardless of the type of detail assessed, remember judgments were linked to more accurate detail recollection. Similar results were observed when participants were asked to rate their confidence in memory accuracy, with high confidence judgments yielding more accurate memory detail. These findings suggest that for neutral events, these subjective mnemonic judgments may help predict memory accuracy across a wide range of contextual details.

What is surprising about the subjective sense of remembering for emotional events is that the judgments of memory vividness and confidence are magnified, whereas accuracy for many memory details is not. In the study by Rimmele et al. (2011) described earlier, in which memory details were manipulated with the presentation of emotional and neutral scenes, accurate memory for details was greater if scenes were paired with scenes judged to be remembered compared to those that were known, replicating the finding of Perfect et al. (1996). This effect was observed for both emotional and neutral scenes. However, even though participants were more likely to remember emotional scenes and judge memory for these scenes with high confidence relative to neutral scenes, they were less likely to accurately identify the peripheral details paired with remembered emotional scenes. It seems as if the enhancement in memory detail accuracy observed for neutral events that are retrieved with a relatively rich recollective experience does not scale up for the emotional events that are often remembered with a much richer recollective experience.

However, as discussed in the previous section, it is not the case that accuracy for all memory details is poor for emotional events. Emotion's impact on attention and perception enables preferential processing of a few details at the cost of others. Studies examining the accuracy of detail memory for emotional scenes routinely find impaired memory for more peripheral details and better memory for more central, intrinsic, or gist details (e.g., Christianson & Loftus; Mather, 2007) compared to neutral events, an effect that depends on the amygdala (Adolphs et al., 2005). For instance, memory accuracy for the contextual details of spatial location and temporal order is often enhanced for emotional stimuli (D'Argembeau & Van der Linden, 2004, 2005; Mather & Nesmith, 2008; Schmidt, Patnaik, & Kensinger, 2011). Space and time are two contextual details that have a special place in our conscious memories in that they help determine episodes in memory and provide a contextual framework in which to organize life events (Ezzyat & Davachi, 2011; Tulving & Markoswitch, 1998). In addition, research on the hippocampus, the brain region most critical for this type of memory, has shown that responses of neurons in this region are specifically tuned to spatial (Nadel, 2008) and temporal order (Macdonald, Lepage, Eden, & Eichenbaum, 2011) information.

In order to examine whether memory for spatial and temporal details is more likely to be accurately linked to the rich recollective experience of emotional events, Rimmele, Davachi, and Phelps (in press) conducted a follow-up study that specifically manipulated three details at scene encoding: spatial location (i.e., the quadrant of the screen in which the scene was presented), temporal order (i.e., which list in a sequence of three the scene was part of), and the color of a set of dots located in the conceptual center of the scene. As in the previous study (Rimmele et al., 2011), at memory test participants were more likely to rate emotional scenes as remembered and retrieved with high confidence relative to neutral scenes. They were also more likely to accurately identify the spatial location and temporal order of the emotional scenes relative to neutral scenes, although the benefit in accuracy for these details was similar if the emotional and neutral scenes were both judged as remembered with high confidence. In contrast, detail accuracy for the color of the dots placed at the conceptual center of the scene was worse for remembered emotional scenes relative to neutral scenes, suggesting that spatially close but conceptually unimportant details are not preferentially encoded for emotional events. Following up on this finding, Rimmele et al. (in press) further investigated whether this relatively enhanced memory for spatial location observed for emotional scenes in the laboratory extends to autobiographical memory for a real-life shocking and consequential event. Using the same survey data for memory of the 9/11 terrorist attacks reported by Hirst et al. (2009) and described earlier, it was found that participants' reported location when learning of the attack was much more likely to be consistent over time than other personal details—with an 11% inconsistency rate for location versus 37% for other details after 1 year and 17% versus 43% after 3 years.

The finding that reports of location at the time of learning about the 9/11 attacks varied for only 11% of participants after 1 year supports the suggestion that the enhanced subjective sense of remembering observed with shocking and traumatic events is tied to enhanced memory accuracy for select details. However, this number still seems high given that all the participants report being extremely confident in these recollections. In fact, most people report being so confident in their vivid memories for these types of shocking and consequential events that it is hard to convince them that they could be wrong about any details, even after being made aware of the extensive scientific literature demonstrating that there are likely inaccuracies. Given the relative importance of spatial and temporal information in autobiographical memory, the boost in accuracy for these details with emotion is understandable because emotion is a cue to the potential relevance of an event for future survival. However, the details that are most likely to be selectively encoded and consolidated with emotion may be critical idiosyncratic details of the event itself.

The question remains, however, of why a very strong memory for a few select critical details would result in a rich and vivid recollective experience that leads one to mistakenly believe in the accuracy of many details. If the adaptive functional role of memory is to guide future actions based on past experience, then confidence in memory should help facilitate faster actions. When there is doubt about the accuracy of a memory, the prudent choice would be to search for additional confirming information before deciding how to act. However, if a memory is particularly vivid and strong, then acting on the basis of that memory is facilitated. Life events that elicit strong emotional responses are more likely to be those that provide important information for future survival. For dangerous situations, encountering a similar event in the future might require fast action to avoid harm. Having strong and vivid memories prevents the need for additional or confirming information before choosing how to act and facilitates fast action. Although memories for many peripheral details may not be correct for highly emotional events, emotion's tuning of memory encoding and consolidation makes it likely that memories of the critical details are enhanced. It is these conceptually important details that will likely provide the most useful information when determining how to act in the future.

FUTURE DIRECTIONS AND POTENTIAL IMPLICATIONS FOR THE LEGAL SYSTEM

The adaptations that make memory useful in everyday life are not necessarily the most advantageous for the legal system. If the purpose of memory is to incorporate lessons learned from past experience to promote adaptive responding in the future, then the flexible and dynamic nature of memory makes sense (Schacter, 2001). However, the goals of the legal system are different, and this same flexibility, and the imperfections that may result, can be problematic. For emotional events in particular, the dissociation between memory vividness and accuracy for some details is surprising, because these events tend to be more vivid in our minds and we generally depend on this subjective sense of remembering to gauge the reliability of our own memories and the memories of others. However, it is important to acknowledge that even though a rich recollection may not be linked to memory accuracy for some details, this does not mean that our memories for highly emotional events are wholly inaccurate. The challenge for legal scholars is to determine when memory may be more or less reliable given what we know about the psychological mechanisms of memory.

For any event, we cannot know the veracity of someone else's memory unless we have additional corroborating information. The best one can hope for when memory is important in legal settings is a consideration of the science of memory in order to make the best possible assessment of its reliability. In this chapter, I have outlined our current understanding of emotion's impact on memory. Based on this research, legal actors may choose to judge some memory details as more reliable than others when a witness is recounting the memory of an emotional event such as a crime. For instance, aside from the occurrence of the crime, location and temporal order may be details that are generally more accurate for an emotional event retrieved with a rich recollective experience, whereas more peripheral details, such as objects in the room at the time, may not be as accurately recalled. In addition, for every highly emotional event there are likely idiosyncratic, conceptually important details for which memory may be quite accurate. Of course, what is conceptually important to one person may not be conceptually important to another. For example, after the fact, a legal professional may be interested in a witness' memory for facial features of a criminal suspect, whereas the most conceptually important detail for the witness during the crime may be the presence of a weapon (Loftus, Loftus, & Messo, 1987). The challenge is determining which details accompanying a rich recollective experience are more likely to be accurate, especially if the person recollecting the event believes many details to be accurate. Although scientists have determined that the intrinsic (Mather, 2007) or central (Burke, Heuer, & Reisberg, 1992; Christianson & Loftus, 1991) details of an emotional event are those that are more likely to be accurately retained, research resulting in a more fine-grained and predictive description of this effect would be useful (e.g., Mather & Sutherland, 2009).

In addition to refining and elaborating our current understanding of the relation between the subjective sense of remembering and memory accuracy, there are many additional factors linked to the relation between emotion and memory that are poorly understood. Some of these are related to the nature of the emotional response. Although in this chapter I have referred to emotion as if it is a unitary concept, it clearly is not. Emotion comprises a number of components (Scherer, 2005), each of which may have unique effects on memory. For example, the vast majority of laboratory studies examining emotion's impact on memory have used stimuli with a negative valence that aim to elicit a physiological arousal response. Studies of flashbulb memories also have focused primarily on negative and traumatic public events. Although most researchers agree that arousal and intensity, which are components of both positive and negative events, play a role in emotion's impact on attention and consolidation, there is debate about whether stimuli with a positive valence exhibit different attentional effects than those with negative valence (Kensinger, 2009; Mather & Sutherland, 2009). As described earlier, any effect of emotion on attention should influence memory encoding for details. In addition, negative and shocking events are often more likely to elicit a strong arousal response, which makes it difficult to disentangle the effects of stimulus arousal and valence on later memory. Although there have been some initial investigations exploring the impact of event valence on memory (e.g., Kensinger, 2009; Ochsner, 2000), there is not yet a detailed understanding of its impact on the different stages of memory formation.

Another component of emotion that is known to impact memory, but is difficult to investigate in humans, is the level of arousal or stress. As outlined above, physiological arousal at encoding may lead to enhanced memory performance in both rats and humans. However, when arousal is extreme, and especially when there is a prolonged arousal or stress response, memory can be impaired. The relation between memory and stress is described as an inverted U-shaped curve (Zoladz & Diamond, 2009). Whereas some stress or arousal can improve memory, extreme or prolonged stress can impair memory. In addition, stress at the time of retrieval may also impact memory performance (Tollenaar, Elzinga, Spinhoven, & Everaerd, 2009). Of course, it is ethically impossible to purposefully create extreme or prolonged stress in human research participants, but research with nonhuman animals has shown that lasting stress can negatively impact the hippocampus, resulting in overall diminished memory performance (McEwen, 1999). How these findings translate into memory accuracy in individuals who undergo extreme emotional events is unclear, but the event's intensity and duration, as well as its lasting psychological consequences, are likely important components of later memory performance. For instance, some forms of psychopathology, such as post-traumatic stress disorder (PTSD) and depression, are known to have negative effects on general memory performance, which is proposed to be one result of the prolonged stress associated with these disorders (Bremner, 1999; Bremner et al., 2000).

Finally, critical in determining the impact of emotion on memory is to consider factors related to the individual. For instance, individuals who are generally more anxious are more likely to show strong attentional capture effects for emotional stimuli (e.g., Fox, Russo, & Georgiou, 2005), thus altering encoding and later memory. In addition, an underappreciated aspect of emotion is the malleability of emotional reactions based on how one approaches or appraises a situation. The ability to change our emotional response is referred to as *emotional regulation*, and one technique is to reappraise the interpretation or meaning of an event (see Gross, 2002, for a review). Emotion regulation techniques can have a profound effect on the nature of the emotional response, which should, in turn, impact later memory. For example, police officers are trained to approach crime scenes in a dispassionate and professional manner. This training, along with exposure to previous crimes and experience, alters their appraisal of situations that most people would find shocking and arousing. As a result, later memory might differ for the trained professional. Of course, it is hard in retrospect to evaluate how any individual appraised or reacted to any specific event. However, it is important to recognize that a legal actor's specific training or experience may play a role in the quality of his or her memory, in part due to its influence on the emotional response.

In addition to research clarifying the role of emotion and other factors in determining the reliability of memory in legal settings, a major challenge is conveying this research to a legal audience in a concise but comprehensive manner that can be easily integrated into memory assessments. With emotion, this is especially difficult because our rich recollective experiences for highly emotion events seem so detailed that it is sometimes hard to imagine that they are not completely accurate, both for ourselves and for others. Learning that memories for details are often inaccurate, especially for shocking and traumatic events, may lead some to conclude that memory can never be relied on in legal proceedings. This would be a mistake, because at times memory is clearly reliable and can provide important information. Instead, legal scholars should work together with scientists to develop a better characterization of how and when memory should, or should not, be considered reliable in legal proceedings.

REFERENCES

Adolphs, R., Tranel, D., & Buchanan, T. W. (2005). Amygdala damage impairs emotional memory for gist but not details of complex stimuli. *Nature Neuroscience, 115,* 512–518.

Anderson, A. K. (2005). Affective influences on the attentional dynamics supporting awareness. *Journal of Experimental Psychology: General, 134,* 258–281.

Anderson, A. K., & Phelps, E. A. (2001). Lesions of the human amygdala impair enhanced perception of emotionally salient events. *Nature, 411,* 305–309.

Bremner, J. D. (1999). Does stress damage the brain? *Biological Psychiatry, 45,* 797–805.

Bremner, J. D., Narayan, M., Anderson, E. R., Staib, L. H., Miller, H. L., & Charney, D. S. (2000). Hippocampal volume reduction in major depression. *American Journal of Psychiatry, 157,* 115–118.

Brown, R., & Kulik, J. (1977). Flashbulb memories. *Cognition, 5,* 73–99.

Burke, A., Heuer, F., & Reisberg, D. (1992). Remembering emotional events. *Memory and Cognition, 20,* 277–290.

Christianson, S. A., & Loftus, E. F. (1987). Memory for traumatic events. *Applied Cognitive Psychology, 1,* 225–239.

Christianson, S. A., & Loftus, E. F. (1991). Remembering emotional events: The fate of detailed information. *Cognition and Emotion, 5,* 81–108.

D'Argembeau, A., & Van der Linden, M. (2004). Influence of affective meaning on memory for contextual information. *Emotion, 4,* 173–188.

D'Argembeau, A., & Van der Linden, M. (2005). Influence of emotion on memory for temporal information. *Emotion, 5,* 503–507.

Davis, M., & Whalen, P. J. (2001). The amygdala: Vigilance and emotion. *Molecular Psychiatry, 6,* 13–34.

Easterbrook, J. A. (1959). The effect of emotion on cue utilisation and the organization of behavior. *Psychological Review, 66,* 183–201.

Eldridge, L. L., Knowlton, B. J., Furmanski, C. S., Bookheimer, S. Y., & Engel, S. A. (2000). Remembering episodes: A selective role for the hippocampus during retrieval. *Nature Neuroscience, 3,* 1149–1152.

Ezzyat, Y., & Davachi, L. (2011), What constitutes an episode in episodic memory? *Psychological Science, 22,* 243–252.

Fox, E., Russo, R., Bowles, R., & Dutton, K. (2001). Do threatening stimuli draw or hold visual attention in subclinical anxiety? *Journal of Experimental Psychology: General, 130,* 681–700.

Fox, E., Russo, R., & Georgiou, G. A. (2005). Anxiety modulates the degree of attentive resources required to process emotional faces. *Cognitive, Affective, and Behavioral Neuroscience, 5,* 396–404.

Gross, J. J. (2002). Emotion regulation: Affective, cognitive, and social consequences. *Psychophysiology, 39,* 281–291.

Heuer, F., & Reisberg, D. (1992). Emotion, arousal and memory for detail. In S. A. Christianson (Ed.), *Handbook of emotion and memory* (pp. 151–180). Hillsdale, NJ: Erlbaum.

Hirst, W., Phelps, E. A., Buckner, R. L., Budson, A. E., Cuc, A., Gabrieli, J. D., et al. (2009). Long-term memory for the terrorist attack of September 11: Flashbulb memories, event memories, and the factors that influence their retention. *Journal of Experimental Psychology: General, 138,* 161–176.

Kensinger, E. A. (2009). Remembering the details: Effects of emotion. *Emotion Review, 1,* 99–113.

Kleinsmith, L. J., & Kaplan, S. (1963). Paired-associate learning as a function of arousal and interpolated interval. *Journal of Experimental Psychology, 65,* 190–193.

Kohler, S., Crane, J., & Milner, B. (2002). Differential contributions of the parahippocampal place area and the anterior hippocampus to human memory for scenes. *Hippocampus, 12,* 718–723.

Kvavilashvili, L., Mirani, J., Schlagman, S., & Kornbrot, D. E. (2003). Comparing flashbulb memories of September 11 and the death of Princess Diana: Effect of time delays and nationality. *Applied Cognitive Psychology, 17,* 1017–1031.

LaBar, K. S., & Phelps, E. A. (1998). Arousal-mediated memory consolidation: Role of the medial temporal lobe in humans. *Psychological Science, 9,* 490–493.

Loftus, E. F., Loftus, G. R., & Messo, J. (1987). Some facts about "weapon focus." *Law and Human Behavior, 11,* 55–62.

Macdonald, C. J., Lepage, K. Q., Eden, U. T., & Eichenbaum, H. (2011). Hippocampal "time cells" bridge the gap in memory for discontiguous events. *Neuron, 71,* 737–749.

Mather, M. (2007). Emotional arousal and memory binding: An object-based framework. *Perspectives in Psychological Science, 2,* 33–52.

Mather, M., & Nesmith, K. (2008). Arousal-enhanced location memory for pictures. *Journal of Memory and Language, 58,* 449–464.

Mather, M., & Sutherland, M. (2009). Disentangling the effects of arousal and valence on memory for intrinsic details. *Emotion Review, 1,* 118–119.

McEwan, B. S. (1999). Stress and hippocampal plasticity. *Annual Review of Neuroscience, 22,* 105–122.

McGaugh, J. L. (2000). Memory—a century of consolidation. *Science, 287,* 248–251.

Most, S. B., Chun, M. M., Widders, D. M., & Zald, D. H. (2005).Attentional rubbernecking: Cognitive control and personality in emotion-induced blindness. *Psychonomic Bulletin and Review, 12,* 654–661.

Nadel, L. (2008). Hippocampus and context revisited. In S. J. Y. Mizumori (Ed.), *Hippocampal place fields: Relevance to learning and memory* (pp. 3–15). New York: Oxford University Press.

Neisser, U., & Harsch, N. (1992a). Phantom flashbulbs: False recollections of hearing the news about *Challenger.* In E. Winograd & U. Neisser (Eds.), *Affect and accuracy in recall* (pp. 9–31). Cambridge: Cambridge University Press.

Neisser, U., & Harsch, N. (1992b). *Affect and accuracy in recall: Studies of flashbulb memories.* New York: Cambridge University Press.

Neisser, U., Winograd, E., Bergman, E. T., Schreiber, C. A., Palmer, S. E., & Weldon, M. S. (1996). Remembering the earthquake: Direct experience vs. hearing the news. *Memory, 4,* 337–357.

Ochsner, K. N. (2000). Are affective events richly recollected or simply familiar? The experience and process of recognizing feelings past. *Journal of Experimental Psychology: General, 129,* 242–261.

Perfect, T. J., Mayes, A. R., Downes, J. J., & Van Eijk, R. (1996). Does context discriminate recollection from familiarity in recognition memory? *Quarterly Journal of Experimental Psychology A., Human Experimental Psychology, 49,* 797–813.

Phelps, E. A. (2006). Emotion and cognition: Insights from studies of the human amygdala. *Annual Review of Psychology, 57,* 27–53.

Phelps, E. A., Ling, S., & Carrasco, M. (2006). Emotion facilitates perception and potentiates the perceptual benefit of attention. *Psychological Science, 17*, 292–299.

Pourtois, G., & Vuilleumier, P. (2006). Dynamics of emotional effects on spatial attention in the human visual cortex. *Progress in Brain Research, 156*, 67–91.

Raymond, J. E., Shapiro, K. L., & Arnell, K. M. (1992). Temporary suppression of visual processing in an RSVP task: An attentional blink?. *Journal of Experimental Psychology: Human Perception and Performance, 18*, 849–860.

Rimmele, U., Davachi, L., Petrov, P., Dougal, S., & Phelps, E. A. (2011). Emotion enhances the subjective feeling of remembering despite lower accuracy for contextual details. *Emotion, 11*, 553–562.

Rimmele, U., Davachi, L., & Phelps, E. A. (in press). Memory for time and place contributes to enhanced confidence in memories for emotional events. *Emotion*.

Schacter, D. L. (2001). *The seven sins of memory*. New York: Houghton Mifflin.

Schacter, D. L. Addis, D. R., & Buckner, R. L. (2008). Episodic simulation of future events: Concepts, data, and applications. *Annals of the New York Academy of Sciences, 1124*, 39–60.

Scherer, K. R. (2005). What are emotions? And how can they be measured? *Social Science Information, 44*, 695–729.

Schmidt, K., Patnaik, P., & Kensinger, E. A. (2011). Emotion's influence on memory for spatial and temporal context. *Cognition and Emotion, 25*, 229–243.

Schmolck, H., Buffalo, E. A., & Squire, L. R. (2000). Memory distortions develop over time: Recollections of the O. J. Simpson trial verdict after 15 and 32 months. *Psychological Science, 11*, 39–45.

Sharot, T., Delgado, M. R., & Phelps, E. A. (2004). How emotion enhances the feeling of remembering. *Nature and Neuroscience, 7*, 1376–1380.

Sharot, T., Martorella, E. A., Delgado, M. R., & Phelps, E. A. (2007). Remembering 9/11: How personal experience modulates the neural circuitry of recollection. *Proceedings of the National Academy of Sciences of the United States of America, 104*, 389–394.

Talarico, J. M., & Rubin, D. C. (2003). Confidence, not consistency, characterizes flashbulb memories. *Psychological Science, 14*, 455–461.

Tollenaar, M. S., Elzinga, B. M., Spinhoven, P., & Everaerd, W. (2009). Immediate and prolonged effects of cortisol, but not propranolol, on memory retrieval in healthy young men. *Neurobiology of Learning and Memory, 91*, 23–31.

Tulving, E., & Markowitsch, H. J. (1998). Episodic and declarative memory: Role of the hippocampus. *Hippocampus, 8*, 198–204.

Vuilleumier, P., Richardson, M. P., Armony, J. L., Driver, J., & Dolan, D. J. (2004). Distant influences of amygdala lesion on visual cortical activation during emotional face processing. *Nature Neuroscience, 7*, 1271–1278.

Zoladz, P. R., & Diamond, D. M. (2009). Linear and non-linear dose-response functions reveal a hormetic relationship between stress and learning. *Dose-Response, 7*, 132–148.

PART TWO

Memory in Eyewitnesses

2

Inconsistencies between Law and the Limits of Human Cognition

The Case of Eyewitness Identification

DEBORAH DAVIS AND ELIZABETH F. LOFTUS

American criminal and civil courts are heavily dependent upon memory-based reports to provide relevant evidence for virtually every kind of case before them. Such reports come from both lay and expert witnesses and span the gamut of memories of all kinds—such as memory for people, or of specifics of events, conversations, objects, timing, and even one's own past thoughts and cognitive processes. Likewise, the courts are dependent upon those who must judge those memories to reasonably assess their accuracy. This double dependency raises the twin issues of (1) the accuracy of human memory and the circumstances under which it can provide sufficiently reliable and probative evidence for the purposes of the courts and (2) the ability of observers to judge the accuracy of witnesses' memories and to weight them appropriately in arriving at their decisions. Are the limits of human cognition—whether those of the witnesses or of those who judge them—adequate to the tasks imposed by the legal system? Or does the law assume more than human cognition can provide, giving more weight than warranted to witnesses' accounts and overestimating the ability of judges and juries to reliably recognize inaccurate accounts when they occur? Here, we address these issues with respect to the specific case of memory for people and witnesses' ability to accurately identify the perpetrator of a crime.

EYEWITNESS EVIDENCE: THE LAW

The U.S. legal system currently allows conviction of criminal charges based solely on the testimony of a single eyewitness. It therefore is of considerable importance to ask whether eyewitness accuracy is sufficient to warrant a conclusion of guilt "beyond a reasonable doubt" based solely on one or more eyewitness identifications. Likewise, it is important to address the conditions under which such identifications should be considered sufficiently probative of guilt to outweigh their potential prejudicial impact and warrant admission as evidence in legal proceedings.

Although some variability exists between jurisdictions in standards of admissibility, the U.S. Supreme Court's ruling concerning the admission of eyewitness evidence was established in *Manson v. Braithwaite* (1977), and recently upheld in *Perry v. New Hampshire* (2012). The Court offered a two-pronged test for exclusion of the identification. The first determination is to be whether the identification procedure was or was not impermissibly suggestive. If not, the identification is to be admissible and the second question is moot. If so, the second determination is to be whether the identification was nevertheless reliable. The Court further specified five reliability criteria to guide the second inquiry: (1) opportunity to view the perpetrator, (2) attention to the perpetrator, (3) the accuracy of the witness's description of the perpetrator (which tends to be interpreted as the degree of detail and consistency of the original description given by the witness with the appearance of his or her lineup choice; Wells & Quinlivan, 2009), (4) delay between the event and the identification, and (5) the certainty in the identification expressed by the witness.

The use of this two-pronged test has recently been reviewed and criticized in detail by Wells and Quinlivan (2009). Their criticisms focus largely on the lack of independence between the two prongs of the test: that is, the fact that suggestive identification procedures directly impact three of the five reliability criteria, leading witnesses to report greater certainty, and better witnessing conditions (view, attention, etc.) than for those not exposed to suggestive procedures. Here, we consider the *Manson* criteria as well but focus largely on two issues.

First, we argue that eyewitness science currently offers sufficient evidence of the limits of eyewitness identification performance to justify exclusion under some circumstances even *in the absence of suggestive identification procedures*. That is, because under the *Manson* test courts can and have admitted "impossible" identifications into evidence (for example, identifications based on witnessing conditions that exceed the limits of basic perceptual abilities), we argue that exclusionary rulings should be addressed in the reverse order such that the first inquiry should be whether the witness could have, under the circumstances, been sufficiently accurate; and if so, whether impermissibly suggestive identification procedures were employed. Either alone should be grounds for exclusion, with no remediation by the other. Second, we consider whether observers can reliably perform the assessments of accuracy and suggestion necessary for both prongs of an admissibility ruling, as well as for proper weighting of eyewitness testimony at trial.

THE WITNESS

When considering whether what the law asks of witnesses is beyond the limits of human cognition, two primary issues come to mind: "What are the limits of witness identification performance in the most ideal circumstances?" and "What are the limits of memory's resistance to distortion?" We address these issues in the following sections, with emphasis on research investigating the ability to identify once-seen strangers rather than known individuals. We discuss existing findings in terms of their implications for the conditions under which eyewitness identification evidence should or should not be admissible in criminal proceedings and suggest avenues for future research to further inform this question.

The Limits of Witness Identification Performance Under Ideal Conditions

To establish the upper limits of eyewitness performance, performance must be examined with original witnessing conditions providing adequate opportunity to observe the target, minimal or no delay between observation and test, witnesses at the peak of their perceptual abilities, a same-race target, and identification procedures that do not bias witnesses' choice. Thus, arguably, the most stringent and relevant tests of the limits of eyewitness lineup performance are provided by studies in which a same-race target is still present and easily observable, and the subject must inspect a lineup to determine whether the target is or is not present, and if so, which lineup member is the target. For witness show-up performance, the most relevant test would be studies in which the target is still present, and the subject must indicate whether a photo is or is not of the target.

Critics of eyewitness science have sometimes argued that performance in eyewitness identification studies does not reflect the circumstances of real-life criminal events sufficiently to provide reliable estimates of performance. Among the reasons offered to support this argument is the proposition that increased importance of the event, increased attention, or increased arousal produces superior encoding of the perpetrator's face compared to common stimuli in eyewitness studies (e.g., Bailey & Mecklenburg, 2009; Flowe, Finklea, & Ebbesen, 2009). To the extent that the target is still present, however, the subject need not even rely on memory, but must simply be able to match the target to his or her photo. Thus, criticisms entailing superior encoding under real-life conditions would not apply, and, arguably, valid estimates of maximum accuracy can be obtained.

Particularly relevant examples of such studies were conducted by Megreya and Burton (2008). In their first study, participants were presented with each of 36 targets for 30 seconds each, followed by a 5-second delay, and then a 10-face target-present or target-absent array. Targets were presented live for half of the participants and in still videos for the other half. Across types of arrays, accuracy (hits plus correct rejections) was roughly 70% for both live and video targets; and for target-absent arrays 20% falsely identified a foil, whereas for target-present arrays 10.6% did so.

The second study tested maximum performance with a still-present target, where the participant could directly compare the target to the array. On each of 36 trials, participants were allowed to look at a live or still photo target and either a target-present or target-absent array until they made their choice. Overall accuracy across live and photo targets was roughly 67%. For target-absent arrays 38% misidentified a foil, and for target-present arrays roughly 16% did so.

The final study tested the ability of participants to determine whether either two photos or a live actor and a photo (with the target and comparison photo shown simultaneously) were or were not the same person—more analogous to a "show-up" identification procedure. Participants were shown 36 comparisons, with 18 matches and 18 no-matches. Overall accuracy rates rose to roughly 85%, with false identification rates of roughly 19% when the target and comparison photo did not actually match.

Together, these three studies suggest poor maximum performance, particularly with regard to identification from lineups. There, overall accuracy across the two studies averaged 68.5% and false identification of foils in target absent arrays averaged 29%, whereas that in target present arrays averaged 13.6%. In the matching task of Experiment 3, a rate of 19% false matches was found for nonmatching pairs. These would seem to be strikingly high rates, particularly for Experiments 2 and 3, where the targets were still present while participants made their choices and the task was simply to accurately compare two visible stimuli.

However, a number of studies have obtained comparably high error rates in matching tasks where participants had to determine whether the target matched a single comparison photo or one in target-present or target-absent arrays of varying size (e.g., Bruce et al., 1999; Burton, Miller, Bruce, Hancock, & Henderson, 2001; Henderson, Bruce, & Burton, 2001; Megreya & Burton, 2006, 2007). Several real-life studies of face matching have also obtained high error rates. For example, in a study of cashiers' ability to match credit card photos to their bearers, Kemp, Towell, and Pike (1977) obtained false-positive error rates of 34%–64%, depending upon the similarity of the comparison photo to the target. Similarly, based on a meta-analysis of 53 studies of the effects of delay on memory for previously unseen faces, Deffenbacher and colleagues concluded that "a plausible upper limit for witness initial memory strength corresponds to a probability of .67 of being correct on a fair six-person lineup" (Deffenbacher, Bornstein, McGorty, & Penrod, 2008, p. 139).

This body of research has been supplemented by meta-analyses of eyewitness performance in both laboratory experiments and archival field studies of real-life eyewitnesses. Three meta-analyses of laboratory experiments revealed poor accuracy (Clark, Howell, & Davey, 2008; Steblay, Dysart, & Wells, 2011; Steblay, Dysart, Fulero, & Lindsay, 2003). In target-present lineups, rates of foil IDs ranged from 17% to 21%; and among all those who did make an ID, from 29.8% to 38.7% identified foils. In target-absent lineups foil IDs ranged from 32% to 57%. Two of the analyses separated simultaneous and sequential lineups (Clark et al., 2008; Steblay et al., 2011). Both found lower rates of foil identifications in target-absent lineups for sequential (32%, 36%) versus simultaneous (49%, 57%) lineups. Thus, though the recommended sequential procedure did reduce the rate of foil identification, it remained substantial at over 30%.

Accuracy was similarly poor across the eight archival studies (Behrman & Davey, 2001; Behrman & Richards, 2005; Horry, Memon, Wright, & Milne, 2011; Memon, Havard, Clifford, Gabbert, & Watt, 2011; Slater, 1994; Valentine, Pickering, & Darling, 2003; Wright & McDaid, 1996; Wright & Skagerberg, 2007). From 36% to 58% of witnesses identified the suspect, and from 15% to 42% identified known innocent foils. However, of all witnesses who did make an identification, from 22.4% to 48.8% identified known innocent foils. Overall accuracy is, of course, unknown in these archival studies, given that the identity of the perpetrator is not subject to absolute verification, but it is likely be less than 70% since many witnesses fail to identify anyone in the lineup and suspects may be chosen although they are actually innocent.

What Happens When the Exposure and Test Targets Are Not Identical?

In part, the low rates of accuracy obtained in the above studies are likely due to the difficulty of matching a specific image of the target to differing specific images in an array of similar targets—a task that has been shown to contribute to error, and yet one that is inherent in real-life eyewitness identification. An eyewitness to real-life crimes will not see an identical presentation of the suspect during the original crime and any identification procedure to follow. Even if the witness participates in a show-up identification soon after the crime, the lighting, angle of view, facial expression of the suspect, and a number of other things will be different. Unfortunately, research has indicated that *any* variation between the exact appearance of the target during exposure versus test results in declining performance. This variation can be as simple as that between two different rather than identical photos of the same person, between the exposure and testing media (live vs. photo, film vs. photo, etc.), or between viewing conditions such as angle of view or lighting (see Bruce, 2009; Burton & Jenkins, 2011 for reviews).

Regarding the simple difference between two photos of the same person, although recognition accuracy (correctly indicating that a particular photo has or has not been seen before) is relatively high when the original and identification photos are identical, performance is highly sensitive to any kind of change between the two. For example, Bruce (1982) showed participants 24 unfamiliar faces, followed by a recognition task 15 minutes later. The hit rate for identical exposure and test photos was high (90%), but declined to 76% when there was a change in either pose or expression and to 61% when there was a change in both. The photos included clothing that could have aided recognition, making the declines due to differences in pose or expression particularly striking.

Given the variety of methods that have produced similarly high rates of error, it seems reasonable to conclude that real-life attempts to match a target face to a single comparison photo or to select it from a fair lineup of similar targets are likely to produce accuracy rates of roughly 70% or below under relatively ideal circumstances entailing few or no demands for memory of the face and adequate opportunity to observe and encode it. But what happens when we make the conditions more comparable to the task of the real-life eyewitness to crime?

Adding to the Burden: Increasing Perceptual Difficulty

Various aspects of *witnessing conditions* can affect the ability of the witness to perceive and encode a target's face. These include aspects that affect basic perception, such as lighting, distance, obstructions, or duration of exposure, as well as those that affect the ability to deploy perceptual resources—such as factors promoting diversion of attention from the target or impairment of cognition through such impairments as acute stress or substance use (see Davis & Follette, 2001; Lindsay, Ross, Read, & Toglia, 2007; Toglia, Read, Ross, &

Lindsay, 2007, for reviews). The latter factors affecting deployment of perceptual resources are difficult to quantify, particularly after the fact. However, those affecting basic perception can be manipulated parametrically and in combination so as to provide limits of performance under varying combinations of relevant conditions. Although we do not currently have such comprehensive parametric studies, we do have evidence of some limits at which identification performance drops to chance.

Several researchers have varied the distance and/or lighting conditions under which participants are exposed to known or unknown faces (e.g., De Jong, Wagenaar, Wolters, & Verstijnen, 2005; Loftus & Harley, 2005; Wagenaar & van der Schrier, 1996). Wagenaar and associates have simulated distance by varying the size of the target image, which shrinks from the observer's perspective such that size is inversely proportional to distance. Loftus and Harley (2005) offered a method of simulating distance based on spatial frequency composition (see Loftus & Harley, 2005, for details), demonstrating that this method of simulation corresponds well to the sizing method. For both known celebrity faces and previously unknown faces, accuracy falls predictably with more distance and less illumination, though the exact numbers have varied across methods of simulation. Regardless of the method, however, accuracy reaches chance levels sooner than is commonly assumed. Loftus and Harley (2005), for example, found across three experiments that the ability to name a celebrity face accurately was roughly 75% at 34 feet, 25% by 77 feet, and zero at approximately 110 feet. Similarly, De Jong et al. (2005) found somewhat higher overall levels of recognition for celebrities, but likewise found decreasing performance with increasing distance as well as decreasing illumination.

Unfortunately, the methods used for the above studies of distance and illumination have relied on simulations of distance and largely on identification of known rather than unknown persons, and otherwise have not resembled the task of real-life witnesses. Moreover, there have been no studies manipulating actual distance and lighting in such parametric fashion. However, a large-scale field study of the effect of distance was conducted by Lindsay, Semmler, Weber, Brewer, and Lindsay (2008). Over 1,300 participants were approached during everyday activities and asked to observe targets at varying distances. Then, either immediately, in person, or after a delay, over the Internet, they were asked to estimate the distance of the target from their location, provide a verbal description of the target, and, finally, inspect a six-person target-present or target-absent lineup. The authors found that participants underestimated distance when actual distance was shorter than 30 meters (98.4 feet) and overestimated distance at actual distances over 30 meters. Estimates were roughly 51% of the actual distance at the lower mean distance of 10.7 meters (35 feet) and rose to 190.4% of the actual distance at the upper mean distance of 34.63 meters (113.6 feet).

For analyses of accuracy, two distance conditions were created: long distances between 20 meters (65.6 feet) and 50 meters (164.04 feet) and short distances between 5 meters (16.4 feet) and 15 meters (49.2 feet). While the ranges both within and between the two distance conditions are too large to obtain meaningful estimates of maximum performance as a function of distance, there were significant effects of distance on performance. Target descriptions were less accurate at longer distances and were generally poor. Accuracy in estimating age within 10 years, for example, was only 47% even at 15 meters or less. Finally, those who were asked to inspect a lineup, even immediately after viewing the target, performed poorly. For those viewing the targets at or below 15 meters, performance was generally somewhat worse than the maximum performance in the matching experiments reported earlier: roughly 62% correctly identified the target in target-present lineups, whereas roughly 51% misidentified a foil in target-absent lineups and roughly 21% did so in target-present lineups. Though witnesses were equally likely to choose someone in the lineup regardless of distance, error rates were higher for the longer distances and after longer delays.

Summary and Conclusions

The results reviewed so far have shown that the maximum initial limits of eyewitness lineup performance in ideal conditions are likely to be about 70% or below, and that these limits will fall as the result of factors impacting basic perception, as well as factors impacting the deployment of perceptual resources. While we do not yet have the parametric studies needed to determine the limits of performance with varying combinations of factors affecting basic perceptual abilities—such as distance, lighting, duration of exposure, angle of view, disguise and obstructions of parts of the face—we do have sufficient data to offer courts information concerning some basic limits of performance, and to aid in preventing the admission of "impossible" eyewitness identifications made under witnessing conditions in which maximum accuracy approaches that of guessing. We also have the methods to perform parametric studies examining greater range within factors and the interactions between them. We strongly encourage eyewitness scientists to perform such studies so that in the future we can provide this information to the courts to aid them in understanding the circumstances in which eyewitness accuracy falls sufficiently low to demand exclusion of the testimony.

As noted earlier, the law currently allows for conviction based solely on the unsupported testimony of one or more eyewitnesses. The evidence reviewed here suggests that even under the best circumstances, eyewitness performance may not justify this practice. Further, a wealth of scientific evidence exists to show that accuracy is decreased by basic perceptual variables, as discussed above, as well as by witnesses' perceptual abilities, and by factors that either affect deployment of perceptual capacities at the time of the event or promote errors of perception and interpretation (see Lindsay et al., 2007, and Toglia et al., 2007, for reviews). This evidence suggests that legal standards for exclusion should not require a finding of suggestive procedures; but rather, they should provide for the exclusion of eyewitness evidence based on insufficient reliability.

Further, such standards need to be evidence-based. As we show in subsequent sections, current treatments of reliability in exclusionary standards, as well as in other indicators of intuitive understanding of witness performance (such as common instructions to juries regarding determinants of reliability), reflect poor understanding of the determinants of witness accuracy. In the next section, we consider such misunderstanding as it applies to the degree to which memory can be distorted over time and circumstances, as well as the degree to which memory can be resilient and self-correcting notwithstanding such distortion.

Limits of Memory: Distortion and Resilience Over Time and Circumstance

In addition to poor upper limits of performance for witness accuracy, memory scientists have shown that the lower limits of performance include not only complete failure to remember, but also complete substitution of false memories for true ones and even complete fabrication of events that never happened at all (see Brainerd & Reyna, 2005, and Loftus, 2005, for reviews). Further, the importance or emotionality of events for which these distortions occur appears to know no limits, as false memories for entire (and allegedly frequently repeated) events as seemingly impossible as satanic ritual abuse involving sacrifice and eating of babies, forced demonic impregnation, abduction and impregnation by aliens, and many others have been documented and litigated (see Clancy, 2005, and Loftus & Davis, 2006, for reviews).

Laboratory science has also examined the nature and impact of distorting influences on eyewitness memory specifically, showing that identification accuracy can be reduced through two classes of influence. The first might be thought of as those that simply interfere with the original image of the perpetrator: for example, attempts to describe the perpetrator, to work with police sketch artists, exposure to multiple images in mug books, and others. The second class of influences operates through effects on the witness's beliefs about the identity of the perpetrator. These include postevent information about the perpetrator's identity acquired through such sources as conversations with other witnesses, media accounts, or suggestive police interviewing or identification procedures. Some entail both processes, such as media accounts including notice of a suspect's arrest, the evidence against him or her, and a mug shot (for reviews of these processes, see Lindsay et al., 2007, and Toglia et al., 2007).

Wells and Quinlivan (2009) argued that the legal system does not fully appreciate the degree to which such suggestive influences can affect eyewitness identifications, nor does it appreciate the permanence of the effects, noting that

> there is an apparent belief that damage from an unfair identification procedure can be undone by simply following it with a fair procedure. Even Justice Marshall, in his dissenting opinion in *Manson v. Braithwaite* claimed, "When a prosecuting attorney learns that there has been a suggestive confrontation, he can easily arrange another lineup under scrupulously fair conditions." (p. 128)
>
> This "retesting" view is diametrically opposed to the dominant view among psychological scientists that, once an eyewitness has mistakenly identified someone, that person "becomes" the witness' memory and the error will simply repeat itself. (pp. 8–9)

In other words, the authors argue that eyewitness memory is both more subject to distortion and less resilient to it than is commonly assumed by the legal system. They go on to review evidence of the distorting effects of a variety of suggestive police procedures, varying in subtlety from simple failure to instruct the witness that the perpetrator may or may not be in the lineup to use of poor foils to feedback confirming that the witness identified the police's suspect and others. Less research, however, has addressed the question of the extent to which, once distorted, memory can be resilient and restored to accuracy.

In part, research showing that once witnesses have identified a particular innocent suspect in one procedure, they are more likely to do so in subsequent procedures can be taken as a demonstration that memory tends to go uncorrected. Recent research by Cook, Kwak, Hoffman, and Loftus (2010) has asked the additional question of whether, once the witness has been led to identify an innocent suspect in a target-absent lineup, he or she will be able to recognize the correct suspect when viewing a target-present lineup. That is, the authors examined Justice Marshall's suggestion that the biasing effects of a suggestive identification procedure can be nullified by having the witness complete a second, presumably unbiased, procedure.

The authors conducted 15 experiments to test this hypothesis. In the first phase, participants studied 20 target faces. After a brief filler task, they then engaged in an initial recognition task in which they were asked to indicate which of two faces they saw in the first phase. Some pairs consisted of one of the original target faces and a previously unshown distractor face. Others consisted of a distractor face and a morph of the original face, in which either external features (such as hair) or internal features (such as eye, nose, or mouth shape and configuration) had been altered (a procedure that tends to result in choosing the morph). Thus, the morphed distractors were similar in some respects to the original. Following a second filler task, participants in seven of the experiments engaged in a final recognition task in which they once again had to choose between two faces consisting of pairs of either (1) an original target and its morph, neither shown in the intervening recognition task, (2) an original target shown in the interim and its morph not shown in the interim, or (3) an original target not shown in the interim and its morph shown in the interim. For the remaining experiments, the final phase consisted of a yes-no recognition task for original targets, morphs, and foils.

Across all 15 experiments, exposure to target morphs during the interim recognition task decreased accuracy, including reduced identification of the original target face and increased false alarms to the morph of the original. Of particular interest, for the seven experiments where participants chose between the original target and its morph in the final recognition task, those exposed to the target morph in the interim recognition task were significantly more likely to choose the morph over the original in the final phase than either those exposed to the original or those not exposed to either in the interim.

Though the study was not conducted in the format of a standard eyewitness identification experiment, these results clearly converge with the more massive literature on misinformation effects to suggest that, once corrupted, the original more accurate memory is less likely to drive subsequent memory reports. Further, although more research on the reversibility of distortion in eyewitness identifications due to suggestion is needed, more than sufficient evidence from both the eyewitness and broader memory literatures clearly indicates that the law should not presume the ability of corrective procedures to eliminate the effects of prior impermissibly suggestive identification procedures.

THOSE WHO MUST JUDGE THEM

Once a witness has identified a suspect, a number of decisions from that point forward are based in whole or part on that identification. These can begin immediately as police decide whether to continue their investigation of the suspect or present him or her as the perpetrator to the prosecutor. The prosecutor must then decide whether to press charges initially, and must also consider how the overall strength of the case (including the strength of the witness identification) should factor into subsequent plea bargaining and the decision to go to trial. Trial judges may then be faced with the need to rule on motions to exclude the witness identification (which appellate judges may later have to second guess), and grand juries and trial juries must judge the likely accuracy of the witness. In some cases these judgments are made in relative isolation, as the witness is sometimes the only evidence against the suspect. But more often, they are made in the context of other evidence. Each situation poses unique challenges for the observers who must judge the witness.

What Is the Relevant Information Needed to Judge Witness Accuracy? "Do observers have it?" and "Do they know what to do with it?"

In a nutshell, the answers to these three questions are: (1) "A lot! Some knowable, some not. Some known, much not," (2) "No," and (3) "No." But how do we know this?

What Is the Necessary Relevant Information?

At minimum, the information needed to determine the probability that a given witness could provide an accurate identification under the circumstances at hand includes the following:

1. Understanding of how memory works, including what factors determine the accuracy of original encoding of the perpetrator's appearance, what factors affect the fidelity versus distortion or fading of that memory over time, and what factors affect memory and/or identification choices at each identification procedure.
2. Understanding of how the individual characteristics of the witness might affect any of the above factors. In addition to the witness's perceptual and memory skills, or characteristics associated with susceptibility to memory loss or distortion over time, this includes the witness's personal approach to the identification task—such as the relative concerns of identifying the perpetrator versus the risk of identifying an innocent, a priori beliefs about the likelihood that police have caught and included the perpetrator in the lineup, and other personal orientations that would affect the witness's criteria for or likelihood of making an identification.
3. Understanding of how the many relevant determinants of accuracy interact with one another and with the characteristics of the witness to determine the likelihood of accuracy.

4. Understanding of what was actually the case for the witness at hand, including
   a. All the factors entailed in 1 and 2, and
   b. The witness's ability to report accurately on factors entailed in 1 or 2 (such as the ability to accurately estimate speed, distance, and duration of exposure; to characterize lighting; to assess and convey the degree of stress experienced during the event or how much his or her identification of the suspect was influenced by various factors; to report how much attention was paid to various aspects of the events, including the perpetrator; and so on).
5. Understanding of how to interpret, weight, and properly integrate the witness's behaviors surrounding identification processes with factors entailed in 1–4. These can include behaviors that occur prior to the process (such as statements reflecting expectations that may impact the process), during the process (such as hesitations or other behavioral reflections of uncertainty, time spent inspecting the lineup before making a choice, statements reflecting use of active comparison processes or other bases of their choice, and so on), or after the process (such as statements regarding confidence in the identification). They can also include statements regarding any aspect of the process given at any time.

Do Observers Have the Necessary Relevant Information?

As might be inferred from the above list of necessary information, the complete answers to questions 1, 2, 3 and 5 above are not known. Perhaps less obviously, the answers to question 4 cannot be known, in part because these answers depend largely on the completeness and accuracy of witness reports concerning the relevant internal and external variables (which are known to suffer from incompleteness, inaccuracy, and systematic distortion, as we discuss further in later sections).

Scientific Understanding of Relevant Information

Beginning with the work of Hugo Munsterberg in the late 1800s (Munsterberg, 1908), eyewitness memory has been subject to intensive scientific investigation for more than 100 years. Nevertheless, scientific knowledge of the determinants of identification accuracy remains patchy—precise in some cases, less so in others.

The most precise scientific knowledge arguably concerns the limits of relevant perceptual abilities. Good indices of the overall likelihood of correctly identifying a once-seen stranger in a fair lineup have been established through several lines of research at roughly 67%–70% (as described in earlier sections).

Further constraints on accuracy have been established by the previously described work of G. Loftus, W. Wagenaar, and others regarding the limits of perception under varying conditions of lighting, distance, and duration of exposure. The effects of these variables and their interactions are amenable to empirical tests and establishment of precise performance curves documenting the upper limits of performance in varying conditions—though the additional effects of other variables in a given case can degrade performance below such limits. Further, to the extent that lighting, distance, and duration of exposure can be determined in a specific case, this knowledge can often provide the basis to determine (1) whether it is even possible at all for the witness to encode the perpetrator's appearance sufficiently to make a reliable identification, and if so, (2) the maximum likelihood of accuracy under the circumstances.

The bulk of the scientific knowledge is less precise, in that it entails demonstrations that a variety of specific influences tend to increase or decrease eyewitness accuracy, but without specification of performance curves reflecting the precise relationship between the variable and performance. In other words, we may know that a particular variable causes a significant decrement in accuracy, but not know how much of a decrement occurs under different levels of the variable or how the degree of decrement produced by one variable might depend upon the status of other relevant variables (see Flowe et al., 2009, for detailed discussion of these limitations). Without this knowledge, it is not possible, based on knowledge of any of these sorts of variables, to provide precise estimates of the likelihood of accuracy for a witness subject to their influence.

Thus, the best scientific knowledge of the determinants of eyewitness identification accuracy specifies some upper limits of the ability to identify a once-seen face in lineups or show-ups under ideal conditions, as well as the degree to which this performance will degrade as a function of basic perceptual variables. In addition, we know a great deal about the effects on accuracy of other variables relating to encoding, to the preservation versus fading or distortion of memory over time, and to the effects of specific police identification procedures—as well as the effects of acute and chronic characteristics of the witness. In some cases, we know how one or more of these variables interact with one another to affect accuracy (see Lindsay et al., 2007, and Toglia et al., 2007, for reviews). But for none of them do we know how they interact with the full range of additional relevant variables, including those specific to the witness. Even with respect to the three basic perceptual variables of time, distance, and lighting, although clear and valid methods exist to study such interactions, we currently do not have databases specifying performance at all levels of the interaction of these variables. Thus, we do not have adequate scientific knowledge to specify the likelihood of witness accuracy under most case-specific combinations of factors. The exception to this would be only where the conditions of encoding are such that the likelihood of accuracy would fall to near chance.

Lay Understanding of Relevant Information

A number of surveys of jury-eligible adults, police, prosecutors, judges, and students have assessed knowledge of the determinants or reflections of witness accuracy (see Read and Desmarais, 2009 for review). These surveys have addressed a number of witnessing conditions (including witness variables such as age or intoxication, and variables reflecting the opportunity to observe, such as lighting, distance, or stress), postevent influences (such as exposure to media, passage of time, etc.), and aspects of police procedure (such as suggestive questions, lineup procedures, etc.). Survey responses of laypersons ranging from jury-eligible adults to trial judges reflect considerable variability in understanding of principles governing witness performance. Although some are widely understood, many variables that influence eyewitness identifications are misunderstood (such as the relatively weak relationship between confidence and accuracy). Knowledge of these issues is poorest among students and jury-eligible adults and best among judges.

Though such surveys reveal some fundamentals of basic knowledge among the participants, they suffer from several problems that limit their ability to reflect the adequacy of knowledge needed to accurately judge witness accuracy in varying case-specific conditions. Perhaps most fundamentally, it is unclear whether the respondents would have thought of much of the content of the surveys without being asked whether they believe the statements presented to them. If not, they would not be expected to apply that content when judging an actual eyewitness identification unless specifically apprised of it by relevant arguments or cross-examination, expert testimony, or jury instructions.

Survey items are also, in many cases, very general and sometimes poorly worded and unclear, rendering the meaning of agreement ambiguous. Finally, the insensitivity to the "main effects" on accuracy of various factors revealed in the surveys can only result in greater error when extended to the many interactions between factors—unfortunately, none of which have been addressed in the surveys of lay knowledge.

Overall, then, although surveys of knowledge of the determinants of eyewitness performance have provided an incomplete and imperfect picture of the level of knowledge among judges and juries, it is nevertheless clear that those in the legal system who must judge eyewitness accuracy possess insufficient knowledge concerning the actual determinants of eyewitness accuracy. But this problem becomes magnified by problems in judging the

What to Make of Others' Reports: Scientific and Lay Knowledge

Those who must judge witness accuracy are inevitably exposed to subjective witness reports of many kinds. Some deal with the originally witnessed events, such as reports of lighting, distance, duration of the event, whether weapons were used, specific actions and sequences of actions, and so on. Many such reports are relevant to the ability of the witness to have accurately encoded the perpetrator's appearance into memory, and are therefore quite important for observers' assessments of witness accuracy. However, at best, they represent only an indirect link to actual accuracy, in that they are an imperfect reflection of the actual events. They are also incomplete, in that some relevant factors tend to be asked about and recorded and others go unmentioned, whether originally noticed by the witness or not.

Further, scientific research has demonstrated that many such judgments are imprecise and/or prone to significant error—such as those of distance, speed, duration, sequence, and others (see Davis & Follette, 2001). Weist and Bell (1985), for example, reported an average of 15% underestimation of distance across 45 studies, and more recent reviews have likewise reported common underestimation of distance (e.g., Witmer & Kline, 1998). Further, Weist and Bell concluded that though remembered distance is less accurate than perceived distance, both conformed well to Steven's power law (Stevens, 1957), indicating that relatively precise estimates of the relationship of reported to actual distance can be provided to the courts.

Moreover, as we discuss further below, witness reports of witnessing conditions such as those entailing opportunity to view the perpetrator or the amount of attention paid to the perpetrator are subject to inflation through post-event influences that increase belief in the alleged perpetrator's guilt. Thus, witness reports that are crucial for assessment of witness accuracy are subjective, error prone, and subject to distortion that would tend to inflate observer judgments of witness accuracy. Unfortunately, we currently have little data regarding lay beliefs concerning the accuracy and susceptibility to distortion of these kinds of witness reports, though there is little reason to expect that most laypersons will be aware of these issues at all, much less have an accurate understanding of determinants of the accuracy of such reports.

Other witness reports entail subjective self-reports of their own past and present internal processes, as well as self-reported judgments of the accuracy of their own memories and judgments. These can be as diverse as when the witness first noticed something or someone or arrived at a judgment; what inferences the witness drew about the intentions, perceptions, or behaviors of others; how the witness felt during the event; whether and how long he or she paid attention to particular persons or actions; whether or how often he or she thought about the event between it and the identification procedure; or how the witness assessed the strength or accuracy of his or her own memories. Some of these memories and judgments go to the opportunity the witness would have had to adequately encode the event or the perpetrator's appearance (such as reports of the focus of attention, fear, or stress). Others go to the strength or distortion of the memories or judgments over time (such as thinking about a memory or talking with others about it in the interim), and still others go indirectly or directly to the issue of accuracy (such as explanations of how the witness arrived at the identification [indirect] or expressions of confidence in the identification [direct]). Almost no evidence exists to assess the degree to which self-reports in hindsight correspond to actual online subjective experiences, to assess the relationship of the self-reports to identification accuracy, or to assess lay beliefs concerning the accuracy of witness self-reports of these sorts. Again, however, there is little reason to believe that lay understanding of these issues is accurate.

The import of one type of self-report, concerning witness confidence, is widely misunderstood, and tends to be misapplied to assessments of witness accuracy. Observers are impressed with expressions of confidence. They give more weight to witness confidence than to the more diagnostic variables concerning the conditions under which the event was witnessed or the identification procedures used for the identification, accounting for as much as 50% of the variance in judgments of accuracy (Wells, Lindsay, & Ferguson, 1979; see Davis & Follette, 2001; Leippe & Eisenstadt, 2007, 2009 for reviews). Further, Cutler, Penrod, and Dexter (1990) found that out of 10 witness variables known to affect actual accuracy, only confidence predicted perceptions of accuracy. Finally, surveys of juror beliefs concerning eyewitness accuracy have shown that the majority believe that witness confidence is associated with accuracy (see Read & Desmarais, 2009, for review). Yet, in laboratory studies, confidence is at best a moderate predictor of actual accuracy among those who make an identification in the context of non-biasing identification procedures. Moreover, it is subject to inflation through a number of influences that can occur in real-life cases before, during, and after identification procedures (see Leippe & Eisenstadt, 2007; Wells & Quinlivan, 2009).

Do Observers Know How to Apply Their Knowledge to Specific Cases?

Those in the legal system clearly have some accurate knowledge concerning determinants of witness accuracy. But how is that knowledge applied when they must address a specific witness in the context of concrete instantiation of the conceptual determinants of accuracy? The sheer number of relevant factors that would have to be considered and integrated is beyond the limits of what human decision makers can and do typically weigh when arriving at their judgments (see Hastie & Dawes, 2010, for a review of the limitations of information use in decision making).

Given the plethora of factors contributing to witness accuracy—combined with the incompleteness, imprecision, and/or unreliability of available scientific information regarding these factors and the lack of adequate relevant observer knowledge of their individual or combined effects on accuracy—in the absence of other valid and significant evidence of the suspect's innocence or guilt, it is unlikely that observers can distinguish between accurate and inaccurate witnesses with a high rate of success. Indeed, research evidence consistent with this expectation has been provided in a number of studies.

Jurors

One series of studies was specifically designed to assess the ability of observers to distinguish between accurate and inaccurate eyewitnesses (Lindsay, Wells, & O'Connor, 1989; Wells, Ferguson, & Lindsay, 1981; Wells & Leippe, 1981; Wells, Lindsay, & Ferguson, 1979; Wells, Lindsay, & Tousignant, 1980). Student witnesses were first exposed to staged events and later attempted to identify the target from photographic lineups. In the second stage, witnesses who did make an identification from the lineups were asked to testify in a mock trial format where they were questioned about the event and their identifications. In the final stage, videotapes of the witnesses were shown to mock jurors, who were asked to judge their accuracy. A major finding was that in the absence of expert testimony on determinants of witness accuracy, mock jurors were unable to distinguish between accurate and inaccurate eyewitnesses.

Further, as noted earlier, Cutler and colleagues (1990) found that out of 10 witness variables known to affect actual accuracy, only confidence predicted perceptions of accuracy. Other studies have shown that judgments of accuracy are insensitive to the effects of many known determinants of accuracy, but show some sensitivity to inconsistency in the witness's testimony and to some issues surrounding lineup procedure (see Devenport, Kimbrough, & Cutler, 2009, for review).

Judges

To our knowledge, only one study has examined the basis of judges' rulings on motions to exclude eyewitness testimony. Stinson, Devenport, Cutler, and Kravitz (1997) presented judges with a written description of a case, including events surrounding the crime and perpetrator, materials regarding the identification procedures (varied to include biased versus unbiased foils, biased or unbiased instructions to the witness, and a sequential versus simultaneous lineup presentation format), a motion to suppress the identification, and a questionnaire assessing their perceptions of the lineup procedures and their likely ruling. Judges were more likely to indicate that they would suppress identifications involving biased foils or biased instructions, but did not differ between simultaneous versus sequential lineup procedures. While somewhat encouraging, this study did not address many other potentially biasing procedural variables, nor did it address the second prong of the admissibility test of whether, notwithstanding the use of biasing identification procedures, the witness was nevertheless accurate (*Manson v. Braithwaite*, 1977).

In practice, however, judges rarely grant motions to suppress eyewitness identifications, apparently due to the tendency to view identifications as reliable, notwithstanding biasing procedures (see Garrett, 2011; Wells & Quinlivan, 2009). Such a pattern reflects lack of appreciation for both the power and irrevocability of the impact of suggestive procedures and for the limits and determinants of witness accuracy.

The Law

The answer to the question of whether the law itself appropriately applies knowledge of the determinants and reflections of eyewitness accuracy can perhaps be best answered with the famous quote of Mr. Bumble from Charles Dickens' *Oliver Twist* that "the law is an ass!"—reflecting the presumed characteristics of the animal of stupidity (in this case, ignorance) and willful stubbornness. That is, the law shows ignorance of the determinants and reflections of eyewitness accuracy, as well as stubbornness in refusing to allow eyewitness science to influence how it treats eyewitness evidence (see Wells & Quinlivan, 2009), or, in many cases, to allow the findings of eyewitness science to be presented to jurors (see Cutler, 2009, for reviews).

The law provides five potential safeguards against convictions resulting from mistaken eyewitness identifications, including the presence of counsel at live post-indictment lineups; motions to suppress eyewitness identifications; voir dire of jurors to establish receptivity to indicators of inaccuracy in witness identifications; cross-examination of witnesses to expose indicators of inaccuracy; and judicial instructions regarding eyewitness identification evidence. Each of these alleged safeguards relies on unmet assumptions, whose invalidity undermines their effectiveness.

Inherent in all of them is the assumption that the actors involved possess sufficient knowledge of the determinants of witness accuracy to be effective—an assumption that all available data soundly contradict, as per our earlier discussion. Many alleged protections further require adequate understanding of such issues as reflections of accuracy in witness reports of confidence or the bases of their identifications, or potential flaws in the many subjective witness reports of witnessing conditions, their emotions, thoughts, and perceptions during the event, and so on. For their presence during identification procedures to be effective, attorneys would need to have sufficient knowledge of potential biases in identification procedures. They would also need to have much broader knowledge of the determinants (and reflections) of accuracy to use voir dire to diagnose probable juror reactions to eyewitness evidence, to cross-examine witnesses, or to write effective motions to exclude a witness.

Jurors would also need such knowledge to react appropriately to information revealed through cross-examination, as would judges (in order to rule appropriately on motions to suppress an identification) and those who craft jury instructions (in order to determine what to include). Adding to the deficits in knowledge that clearly undermine these alleged protections are a variety of other unmet assumptions: for example, that identification procedures occur after the attorney has been appointed and that he or she will be willing and able to attend identification procedures or that judges will allow sufficient time to cover eyewitness issues in voir dire (see Devenport et al., 2009, for detailed discussion of other unmet assumptions entailed in the five alleged protections).

Brandon Garrett (2011) has provided a stunning and revealing look at the many ways these protections failed in the cases of 190 wrongfully convicted innocents (76% of the 250 wrongful convictions he examined). Garrett obtained trial records for 161 of these cases and examined them in detail for evidence of the original witnessing conditions, police procedures, and testimony in previous hearings as well as in trial. These witnesses were all wrong, and yet all were believed. Their records revealed indicators of unreliability that would seem definitive to eyewitness scientists—such as impossible witnessing conditions, initial reports that they never saw the perpetrator's face, initial failures to identify the suspect, misidentifications of foils that were transformed into 100% confident identifications of the suspect in the context of strong police suggestion and at trial, and many others. Witnesses explained away their initial uncertainty or mistakes and judges and juries believed them, notwithstanding all evidence that they should not have done so. Defense attorneys filed motions for suppression, cross-examined the mistaken witnesses, and argued before the juries that the witnesses were inaccurate. But judges and juries frequently allowed flawed assumptions about how to diagnose accuracy—such as through the witnesses' confidence in the identifications, or the emotion expressed by the witness at the sight of the defendant—to outweigh all other concerns. Neither John Henry Wigmore's "greatest legal engine ever invented for the discovery of truth" (i.e., cross-examination; Wigmore, 1974, vol. 5, 1367 at 32) nor any other of the five alleged protections prevailed.

Clearly, the presumed protections against wrongful conviction based on eyewitness error are inadequate, and are based on the assumption that determinants of eyewitness accuracy are well understood. But what, specifically, does the law state explicitly about eyewitness performance?

Law and Expressed Beliefs Regarding Eyewitness Performance

The law provides specific criteria for evaluation of eyewitness testimony largely in two contexts: case law specifying criteria for exclusion of an identification and judicial instructions to jurors.

CRITERIA FOR EXCLUSIONARY RULINGS

Wells and Quinlivan (2009) have recently reviewed the criteria for exclusionary rulings as established in U.S. Supreme Court rulings in *Neil v. Biggers* (1972) and reaffirmed in *Manson v. Braithwaite* (1977) and *Perry v. New Hampshire* (2012), criteria that have remained unchanged for decades and in the face of an exponentially expanding eyewitness science. As noted earlier, based on a reliability test from *Neil v. Biggers,* the Court articulated five criteria for assessing reliability: opportunity to view the perpetrator, attention to the perpetrator, whether the witness offered an accurate description of the perpetrator (the suspect they later identified), delay between the event and the identification, and the certainty of the witness in the identification.

Wells and Quinlivan (2009) summarized three general concerns with the *Manson* two-pronged assessment. First, three of the five reliability criteria (view, attention, certainty) are self-reports, which must be viewed with skepticism due to well-known problems with imprecision, inaccuracy, malleability in response to suggestive questioning, social influence, reconstructive effects of hindsight, and motives such as the need to look good or the desire to see the defendant convicted (see Davis & Loftus, 2007, and Wells & Quinlivan, 2009, for reviews).

Second, the nature of the relationship of the five reliability criteria to actual witness accuracy is in most cases imprecise (e.g., attention), in some cases subject to significant error in reporting (e.g., opportunity to view), and, in some, poorly related to accuracy (e.g., confidence). Aspects of the view of the perpetrator, for example, are clearly related to accuracy. But in the case of distance, the relationship is not linear and not necessarily intuitive. The reliability test specifies no limit, however, and thus identifications at over 400 feet (which are impossible other than by guessing) have been admitted under the *Manson* criteria. Further, other aspects of opportunity to view the perpetrator, while related to witness accuracy, are self-report variables shown to be subject to either systematic overestimation (such as duration of exposure to the perpetrator) or underestimation (such as distance or the portion of time the perpetrator's face was occluded; see Wells & Quinlivan, 2009).

The validity of the *Manson* criteria of attention is also complex. The issue of what kind of attention is devoted to what aspects of the scene is crucial. Self-reports of attention are not typically so precise with respect to specific targets and are subject to distortion due, in part, to failures to pay attention to attention itself: that is, a form of metacognition. The question of what exactly the witness was attending to at the time of the crime is something that would not likely be the focus of the witness's attention at the time of the event. Since memory follows the focus of attention, a complete and valid account of where attention was deployed at the time is not likely to be encoded into memory. When asked after the fact, the witness will attempt to review the memory of his or her own cognitive processes at the time to answer, but such after-the-fact searches cannot retrieve accurately what was never specifically encoded. Perhaps in part for this reason, retrospective accounts of attention are highly malleable in response to post-event influences such as conversations with other witnesses or suggestive police procedures (see below).

In addition to problems related to reporting of attention, its relationship to witness accuracy is not always obvious. While generally beneficial, attention can be counterproductive under some circumstances, such as when aspects of the scene other than the perpetrator's face divert attention from the face, or when the witness focuses attention on specific features of the face (known to result in less identification accuracy; see Bruce, 2009, for review) rather than on the holistic configuration of the face.

The remaining three reliability criteria are also more complex than is reflected in *Manson*. Regarding consistency between the witness's description and the characteristics of the person identified, there are minimal relationships between witness accuracy and either the consistency of witness descriptions of a perpetrator with the perpetrator's actual appearance or the completeness of the description. Regarding the passage of time, accuracy does fade with time, although the rate of decay varies across situations. Thus, these two criteria are either weak or imprecise.

The remaining criterion of certainty is one of the most researched variables in eyewitness psychology and, as discussed earlier, has been shown to only modestly predict accuracy under the least biasing circumstances (immediately after an identification made without suggestion from other sources prior to or during the procedure). However, the susceptibility of witness confidence to influence from forces within and outside police procedure is also one of the most well-documented phenomena in the field. Particularly at the time judges or juries are exposed to the witness, the witness is likely to have suffered inflated confidence due to conversations with other witnesses, accounts in the media, one or more biasing police procedures, the very fact that the suspect was charged and brought to trial, or generally from a variety of forces that increase confidence in the suspect's guilt. Thus, the natural tendency to give great weight to witness confidence should be discouraged rather than encouraged in legal tests of reliability.

Generally, as the foregoing discussion suggests, the *Manson* reliability tests are sometimes minimally predictive of accuracy and sometimes predictive but imprecisely specified—and sometimes based on self-reports subject to serious error. Thus, it is no surprise, in light of the additional problems of understanding documented earlier, that the courts have made a number of spectacularly inappropriate rulings (from the perspective of relevant science) based on these criteria.

The third general concern regarding the *Manson* reliability factors is that at least three of the criteria are affected by suggestive procedures, rendering the second prong of the admissibility test non-independent of the first. As noted by Wells and Quinlivan (2009), "the use of suggestive procedures can lead the eyewitness to enhance (distort) his or her retrospective self-reports in ways that help ensure the witness' high standing on the *Manson* criteria, thereby leading to a dismissal of the suggestiveness concern. We will call this latter process, in which suggestiveness causes inflated status on the *Manson* factors, which in turn causes courts to discount the suggestiveness, the *suggestiveness augmentation effect*" (p. 9).

For several suggestive procedures (including post-identification verification of the witness's identification choice by the administrator, use of a lineup with poor foils, and others), this "suggestiveness augmentation effect" has been shown for reports of three of the *Manson* reliability criteria: opportunity to observe, attention to the perpetrator, and certainty (see Wells & Quinlivan, 2009).

Discussing the import of such findings for use of the *Manson* criteria, Wells and Quinlivan (2009) observe that "Because the *Manson* reliability factors come into consideration once it is already determined that a procedure was suggestive, courts are using the *Manson* reliability factors under precisely the conditions that make the *Manson* criteria questionable and likely misleading" (p. 12). We would only add that they are also woefully incomplete and do not recognize that even in the absence of suggestive procedures, a more valid test of reliability would identify conditions under which poor reliability should be sufficient grounds for exclusion.

The Adequacy of Jury Instructions

As noted earlier, the law assumes that instructing juries regarding what to consider in arriving at their determination of the accuracy of a witness will help them distinguish between accurate and inaccurate witnesses. But do commonly used jury instructions offer sufficiently accurate and comprehensive instructions to accomplish this purpose?

Generally, the answer is "No." Jury instructions suffer from essentially the same problems as criteria for exclusionary rulings in that they are incomplete, imprecise, and sometimes wrong. The instructions in *United States v. Telfaire* (1972) are designed to instruct jurors with respect to the dangers of mistaken identifications, to advise jurors to evaluate eyewitness evidence with caution, to remind them of the necessity of proof of guilt beyond a reasonable doubt, and to provide guidance as to factors to consider in arriving at their decisions. The factors listed in *Telfaire*, however, are based on those in *Neil v. Biggers* (1972) and *Manson v. Braithwaite* (1977) and therefore suffer from the same problems. The *Telfaire* instructions, as is typical of others as well, fail to tell jurors *how* the factors are related to accuracy. Thus, it is perhaps no surprise that they appear to function more to produce juror skepticism of eyewitnesses than to help them discriminate between accurate and inaccurate witnesses (see Devenport et al., 2009 for a review).

Notwithstanding the common use of imprecise and/or incomplete instructions, there have been attempts to improve them. The Utah Model Jury Instruction CR404, for example, is a substantial improvement over the *Telfaire* instructions with regard to comprehensiveness, and the instructions set forth by the California Supreme Court in *People v. Wright* (1987) improve upon the *Telfaire* instructions in both precision and completeness. Unlike others, the *Wright* instructions do inform jurors of the nature of the effects of the factors, rather than leaving jurors to guess how to apply them. Still, though the completeness and precision of instructions such as those of Utah or California have improved, they are not yet comprehensive or sufficiently precise. Additional possibilities are posted at the website EyeID, which has a comprehensive collection of jury instructions.

To our knowledge, however, there has yet to be sufficient research examining the effectiveness of alternatives to the *Telfaire* instructions in producing greater juror discrimination between accurate and inaccurate witnesses rather than simply enhancing the skepticism of witnesses. Further, the extent to which improved instructions are used is unknown. We have worked on many cases, even in California (where the *Wright* instructions might be expected to be standard), involving woefully incomplete, imprecise, and misleading (often nonstandard) instructions. For the foreseeable future, many, if not most, jurors across the United States will be offered subpar "help" from jury instructions.

And All of This Is Common Sense....

The final reflection of the law's beliefs concerning witness performance is the common objection to the admission of testimony by eyewitness scientists that such testimony is not beyond the common knowledge of jurors and is therefore unnecessary and potentially prejudicial (see Bailey & Mecklenburg, 2009; Epstein, 2009; Read & Desmarais, 2009). Such objections are clearly based on both underestimation of the available science and overestimation of common knowledge.

CONCLUSIONS AND POLICY RECOMMENDATIONS

After declaring the law an ass, Charles Dickens' Mr. Bumble from *Oliver Twist* went on to say, "the worst I wish the law is that his eye may be opened by experience—by experience" (Dickens, Mitchell, Calder, & Cardwell, 1970, p. 489). But if its eye could be opened, what should the law then see and do?

First and foremost, the legal system would see that the assumptions upon which it has been operating are woefully incomplete and often wrong, and that it must finally put aside the pervasive but clearly mistaken idea that determinants of witness accuracy are a matter of common sense. If nothing else, the forgoing discussion has made it clear that eyewitness identifications are generally less reliable than is commonly assumed; that determinants of accuracy are more complex than is commonly recognized, generally poorly understood (in some respects even by eyewitness scientists), and incorrectly applied in actual cases; and that the subjective reports given by witnesses regarding the many variables that might affect accuracy are often inaccurate and incomplete.

Second, the established upper limits on the likelihood of a correct identification of a once-seen stranger clearly suggest that eyewitness identification alone cannot meet the standard of proof beyond a reasonable doubt. A number of researchers have surveyed members of the public or the judiciary to determine what probability of guilt constitutes, in their minds, beyond a reasonable doubt. These studies have demonstrated that there is wide individual variability in probability standards, that mean probability estimates tend to fall in the 80%–99% range, and that they can be affected by judges' instructions regarding the meaning of reasonable doubt such that they can fall below 70% (a level legal scholars view as unacceptably low; see Dhami, 2008, and Horowitz, 1997, for reviews). The upper limits of eyewitness performance do not appear to approach even the lower bounds of reasonable doubt found in these studies—much less the more stringent boundaries of 90% and above. Therefore, the law should not permit conviction based solely on eyewitness testimony, and instead should require at least one other form of credible evidence to support a conviction.

Third, eyewitness scientists should run parametric studies plotting average accuracy under varying combinations of basic perceptual variables such as lighting, distance, duration of exposure, angle of view, and so on under conditions where the target is present during the identification attempt. Clear and valid methods exist for doing such studies, and they can provide much-needed information on upper limits of accuracy for conditions commonly encountered by eyewitnesses across a variety of cases. Though other factors will affect accuracy in any given case, upper limits on performance will provide a valuable starting point for evaluating the accuracy of the witness at hand.

Fourth, the law should use such parametric work to establish clear guidelines for exclusion of identifications based on witnessing conditions where maximum accuracy fails to meet basic standards for probative value. While some may view the problem of impossible or highly improbable identifications as rare, offering such arguments as offered by prosecutors Bailey and Mecklenburg (2009) that "in the real world, witnesses who are unreliable because they did not see or remember enough, or who had poor viewing conditions or have some bias, are weeded out" (p. 225), our own experiences as expert witnesses soundly contradict this view. We have served in cases where witnesses have made identifications when they viewed the perpetrator from distances ranging from 100 to 500 feet, more often than not at night, sometimes only from a side angle with a hoodie covering the hair and most of the side of the face, or with only the eyes visible because the face was fully masked. They claim that they will never forget the eyes but then make their identifications from full-face photos. These and other situations commonly involving real-life witnesses are, indeed, situations where identification accuracy will fall below chance.

Fifth, the legal system more generally must be willing to admit to the magnitude of the problem with eyewitness identification accuracy, and to recognize and incorporate the available science into its understanding of contributors to inaccuracy as well as of how to recognize inaccuracy.

Sixth, as frequently recommended by eyewitness scientists (e.g., Wells, Memon, & Penrod, 2006; Wells & Quinlivan, 2009), the legal system must be willing to cast aside inappropriate procedures or criteria for rulings and to grapple with how to guard more effectively against the production of inaccurate identifications through biasing police procedures, as well as how to minimize the contribution of inaccurate identifications to wrongful convictions of the innocent. This would entail appellate courts establishing sufficiently suggestive police procedures as grounds for automatic exclusion to discourage continued use of such practices, as well as establishing evidence-based criteria for deeming likely witness accuracy sufficiently low to prompt exclusion (independent of the issue of suggestive procedures). Further, it would entail increased receptivity and training of law enforcement officers regarding the use of nonbiasing procedures.

Finally, the law must continually evolve in response to developing knowledge. Though eyewitness science has offered a wealth of relevant knowledge of how, why, and under what circumstances eyewitness accuracy tends to fail, the law has remained largely unresponsive to this information. Though available scientific knowledge remains admittedly incomplete, new findings regularly add important information that should be incorporated more readily than has been the case in the past.

REFERENCES

Bailey, P. J., & Mecklenburg, S. H. (2009). The prosecutor's perspective on eyewitness experts in the courtroom. In B. L. Cutler (Ed.), *Expert testimony on the psychology of eyewitness identification* (pp. 223-248). New York: Oxford University Press.

Behrman, B. W., & Davey, S. L. (2001). Eyewitness identification in actual criminal cases: An archival analysis. *Law and Human Behavior, 25*(5), 475-491.

Behrman, B. W., & Richards, R. E. (2005). Suspect/foil identification in actual crimes and in the laboratory: A reality monitoring analysis. *Law and Human Behavior, 29*(3), 279-301.

Brainerd, C. J., & Reyna, V. F. (2005). *The science of false memory.* New York: Oxford University Press.

Bruce, V. (1982). Changing faces—visual and non-visual coding processes in face recognition. *British Journal of Psychology, 73*, 105-116.

Bruce, V. (2009). Remembering faces. In J. R. Brockmole (Ed.), *The visual world in memory* (pp. 66-88). New York: Psychology Press.

Bruce, V., Henderson, Z., Greenwood, K., Hancock, P. J. B., Burton, A. M., & Miller, P. (1999). Verification of face identities from images captured on video. *Journal of Experimental Psychology: Applied, 5*, 339-360.

Burton, A. M., Miller, P., Bruce, V., Hancock, P. J. B., & Henderson, Z. (2001). Human and automatic face recognition: A comparison across image format. *Vision Research, 41*, 3185-3195.

Burton, A. M., & Jenkins, R. (2011). Unfamiliar face perception. In A. J. Calder, G. Rhodes, M. H. Johnson & J. V. Haxby (Eds.), *The oxford handbook of face perception.* New York, NY: Oxford University Press.

Clancy, S. (2005). *Abducted: How people come to believe they were kidnapped by aliens.* Cambridge, MA: Harvard University Press.

Clark, S. E., Howell, R. T., & Davey, S. L. (2008). Regularities in eyewitness identification. *Law and Human Behavior, 32*(3), 187-218.

Cook, M. B., Kwak, J. Y., Hoffman, D. D., & Loftus, E. F. (2010). False memory for faces: How misinformation disrupts face identification. Unpublished manuscript, University of California, Irvine.

Cutler, B. L. (Ed.). (2009). *Expert testimony on the psychology of eyewitness identification.* New York: Oxford University Press.

Cutler, B. L., Penrod, S. D., & Dexter, H. R. (1990). Juror sensitivity to eyewitness identification evidence. *Law and Human Behavior, 14*, 185-191.

Davis, D., & Follette, W. C. (2001). Foibles of witness memory for traumatic/high profile events. *Journal of Air Law and Commerce, 66*(4), 1421–1549.

Davis, D., & Loftus, E. F. (in press). The dangers of eyewitnesses for the innocent: Learning from the past and projecting into the age of social media. *New England Law Review*.

Davis, D., & Loftus, E. F. (2007). Internal and external sources of misinformation in adult witness memory. In M. P. Toglia, J. D. Read, D. F. Ross & R. C. L. Lindsay (Eds.), *The handbook of eyewitness psychology, Vol I: Memory for events* (pp. 195–237). Mahwah, NJ US: Lawrence Erlbaum Associates Publishers.

De Jong, M., Wagenaar, W. A., Wolters, G., & Verstijnen, I. M. (2005). Familiar face recognition as a function of distance and illumination: A practical tool for use in the courtroom. *Psychology, Crime & Law, 11*(1), 87–97.

Deffenbacher, K., Bornstein, B. H., McGorty, E. K., & Penrod, S. D. (2008). Forgetting the once-seen face: Estimating the strength of an eyewitness's memory representation. *Journal of Experimental Psychology: Applied, 14*(2), 139–150.

Devenport, J. L., Kimbrough, C. D., & Cutler, B. L. (2009). Effectiveness of traditional safeguards against erroneous conviction arising from mistaken eyewitness identification. In B. L. Cutler (Ed.), *Expert testimony on the psychology of eyewitness identification* (pp. 51–68). New York: Oxford University Press.

Dhami, M. K. (2008). On measuring quantitative interpretations of reasonable doubt. *Journal of Experimental Psychology: Applied, 14*(4), 353–363.

Dickens, C., Mitchell, C., Calder, A., & Cardwell, M. (1970). Great expectations (Charles Dickens Complete Works (Centennial Edition). Edito-Service S. A.

Epstein, J. (2009). Expert testimony: Legal standards for admissibility. In B. L. Cutler (Ed.), *Expert testimony on the psychology of eyewitness identification* (pp. 69–89). New York: Oxford University Press.

Flowe, H. D., Finklea, K., M., & Ebbesen, E. B. (2009). Limitations of expert psychology testimony on eyewitness identification. In B. L. Cutler (Ed.), *Expert testimony on the psychology of eyewitness identification* (pp. 201–221). New York: Oxford University Press.

Garrett, B. L. (2011). *Convicting the innocent: Where criminal prosecutions go wrong*. Cambridge, MA: Harvard University Press

Hastie, R. K., & Dawes, R. M. (2010). *Rational choice in an uncertain world: The psychology of judgment and decision making*. Thousand Oaks, CA: Sage.

Henderson, Z., Bruce, V., & Burton, A. M. (2001). Matching the faces of robbers captured on video. *Applied Cognitive Psychology, 15*, 445–464.

Horowitz, I. A. (1997). Reasonable doubt instructions: Commonsense justice and standard of proof. *Psychology, Public Policy, and Law, 3*(2–3), 285–302.

Horry, R., Memon, A., Wright, D. B., & Milne, R. (2011). Predictors of eyewitness identification decisions from video lineups in England: A field study. *Law and Human Behavior*.

Kemp, R., Towell, N., & Pike, G. (1997). When seeing should not be believing: Photographs, credit cards and fraud. *Applied Cognitive Psychology, 11*, 211–222.

Leippe, M. R., & Eisenstadt, D. (2007). Eyewitness confidence and the confidence-accuracy relationship in memory for people. In R. C. L. Lindsay, D. F. Ross, J. D. Read, & M. P. Toglia (Eds.), *The handbook of eyewitness psychology, Vol. II: Memory for people* (pp. 377–425). Mahway, NJ: Erlbaum.

Leippe, M. R., & Eisenstadt, D. (2009). The influence of eyewitness expert testimony on jurors' beliefs and judgments. In B. L. Cutler (Ed.), *Expert testimony on the psychology of eyewitness identification* (pp. 169–199). New York: Oxford University Press.

Lindsay, R. C. L., Ross, D. F., Read, J. D., & Toglia, M. P. (Eds.). (2007). *Handbook of eyewitness psychology, Vol II: Memory for people*. Mahwah, NJ: Erlbaum.

Lindsay, R. C. L., Semmler, C., Weber, N., Brewer, N., & Lindsay, M. R. (2008). How variations in distance affect eyewitness reports and identification accuracy. *Law and Human Behavior, 32*(6), 526–535.

Lindsay, R. C., Wells, G. L., & O'Connor, F. J. (1989). Mock-juror belief of accurate and inaccurate eyewitnesses: A replication and extension. *Law and Human Behavior, 13*(3), 333–339.

Loftus, E. F. (2005). Planting misinformation in the human mind: A 30-year investigation of the malleability of memory. *Learning & Memory, 12*, 361–366.

Loftus, E. F., & Davis, D. (2006). Recovered memories. *Annual Review of Clinical Psychology, 2*, 469–498.

Loftus, G. R., & Harley, E. M. (2005). Why is it easier to identify someone close than far away? *Psychonomic Bulletin & Review, 12*(1), 43–65.

Manson v. Brathwaite (432 U.S. 98 1977).

Memon, A., Havard, C., Clifford, B., Gabbert, F., & Watt, M. (2011). A field evaluation of the VIPER system: A new technique for eliciting eyewitness identification evidence. *Psychology, Crime & Law, 17*(8), 711–729.

Megreya, A. M., & Burton, A. M. (2006). Unfamiliar faces aren't faces: Evidence from a matching task. *Memory and Cognition, 34*, 865–876.

Megreya, A. M., & Burton, A. M. (2007). Hits and false positives in face matching: A familiarity-based dissociation. *Perception & Psychophysics, 69*(7), 1175–1184.

Megreya, A. M., & Burton, A. M. (2008). Matching faces to photographs: Poor performance in eyewitness memory (without the memory). *Journal of Experimental Psychology: Applied, 14*(4), 364–372.

Munsterberg, H. (1908). *On the witness stand: Essays on psychology and crime*. New York: The McClure Company.

Neil v. Biggers (409 U.S. 188 1972).

People v. Wright, 43 Cal.3d 399 (1987).

Perry v. New Hampshire, 565 U.S. (2012).

Read, J. D., & Desmarais, S. L. (2009). Expert psychology testimony on eyewitness identification: A matter of common sense? In B. L. Cutler (Ed.), *Expert testimony on the psychology of eyewitness identification* (pp. 115–141). New York: Oxford University Press.

Slater, A. (1994). Identification parades: A scientific evaluation *Police Research Award Scheme*. London: Police Research Group, Home Office.

Steblay, N., Dysart, J., Fulero, S., & Lindsay, R. C. L. (2003). Eyewitness accuracy rates in police showup and lineup presentations: A meta-analytic comparison. *Law and Human Behavior, 27*(5), 523–540.

Steblay, N. K., Dysart, J. E., & Wells, G. L. (2011). Seventy-two tests of the sequential lineup superiority effect: A meta-analysis and policy discussion. *Psychology, Public Policy, and Law, 17*(1), 99–139.

Stevens, S. S. (1957). On the psychophysical law. *Psychological Review, 64*, 153–181.

Stinson, B., Devenport, J. L., Cutler, B. L., & Kravitz, D. A. (1997). How effective is the motion-to-suppress safeguard? Judges' perceptions of the suggestiveness and fairness of biased lineup procedures. *Journal of Applied Psychology, 82*, 211–220.

Toglia, M. P., Read, J. D., Ross, D. F., & Lindsay, R. C. L. (Eds.). (2007). *Handbook of eyewitness psychology, Vol I: Memory for events*. Mahwah, NJ: Erlbaum.

United States v. Telfaire, 469 F.2d 552, 558-59 (D.C.Cir. 1972).

Valentine, T., Pickering, A., & Darling, S. (2003). Characteristics of eyewitness identification that predict the outcome of real lineups. *Applied Cognitive Psychology, 17*(8), 969–993.

Wagenaar, W. A., & van der Schrier, J. H. (1996). Face recognition as a function of distance and illumination: A practical tool for use in the courtroom. *Psychology, Crime & Law, 2*(4), 321–332.

Weist, W. M., & Bell, B. (1985). Steven's exponent for psychophysical scaling of perceived, remembered, and inferred distance. *Psychological Bulletin, 98*, 457–470.

Wells, G. L., Ferguson, T. J., & Lindsay, R. C. (1981). The tractability of eyewitness confidence and its implications for triers of fact. *Journal of Applied Psychology, 66*(6), 688–696.

Wells, G. L., & Leippe, M. R. (1981). How do triers of fact infer the accuracy of eyewitness identifications? Using memory for peripheral detail can be misleading. *Journal of Applied Psychology, 66*, 682–687.

Wells, G. L., Lindsay, R. C., & Ferguson, T. J. (1979). Accuracy, confidence, and juror perceptions in eyewitness identification. *Journal of Applied Psychology, 64*(4), 440–448.

Wells, G. L., Lindsay, R. C., & Tousignant, J. P. (1980). Effects of expert psychological advice on human performance in judging the validity of eyewitness testimony. *Law and Human Behavior, 4*, 275–285.

Wells, G. L., Memon, A., & Penrod, S. D. (2006). Eyewitness evidence: Improving its probative value. *Psychological Science in the Public Interest, 7*(2), 45–75.

Wells, G. L., & Quinlivan, D. S. (2009). Suggestive eyewitness identification procedures and the Supreme Court's reliability test in light of eyewitness science: 30 years later. *Law and Human Behavior, 33*(1), 1–24.

Wigmore, J. H. (1974, revised by Chadbourn, J. H.). *Evidence in trials at common law*. Boston: Little, Brown.

Witmer, B. G., & Kline, P. B. (1998). Judging perceived and transversed distance in virtual environments. *Presence, 7*, 144–167.

Wright, D. B., & McDaid, A. T. (1996). Comparing system and estimator variables using data from real line-ups. *Applied Cognitive Psychology, 10*(1), 75–84.

Wright, D. B., & Skagerberg, E. M. (2007). Postidentification feedback affects real eyewitnesses. *Psychological Science, 18*(2), 172–178.

3

Lineup Procedures in Eyewitness Identification

SCOTT D. GRONLUND, CHARLES A. GOODSELL, AND SHANNON M. ANDERSEN

LINEUP PROCEDURES IN EYEWITNESS IDENTIFICATION

On September 2, 2010, Ohio Governor Ted Strickland commuted Kevin Keith's sentence. Two weeks short of execution, Keith now will spend the rest of his life in prison unless his attorney, Rachel Troutman, can get him a new trial and prove his innocence. Keith had a motive in 1994 for the killing of Marichell Chatman, Marchae Chatman, and Linda Chatman and the shooting of three more people: A relative of the victims was a police informant for a prior crime committed by Keith and several accomplices. But Keith also had an alibi. Moreover, much of the evidence originally used to convict Keith is thought to be problematic. This includes how one of the eyewitnesses, Richard Warren, came to know the name *Kevin Keith*, whether a bullet casing from the murder weapon was found at a location where Keith admitted to picking up his girlfriend or was found several miles away from that location, and whether a partial license plate imprint in the snow matches a car to which Keith had access.[1] If Ms. Troutman can convince a jury that this evidence is faulty, the only evidence remaining is the eyewitness evidence.

There were three eyewitnesses. Seven-year-old Quanita Reeves was shot along with her 4-year-old brother, Quinton. Quanita did not identify Keith, stating that Daddy's friend Bruce shot her. Quanita Reeves' nonidentification provided evidence of Keith's innocence (see Clark, Howell, & Davey, 2008). A neighbor, Nancy Smathers, told the police at the scene of the crime that she could not make an identification. And she did not, until she saw Keith on television after he was arrested. Ms. Smathers' identification should have been discounted because she likely misattributed her familiarity with Keith's lineup photo to the crime rather than to viewing him on television. That leaves only Richard Warren. Warren was shot multiple times and, once the perpetrator fled the scene, heroically took off after him and was shot again. Once his condition was stabilized, Warren chose Keith from a lineup. We shall use the lineup identification of Kevin Keith by Richard Warren to frame our discussion.

Lineup procedures involve the retrieval phase of memory. Before discussing lineup procedures, we briefly review the encoding and maintenance phases of memory that precede the retrieval phase. In the case of a crime, the events to be encoded include the face of the perpetrator, a description (face, clothing, gait, voice, etc.), the weapon, and other relevant details (e.g., where the crime took place, who else was present). In such a situation, as in most situations, there is more information available than can be encoded, given our limited cognitive capacity (Engle, Kane, & Tuholski, 1999; Simons & Ambinder, 2005). Other factors present during this particular crime also harmed encoding, including stress (Deffenbacher, Bornstein, Penrod, & McGorty, 2004), a focus on the weapon (Steblay, 1992), cross-race identifications (Meissner & Brigham, 2001), and a disguise or hiding of the perpetrator's appearance (Cutler, Penrod, & Martens, 1987). Warren's and Smathers' descriptions of the perpetrator ("big black guy" and "husky black man," respectively) reflected the resulting poor encoding.

Once an event is encoded, it must be maintained throughout a retention interval. Two primary changes happen to an event during this period. One is that the encoded event weakens. The other is that the memory for the original event can be modified. A suggestion by another witness, the police, or the media, or an inference made by the witness, can modify or influence memory for an existing event (see Schacter, 1999, 2002). There are countless studies that demonstrate this phenomenon (e.g., Loftus, 1997; Loftus & Ketcham, 1994; Loftus & Palmer, 1974). The issues surrounding the maintenance of a memory revolve around how Warren acquired the first name *Kevin* and the last name *Keith*, but neither is of primary interest here. Instead, our focus is on a lineup of faces and how it is constructed, the instructions given to a witness, who administers the lineup, and how it is presented. A lineup is a system variable (Wells, 1978) because how it is conducted is under the control of the criminal justice system. Wells and Olson (2003) divided system variable research on lineups into four categories: content, instructions, behavioral influence, and presentation method. We will review each of these and update the best practices for conducting a lineup (Wells et al., 1998).

LINEUP CONTENT

A proper lineup should contain a single suspect along with some number of nonsuspect or filler faces. In the real world, law enforcement is uncertain about a suspect's guilt or innocence. Therefore, we mimic this situation in the laboratory by creating two types of lineups: perpetrator-present lineups that contain the guilty suspect and perpetrator-absent lineups that replace the guilty suspect with an innocent suspect. Examining both types is crucial because procedural manipulations that decrease the likelihood of a false identification of an innocent suspect also may decrease the likelihood of correctly identifying a guilty suspect (Clark & Godfrey, 2009).

There are two ways in which filler faces can be chosen. Suspect-matched fillers are selected based on their physical resemblance to a suspect. This results in different fillers in perpetrator-present and perpetrator-absent lineups because these lineups include different suspects (guilty or innocent suspect, respectively). Using a suspect-matched strategy may result in a bias toward an innocent suspect (Clark & Tunnicliff, 2001; Navon, 1992). The problem is that the innocent suspect matches the description of the perpetrator, but the fillers matched to that innocent suspect may not. Rather, the fillers may approximate exemplars arrayed around a prototype. Consequently, the innocent suspect stands out because he or she is the prototype (e.g., Posner & Keele, 1968) of the lineup.

An alternative strategy is to select fillers according to whether they match a witness' description of the suspect. This method has been championed as a better alternative to the suspect-matched strategy because a suspect will not stand out relative to the fillers (Malpass, Tredoux, & McQuiston-Surrett, 2007). Some research showed that using description-matched lineups increased witness accuracy (Tunnicliff & Clark, 2000; Wells, Rydell, & Seelau, 1993), but Valentine, Darling, and Memon (2007) found that the filler selection strategy did not have a significant effect on lineup performance (see also Clark & Godfrey, 2009).

There is no clear-cut recommendation to make regarding how to select fillers. Suspect-matched fillers can backfire against the innocent suspect (Clark & Tunnicliff, 2001). But a witness's description of the suspect may not be detailed enough to construct a reasonable lineup. The case of Kevin Keith is one such example. Police constructed a lineup of men who were black and big. But Keith's photo was cropped so that he was clearly the biggest man. He also stood out as the only bald man in the lineup. The ultimate choice regarding how to select fillers may depend on the level of detail in a description. Valentine et al. (2007) could have examined this question because they constructed different lineups for each participant based on his or her description. Of interest would be whether lineup identification was better for those participants who gave a more detailed description. The problem, however, is that having a detailed description likely is confounded with having a better memory for the perpetrator. What is needed is to match participants by the level of detail in their description, and then randomly assign participants to view lineups that contain fillers that match the entire description or lineups that contain fillers that match only a portion of the description.

If we select fillers that match all versus only a portion of a description, we are modifying the fairness of a lineup. We measure the fairness of a lineup as follows: Naive participants with no knowledge of the crime are asked to choose the likely perpetrator from the lineup. Lineup fairness—the effective size of the lineup—is based on the proportion of these participants who choose the guilty suspect relative to what would be expected by chance (Malpass & Lindsay, 1999). The more reasonable competitors there are, the fairer is the lineup and the greater its effective size. For example, in the Kevin Keith lineup, a naive participant given the description should choose at random because every lineup member should match the description. But in fact, informal evaluation showed that over 80% of the naive participants shown the lineup picked Keith, making the effective size of Keith's lineup approximately 1.0. Clark and Godfrey (2009) showed that biased lineups (i.e., lineups containing few fillers that are reasonable competitors) produced fewer accurate identifications.

The current consensus is that description-matched fillers are preferred because they allow for greater heterogeneity among fillers; a suspect-matched approach runs the risk of filling a lineup with clones (Wells et al. 1998). However, the evidence on this point is still incomplete. But the evidence does indicate that a more accurate identification will result from a lineup that contains multiple individuals who are reasonable competitors for the suspect. In other words, the suspect should not unduly stand out. Step 1 is complete—we have constructed a fair lineup; the next step is to determine how to instruct the witness prior to viewing the lineup.

INSTRUCTIONS

Witnesses may feel it is their duty to pick someone from a lineup and may consider it a failure when they cannot. That is why we must instruct witnesses carefully so that they do not assume that the perpetrator is always present and therefore they should always choose. Malpass and Devine (1981) had participants observe a staged theft followed by a perpetrator-present or perpetrator-absent lineup. Participants received either biased or unbiased instructions. Those in the biased instruction condition were told that the experimenter believed the perpetrator was in the lineup and were given a response sheet that did *not* contain an option to indicate that the perpetrator was absent. Those in the unbiased instruction condition were informed that the perpetrator might or might not be present, and their response sheet contained the option to respond that the perpetrator was not present. The biased instructions led to a high (erroneous) choosing rate in the perpetrator-absent condition compared to the unbiased instructions.

Subsequent research indicated that biased instructions can lead to increased choosing of the innocent suspect from a perpetrator-absent lineup without decreasing correct identifications from a perpetrator-present lineup (Cutler et al., 1987; O'Rourke, Penrod, Cutler, & Stuve, 1989; see the meta-analysis by Steblay, 1997). However, this conclusion was challenged by Clark (2005), who demonstrated that this asymmetric pattern captured in the Steblay (1997) meta-analysis was due to a ceiling effect in several studies (the correct identification rate was extremely high in the unbiased conditions and thus had no room to increase) and the inclusion of an unpublished study identified as an outlier. After eliminating these studies from consideration, Clark concluded that providing unbiased instructions decreased choosing rates in general, resulting in fewer false identifications of innocent suspects but also fewer correct identifications of guilty suspects.

If instructions affect choosing rates but not identification accuracy, some might argue that it does not matter how we instruct witnesses. That would be an incorrect conclusion. Instructions would not matter only if the increased choosing rate gets spread out across all lineup members. However, biased instructions are a big problem if the bias is directed at a particular individual. In the Kevin Keith case the detective gave Richard Warren biased instructions, telling him to "pick him out." Because Keith stood out in the lineup, the use of biased instructions was problematic, as evidenced by the high proportion of naive participants who selected Keith in our informal evaluation.

We now have described how to construct a lineup in which the suspect does not unduly stand out. We have instructed the witness that the perpetrator may or may not be present. Does it matter who administers this lineup to the witness? We turn to that question next.

BEHAVIORAL INFLUENCES

Lineup administrators can influence a witness. Phillips, McAuliff, Kovera, and Cutler (1999) had participants play the role of witness or lineup administrator. Witnesses viewed a staged crime involving two perpetrators and later made two separate identifications from perpetrator-absent lineups. The lineups were presented simultaneously or sequentially; an observer was present or absent. Phillips et al. hypothesized that an observer might limit the biasing influence of the administrator. False identifications of the innocent suspect were highest when the lineup administrator knew the identity of the suspect; however, this occurred only in the sequential lineup when an observer was present. No differences were found for the simultaneous lineup. Phillips et al. concluded that having an observer present made the lineup administrator feel pressure to get a suspect identification and that it was easier to do this in the sequential lineup.

Greathouse and Kovera (2009) had witnesses view a mock crime. Lineup administrators delivered biased or unbiased instructions, presented sequential or simultaneous lineups, and were informed or not informed of the identity of the suspect. All administrators were told that they would receive $20 if their witness chose the suspect. Results showed that identifications made when the lineup administrator did not have knowledge of the suspect were more diagnostic of guilt than when they did have knowledge. That is, the ratio of guilty to innocent suspect identifications was greater (Wells & Lindsay, 1980). The least diagnostic decisions occurred when administrator knowledge of the suspect was coupled with biased instructions and simultaneous lineups.

One of the recommendations for conducting lineups proposed by Wells et al. (1998) was that a lineup administrator should have no knowledge of who the suspect is. However, double-blind lineup administration will not eliminate all administrator influences that affect witness choosing. Clark, Marshall, and Rosenthal (2009) had participants view a staged crime and, following a short distractor task, a lineup. Lineup administrators, who were blind to the presence of the perpetrator and the position of the suspect, gave one of three instructions to a witness. In the no-influence condition the lineup administrator remained silent while the witness viewed the lineup. In the subtle-influence condition the lineup administrator waited for 12 seconds and then (assuming that the witness had not already chosen) made innocuous statements like "Take your time" or "There's no rush." Finally, in the similarity-influence condition the lineup administrator waited for 12 seconds and asked the witness if any lineup member resembled the perpetrator more than any other lineup member. Note that there was never any direct declaration that the suspect was present or which position he was in. Witnesses in the similarity-influence condition showed an increased choosing rate for both perpetrator-present and perpetrator-absent lineups relative to those in the no-influence condition, consistent with an increased willingness to choose. Witnesses in the subtle-influence condition exhibited increased choosing in the perpetrator-absent but not the perpetrator-present condition. As a result, the false but not the correct identification rate increased, harming performance. Also of concern was the fact that the witnesses generally did not notice that the administrator had influenced them. In sum, a lineup administrator can influence how an eyewitness chooses from a lineup. Double-blind administration will eliminate most but not all sources of influence related to the identification decision. However, double-blind administration will eliminate the influence that takes place after a decision has been made—postidentification feedback.

Wells and Bradfield (1998) were the first to demonstrate that providing feedback to a witness after a lineup selection can affect retrospective judgments about the witnessing experience. Participants viewed a store security camera video and subsequently were shown a perpetrator-absent lineup and told that that their task was to identify the perpetrator. As a consequence, everyone chose and no one made a correct decision. The experimenter then either told the witness that his or her choice was correct, or incorrect, or said nothing. Those who were told they were correct (i.e., received confirming feedback) displayed enhanced confidence in their choice, judged that they had a better view of the perpetrator, and were more willing to testify in court compared to those who received disconfirming or no feedback.

This was problematic for two reasons. First, a police officer could unintentionally influence the witnesses' belief in their memory/choice simply by indicating that they had chosen the suspect. Second, research shows that eyewitness testimony is one of the most powerful forms of evidence a juror can consider, and this is especially true if a witness displays confidence in his or her testimony (Cutler, Penrod, & Dexter, 1990; Fox & Walters, 1986; Wells, Ferguson, & Lindsay, 1981). Thus, if a witness who has chosen an innocent suspect is given confirming feedback, the suspect is in greater jeopardy of being falsely convicted.

The postidentification feedback effect is a robust finding (see the meta-analysis by Douglass & Steblay, 2006) and has been found with children (Hafstad, Memon, & Logie, 2004), young and older eyewitnesses (Neuschatz et al., 2005), earwitnesses (Quinlivan et al., 2009), after a 1-week delay (Neuschatz et al., 2005), and, in some cases, even persists when the witness is warned about the influence of the feedback (Lampinen, Scott, Pratt, Leding, & Arnal, 2007). Most importantly, the effect has been found in real eyewitnesses (Wright & Skagerberg, 2007). Wells and Bradfield (1998) demonstrated that requiring a witness to think about the witnessing experience (i.e., his or her view, certainty, confidence) after the identification but before receiving feedback mitigated the postidentification feedback effect. They called this the *confidence prophylactic effect*. However, Neuschatz et al. (2007) showed that the prophylactic effect disappeared after a 1-week interval.

We now know how to construct a lineup, how to deliver instructions, and who should administer the lineup. But we have yet to consider the two primary ways in which the members of the lineup are presented: all at once or one at a time. The next section begins with an overview of research comparing simultaneous and sequential lineup presentation methods. That will be followed by consideration of the role of theory in adjudicating between these two presentation methods. Finally, we will consider several alternative methods for conducting lineups and evaluating the memory of an eyewitness.

PRESENTATION METHODS

Simultaneous and Sequential Lineups

There are two primary means by which lineups are conducted. In a simultaneous lineup, all lineup members are presented at once and only one decision is required: Which, if any of these individuals, is the perpetrator? In a sequential lineup, lineup members are presented one at a time. A witness must make a decision about the first one ("yes" or "no": is this the perpetrator?) before viewing the second one. If the witness rejects the first individual, that individual cannot subsequently be chosen. The lineup typically terminates with the first "yes" response. Also, when the lineup begins, a witness does not know how many individuals will be viewed. McQuiston-Surrett, Malpass, and Tredoux (2006) pointed out that these two lineup types differ by more than just method of presentation. A witness knows how many individuals need to be considered in the simultaneous lineup, but that is not known in the sequential lineup. Also, only one decision is made in the simultaneous lineup, and an explicit reject decision is made. The sequential lineup requires a series of decisions (unless the first individual is selected) and a reject decision results from a witness's not having chosen anyone when the lineup terminates.

Lindsay and Wells (1985; Wells, 1984) argued that simultaneous lineups tend to induce relative judgments. That is, there is a tendency to compare lineup members to one another and choose the one who most closely resembles the perpetrator. This is an acceptable strategy if the guilty suspect is in the lineup, but obviously it is a problem if an innocent suspect who resembles the perpetrator is in the lineup. Sequential lineups are thought to be more likely to induce absolute judgments. An absolute judgment involves a comparison of each lineup member to the witness's memory for the perpetrator. If a match is sufficiently strong, that lineup member is selected.

Most lineups in the United States are simultaneous lineups (Wogalter, Malpass, & McQuiston, 2004). But there is a movement toward conducting lineups in a sequential manner because they purportedly enhance the accuracy of eyewitness identification evidence. The states of New Jersey, North Carolina, Ohio, and Wisconsin conduct sequential lineups, as do the cities of Boston, Dallas, Denver, Minneapolis/St. Paul, and Tampa, among others. California, Georgia, Texas, New Mexico, West Virginia, and Vermont have considered legislation to make the switch (Jonsson, 2007). The merits of sequential lineups have made it into the textbooks (e.g., Esgate & Groome, 2005; Goldstein, 2008; Reisberg, 2001; Robinson-Riegler & Robinson-Riegler, 2004). The superiority of sequential lineups even has reached the popular culture. In Robert Ludlum's novel *The Ambler Warning*, one of the characters talks about the dangers of relative judgment. This character goes on to state, "Now, there's a way to elicit what an eyewitness saw without that distortion: you do it seriatim. Show them photographs of people, not at the same time, but one after another" (Ludlum, 2005, pp. 570–571). Does conducting lineups seriatim or sequentially really enhance witness accuracy? Is there truly a performance advantage for sequential lineups?

Before addressing these questions, we need to define what we mean by a *sequential advantage*. To do so, we need to consider the costs and benefits of conducting a sequential lineup. As we shall see, sequential lineups produce more conservative choosing than do simultaneous lineups. That means that the benefits of reduced false identifications in sequential perpetrator-absent lineups are balanced by the costs of reduced correct identifications in sequential perpetrator-present lineups. We call this the *sequential shift*, and it is commonly observed. However, a true sequential *advantage* requires that the benefits outpace the costs (Clark & Godfrey, 2009). But to further complicate matters, the utilities assigned to benefits (reduced false identifications) and costs (missed correct identifications) are not equal if it is "better that ten guilty persons escape than that one innocent suffer" (Blackstone, 1769, p. 352). Consideration of the unequal weighting of costs versus benefits moves the decision about what lineup presentation method is best out of the laboratory and into the policy domain (Malpass, 2006) and beyond the scope of this chapter. Consequently, our focus in this chapter will remain on a numerical sequential advantage that assumes an equal weighting of costs and benefits, and the question we answer is whether the benefits outpace the costs. We contrast that with the decision that policymakers must make, which we call an *evaluative sequential advantage*.

Lindsay and Wells (1985) had participants view a mock crime and subsequently try to pick the perpetrator out of a perpetrator-present or a perpetrator-absent lineup. Lineup members were presented simultaneously or sequentially. Lindsay and Wells found a slight decrease in the correct identification rate in the perpetrator-present lineup from .58 (simultaneous) to .50 (sequential) but a larger decrease in the false identification rate in the perpetrator-absent lineup (selecting the innocent suspect) from .43 (simultaneous) to .17 (sequential). Most importantly, the conditional probability of a guilty suspect selection (i.e., given that the witness chose a suspect, what was the probability that the suspect was guilty?) favored the sequential lineup. Since that first study, others have found similar results, culminating in a meta-analysis by Steblay, Dysart, Fulero, and Lindsay (2001) that concluded that sequential lineups were superior. Steblay, Dysart, and Wells (2011) recently updated that meta-analysis and reached the same conclusion.

But the move to sequential lineups has its critics (e.g., Malpass, Tredoux, & McQuiston-Surrett, 2009; McQuiston-Surrett et al., 2006; Valentine et al., 2007), and questions have been raised about the robustness of the sequential lineup advantage. Carlson, Gronlund, and Clark (2008) conducted a replication of the study by Lindsay and Wells (1985), with the only change being the selection of an innocent suspect who was less similar to the perpetrator. No sequential advantage materialized. McQuiston-Surrett et al. suggested that the space of possible experiments and possible manipulations exploring simultaneous and sequential lineups might be insufficient: It was possible that studies have been finding similar results (a sequential advantage) because researchers have been conducting similar experiments. This is problematic for a meta-analysis because a meta-analysis can only summarize existing data.

Gronlund, Carlson, Dailey, and Goodsell (2009) completed a large empirical study exploring the robustness of the sequential advantage across a wide range of factors. Over 2,500 participants (recruited online plus a college sample) viewed a mock crime video, completed a short distracter task, and then viewed a single simultaneous or sequential lineup. In addition to varying the lineup type and the presence or absence of the perpetrator, the researchers manipulated the quality of the memory for the perpetrator (good- or poor-quality photograph of the guilty suspect), a good- or poor-matching innocent suspect, three levels of lineup fairness, and the positioning of the suspect in the lineup—second or fifth position in the sequential lineup or top middle or bottom middle position in the simultaneous lineup. They evaluated 24 simultaneous-sequential comparisons, holding lineup fairness and suspect position constant across comparisons. The sequential lineup resulted in superior performance in only 2 of the 24 comparisons; the simultaneous lineup was superior in 3 of the 24 comparisons. Both sequential advantages occurred when the suspect (guilty or innocent) was in the fifth position in the sequential lineup, and all three simultaneous advantages occurred when the suspect was in the second position in the sequential lineup. We will discuss the role suspect position plays in producing a sequential advantage in the "Contributions of Theory" section.

To reiterate, Gronlund et al. (2009) examined the data across a wide range of conditions and found that a sequential advantage was a rare occurrence. Therefore, because a new meta-analysis now will include a wider range of data, it can summarize the state of the research in the field. But Steblay et al. (2011) excluded these data from their meta-analysis. They argued that the

Gronlund et al. data did not meet their inclusion criteria. Their inclusion criteria required either that the guilty suspect needed to be chosen at least 10% more often than the innocent suspect (in either the simultaneous or the sequential lineup) or that the correct rejection rate had to be at least 10% greater than the false rejection rate (in either the simultaneous or the sequential lineup). In the aggregate, the Gronlund et al. data just failed to meet these criteria. But if the purpose of the .10 criterion was to exclude data at or below chance, Clark (in press) showed that the correct versus false suspect identifications in simultaneous and sequential lineups and the correct versus false rejections in simultaneous and sequential lineups all were above chance according to chi-square analyses.

Clark (in press; for more detail see Clark, Gronlund, Carlson, & Goodsell, under review) meta-analyzed 51 comparisons, all of which involved a 2 × 2 fully randomized factorial design (Sequential/Simultaneous × Perpetrator-Present/Absent), were published, and had adult witness/participants. The majority of these tests overlapped those considered by Steblay et al. (2011), although Clark excluded one confounded study, disaggregated tests that had been collapsed over other independent variables, and included several tests that had been excluded. This included six tests from Gronlund et al. (2009: GuiltyStrong paired with InnocentWeak), all of which exceeded Steblay et al.'s .10 performance criterion.

Clark (in press) examined several measures of lineup performance. Many of these measures favored the sequential lineup, but none of these advantages were statistically significant. In contrast, both the correct and false identification rates were significantly reduced by the sequential lineup, consistent with a conservative sequential shift. Also consistent with a sequential shift, an assessment of the decision criterion ($\log(\beta)$) was significantly more conservative for the sequential lineup. The conclusion is clear: The sequential lineup produces a trade-off between correct and false identifications that, based on the lineup performance measures, balance out. Palmer and Brewer (in press) reached the same conclusion using a subset of the data considered by Steblay et al. (2011).

As a result of more conservative choosing in the sequential lineup, the false identification rate is reduced and an innocent suspect in a perpetrator absent lineup is less likely to be put at risk. This is a laudable accomplishment given that faulty eyewitness evidence played a role in over 75% of the 289 DNA exoneration cases to date (http://www.InnocenceProject.org; retrieved March 1, 2012). But there is a cost to this benefit. The reduced willingness to choose from a sequential lineup also results in a reduced correct identification rate. If policymakers believe it is more important to protect the innocent than inculpate the guilty, a sequential shift might be sufficient to favor an evaluative sequential advantage. However, our focus remains on a numerical sequential advantage and whether the benefits outpace the costs.

One factor that has been identified that contributes to creating a sequential advantage is the late placement of the suspect (guilty or innocent) in the sequential lineup. Both of Gronlund et al.'s (2009) sequential advantages were found when the suspect was in position 5 and all three simultaneous advantages were found when the suspect was in position 2. Carlson et al. (2008, Experiment 2) found that the sequential lineup was superior when the suspects were placed in the fifth or sixth position. Two of the three largest sequential lineup advantages found in the literature (Lindsay, Lea, & Fulford, 1991a; Lindsay et al., 1991b)[2] placed the suspect in the eighth position. Perfect, Dennis, and Snell (2007, Experiment 4) compared sequential perpetrator-present lineups with the guilty suspect in position 1 versus position 4. The correct identification rate was marginally better ($p < .07$) when the suspect was placed in position 4.

Gronlund et al. (2009) proposed two possible reasons why performance might improve as the sequential lineup unfolds. One possibility involves decision aspects of the task. After viewing several fillers in the sequential lineup, a witness might shift from making absolute judgments to making relative judgments. Specifically, after viewing and rejecting several lineup members, a witness might begin to compare the match value of the next lineup member to an estimate of the match values of the lineup members viewed so far. If the difference between these two quantities is sufficiently large, a witness would decrease the decision criterion and choose. The second possibility is that participants develop a better memory probe as the lineup unfolds. For example, upon seeing the first lineup member, a witness might decide that the eyes are right but the perpetrator's nose was narrower. Upon rejecting this first lineup member and viewing the next, the witness might develop a better sense of the nose or remember something about face shape, and so on. Goodsell, Gronlund, and Carlson (2010) instantiated these two possibilities in a computational memory model (WITNESS; Clark, 2003). A theory of the underlying memory and decision contributions to eyewitness identification is needed to understand why suspect position plays the role it does in producing a sequential advantage.

Contributions of Theory

In 2008, *Applied Cognitive Psychology* devoted an entire issue to the discussion of eyewitness identification, arguing that there has been an "overemphasis on practical questions, accompanied by a lack of theoretical relevance" (Bornstein & Meissner, 2008, p. 734). Lane and Meissner (2008) argued that the field of eyewitness identification has failed to incorporate what has been learned from basic cognitive and social psychological research and theory. Instead, the field has relied on an ecological or practical perspective. Lane and Meissner agree that real-world application is the goal of most research in this domain but argued that it should be the setting for which theories are tested, not the foundation of research. Clark (2008) stated that the best way to advance our understanding of eyewitness decision making is through the use of formal computational models (see also Wells, 2008). We agree. But before discussing our work on the sequential advantage, we describe the computational model of eyewitness decision making we used, Clark's (2003) WITNESS model. Clark developed the WITNESS model as the first formal model designed for eyewitness identification. It is ideal for this purpose because its parameters are tied directly to key components of the eyewitness task. We will describe how the model represents memory for a perpetrator, how lineups are constructed, and how the model evaluates lineup members and makes decisions.

In WITNESS, faces are represented as vectors of features. These are abstract features and are not meant to represent specific features like the shape of a nose or the color of the eyes. Most memory models make similar representational assumptions. To start, the model creates a perpetrator, which is a 100-item vector of features. Memory is not perfect; therefore, the degree of overlap between the perpetrator and the memory for the perpetrator is governed by the parameter a. Each feature of the perpetrator vector is encoded correctly into memory with probability a or replaced with a random feature with probability $1-a$. The better the encoding, the higher the value of a, the more the memory for the perpetrator resembles the actual perpetrator. To create a lineup, the model places the perpetrator in the perpetrator-present lineup and surrounds it with fillers. These fillers are generated using another parameter that governs the similarity of these fillers to the perpetrator. To generate the perpetrator-absent lineup, the perpetrator is replaced with an innocent suspect. The degree to which the innocent suspect resembles the perpetrator is governed by another parameter.

Now that we have described how the lineups are represented, we need to specify how retrieval takes place and we need the model to make a decision. The degree of match between each lineup member and the perpetrator's approximation stored in memory is based on the dot product of these two vectors—a sum of the products obtained by multiplying the values of corresponding features in the two vectors. A large match value signals strong overlap between a lineup member and memory for the perpetrator; a small match value signals that the lineup member bears little resemblance to memory for the perpetrator.

Once a match value(s) is determined, it must be translated into a decision (i.e., make a choice or reject the lineup). We begin with the sequential lineup. The model begins by comparing the first lineup member to memory.

The resulting match value is compared to a decision criterion, and if it exceeds criterion the model chooses that lineup member and the lineup is done. If the first member is not above criterion, the model proceeds to the second member, and so on. If the model evaluates all lineup members without choosing, the model records a rejection. The simultaneous lineup is more complex, jointly considering both absolute and relative judgment contributions. The model first identifies which lineup member yields the highest match value (called BEST) and which member yields the second highest value (called NEXT). The BEST is chosen if the weighted sum of wa * BEST + wr * (BEST−NEXT) exceeds a decision criterion; wa represents the weight given to the absolute contribution and wr represents the weight given to the relative contribution; $wa + wr = 1$.

Goodsell et al. (2010) viewed an array of simultaneous and sequential lineup data through the lens of the WITNESS model to see what could be learned about explicating the sequential advantage. Five of the 10 datasets considered showed no sequential advantage; WITNESS did a good job of approximating these data. However, the remaining five experiments showed a sequential advantage, and these data were problematic. WITNESS can create a sequential advantage only by pairing less stringent simultaneous choosing with more stringent sequential choosing. However, an adjustment of decision criteria only fit one of these five datasets (Melara, DeWitt-Rickards, & O'Brien, 1989). Goodsell et al focused their efforts on the Lindsay et al. (1991a) and the Lindsay et al. (1991b) data because these experiments placed the suspect in only one position (the eighth). Other studies (Kneller, Memon, & Stevenage, 2001; Lindsay & Wells, 1985) counterbalanced suspect position but pooled the data over that factor. Although neither found significant suspect position effects, they might not have had the statistical power to detect suspect position effects in their data. Smith and Batchelder (2008) showed that it was misleading to fit a formal model to pooled data that differed over items (i.e., the suspect in different positions). This made the two Lindsay et al. experiments ideal because these data were uncontaminated by suspect position effects.

Goodsell et al. (2010) developed two modifications to WITNESS that explained the two Lindsay sequential advantages. As mentioned above, a witness might shift from making absolute judgments to making relative judgments after viewing several fillers in the sequential lineup. After viewing and rejecting several lineup members, the model compares the match value of the next lineup member to the average of the match values of the lineup members viewed so far. If the difference between these two quantities exceeded a parameter we called *popout*, the model would decrease the decision criterion and choose. This idea was instantiated in WITNESS, and it produced a sequential advantage and a very good fit to the data. We also implemented the idea that a witness constructs a better memory probe as the sequential lineup unfolds. This was done by increasing the length of the memory vector as the lineup unfolded, allowing for a greater degree of match. As a result, the model is better able to discriminate between guilty and innocent suspects when they occur late in the sequential lineup than if they occur early.

Computational models allow one to think about the existing data in a more rigorous manner and can help resolve the simultaneous-sequential lineup debate by developing explanations for further testing. In the meantime, Gronlund and colleagues have demonstrated that the sequential advantage is not as robust as has been reported. Rather, it depends in part on the late positioning of a suspect in the sequential lineup. We have concerns about recommending that a suspect always be placed late in a sequential lineup; the police, attorneys, and even eyewitnesses will figure this out. But there might be alternative procedures that could be developed that would mitigate suspect position effects and enhance the robustness of the sequential advantage. In the final section, we describe preliminary work on one such procedure, as well as several other alternative approaches that might enhance the veracity of eyewitness evidence.

Alternative Approaches

Conducting a lineup in a simultaneous versus sequential manner hardly exhausts all the possible ways that a witness' memory can be probed. We begin with a discussion of several variations on the traditional lineup. We follow that with an alternate response format involving confidence decisions. Finally, we consider two techniques that a witness could engage in prior to viewing a lineup that may enhance the accuracy of eyewitness identification. This will include the aforementioned procedure that has grown out of our attempts to explain the sequential advantage.

Levi (1998) examined larger (20-person) sequential lineups and allowed multiple selections to be made. He concluded that this reduced the chance of mistakenly identifying the innocent suspect, but the lineups were atypical because guilty suspects were very prominent: 69% of the participants selected a guilty suspect either singly or plus one or two fillers, and innocent suspects very rarely were chosen. Would a similar conclusion be reached with fairer lineups? Dillon, McAllister, and Vernon (2009) compared sequential and simultaneous lineups to hybrid lineups that presented two individuals at a time. These data showed no differences in the correct or false identification rates as a function of how the lineup was conducted. Another procedure, the elimination lineup, was developed to aid children in making eyewitness decisions because children are prone to false identifications (Pozzulo & Lindsay, 1999). In the elimination lineup, a witness first views a simultaneous lineup and is required to select one lineup member who most closely resembles the perpetrator (a relative judgment). Next, the selected photo is presented to the witness, who is asked to make an absolute judgment: "Is this the man who robbed you?" Pozzulo et al. (2008) compared simultaneous, sequential, and elimination lineups. Despite fairly large differences, they found no significant differences among the correct identification rates (simultaneous = .48; sequential = .40; elimination = .32). However, the simultaneous correct rejection rate was less than either of the other two, which did not differ. But an estimate of the conditional probability of a suspect choice showed little difference among the three types of lineups, which is consistent with a criterion shift across conditions. More research is needed to evaluate the effectiveness of alternate lineup presentation methods.

Other ideas have been proposed that might enhance eyewitness identification accuracy. Wells and Olson (2003) argued that police should have probable cause before they put someone at risk in a lineup, which likely would reduce the incidence of perpetrator-absent lineups. Wells (1984) suggested a dual-lineup approach to help eliminate witnesses who are too willing to choose or rely too much on relative judgments. The first lineup would be a blank lineup that would not contain a suspect. Participants who made a selection from the blank lineup were more likely to make false identifications in a second lineup. Dunning and Perretta (2002) proposed that identification decisions made within 10–12 seconds maximally discriminated accurate from inaccurate identifications. Although it is true that accurate identifications tend to be faster, Weber, Brewer, Wells, Semmler, and Keast (2004) found no support for a sacrosanct 10- to 12-second cutoff. Weber and Perfect (in press) showed that allowing uncertain witnesses to opt out of making an identification by providing an explicit "Don't Know" option resulted in decisions more diagnostic of a suspect's guilt, with no reduction in the number of correct decisions. Although Weber and Perfect used a showup (a one-person lineup), the recommendation should apply to lineups.

Subjective aspects of a witness's memory report might differentiate between more versus less accurate decisions (Palmer, Brewer, McKinnon, & Weber, 2010). Dunning and Stern (1994) found that identifications judged as automatic ("the face popped out") were more accurate than more deliberative decisions; Lindsay and Bellinger (1999) found that self-reported absolute judgments were associated with accurate identification more often than were relative judgments. A more rigorous technique for collecting subjective reports involves making confidence judgments. There exists a relatively robust, positive relationship between confidence and accuracy for lineup choosers (Brewer & Wells, 2006). Sauer, Brewer, and Weber (2008) capitalized on this by having participants rate their confidence (0–100%: "Was this the perpetrator?") to each individual in the lineup. Then, they fashioned algorithms that combined these confidence judgments to specify if a selection should be made, and if so, whom to select from the lineup. Generally speaking, the algorithms outperformed binary choice decisions in the perpetrator-absent lineups, and more sophisticated algorithms achieved the same goal for the perpetrator-present lineups, with some loss of perpetrator-absent accuracy. Sauer et al.'s confidence estimation procedure is a promising approach: A witness may have more nuanced information about a perpetrator than can be captured by a binary decision.

Pryke, Lindsay, Dysart, and Dupuis (2004) devised a technique that allowed a witness to utilize nuanced information beyond what a perpetrator looked like. They proposed that different characteristics of a perpetrator be tested in separate lineups. For example, there would be a lineup of faces, a lineup of voice samples, a lineup of clothing, and so on. The more times a witness selected the suspect (his or her face, voice, clothing) rather than a filler, the more likely the suspect was guilty. In other words, a witness with a weak memory who is guessing has a 1 in 6 chance of selecting the innocent suspect's face but a 1 in 36 chance (1/6 * 1/6) that the witness also selects that same individual's voice. However, Nairne (2002) would have a different view of this procedure. The effectiveness of a retrieval cue is determined by the extent to which it provides diagnostic (distinctive) information about a target. That is, we are more likely to retrieve the memory we are searching for if we use the available cues in a multiplicative manner to focus the search rather than in an additive manner.

The final two alternative approaches we consider involve having a witness perform an ancillary task prior to making a lineup decision. In one such technique proposed by Macrae and Lewis (2002), participants were randomly assigned to complete one of three tasks. The two experimental groups made a series of decisions about Navon (1977) stimuli. A Navon stimulus is a large letter composed of many smaller letters (e.g., a large T composed of small Rs). Participants either made a series of global judgments (e.g., respond "T"), made a series of local judgments (respond "R"), or completed a control task. After completion of the ancillary task, all participants viewed an eight-person perpetrator-present simultaneous lineup. The guilty suspect was selected 60% of the time in the control condition. Surprisingly, global processing increased accuracy to 83% while local processing decreased accuracy to 30%. Perfect et al. (2007) extended these findings. Their participants interacted with a female confederate and subsequently tried to find this individual in a perpetrator-present or perpetrator-absent lineup. Before viewing the lineup, participants completed an ancillary task. In Experiment 2 this involved making local or global decisions to Navon stimuli. In Experiment 3 it involved viewing a series of faces and rating how honest each individual was (global processing) or how distinctive the eyes were (local processing). In both studies the percentage correct after global processing was superior to the control condition. This was true in both the perpetrator-present and perpetrator-absent lineups. For possible explanations of the beneficial effect of viewing Navon stimuli, see Perfect, Weston, Dennis, and Snell (2008).

A second technique proposed by Goodsell, Gronlund, and Buttaccio (2010) used ideas developed to explain the learning that took place during a sequential lineup. They had participants ($N = 1,721$) view a mock crime video. After completing a distractor task, participants viewed six faces in succession. They were told that these individuals would not include the suspect. The idea was that allowing a participant to "learn" prior to beginning the lineup might mitigate the suspect position effects in the sequential lineup. If successful, it would allow a suspect to be placed in a random position. However, this initial study did not vary the positioning of the suspect (always in the fourth position) and instead focused on whether evaluating the so-called pre-ID (identification) faces would affect performance. Across groups Goodsell et al. varied how closely the six pre-ID faces matched the perpetrator. The faces were either a close match, a moderate match, or irrelevant (wrong age, wrong race). Then participants viewed either a perpetrator-present or a perpetrator-absent lineup presented in either a simultaneous or sequential manner. Goodsell et al. found one sequential advantage for the irrelevant face group. However, the best-performing combination was the simultaneous lineup after viewing the closely matching faces. Perhaps the success of this particular combination arose from the contrast of the serial evaluation of the pre-ID faces followed by the concurrent comparisons allowed by the simultaneous lineup. We need to try the converse: simultaneous pre-ID evaluation followed by a sequential lineup. More research is needed to evaluate the merits of the pre-ID technique and determine if it will mitigate suspect position effects and enhance the robustness of the sequential advantage.

SUMMARY AND CONCLUSIONS

We reviewed four categories of system variable research: lineup content, instructions, behavioral influence, and presentation method. The first three correspond to recommendations made over 10 years ago by Wells et al. (1998). Specifically, lineups should include description-matched fillers, unbiased instructions, and be administered in a double-blind manner. Research since 1998 generally has supported these recommendations. As we discussed, description-matched fillers generally lead to lineups that are less biased toward a suspect. If that suspect is innocent, this can protect against a false identification. Unbiased instructions reduce the rate at which anyone is chosen from a lineup. As a consequence, although they can reduce the rate at which a guilty suspect is chosen, unbiased instructions provide important protection if a bias exists that isolates an innocent suspect. Double-blind administration will eliminate most instances of administrator bias as well as prevent postidentification feedback effects.

Wells et al. (1998) favored sequential presentation of the lineup but did not make that a recommendation. Since then, however, there has been a national movement toward conducting lineups in this manner. Our take on this literature is that there is strong support for the existence of a sequential shift that makes witnesses more conservative and less willing to choose when viewing a sequential lineup. On the plus side, fewer false identifications occur, making the use of sequential lineups consistent with an adherence to Blackstone's ratio. In addition, given that many of the innocent people in prison were put there largely or in part due to faulty eyewitness identification, the benefit of a sequential shift should not be underestimated. But a countervailing factor is the base rate at which the police put an innocent suspect in a lineup (Wells & Olson, 2002). Penrod (2003) estimated a 2:1 ratio of guilty to innocent suspects for the 271 Behrman and Davey (2001) lineups. If actual lineups are twice as likely to contain a guilty suspect (and our hunch is that the ratio generally is greater than this), a reduced sequential correct identification rate might give one pause.

It is up to policymakers to make the call about the trade-offs between the costs and benefits that arise from sequential lineups, the utilities attached to those costs and benefits, and the base rate of innocent people in lineups. Given that sequential lineups are becoming the norm at various places around the country, it appears that some policymakers already have decided that the evidence favors an evaluative sequential advantage. But those decisions were made presuming the existence and robustness of a numerical sequential advantage, and we believe that the evidence in favor of a numerical sequential advantage is deficient (see also Clark, in press). The research by Gronlund and colleagues shows that a sequential advantage is real but not robust. One factor that tends to produce a sequential advantage is the late placement of a suspect in the sequential lineup. A theory-driven approach to this issue has resulted in proposed explanations that assume that a witness can learn something as the lineup unfolds. More theory-driven research is needed to resolve the sequential lineup debate, evaluate the limitations we have observed, and test the explanations we have proposed.

In April 2010, Ohio passed the Innocence Protection Act. In addition to various reforms involving DNA evidence, the act mandated double-blind lineup administration, unbiased instructions, and description-matched fillers with an assurance that the suspect not stand out. It also stated that lineups should be conducted in a sequential manner using a *folder system*. Each of six folders contains one photo. The suspect's picture should not be placed in the first folder, with four empty folders placed at the bottom of the stack so that a witness would not know how many pictures will be presented. A witness is allowed to go through the folders twice and must report his or her confidence at the time of making a selection. In addition, there are extensive documentation requirements concerning the conduct of the lineup. If the police had followed these procedures back in 1994, would we still be debating the innocence of Kevin Keith? Eyewitness identification will never be perfect; but following the recommendations we have reviewed, coupled with the continued interplay of theory and data to guide future research, can enhance the quality of eyewitness evidence and reduce the risk of convicting the innocent.

NOTES

1. More details about the case can be found at http://opd.ohio.gov/DP_Kevin_Keith/DP_Kevin_Keith_eyewitness_report.pdf
2. Lindsay et al. (1991b) did not indicate the position of the suspect, but we assumed it was the eighth position given that this paper and the one by Lindsay et al. (1991a) were published at about the same time.

REFERENCES

Behrman, B. W., & Davey, S. L. (2001). Eyewitness identification in actual criminal cases: An archival analysis. *Law and Human Behavior, 25*(5), 475–491.

Blackstone, W. (1769). *Commentaries on the Laws of England, Vol II, Book IV.*

Bornstein, B. H., & Meissner, C. A. (2008). Introduction: Basic and applied issues in eyewitness research: A Münsterberg centennial retrospective. *Applied Cognitive Psychology, 22*(6), 733–736.

Brewer, N., & Wells, G. L. (2006). The confidence-accuracy relationship in eyewitness identification: Effects of lineup instructions, foil similarity, and target-absent base rates. *Journal of Experimental Psychology: Applied, 12*(1), 11–30.

Carlson, C. A., Gronlund, S. D., & Clark, S. E. (2008). Lineup composition, suspect position, and the sequential lineup advantage. *Journal of Experimental Psychology: Applied, 14*(2), 118–128.

Clark, S. D. (in press). Costs and benefits of eyewitness identification reform: Psychological science and public policy. *Perspectives on Psychological Science.*

Clark, S. E. (2003). A memory and decision model for eyewitness identification. *Applied Cognitive Psychology, 17*(6), 629–654.

Clark, S. E. (2005). A re-examination of the effects of biased lineup instructions in eyewitness identification. *Law and Human Behavior, 29*(4), 395–424.

Clark, S. E. (2008). The importance (necessity) of computational modelling for eyewitness identification research. *Applied Cognitive Psychology, 22*(6), 803–813.

Clark, S. E., & Godfrey, R. D. (2009). Eyewitness identification evidence and innocence risk. *Psychonomic Bulletin & Review, 16*(1), 22–42.

Clark, S. E., Gronlund, S. D., Carlson, C. A., & Goodsell, C. A. (under review). Deconstructing the sequential lineup superiority effect.

Clark, S. E., Howell, R. T., & Davey, S. L. (2008). Regularities in eyewitness identification. *Law and Human Behavior, 32*(3), 187–218.

Clark, S. E., Marshall, T. E., & Rosenthal, R. (2009). Lineup administrator influences on eyewitness identification decisions. *Journal of Experimental Psychology: Applied, 15*(1), 63–75.

Clark, S., & Tunnicliff, J. L. (2001). Selecting lineup foils in eyewitness identification experiments: Experimental control and real-world simulation. *Law and Human Behavior, 25*(3), 199–216.

Cutler, B. R., Penrod, S., & Dexter, H. R. (1990). Juror sensitivity to eyewitness identification evidence. *Law and Human Behavior, 14*, 185–191.

Cutler, B. L., Penrod, S. D., & Martens, T. K. (1987). The reliability of eyewitness identification: The role of system and estimator variables. *Law and Human Behavior, 11*(3), 233–258.

Deffenbacher, K. A., Bornstein, B. H., Penrod, S. D., & McGorty, E. K. (2004). A meta-analytic review of the effects of high stress on eyewitness memory. *Law and Human Behavior, 28*(6), 687–706.

Dillon, J. M., McAllister, H. A., & Vernon, L. L. (2009). The hybrid lineup combining sequential and simultaneous features: A first test. *Applied Psychology in Criminal Justice, 5*(1), 90–108.

Douglass, A. B., & Steblay, N. (2006). Memory distortion in eyewitnesses: A meta-analysis of the post-identification feedback effect. *Applied Cognitive Psychology, 20*(7), 859–869.

Dunning, D., & Perretta, S. (2002). Automaticity and eyewitness accuracy: A 10- to 12-second rule for distinguishing accurate from inaccurate positive identifications. *Journal of Applied Psychology, 87*(5), 951–962.

Dunning, D., & Stern, L. B. (1994). Distinguishing accurate from inaccurate eyewitness identifications via inquiries about decision processes. *Journal of Personality and Social Psychology, 67*(5), 818–835.

Engle, R. W., Kane, M. J., & Tuholski, S. W. (1999). Individual differences in working memory capacity and what they tell us about controlled attention, general fluid intelligence, and functions of the prefrontal cortex. In A. Miyake & P. Shah (Eds.), *Models of working memory: Mechanisms of active maintenance and executive control.* (pp. 102–134). New York: Cambridge University Press.

Esgate, A., & Groome, D. (2005). *An introduction to applied cognitive psychology.* New York: Psychology Press.

Fox, S. G., & Walters, H. A. (1986). The impact of general versus specific expert testimony and eyewitness confidence upon mock juror judgment. *Law and Human Behavior, 10*(3), 215–228.

Goldstein, E. B. (2008). *Cognitive psychology: Connecting mind, research, and everyday experience* (2nd ed.). Belmont, CA: Thomson Wadsworth.

Goodsell, C. A., Gronlund, S. D., & Buttaccio, D. R. (2010). *Enhancing eyewitness identification accuracy: Sequential lineups and a new procedure.* Presented at the 21st annual convention of the American Psychology-Law Society (AP-LS), Vancouver, BC, Canada.

Goodsell, C. A., Gronlund, S. D., & Carlson, C. A. (2010). Exploring the sequential lineup advantage using WITNESS. *Law and Human Behavior*, 34(6), 445–459.

Greathouse, S. M., & Kovera, M. B. (2009). Instruction bias and lineup presentation moderate the effects of administrator knowledge on eyewitness identification. *Law and Human Behavior*, 33(1), 70–82.

Gronlund, S. D., Carlson, C. A., Dailey, S. B., & Goodsell, C. A. (2009). Robustness of the sequential lineup advantage. *Journal of Experimental Psychology: Applied*, 15(2), 140–152.

Hafstad, G. S., Memon, A., & Logie, R. (2004). Post-identification feedback, confidence and recollections of witnessing conditions in child witnesses. *Applied Cognitive Psychology*, 18(7), 901–912.

Jonsson, P. (2007, February 6). The police lineup is becoming suspect practice. *Christian Science Monitor*. Retrieved March 4, 2012, from http://www.csmonitor.com/2007/0206/p01s02-usju.html

Kneller, W., Memon, A., & Stevenage, S. (2001). Simultaneous and sequential lineups: Decision processes of accurate and inaccurate eyewitnesses. *Applied Cognitive Psychology*, 15(6), 659–671.

Lampinen, J. M., Scott, J., Pratt, D., Leding, J. K., & Arnal, J. D. (2007). "Good, you identified the suspect…but please ignore this feedback": Can warnings eliminate the effects of post-identification feedback? *Applied Cognitive Psychology*, 21(8), 1037–1056.

Lane, S. M., & Meissner, C. A. (2008). A "middle road" approach to bridging the basic-applied divide in eyewitness identification research. *Applied Cognitive Psychology*, 22(6), 779–787.

Levi, A. M. (1998). Protecting innocent defendants, nailing the guilty: A modified sequential lineup. *Applied Cognitive Psychology*, 12(3), 265–275.

Lindsay, R. C. L., & Bellinger, K. (1999). Alternatives to the sequential lineup: The importance of controlling the pictures. *Journal of Applied Psychology*, 84(3), 315–321.

Lindsay, R. C., Lea, J. A., & Fulford, J. A. (1991a). Sequential lineup presentation: Technique matters. *Journal of Applied Psychology*, 76(5), 741–745.

Lindsay, R. C. L., Lea, J. A., Nosworthy, G. J., Fulford, J. A., Hector, J., LeVan, V., et al. (1991b). Biased lineups: Sequential presentation reduces the problem. *Journal of Applied Psychology*, 76(6), 796–802.

Lindsay, R. C., & Wells, G. L. (1985). Improving eyewitness identifications from lineups: Simultaneous versus sequential lineup presentation. *Journal of Applied Psychology*, 70(3), 556–564.

Loftus, E. F. (1997). Creating false memories. *Scientific American*, 277, 70–75.

Loftus, E. F. & Ketcham, K. (1994). *The myth of repressed memory*. New York: St. Martin's Press.

Loftus, E. F., & Palmer, J. C. (1974). Reconstruction of automobile destruction: An example of the interaction between language and memory. *Journal of Verbal Learning & Verbal Behavior*, 13(5), 585–589.

Ludlum, R. (2005). *The ambler warning*. New York: St. Martin's Press.

Macrae, C. N., & Lewis, H. L. (2002). Do I know you?: Processing orientation and face recognition. *Psychological Science*, 13(2), 194–196.

Malpass, R.S. (2006). A policy evaluation of simultaneous and sequential lineups. *Psychology, Public Policy, and Law, 12*, 394–418.

Malpass, R. S., & Devine, P. G. (1981). Eyewitness identification: Lineup instructions and the absence of the offender. *Journal of Applied Psychology, 66*(4), 482–489.

Malpass, R. S., & Lindsay, R. C. L. (1999). Measuring line-up fairness. *Applied Cognitive Psychology, 13*(Spec Issue), S1–S7.

Malpass, R. S., Tredoux, C. G., & McQuiston-Surrett, D. (2007). Lineup construction and lineup fairness. In R. C. L. Lindsay, D. F. Ross, J. D. Read, & M. P. Toglia (Eds.), *The handbook of eyewitness psychology, Vol II: Memory for people* (pp. 155–178). Mahwah, NJ: Erlbaum.

Malpass, R. S., Tredoux, C. G., & McQuiston-Surrett, D. (2009). Public policy and sequential lineups. *Legal and Criminological Psychology, 14*(1), 1–12.

McQuiston-Surrett, D., Malpass, R. S., & Tredoux, C. G. (2006). Sequential vs. simultaneous lineups: A review of methods, data, and theory. *Psychology, Public Policy, and Law, 12*(2), 137–169.

Meissner, C. A., & Brigham, J. C. (2001). A meta-analysis of the verbal overshadowing effect in face identification. *Applied Cognitive Psychology, 15*(6), 603–616.

Melara, R. D., DeWitt-Rickards, T. S., & O'Brien, T. P. (1989). Enhancing lineup identification accuracy: Two codes are better than one. *Journal of Applied Psychology, 74*(5), 706–713.

Nairne, J. S. (2002). Remembering over the short-term: The case against the standard model. *Annual Review of Psychology, 53*(1), 53–81.

Navon, D. (1977). Forest before trees: The precedence of global features in visual perception. *Cognitive Psychology, 9*, 353–383.

Navon, D. (1992). Selection of lineup foils by similarity to the suspect is likely to misfire. *Law and Human Behavior, 16*(5), 575–593.

Neuschatz, J. S., Neuschatz, J. S., Lawson, D. S., Powers, R. A., Fairless, A. H., Goodsell, C. A., et al. (2007). The mitigating effects of suspicion on post-identification feedback and on retrospective eyewitness memory. *Law and Human Behavior, 31*(3), 231–247

Neuschatz, J. S., Preston, E. L., Burkett, A. D., Toglia, M. P., Lampinen, J. M., Neuschatz, J. S., et al. (2005). The effects of post-identification feedback and age on retrospective eyewitness memory. *Applied Cognitive Psychology, 19*, 435–453.

O'Rourke, T. E., Penrod, S. D., Cutler, B. L., & Stuve, T. E. (1989). The external validity of eyewitness identification research: Generalizing across subject populations. *Law and Human Behavior, 13*(4), 385–395.

Palmer, M. A., & Brewer, N. (in press). Sequential lineup presentation promotes less biased criterion setting but does not improve discriminability. *Law & Human Behavior.*

Palmer, M. A., Brewer, N., McKinnon, A. C., & Weber, N. (2010). Phenomenological reports diagnose accuracy of eyewitness identification decisions. *Acta Psychologica, 133*, 137–145.

Penrod, S. (2003, Spring). Eyewitness identification evidence: How well are witnesses and police performing? *Criminal Justice Magazine, 18*, 36–47.

Perfect, T. J., Dennis, I., & Snell, A. (2007). The effects of local and global processing orientation on eyewitness identification performance. *Memory, 15*(7), 784–798.

Perfect, T. J., Weston, N., Dennis, I., & Snell, A.. (2008). The effects of precedence on Navon-induced processing bias in face recognition. *Quarterly Journal of Experimental Psychology, 61*, 1479–1486.

Phillips, M. R., McAuliff, B. D., Kovera, M. B., & Cutler, B. L. (1999). Double-blind photoarray administration as a safeguard against investigator bias. *Journal of Applied Psychology, 84*(6), 940–951.

Posner, M. I., & Keele, S. W. (1968). On the genesis of abstract ideas. *Journal of Experimental Psychology, 77*, 353–363.

Pozzulo, J. D., Dempsey, J., Corey, S., Girardi, A., Lawandi, A., & Aston, C. (2008). Can a lineup procedure designed for child witnesses work for adults? Comparing simultaneous, sequential, and elimination lineup procedures. *Journal of Applied Social Psychology, 38*(9), 2195–2209.

Pozzulo, J. D., & Lindsay, R. C. L. (1999). Elimination lineups: An improved identification procedure for child eyewitnesses. *Journal of Applied Psychology, 84*(2), 167–176.

Pryke, S., Lindsay, R. C. L., Dysart, J. E., & Dupuis, P. (2004). Multiple independent identification decisions: A method of calibrating eyewitness identifications. *Journal of Applied Psychology, 89*(1), 73–84.

Quinlivan, D. S., Neuschatz, J. S., Jimenez, A., Cling, A. D., Douglass, A. B., & Goodsell, C. A. (2009). Do prophylactics prevent inflation? Post-identification feedback and the effectiveness of procedures to protect against confidence-inflation in ear-witnesses. *Law and Human Behavior, 33*(2), 111–121.

Reisberg, D. (2001). *Cognition: Exploring the science of the mind* (2nd ed.). New York: W. W. Norton.

Robinson-Riegler, G., & Robinson-Riegler, B. (2004). *Cognitive psychology: Applying the science of the mind*. Boston: Pearson Education.

Sauer, J. D., Brewer, N., & Weber, N. (2008). Multiple confidence estimates as indices of eyewitness memory. *Journal of Experimental Psychology: General, 137*(3), 528–547.

Schacter, D. L. (1999). The seven sins of memory: Insights from psychology and cognitive neuroscience. *American Psychologist, 54*(3), 182–203.

Schacter, D. L. (2002). *The seven sins of memory: How the mind forgets and remembers*. Boston: Houghton Mifflin Harcourt.

Simons, D. J., & Ambinder, M. S. (2005). Change blindness: Theory and consequences. *Current Directions in Psychological Science, 14*(1), 44–48.

Smith, J. B., & Batchelder, W. H. (2008). Assessing individual differences in categorical data. *Psychonomic Bulletin & Review, 15*(4), 713–731.

Steblay, N. M. (1992). A meta-analytic review of the weapon focus effect. *Law and Human Behavior, 16*(4), 413–424.

Steblay, N. M. (1997). Social influence in eyewitness recall: A meta-analytic review of lineup instruction effects. *Law and Human Behavior, 21*(3), 283–297.

Steblay, N., Dysart, J., Fulero, S., & Lindsay, R. C. L. (2001). Eyewitness accuracy rates in sequential and simultaneous lineup presentations: A meta-analytic comparison. *Law and Human Behavior, 25*(5), 459–473.

Steblay, N., Dysart, J., & Wells, G. L. (2011). Seventy-two tests of the sequential lineup superiority effect: A meta-analysis and policy discussion. *Psychology, Public Policy, and Law, 17*, 99–139.

Tunnicliff, J. L., & Clark, S. E. (2000). Selecting foils for identification lineups: Matching suspects or descriptions? *Law and Human Behavior, 24*(2), 231–258.

Valentine, T., Darling, S., & Memon, A. (2007). Do strict rules and moving images increase the reliability of sequential identification procedures? *Applied Cognitive Psychology, 21*(7), 933–949.

Weber, N., Brewer, N., Wells, G. L., Semmler, C., & Keast, A. (2004). Eyewitness identification accuracy and response latency: The unruly 10–12 second rule. *Journal of Experimental Psychology: Applied, 10,* 139–147.

Weber, N., & Perfect, T. J. (in press). Improving eyewitness identification accuracy by screening out those who say they don't know. *Law & Human Behavior.*

Wells, G. L. (1978). Applied eyewitness-testimony research: System variables and estimator variables. *Journal of Personality and Social Psychology, 36*(12), 1546–1557.

Wells, G. L. (1984). The psychology of lineup identifications. *Journal of Applied Social Psychology, 14*(2), 89–103.

Wells, G. L. (2008). Theory, logic and data: Paths to a more coherent eyewitness science. *Applied Cognitive Psychology, 22*(6), 853–859.

Wells, G. L., & Bradfield, A. L. (1998). "Good, you identified the suspect": Feedback to eyewitnesses distorts their reports of the witnessing experience. *Journal of Applied Psychology, 83*(3), 360–376.

Wells, G. L., Ferguson, T. J., & Lindsay, R. C. (1981). The tractability of eyewitness confidence and its implications for triers of fact. *Journal of Applied Psychology, 66*(6), 688–696.

Wells, G. L., & Lindsay, R. C. (1980). On estimating the diagnosticity of eyewitness nonidentifications. *Psychological Bulletin, 88*(3), 776–784.

Wells, G. L., & Olson, E. A. (2002). Eyewitness identification: Information gain from incriminating and exonerating behaviors. *Journal of Experimental Psychology: Applied, 8*(3), 155–167.

Wells, G. L., & Olson, E. A. (2003). Eyewitness testimony. *Annual Review of Psychology, 54,* 277–295.

Wells, G. L., Rydell, S. M., & Seelau, E. P. (1993). The selection of distractors for eyewitness lineups. *Journal of Applied Psychology, 78*(5), 835–844.

Wells, G. L., Small, M., Penrod, S., Malpass, R. S., Fulero, S. M., & Brimacombe, C. A. E. (1998). Eyewitness identification procedures: Recommendations for lineups and photospreads. *Law and Human Behavior, 22*(6), 603–647.

Wogalter, M. S., Malpass, R. S., & Mcquiston, D. E. (2004). A national survey of U.S. police on preparation and conduct of identification lineups. *Psychology, Crime & Law, 10*(1), 69–82.

Wright, D. B., & Skagerberg, E. M. (2007). Postidentification feedback affects real eyewitnesses. *Psychological Science, 18*(2), 172–178.

4

The Curious Complexity between Confidence and Accuracy in Reports from Memory

HENRY L. ROEDIGER III, JOHN H. WIXTED, AND K. ANDREW DESOTO

The relation between the probability of remembering an event and one's confidence in it seems obvious: The more confident a person is in remembering an event, the more accurate he or she will be (and vice versa). Imagine giving people a series of events to remember every day for a week, say 10 per day. The events could be sentences such as "The hippie touched the debutante in the park" or "The policeman arrested the homeless woman near the movie theater." Then, on the seventh day, people could be asked to recall (or recognize) all the sentences that had been presented that seventh day, and those from the third day of the experiment, and to rate the confidence of each reported memory. It would surprise no one to learn that people would correctly remember more sentences from the seventh day than from the third day; surely they would be more accurate for the recent memories. In addition, there is no doubt that their confidence would track their accuracy if confidence were measured on, say, a 7-point rating scale (from 7 = sure the event happened to 1 = sure the event did not happen). People would be much more confident for the recently presented sentences than for those heard 4 days previously. The reason people can intuit the result of this experiment so accurately is that we essentially live this experiment every day of our lives. We can tell an inquirer what events happened to us today with reasonable accuracy and certainty, but if we are asked to retrieve events from a particular day even a few days ago, they would be much hazier to us—we would be less accurate and less confident.

If the conclusion from this first paragraph were correct—that accuracy and confidence of retrieval were always strongly linked—then this could be a short chapter. In fact, the editors would not have asked for a chapter about this topic. However, as we shall see, the situation is much more complex—even, as the title has it, curiously so. This chapter is about that complexity and how to understand it.

The chapter is divided into several sections. In the next section, we note why the relation between accuracy and confidence in memory retrieval matters for the legal system and how the simple assumption usually made—that confidence and accuracy are always tightly linked—is wrong. In the following section, we outline a simple theory of memory that seems implicit in lay (and judicial) assumptions about remembering, but one that is at best incomplete and at worst wrong. In the next section we consider the widely varying opinions that psychologists have offered about the relation between confidence and accuracy. We also sketch out how those making strong claims about confidence and accuracy of retrieval are both partly right and partly wrong. As in most issues concerning remembering, the correct answer is "it depends" (Roediger, 2008); in this case, the relation between confidence and accuracy depends on the method of analysis, on the target material being remembered, on who is doing the remembering, and (in situations where memory is tested by recognition) on the nature of the lures and distractors. In addition, there is more than one way to measure the relationship between confidence and accuracy, and not every way is equally relevant to what courts of law would like to know about the issue.

The main part of our chapter is oriented around five different ways of analyzing the relation between confidence and accuracy of retrieval, which can lead to different conclusions depending on a host of factors. We will also consider other factors, such as individual differences among rememberers that might affect the confidence-accuracy relation. The final part of the chapter provides recommendations about confidence and accuracy that might be considered guidelines. To presage our conclusions, confidence and accuracy can be positively related, they can be unrelated, and they can even be negatively related (that is, in certain situations, factors that lead to greater numbers of errors also lead to greater confidence in those errors). Even so, it would be a mistake to conclude that confidence ratings are uninformative. But we are getting ahead of the game. First, why is this topic important?

CONVICTION OF THE INNOCENT

In criminal courts of law, eyewitness testimony is critical in many cases. Often there is little physical evidence and the jury and judge must base their decision about guilt or innocence on the testimony of an eyewitness to the crime. Even if we assume the best intentions of all parties involved to seek the truth—the eyewitness, the police, the prosecutors, the judge and jury— mistakes can occur. Innocent people can be convicted of crimes they did not commit (and guilty people can walk free) because of memory errors made by an eyewitness. Psychologists have argued this point for 100 years, since the pioneering work of Hugo Münsterberg in his book about the psychology of the witness (*On the Witness Stand*, 1908). In the last 40 years, since publication of the groundbreaking work of Elizabeth Loftus (e.g., 1975; Loftus & Palmer, 1974) and Robert Buckhout (1974), a huge volume of research has arisen on factors that affect eyewitness testimony and memory errors in general (see Roediger & Gallo, 2002, for a brief overview and Brainerd & Reyna, 2005, for a fuller treatment).

One critical factor that can taint testimony is information that the witness is exposed to after he or she witnesses a crime, although the same principle is true for any event and not just crimes. Information occurring after an event can supply retroactive interference (McGeoch, 1932) and disrupt retention of the original event. If erroneous information about details of the crime (or its perpetrator) is provided by other witnesses, by police, or even by erroneous recollections of the witness himself or herself, this can serve as a potent force to shape the recollection of the crime scene (or the perpetrator). This erroneous information will often be incorporated in the witness's recollections, leading the witness to confidently remember events differently from the way they happened. Loftus (e.g., 1975, 1992) has extensively studied the process by which misinformation delivered by others can be incorporated into a witness's recollection (see the chapter by Davis & Loftus in this volume, too). Further, the witness's act of recalling wrong information makes it even more likely to be misremembered in the future (Roediger, Jacoby, & McDermott, 1996). This is not the place to review the types of errors that eyewitnesses can make, but much laboratory research as well as forensic experience shows the validity of the claims. Loftus's (1996) book, *Eyewitness Testimony*, still provides a fine introduction to the basic issues involved in understanding eyewitness testimony and how it can go awry.

The point to take away for present purposes is that eyewitness testimony can be wrong—even in the absence of misleading postevent information— and yet the witness can be highly confident in her or his recollections. Thus, high confidence does not always mean that the witness is accurate, and this is a point the legal system has not adequately appreciated in years gone by. Instead, high-confidence eyewitness testimony, by virtue of the fact that it constitutes *direct* evidence (as opposed to *circumstantial* evidence), is often considered to be essentially infallible. As a result, people have been convicted and sentenced to long jail terms based solely on high-confidence eyewitness testimony.

Of course, in thousands of cases decided on the basis of eyewitness testimony there is no way to tell if an error has been made. A suspect who actually committed a crime but who has been freed because an eyewitness confidently reported that a lineup did not contain the perpetrator is unlikely to later reveal the truth of the matter, so this kind of error (a miss) is unlikely to ever be detected unless other evidence comes to light to implicate the person. Similarly, an individual who is convicted on the basis of high-confidence eyewitness testimony may naturally protest his or her innocence, but how can the legal system know what the truth is? Occasionally, some other person may eventually be caught (usually for an unrelated crime) and then confess to the crime for which another person had been wrongfully convicted. Such events are rare. However, since the late 1980s, another source of information has come into play: DNA evidence. Scientists in the United Kingdom perfected technologies that make *DNA fingerprinting* (as it is often called) highly reliable (except for identical twins, since they share 100% of their DNA). Because DNA is associated with at least some crimes for which people have been convicted (e.g., rapes, some murders), if a court permits a test of the convicted person's DNA, it can be matched against the DNA left by the perpetrator at the crime scene. If the evidence shows a mismatch, then the person who has been convicted of the crime almost certainly did not commit it. However, even the legal process leading to testing of DNA is often fraught with difficulty (that is, often there is a legal battle over retrospective testing of a convicted person's DNA). Another difficulty is that often DNA evidence is disposed of after a conviction. Nonetheless, sometimes DNA testing is permitted and sometimes the conviction of a person for a crime is shown to have been in error.

The Innocence Project (affiliated with the Benjamin N. Cardozo School of Law at Yeshiva University) was founded by Barry Scheck and Peter Neufeld to help convicted prisoners seeking to establish their innocence from crimes through DNA testing and other means. As of this writing (April 2012), 289 people have been exonerated by the Innocence Project, many by DNA testing, including 17 who had spent time on death row. These innocent people served an average of 13 years in prison before their convictions were overturned. Brandon Garrett (2011) examined the first 250 DNA exonerations in his book, *Convicting the Innocent*, and concluded that 190 of the convictions (76%) were the result of eyewitness misidentification. (Other causes include improper forensics, false or coerced confessions, and use of informants who gave wrong testimony.)

Most cases of eyewitness identification come from people who are highly confident and believe they are correctly identifying the right person.

Identifications made with low confidence generally never make it to a court of law and are given little weight if they do. (If a witness said "that might be the man who robbed me, but it might not be. I'm just not sure" the case would never go to court.) Thus, if there was ever any doubt that high-confidence eyewitness errors can occur, such DNA exonerations establish beyond any reasonable doubt that they do. This fact, perhaps more than any other, has contributed to the impression that the relationship between confidence and accuracy is hopelessly weak. As we shall see, however, despite the occurrence of an uncomfortably large number of high-confidence errors in eyewitness testimony, the relationship between confidence and accuracy is not always so poor. The issue of confidence and memory is complex, and in some situations the relation can be quite high.

As indicated above, eyewitness errors made with high confidence have led to the conviction of over 200 innocent people. Of course, 200 erroneous convictions over many years out of the thousands of people convicted each year may not seem great. However, the danger is that this number represents the tip of the iceberg, a small proportion of the people who have been wrongly convicted. Wrongful convictions are obviously of paramount concern even if it could also be true that a much larger number of criminals have been rightly convicted (and innocent suspects rightly exonerated) on the basis of eyewitness testimony made with high confidence.

DNA evidence does not exist in most criminal cases, and exonerations are extremely difficult without such evidence (although some do occur). According to The Innocence Project website (http://www.innocenceproject.org), "Those exonerated by DNA testing aren't the only people who have been wrongly convicted in recent decades. For every case that involves DNA, there are thousands that do not." Although it is hard to defend the last claim rigorously, the point here is that every precaution should be taken beforehand to limit erroneous eyewitness testimony and to understand situations in which it may arise. As the English jurist William Blackstone argued, it is "better that ten guilty persons escape than that one innocent suffer." In order to satisfy this maxim, and due to the fact that so many have been wrongly convicted, we must ask: Under what conditions are eyewitnesses likely to make high-confidence errors? The aim of the remainder of this chapter is to provide answers to this question.

TRACE THEORIES OF REMEMBERING

Both Plato and Aristotle used an analogy of traces left on memory to impressions created in a wax tablet. It is worthwhile to quote a few lines here from

Plato's dialog *Theaetetus* because, we will argue, the same assumptions used by Socrates (or Plato) in the dialog are still surprisingly common today:

> Imagine, then, for the sake of argument, that our minds contain a brick of wax, which in this or that individual may be larger or smaller, and composed of wax that is...harder in some, softer in others, and sometimes of just the right consistency.... Let us call it...Memory, and say that whenever we wish to remember something we hear or conceive in our own minds, we hold this wax under the perceptions or ideas and imprint on it as we might stamp the impression of a seal ring. What is so imprinted we remember and know so long as the image remains; what is rubbed out or has not succeeded in leaving an impression we have forgotten and do not know. (Translated by Hamilton, 1961, p. 897)

The metaphor was continued in *Theaetetus* in other interesting ways (Roediger, 1980).

No one today believes that memory works like the imprint of a seal on wax, but one dominant class of theories, called *trace-dependent theories* (Tulving, 1974) or *trace access theory* (King, Zechmeister, & Shaughnessy, 1980), is very much like Aristotle's and Plato's conception. These trace theory ideas are still found today in some accounts (perhaps especially in neurobiological theories) of memory. The basic ideas are straightforward: First, events and experiences change the nervous system, and these changes are referred to as the creation of memory traces or *engrams*. (Every theory of memory has some version of this assumption.) Second, memory traces vary in strength from weak to strong. In terms of Plato's metaphor, some impressions are deep and some are shallow. In terms of one popular modern theory, the *levels of processing framework* (Craik & Lockhart, 1972), processing of information can be either shallow (or superficial) or deep (involving meaning), leaving traces that, like Plato's, are more or less robust. If traces vary in strength, such variations determine accuracy. Memories with stronger traces are more likely to support later memory performance (recall, recognition, transfer) than are weaker traces. The theory can further assume that trace strength determines confidence—a person will be more confident in a memory underlain by a strong trace than one that arises from a weak trace. Thus, the trace strength account of the relation between accuracy and confidence is neat and tidy; according to this theory, both accuracy and confidence are supported by the same underlying entity, the strength of memory traces (and nothing more).

The trace theory of memory is straightforward and intuitive and accords well with common sense. Insofar as laypeople think about memory at all, it is probably their theory, because we use the language of strength theory in speaking of memory. If I say I have a strong memory of the basketball game last week, everyone knows what I mean. One reason people generally believe that accuracy and confidence are tightly linked is probably that they subscribe to some version of trace theory.

The problem is that trace theory is wrong—not completely wrong, but still wrong. At the very least, the theory is incomplete in postulating that memory performance is totally determined by the strength of memory traces. The problem is that trace theory—the idea that remembering involves a direct readout from memory traces—ignores retrieval processes, and much evidence indicates that remembering is a cue-dependent process (Tulving, 1974). Toward the end of his great book *Remembering*, published 80 years ago, Sir Frederic Bartlett (1932) wrote:

> If there be one thing upon which I have insisted more than another throughout all the discussions of this book, it is that the description of memories as 'fixed and lifeless' [traces] is merely an unpleasant fiction. That views implying this are still very common is evidence of the astonishing way in which many psychologists, even the most deservedly eminent, often appear to decide what are the characteristic marks of the process they set out to study, before they ever begin to actually study it. (pp. 311–312)

What is missing from trace theory? Quite a bit, actually. For now, let us be content to fill out the point above about the critical omission of retrieval processes. The weakness or strength of memory traces is just one factor determining the memorability of an event. Another important set of processes concern retrieval, because the same trace may or may not eventuate in successful remembering, depending on many other factors occurring during access of stored information. The nature of cues the rememberer has (or can generate) when trying to remember is also crucial, as are the processes through which these cues are used. The *mental set* or instructions about retrieval with particular cues and traces also matter. For example, you may see the word *lamp* and no particular memory may come to mind. However, if you are told, "Recall an experience from your past involving a lamp," a specific episode may come rushing back. One key issue concerns how strong or vivid the experienced sense of remembering is once a memory is retrieved. The experience is partly determined by the cues in the retrieval environment, partly by the trace, partly by the interaction of these two factors, and partly by other considerations such as the instructions given for retrieval (the mental set or the retrieval mode; Tulving, 1974, 1983; Wixted & Mickes, 2010). Such retrieval experience probably gives rise to the sense of confidence that people have in their specific memories. The strength of the trace or engram (which, of course, can never be measured—it is a hypothetical concept for psychologists) is just one component in the process of remembering. That, in a nutshell, is why trace theories are incomplete or wrong—they leave out other factors that determine remembering, especially ones arising during retrieval.

Whether or not an event is retrieved from memory is determined powerfully by the nature of retrieval cues used to prompt the memory. Suppose I want people to retrieve a specific word from the English language, one they usually do not use much, like *ghost*. The strength of the word's representation (trace) may not help. In an experiment, Rubin and Wallace (1989) gave one group the cue "a mythical being" and no one retrieved *ghost*. They gave another group the cue "the word ends in *ost*," and again, no one recalled the word. However, when they gave a third group the cue "a word naming a mythical being that ends in *ost*," 100% of the people were able to produce *ghost*. Two cues that were individually ineffective produced perfect retrieval when used together, all with the same trace.

The power of cues also matters in remembering events from one's life. Traces of experience that are inaccessible with one type of cue may be easily retrieved with another type of cue (e.g., Barclay, Bransford, Franks, McCarrell, & Nitsch, 1974; Roediger & Payne, 1982; Tulving & Pearlstone, 1966). As Tulving (1974) has written:

> Memory for an event is always a product of information from two sources. The first is conceptualized as the memory trace—information laid down and retained in a person's memory store as a result of the original perception of the event. Its postulation is necessary to account for the residual effects of the event. The other source is the retrieval cue—information that is present in the individual's cognitive environment at the time retrieval occurs. (p. 74)

Thus, to the extent that the concept of memory strength is applicable to the understanding of the relationship between confidence and accuracy, it is the strength of memories *as retrieved*, not the strength of memories as encoded (i.e., not the strength of the memory trace), that is critical. Because remembering is reconstructive (Bartlett, 1932), retrieval processes are crucial: We usually take the traces of experience and weave them together into a more or less coherent description of a remembered event, a description that depends heavily on the cues used during retrieval. We shall have more to say on this topic later in the chapter, but now we turn to a survey of opinions psychologists have provided about the relation between confidence and accuracy of memories.

CONFLICTING CLAIMS OF PSYCHOLOGISTS

Psychologists have issued a variety of pronouncements about the relation between confidence and accuracy of memory reports. Cognitive psychologists tend to perform experiments in which a list of unrelated words is presented for study and then twice as many are presented during the test (say, 100 studied and 200 tested). Subjects in the experiments are asked to judge whether each tested item is old (studied) or new (nonstudied) and to rate their confidence on a straightforward scale (say, 1–7, with 7 being most confident). In considering research mostly of this kind, Dunlosky and Metcalfe (2009) wrote, "The relative accuracy of people's confidence is high. Higher confidence ratings almost inevitably mean that the item had been previously presented. Low ratings correlate very well with the item being new" (p. 176). In commenting on others' research, Wixted and Mickes (2010, p. 1030) remarked that confidence "is a useful proxy for memory strength" (with "memory strength" construed as the strength of a retrieved memory, not the strength of an encoded trace). The authors cited here have a powerful ally: The U.S. Supreme Court ruled in the case of *Neil v. Biggers* (1972) that highly confident eyewitness identifications (ones that meet certain criteria) are likely to be accurate, although not all outside observers were convinced of the Court's argument (see Wells & Murray, 1983).

In striking contrast, researchers from a different tradition of research (mostly investigating memory for faces in eyewitness situations) have sometimes reached a quite different conclusion. Surveying the evidence in 1989, Smith, Kassin, and Ellsworth concluded that "confidence is neither a useful predictor of the accuracy of a particular witness or of the accuracy of particular statements made by the same witness" (p. 358). Kassin, Ellsworth, and Smith (1989) surveyed forensic psychologists and reported that 80% of respondents believed that confidence and accuracy were actually unrelated. Similarly, a 1995 article in *The New York Times* that covered research on eyewitness identification arrived at the same conclusion: "there is little or no relationship between the accuracy of the witness identification and his or her confidence in it" (January 17, 1995, cited by Juslin, Olsson, & Winman, 1996, p. 1304). More recently, Odinot, Wolters, and van Koppen (2009) argued that the relationship between confidence and accuracy is so weak that confidence ratings "should never be allowed as evidence for memory accuracy in the courtroom" (p. 513).

The statements in the first paragraph of this section arguing that confidence and accuracy are highly related came from cognitive psychologists surveying their type of research (as well as from Supreme Court justices). The statements in the second paragraph were derived from social and applied (forensic) psychologists examining research in a different tradition. What are we to make of these conflicting statements? We will argue that both groups have a legitimate point to make with respect to how expressions of confidence should be interpreted in the legal system. However, we shall argue that the conclusions cited above by social and forensic psychologists about confidence never being related to accuracy are far too strong. Often, as cognitive psychologists maintain, confidence and accuracy are positively correlated. Nevertheless, this does not change the fact that confidence is clearly malleable or the fact that high-confidence errors occur considerably more often than was once believed (as long argued by eyewitness memory researchers). The aim of this chapter is to lead toward a more nuanced view of the relation between confidence and accuracy.

Complicating any inquiry into this issue is the fact that the relation between confidence and accuracy can be measured in very different ways. Indeed, different analyses answer different questions about that relationship. Here are some questions that have been asked: Are experimental conditions that are associated with high accuracy also associated with higher confidence compared to conditions that are associated with low accuracy? Are people who are more confident also more accurate than people who are less confident? When individuals express high confidence, are they usually more accurate than when they express low confidence? Because these are different questions, they need not have the same answers. For that reason alone, one cannot make blanket statements about the way in which confidence and accuracy are related in memory reports.

Actually, the situation is even more complex than the preceding paragraphs indicate. Even when the question asked is held constant (e.g., Are experimental conditions that are associated with high accuracy also associated with higher confidence compared to conditions that are associated with low accuracy?), there are different ways of computing the statistic of interest. The different computational methods can yield wildly different answers, and this has contributed to the impression that there is widespread disagreement about the relation between confidence and accuracy. However, it turns out that some computational methods that have been influential in the debate over the confidence-accuracy relationship are not as relevant as was once thought, and those methods have been largely replaced by newer and more useful methods that yield a different answer.

Finally, even when the question that is asked and the computational method of analyzing the relationship between confidence and accuracy are both held constant, it is possible to find data showing both positive correlations and zero correlations between confidence and accuracy, and several experiments have even shown that negative correlations can exist. That is, one can find conditions in which the more errors people make, on average, the more confident they are, on average, in those errors (Brewer & Sampaio, 2005; DeSoto &

Roediger, 2011; Roediger & DeSoto, 2011; Sampaio & Brewer, 2009). By the end of the chapter, we will have explained how all these relationships are possible and try to make sense of them.

ANALYZING THE RELATION BETWEEN ACCURACY AND CONFIDENCE IN MEMORY: FIVE ANALYSES

Psychologists often ask for confidence judgments in studies of perceiving, remembering, decision making, and social behavior. Subjects in experiments readily supply such judgments, but their basis is not well understood. Still, it seems a natural judgment to make. For the purposes of this chapter, we consider only what are called *retrospective confidence judgments*; that is, after events have happened and a person is given some form of test, what is the confidence that the answer provided is correct? Confidence can be measured on various sorts of scales: 1–4, 1–7, 1–20, or even 1–100. In calibration studies, the 1–100 confidence scale has a specific meaning: Subjects are instructed to give a confidence rating of X when they believe that their chances of being correct are X%. Although the measurement scale may have subtle effects on judgments, we think this factor does not play a big role for our points below.

In an excellent paper, Busey, Tunnicliff, Loftus, and Loftus (2000) outlined three different ways of analyzing the confidence-accuracy relation in recognition memory. We partly use their framework here, although we extend it to recall and we describe one type of analysis that Busey et al. did not mention (and we discuss a variant of two methods that they did describe). As we shall see, this analysis is critical to understanding zero and negative correlations between confidence and accuracy. The five methods address different questions about the relationship between confidence and accuracy. All of these methods are relevant to psychological theory, but some methods have more direct implications for the legal setting than other methods. Here are the five methods in brief; we consider each one at length in succeeding sections.

1. *Manipulating an independent variable*: An independent variable is manipulated in an experiment (e.g., the retention interval is 1 day or 1 week), and measures of both confidence and accuracy of memory reports are obtained in the various conditions. The question of interest is whether average confidence and average accuracy are correlated across conditions (e.g., are confidence and accuracy both higher, on average, in the 1-day condition compared to the 1-week condition?).

2. *Between-events correlations*: A second type of analysis one can perform (one not described by Busey et al., 2000) is to make the events or items to be remembered the unit of analysis. That is, if people study 100 pictures or

100 words or 100 faces, then a researcher can average across people to determine the accuracy and the confidence with which the events are recollected. Are there some sets of events for which average confidence and average accuracy are highly correlated (say, words) and other sets for which the correlation is zero or even negative (say, faces)?

3. *Between-subjects correlations*: In this case, for each participant, confidence and accuracy are averaged over the events studied. The question then asked of the data is: Are people who are more accurate in their recollections, on average, also more confident in their recollections, on average? Using this method, we can also compare groups: Are confident children no more accurate in their memories than other children, on average, whereas average confidence is a reliable predictor of average accuracy in young adults?

4. *Within-subjects correlations*: In this method, individual subjects are exposed to materials for later recognition or recall. On the test, they are asked to recall or recognize the target items and to give a confidence judgment for each one. The question of interest here is whether items on which subjects are more confident are also items on which they are more accurate (compared to items on which they express low confidence). That is, this analysis asks whether an individual who expresses high confidence in a decision is more likely to be correct than when that same individual expresses low confidence in a decision. This type of analysis can be performed when participants recall or recognize multiple items (e.g., from a list) or multiple details (when eyewitnesses are asked about many different aspects of a crime).

5. *Within/between hybrid analysis*: The last method is the one that is most commonly used in applied research investigating the relationship between confidence and accuracy. It involves elements of both the between-subjects analysis and the within-subjects analysis. In this method, each subject watches a single event (e.g., a video of an individual committing a crime). Later, memory for the culprit is tested (e.g., using a photo lineup), and a confidence rating is taken. The data for each subject consist of one particular accuracy score (with "incorrect" and "correct" coded as 0 or 1) and one particular confidence rating. Under these conditions, the confidence rating could be a function of both (a) the subject's general inclination to express high confidence (an individual difference, between-subjects variable) and (b) the clarity of the subject's memory for that particular episode (a within-subjects variable because the subject would have made a lower confidence rating if, for example, he or she had paid less attention to the video and had a less clear memory of it). Both play a role because neither source of variance has been averaged out.

We orient the remainder of our review of the literature around these five types of analyses. All five are perfectly legitimate ways of asking about the relation between confidence and accuracy, and they need not (and, in fact, do not) lead to the same answer in all cases. However, the way in which the different answers inform the legal system is not entirely straightforward. As a first step, computing a correlation coefficient between confidence and accuracy is a useful and informative technique, though it can also be misleading (as we shall see later in the chapter). Moreover, regardless of what a correlation coefficient suggests, a particularly informative way of analyzing the relationship for its implications with respect to the legal system does not involve computing a correlation coefficient at all. Instead, it involves plotting the accuracy associated with each level of confidence. Courts of law mainly need to know if accuracy is higher for eyewitnesses who express high confidence compared to eyewitnesses who express low confidence (or, when a witness provides multiple details, whether the high-confidence recollections of the witness should be given more weight than the low-confidence recollections of that same witness).

The most straightforward way to address this question about confidence and accuracy in a research study is to simply compute the probability of making a correct decision for each level of confidence. For example, imagine that confidence ratings in recognition decisions were taken using a 5-point scale (1 = guessing, 5 = certain). For each subject, an accuracy score would be computed for each level of confidence. For example, for all ratings of 5—the highest possible confidence—the percent correct score would equal [correct 5s/(correct 5s + incorrect 5s)] × 100% to answer the question "What percentage of items given the highest confidence rating are actually correct?" The same approach would be used to compute accuracy scores for the remaining levels of confidence. The confidence-accuracy scores for the five levels of confidence would then be averaged across subjects and plotted. A weak relation between confidence and accuracy would be indicated if accuracy for ratings of 1 were similar to accuracy for ratings of 5. A strong relationship would be implied if the accuracy associated with ratings of 5 far exceeds the accuracy associated with ratings of 1. The strength of the relation can, of course, be captured in a correlation coefficient, such as the gamma statistic, and it is important to consider which approach is more informative (e.g., for the legal system). For example, one question that is quite informative is the percentage correct of judgments given the highest level of confidence. If this is, say, 75%, that would mean that 25% of the time the subject gave the highest confidence rating, he or she was wrong. So, even if the overall correlation between confidence and accuracy is high (say, +.80), the most highly confident cases could still often be in error. This fact would still be quite troubling and, in the case of eyewitness confidence in legal settings, could still lead to many wrongful convictions.

In many studies, called *calibration experiments*, the confidence rating scale that is used for each recognition decision is meant to provide more than just an ordinal scale (which is all that the 1–5 scale mentioned above provides). In these studies, subjects are asked to give a confidence rating of X when they believe that their chances of being correct are X%. Thus, a confidence rating of 80% means that the subject believes that across all items given this rating, 80% of the decisions will be correct. As when a 1–5 scale is used, accuracy can be plotted for each level of confidence, but in this new analysis the confidence and accuracy scores are meaningfully related. This kind of plot is known as a *calibration plot*, and it allows for further considerations (e.g., one can see from such a plot whether subjects are generally overconfident or underconfident). But the key point for present purposes is that this kind of analysis (whether on a 1–5 scale or a 1–100 scale) is probably most pertinent to the legal system. Sauer, Brewer, Zweck, and Weber (2010) put it this way:

> The forensic utility of the calibration approach, when compared to correlation, lies in its indication of probable accuracy for each level of confidence. As Juslin et al. (1996) note, the knowledge that the CA [confidence-accuracy] correlation is, for example, .28 does not help assess the accuracy of an individual identification made with 80% confidence. On the other hand, knowing that 80% (or 70, or 90%) of identifications made with 80% confidence are correct provides a guide for assessing the likely reliability of an individual identification decision. (p. 338)

As noted above, the correlation could be very high between confidence and accuracy, and the correctness of the highest confidence accuracy scores might still not be that great if the task is difficult (e.g., 75% correct for the highest level of confidence).

In what follows, we refer to any plot showing the accuracy associated with each level of confidence as a *calibration plot* whether the confidence scale is an ordinal scale (e.g., 1–5) or a probability scale (though, technically, only the latter is a true calibration plot).

Manipulation of Independent Variables

This tactic is the grist for the experimental cognitive psychologist's mill: Select an independent variable that is known (or strongly suspected) to increase accuracy on some measure of memory, manipulate it, and see (1) if the variable does affect the memory measure and (2) whether confidence is affected in a similar manner as the accuracy measure. Many experiments have tried this tactic. A related strategy is to manipulate a variable that is thought to affect confidence in memory judgments and see if accuracy is also affected. We consider each in turn.

Busey et al. (2000) reported three experiments using the first strategy. They had subjects study 30 faces (pictures of bald men, some with facial hair and some without), and they manipulated several variables. In Experiment 1 the faces were presented three times for varying amounts of time (ranging from 230 to 930 milliseconds), and after each picture was presented, 15 seconds were permitted for possible rehearsal or, in a different condition, for math problems (to block rehearsal of those items). Experiments 2 and 3 were similar, except that instead of manipulating presentation duration of the faces, Busey et al. manipulated their luminance (from low to high, or relatively dark to relatively bright). Considering analogs to these variables outside the lab, as in witnessing the perpetrator of a crime, the variables correspond to how long a look the witness had, how bright the scene was, and whether the witness could reflect on (rehearse) the face or was distracted by something else (math problems in the experiment). After viewing the 30 faces, subjects took a test on 60 faces, the 30 previously viewed ones and 30 similar distractors, presented in a random order. They judged each face to be old or new (studied or not studied in the previous phase), and then they gave a confidence judgment on a 5-point scale (from "not at all certain" to "100% certain"). We are considering only part of their experiments here, the part concerned with retrospective confidence judgments (the focus of our chapter). The full experiments are more complex than the portions of interest for present purposes.

The results across the three experiments were highly consistent. Duration of presentation of the faces, luminance, and whether or not time was given for rehearsal of the faces all affected both recognition accuracy and confidence in the same way. We need not go through the details of the results, because the retrospective confidence judgments always followed accuracy. The two measures were tightly bound. The bottom line of the story from Busey et al. is that when an independent variable is manipulated that affects accuracy of memory reports, confidence comes along for the ride. More generally, confidence and accuracy seem well correlated in this kind of experiment in which independent variables are manipulated. In fact, the exceptions are sufficiently few that we can safely conclude that when an independent variable affects accuracy of memory reports, subjects' confidence in those reports will virtually always be affected the same way (however, see Tulving, 1981, for a somewhat different case).

But what about the other type of manipulation described above? If a variable is manipulated that is expected to affect confidence, will it always affect accuracy? The answer here is "no," or at least "not always," because it is possible to manipulate a person's retrospective confidence without influencing his or her accuracy. In the cognitive psychology lab, this is commonly done in the context of Receiver Operating Characteristic (ROC) analysis, in which the hit rate is plotted on the ordinate against the false alarm rate on the abscissa. For example, in a standard list-learning paradigm, Mickes, Hwe, Wais, and Wixted (2011) provided error feedback to subjects who supplied confidence ratings for their old/new recognition decisions using a 20-point confidence scale. In response, the subjects became more cautious about supplying ratings of high confidence on both ends of the confidence scale (i.e., they produced fewer high-confidence old judgments at or near 20 and fewer high-confidence new judgments around 1). The data are shown in Figure 4.1 for the subjects who did not receive feedback and for those who did (and became less likely to give extreme ratings). Each point on the ROC represents the hit rate and the false alarm rate associated with a particular level of confidence. The lower left point represents the hit and false alarm rates associated with the highest confidence rating of 20—the false alarm rate is quite low. Moving up and to the right, the next point represents the hit and false alarm rates associated with confidence ratings of 19 or 20, and so on. As shown in Figure 4.1, overall accuracy remained unchanged between the two conditions; that is, the ROC curve did not move further from the diagonal when subjects became more cautious

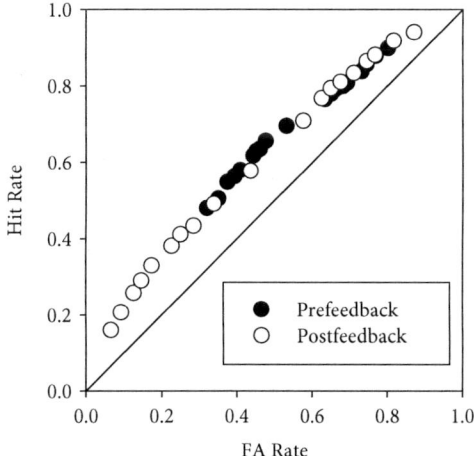

Figure 4.1 In an experiment, subjects made recognition memory judgments and gave confidence ratings. They either did or did not receive feedback. Subjects tended to use the entire range of the confidence scale (open circles) when they did not get feedback. However, with feedback, they were much less likely to use the whole range of the scale. Nonetheless, all the points fall on the same ROC curve, showing that accuracy did not differ between the two conditions despite the variations in confidence. Data are from Mickes, Hwe, Wais, and Wixted (2011).

about using the extreme ratings (e.g., for confidence ratings of 20, both the hit rate and the false alarm rate are lower postfeedback compared to prefeedback). Instead, the points shifted along the same ROC curve after error feedback was provided. Thus, confidence was affected but accuracy (measured by d' in signal detection theory or the distance of the ROC curve from the diagonal) was not in this experiment.

Using an eyewitness memory paradigm in which subjects saw a crime scene, Shaw (1996) had subjects give answers to forced-choice questions during a test of their memories for target items from the scene. That means they had to respond, even if they knew they were guessing. Later, they were exposed to some of their forced-choice answers via questioning. Shaw found that such exposure greatly inflated subjects' confidence in their answers but had no effect on their accuracy. In a related study, Shaw and McClure (1996) showed that repeated questioning influenced witnesses' confidence without increasing their accuracy. This effect was also replicated by Odinot et al. (2009; but see Ebbesen & Rienick, 1998, and a review by Knutsson, Allwood, & Johansson, 2011, that shows that the issue is still in some doubt).

Similarly, an experiment by Wells and Bradfield (1999) revealed that merely introspecting on one's own confidence affects confidence without affecting accuracy. In this study, subjects watched actual security camera footage of a gunman who shot a security guard while off camera. After watching the footage, subjects were asked to identify the gunman from a spread of five photos. Unknown to the subjects, the gunman never appeared in the lineup, yet all 156 subjects in the experiment made a (false) identification.

Two of five experimental conditions are relevant to the present discussion. In one condition, subjects waited 6 minutes after making their identification before they rated their confidence in their identification. In a second condition, an experimenter gave the subjects written instructions prompting them to consider how sure they were that they identified the right person in the photo spread. These subjects waited 6 minutes and were then asked to rate their confidence (on a 100-point scale) in the same fashion as in the first condition.

This study revealed a striking finding: Subjects in the first condition were roughly 50% confident that their identifications were accurate, but subjects who were asked to consider their own confidence were, on average, 70% confident in their false identifications. Wells and Bradfield (1999) dubbed this finding the "thought-alone effect," concluding that "merely thinking about one's confidence, view, and so on, itself seems to produce confidence inflation" (p. 142).

Assuming that Shaw and McClure (1996) and Wells and Bradfield (1999) are correct, then unlike manipulations that affect accuracy and then induce a correlation with confidence, one can manipulate confidence without accuracy showing a corresponding increase. Obviously, to the extent that this latter finding occurs, problems can be created for the criminal justice system. Witnesses who are frequently questioned about a point may become increasingly confident in their answer, even if they are wrong (Shaw, 1996). On the positive side, it might be possible to train witnesses to be more cautious about making high-confidence judgments, thereby increasing their high-confidence accuracy and decreasing their high-confidence false alarm rate (as Mickes et al., 2011, found in the cognitive laboratory). However, in most legal settings, such a suggestion is impractical. People do not practice being witnesses to a crime; by definition, they become witnesses unexpectedly.

To further inform the legal system, a useful issue to consider is what effect postevent questioning and other experimental manipulations (such as retention interval) have on the accuracy associated with different levels of confidence (e.g., using a calibration approach). Counterintuitively, it is possible that the accuracy associated with each level of confidence could decrease even if, as Shaw (1996) observed, the average level of accuracy remained unchanged and average confidence increased with postevent questioning. This could happen if correct and incorrect decisions that were made with low confidence in one condition were made with high confidence in a different condition. Overall accuracy would remain the same if the number of correct and incorrect decisions did not change, but average confidence would increase because more decisions were made with high confidence. At the same time, accuracy for high-confidence decisions could selectively decrease. For example, using a 2-point confidence scale (1 = low, 2 = high), imagine that a subject in condition A made 20 high-confidence decisions, all of which were correct (high-confidence accuracy = 1.0) and 20 low-confidence decisions, 10 of which were correct and 10 of which were incorrect (low-confidence accuracy = 0.50). In this condition, overall accuracy would be 0.75 because 30 out of 40 decisions were correct, and average confidence would be 1.5 because 20 decisions were made with high confidence (2) and 20 decisions were made with low confidence (1). In condition B, suppose this same subject now made 30 high-confidence decisions, 25 of which were correct and 5 of which were incorrect (high-confidence accuracy = 0.83) and also made 10 low-confidence decisions, 5 of which were correct and 5 of which were incorrect (low-confidence accuracy = 0.50). Compared to performance in condition A, high-confidence accuracy selectively decreased in condition B (from 1.0 in A to .83 in B). Even so, overall accuracy remained unchanged at 0.75 (because, again, 30 out of 40 decisions were correct), and average confidence increased to 1.75 (because 30 decisions were made with a high-confidence rating of 2 and 10 were made with a low-confidence rating of 1). Admittedly, this is a hypothetical example, although it is perfectly plausible.

Alternatively, if the overall level of confidence and the overall level of accuracy decreased in response to an experimental manipulation (e.g., as the retention interval increased), the accuracy associated with each individual level of confidence could remain unchanged. In fact, this is essentially the pattern of data reported by Sauer et al. (2010). When subjects identified a suspect as being in the lineup with greater than 50% confidence, the accuracy associated with ratings of 50% to 90% ranged from approximately 50% (not very accurate) to approximately 80% (reasonably accurate). As shown in Figure 4.2, this outcome held true for both short and long retention intervals even though, in the long retention interval condition, average confidence and average accuracy were both lower than in the short retention interval condition. Thus, retention interval, per se, did not have a dramatic effect on calibration. In either condition, if a subject expressed high confidence, accuracy was approximately 80% correct. Ratings of high confidence occurred more often in the short retention interval condition than in the long retention interval condition, but accuracy for high-confidence responses was approximately the same in both cases (though accuracy for low-confidence responses was higher in the short retention interval condition).

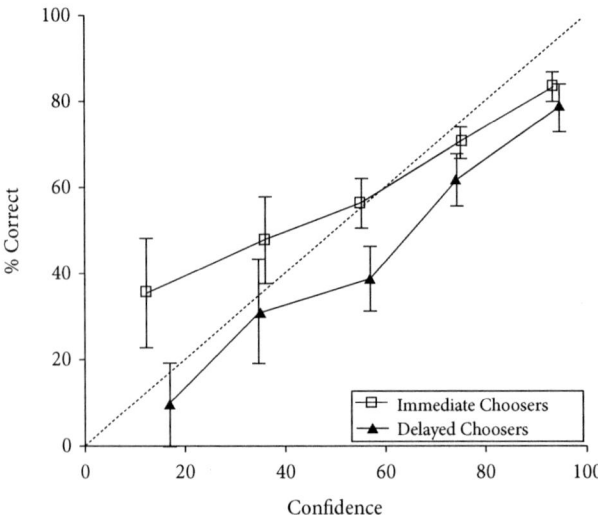

Figure 4.2 Subjects chose a face from a lineup either shortly after seeing the person in a simulated crime or after a delay. Both confidence and accuracy were poorer after the delay, but the calibration plot showed that the relation between confidence and accuracy did not much change. Subjects were somewhat underconfident (i.e., their data are below the diagonal line) after the delay. Data are from Sauer, Brewer, Zweck, and Weber (2010). With kind permission from Springer Science + Business Media: *Law and Human Behavior*, "The Effect of Retention Interval on the Confidence-Accuracy Relationship for Eyewitness Identification," 34, 2009, 343, James Sauer, Fig. 1.

Between-Events Correlations

A surprisingly overlooked type of analysis is that in which *memory events* or *items to be remembered* is the unit of analysis. The question can be posed in various ways. Is the confidence-accuracy relation (say, in a calibration plot) different across faces than across, say, sentences? For Caucasian viewers of faces, is the confidence-accuracy correlation different when they viewed a crime committed by Caucasians relative to Asians relative to African Americans? We cannot know the answers to these questions, for the good reason that no one seems to have asked them. Researchers have shown that there is an effect of race on accuracy, with people better able to recognize and differentiate people of their own race (e.g., Meissner & Brigham, 2001), but surprisingly, no one seems to have addressed the confidence-accuracy relationship in these cases.

Some evidence exists on the between-events correlations with verbal materials, primarily sentences and categorized word lists, and the results are unlike those we have observed to this point. Sampaio and Brewer (2009) used a sentence recognition task and looked at normal (nondeceptive) sentences (ones that generally were meaningful and straightforward) and what they called "deceptive" sentences. The latter consisted of sentences such as "The baby stayed awake all night" or "The karate champion hit the cinder block." In a later sentence recognition test, subjects could be given either the sentence they studied or a changed sentence. Subjects rated the sentence as old or new (studied or not studied), and they rated the confidence in their judgments. For the deceptive sentences the lures were "The baby cried all night" or "The karate champion broke the cinder block." These deceptive variations employ what are called *pragmatic implications*, because the studied sentences do not logically require the implication (the baby could have watched TV all night; the karate champion could have broken her hand), but nonetheless, most people draw the inference that the baby cried and the karate champion broke the cinder block. Sampaio and Brewer compared the correlation of accuracy and confidence for the two types of sentences. They found a modest positive correlation (+.30) between the two for the normal (nondeceptive) sentences, but they obtained a strongly negative correlation (−.61) for the deceptive sentences. That is, the more likely subjects were to false alarm to the sentence, the more confident they were in making the error (across sentences). Sampaio and Brewer concluded:

> With a list of nondeceptive items, one can have a strong positive relationship between confidence and accuracy. With a list including a mixture of deceptive and nondeceptive items, one can have no relationship between confidence and accuracy. With a list of only deceptive items, one can have a strong negative relation between confidence and accuracy. (p. 162)

DeSoto and Roediger (2011) showed a similar pattern in recognition of categorized word lists (that is, words belonging to common categories like birds or articles of clothing). Norms exist for categories that list members of the category in terms of their output dominance, or how likely people are to produce the word when asked to produce members of the category. For birds, *eagle* and *robin* are high-dominance members (likely to be produced by most people), whereas *kiwi* and *penguin* are lower dominance. DeSoto and Roediger had subjects study 10 items from a category like birds (some high dominance and some low dominance among the first 20 birds in the category) and then later gave them a recognition test. The subjects had studied 120 items (10 words from each of 12 categories), and the test provided them with 240 items (the 120 studied items and 120 distractors or lures—nonstudied items from the same categories). Subjects judged each word as old or new and then gave a confidence rating on a 100-point scale so that calibration curves could be plotted. DeSoto and Roediger were especially interested in false recognition to the lures, words from the same categories as studied words but ones that had not been studied. They found that false recognition was much greater for items of high dominance (like *eagle* and *robin*) than for those of low dominance (like *kiwi* and *penguin*). Further, confidence followed the same trend. The items on which subjects were most likely to produce a false alarm also led to false alarms with highest confidence. Thus, they also obtained a negative correlation between confidence and accuracy with related lures, much like Sampaio and Brewer (2009) with their deceptive sentences. Roediger and McDermott (1995) also showed high-confidence false alarms using somewhat different types of word lists.

This type of negative relation between confidence and accuracy is especially troublesome for issues of courtroom testimony—what if eyewitnesses are more likely to be in error the more confident they are? Does this ever happen? Thus, we need to ask if the situation often faced by witnesses is at all like the situation in these experiments. After all, the experiments just described were conducted with verbal materials, whereas eyewitness cases often involve faces. Although evidence is sparse, certainly a case can be made that eyewitness situations may have this character of high similarity between the target person and the members of a lineup. Take an extreme case: A man commits a robbery and his identical twin is arrested for committing it. The witness views a lineup and decides that the man in the lineup is the perpetrator; in addition, she is sure that she is right. It is easy to understand how this situation could occur; the two people look very much alike (unless their hairstyles or other surface features are dissimilar), so a highly confident judgment is understandable, even if it turns out to be false.

The case of the lineup can be a less extreme version of the situation just described: A person witnesses a crime and sees the perpetrator. She gives the police a general description. The police catch a suspect who fits the general description and construct a lineup. If the lineup is constructed properly according to most protocols, the people in the lineup will usually fit the perpetrator's general description. For example, if the perpetrator is described as an Asian American male, no African Americans or Caucasians would be in the lineup. Thus, by design, the members of the lineup will be somewhat similar to the perpetrator, and perhaps the suspect might be most similar. If so, this situation might lead to an erroneous identification. It seems plausible that this situation can arise in true lineups.

Consider the three men whose pictures appear in Figure 4.3. The man on the left was arrested in New York City and accused of committing a rape. He was picked out in a lineup by the victim. The man on the right was arrested for a robbery and also picked out in a lineup by a different witness. Both men spent time in jail before being exonerated. Eventually, the police captured the man in the middle, and he was convicted of both crimes. Obviously, the similarity among the three men is great. Most of us looking at Figure 4.3 could see how the first and third men might be mistakenly identified as the one in the middle. This case (a true case, from New York City in the early 1970s) shows how similarity relations can often affect recognition (the case comes from Buckhout, 1974).

Similarity relations in recognition are, in a way, obvious (but see Tulving, 1981, for a principled exception). Every student knows that a multiple-choice test with highly similar response alternatives is tricky. Lineups with "filler" people who are highly similar to the perpetrator can be viewed as tricky multiple-choice tests where the task is to pick a person from among similar alternatives

 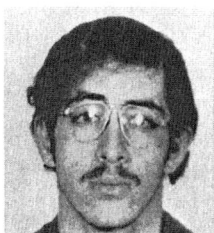 

Lawrence Berson Richard Carbone George Morales

Figure 4.3 Lawrence Berson was arrested for a rape and picked out by the victim in a lineup. The same thing happened to George Morales for a robbery. Later, Richard Carbone was arrested for another crime and confessed to the first two. This example illustrates the problem of similarity in recognition memory. The suspect in the lineup may be judged to be the perpetrator of the crime just because he looks like the perpetrator.

or to say "none of the above." Because of high similarity, sometimes people can make high-confidence false identifications. The results described above by Sampaio and Brewer (2009) and DeSoto and Roediger (2011) show similar results, albeit with verbal materials.

One recent study to show similarity relations in recognition for faces is found in experiments by Carlson, Gronlund, and Clark (2008). In Experiment 2, 619 college students watched a video of a carjacking and then were asked to pick the perpetrator's face out of either a simultaneous or sequential lineup. In a simultaneous lineup, all the faces (both target and lures) are shown to the chooser at the same time; in a sequential lineup, however, only one face is shown at a time. Whether the perpetrator was present or absent in the lineup varied between conditions. The similarity of the different faces in the lineup also varied such that some subjects were presented with extremely similar faces and others were presented with dissimilar faces. Carlson et al. found that false identification in simultaneous lineups was dramatically affected by similarity, such that witnesses were much more likely to falsely identify an innocent face when all the faces presented were similar. In contrast, false identification was low when the faces were not overly similar. Similarity also appeared to have a reduced effect on false identification in sequential lineups. Although Carlson et al. did not collect confidence ratings in their experiment, confidence would probably have increased as a result of visual similarity as well.

Between-Subjects Correlations

A different approach to understanding the relation between confidence and accuracy has been to ask whether there are individual differences in that relationship. That is, are people who generally express high confidence in their decisions also more accurate than those who express low confidence? Conversely, are those who are more accurate also more confident (relative to those who are less accurate)? To answer these questions, subjects might respond to a series of general knowledge questions, expressing confidence in each answer. At the end of the test, an average accuracy score and an average confidence score can be computed for each subject, and then a correlation across subjects can be computed. Of course, the same type of experiment can be done with any sort of material, so long as each subject is assessed on both accuracy and confidence for many events.

Robinson and Johnson (1996) provide a relevant example of the between-subjects approach. In this research, subjects watched a 3-minute video depicting a thief taking money from a woman's purse. After performing a neutral distractor task, subjects answered a questionnaire containing 32 multiple-choice or short-answer questions (e.g., "What was the thief doing before the female teacher entered the snack bar?"). Subjects rated their confidence on a scale from 1 to 9 (1 = not at all confident, 9 = extremely confident). The researchers correlated mean confidence and percent correct for each subject over the 32 questions. Across a variety of recall and recognition conditions, a strong Pearson correlation was found, leading the researchers to conclude that eyewitnesses who tend to be more accurate also tend to be more confident. However, the strength of this between-subjects correlation varied depending on the experimental condition; for instance, the confidence-accuracy relation for subjects making confidence ratings immediately after they had made recognition judgments was nonsignificant ($r = .24$), but the confidence-accuracy relation when confidence ratings were made after all recall responses had been offered was quite strong ($r = .63$). Obviously, this consideration tempers general conclusions about the correlation between confidence and accuracy across people.

A second example of this type of analysis comes from a paper by Perfect, Watson, and Wagstaff (1993). In this experiment, subjects either answered 35 general knowledge questions or watched a forensically relevant 30-minute clip (from the film *Midnight Express*) and answered 35 questions about the clip. After each response, subjects indicated their confidence on a scale from 1 to 5 (1 = very confident, 5 = no idea). For each subject, mean confidence was calculated across all 35 responses, and the proportion correct of the 35 responses was obtained. Then, Pearson product-moment correlation coefficients were calculated between confidence and proportion correct for each individual subject.

Perfect et al. (1993) used the between-subjects approach to compare the confidence-accuracy relation for general knowledge responses and for the forensically relevant responses. They found that for general knowledge questions, there was a strong relation between confidence and proportion correct—subjects who were more confident on average were also more accurate. No relationship, however, was found between confidence and proportion correct for responses to the forensically relevant responses. This effect has been replicated in additional research (e.g., Perfect & Hollins, 1996). These researchers explained this effect by suggesting that significant between-subjects confidence-accuracy correlations can only result when the use of confidence is consistent across people—which is more likely for general knowledge questions than in eyewitness memory (Perfect, Hollins, & Hunt, 2000). Obviously, this research raises doubt about whether courts of law should give more weight to witnesses who are known to express (on average) high confidence in their decisions compared to witnesses who are known to express (on average) lower confidence in their decisions. It may be that highly accurate people are sometimes often lacking in confidence of their knowledge and/or that highly confident people may not be as accurate as they think.

In short, the low correlations between confidence and accuracy when measured between subjects in forensically relevant situations seem to argue that one need not necessarily believe in the accuracy of a witness who displays great confidence. It may well be that other individuals, less confident in their own abilities, may exhibit accuracy just as great as that of the highly confident person. This point essentially says that there are general individual differences in response bias and confidence that may inflate or deflate correlations, depending on their nature.

Although not strictly relevant to the issue at hand, bringing the qualities of subjects into the issue of eyewitness accountability leads to the issue of individual differences in eyewitness memory and testimony. Are children less reliable witnesses than adults? Are older adults less reliable than younger adults? We could add many more questions like this for other groups of people (e.g., people suffering from severe depression who also have poorer memories than matched controls). Reviewing this voluminous literature is beyond the bounds of this chapter, although readers could get a start on the question of children as witnesses from Ceci and Bruck's (1995) book and about older adults from a chapter by Roediger and McDaniel (2007).

Within-Subjects Correlations

A within-subjects analysis asks whether different levels of confidence expressed by an individual are associated with different levels of accuracy. In the metacognition literature, this sort of analysis is referred to as *resolution* (Dunlosky & Metcalfe, 2009). This kind of analysis has been performed in studies in which witnesses provide answers to a variety of questions about the incident they witnessed. For example, Odinot et al. (2009) interviewed 14 witnesses to an actual armed robbery at a supermarket 3 months after the event. The crime was recorded on multiple security cameras, so the accuracy of witness recollections could be assessed. The witnesses were asked a variety of questions (e.g., to provide a full description of the robbers, the guns, the bag used, the position and acts of the robbers, the position and acts of the witness and his or her colleagues). For each answer, a confidence rating was taken using a 7-point scale (1 = very uncertain, 7 = absolutely certain). For each subject, a gamma correlation was computed between confidence and accuracy, and the obtained values ranged from .09 to .96. The mean value was only .38, which seems low. On that basis, the authors concluded that the relationship between confidence and accuracy is so weak that confidence ratings should never be taken into consideration in a court of law.

Does an intrasubject correlation coefficient provide the information that is needed to make such a recommendation? Possibly not. Odinot et al. (2009)

also provided information that allowed one to compute a calibration-like plot of the relationship between confidence and accuracy. Of the 14 witnesses in their study, 9 were centrally involved and were interviewed by the police (the other 5 were not). For the 9 central witnesses, the accuracy of recall associated with ratings of low confidence (1 through 3) was 61% correct. For intermediate confidence ratings (4 through 6), accuracy was 71% correct. For ratings of high confidence (7, which is the confidence rating that was most frequently supplied), accuracy was 85% correct. Thus, for low-confidence ratings, the witness's recollections were only 1.6 times more likely to be correct than incorrect. For high-confidence ratings, they were 5.7 times more likely to be correct than incorrect. This indicates that the relationship between confidence and accuracy is meaningful. At the same time, expressions of high confidence were associated with a 15% error rate. Thus, as we observed in an earlier analysis, a meaningful relationship between confidence and accuracy does not by any means imply that high-confidence memories are even close to being error free. Still, contrary to Odinot et al.'s (2009) conclusion, confidence does seem useful in forensic cases, including the real-life case they investigated.

Within/Between Hybrid Correlations

In the eyewitness domain, it is often the case that the correlation between confidence and accuracy is based on a single accuracy score for a test item and a single confidence rating associated with that item for each subject. For example, subjects might watch a video of a staged crime scene. Later, the subjects would be asked to try to identify the suspect from a photo lineup. Each subject would provide a confidence rating using a numeric scale (e.g., 1 = low confidence, 5 = high confidence), and his or her accuracy would be scored as either being correct (1) or incorrect (0). A point-biserial correlation would then be computed between the confidence and accuracy scores across subjects. This approach is actually a hybrid within/between-correlational approach because the point-biserial correlation computed in this manner is sensitive to both within-subjects variation in confidence and accuracy (if subjects are more accurate when they are more confident) and between-subjects variation in confidence and accuracy (if subjects who are more confident, on average, are also more accurate, on average).

Most of the claims in the eyewitness literature to the effect that the relationship between confidence and accuracy is weak or nonexistent used the hybrid within/between correlational method. The hybrid design of these experiments seems reasonable if the goal is to generalize to courts of law, which are often faced with different individuals who have each been exposed to a single event and who are then asked to make an eyewitness identification.

In studies that have used the hybrid approach, the obtained point-biserial correlation between confidence and accuracy is often very weak, and this created the once-widespread impression that "Witnesses who are confident in their testimony are not substantially more accurate than those who are not" (Smith et al., 1989, p. 358). However, it has since become clear that this conclusion may have been premature because it was based on the point-biserial correlation coefficient, which is not well suited to answering the question of whether witnesses who are more confident in their testimony are also more accurate in one-shot situations. As indicated above, a much more straightforward way to answer this question is to simply compute the likelihood of being correct as a function of confidence expressed (Juslin et al., 1996). Theoretical considerations based on signal-detection theory suggest that, when computed in this more direct way, a substantial relationship between confidence and accuracy should be evident (even if the point-biserial correlation often suggests otherwise). Juslin et al. first showed that for data that exhibit a very strong relationship between confidence and accuracy (in that expressions of high confidence are associated with high accuracy and expressions of low confidence are associated with low accuracy), the point-biserial correlation is nevertheless rather low. This indicates that the point-biserial correlation is problematic (not that the relationship between confidence and accuracy is weak).

Summary of the Various Analyses of Confidence and Accuracy

What is the relationship between confidence and accuracy in reports from memory? The preceding analyses show why this question, as stated, is not really meaningful because it could be asking about the relationship between confidence and accuracy across different conditions or across different people or across different responses made by an individual or across different items within a condition. The answers need not be the same in each domain, so no single answer is possible. Thus, for example, there is no contradiction between the statement that the relationship between confidence and accuracy across different individuals is weak and the statement that the relationship between confidence and accuracy across different responses made by individuals is strong. Consider, for example, a confident person (one who averages 4 on a 5-point confidence scale) whose average accuracy in memory decisions is relatively low (e.g., 59% correct) versus a less confident person (one who averages 3 on a 5-point scale) whose average accuracy is somewhat higher (e.g., 65% correct). In this case, we would be rather unimpressed by the relationship between confidence and accuracy (across people). However, for those same two people, it might also be true that when they express low confidence, their accuracy tends to be low, whereas when they express high confidence, their accuracy tends to be much higher.

Table 4.1 illustrates this situation with hypothetical data for subjects with varying levels of accuracy (percent correct) and confidence (measured on a 1–5 scale). For both subjects in this example, accuracy is very low when confidence is low (1) but accuracy is much higher when confidence is high (5). Even so, the average accuracy for the relatively confident Subject 1 (89 out of 150 correct) is only 59%, whereas the average accuracy of the less confident Subject 2 (97 out of 150 correct) is 65%. The average confidence for Subject 1 is higher because most decisions were made with high confidence (5), whereas most of Subject 2's were made with medium confidence (3).

Every approach to assessing the relationship between confidence and accuracy is relevant to psychological theory, whether that relationship is measured by a correlation coefficient or by a calibration curve. For example, why is the relationship between confidence and accuracy higher for some stimulus materials than for others? Such questions are important for the experimental psychologist to answer to inform theory development, but the answers are potentially relevant to the legal system as well. For example, if the events of interest in a particular crime happen to be stimuli for which ratings of confidence in the laboratory have been found to be especially poor indicators of accuracy, such information would be important to know. However, at the present time, we know precious little about how to characterize the stimuli that are encountered in real-world crime situations in terms of how they might influence the relationship between confidence and accuracy in later reports

Table 4-1 HYPOTHETICAL ILLUSTRATION OF CORRECT AND INCORRECT RESPONSES AS A FUNCTION OF CONFIDENCE MADE USING A 5-POINT SCALE FOR TWO SUBJECTS

	CONFIDENCE	TOTAL RESPONSES	CORRECT	INCORRECT	% CORRECT
Subject 1	1	10	1	9	10%
	2	15	3	12	20%
	3	20	6	14	30%
	4	25	15	10	60%
	5	80	64	16	80%
	Σ	**150**	**89**	**61**	
Subject 2	1	30	9	21	30%
	2	20	10	10	50%
	3	50	35	15	70%
	4	20	16	4	80%
	5	30	27	3	90%
	Σ	**150**	**97**	**53**	

from memory. Thus, for the time being, the best we can do in order to generalize conclusions about the relationship between confidence and accuracy to the legal setting is to arrange ecologically valid experiments that seem to be as closely modeled on real-world situations as possible. Many experiments in the applied literature have followed that approach, and some general conclusions for the legal system can be drawn from them.

PRACTICAL IMPLICATIONS FOR THE LEGAL SYSTEM

Of the various questions that have been asked about the relationship between confidence and accuracy, the two that seem most relevant to the legal setting are the within-person measures (e.g., when a witness recounts multiple crime-scene details, each accompanied by a confidence rating) and the within/between hybrid measures (e.g., when different witnesses make a single eyewitness judgment accompanied by a confidence rating). Ideally, studies of these questions would be conducted in the real world and would involve events associated with real crimes, known perpetrators, and real police lineups. Obviously, this ideal is rather hard to achieve, but in studies that have attempted to match reality as closely as possible, two points seem to emerge (from both within-person and within/between hybrid studies):

1. Confidence is a reliable indicator of accuracy in the sense that reports from memory made with low confidence are generally associated with low accuracy, whereas reports made with high confidence are generally associated with higher accuracy. This is true even though point-biserial and gamma correlation coefficients are often low. Whereas the correlation coefficient offers little useful information for courts of law, the descriptive relationship between levels of confidence and associated levels of accuracy provides more intelligible and (therefore) useful information (Juslin et al., 1996). Although it is contrary to the legal testimony of many expert witnesses in recent years, the evidence suggests that, in the absence of known contamination (e.g., exposure to misleading postevent information), it is reasonable to regard the confidence expressed by eyewitnesses as a useful indicator of the reliability of the memory decision. This is especially so for more immediate tests of memory and not necessarily for courtroom testimony that often occurs much later. The reason is that we base our conclusions on experiments in which confidence and accuracy are assessed shortly after the witnessed event and without repeated testing. Thus, our recommendation that confidence should be taken into account applies most strongly to police interrogations. Repeated questioning of witnesses has sometimes been found to increase confidence without increasing accuracy (Shaw & McClure, 1996). By the time a witness arrives in court (often months or even years after

the occurrence of the crime), confidence may be relatively fixed by prior tests. If the witness has been confident in his or her judgment ever since the first examination by police, then the high confidence may be warranted. However, if confidence was low on the initial examination (say, a photo lineup) but then grew over time and repeated testing (more photo lineups, a real lineup, identification in court), then the confidence may be less trustworthy. Certainly, even on an immediate test, confidence is not infallible, which leads to the next point.

2. Ratings made with high confidence can be associated with an error rate that is far too high for someone to be considered guilty of a crime solely on the basis of high-confidence identification by a single eyewitness. Indeed, it is not uncommon to find accuracy rates associated with high confidence in the range of 80% to 90% correct (i.e., a 10% to 20% error rate) even in situations that do not involve misleading postevent information or potentially confidence-inflating activities such as repeated postevent questioning (Wells, Memon, & Penrod, 2006). Thus, in light of the evidence, convicting a defendant solely on the basis of the high-confidence memory-based testimony of one witness who is identifying a previous stranger should itself be a crime (or at least it is wrong). Reports from memory—including ones with high confidence—are simply not a reliable enough indicator of truth to unilaterally adjudicate guilt or innocence. The situation is different if one is identifying a well-known person rather than a stranger. Nonetheless, the point is that eyewitness testimony should be considered one piece of evidence in a complex web of information (direct or circumstantial) that would indicate a person's guilt or innocence in criminal situations. We believe it is a mistake to convict someone based on this single piece of evidence because of the many problems discussed in this chapter.

CONCLUSION

The main point of our chapter is that eyewitness memory confidence is a useful but imperfect indicator of the truth. In that sense, it is much like all other forms of evidence that courts must deal with on a daily basis. With the possible exception of DNA evidence, which can approach the ideal of infallibility, evidence in the real world is almost invariably fallible, including fingerprint evidence, fiber evidence, microscopic hair analysis, bloodstain pattern analysis, handwriting analysis, and so on. Even DNA evidence is not as simple as it is often portrayed (see Lindsey, Hertwig, & Gigerenzer, 2003). In a recent report to Congress on the subject of forensic analysis, the National Research Council (2009) observed:

> A body of research is required to establish the limits and measures of performance and to address the impact of sources of variability and potential

bias. Such research is sorely needed, but it seems to be lacking in most of the forensic disciplines that rely on subjective assessments of matching characteristics. These disciplines need to develop rigorous protocols to guide these subjective interpretations and pursue equally rigorous research and evaluation programs. (p. S-6)

Subjective interpretation is an inescapable component of many forms of evidence evaluation, not just when the evidence consists of eyewitness memory. Whether the evidence consists of eyewitness memory or expert fingerprint analysis, confidence ratings can help to provide an indication of its reliability. With regard to fingerprint evidence, for example, Mnookin (2008) argued that fingerprint examiners would do well to provide graded expressions of confidence in their analyses instead of always expressing certainty so that courts of law could better appreciate how reliable the analysis is:

Given the general lack of validity testing for fingerprinting; the relative dearth of difficult proficiency tests; the lack of a statistically valid model of fingerprinting; and the lack of validated standards for declaring a match, such claims of absolute, certain confidence in identification are unjustified, the product of hubris more than established knowledge. (p. 139)

Fingerprint analysts presumably have the training and experience to judge the confidence of their analyses in a way that corresponds to the accuracy of their analyses. However, it seems reasonable to suppose that research would show that while their expressions of confidence are indicative of accuracy, expressions of certainty would not indicate 100% accuracy. Whether or not that is true of fingerprint analysts, it does appear to be true of eyewitnesses. By virtue of a lifetime of training and experience in the use of memory, eyewitnesses appear to have acquired some degree of expertise in judging the reliability of their own recollections. Even so, that expertise has its limits, with the most important one being that expressions of 100% certainty or confidence do not reflect 100% accuracy.

Because virtually all forms of evidence are fallible (even when accompanied by expressions of 100% certainty), multiple indicators of guilt should be combined to eliminate reasonable doubt, as might happen if all of the indicators point strongly in the direction of guilt. High-confidence eyewitness testimony alone can never do that, for the simple reason that virtually all studies show that ratings of high confidence occur with significant probabilities of error (often 10%–20% in experimental settings). At the same time, ignoring confidence ratings altogether is chucking the baby out with the bathwater. A witness who is highly confident about some details of an event almost certainly is more accurate on these details than on those details provided with low confidence. Precisely because evidence is fallible, every reliable indicator should be made available to the court, and confidence in reports from memory should be no exception.

ACKNOWLEDGMENTS

We thank Pooja Agarwal, Sean Kang, Kathleen McDermott, Laura Mickes, Lynn Nadel, John Nestojko, Adam Putnam, Walter Sinnott-Armstrong, and Yana Weinstein for comments on prior drafts of this chapter.

REFERENCES

Barclay, J. R., Bransford, J. D., Franks, J. J., McCarrell, N. S., & Nitsch, K. (1974). Comprehension and semantic flexibility. *Journal of Verbal Learning and Verbal Behavior*, 13, 471–481.

Bartlett, F. C. (1932). *Remembering: A study in experimental and social psychology*. Cambridge: Cambridge University Press.

Brainerd, C. J., & Reyna, V. F. (2005). *The science of false memory*. New York: Oxford University Press.

Brewer, W. F., Sampaio, C., & Barlow, M. R. (2005). Confidence and accuracy in the recall of deceptive and nondeceptive sentences. *Journal of Memory and Language*, 52, 618–627.

Buckhout, R. (1974). Eyewitness testimony. *Scientific American*, 231, 23–31.

Busey, T. A., Tunnicliff, J., Loftus, G. R., & Loftus, E. F. (2000). Accounts of the confidence-accuracy relation in recognition memory. *Psychonomic Bulletin & Review*, 7, 26–48.

Carlson, C. A., Gronlund, S. D., & Clark, S. E. (2008). Lineup composition, suspect position, and the sequential lineup advantage. *Journal of Experimental Psychology: Applied*, 14, 118–128.

Ceci, S. J., & Bruck, M. (1995). *Jeopardy in the courtroom: A scientific analysis of children's testimony*. Washington, DC: American Psychological Association.

Craik, F. I. M., & Lockhart, R. S. (1972). Levels of processing: A framework for memory research. *Journal of Verbal Learning and Verbal Behavior*, 11, 671–684.

DeSoto, K. A., & Roediger, H. L. (2011). *Often wrong but never in doubt: Typicality relates to confident false memories*. Manuscript in preparation, Psychology Department, Washington University, St. Louis, MO.

Dunlosky, J., & Metcalfe, J. (2009). *Metacognition*. Thousand Oaks, CA: Sage Publications.

Ebbesen, E. B., & Rienick, C. B. (1998). Retention interval and eyewitness memory for events and personal identifying attributes. *Journal of Applied Psychology*, 83(5), 745–762.

Garrett, B. F. (2011). *Convicting the innocent*. Cambridge, MA: Harvard University Press.

Hamilton, E. (1961). *Plato: The collected dialogues.* New York: Bollingen Foundation.

Juslin, P., Olsson, N., & Winman, A. (1996). Calibration and diagnosticity of confidence in eyewitness identification: Comments on what can be inferred from the low confidence–accuracy correlation. *Journal of Experimental Psychology: Learning, Memory, and Cognition, 22,* 1304–1316.

Kassin, S. M., Ellsworth, P. C., & Smith, V. L. (1989). The "general acceptance" of psychological research on eyewitness testimony: A survey of the experts. *American Psychologist, 44,* 1089–1098.

King, J. F., Zechmeister, E. B., & Shaughnessy, J. J. (1980). Judgments of knowing: The influence of retrieval practice. *The American Journal of Psychology, 93,* 329–343.

Knutsson, J., Allwood, C. M., & Johansson, M. (2011). Child and adult witnesses: The effect of repetition and invitation-probes on free recall and metamemory realism. *Metacognition and Learning, 3,* 213–228.

Lindsey, S., Hertwig, R., & Gigerenzer, G. (2003). Communicating statistical DNA evidence. *Jurimetrics, 43,* 147–163.

Loftus, E. F. (1975). Leading questions and the eyewitness report. *Cognitive Psychology, 7,* 550–572.

Loftus, E. F. (1992). When a lie becomes memory's truth: Memory distortion after exposure to misinformation. *Current Directions in Psychological Science, 1,* 121–123.

Loftus, E. F. (1996). *Eyewitness testimony.* Cambridge, MA: Harvard University Press.

Loftus, E. F., & Palmer, J. C. (1974). Reconstruction of automobile destruction: An example of the interaction between language and memory. *Journal of Verbal Learning and Verbal Behavior, 13,* 585–589.

McGeoch, J. A. (1932). Forgetting and the law of disuse. *Psychological Review, 39,* 352–370.

Meissner, C. A., & Brigham, J. C. (2001). Thirty years of investigating the own-race bias in memory for faces: A meta-analytic review. *Psychology, Public Policy, and Law, 7,* 3–35.

Mickes, L., Hwe, V., Wais, P. E., & Wixted, J. T. (2011). Strong memories are hard to scale. *Journal of Experimental Psychology: General, 140,* 239–257.

Mnookin, J. L. (2008). The validity of latent fingerprint identification: Confessions of a fingerprinting moderate. *Law, Probability and Risk, 7,* 127–141.

Münsterberg, H. (1908). *On the witness stand.* New York: Doubleday.

National Research Council (2009). *Strengthening forensic science in the United States: A path forward.* Washington, DC: National Academies Press.

Neil v. Biggers, 409 U.S. 188 (1972).

Odinot, G., Wolters, G., & van Koppen, P. J. (2009). Eyewitness memory of a supermarket robbery: A case study of accuracy and confidence after 3 months. *Law and Human Behavior, 33,* 506–514.

Perfect, T. J., & Hollins, T. S. (1996). Predictive feeling of knowing judgments and postdictive confidence judgments in eyewitness memory and general knowledge. *Applied Cognitive Psychology, 10,* 371–382.

Perfect, T. J., Hollins, T. S., & Hunt, A. L. (2000). Practice and feedback effects on the confidence-accuracy relation in eyewitness memory. *Memory, 8,* 235–244.

Perfect, T. J., Watson, E. L., & Wagstaff, G. F. (1993). Accuracy of confidence ratings associated with general knowledge and eyewitness memory. *Journal of Applied Psychology, 78*, 144–147.

Robinson, M. D., & Johnson, J. T. (1996). Recall memory, recognition memory, and the eyewitness confidence-accuracy correlation. *Journal of Applied Psychology, 81*, 587–594.

Roediger, H. L. (1980). Memory metaphors in cognitive psychology. *Memory & Cognition, 8*, 231–246.

Roediger, H. L. (2008). Relativity of remembering: Why the laws of memory vanished. *Annual Review of Psychology, 59*, 225–254.

Roediger, H. L., & DeSoto, K. A. (2011). *Complexities in the relation between confidence and accuracy in recognition memory.* Manuscript in preparation, Psychology Department, Washington University, St. Louis, MO.

Roediger, H. L., & Gallo, D. A. (2002). Processes affecting accuracy and distortion in memory: An overview. In M. L. Eisen, G. S. Goodman, & J. A. Quas (Eds.), *Memory and suggestibility in the forensic interview* (pp. 3–28). Mahwah, NJ: Erlbaum.

Roediger, H. L., Jacoby, J. D., & McDermott, K. B. (1996). Misinformation effects in recall: Creating false memories through repeated retrieval. *Journal of Memory and Language, 35*, 300–318.

Roediger, H. L. & McDaniel, M. A. (2007). Illusory recollections in older adults: Testing Mark Twain's conjecture. In M. Garry & H. Hayne (Eds.), *Do justice and let the sky fall: Elizabeth F. Loftus and her contributions to science, law, and academic freedom* (pp. 105–136). Hillsdale, NJ: Erlbaum.

Roediger, H. L., & McDermott, K. B. (1995). Creating false memories: Remembering words not presented in lists. *Journal of Experimental Psychology: Learning, Memory and Cognition, 21*, 803–814.

Roediger, H. L., & Payne, D. G. (1982). Hypermnesia: The role of repeated testing. *Journal of Experimental Psychology: Learning, Memory, and Cognition, 8*, 66–72.

Rubin, D. C., & Wallace, W. T. (1989). Rhyme and reason: Analyses of dual retrieval cues. *Journal of Experimental Psychology: Learning, Memory, and Cognition, 15*, 698–709.

Sampaio, C., & Brewer, W. F. (2009). The role of unconscious memory errors in judgments of confidence for sentence recognition. *Memory & Cognition, 37*, 158–163.

Sauer, J., Brewer, N., Zweck, T., & Weber, N. (2010). The effect of retention interval on the confidence-accuracy relationship for eyewitness identification. *Law and Human Behavior, 34*, 337–347.

Shaw, J. S. (1996). Increases in eyewitness confidence resulting from postevent questioning. *Journal of Experimental Psychology: Applied, 2*, 126–146.

Shaw, J. S., & McClure, K. A. (1996). Repeated postevent questioning can lead to elevated levels of eyewitness confidence. *Law and Human Behavior, 20*, 629–653.

Smith, V. L., Kassin, S. M., & Ellsworth, P. C. (1989). Eyewitness accuracy and confidence: Within- versus between-subjects correlations. *The Journal of Applied Psychology, 74*, 356–359.

Tulving, E. (1974). Cue-dependent forgetting. *American Scientist, 62*, 74–82.

Tulving, E. (1981). Similarity relations in recognition. *Journal of Verbal Learning and Verbal Behavior, 20*, 479–496.

Tulving, E. (1983) *Elements of episodic memory.* New York: Oxford University Press.

Tulving, E., & Pearlstone, Z. (1966). Availability versus accessibility of information in memory for words. *Journal of Verbal Learning and Verbal Behavior, 5,* 381–391.

Wells, G. L., & Bradfield, A. L. (1999). Distortions in eyewitnesses' recollections: Can the postidentification-feedback effect be moderated? *Psychological Science, 10,* 138–144.

Wells, G. L., Memon, A., & Penrod, S. D. (2006). Eyewitness evidence: Improving its probative value. *Psychological Science in the Public Interest, 7,* 45–75.

Wells, G. L., & Murray, D. M. (1983). What can psychology say about the *Neil v. Biggers* criteria for judging eyewitness accuracy? *Journal of Applied Psychology, 68,* 347–362.

Wixted, J. T., & Mickes, L. (2010). A continuous dual-process model of remember/know judgments. *Psychological Review, 117*(4), 1025–1054.

5

Evaluating Confidence in Our Memories

Results and Implications from Neuroimaging and Eye Movement Monitoring Studies of Metamemory

ELIZABETH F. CHUA

Eyewitness misidentifications are the most common cause of wrongful convictions, playing a role in over 75% of cases that are overturned by DNA evidence (http://www.innocenceproject.org/understand/Eyewitness-Misidentification.php; Wells, et al., 1998). These misidentifications are likely the result of the fact that our memory is constructive in nature and not a verbatim recording of the past (Schacter & Dodson, 2001; Schacter, Norman, & Koutstaal, 1998) rather than a malicious intent to wrongfully accuse another individual. However, if eyewitness identifications are susceptible to distortions, then how do we evaluate the validity of an eyewitness's identification? Confidence in the eyewitness identification is the most common way accuracy is assessed, and confident witnesses are very convincing to jurors (Wells & Olson, 2003). Indeed, several court cases have indicated that confidence is a good indicator of accuracy and should be used to evaluate the accuracy of the eyewitness's identification (*Manson v. Braithwaite*, 1977; *United States v. Telfaire*, 1979). However, 87% of experimental psychologists surveyed would testify that confidence is *not* necessarily a good indicator of accuracy (Kassin, Ellsworth, & Smith, 1989; Kassin, Tubb, Hosch, & Memon, 2001). What do these psychologists know that the courts do not?

Let's consider the following case: On the witness stand, Roberta Ingrado was 100% confident that Dror Goldberg was the man who brutally stabbed Manuel Silverio to death (*Goldberg v. State*, 2002). Most people would find her certainty convincing (Cutler, Penrod, & Stuve, 1988; Wells & Olson, 2003). However, at the time of the lineup, which in this case occurred years earlier, she was only 80% confident in her identification (*Goldberg v. State*, 2002; Rubenzer, 2002). Many fewer people would be willing to convict on the basis of an identification made with only 80% confidence (Cutler et al., 1988). Would you trust her identification, especially given this change in confidence? At the very least, the change in confidence should raise a warning flag that something other than memory for the original event is contributing to her confidence. Thus, understanding what sources of information people use to make their confidence judgments is critical for being able to evaluate the validity of a confidence judgment. When individuals make a confidence judgment, they monitor the contents of their memory for relevant information and then make a final response. Researchers in the field of metamemory study people's knowledge of their own memory, including the monitoring processes that lead to a final judgment. One purpose of metamemory research is to characterize the accuracies and inaccuracies of people's introspective reports about their memory. In this chapter, I will discuss some of the theoretical and empirical work that focuses on how people make retrospective confidence judgments about their memory. I will then turn to whether particular methods, namely neuroimaging and eye tracking, might be useful in (1) distinguishing highly confident accurate and highly confident inaccurate memory and (2) determining what sources of information people use to make their confidence judgments.

HOW DO WE MAKE OUR CONFIDENCE JUDGMENTS?

The most common assumption is that memory confidence is strongly correlated with the strength or quality of the individual's internal memory representation (Stretch & Wixted, 1998; Yonelinas, 1994). In some cases, this may be the dominant source for confidence, but numerous studies have shown that there are also other factors that influence memory confidence (Bradfield, Wells, & Olson, 2002; Lindsay, Read, & Sharma, 1998; Perfect, Hollins, & Hunt, 2000; Sporer, 1993; Wells & Olson, 2003; Wells, Olson, & Charman, 2002, 2003). Almost everyone who has taken a multiple-choice test and used the process of elimination has experienced how confidence in an answer can be based on factors other than memory for the sought-after information. In such cases, even if an individual does not remember the correct answer to the question, but knows that all but one of the alternatives are wrong, that person should be confident that the remaining answer is correct, even though he or she does not have direct knowledge that the answer is correct. This is just one example of a reasoned, analytical process that can influence confidence judgments, and there are many others. Theoretical conceptions of the types of influences on confidence judgments, as well as other metamemory judgments, have divided them into two types: *experience-based* and *information-based* (Koriat, Nussinson, Bless, & Shaked, 2008). Information-based judgments, as exemplified by but not limited to the process of elimination, are based on declarative knowledge and are the result of a deliberate, reasoned process. In contrast, experience-based judgments are made on the basis of a subjective feeling that arises from the mnemonic experience of the individual. Most people assume that memory confidence is experience-based and that the experience is directly tied to an accurate underlying memory representation. Of course, confidence judgments do not have to be, and are not likely to be, entirely experience-based or entirely information-based. Instead, they are likely to be based on a combination of experience- and information-related factors (Koriat, et al., 2008). However, it is useful to consider them separately to understand their influences on memory confidence.

Experience-based retrospective confidence judgments are based on the online experience of remembering (Koriat et al., 2008). The accuracy of experience-based judgments is often, but not always, similar to memory accuracy (Koriat et al., 2008; Yonelinas, 1994), especially if the mnemonic experience is based on the initial recollection. Research has shown that confidence judgments can be influenced by familiarity (Yonelinas, 1994), vividness of recollected details (Robinson, Johnson, & Robertson, 2000), and how quickly or easily the target information is retrieved (Kelley & Lindsay, 1993; Robinson, Johnson, & Herndon, 1997). In other words, memories that are retrieved more quickly and easily are often associated with higher confidence than memories that are more effortful to retrieve, and these factors also tend to be associated with the underlying memory trace. Thus, it is not surprising that in everyday situations memory confidence judgments based on these experience-based factors are often more accurate (Brewer, Keast, & Rishworth, 2002; Robinson et al., 2000; Sporer, Penrod, Read, & Cutler, 1995). Experience-based confidence judgments may be more desirable than information-based judgments because they tend to be more accurate and because they are thought to be related to the quality of the memory for the event.

However, it is important to note that most research procedures investigating experience-based judgments in the laboratory are very different from the circumstances under which eyewitnesses retrieve their memories, and the content is also quite different. Most laboratory studies on experience-based confidence judgments involve participants retrieving a single episode, but this is not the case with eyewitnesses, who are often repeatedly recalling the same event over a long period of time. It is well established that repetition enhances the ease with which information is retrieved (e.g., Kelley & Lindsay, 1993), so an eyewitness's experience of remembering the event may be related to factors other than the strength of the original memory. Indeed, repeated recall has been shown to increase false memories and the confidence in those memories (e.g., Roediger, Jacoby, & McDermott, 1996; Zaragoza & Mitchell, 1996). In other words, experience-based confidence judgments, although likely more accurate than information-based judgments, are still fallible and may not be able to distinguish between accurate memory and certain kinds of memory distortions, such as source misattributions. Source misattributions are a kind of memory error that occurs when the information remembered is associated with the wrong context (e.g., mistakenly remembering seeing someone in person instead of hearing someone else say he had seen someone in person).

Information-based confidence judgments, on the other hand, have a less consistent relationship to memory accuracy and the underlying memory trace for the event in question. As one might expect, the relationship of information-based confidence judgments to accuracy depends on the accuracy of the premises on which they are based (Koriat et al., 2008). As such, confidence judgments that are information-based, completely or in part, are more likely to be less accurate as a whole. Importantly for the legal system and eyewitness confidence, information-based judgments are less likely to be grounded in the individual's memory for the event and may be contaminated by other individuals' perspectives and beliefs (Luus & Wells, 1994; Shaw, Appio, Zerr, & Pontoski, 2007). However, there are types of information, such as the witness's knowledge of how good or bad his or her view of the crime was, that are relevant for eyewitness confidence and are not necessarily sources of contamination.

Much of the eyewitness confidence research has focused on the impact of information-based judgments on the confidence-accuracy relationship. There has been particular interest in how factors called *system variables*, which can be controlled by the judicial system (Wells & Seelau, 1995), influence confidence. Indeed, based on eyewitness research, some researchers have even made recommendations on how to conduct lineups so as to get the best relationship between confidence and accuracy possible (Wells et al., 1998). One example is *sequential* versus *simultaneous* lineups (Lindsay & Wells, 1985). The simultaneous lineup is the traditional lineup, in which several individuals are viewed together. By seeing multiple individuals together, the eyewitness may make a *relative* judgment in which the eyewitness weighs the evidence for one suspect over another, much as in a multiple-choice test. In contrast, the sequential lineup, in which suspects are presented one after another, minimizes the ability to make comparisons among the suspects and encourages the eyewitness to make a more experience-based or absolute judgment. Indeed, several studies have shown that sequential lineups show reduced rates of mistaken identifications (Clark & Davey, 2005; Kneller, Memon, & Stevenage, 2001; Sporer, 1993; Steblay, Dysart, Fulero, & Lindsay, 2001).

Another example of information-based confidence judgments causing inflated confidence in an identification comes from studies on postidentification feedback. Witnesses who were told, after making an identification from a lineup, "Good, you identified the actual suspect" showed increased confidence in their memory compared to those who heard no feedback or were given disconfirming feedback (Lindsay & Wells, 1985). Furthermore, positive feedback has been shown to inflate confidence in both accurate and mistaken identifications (Semmler, Brewer, & Wells, 2004). This effect is robust, and a recent meta-analysis of studies investigating postidentification feedback showed large effects of feedback on eyewitness confidence (Douglass & Steblay, 2006). In such cases, individuals are acknowledging the feedback and are incorporating this declarative knowledge into their confidence decisions. If this feedback is accurate, then confidence and accuracy will be related. However, in a courtroom setting, establishing a strong confidence-accuracy relationship is not the only goal. In the courtroom, a defendant deserves a fair trial; therefore, witness confidence should not be contaminated by someone who has a priori knowledge of the suspect. A proposed way to combat this issue is to have double-blind lineup procedures, in which neither the witness nor the administrator knows who the suspect is (Wells et al., 1998).

Another issue that often comes up in the eyewitness research literature is the malleability of confidence. *Confidence malleability* refers to the finding that an eyewitness becomes more or less confident about his or her identification based on events that occur after the identification (Wells & Seelau, 1995). Indeed, this was illustrated by the case of Roberta Ingrado going from 80% to 100% confident in her identification of Dror Goldberg (*Goldberg v. State*, 2002). One way to think about this issue is to think about the difference between "I am confident that I *remember and saw* that the suspect committed the crime" and "I am confident that the suspect committed the crime." In the latter case, factors other than memory for the event come into play, and these may be biased against the accused. An example of a variable that can lead to changes in confidence is the identification of a co-witness (Luus & Wells, 1994) or even social pressure (Shaw et al., 2007). For example, Luus & Wells (1994) showed that when witnesses were told that a co-witness identified the same suspect, they increased their confidence; similarly, when the co-witness reported a conflicting identification, they decreased their confidence. What a co-witness does should not influence the original witness' memory, but it does influence his or her confidence. This is related to several studied phenomena. For example, this tendency to change a previous judgment in light of new information has been referred to as the *hindsight bias* (for review, see Blank,

Musch, & Pohl, 2007), and has been studied extensively in terms of memory and metacognitive judgments (e.g., Mazzoni & Vannucci, 2007; Sanna & Schwarz, 2007). Another example is the *illusion of knowledge*, in which more knowledge can lead to increased confidence, even when accuracy is reduced (e.g., Hall, Ariss, & Todorov, 2007). New information based on a co-witness is one example of a factor that can change a witness's confidence, and it is yet another example of an information-based judgment that can be dangerous in the courtroom. Based on the finding that confidence is malleable, one recommendation has been to record the witness' confidence immediately after the identification is made (Wells et al., 1998) in the hope that this confidence judgment will be less contaminated by extraneous factors. Recording witness confidence immediately after the identification is made is also useful in combatting inflation in confidence due to repetition.

In addition to understanding what variables could lead to overconfidence in an identification, much research has been directed at finding *markers* or *assessment variables* to help distinguish between accurate and mistaken eyewitness identifications (Sporer, 1993). Examples of potential markers that have been investigated include confidence-accuracy calibration curves (Weber & Brewer, 2003) and response latency cutoffs (Weber, Brewer, Wells, Semmler, & Keast, 2004). Thus far, these curves have led to some statistically significant and insignificant findings, but they have not been found to be robust enough to use as a marker. In the remainder of the chapter, I focus on two methods, neuroimaging and eye tracking, and their potential use as a marker for (1) distinguishing confident accurate and inaccurate memory and (2) identifying the sources of information used to make confidence judgments.

WHAT CAN NEUROIMAGING TELL US ABOUT CONFIDENCE AND ACCURACY IN MEMORY?

Neuroimaging studies of metamemory are still in their infancy, especially those related to retrospective confidence judgments (for review, see Schwartz & Bacon, 2008). Although numerous neuroimaging studies have used confidence as a measure of memory quality or memory strength (Ranganath et al., 2004; Yonelinas, Otten, Shaw, & Rugg, 2005), we will focus here primarily on studies examining brain activations that inform the basis of retrospective confidence judgments and can distinguish between confident accurate and inaccurate memory. There are three main ways that neuroimaging studies have examined metacognition: (1) by investigating which brain regions are involved in the process of making the metacognitive judgment, (2) by determining those brain regions in which activity is modulated by the subjective level of confidence expressed for both accurate and inaccurate memory, and

(3) by examining those brain regions in which activity is modulated based on metacognitive accuracy.

A fundamental question to ask is whether the same cognitive processes are engaged when people make confidence judgments and when people make recognition judgments. If explicit confidence is tied to the recognition judgment and happens automatically as people are retrieving memory, or if the judgments were solely experience-based, then we might expect similar patterns of brain activity when people make confidence and recognition judgments. If people engage in additional cognitive processes beyond any automatic memory monitoring that occurs, such as incorporating information-related factors, then we would expect to see different patterns of brain activity when people make recognition and confidence judgments. As mentioned previously, behavioral evidence that confidence and accuracy can be dissociated suggests that there are additional influences on making confidence judgments besides just the recognition experience (Koriat, 2008a, 2008b; Koriat et al., 2008). In our own neuroimaging study, we directly contrasted brain activity, as measured by functional magnetic resonance imaging (fMRI), and showed that there were many brain regions that showed greater activity when participants made confidence judgments about their recognition performance than when they performed a forced-choice recognition task (Chua, Schacter, Rand-Giovannetti, & Sperling, 2006). The brain regions that showed greater activity when individuals made confidence judgments compared to recognition judgments, including medial prefrontal, medial parietal, and lateral parietal cortices, have been shown to be involved in self-reflection and self-related processing (Gusnard, Akbudak, Shulman, & Raichle, 2001; Raichle et al., 2001). This is consistent with the idea that when people are explicitly asked to make confidence judgments, they engage in additional internal and self-reflective processes to make their judgments.

The next question to ask is whether neuroimaging can distinguish between highly confident accurate and inaccurate memories, and in what circumstances it can distinguish between them. We used fMRI to compare brain activity for high-confidence and low-confidence decisions using a face-name relational memory task (Chua et al., 2006). Participants learned face-name pairs and then were tested on their memory while being scanned. They saw the face with three names written underneath it and were instructed to choose which of the three names had been paired with that face previously, and one of the names was always correct. They were then asked to indicate whether they had high or low confidence that they chose correctly. We then examined which brain regions showed greater activity for all high-confidence decisions (correct and incorrect name choices) compared to all low-confidence decisions (correct and incorrect name choices). We showed that the anterior and posterior cingulate, as well as the medial temporal lobes (including the hippocampus, perirhinal cortex, and parahippocampal cortex) showed greater activity for high- versus low-confidence responses regardless of accuracy (Chua et al., 2006; Chua, Schacter, & Sperling, 2009). In contrast, a network of frontoparietal regions showed greater activity for low- compared to high-confidence responses (Chua et al., 2009). In another study, Moritz, Glascher, Sommer, Buchel, and Braus (2006) reported similar findings using a different paradigm. They used a modified version of the Deese-Roediger-McDermott (DRM) paradigm (Roediger & McDermott, 1995), in which participants saw several lists of 12 related words during study, and then at test saw the studied words as well as 4 additional semantically related words and 6 nonrelated, nonstudied words. This paradigm is known to elicit high rates of false recall and recognition, often accompanied by high confidence (Gallo, 2006; Roediger & McDermott, 1995). Moritz et al. (2006) were then able to use fMRI to examine which brain regions were modulated by confidence (high, medium, and low levels) for hits (correctly identifying a studied item as studied), false alarms (incorrectly endorsing a nonstudied item as studied), misses (incorrectly endorsing a studied item as nonstudied), and correct rejections (correctly identifying a nonstudied item as nonstudied). Similar to Chua et al. (2006, 2009), they found that the anterior and posterior cingulate, as well as the medial temporal lobe, showed greater activity for high- compared to low-confidence responses regardless of whether they were hits, false alarms, misses, or correct rejections. These findings suggest that in these two paradigms, the fMRI signal is dominated by subjective confidence signals rather than objective accuracy. This may be an example of how experience-based judgments can still be inaccurate under certain kinds of memory distortions, such as source misattributions.

However, subsequent work by Kim and Cabeza (2007) was able to distinguish between high and low confidence for both true and false recognition. In this study, they used a modified version of the DRM paradigm (Roediger & McDermott, 1995) to elicit high levels of false recognition. At study, participants viewed four words along with a category name and were asked to indicate whether three or four words on the list belonged to the category. At test, they viewed studied words and nonstudied words that belonged to the same category. They then compared high- and low-confidence responses for both true and false recognition. Similar to the Chua et al. (2006, 2009) and Moritz et al. (2006) studies, they showed greater activity in the posterior cingulate for high- and low-confidence responses for both true and false recognition. However, they showed greater anterior cingulate activity for high- compared to low-confidence responses for true recognition only. Within the medial temporal lobes, they observed differential patterns related to confidence for true and false recognition. The hippocampus, which is believed to be important in recollecting an item and its context (Davachi, 2006; Davachi, Mitchell, & Wagner, 2003; Diana, Yonelinas, & Ranganath, 2007), showed greater activity for high-confidence compared to low-confidence true recognition. In contrast, the perirhinal cortex, another structure within the medial temporal lobes, which is thought to be important in item memory or familiarity-based memory (Davachi, 2006; Davachi et al., 2003; Diana et al., 2007), showed greater activity for high- compared to low-confidence false recognition. Furthermore, additional frontoparietal regions, which are also thought to subserve recognition based on a feeling of familiarity (Henson, Rugg, Shallice, & Dolan, 2000; Henson, Rugg, Shallice, Josephs, & Dolan, 1999; Yonelinas et al., 2005), also showed greater activity for high- compared to low-confidence false recognition. In such a case, we see brain-based evidence that confidence for true and false recognition is based on different sources of information. High confidence for true recognition appears to be based on recollective information, whereas high confidence for false recognition appears to be based on stronger feelings of familiarity. Although there are similarities between the above-mentioned studies, the differences merit discussion.

In order for fMRI to have some potential utility in distinguishing highly confident accurate and inaccurate memory, we need to know the circumstances in which it is capable of doing this. The above-mentioned studies suggest that there are limits to the potential of fMRI to detect differences, and the variety of paradigms raises some possibilities for future testing. One likely possibility is that fMRI is useful for distinguishing highly confident accurate and inaccurate recognition only when the confidence judgments are based on different enough information. In the Kim and Cabeza (2007) study, the authors suggested that the patterns of brain activity seen for high-confidence compared to low-confidence true recognition versus the pattern of brain activity seen for high-confidence compared to low-confidence false recognition indicated that confidence for true recognition was based on recollection and confidence for false recognition was based on familiarity. The question remains whether this was also the case in the Moritz et al. (2006) and Chua et al. (2006, 2009) studies. Chua et al. used a face-name relational memory task, in which performance is less likely to be based on familiarity (Cohen, Poldrack, & Eichenbaum, 1997; Cohen et al., 1999), and errors are likely due to source misattributions. If fMRI can only detect differences between confidence decisions based on different qualities of memory, we would not expect it to distinguish between highly confident accurate memory based on recollection and highly confident inaccurate memory based on misattributions. The Moritz et al. and Kim and Cabeza studies used similar procedures, though it is possible that the specific manipulation used by Kim and Cabeza is more likely to elicit familiarity-based responses. Kim and Cabeza presented a category name with the individual list items, whereas Moritz et al. did not, and it is possible that this led to more familiarity-based false recognition responses made with high confidence. One possibility is that the category label made other exemplars from the category more familiar, and thus false recognition was based on this increase in familiarity. Of course, hearing many exemplars from the category (even without seeing the category label) could also lead to increased familiarity of the nonstudied exemplar in the Moritz et al. study. However, the longer lists used in the Moritz et al. study could also have led to increased generation of related exemplars during study. In such a case, participants may recall thinking of the word during study, but misattribute it to being studied rather than internally generated, and this would lead to a high-confidence response based on a false recollection. In summary, there are consistencies in the literature regarding which brain regions are modulated by confidence, and some promise that fMRI may be useful in distinguishing high-confidence responses based on different sources of information. However, further research is needed to precisely delineate when fMRI is and is not sensitive to different types of confidence judgments.

Although distinguishing highly confident accurate and highly confident inaccurate memory is useful, another potentially useful marker would be one for metacognitive accuracy. *Metacognitive accuracy* refers to whether or not the subjective confidence judgment is congruent with objective accuracy. In other words, correct recognition judgments made with high confidence and incorrect recognition judgments made with low confidence are metacognitively accurate, whereas incorrect recognition judgments made with high confidence and correct recognition judgments made with low confidence are metacognitively inaccurate. Broadly speaking, two kinds of measures are typically used to assess metacognitive accuracy, and they are referred to as *absolute* and *relative* measures (Nelson, 1996; Pannu & Kaszniak, 2005). Absolute measures, such as the Hamann index, measure whether the confidence judgment and recognition judgment are congruent and are tied to the scale used, such that a metacognitively accurate judgment is one made with, for example, 25% confidence and has a 25% likelihood of being a correct recognition judgment. Relative measures, such as the gamma statistic, provide a measure of whether the confidence judgment given to a recognition judgment is consistently ordered, such that higher-confidence judgments are more likely to be accurate than lower-confidence judgments but are not tied to the scale used. Few neuroimaging studies have examined whether there are brain regions whose activity correlates with metacognitive accuracy for retrospective confidence ratings, and the results have been somewhat mixed. In our own studies, we showed no brain regions in which activity correlated with metacognitive accuracy, using a measure of absolute accuracy (Chua et al., 2009). However, recent work showed that activity in the right frontopolar cortex, as measured by fMRI, correlated with the gamma coefficient, indicating that this region was sensitive to metacognitively accurate confidence ratings (Yokoyama et al., 2010). Clearly, more research needs to be done and these findings need to be replicated to determine how robust they are before determining whether there are brain regions sensitive to the metacognitive accuracy of confidence judgments. However, there is reason to be optimistic because several studies using other types of metacognitive judgments that require participants to predict their future memory performance (e.g., feeling-of-knowing, tip-of-the-tongue, and judgments of learning) have suggested that various prefrontal brain regions are important for metacognitive accuracy (Pannu & Kasniak, 2005; Schwartz & Bacon, 2008). By extension, it may be that similar prefrontal regions are also involved in metacognitive accuracy for confidence judgments.

The question of whether fMRI is capable of distinguishing highly confident accurate memories from highly confident inaccurate memories, however, is not the only question to be asked. Another important question is whether it *should* be used in a legal context. Indeed, there is some evidence that certain types of fMRI evidence may be *too* convincing and could potentially lead to prejudicial judgments (McCabe & Castel, 2008; Weisberg, Keil, Goodstein, Rawson, & Gray, 2008). Neuroimaging studies are often accompanied by striking visual images showing bright blobs of activity overlaid on a brain image, and research has shown that information accompanied by these types of images is rated as based on sounder scientific reasoning than the same information presented without these kinds of images (McCabe & Castel, 2008). Thus, it is possible that jurors could give more weight to the brain evidence than is warranted. Furthermore, explanations containing information about neuroscience are more satisfying to nonexperts, even when the neuroscience information is irrelevant (Weisberg et al., 2008). Thus, adding neuroscientific information has the potential to hinder jurors' ability to evaluate the evidence accurately. Accordingly, alternative methods may be more appropriate for a legal setting, and the next section addresses relevant research using eye movement monitoring.

EYE MOVEMENTS, MEMORY ACCURACY, AND MEMORY CONFIDENCE

Another method that may eventually prove useful for distinguishing highly confident accurate and highly confident inaccurate memory, and for understanding the basis for confidence judgments, is eye movement monitoring. Many studies have shown that viewers' eye movements are indicative of their previous mnemonic experiences (for review, see Hannula et al., 2010) and can be used to examine what information is being used to make confidence judgments (Chua, Hannula, & Ranganath, 2012). Eye movement monitoring studies of memory capitalize on the fact that we live in a visual world and that our eye movements are not random, but are influenced by our previous experiences, expectations, and knowledge. For example, if we are expecting a visitor, we might look out the window more often for his or her arrival. Alternatively, if we see something surprising, such as a pig walking down a city street, our eyes may be drawn to it because it is unexpected. Although eye movement monitoring may not have the same explanatory appeal to the layperson that fMRI does (McCabe & Castel, 2008; Weisberg et al., 2008), eye movement monitoring can provide an indirect measure of the underlying brain activity. In memory studies, amnesic patients with hippocampal damage do not show the same eye movement–based memory effects as intact controls (Hannula, Ryan, Tranel, & Cohen, 2007; Ryan, Althoff, Whitlow, & Cohen, 2000), and eye movement indices of relational memory correlate with hippocamal activity as measured by fMRI (Hannula & Ranganath, 2009). As such, eye movement monitoring has the potential to reveal information about our memory and cognition. In evaluating the utility of eye movement monitoring and fMRI, several benefits to eye movement monitoring exist. It has the virtue of being less costly than fMRI and potentially less prejudicial (McCabe & Castel, 2008). Both fMRI and eye movements provide indirect measurements of the underlying neural activity; fMRI is a technique that measures the downstream metabolic consequences of neural activity and is therefore considered indirect. However, fMRI is arguably a step closer to the underlying neural activity than eye movements and has been correlated with measures of neural activity (e.g., Goense & Logothetis, 2008; Logothetis, Pauls, Augath, Trinath, & Oeltermann, 2001). Nevertheless, the many benefits of eye movement monitoring may be particularly appealing for potential use in evaluating eyewitness identifications because it allows memory to be assessed without relying only on verbal reports or introspective judgments.

There is a growing body of research examining eye movement–based memory effects (for review, see Hannula et al., 2010). Although there have been many types of eye movement and memory studies, I will focus here on differential viewing behavior for item memory and relational memory. Relational memory is the memory for an item and its context. The classic paradigm for studying item memory using eye movements is to compare viewing behavior between familiar and unfamiliar items. There have been robust eye movement–based item memory effects, with participants showing fewer fixations and less constrained viewing for familiar compared to unfamiliar faces (e.g., Althoff & Cohen, 1999) and scenes (e.g., Ryan et al., 2000). Other studies have focused on relational aspects of memory and have shown that eye movements were sensitive to the memory of spatial positions of elements within a scene (Ryan et al., 2000), that eye movements reflected the temporal sequence in which objects were studied (Ryan & Villate, 2009), and that participants spent more time viewing a face that had been presented with a specific scene compared to faces that were presented with other scenes (Hannula & Ranganath, 2009; Hannula et al., 2007). Thus, eye movement indices of item and/or relational memory have the potential to be used in eyewitness procedures. However, first we need to consider their relationship to memory confidence.

In a laboratory study, we examined the relationship between eye movements, recognition accuracy, and recognition confidence (Chua et al., 2012). We showed participants a scene, followed by a face superimposed on that scene, which formed a face-scene pair, and participants were instructed to try to remember these face-scene pairs for later testing. We then tested their memory for these face-scene pairs and monitored their eye movements during testing. The recognition test consisted of viewing a scene, which served as a *cue* that would elicit attempted retrieval of the face that had previously been paired with that scene. After viewing the scene cue, participants saw three faces superimposed on the scene (three-face display) and were asked to choose which of the three faces had been paired with the scene previously. One of these faces was the *target* face that had previously been paired with that scene, and if chosen, it meant that the participant correctly recognized the face-scene pair. The other two faces were considered distracters and had been previously paired with different scenes; choosing either of these faces meant that the participant forgot the face-scene pair or had a source misattribution. After choosing a face during the three-face display, participants indicated their confidence that they had correctly chosen the face paired with the scene. We monitored eye movements both when participants viewed the scene cue and when they viewed the three-face display. We therefore had independent measures of the cueing period and the target recognition period and could examine how eye movements during these different stages related to confidence and accuracy.

We investigated two main types of influences on confidence judgments in this study (Chua et al., 2012). The first is the *target recognition experience*, which is an experience-based influence on confidence. Again, this is probably what most people assume forms the entire basis of confidence judgments. After all, we make confidence judgments about our ability to recognize a target, so therefore our mnemonic experience and the quality of the memory retrieved during recognition should influence our confidence. Examples of things that fall under this category, and have been shown to influence confidence (and typically accuracy as well), are target familiarity (Yonelinas, 1994), vividness of retrieval (Robinson et al., 2000), and speed/ease of retrieval (Kelley & Lindsay,

1993; Robinson et al., 1997). Many of these overlap with what would influence accurate memory as well; therefore, we expected that confidence judgments based on target recognition experience were more related to accuracy and that this was a relevant source of information for confidence. Another potential factor is *relative evidence* for one alternative over another; this is particularly important in forced-choice tasks, in which participants are shown many alternatives and are forced to choose one of them. This would be an information-based influence on confidence and is different from the target recognition experience, which involves considering a single item, whereas relative evidence involves weighing evidence among multiple alternatives and is a reasoned, analytic process (Koriat et al., 2008). Again, the most familiar example is the process of elimination in multiple-choice tests. One may not remember the answer but still succeed in answering the question correctly if choices can be eliminated. Relative evidence is expected to be less diagnostic of accuracy than target recognition experience, but its relation to accuracy really depends on the validity of the beliefs held and thus is potentially relevant. Finally, the other potential influence we investigated was *cue familiarity or cue utilization*. When an individual is given a cue to elicit retrieval of a sought-after target, there may be influences related to that cue that affect confidence. Of course, the confidence judgments are not made about the cue, they are made about the sought-after target, so it may be surprising that this could have an influence. However, it has been shown in the semantic memory domain that cue familiarity can influence confidence (e.g., a computer expert is more confident about giving answers to computer questions than a nonexpert; for review, see Koriat et al., 2008). However, given that the confidence judgments are about the target, we expected these influences to be irrelevant and nonoverlapping with accuracy.

The target recognition experience, as measured by eye movements, influenced confidence for accurate but not inaccurate memory (Chua et al., 2012). We compared the proportion of time spent viewing each of the faces during the three-face display. For accurate memory, in which participants correctly chose the face that was paired with the scene cue, there was a linear increase in viewing of the correctly chosen face with increasing confidence. This suggests that one factor influencing confidence in accurate memory is the target recognition experience. In contrast, there was no such effect of confidence on viewing of the incorrectly chosen face for inaccurate recognition trials. This suggests that something other than the target recognition experience is driving confidence for inaccurate memory.

We next examined effects of relative *evidence assessment* on confidence judgments (Chua et al., 2012). We used the number of *transitions,* or movement of the eyes, from one face to another as an index of relative evidence assessment based on previous findings from the decision-making literature (Pochon, Riis, Sanfey, Nystrom, & Cohen, 2008; Reutskaja, Nagel, Camerer, & Rangel, 2011). We did not see evidence of an effect of relative evidence assessment, as indexed by eye movements, on confidence, but instead observed slightly more transitions during inaccurate trials compared to accurate trials. Thus, it does not appear that relative evidence assessment was driving confidence for inaccurate memory in this study.

We then examined viewing behavior during the scene cueing period (Chua et al., 2012). We used the number of fixations made during the scene cueing period as our index of cue familiarity, or other cue-related processing, because several studies have shown fewer fixations to repeated stimuli compared to novel stimuli (e.g., Althoff & Cohen, 1999; Ryan et al., 2000). Our results showed that for both highly confident accurate and highly confident inaccurate memory, fewer fixations were made during the scene cueing period compared to during their medium-confidence counterpart. Taken together with the analyses based on the target recognition experience, it appears that highly confident accurate memories show eye movement–based memory effects during both the scene cue and the three-face display, whereas highly confident inaccurate memories show eye movement–based memory effects only during the scene cueing period. This suggests that confidence in inaccurate memory may be related to overreliance on cue-related information without proper regard for the target recognition experience. Furthermore, these results show the power of eye movement monitoring in distinguishing memories of different qualities, particularly highly confident accurate and highly confident inaccurate memories, and in delineating what factors are influencing confidence judgments. These results are exciting and intriguing, with implications for evaluating confidence in eyewitnesses. However, these results are far from meeting the standard established in *Daubert v. Merrell Dow Pharmaceuticals* (1993) for admission of scientific evidence in courts. Further research is needed to replicate these findings and delineate limitations, or boundary conditions, in using this technique.

At least one other study has shown an effect of memory confidence on eye movements (Smith & Squire, 2008). In their paradigm, Smith and Squire showed novel and repeated scenes to younger and older adults while monitoring their eye movements. During test, participants indicated whether a scene was "definitely new," "probably new," "maybe new," "maybe old," "probably old," or "definitely old." Younger adults showed less sampling of repeated scenes compared to novel scenes (collapsed across correct and incorrect trials) that were given "definitely" and "probably" ratings but not "maybe" ratings. Older adults showed less sampling of repeated scenes only for those given a "definitely" rating. Both younger and older adults showed less sampling of repeated scenes compared to novel scenes for correct trials but not incorrect trials (collapsed across confidence levels). Because they did not separately examine correct and incorrect trials across different levels of confidence, it is difficult to know if eye movements would be useful for distinguishing highly confident correct and incorrect recognition with this kind of setup and materials. Nevertheless, their findings, in combinations with those of Chua et al. (2012) mentioned earlier, suggest that there is a relationship between viewing behavior and confidence using multiple types of paradigms and that further delineation of these effects is warranted. Importantly, it is worth noting that in the Smith and Squire study, there are slightly different results from the two populations (younger and older adults). Given that eyewitnesses come from diverse age groups, future studies involving populations across a range of ages would be useful.

In addition to distinguishing highly confident accurate from highly confident inaccurate memory, another area of interest may be in distinguishing correct guesses from incorrect guesses. In other words, can eye movements reveal memory in the absence of awareness? We examined this issue in the above-mentioned face-scene paradigm (Chua et al., 2012) by examining viewing behavior during incorrect recognition trials. Specifically, we investigated whether or not participants spent more time viewing the correct face than would be expected by chance, even though participants failed to choose it during the explicit recognition task. In this paradigm, we did not see such an effect either collapsed across the entire trial or even in the earliest portions of the trial, suggesting that eye movements may be less useful for weak memories.

Whether or not eye movements reveal evidence of memory in the absence of awareness has been controversial, with some studies demonstrating effects in the absence of awareness (Ryan et al., 2000) and other studies showing eye movement–based memory effects only for aware memory (Smith, Hopkins, & Squire, 2006; Smith & Squire, 2008). The canonical paradigm in these studies involves comparing eye movements during repeated and manipulated scenes. In the manipulated scenes, an element of the scene was removed, and viewing behavior to this critical region, where the element was previously located, was measured. This was then compared to viewing of this same region in the repeated condition, when the scene was viewed both initially and at test without an element in the critical region. Some studies show that participants spend more time viewing the critical region in the manipulated condition only when they are aware of the change (Smith et al., 2006; Smith & Squire, 2008), and others show that this occurs regardless of awareness (Ryan et al., 2000). The major difference in these paradigms is the task instructions given to the participants. Although these results may have future applications, given that eye movement-based memory effects in the absence of awareness are less robust and the emphasis of the legal system is on "innocent until proven guilty," it would be imprudent to use eye movements for identifications that were not endorsed by the witness at this time. Further research is needed to determine the specific conditions under which eye movements reliably reveal memory effects in the absence of awareness.

GENERAL LIMITATIONS OF NEUROIMAGING AND EYE MOVEMENT STUDIES

Although there have been promising findings from neuroimaging (Chua et al., 2006, 2009; Kim & Cabeza, 2007; Moritz et al., 2006) and eye movement studies (Chua et al., 2012) of memory confidence that shed light on how people make confidence judgments on their memory, there are several limitations with these methods in terms of courtroom and lineup applications.

The first limitation is that the research findings reported are based on averaging across study participants and across trials; therefore, further work must be done to see if these findings are robust for eyewitness cases that would only involve a single trial and one individual. This is a greater problem for neuroimaging than for eye tracking because neuroimaging has a relatively poor signal-to-noise ratio. Indeed, researchers typically average over many trials across groups of subjects in order to have enough power to detect significant results. The eye movement monitoring study focused on in this chapter (Chua et al., 2012) also averages across subjects and trials; thus, it is unclear how robust the eye movement patterns related to confidence would be on an individual level. However, some eye tracking studies have reported results from single trials (Smith & Squire, 2008), suggesting that this method may be feasible for single trials. However, further testing is needed to determine the relationship between confidence, accuracy, and eye movements on a single-trial level.

Another limitation is that very few types of stimuli have been used to systematically examine confidence and accuracy in memory, and while these stimuli are appropriate for the laboratory, they are quite different from the experience of an eyewitness. First, the stimuli are quite simple and emotionally neutral. Although pictures of faces paired with names or scenes bear some similarity to photo lineups, the conditions under which study participants first encoded these faces is not. In the study, people viewed static images, but eyewitnesses viewed complex scenes and interactions. Indeed, there is some evidence that there are key differences in brain activation for autobiographical memories compared to laboratory memories (Cabeza et al., 2004). Furthermore, eyewitnesses likely viewed highly emotional events, whereas the studies here used emotionally neutral events. Indeed, emotion has been shown to enhance the subjective feeling of remembering, which is related to confidence (Sharot, Delgado, & Phelps, 2004). There is substantial evidence that emotional memories show some differences in brain activation (Kensinger & Corkin, 2004; Kensinger & Schacter, 2005), although eye movement studies showed no significant difference in viewing behavior for emotional versus neutral scenes (Sharot, Davidson, Carson, & Phelps, 2008). Further work is needed involving testing participants under conditions that are more similar to eyewitness conditions.

CONCLUDING REMARKS

Let's return to the case of Dror Goldberg. After reading this chapter, would you convict him on the basis of Roberta Ingrado's confident testimony? What would you want to know about her confidence in order to trust her reports? Dror Goldberg was convicted in 2000 and to date remains in prison. However, there is a task force consisting of people who believe he is innocent and are dedicated to appealing and overturning his conviction (http://drorgoldberg.org/). Eyewitness testimony was obviously not the only factor in his conviction, but it did have a role.

In 1996, the American Psychology/Law Society and Division 41 of the American Psychological Society appointed a subcommittee to review scientific research findings and make suggestions on the proper way to conduct lineups to minimize eyewitness misidentifications. The committee made three main recommendations: (1) conduct sequential lineups, (2) use a double-blind procedure, and (3) assess and record confidence at the time of the identification (Wells et al., 1998). These modifications to the traditional lineup have the potential to reduce overconfidence in faulty identifications, and although they were formed based on decades of applied eyewitness research, they are consistent with the metacognitive framework and evidence presented above, and they reduce potential contamination of confidence judgments from irrelevant sources. These recommendations have been implemented in some states, such as Wisconsin, New Jersey, and North Carolina (http://www.innocenceproject.org/fix/Eyewitness-Identification.php), which is a testimony to the benefits of research-based policy.

Efforts to reduce eyewitness misidentifications and overconfidence through policy are necessary early steps, and identifying markers of misidentifications and overconfidence is a good later step. In this chapter, I reviewed studies on memory confidence and accuracy using fMRI and eye tracking methods, and evaluated their potential utility for (1) distinguishing highly confident accurate and inaccurate memory and (2) identifying the factors that influence memory confidence. Both fMRI and eye tracking show promising results, but significantly more research will need to be conducted over the next several years to validate their use in evaluation eyewitness confidence.

REFERENCES

Althoff, R. R., & Cohen, N. J. (1999). Eye-movement-based memory effect: A reprocessing effect in face perception. *Journal of Experimental Psychology: Learning, Memory and Cognition, 25*(4), 997–1010.

Blank, H., Musch, J., & Pohl, R. F. (2007). Hindsight bias: On being wise after the event. *Social Cognition, 25*(1), 1–9.

Bradfield, A. L., Wells, G. L., & Olson, E. A. (2002). The damaging effect of confirming feedback on the relation between eyewitness certainty and identification accuracy. *Journal of Applied Psychology, 87*(1), 112–120.

Brewer, N., Keast, A., & Rishworth, A. (2002). The confidence-accuracy relationship in eyewitness identification: The effects of reflection and disconfirmation on correlation and calibration. *Journal of Experimental Psychology: Applied, 8*(1), 44–56.

Cabeza, R., Prince, S. E., Daselaar, S. M., Greenberg, D. L., Budde, M., Dolcos, F., et al. (2004). Brain activity during episodic retrieval of autobiographical and laboratory events: An fMRI study using a novel photo paradigm. *Journal of Cognitive Neuroscience, 16*(9), 1583–1594.

Chua, E. F., Hannula, D. E., & Ranganath, C. (2012). Distinguishing highly confident accurate and inaccurate memory: Insights about relevant and irrelevant influences on memory confidence. *Memory, 20*(1), 48–62.

Chua, E. F., Schacter, D. L., Rand-Giovannetti, E., & Sperling, R. A. (2006). Understanding metamemory: Neural correlates of the cognitive process and subjective level of confidence in recognition memory. *Neuroimage, 29*(4), 1150–1160.

Chua, E. F., Schacter, D. L., & Sperling, R. A. (2009). Neural basis for recognition confidence in younger and older adults. *Psychology of Aging, 24*(1), 139–153.

Clark, S., & Davey, S. (2005). The target-to-foils shift in simultaneous and sequential lineups. *Law and Human Behavior, 29*(2), 151–172.

Cohen, N. J., Poldrack, R. A., & Eichenbaum, H. (1997). Memory for items and memory for relations in the procedural/declarative memory framework. *Memory, 5*(1–2), 131–178.

Cohen, N. J., Ryan, J., Hunt, C., Romine, L., Wszalek, T., & Nash, C. (1999). Hippocampal system and declarative (relational) memory: Summarizing the data from functional neuroimaging studies. *Hippocampus, 9*(1), 83–98.

Cutler, B., Penrod, S., & Stuve, T. (1988). Juror decision making in eyewitness identification cases. *Law and Human Behavior, 12*(1), 41–55.

Daubert v. Merrell Dow Pharmaceuticals, 509 U.S. 1993.

Davachi, L. (2006). Item, context and relational episodic encoding in humans. *Current Opinion in Neurobiology, 16*(6), 693–700.

Davachi, L., Mitchell, J. P., & Wagner, A. D. (2003). Multiple routes to memory: Distinct medial temporal lobe processes build item and source memories. *Proceedings of the National Academy of Sciences of the United States of America, 100*(4), 2157–2162.

Diana, R. A., Yonelinas, A. P., & Ranganath, C. (2007). Imaging recollection and familiarity in the medial temporal lobe: A three-component model. *Trends in Cognitive Science, 11*(9), 379–386.

Douglass, A., & Steblay, N. (2006). Memory distortion in eyewitnesses: A meta-analysis of the post identification feedback effect. *Applied Cognitive Psychology, 20*(7), 859–869.

Gallo, D. A. (2006). *Associative illusions of memory: False memory research in DRM and related tasks.* New York: Psychology Press.

Goldberg v. State, 95 SW 3d.345—Tex: Court of Appeals, 2002.

Goense, J., & Logothetis, N. K. (2008). Neurophysiology of the BOLD fMRI signal in awake monkeys. *Current Biology, 18*(9), 631–640.

Gusnard, D. A., Akbudak, E., Shulman, G. L., & Raichle, M. E. (2001). Medial prefrontal cortex and self-referential mental activity: Relation to a default mode of brain function. *Proceedings of the National Academy of Sciences of the United States of America, 98*(7), 4259–4264.

Hall, C. C., Ariss, L., & Todorov, A. (2007). The illusion of knowledge: When more information reduces accuracy and increases confidence. *Organizational Behavior and Human Decision Processes, 103*(2), 277–290.

Hannula, D. E., Althoff, R. R., Warren, D. E., Riggs, L., Cohen, N. J., & Ryan, J. D. (2010). Worth a glance: Using eye movements to investigate the cognitive neuroscience of memory. *Frontiers in Human Neuroscience, 4*, 1–17.

Hannula, D. E., & Ranganath, C. (2009). The eyes have it: Hippocampal activity predicts expression of memory in eye movements. *Neuron, 63*(5), 592–599.

Hannula, D. E., Ryan, J. D., Tranel, D., & Cohen, N. J. (2007). Rapid onset relational memory effects are evident in eye movement behavior, but not in hippocampal amnesia. *Journal of Cognitive Neuroscience, 19*(10), 1690–1705.

Henson, R. N., Rugg, M. D., Shallice, T., & Dolan, R. J. (2000). Confidence in recognition memory for words: Dissociating right prefrontal roles in episodic retrieval. *Journal of Cognitive Neuroscience, 12*(6), 913–923.

Henson, R. N., Rugg, M. D., Shallice, T., Josephs, O., & Dolan, R. J. (1999). Recollection and familiarity in recognition memory: An event-related functional magnetic resonance imaging study. *Journal of Neuroscience, 19*(10), 3962–3972.

Kassin, S., Ellsworth, P., & Smith, V. (1989). The "general acceptance" of psychological research on eyewitness testimony. *American Psychologist, 44*(8), 1089–1098.

Kassin, S., Tubb, V., Hosch, H., & Memon, A. (2001). On the "general acceptance" of eyewitness testimony research. *American Psychologist, 56*(5), 405–416.

Kelley, C. M., & Lindsay, D. S. (1993). Remembering mistaken for knowing: Ease of retrieval as a basis for confidnece in answers to general knowledge questions. *Journal of Memory and Language, 32*(1), 1–24.

Kensinger, E. A., & Corkin, S. (2004). Two routes to emotional memory: Distinct neural processes for valence and arousal. *Proceedings of the National Academy of Sciences of the United States of America, 101*(9), 3310.

Kensinger, E. A., & Schacter, D. L. (2005). Retrieving accurate and distorted memories: Neuroimaging evidence for effects of emotion. *Neuroimage, 27*, 167–177.

Kim, H., & Cabeza, R. (2007). Trusting our memories: Dissociating the neural correlates of confidence in veridical versus illusory memories. *Journal of Neuroscience, 27*(45), 12190–12197.

Kneller, W., Memon, A., & Stevenage, S. (2001). Simultaneous and sequential lineups: Decision processes of accurate and inaccurate eyewitnesses. *Applied Cognitive Psychology, 15*(6), 659–671.

Koriat, A. (2008a). Subjective confidence in one's answers: The consensuality principle. *Journal of Experimental Psychology: Learning, Memory and Cognition, 34*(4), 945–959.

Koriat, A. (2008b). When confidence in a choice is independent of which choice is made. *Psychonomic Bulletin Review, 15*(5), 997–1001.

Koriat, A., Nussinson, R., Bless, H., & Shaked, N. (2008). Information-based and experience-based metacognitive judgments: Evidence from subjective confidence. In J. Dunlosky & R. A. Bjork (Eds.), *Handbook of metamemory and memory* (pp. 117–135). New York: Psychology Press.

Lindsay, D. S., Read, J. D., & Sharma, K. (1998). Accuracy and confidence in person identification: The relationship is strong when witnessing conditions vary widely. *Psychological Science, 9*(3), 215–218.

Lindsay, R. C. L., & Wells, G. L. (1985). Improving eyewitness identifications from lineups: Simultaneous versus sequential lineup presentation. *Journal of Applied Psychology, 70*(3), 556–564.

Logothetis, N. K., Pauls, J., Augath, M., Trinath, T., & Oeltermann, A. (2001). Neurophysiological investigation of the basis of the fMRI signal. *Nature, 412*(6843), 150–157.

Luus, C. A., & Wells, G. L. (1994). The malleability of eyewitness confidence: Co-witness and perseverance effects. *Journal of Applied Psychology, 79*(5), 714–723.

Manson v. Braithwaite, 432 U.S. 98 (1977).

Mazzoni, G., & Vannucci, M. (2007). Hindsight bias, the misinformation effect, and false autobiographical memories. *Social Cognition, 25*(1), 203–220.

McCabe, D. P., & Castel, A. D. (2008). Seeing is believing: The effect of brain images on judgments of scientific reasoning. *Cognition, 107*(1), 343–352.

Moritz, S., Glascher, J., Sommer, T., Buchel, C., & Braus, D. F. (2006). Neural correlates of memory confidence. *Neuroimage, 33*(4), 1188–1193.

Nelson, T. O. (1996). Gamma is a measure of the accuracy of predicting performance on one item relative to another item, not of the absolute performance on an individual item. *Applied Cognitive Psychology, 10*(3), 257–260.

Pannu, J. K., & Kaszniak, A. W. (2005). Metamemory experiments in neurological populations: A review. *Neuropsychology Review, 15*(3), 105–130.

Perfect, T. J., Hollins, T. S., & Hunt, A. L. (2000). Practice and feedback effects on the confidence-accuracy relation in eyewitness memory. *Memory, 8*(4), 235–244.

Pochon, J. B., Riis, J., Sanfey, A. G., Nystrom, L. E., & Cohen, J. D. (2008). Functional imaging of decision conflict. *Journal of Neuroscience, 28*(13), 3468–3473.

Raichle, M. E., MacLeod, A. M., Snyder, A. Z., Powers, W. J., Gusnard, D. A., & Shulman, G. L. (2001). A default mode of brain function. *Proceedings of the National Academy of Sciences of the United States of America, 98*(2), 676–682.

Ranganath, C., Yonelinas, A. P., Cohen, M. X., Dy, C. J., Tom, S. M., & D'Esposito, M. (2004). Dissociable correlates of recollection and familiarity within the medial temporal lobes. *Neuropsychologia, 42*(1), 2–13.

Reutskaja, E., Nagel, R., Camerer, C. F., & Rangel, A. (2011). Search dynamics in consumer choice under time pressure: An eye-tracking study. *The American Economic Review, 101*(2), 900–926.

Robinson, M. D., Johnson, J. T., & Herndon, F. (1997). Reaction time and assessments of cognitive effort as predictors of eyewitness memory accuracy and confidence. *Journal of Applied Psychology, 82*(3), 416–425.

Robinson, M. D., Johnson, J. T., & Robertson, D. A. (2000). Process versus content in eyewitness metamemory monitoring. *Journal of Experimental Psychology: Applied, 6*(3), 207–221.

Roediger, H. L., Jacoby, J. D., & McDermott, K. B. (1996). Misinformation effects in recall: Creating false memories through repeated retrieval. *Journal of Memory and Language, 35*, 300–318.

Roediger, H. L., 3rd, & McDermott, K. B. (1995). Creating false memories: Remembering words not presented on lists. *Journal of Experimental Psychology: Learning, Memory and Cognition, 21*, 803–814.

Rubenzer, S. J. (2002). Eyewitness identification: Challenging a confident witness and common misconceptions. *Voice for the Defense (Journal for the Texas Criminal Defense Lawyers Association),31*(4), 20–23.

Ryan, J. D., Althoff, R. R., Whitlow, S., & Cohen, N. J. (2000). Amnesia is a deficit in relational memory. *Psychology and Science, 11*(6), 454–461.

Ryan, J. D., & Villate, C. (2009). Building visual representations: The binding of relative spatial relations across time. *Visual Cognition, 17*(1), 254–272.

Sanna, L. J., & Schwarz, N. (2007). Metacognitive experiences and hindsight bias: It's not just the thought (content) that counts! *Social Cognition, 25*(1), 185–202.

Schacter, D. L., & Dodson, C. S. (2001). Misattribution, false recognition and the sins of memory. *Philosophical Transactions of the Royal Society of London B: Biological Science, 356*(1413), 1385–1393.

Schacter, D. L., Norman, K. A., & Koutstaal, W. (1998). The cognitive neuroscience of constructive memory. *Annual Review of Psychology 49*, 289–318.

Schwartz, B. L., & Bacon, E. (2008). Metacognitive neuroscience. In J. Dunlosky & R. A. Bjork (Eds.), *Handbook of metamemory and memory* (pp. 355–371). New York: Psychology Press.

Semmler, C., Brewer, N., & Wells, G. L. (2004). Effects of postidentification feedback on eyewitness identification and nonidentification confidence. *Journal of Applied Psychology, 89*(2), 334–345.

Sharot, T., Davidson, M. L., Carson, M. M., & Phelps, E. A. (2008). Eye movements predict recollective experience. *PLoS One, 3*(8), e2884.

Sharot, T., Delgado, M. R., & Phelps, E. A. (2004). How emotion enhances the feeling of remembering. *Nature Neuroscience, 7*(12), 1376–1380.

Shaw, J., III, Appio, L., Zerr, T., & Pontoski, K. (2007). Public eyewitness confidence can be influenced by the presence of other witnesses. *Law and Human Behavior, 31*(6), 629–652.

Smith, C. N., Hopkins, R. O., & Squire, L. R. (2006). Experience-dependent eye movements, awareness, and hippocampus-dependent memory. *Journal of Neuroscience, 26*(44), 11304–11312.

Smith, C. N., & Squire, L. R. (2008). Experience-dependent eye movements reflect hippocampus-dependent (aware) memory. *Journal of Neuroscience, 28*(48), 12825–12833.

Sporer, S. L. (1993). Eyewitness identification accuracy, confidence, and decision times in simultaneous and sequential lineups. *Journal of Applied Psychology, 78*(1), 22–33.

Sporer, S. L., Penrod, S., Read, D., & Cutler, B. (1995). Choosing, confidence, and accuracy: A meta-analysis of the confidence-accuracy relation in eyewitness identification studies. *Psychological Bulletin, 118*(3), 315–327.

Steblay, N., Dysart, J., Fulero, S., & Lindsay, R. (2001). Eyewitness accuracy rates in sequential and simultaneous lineup presentations: A meta-analytic comparison. *Law and Human Behavior, 25*(5), 459–473.

Stretch, V., & Wixted, J. T. (1998). Decision rules for recognition memory confidence judgments. *Journal of Experimental Psychology: Learning, Memory and Cognition, 24*(6), 1397–1410.

United States v. Telfaire, 469 F.2d 552, 558-59 (D.C.Cir. 1979).

Weber, N., & Brewer, N. (2003). The effect of judgment type and confidence scale on confidence-accuracy calibration in face recognition. *Journal of Applied Psychology, 88*(3), 490–499.

Weber, N., Brewer, N., Wells, G. L., Semmler, C., & Keast, A. (2004). Eyewitness identification accuracy and response latency: The unruly 10–12-second rule* 1. *Journal of Experimental Psychology: Applied, 10*(3), 139–147.

Weisberg, D. S., Keil, F. C., Goodstein, J., Rawson, E., & Gray, J. R. (2008). The seductive allure of neuroscience explanations. *Journal of Cognitive Neuroscience, 20*(3), 470–477.

Wells, G. L., & Olson, E. A. (2003). Eyewitness testimony. *Annual Review of Psychology, 54*(1), 277–295.

Wells, G. L., Olson, E. A., & Charman, S. D. (2002). The confidence of eyewitnesses in their identifications from lineups. *Current Directions in Psychological Science, 11*(5), 151–154.

Wells, G. L., Olson, E. A., & Charman, S. D. (2003). Distorted retrospective eyewitness reports as functions of feedback and delay. *Journal of Experimental Psychology: Applied, 9*(1), 42–52.

Wells, G. L., & Seelau, E. (1995). Eyewitness identification: Psychological research and legal policy on lineups. *Psychology, Public Policy, and Law, 1*(4), 765.

Wells, G. L., Small, M., Penrod, S., Malpass, R., Fulero, S., & Brimacombe, C. (1998). Eyewitness identification procedures: Recommendations for lineups and photospreads. *Law and Human Behavior, 22*(6), 603–647.

Yokoyama, O., Miura, N., Watanabe, J., Takemoto, A., Uchida, S., Sugiura, M., et al. (2010). Right frontopolar cortex activity correlates with reliability of retrospective rating of confidence in short-term recognition memory performance. *Neuroscience Research, 68*(3), 199–206.

Yonelinas, A. P. (1994). Receiver-operating characteristics in recognition memory: Evidence for a dual-process model. *Journal of Experimental Psychology: Learning, Memory and Cognition, 20*(6), 1341–1354.

Yonelinas, A. P., Otten, L. J., Shaw, K. N., & Rugg, M. D. (2005). Separating the brain regions involved in recollection and familiarity in recognition memory. *Journal of Neuroscience, 25*(11), 3002–3008.

Zaragoza, M. S., & Mitchell, K. J. (1996). Repeated exposure to suggestion and the creation of false memories. *Psychological Science, 7*(5), 294–300.

6

Evidentiary Independence

How Evidence Collected Early in an Investigation Influences the Collection and Interpretation of Additional Evidence

LISA E. HASEL

Two men—Gary Dotson and David Vasquez—exonerated in 1989 were the first people exonerated because postconviction DNA testing proved their innocence. Two decades later, in 2009, 22 people—too many to name—were exonerated because DNA testing proved their innocence. Although the number of people exonerated each year fluctuates, there has been a strong positive correlation between the number of DNA exonerations and the year they were exonerated, $r(22) = .838$, $p < .001$. By the beginning of 2012, over 280 people had been exonerated based on postconviction DNA testing; they had collectively spent over 3,500 years behind bars for crimes they did not commit (see http://www.innocenceproject.org for an updated count). With the growing number of proven wrongful convictions, some legal practitioners are turning to psychological scientists for help in detecting errors in past cases and preventing such errors from happening in the future.

The DNA exoneration cases handled by the Innocence Project are a unique subset of cases for which the ground truth has been discovered after an innocent person has been wrongfully convicted. Psychological scientists often focus on the causes of wrongful conviction in DNA exoneration cases because those are cases of known, undisputed error. These cases represent merely the tip of the iceberg of wrongful convictions across the United States because DNA evidence is only available in approximately 5%–10% of cases (http://www.innocenceproject.org). Cases for which DNA evidence exists almost exclusively involve rape or rape-murder, so it has been suggested that they may not be representative of all crimes or even all wrongful convictions (e.g., Hoffman, 2007). However, a recent study looked at the prevalence of over 20 potential issues raised at successful appeals of DNA and non-DNA exoneration cases (Wechsler, Garcia-Dubus, & Kucharski, 2011). The only significant difference between them was that in DNA exoneration cases, the "presence of biological evidence at the scene that was not tested" was cited more frequently than in non-DNA exoneration cases.

The leading contributor to wrongful conviction in DNA exoneration cases is eyewitness misidentification, present in over 77% of cases; the second greatest contributor is unvalidated or improper forensics, present in 52% of cases; the third greatest contributor is false confessions, present in 23% of cases; and the fourth greatest contributor is informants or snitches, present in 16% of the (http://www.innocenceproject.org). It is clear from these numbers that there are often multiple problematic pieces of evidence leading to wrongful conviction.

This chapter will examine the potential cognitive biases that can occur during criminal investigations that can lead to the presence of multiple pieces of faulty evidence. Decisions made by people investigating a crime occur in a social milieu and are, therefore, not always objective. When investigating a crime, detectives attempt to determine what occurred during the crime and who was involved in that crime. During this process, the detectives must form and test hypotheses about what happened and about the identity of the perpetrator. These hypotheses are often largely shaped by evidence that was collected early in the investigation. The detectives might, intentionally or unintentionally, convey information about this early evidence to other people who are essential to the evidence collection and interpretation process, such as forensic scientists or eyewitnesses. However, decisions made by forensic scientists about whether a sample from a suspect matches a sample from the crime scene can be influenced by factors outside of the objective features of the samples, and decisions made by eyewitnesses about whether or not the suspect is the person they saw commit a crime can also be influenced by factors outside of the eyewitness's memory for the perpetrator. Pertinent to this chapter, these decisions can be influenced by information about other evidence that has been collected. Therefore, this chapter will examine how the presence of one piece of faulty evidence might lead to the presence of multiple pieces of faulty evidence. Because of its prevalence in the DNA exoneration cases and its implications for memory, the majority of the chapter will largely focus on how eyewitnesses' memories can be influenced during an investigation, and it will conclude with a discussion of how confirmation biases can occur throughout entire criminal investigations and lead to wrongful convictions.

CRIMINAL INVESTIGATORS

On November 17, 1989, the body of Angela Correa, a 15-year old girl, was found; she had been raped, strangled, and beaten (http://www.innocenceproject.org). One of her classmates, Jeffrey Deskovic, was very interested in the case and actively tried to assist the detectives in their investigation. Deskovic became a suspect because an "offender profile" provided by the New York Police Department matched Deskovic in many ways, and this led the detectives to view Deskovic's interest in the case as suspicious (Synder, McQuillan, Murphy, & Joselson, 2007). Therefore, detectives proceeded to question Deskovic over several days, asked him to submit to three polygraph examinations, and treated him in ways that laid the groundwork for a false confession. Ultimately, Deskovic falsely confessed to the rape and murder of Correa because he was trying to escape the situation and because detectives told him that they had found DNA evidence—which Deskovic knew would not match his because he was innocent. DNA testing was conducted, and it showed that Deskovic was not the source of the semen in the rape kit. However, because Deskovic had confessed, prosecutors claimed that Correa must have had consensual sex with an unknown person before Deskovic killed her. Deskovic was convicted and spent over 16 years in prison until the DNA was run through the CODIS DNA databases. The semen was found to match Steven Cunningham, a man who was serving a life sentence for an unrelated murder and who subsequently confessed to raping and killing Correa.

How did the confession of a teenage boy trump DNA evidence in the investigators' minds? It is probable that tunnel vision, a form of cyclical reasoning related to confirmation bias, was occurring in this situation. Tunnel vision occurs when an investigator will "focus on a suspect, select and filter evidence that will 'build a case' for conviction, while ignoring or suppressing evidence that points away from guilt" (Martin, 2001, p. 848), and it is a theme that runs through almost every case of wrongful conviction (Findley & Scott, 2006). The first piece of evidence an investigator reviews has the potential to anchor the investigator's belief in a suspect's guilt or innocence that might be insufficiently adjusted after the investigator reviews additional evidence in the case (Lisuzzo & Hasel, 2011). In one study, investigators who received information indicating that a suspect was guilty rated a facial composite created of the perpetrator as more similar to the suspect than did investigators who received information indicating that the suspect was innocent (Charman, Gregory, & Carlucci, 2009). In another study, investigators who received a potentially incriminating piece of evidence and a potentially exonerating piece of evidence thought that the evidence against the suspect was much stronger if they received the potentially incriminating evidence before the potentially exonerating evidence (Lisuzzo & Hasel, 2011).

The malleability of investigators' opinions of a suspect's guilt, however, depends on how strong they perceive the evidence to be, which itself depends on whether the evidence supports their belief in a suspect's guilt or innocence (Ask, Rebellius, & Granhag, 2008). Police trainees were given information about a case indicating that the suspect was guilty and were later given additional evidence that either confirmed or disconfirmed their hypothesis of guilt. This evidence was strong (i.e., DNA match or exclusion), moderate (i.e., pictures of the suspect in a taxi security camera), or weak (i.e., an eyewitness' identification or nonidentification of the suspect). Evidence that was consistent with the investigators' initial beliefs was rated as more reliable than evidence that was inconsistent with their initial beliefs. However, these changed opinions about the reliability of evidence differed across the types of evidence. When the evidence was consistent with the hypothesis of guilt, the investigators thought the three types of evidence were equally reliable. However, when the evidence was inconsistent with the hypothesis of guilt, the weak evidence was rated as less reliable than the moderate evidence, and the moderate evidence was rated as less reliable than the strong evidence. This demonstrates how investigators might overlook or discount exonerating evidence, especially evidence that has the potential to be malleable in certain situations, if they have a preconceived notion of a suspect's guilt. However, an investigator might only view evidence that has been provided by others, such as forensic scientists. Is it possible that forensic scientists' judgments might be biased by initial evidence as well?

FORENSIC SCIENTISTS

Following the bombing of a train in Madrid in 2004, Brandon Mayfield's fingerprint was identified by a fingerprint examiner from the FBI as matching one found on the bomb (U.S. Department of Justice, 2006). After this initial match was made by one examiner, it was confirmed by two other FBI fingerprint examiners as well as an independent examiner appointed by the court. However, the Spanish National Police later informed the FBI that *they* had identified the fingerprint as a match to another person—an Algerian national named Ouhnane Daoud. After the FBI examiners reviewed the match found by the Spanish police, Mayfield was released from jail.

How did four trained fingerprint examiners all make the same mistake? The FBI convened an international panel of fingerprint experts who determined that the first mistaken "identification" of Mayfield's print was a result of errors made by the initial examiner under the pressure of working on a high-profile case (U.S. Department of Justice, 2006). They also concluded "that the verification was 'tainted' by knowledge of the initial examiner's conclusion" and that the subsequent examiners engaged in "circular thinking" by emphasizing the parts of the print that did match and deemphasizing the parts of the print that did not match because of having the hypothesis that the fingerprint was a match (p.4). Therefore, the evaluation of one piece of evidence by one fingerprint examiner tainted multiple other fingerprint examiners' later evaluations of that same evidence. The potential for the tainting of evidence evaluations is especially strong in fields that rely on subjective assessments of matching characteristics, such as fingerprint, firearm, tool print, or bite mark evidence (National Research Council, 2009).

Dror and Charlton (2006) systematically examined this effect by presenting five latent fingerprint experts with pairs of prints from a crime scene and from a suspect in actual cases for which they had previously made a match or exclusion judgment. The prints were accompanied either by no extraneous information, an instruction that the suspect had confessed (suggesting a match), or an instruction that the suspect was in custody at the time of the crime (suggesting an exclusion). This extraneous information always suggested a different conclusion than the examiners' previously correct judgments, and the misinformation led the fingerprint examiners to change 17% of their original, previously correct judgments. Overall, 66% of the experts changed at least one of their decisions as a result of the extraneous information.

Fingerprint and other forms of forensic pattern-matching evidence can be kept and evaluated by independent examiners at a later time if necessary. However, if evidence provided by humans, such as eyewitnesses or alibi corroborators, is tainted, it is impossible to determine subsequently whether or not their memories of the event are based on their actual memories for the event or on information obtained later. Therefore, it is important to understand the conditions under which eyewitness memories might be tainted in ways similar to those in which the forensic scientists' judgments can be tainted. Is it possible that eyewitnesses' memories might be biased by initial evidence as well?

EYEWITNESSES

Misinformation Effect

Memory is extremely malleable and can be shaped by a large number of influences outside of the memory itself (e.g., Loftus, 2005; Loftus & Palmer, 1974). One of the most widely examined aspects of the malleability of memory in forensic contexts is the misinformation effect (see Davis and Loftus, this volume, for a detailed discussion of this phenomenon). The misinformation effect occurs when memory for an event in the past is impaired or altered after exposure to misleading information. Although misinformation paradigms are now frequently used to demonstrate how rich false memories about autobiographical events from childhood can be implanted in individuals, the first examinations of the misinformation effect focused on how biasing information influences eyewitnesses. Early researchers of this effect studied how people's memories could be changed for occurrences such as a car accident (Loftus, 1975, 1977; Loftus & Palmer, 1974), an auto-pedestrian accident (Bekerian & Bowers, 1983; Loftus 1975), a class disruption (Loftus, 1975, 1977), a wallet snatching (Christiaansen & Ochalek, 1983; Loftus, 1979), a person shoplifting (Christiaansen & Ochalek), or a person stealing multiple items from a room (McCloskey & Zaragoza, 1985). In each of these situations, misleading information provided after an event influenced what witnesses reported remembering. However, will misinformation lead eyewitnesses to change their memories about what they personally experienced during an event, not just what they saw?

Postidentification Feedback Effect

In *Missouri v. Huchting* (1996) a victim-witness spent over 30 minutes looking at a lineup before very tentatively identifying Huchting as the perpetrator, saying, "I don't know…number two?" (p. 202). The officer administering the lineup affirmed that decision, and the case went to trial. During the trial, which occurred months later, the eyewitness claimed, "There was no maybe about it…I was absolutely positive" (p. 202). The confirming feedback that the eyewitness received from the officer immediately after her identification and from the fact that the case went to trial appears to have changed her memory of the identification process. Laboratory and field studies have consistently confirmed that feedback given to an eyewitness after an identification can alter the eyewitness's memory for the identification procedure and for the crime itself (e.g., Wells & Bradfield, 1998, 1999; Wright & Skagerberg, 2007; see Douglass & Steblay, 2006, for a meta-analysis of this effect).

In the classic postidentification feedback paradigm, eyewitnesses view a crime and make an identification from a target-absent lineup. Therefore, any identification that is made is incorrect. They are then given feedback about their decision that is either positive (e.g., "Good job. You identified the suspect.") or negative (e.g., "Nice try. But the person you identified is not the suspect."). After receiving that information, participants are asked about different aspects of their memory for the crime and identification as well as about their current evaluations of the quality of their identification. Eyewitnesses who receive positive feedback, which is necessarily misinformation because any identification from a target-absent lineup is inaccurate, not only report a better current evaluation of their identification but also recall the event and the identification procedure differently than control participants (e.g., Wells & Bradfield, 1998, 1999). Specifically, witnesses who received positive feedback report having a better view at the time of the crime and paying more attention during the crime than witnesses who did not receive feedback. They also claim to have been more confident than control participants in their identification at the time that they made the identification. Therefore, a simple confirmation from the investigator that the eyewitness identified the suspect can render eyewitnesses unable to recall the witnessing experience and the identification experience in a manner that reflects how they actually experienced these events.

The dominant explanation for why postidentification feedback alters eyewitnesses' memories of a crime and their identification experience is that memories of their cognitive processes are, like other memories, reconstructions (e.g., Quinlivan, Wells, & Neuschatz, 2010; Wells, Olson, & Charman, 2003). Eyewitnesses appear to have little or no access to the cognitive traces formed at the time of witnessing (e.g., how good their view was) or at the time of the identification (e.g., how certain they were). Therefore, if they are given postidentification feedback before answering questions about their memory for the event or for the identification, they infer what their view was and how confident they were, given the information that they have at that point. For example, if given positive feedback, they infer that they were correct and, therefore, must have had a good view and must have been confident in the identification. In order to examine this, researchers have asked participants to access the cognitive traces from the time when witnessing the crime or making the identification by thinking privately about, for example, how good their view was or how certain they were *before* being given feedback about their identification (e.g., Bradfield &Wells, 2005; Wells & Bradfield, 1998). This prefeedback, private thought manipulation significantly reduces the effect of feedback on subsequent public answers to the same questions.

Negative feedback has an effect similar to that of positive feedback but in the opposite direction; eyewitnesses who receive negative feedback report having been less confident at the time of the identification, paying less attention during the crime, having a worse view of the crime, and having a worse current evaluation of the quality of their identification than control participants. Laboratory studies have shown that negative feedback results in less memory distortion than positive feedback (e.g., Wells & Bradfield, 1998, 1999), but a field study of the postidentification feedback effect found that real witnesses' memories are influenced more by negative feedback than by positive feedback (Wright & Skagerberg, 2007). This is possibly due to the nature of the task. In the classic postidentification feedback paradigm in the laboratory, eyewitnesses are induced to make a false identification from a target-absent lineup. Because they have made an identification, it can be concluded that their internal cues of recognition were weak. Therefore, they must rely on external cues in order to infer their accuracy. In fact, in studies of the postidentification feedback effect that included the culprit in the lineup—instances in which the internal recognition cues would be stronger than if the culprit was absent—it has been found that the effect of feedback is weaker in accurate than inaccurate witnesses (e.g., Bradfield, Wells, & Olson, 2002; Quinlivan, Neuschatz, Douglass, Wells, & Wetmore, 2011; Semmler, Brewer, & Wells, 2004). In the field, the witnesses who were most affected by positive feedback were those who identified the suspect but thought that the task was very difficult, which provides additional support for the idea that postidentification feedback might have the greatest effect on witnesses whose internal cues are weak (Wright & Skagerberg, 2007).

Postidentification feedback is one manner in which detectives who have a hypothesis about who the perpetrator is might influence an eyewitness's confidence in his or her identification. But is it possible that one piece of evidence might influence who an eyewitness chooses to identify in a lineup?

Evidence Interactions

Michael Evans was convicted and sentenced to 400 years in jail for the rape and murder of Lisa Cabassa (*People v. Evans*, 1979). Prior to this, Evans had never been arrested for anything in his life. The case against Evans rested almost exclusively on the mistaken identification that a lone eyewitness made of him after seeing the perpetrator with the victim on the night of the crime from a distance of 75–100 feet. The conviction against Evans was vacated in 2003 based on DNA testing that proved his innocence. In 2005, during a deposition in preparation for a civil suit on behalf of Evans against the City of Chicago, the eyewitness stated that at the time of the original trial she did not want to testify and said this to "anybody [she] knew would talk to [her]" about the case (*Evans v. City of Chicago et al.*, 2006, p. 274). When asked why she did not want to testify, the eyewitness stated that it was "Because I didn't believe that what I saw was enough. But then I was told there was a confession. And that's how they convinced me that there was more to it than just me" (p. 274). Interestingly, Evans had not actually confessed. It is probable that the false information about his "confession" was provided to the eyewitness so that she would express confidence about her identification when testifying, which she did.

How did this false evidence that the eyewitness was told about influence her testimony about an unrelated piece of evidence—her memory? And how strong does information about other evidence in a case have to be in order to influence an eyewitness's testimony? A relatively weak form of other evidence is what a co-witness to a crime reports having seen (see Hirst, Coman, & Stone, this volume, for a detailed discussion of group influences on memories).

Information from a Co-witness

Even before making an identification, information about a co-witness's actions can influence an eyewitness's decision-making process. Witnesses who learn that a co-witness identified somebody in a lineup are more likely to make an identification than witnesses who learn that a co-witness said that the perpetrator was not in the lineup (Levett & Driest, 2008). Additionally, if an eyewitness is informed of a co-witness's specific identification decision before making his or her own identification, the eyewitness has a tendency to conform to the co-witness's decision (Hasel & Wells, 2008). This is true even if the person the co-witness identifies is the lineup member who looks the least like the perpetrator. In one study, eyewitnesses viewed a crime and were asked to make an identification from a target-absent lineup (Hasel & Wells). In the control condition, none of the eyewitnesses identified Lineup Member #2 as the perpetrator. However, if participant-witnesses learned that a co-witness had identified Lineup Member #2, 15% of them decided to identify that lineup member, and did so with confidence.

If eyewitnesses believe that a co-witness has a different memory than their own, it has been found that they may conform to the co-witness's memory for one of three reasons—normative influence, informational influence, or memory distortion (Wright, Memon, Skagerberg, & Gabbert, 2009). *Normative influence* (e.g., Asch, 1955) occurs when people believe that the cost of disagreeing is high and the cost of being wrong is low and, therefore, knowingly report incorrect information. In one study, participant-witnesses often conformed to a group of three confederates' incorrect identifications on an easy task if they were told that data from their session were being used as pilot data (i.e., the results were of little importance), but they conformed much less frequently if they were told that data from their session would be used by police and courts (i.e., the results were important; Baron, Vandello, & Brunsman, 1996).

Informational influence (e.g., Sherif, 1936) occurs when there is an ambiguous situation and a person looks to others around him or her to resolve the uncertainty. With eyewitnesses, this occurs when they believe that it is likely that they are incorrect and the other person is correct because the other person had, for example, a better view or a better memory for the event and, therefore, believe and report incorrect information. In the study described above, Baron and colleagues (1996) manipulated not only the perceived importance of the task but also the task difficulty. When participants were given a difficult task and told that the results were important, they were more likely to conform to the decisions of the three confederates—who cumulatively should have a better memory than one person—than if they were told that the results were of little importance. When the task was important *and* difficult, the participants looked to the confederates to help determine the correct answer instead of relying on their own memories.

Memory distortion occurs when eyewitnesses encounter information suggested by another person that eventually becomes part of the eyewitnesses' own memories, and they, therefore, believe and report incorrect information. Cognitive psychologists differentiate between *semantic memory*—simply knowing that something is true—and *episodic memory*—having an autobiographical memory for an event (e.g., Tulving & Schacter, 1990). When memory distortion occurs in eyewitnesses, they incorporate misinformation from another source, like a co-witness, into their own memories for events, thus creating a false episodic memory. In one study, participants were shown a video in a group and were asked to recall the contents of the scene; (Edelson, Sharot, Dolan, & Dudai, 2011). Later, participants performed two other recall tests while being scanned with function magnetic resonance imaging (fMRI). Before the second recall test, participants were shown some of the answers that were supposedly given by their four co-witnesses—some of which were false—and before the third recall test, participants were told that the co-witnesses' information had been randomly determined. By examining the differences in responses to these tests, researchers could determine which items the participants conformed to in the previous session because of explicit social influences (i.e., public conformity) and which items participants conformed to because of memory distortion. It was found that participants conformed to their co-witnesses' answers on almost 70% of the items and that conforming persisted for about 40% of the items even after participants were told that the co-witnesses' answers were randomly determined, indicating memory distortion. Interestingly, when participants had memory distortion, as opposed to conforming publicly, there was increased activity in the amygdala, which is important in social and emotional processing, and in the hippocampus, which is involved with memory processing. Therefore, there are underlying biological mechanisms that function when memory distortion is occurring.

INFORMATION FROM AN INVESTIGATOR

The above research demonstrates how eyewitnesses may be influenced by other eyewitnesses, but what other types of evidence can influence eyewitness identification decisions? Hasel and Kassin (2009) demonstrated that eyewitness identification decisions could be influenced by information about the results of a series of interrogations. In their study, eyewitnesses viewed a staged crime and were asked to make an identification from a target-absent lineup. A few days later, the eyewitnesses were either told that the person they identified *denied* committing the crime or that a different lineup member than the one they identified had *confessed* to the crime. When asked what identification decision they would like to make after having received this information, 28% and 61% of the eyewitnesses, respectively, chose to identify a *different* lineup member than the one they had originally identified. When asked to express their confidence in their final identification in words, most participants spontaneously gave explanations for why they changed their identification decision. Of those who changed their decision and provided an explanation as to why they did so, a little less than half reported that they had changed their mind because of belief in the power of the confession (e.g., "He doesn't seem like the guy I think I remember, but a signed confession is pretty hard to beat"; "I was told that number five confessed. GUILTY!"). However the remaining eyewitnesses who changed their identifications reported that they had changed their mind because they reconsidered their own observations and memories in light of the feedback (e.g., "His face now looks more familiar than the one I chose before"; "This person's face matches more of the face I envision in my mind"). Similarly to when eyewitnesses change their testimony because of information about a co-witness's testimony, in this situation the eyewitnesses seemed to be changing their identifications because of normative influence or because of memory distortion prompted by informational influence.

Of course, this study might simply attest to the overwhelming power of confession evidence and might overestimate the extent to which one piece of evidence can influence an eyewitness's memory for an event. What would happen if the potentially influencing evidence suggesting a suspect's guilt or innocence was typically perceived as weak, such as an alibi? In another study, similar to the procedures in Hasel and Kassin's (2009) work, witnesses viewed a staged crime, made an identification from a target-absent lineup, and returned a few days later to discuss their identification with a researcher who provided them with information about the status of the investigation (Smith & Hasel, 2011). However, in this study, witnesses were told that all members of the lineup had provided an alibi and were told the specific alibi of the person that the witness had identified. Witnesses were then given the opportunity to change their identification to another lineup member. If the alibi contained information about physical evidence corroboration that was easy to fabricate (e.g., a taxi receipt or a cash receipt), 44% of witnesses chose to change their identification, and if the alibi contained information about physical evidence corroboration that was difficult to fabricate (e.g., security camera footage at a bank), 59% of witnesses chose to change their identification. After changing their identification to a different lineup member, the witnesses expressed confidence in their second identification that was very similar to the confidence they had expressed in their initial identification. It appears that even relatively weak evidence has the potential to change an eyewitness's decision of who in a lineup looks most like the perpetrator, which can then change the eyewitness's memory trace of the perpetrator as well (e.g., Loftus & Greene, 1980).

The results discussed above demonstrate the potentially pernicious interactions between seemingly discrete pieces of evidence. The changes found in eyewitnesses' memories of the crime (Hasel & Kassin, 2009; Smith & Hasel, 2011) were a result of cognitive biases created by the extraneous information about other pieces of evidence. A voluminous body of research on confirmation biases indicates that people tend to overlook, discount, or assimilate new information that contradicts their existing beliefs (see Nickerson, 1998). In the research discussed in this chapter, the new information, suggesting that a suspect was the perpetrator or that a suspect was innocent, led the eyewitnesses to consider the hypothesis suggested by the new information. The new information was provided by a trustworthy source, such as an investigator, which made the information that was given to them appear valid, thereby making the suggested hypothesis a viable option. Because people are biased to look for information that confirms rather than invalidates their hypotheses (e.g., Ask et al., 2008; Nickerson, 1998), the eyewitnesses looked for aspects of the facial features that confirmed the hypothesis suggested by the information.

The behavior exhibited by the eyewitnesses is known as the *confirmation bias*, which is a preference that people have for confirming evidence over disconfirming evidence and that can lead to an overreliance on confirming evidence when making decisions (Ask et al., 2008; Burke & Turtle, 2003). Hence, if evidence—whether it is accurate or not—exists that supports an eyewitness's preconceived beliefs about a suspect's guilt, then the eyewitness may "cognitively adopt" a conclusion that the suspect is guilty and then be perpetually biased toward information that supports that conclusion (Dror & Fraser-Mackenzie, 2008, p. 57). The erroneous conclusions reached by eyewitnesses who have been biased in this manner are all the more convincing because the eyewitnesses are usually unaware that they have been biased.

HOW CAN LEGAL PRACTITIONERS INCORPORATE CURRENT KNOWLEDGE IN THEIR PRACTICES?

It has been suggested that forensic science has historically dismissed these cognitive biases by viewing bias as an ethical issue as opposed to an inherently cognitive issue (e.g., Risinger, Saks, Thompson, & Rosenthal, 2002). The practical solution to the problem of evidence interactions is rather obvious: keep investigators and forensic scientists blind to the identity of the suspect when conducting the investigation. Clinical trials are double blind, and investigative practices in science could be incorporated by law enforcement officers in their investigations to address the problem of bias, including how to control and correct for it.

The National Academy of Sciences (2009) recently published a report on forensic sciences in which they recommend that additional research should be conducted specifically on "human observer bias and sources of human error in forensic investigations" (p. 45). The National Academy also recommends that guidelines should be developed for standard operating procedures that would minimize the potential for such bias and error. In some jurisdictions, steps have been taken to decrease the potential for contamination of eyewitness evidence, such as mandating that the person conducting the lineup be unaware of the identity of the suspect (e.g., Gronlund, Goodsell, & Andersen, this volume).

To date, most changes in eyewitness identification procedures have been framed as suggested guidelines, such as those created by the Technical Working Group for Eyewitness Evidence, which was convened on behalf of the National Institute of Justice by then United States Attorney General Janet Reno (1999). Similar guidelines have been created in states or jurisdictions, such as Wisconsin (Van Hollen, 2005) and Florida (Florida Department of Law Enforcement, 2011). However, the extent to which legal practitioners are adopting or will adopt these recommendations is still not clear (Cole, 2010). It is possible that these recommendations for forensic scientists will be dismissed as the efforts of academics who do not have any practical experience in the field (Cole, 2010).

Although the movement to adopt eyewitness identification procedures that are supported by psychological scientists has been rather slow, some large-scale reforms have occurred throughout the United States. In 2001, the New Jersey State Attorney General ordered the implementation of eyewitness identification reforms throughout the state (Farmer, 2001), and the reforms have been recently upheld by the New Jersey Supreme Court (*State of New Jersey v. Larry R. Henderson*, 2011). In addition to supporting the procedures outlined by the Attorney General, this decision gives judges tools to effectively evaluate the reliability of eyewitness identification and includes instructions to juries that might help them when evaluating the veracity of eyewitness testimony. Additionally, the West Virginia legislature passed the Eyewitness Identification Act in 2007 and the North Carolina legislature enacted the Eyewitness Identification Reform Act in 2009, which both mandate procedures that would help keep eyewitness identification evidence separate from other evidence.

Another potential solution to the problem is to inform juries about the potential for interactions between different sources of evidence. This could be accomplished through judicial instructions in cases where it was known that there was a situation in which investigators and forensic scientists were not blind to the identity of the suspect when conducting the investigation. However, there is a large body of research demonstrating that jurors do not remember, understand, or apply judges' instructions correctly (e.g., Ellsworth & Reifman, 2000; Lieberman & Sales, 1997). Additionally, there is some evidence that even if juries know that a particular piece of evidence was contaminated, they do not necessarily discount that evidence (e.g, Douglass, Neuschatz, Imrich, & Wilkinson, 2010). One study showed that eyewitness evidence that is contaminated by postidentification feedback is still convincing to jurors, even if they are made aware of the contamination (Douglass et al., 2010). Therefore, it is unclear how effective judicial instructions would be to reduce the impact of evidence interactions at trial.

CONCLUSION

It is clear, both from case examples and from psychological research, that evidence that is collected early in an investigation has the potential to affect the collection and interpretation of evidence later in an investigation. It is also clear that these evidence interactions have the potential to result in very wrongful convictions when an early piece of evidence is faulty. Nevertheless, only a handful of studies have attempted to examine the cognitive and perceptual processes that allow forensic pattern recognition and eyewitness identification decisions to be influenced by prior evidence. Therefore, it is essential to continue to build this body of work that examines these how evidence interactions might function outside of the laboratory during an investigation.

REFERENCES

Asch, S. E. (1955). Opinions and social pressure. *Scientific American, 193*, 31–35.

Ask, K., Rebellius, A. & Granhag, P. A. (2008). The "elasticity" of criminal evidence: A moderator of investigator bias. *Applied Cognitive Psychology, 22*, 1245–1259

Baron, R. S., Vandello, J. A., & Brunsman, B. (1996). The forgotten variable in conformity research: Impact of task importance on social influence. *Journal of Personality and Social Psychology, 71*, 915–927

Bekerian, D. A., & Bowers, J. N. (1983). Eyewitness testimony: Were we misled? *Journal of Experimental Psychology: Learning, Memory, and Cognition, 1*, 139–145.

Bradfield, A. L., & Wells, G. L. (2005). Not the same old hindsight bias: Outcome information distorts a broad range of recollections. *Memory and Cognition, 33*, 120–130.

Bradfield, A. L., Wells, G. L., & Olson, E. A. (2002). The damaging effect of confirming feedback on the relation between eyewitness certainty and accuracy. *Journal of Applied Psychology, 87*, 112–120.

Burke, T. M., & Turtle, J. W. (2003). Alibi evidence in criminal investigations and trials: Psychological and legal factors. *The Canadian Journal of Police and Security Services, 1*(2), 286–294.

Charman, S. D., Gregory, A. M., & Carlucci, M. (2009). Exploring the diagnostic utility of facial composites: Beliefs of guilt can bias perceived similarity between composite and suspect. *Journal of Experimental Psychology: Applied, 15,* 76–90.

Christiaansen, R. E., & Ochalek, K. (1983). Editing misleading information from memory: Evidence for the coexistence of original and post-event information. *Memory & Cognition, 11,* 467–475

Cole, S. A. (2010). Who speaks for science? A response to the National Academy of Sciences report on forensic science. *Law, Probability, and Risk, 9,* 25–46.

Douglass, A. B., Neuschatz, J. S., Imrich, J., & Wilkinson, M. (2010). Does post-identification feedback affect evaluations of eyewitness testimony and identification procedures? *Law and Human Behavior, 34,* 282–294.

Douglass, A. B., & Steblay, N. (2006). Memory distortion in eyewitnesses: A meta-analysis of the post-identification feedback effect. *Applied Cognitive Psychology, 20,* 859–869.

Dror, I. E., & Charlton, D. (2006). Why experts make errors. *Journal of Forensic Identification, 56,* 600–616.

Dror, I. E., & Fraser-Mackenzie, P. A. (2008). Cognitive biases in human perception, judgment, and decision making: Bridging theory and the real world. In K. Rossmo (Ed.), *Criminal investigative failures* (pp. 53–67). Boca Raton, FL: Taylor & Francis.

Edelson, M., Sharot, T., Dolan, R. J., & Dudai, Y. (2011). Following the crowd: Brain substrates of long-term memory conformity. *Science, 333,* 108–111.

Ellsworth, P. C., & Reifman, A. (2000). Juror comprehension and public policy: Perceived problems and proposed solutions. *Public Policy, and Law, 6,* 788–821.

Evans v. City of Chicago et al. www.ilnd.uscourts.gov, Case No. 04-cv-3570, Docket No. 219 (N.D. Ill., 2006).

Eyewitness Identification Act., West Virginia. (2007). Retrieved March 15, 2012 from http://www.nacdl.org/sl_docs.nsf/freeform/EyeID_attachments/$FILE/WV07_82.pdf

Eyewitness Identification Reform Act., North Carolina. (2009). Retrieved March 15, 2012from http://www.ncga.state.nc.us/EnactedLegislation/Statutes/PDF/ByArticle/Chapter_15A/Article_14A.pdf

Farmer, J. J. (2001). *Attorney General guidelines for preparing and conducting photo and live lineup identification procedures.* Retrieved March 15, 2012 from http://www.state.nj.us/lps/dcj/agguide/photoid.pdf

Findley, K. A., & Scott, M. S. (2006).The multiple dimensions of tunnel vision in criminal cases. *Wisconsin Law Review, 2,* 291–397.

Florida Department of Law Enforcement (2011). *Standards for Florida state and local law enforcement agencies in dealing with photographic or live lineups in eyewitness identification.* Retrieved March 15, 2012 from http://www.fdle.state.fl.us/Content/getdoc/bf5b87fb-82e6-43ec-b81f-63d6f36b72a5/Eyewitness-Guideliness.aspx

Hasel, L. E., & Kassin, S. M. (2009) On the presumption of evidentiary independence: Can confessions corrupt eyewitness identifications? *Psychological Science, 21,* 122–126.

Hasel, L. E., & Wells, G. L. (2008, May) *Does order matter when eyewitnesses must negotiate memorial and extra-memorial information?* Paper presented at the Association for Psychological Science Annual Convention, Chicago.

Hoffman, M. B. (2007). The myth of factual innocence. *Chicago-Kent Law Review, 82,* 663–690. Retrieved March 15, 2012 from http://www.innocenceproject.org/

Levett, L. M., & Driest, J. (2008, March). *Social psychological factors in eyewitness behavior: Conformity in choosing behavior.* Paper presented at the American Psychology-Law Society Conference, Jacksonville, FL.

Lieberman, J., & Sales, B. (1997). What social science teaches us about the jury instruction process. *Public Policy and Law, 3,* 589–644.

Lisuzzo, M. C., & Hasel, L. E. (2011, November). *Tunnel vision in investigators: The effects of evidence order on perceptions of guilt.* Poster presented at the American Society of Criminology meeting, Washington, DC.

Loftus, E. F. (1975). Leading questions and the eyewitness report. *Cognitive Psychology, 7,* 560–572.

Loftus, E. F. (1977). Shifting human color memory. *Memory & Cognition, 5,* 696–699.

Loftus, E. F. (1979). *Eyewitness testimony.* Cambridge, MA: Harvard University Press.

Loftus, E. F. (2005). A 30-year investigation of the malleability of memory. *Learning and Memory, 12,* 361–366.

Loftus, E. F., & Greene, E. (1980). Warning: Even memory for faces may be contagious. *Law and Human Behavior, 4,* 323–334.

Loftus, E. F., & Palmer, J. C. (1974). Reconstruction of an automobile destruction: An example of the interaction between language and memory. *Journal of Verbal Learning and Verbal Behavior, 13,* 585–589.

Martin, D. (2001). Lessons about justice from the "laboratory" of wrongful convictions: Tunnel vision, the construction of guilt and informer evidence. *University of Missouri-Kansas City Law Review, 70,* 847–864.

McCloskey, M., & Zaragoza, M. (1985). Misleading postevent information and memory for events: Arguments and evidence against memory impairment hypotheses. *Journal of Experimental Psychology: General, 114,* 3–18.

Missouri v. Huchting, 927 S.W. 2d 411 (1996).

National Academy of Sciences/National Research Council. (2009). *Strengthening forensic science in the United States: A path forward.* Washington, DC: National Academies Press.

Nickerson, R. S. (1998). Confirmation bias: A ubiquitous phenomenon in many guises. *Review of General Psychology, 2,* 175–220.

People v. Evans, 80 Ill. App. 3d 444 (1979), § 725 ILCS 5/116-3

Quinlivan, D. S., Neuschatz, J. S., Douglass, A. B., Wells, G. L., & Wetmore, S. A. (2011). The effect of post-identification feedback, delay, and suspicion on accurate eyewitnesses. *Law and Human Behavior.* doi: 10.1037/h0093970

Quinlivan, D. S., Wells, G. L., & Neuschatz, J. S. (2010). Is manipulative intent necessary to mitigate the eyewitness post-identification feedback effect? *Law and Human Behavior, 34,* 186–197.

Risinger, D. M., Saks, M. J., Thompson, W. C., & Rosenthal, R. (2002). The *Daubert/ Kumho* implications of observer effects in forensic science: Hidden problems of expectation and suggestion. *California Law Review, 90,* 1–56.

Semmler, C., Brewer, N., & Wells, G. L. (2004). Effects of postidentification feedback on eyewitness identification and nonidentification confidence. *Journal of Applied Psychology, 89,* 334–346.

Sherif, M. (1936). *The psychology of social norms.* New York: HarperCollins.

Smith, A., & Hasel, L. E. (2011, March). *"I must have been mistaken": How information about an alibi can corrupt eyewitness identification decisions.* Paper presented at the 4th International Congress on Psychology and Law, Miami, FL.

State of New Jersey v. Larry R. Henderson. (2011). Retrieved March 15, 2012 from http://www.innocenceproject.org/docs/2011/StatevLarryHenderson.pdf

Synder, L. C., McQuillan, P. J., Murphy, W. L., & Joselson, R. (2007). *Report on the conviction of Jeffrey Deskovic. Westchester County District Attorney's Office. White Plains, New York.* Retrieved March, 15, 2012 from http://www.westchesterda.net/Jeffrey%20Deskovic%20Comm%20Rpt.pdfTechnical Working Group for Eyewitness Evidence. (1999). *Eyewitness evidence: A guide for law enforcement.* Washington, DC: U.S. Department of Justice, Office of Justice Programs.

Tulving, E., & Schacter, D. L. (1990). Priming and human memory systems. *Science, 247,* 301–306.

U.S. Department of Justice, Office of the Inspector General. (2006). *A review of the FBI's handling of the Brandon Mayfield case (unclassified and redacte* Retrieved March, 15, 2012 from http://www.justice.gov/oig/special/s0601/PDF_list.htm

Van Hollen, J. B. (2005). *Model policy and procedure for eyewitness identification.* State of Wisconsin Office of the Attorney General. Retrieved from http://www.doj.state.wi.us/dles/tns/eyewitnesspublic.pdf

Wechsler, H., Garcia-Dubus, E., & Kucharski, L. T. (2011,March). *Comparison of DNA and non-DNA exonerations.* Poster presented at the 4th International Congress on Psychology and Law, Miami, FL.

Wells, G. L., & Bradfield, A. L. (1998). "Good, you identified the suspect": Feedback to eyewitnesses distorts their reports of the witnessing experience. *Journal of Applied Psychology, 83,* 360–376.

Wells, G. L., & Bradfield, A. L. (1999). Distortions in eyewitnesses recollections: Can the postidentification-feedback effect be moderated. *Psychological Science, 10,* 138–144.

Wells, G. L., Olson, E. A., & Charman, S. D. (2003). Distorted retrospective eyewitness reports as functions of feedback and delay. *Journal of Experimental Psychology: Applied, 9,* 42–52.

Wright, D. B., Memon, A., Skagerberg, E. M., & Gabbert, F. (2009). When eyewitnesses talk. *Current Directions in Psychological Science, 18,* 174–178.

Wright, D. B., & Skagerberg, E. M. (2007). Post-identification feedback affects real eyewitnesses. *Psychological Science, 18,* 172–176.

PART THREE

Memory in Jurors

7

Memory and Jury Deliberation

The Benefits and Costs of Collective Remembering

WILLIAM HIRST, ALIN COMAN, AND CHARLES B. STONE

As the chapters in this volume make clear, the psychological study of memory can have a profound impact on the law, particularly with respect to the veracity of eyewitness testimony (see also Loftus, 1996; Wells, Memon, & Penrod, 2006). Less appreciated is the role the psychology of memory might play in understanding how juries remember the testimony presented in a trial during their deliberations. Even though, as one study suggests, almost 10% of what juries talk about is trial evidence (Warren & Kuhn, 2010), the large literature on the psychology underlying jury judgment-making barely addresses how this jury-based remembering might unfold (see Kapardis, 2010, for a review of the research on jury decision making). This lacuna is unfortunate. Jurors must remember what they heard during the trial in order to make a reasoned decision, and courts often instruct jurors about how they should treat what they recall during deliberation. The extant judicial rulings suggest that the courts have a bias toward instructing the jury to rely on their "human memory" rather than on mnemonic technology, such as notes or written transcripts. The courts appear to believe that, even if human memory is unreliable, the collaborative efforts of the jury will compensate for its flaws and produce, through the collaboration, a fairly accurate representation of what took place during the trial.

This chapter explores whether the psychological assumptions of the courts are reasonable. The final judgment of a jury is tethered tightly to the collaborative remembering taking place during deliberation. If the courts are wrong, what is remembered may diverge in critical ways from the original testimony and, in doing so, may lead to a flawed final judgment. It is important to determine not only if the courts are correct in their reliance on collective remembering to produce accurate recollection, but also whether a psychological understanding of the dynamics of collaborative remembering might help the courts devise instructions that could mitigate any memory errors that might arise from the collaboration. In what follows, we will first discuss the relevant judicial decisions and then turn to the psychological work on collaborative remembering.

RELEVANT COURT RULINGS ON ISSUES CONCERNING REMEMBERING DURING JURY DELIBERATION

The Sixth Amendment of the Constitution provides that an individual accused of a crime has a right to a trial by an impartial jury. Claims of jury bias are subject to "harmless error analysis," with appellate courts required to consider an appeal only if an error of law was made that is deemed "serious" rather than "harmless" (Traynor, 1970). As a result, habeas corpus relief is granted only when constitutional trial errors have a "substantial effect or influence in determining the jury's verdict." The courts have utilized harmless error analysis when dealing with issues of memory as they apply to jury deliberations.

Generally, the courts have asked jurors to rely on their own memories rather than on mnemonic technologies when trying to remember testimony individually or collectively. Until recently, for instance, there has been resistance to allowing jurors to take notes during the trial and use them as memory aids during deliberations (Heuer & Penrod, 1994; Petroff, 1965). This hesitancy can be traced back to a period when illiteracy was prevalent. The courts feared, and still worry, that jurors who take notes will have greater credibility during deliberations than those who do not or cannot. They also fret that note taking may distract jurors during the trial. They are acutely aware that notes can be inaccurate and that they could focus on details and irrelevancies in a way ordinary recollection might not. Today, the courts generally allow note taking, though there are exceptions. According to a study of the National Center for States Courts (Mize, Hannaford-Agor, & Waters, 2007), 29% of the federal courts and 31% of the state courts prohibit note taking. The attitude of the courts can be captured by two quotes. The Chief Judge of the State of New York (Lippman, 2009) cautions: "Judges [should] be permitted to allow jurors to take notes as a matter of judicial discretion, so long as the jurors are instructed not to rely unduly on their own or others notes" (p. 9) The State of Connecticut offers the following instructions for judges to give to juries:

> Notes are a sound tool to help you refresh your recollections during the deliberative process of this trial. However, notes, by themselves, are not

foolproof. If there is a conflict between your notes and your recollections, *it is your recollection that must prevail.* (Criminal Jury Instructions on Note-taking, State of Connecticut, revised June 12, 2009; retrieved from http://www.jud.ct.gov/ji/criminal/part1/1.2-11.htm on September 1, 2011; italics added by the present authors)

As an aid to memory, jurors can, of course, ask for readbacks. These can take the form of the judge or a court reporter reading to the jurors the requested portion of the court record. A written version of this court record can also be provided, as an alternative. (Courts generally do not allow the use of videotapes of the trials proceedings as a form of readbacks.) In most states, a judge is not required to supply a readback, even when it is requested (*U.S. v. Escotto*, 1997). The judge should consider (1) the length of the trial, (2) the complexity of the issues, (3) the number of witnesses, (4) the amount of testimony requested, (5) importance of the requested testimony, (6) the inconvenience to the court, (7) whether confusion or boredom will result, and (8) whether the request will take the testimony out of context. According to *U.S. v. Escotto*, if there is a close call, a judge should lean toward a readback. Generally, the preference is for verbal readbacks over written transcripts because the courts cannot control what is done with the written transcript once it is handed to the jury. One person may read it and summarize it to the others, or there may be multiple readings of some but not all of the transcripts. Both of these uses of the transcripts could bias the deliberations. This preference for oral readbacks cannot be viewed as a perfect solution to the memory problems that led to the request for a readback, in that jurors must now remember the verbal readback. At no point will the entire written transcript of the court records be accessible to the jury.

As with note taking, when written transcripts are provided, court rulings urge judges to instruct jurors to rely on their memory over the written transcript when there is a conflict. Suggested instructions specifically refer to the jury's "collective memory." For instance, the jury instructions suggested by *U.S. v. Montgomery* (1998) state:

> I want you to bear in mind that the testimony at trial is the evidence, not the transcript. The transcript is not authoritative. If you remember something different from what appears in the transcript, your collective recollections is controlling. In other words, the transcripts may not serve as a substitute for the collective memories of the jury....

Presumably, the reasoning here is that if 12 jurors all agree on what was said during the trial, then they must be right, even if the written transcript, which is also subject to human error, differs.

This reliance on the jurors' memory during deliberation, especially their collective memory, might be legitimate if collective remembering produced the accurate and complete recollections that individual acts of remembering cannot. The psychological literature suggests otherwise.

PSYCHOLOGICAL LITERATURE ON COLLABORATIVE REMEMBERING AND ITS MNEMONIC CONSEQUENCES: ON THE NATURE OF COLLABORATIVE REMEMBERING AND COLLECTIVE MEMORIES

Even though collaborative remembering has not been studied in the jury setting to date, there is a sufficient body of work on collaborative remembering in more neutral contexts to bring into question some of the courts' declarations. This burgeoning literature on collaborative remembering and collective memory can be divided into two areas: (1) research addressing the issue of what is remembered during the collaboration and (2) research exploring how the collaborative remembering affects subsequent memory (see Hirst & Echterhoff, 2012). Both are relevant to any study of remembering in the jury setting. The former, for instance, addresses the issue of whether collaboration leads jurors to remember more during the collaboration than they might as individuals. The latter explores whether the memory that group members hold after the collaboration is more complete or accurate than the memory they might hold if the collaboration never took place.

THE EFFECT OF COLLABORATION ON REMEMBERING DURING COLLABORATION

Groups, as a unit, remember collaboratively more than any group member might remember alone (*collaborative facilitation*). This facilitation can be clearly observed when the group forms a transactive memory system, in which group members distribute among themselves the job of memorizing and remembering (see Andersson & Rönnberg, 1997; Wegner, 1986) But transactive memory systems are unlikely to exist among unrelated individuals, such as jury members. When psychologists consider remembering within groups of unrelated individuals, the benefits of collaborative remembering appear to be limited.

One reason for this limitation is that one putative source of benefit, the cross-cueing that might arise in conversations, does not occur as frequently as one might expect (Meudell, Hitch, & Boyle, 1995; Meudell, Hitch, & Kirby, 1992). But there are other explanations. For instance, even though a group might remember more than any individual would alone, it does not recount the sum of all that its individual members are capable of remembering (*collaborative inhibition*; see Rajaram & Pereira-Pasarin, 2010, for a review). Selective remembering may be typical of all acts of remembering (Marsh, 2007). The presence of collaborative inhibition, however, suggests that collaborative remembering does not improve the situation; rather, it can exacerbate it. It does so for several reasons. First, individuals communicating with others will tune what they say to their expectation about what their audience wants or expects, selecting from a range of possible memories the relevant or desired ones (Echterhoff, Higgins, & Levine, 2009; Marsh & Tversky, 2004; Pasupathi, 2001). Second, some group members may loaf, leaving the task of remembering to others. Third, the collaboration may lead to retrieval blockage (Basden, Basden, Bryner, & Thomas, 1997; Weldon, 2001; Weldon, Blair, & Heubsch, 2000). That is, one person in a conversation may pursue a retrieval strategy that is effective for her but not necessarily ideal for other conversational participants. As a result, the other participants may have difficulty recalling material they might have easily recalled alone. Various experimenters have shown that collaborative inhibition cannot be accounted for by audience tuning or social loafing alone (Weldon et al., 2000). Retrieval blockage plays a critical role (Basden et al., 1997).

Collaborative inhibition can be effectively diminished in group recountings, but the jury setting seems designed to promote rather than limit it. For instance, collaborative inhibition depends on the relationships among group members, with collaborative inhibition all but disappearing in long-term couples (Harris, Paterson, & Kemp, 2008; Johansson, Andersson, & Rönnberg, 2005). But juries consist of unrelated individuals. Moreover, group size matters. Groups of two, for instance, often do not exhibit collaborative inhibition (Thorley & Dewhurst, 2007). Juries, however, are quite large, at least in comparison to the size of the groups in all extant studies of collaborative inhibition. Ranging from 6 to 12 in the United States, their size almost guarantees collaborative inhibition.

Limits on the efficacy of collaborative remembering can also arise because of the *information sampling bias* that exists in what conversational participants recall. As a result of this bias, unshared information (unique to one participant) is less likely than shared information to surface in a group recounting (Wittenbaum & Parks, 2001; Wittenbaum & Stasser, 1996). Accordingly, jurors should be more likely to recollect what each of their fellow jurors encoded about the testimony rather than something that they themselves alone may have noticed.

In other words, collaboration during deliberation may actually prevent critical testimony from surfacing into the jury's discussion that, under other circumstances, would be remembered. Although the limits of cross-cueing, collaborative inhibition, and information sampling biases have not been explicitly studied in a jury setting, several studies of memory and juries reinforce what these phenomena suggest: There are limits to the role deliberation may play in facilitating recall. When individuals were asked to act as if they were jurors, their memory of the testimony they heard previously was, as expected, selective, with jurors individually remembering information consistent with the "story" they constructed around the testimony rather than the testimony in a complete, unbiased form (e.g., Pennington & Hastie, 1992). Moreover, in work more directly related to our concerns about deliberation, Pritchard and Keenan (1999, 2002) contrasted the memories of jurors before and after a mock jury deliberation, probing in each instance for memories of specific aspects of the testimony. They found no improvement in memory after the deliberation of testimony central to the verdict and only a 10% improvement for peripheral information.

THE EFFECT OF COLLABORATION ON SUBSEQUENT MEMORY

The current literature clearly establishes that what speakers and listeners say to each other as they collectively remember changes their subsequent individual memories (Cuc, Ozuru, Manier, & Hirst, 2006; Gabbert, Memon, & Allan, 2003; Gabbert, Memon, Allan, & Wright, 2004; Wright, Self, & Justice, 2000). Most of the experimental work supports this conclusion by placing a memory probe after the conversation. Nevertheless, the findings are important for understanding the consequences of jury deliberation because they suggest that the memory jurors hold as they make their final judgment may differ from the one they possessed as the deliberations began. Indeed, if conversations alter memories, as studies claim, then they probably do so "on-line," reshaping memories as they proceed. These conversational shifts may be quite dramatic when it comes to jury deliberations, in that the deliberations can last for hours, if not days, and are frequently punctuated with breaks.

The experimental literature suggests that conversations can alter memory in at least four ways: social contagion, rehearsal, cueing/retrieval-induced facilitation, and retrieval-induced forgetting. In each instance, effects on memory can be divided into two general classes: (1) effects of what a speaker says on the speaker's own memory and (2) effects of what a speaker says on the listener's memory.

Social Contagion: Postevent Misinformation Effects and Source Monitoring Problems

When two people jointly recount previously studied material, one of the recounters may introduce misinformation into the recounting. In turn, other participants may subsequently remember this misleading information as though it occurred in the originally studied material (see Chapter 2 in this volume by Davis and Loftus for a review of this work). This postevent misinformation effect is often interpreted as a source monitoring error (Johnson, Hashtroudi, & Lindsay, 1993). The misinformation effect has been shown when the source was not a person—for instance, when it was written text. It was stronger, however, when the source was social—for instance, a person in a conversation (Cuc et al., 2006; Echterhoff, Groll, & Hirst, 2007; Echterhoff, Hirst, & Hussy, 2005; Gabbert et al., 2003; Gabbert et al., 2004; Meade & Roediger, 2002; Reysen & Adair, 2008; Wright et al., 2000). When a social source implants misinformation, it is often referred to as *social contagion*.

At least in regard to the law, social contagion and the postevent misformation effect have mainly been studied in terms of the reliability of eyewitness testimony. A lawyer's leading questions, for instance, may alter existing memories or implant misinformation in a way that could lead to false testimony (Loftus & Zanni, 1975). Such work underscores the need for judges and jurors to take into account the malleability and unreliability of memory when arriving at a judgment. Similarly, it is theoretically possible that misleading information could surface in the discussions juries have during deliberation. One juror may incorrectly remember what occurred in the trial, and this misleading recollection could spread through the jury until most, if not all jurors come to remember the trial in the same erroneous way (Brown, Coman, & Hirst, 2009; Cuc et al., 2006). Although such contagion could occur, we suspect that it does so infrequently. First, the number of errors of commission may be small during jury deliberations. Jurors may omit some details, but they are unlikely to introduce information that never appeared in the trial. Many experimental studies report that misleading information was introduced into a recollection around 5% of the time. Moreover, when misleading information was introduced by one jury member, it was likely to be corrected by other jury members (Tschuggnall & Welzer, 2002). Experimental studies have demonstrated that a corrective tendency increases with the size of the group (Thorley & Dewhurst, 2007). The self-corrective nature of groups probably makes the proportion of uncontested errors of commission significantly smaller than 5%. Finally, even when a small number of errors of commission remain uncorrected, the chance of these errors spreading through the jury is also limited. Misleading information is implanted in experimental participants about 30% of the time (Lindsay, Hagen, Read, Wade, & Garry, 2004; Loftus, 2005). Similar rates are thus likely to occur in a jury setting as well. Pritchard and Keenan (2002), for instance, found that when members of a mock jury were probed for what they could remember prior to deliberation, they were more likely to fail to answer a question than to answer it incorrectly. Moreover, around 50% of the time, *errors of commission* in the predeliberation memory test were, in turn, correctly discussed during deliberation. We suspect that an extremely small proportion of what is remembered during a deliberation might be construed as errors of commission. Of course, any widely held false memory is troubling, especially if the error is dispositive. Nevertheless, as we shall see, there are other, more likely candidates for how collaborative remembering during jury deliberations may distort both the jury's memory and also their final judgment. These should be of more concern to the courts when they consider how to facilitate accurate and complete recall as juries deliberate.

Rehearsal

When a speaker in a conversation repeats something already known to the listener, by virtue of the repetition, one would expect and indeed finds an improvement on subsequent memory tests for both speaker and/or listeners (Blumen & Rajaram, 2008; Rajaram & Pereira-Pasarin, 2007; Weldon & Bellinger, 1997). This effect is stronger for speakers than for listeners (Cuc et al. 2006). As Karpicke and Roediger (2007, 2008) have averred, the speaker may have an advantage because retrieval is "key to long-term retention" (see also Slamecka & Graf, 1978; see Mulligan & Lozito, 2004, for a review of the generation effect). Interestingly, because speakers and listeners do not equally share the burden of retrieval and generation, it is possible for joint encoding of material to work against facilitation and produce worse subsequent individual recall than would individual encoding (Barber, Rajaram, & Aron, 2010). Nevertheless, jurors are probably more likely to retain over time information mentioned during their deliberations than information that goes unmentioned.

Information mentioned during deliberations, then, might be expected to have a stronger bearing on the final judgment than information that goes unmentioned. What emerges during deliberations, and hence what becomes more accessible as the deliberations proceeds, depends on several factors. For instance, Pennington and Hastie (1992) suggested that what people remember during deliberation is the material consistent with the "story" developed during the trial. However, how the deliberation itself unfolds may also determine what is remembered, as the work on collaborative inhibition and informational sampling biases indicates (Stasser & Titus, 1987; Weldon & Bellinger, 1997; Weldon et al., 2000; Wittenbaum & Stasser, 1996). Cuc et al. (2006) observed that one person often dominates a conversation, and we see no reason why this would not also apply to jury deliberations. As Cuc et al. demonstrated, this "dominant Narrator" has a large influence on subsequent remembering. For instance, one juror's domination of the conversation may lead the jury to rehearse one set of memories to the exclusion of others. As a result, the final recollections of the jury may reflect the rendering of the trial offered by this dominant Narrator and not necessarily the rendering originally held by others. It is presently unclear why one member of a group might become a dominant Narrator or what instructions might be given to a jury that would lessen this possibility. What is certain is that, without the appropriate instructions, a dominant Narrator could emerge during deliberations.

Cueing and Retrieval-Induced Facilitation

In instances in which cross-cueing does occur, the cued memory should offer an unexpected chance for rehearsal, thereby increasing the probability that this newly remembered item will be subsequently remembered by all group members. The cue could elicit a memory that is not shared with others. The phenomenon of *retrieval-induced facilitation* could be viewed as an example of such cued covert remembering.[1] Here, selective remembering by a person appears to trigger covert remembering of related but unrecalled information by the same individual. The experimental evidence clearly demonstrates that the unmentioned but related memory was better remembered on a subsequent memory test than it would have been if the selective remembering had never occurred. However, just as jury deliberation may not be an ideal environment for cross-cueing generally, it may also not be conducive for retrieval-induced facilitation. Chan and his colleagues (e.g., Chan, McDermott, & Roediger, 2006) have stressed that retrieval-induced facilitation requires a broad retrieval search on the part of the rememberer. The rapid give-and-take of a conversation, including the conversation taking place during jury deliberations, may not allow enough time for the broad search needed to elicit retrieval-induced facilitation.

It would appear, then, that possible positive outcomes of collaborative remembering—cross-cueing, retrieval-induced facilitation, and the rehearsal benefits they accrue—may not occur frequently enough to compensate for any negative outcomes of collaborative remembering. There may be, of course, ways to encourage the use of cross-cueing and retrieval-induced facilitation. For instance, a jury might be instructed to use what their fellow jurors say to jog their memory as they attempt to reconstruct what occurred during the trial. However, the implications of such instructions for the way jurors evaluate evidence and their effect on the final judgment is unclear and needs further investigation.

Retrieval-Induced Forgetting

As we have emphasized, collaborative remembering produces selective remembering. Recent research indicates that, in a conversation, this selective remembering may induce forgetting in speakers (the person doing the remembering; *within-individual retrieval-induced forgetting*, WI-RIF) and listeners (the person listening to the speaker express his or her memories; *socially shared retrieval-induced forgetting*, SS-RIF; see Hirst & Echterhoff, 2008, 2012). These two types of induced forgetting could play a substantial role in shaping the memories of individual jury members. In both instances, what is forgotten is the unmentioned (or unrecalled) material, but, importantly, the rate of forgetting is not the same for all unmentioned material: Unmentioned material related to what was remembered is forgotten at a greater rate than unmentioned and unrelated material. In a way, this pattern suggests that it may be better not to remember at all than to remember selectively.

In the original RIF paradigm of Anderson and his colleagues (Anderson, Bjork, & Bjork, 1994), participants studied category-exemplar pairs such as *animal-cat, animal-dog, vegetable-broccoli,* and *vegetable-pea.* They then retrieved selectively some of these pairs by completing cued words (e.g., *animal-d_____*). This additional practice focused on some pairs (e.g., *animal-dog*) but not other related pairs (e.g., *animal-cat*) and did not involve whole sets of pairs (e.g., all the vegetable pairs). A final recall or recognition test for the original word list followed. This design established three types of retrieval items: practiced items (Rp+), unpracticed items related to practiced items (Rp−), and unpracticed items unrelated to practiced items (Nrp) (see Table 7.1).

Using this paradigm, researchers have found, as the previous summary of results indicated, that (within-individual) retrieval-induced forgetting is indicated by the telltale pattern of Nrp > Rp− (see Anderson & Levy, 2002, for a review). This mnemonic pattern suggests that the forgetting here is not merely a matter of decay but also, at least as some researchers have suggested, inhibition induced by selective practice (Anderson & Levy, 2002; but see, for example, Perfect et al., 2004, for alternative explanations). WI-RIF can be found for a wide range of material, such as visuospatial stimuli, paired associates, stories, and autobiographical memories (Anderson et al., 1994; Barnier,

Table 7-1 Design of Retrieval-Induced Forgetting Experiments

Study Phase	Practice Phase	Testing Phase	Condition
Fruit–Apple	Fruit–Ap_____	List words paired with Fruit	Rp+
Fruit–Orange			Rp−
Vegetable–Broccoli		List words paired with Vegetable	Nrp
Vegetable–Pea			Nrp

Hung, & Conway, 2004; Ciranni & Shimamura, 1999; MacLeod & Saunders, 2008). Moreover, although in some instances it lasts for 24 hours (Migueles & Garcia-Bajos, 2007), in other instances it can last for over 1 week (Garcia-Bajos, Migueles, & Anderson, 2009; Storm, Bjork, Bjork, & Nestojko, 2006; Tandoh & Naka, 2007; but see MacLeod & Macrae, 2001). Either time frame suggests that RIF may be at play during jury deliberations.

Recently, Hirst and his colleagues have extended the WI-RIF paradigm to capture induced forgetting in a social context. They modified the paradigm to include both a speaker (the person doing the remembering) and a listener. In doing so, they directly probed for the way collaborative remembering might elicit RIF. In a representative experiment, Cuc, Koppel, and Hirst (2007) followed the procedure of Anderson et al. (1994) but now asked two participants to study the material. During the retrieval practice phase, one participant selectively recalled the material, while the other listened. Finally, both participants individually recalled the original list. Under certain conditions—more specifically, when monitoring for accuracy—Cuc et al. found RIF for both speakers and listeners. They argued that SS-RIF occurs because the listener concurrently, albeit covertly, recalled the material along with the speaker. As a result, the conditions for retrieval-induced forgetting hold for both speaker and listener.

As with WI-RIF, this covert, concurrent remembering, and the subsequent SS-RIF, occur in a free-flowing conversation in which speaker and listener seek to jointly recount a previously studied story. In some SS-RIF experiments examining free-flowing conversations, two participants individually studied a story. The stories were structured around episode-event pairs; for example, the episode *going to Coney Island* contained the events *eating hot dogs* and *riding the roller coaster*. Formally, the stories do not differ structurally from the category-exemplar pairs used in other retrieval-induced forgetting experiments. After studying the stories (with an appropriate delay), the two participants jointly recounted the story to each other. No instructions were given about how the conversation should unfold other than to jointly recount the story. In the final memory test, following the conversation after 10 or more minutes' delay, each person individually recalled the story. The conversation was transcribed and then classified in terms of practice type (Rp+, Rp−, and Nrp) and conversational role (speaker, listener).

Cuc et al. (2007) observed robust within-individual and socially shared retrieval-induced forgetting following the free-flowing conversation. They argued that when participants are asked to recount jointly a previously studied story, listeners in the conversation value accuracy and hence are inclined to concurrently, albeit covertly, retrieve. Like WI-RIF, SS-RIF can be found for a wide range of material, including highly memorable, schema-consistent elements of a story (Stone, Barnier, Sutton, & Hirst, 2010a), autobiographical memories (Coman, Manier, & Hirst, 2009; Stone, Barnier, Sutton, & Hirst, 2010b), and science articles and textbooks (Koppel, Wohl, Meksin, & Hirst, 2012). Moreover, as Hirst and Ecterhoff (2008) recently observed, studies of retrieval-induced forgetting and conversations tended to report higher levels of retrieval-induced forgetting than do those that employ a structured retrieval practice phase, an observation that probably reflects the claims of Chan et al. (2006) that the counterpoint to retrieval-induced forgetting, retrieval-induced facilitation, needs sufficient retrieval time to emerge. As already noted, the rapidity of conversations often does not supply the needed time.

These remarks suggest that jury deliberation may be an effective medium for induced forgetting. The selective remembering at the beginning of a process might induce not just the rememberer, but all jurors, to have difficulty remembering related but unmentioned memories at a later time in the deliberations. Each juror, after all, hears the same material recalled and the same material left unstated. It is not hard to imagine how such induced forgetting could be detrimental to a balanced consideration of the testimony. Jurors who figure critically at the beginning of a deliberation could not only reinforce some testimony, but also increase the chance that other possibly relevant testimony might not arise as the deliberations proceed. The notion that the collective efforts of the jurors will lead to more complete and unbiased recollection of the testimony may simply not hold true.

SS-RIF as a Mechanism for Collective Forgetting

The judgments of juries are arrived at collectively, even if the voting is done individually. This collective judgment could move more quickly to conclusion if there was agreement among jurors about their recollections of the trial. We will refer to shared individual memories as *collective memories* (Hirst & Echterhoff, 2008; Hirst & Manier, 2008; Rajaram, 2010). Inasmuch as conversations can collectively facilitate the subsequent recall for some information and induced forgetting for other information, they provide one means of promoting the formation of collective memories. Cuc et al. (2006) contrasted the degree to which the memories of previously studied material overlapped prior to a conversation with the overlap subsequent to the conversation. During the conversation, four participants recounted what they could remember of the studied material. Cuc et al. found an increase in overlap from preconversation to postconversation assessments. Moreover, they found that when conversational participants studied slightly different versions of the story, with different *contrasting details*, the overlap could be accounted for, in part, by the social contagion that led different participants to adopt the same contrasting details. This latter finding underscores the role social contagion could play in the formation of collective memories.

As we noted, the role of rehearsal and retrieval-induced forgetting might be more critical when considering jury deliberations than social contagion. Roediger, Zaromb, and Butler (2009) have described in detail the role retrieval and rehearsal can play in the formation of collective memories. Reexposure during deliberation to an aspect of the original testimony, for instance, will not only make it more likely that the speaker will subsequently find this aspect more accessible, but that other jurors will as well. This increase in shared accessibility should increase with the number of reexposures.

As for RIF, because the pattern of remembering and induced forgetting is the same in both speaker and listener, we should also find not just an increase in accessibility for the mentioned material among jurors, but also a decrease in accessibility for the unmentioned but related material. Stone et al. (2010a) assessed this possibility by calculating the proportion of previously studied material *remembered* individually, but in common, by two participants (RR) and the proportion *forgotten* individually, but in common, by the two participants (FF). He then contrasted the overlap scores in a cued recall test prior to a conversation between the two participants with the overlap scores in a cued recall test subsequent to the conversation. Both RR and FF increased subsequent to the conversation. Conversational participants came to remember and forget similar material as a result of the selective practice embedded in the conversation.

A Closer Look at SS-RIF: Moderating Factors

If SS-RIF can promote collective forgetting, are there ways to diminish the level of induced forgetting or, worse yet, increase it? The presence of SS-RIF depends on the goals of the participants when remembering in a social context. For instance, Cuc et al. (2007) manipulated how listeners monitored speakers and found SS-RIF when the listener was asked to judge the accuracy of what the speaker remembered; they showed greater SS-RIF than when they were asked to judge the fluency with which the listener remembered. The former presumably encouraged concurrent retrieval on the part of the listener, whereas the latter did not. As noted, Cuc et al. also argued that instructions to jointly recount a story emphasize accuracy.

What are the goals of the jurors during deliberations? As we saw in the section on judicial rulings and instructions, jurors are asked to rely on their collective memory. How this instruction translates into specific ways jurors monitor each other's recollections is unclear, but, no doubt, jurors may be more inclined to monitor for accuracy than, for instance, people in idle conversation at a dinner party. As a result, jurors should be susceptible to SS-RIF. The need for accuracy may also be accompanied by a need to remember the trial as completely as possible. Although the presence of such a goal would suggest that the usual selective remembering characteristic of conversation may not hold for jury deliberations, the available literature, scant as it is, suggests otherwise. The failure of Pritchard and Keenan (1999, 2002) to find any improvement in memory after a deliberation suggests that the recounting during the deliberation was far from complete. These conclusions must be tentative, however. As yet, no one has studied RIF effects in the context of a jury deliberation.

One concern of the courts is to ensure that no juror is perceived as an expert or more credible than others. Juries should be, at least in theory, a collectivity of peers, and as such, each member's opinion or recommendation should be given equal weight. In reality, of course, one member may project greater authority, expertise, or credibility than others. This level of expertise should not be confused with the level of expertise shown to minimize collaborative inhibition in at least one study of conversational remembering (Meade, Nokes, & Morrow, 2009). In this study, the experts were seasoned air pilots. Jury selection ensures that no one on a jury has that level of expertise. Nevertheless, the courts are correct when they worry that one person may be perceived as having a greater level of authority, even if that person does not demonstrate a professional level of expertise. This perception may be enough to allow the individual to adopt the role of dominant Narrator, which in turn would give this person greater influence on subsequent memory (Brown et al., 2009; Wegner, 2006)—a clear cost. On the other hand, when a speaker is perceived as an expert, the level of SS-RIF is diminished (Koppel et al., 2012), in that listeners are less likely to assess the accuracy of what the speaker says if the speaker is viewed as an expert. Unfortunately, only one member (or a few members) of a jury can play the role of an expert, leaving the degree to which others may induce socially shared forgetting intact. Moreover, social contagion is more robust if the speaker is perceived as an expert (Dodd & Bradshaw, 1980; Smith & Ellsworth, 1987).

COLLECTIVE MEMORY AND DECISION MAKING

As we have emphasized, the courts are concerned about how jurors remember while deliberating because their recollections could shape their judgments concerning acquittal. According to retrospective reports, in most instances, jurors form their opinions during the deliberation, not prior to the deliberation (Hannaford-Agor, Hans, Mott, & Munsterman, 2002). Moreover, predeliberation voting is of low frequency (Devine et al., 2004; Diamond & Casper, 1992) and, unless there is a strong initial sentiment for conviction, the initial vote does not predetermine the outcome of the deliberation (Salerno &

Diamond, 2010). Clearly, the deliberation, and presumably what is remembered in the deliberation, plays a significant role.

Psychological work on decision making outside of the jury setting indicates that mnemonic accessibility can guide decision making (Hastie, 1993; Hastie & Park, 1986; Iglesias-Parro & Gomez-Ariza, 2006; Pennington & Hastie, 1992; Weber & Johnson, 2009). However, the needed work with actual or mock juries has not been done. Pritchard and Keenan (1999, 2002) have shown that what individual jury members remembered after deliberation (actual collaborative deliberation) determined, in part, their judgment, but they failed to investigate the effect of what juries remember collaboratively *during* the deliberation on judgments.

As to the specific mechanisms we have been discussing, Bernstein and Loftus (2009) have shown that an implanted memory can shape subsequent decisions. They studied this issue in the context of food selection. They implanted a memory of a food poisoning incident in childhood and then gave participants the chance to consume the now tainted food. The implanted memory led participants to avoid the tainted food.

As to RIF, in a study that bears only indirectly on the relation between RIF and decision making, Storm, Bjork, and Bjork (2005) failed to find a relation between the forgetting effect and likeability ratings in an RIF paradigm that induced forgetting for either positive or negative traits of a person's description. In a more relevant study, Iglesias-Parro and Gómez-Ariza (2006) found that RIF guided the decision-making process of selecting job applicants. More recently, Coman, Coman, and Hirst (2012) taught participants about a fictitious disease, Wheeler's syndrome, its symptoms, and the strengths and weaknesses of various treatments. After a delay, they asked participants to read a brochure about the disease, which only selectively covered the treatment's strengths and weaknesses. Not only did they find that reading the brochure induced forgetting in a manner found in other RIF experiments, but also that it influenced the decisions participants made about which treatment to pursue: What participants were induced to forget by the brochure influenced their decision about the course of treatment. Their final decision could not be predicted by what was practiced as a result of the brochure, only by the pattern of induced forgetting.

Although these studies suggest that any shift in memory accessibility due to social contagion, practice, or RIF should affect the final judgment of a jury, again, this claim has not been explicitly studied in this setting.

FURTHER INVESTIGATIONS OF PRACTICE EFFECTS AND RIF

A trial usually proceeds with the presentation of the evidence, followed by biased summary statements and then deliberation. This sequence could be viewed as involving a study phase (the presentation of the evidence), an initial social interaction involving a one-way exchange about what was previously studied (the summary statement), and, finally, a second social interaction among individuals who were exposed to both the original material and the biased presentation (the deliberation). Recently, Coman and Hirst (2012) studied how memories can be altered by such a sequence of exchanges. Their study is not an exact analog to a trial because the adversarial nature of a trial is not captured by the sequence they investigated. Moreover, they asked participants to learn arguments for and against the legalization of euthanasia rather than to hear evidence. Finally, they examined the effects of attitudes. Judges, prosecutors, and defendants usually dismiss all potential jurors with strong attitudes toward the case or the issues involved in the case. It is difficult, however, to find individuals without a prior attitude; hence, the role of attitude on jurors' memory is relevant to any consideration of memory and jury decision making.

As Figure 7.1 indicates, Coman and Hirst (2012) first assessed participants' attitude toward the legalization of euthanasia and then exposed them to a range of arguments for and against legalization. The arguments were grouped into general categories, such as scientific, legal, and ethical. As a result, there was a category-exemplar structure to the material the participants studied. Following the study period, in what might be viewed as equivalent to a speech, participants were exposed to a biased slide presentation, which contained only arguments for euthanasia and then only a selected set of these arguments. Participants were told that a proponent of legalization prepared the slide presentation, whom we call PERSON-PRO. After the presentation was completed, Coman and Hirst paired participants and asked them to discuss as many arguments for and against euthanasia as they could remember. They studied all possible configurations of attitude pairings. Following the conversation, there was an individual final recall test.

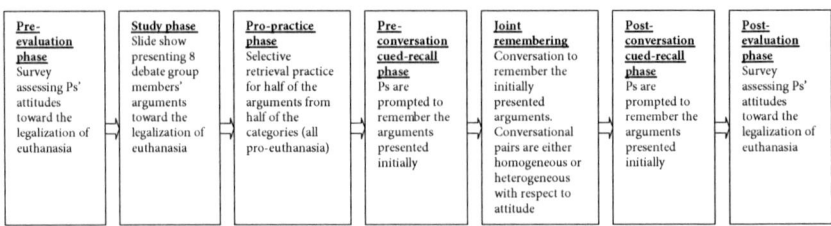

Figure 7.1 Phase of the procedure of an experiment studying mnemonic propagation. From "Cognition through a social network: The propagation of induced forgetting and practice effects" by A. Coman and W. Hirst, [2012], Journal of Experimental Psychology: General [Advance online publication. doi: 10.1037/a0025247.] Copyright 2012 by American Psychological Association. Reprinted by permission of the author.

There are two social influences in this sequence: the presentation in the pro-practice phase and the conversation in the joint remembering phase (see Figure 7.1). Coman and Hirst (2012) considered the presentation in the pro-practice phase as a social influence because participants were told that a person put together the presentation to convey her views on legalization. In a way, the presentation is similar to a PowerPoint slide accompanying a summary statement. There are also three memory assessments (the preconversation individual recall, the postconversation individual recall, and what is remembered in the conversation) and at least two attitude assessments (the preevaluation and postevaluation phases). The first social interaction—exposure to PERSON-PRO's presentation—can affect all three subsequent memory assessments, whereas the second social interaction—the conversation—can affect only the postconversation individual recall. Each of these social interactional effects on memory can be moderated by the attitudes of the participants. In the case of the lecture, the content was always positive about legalization, whereas the participant attending to the presentation could be either for or against legalization. In the case of the conversation, what matters is the pairing of attitudes, with some pairs being homogeneous (Pro-Pro and Anti-Anti) and others heterogeneous (Pro-Anti).

As one might expect, the results are complex, yet a few are quite relevant to our concerns here. First, when attitudes were moderate, Coman and Hirst (2012) failed to find an effect of attitude on practice effects or RIF, as assessed in the first, preconversational memory test. That is, the size of the RIF and practice effects elicited by PERSON-PRO was the same for attendees who agreed with the biased presentation in the pro-practice phase and for those who disagreed with it. This finding suggests that one person (the defendant's lawyer or the prosecutor) might be able to influence the memory of jurors, even in instances in which the jurors might be inclined to disagree with the sentiments of the summary statement.

Second, the effects of PERSON-PRO at the pre-conversational phase propagated into the conversation in a manner that depended on the way the pairs were constructed. When the conversing members of a pair held different attitudes, the RIF and practice effects found prior to the conversation did not shape what was remembered in the conversation. Moreover, the preconversational effects did not, in turn, shape what was eventually remembered subsequent to the conversation in the final memory assessment. In other words, when members of a pair had differing attitudes, their final recollections did not show the influence of PERSON-PRO. In terms of a trial, the efforts of the prosecutor and the lawyer for the defense to shape the memories of the jurors would probably fail if the jurors had differing attitudes.

But, as we noted, everything is done to ensure that jurors have neutral—in effect, similar—attitudes. Coman and Hirst (2012) found that when a pair with similar attitudes conversed, the RIF and practice effects observed in the preconversational memory test shaped what was remembered in both the conversation and the final memory test. Moreover, the presence of RIF and practice effects in both the preconversational test and the conversation accumulated with their repetition, producing even greater RIF and practice effects in the final recall. These cumulative effects led to a convergence of the homogeneous pairs on the rendering of the original material expressed by PERSON-PRO. In terms of a trial, when jurors begin the trial with similar attitudes toward the issue raised by the trial, the presumably biased summary statement of the prosecutor or defendant may then shape both what is remembered in the deliberations and the memories that last beyond the deliberations. To be sure, both legal teams in a trial are competing to grab jurors' attention and their memory. The particular configuration of accessibility that they affect may be a complex combination of these individual influences. Whatever the result, Coman and Hirst's findings suggest that this combination may have a lasting effect, given the desired neutral attitudes of the jurors.

CONCLUDING REMARKS

Two impressions have emerged after this review of the psychological work on social aspects of memory as they apply to jury deliberations: First, the number of studies that specifically look at memory as it emerges during jury deliberation is small, making any strong conclusions difficult. But, second, and perhaps more critically, there is a growing body of research relevant to the issue of remembering during jury deliberation, even if its hypotheses have not been specifically tested in the desired context. This work indicates that the courts' belief that juries should treat their collective memory as more reliable than, for instance, a written transcript must be carefully reconsidered. There is no reason to believe that 12 people working together to remember the testimony from a trial will remember it more accurately than 1 person remembering on his or her own. The recollection will be selective and rarely, if ever, complete. This selectivity will reinforce some memories while simultaneously inducing forgetting in others. The final memory may not impact negatively on the jury's judgment, but it may. It is this possibility that courts must work to avoid.

Is there anything in the literature reviewed herein that could help guide judges as they instruct jurors? It may not be enough to eliminate language that privileges collective memories over mnemonic technology. Rather, one must work toward obtaining more complete memories and less induced forgetting. Simple instructions about the risks of selective remembering may encourage jurors to remember more, but there is no guarantee that their recollection will be complete. Moreover, as a result of the instructions, jurors may be more likely to forget the few unmentioned but related items, in that the instructions may encourage them to monitor more vigorously for accuracy. More detailed instructions about the need for as broad a search as possible may eliminate induced forgetting as well, but there may be a limit here too, especially if the testimony is long and complex. In the end, what the courts seem to want to avoid—a reliance on mnemonic technology—may be preferable. Clearly, more research needs to be done to provide greater insight into the consequences of judicial instructions and the balance between a reliance on collective memory and the use of mnemonic technology.

ACKNOWLEDGMENTS

The support of National Science Foundation Grant #BCS-0819067 is gratefully acknowledged.

NOTE

1. By *covert remembering*, we mean that the rememberer retrieves the item, is personally aware of the memory, but does not share it with others—for example, remaining silent and keeping it to herself (see Stone, Coman, Brown, Koppel, & Hirst, 2011).

REFERENCES

Anderson, M. C., Bjork, R. A., & Bjork, E. L. (1994). Remembering can cause forgetting: Retrieval dynamics in long-term memory. *Journal of Experimental Psychology: Learning, Memory, and Cognition, 20*, 1063–1087.

Anderson, M. C., & Levy, B. J. (2002). Inhibitory processes and the control of memory retrieval. *Trends in Cognitive Science, 6*, 299–305.

Andersson, J., & Rönnberg, J. (1997). Cued memory collaboration: Effects of friendship and type of retrieval cue. *European Journal of Cognitive Psychology, 9*, 273–287.

Barber, S., Rajaram, S., & Aron, A. (2010). When two is too many: Collaborative encoding impairs memory. *Memory & Cognition, 38*, 255–264.

Barnier, A. J., Hung, L., & Conway, M. A. (2004). RIF of emotional and unemotional autobiographical memories. *Cognition & Emotion, 18*, 457–477.

Basden, B. H., Basden, D. R., Bryner, S., & Thomas, R. L. (1997). A comparison of group and individual remembering: Does collaboration disrupt retrieval strategies? *Journal of Experimental Psychology: Learning, Memory, and Cognition, 23*, 1176–1191.

Bernstein, D. M., & Loftus, E. F. (2009). The consequences of false memories for food preferences and choices. *Perspectives on Psychological Science, 4*, 135–139.

Blumen, H. M., & Rajaram, S. (2008). Influence of re-exposure and retrieval disruption during group collaboration on later individual recall. *Memory, 16*, 231–244.

Brown, A., Coman, A., & Hirst, W. (2009). The role of expertise in social remembering. *Social Psychology, 40,* 119–129.

Chan, J. C. K., McDermott, K. B., & Roediger, H. L. (2006). Retrieval-induced facilitation: Initially nontested material can benefit from prior testing of related material. *Journal of Experimental Psychology: General, 135,* 553–571.

Ciranni, M. A., & Shimamura, A. P. (1999). Retrieval-induced forgetting in episodic memory. *Journal of Experimental Psychology: Learning, Memory, and Cognition, 25,* 1403–1414.

Coman, A., & Hirst, W. (2012). Cognition through a social network: The propagation of induced forgetting and practice effects. *Journal of Experimental Psychology: General.* Advance online publication. doi: 10.1037/a0025247.

Coman, A., Manier, D., & Hirst, W. (2008). Socially-shared retrieval-induced forgetting of associated memories: Creating accessibility difficulties for memories of 9/11. *Psychological Science, 20,* 627–633.

Coman, D., Coman, A., & Hirst, W. (2012). *Medical decision-making and retrieval-induced forgetting.* Manuscript submitted for publication.

Cuc, A., Koppel, J., & Hirst, W. (2007). Silence in not golden: A case for socially-shared, retrieval-induced forgetting. *Psychological Science, 18,* 727–733.

Cuc, A., Ozuru, Y., Manier, D., & Hirst, W. (2006). On the formation of collective memories: The role of a dominant narrator. *Memory & Cognition, 34,* 752–762.

Devine, D. J., Clayton, L. D., Dunfor, B. B., Syeing, R., & Pryce, J. (2004). Explaining jury verdicts: Is leniency bias for real? *Journal of Applied Social Psychology, 34,* 2069–2098.

Diamond, S. S., & Caspar, J. D. (1992). Blindfolding the jury to verdict consequences: Damages, experts, and the civil jury. *Law & Society Review, 26,* 513–557.

Dodd, D. H., & Bradshaw, J. T. (1980). Leading questions and memory: Pragmatic constraints. *Journal of Verbal Learning and Verbal Behavior, 19,* 695–704.

Echterhoff, G., Groll, S., & Hirst, W. (2007). Tainted truth: Overcorrection for misinformation influence on eyewitness testimony. *Social Cognition, 25,* 367–409.

Echterhoff, G., Higgins, E. T., & Levine, J. M. (2009). Shared reality: Experiencing commonality with others' inner states about the world. *Perspectives on Psychological Science, 4,* 496–521.

Echterhoff, G., Hirst, W., & Hussy, W. (2005). How eyewitnesses resist misinformation: Social postwarnings and the monitoring of memory characteristics. *Memory & Cognition, 33,* 770–783.

Gabbert, F., Memon, A., & Allan, K. (2003). Memory conformity: Can eyewitnesses influence each other's memory for an event? *Applied Cognitive Psychology, 17,* 533–543.

Gabbert, F., Memon, A., Allan, K., & Wright, D. (2004). Say it to my face: Examining the effects of socially encountered misinformation. *Legal and Criminological Psychology, 9,* 215–227.

Garcia-Bajos, E., Migueles, M., & Anderson, M. C. (2009). Script knowledge modulates retrieval-induced forgetting for eyewitness events. *Memory, 17,* 92–103.

Hannaford-Agor, P. L., Hans, V. P., Mott, N. L., & Munsterman, G. T. (2002). *Are hung juries a problem? The National Center for State Courts.*

Harris, C. B., Paterson, H. M., & Kemp, R. I. (2008). Collaborative recall and collective memory: What happens when we remember together? *Memory, 16*, 213–230.

Hastie, R. (Ed.). (1993). *Inside the juror: The psychology of juror decision making*. New York: Cambridge University Press.

Hastie, R., & Park, B. (1986). The relationship between memory and judgment depends on whether the judgment task is memory-based or on-line. *Psychological Review, 93*, 258–268.

Heuer, L., & Penrod, S. (1994). Juror notetaking and question asking during trials. *Law and Human Behavior, 18*, 121–150.

Hirst, W. (2010). A virtue of memory: The contribution of mnemonic malleability to collective memory. In P. A. Reuter-Lorenz, K. Baynes, G. R. Mangun, & E. A. Phelps (Eds.), *The cognitive neuroscience of the mind: A tribute to Michael. S. Gazzaniga* (pp. 139–154). Cambridge, MA: MIT Press.

Hirst, W., & Echterhoff, G. (2008). Creating shared memories in conversation: Towards a psychology of collective memory. *Social Research, 75*, 183–216.

Hirst, W., & Echterhoff, G. (2012). Remembering in conversation: The social sharing and reshaping of memory. *Annual Review of Psychology, 63*, 55–79.

Hirst, W., & Manier, D. (2008). Towards a psychology of collective memory. *Memory, 17*, 183–200.

Iglesias-Parro, S., & Gomez-Ariza, C. J. (2006). Biasing decision making by means of retrieval practice. *European Journal of Cognitive Psychology, 18*, 899–908.

Johansson, N. O., Andersson, J., & Rönnberg, J. (2005). Compensating strategies in collaborative remembering in very old couples. *Scandinavian Journal of Psychology, 46*, 349–359.

Johnson, M. K., Hashtroudi, S., & Lindsay, D. S. (1993). Source monitoring. *Psychological Bulletin, 114*, 3–28.

Kapardis, A. (2010). Jury decision-making. In G. J. Towl & D. A. Crighton (Eds.), *Forensic psychology* (pp. 228–243). New York: Wiley-Blackwell.

Karpicke, J. D., & Roediger, H. L. (2007). Repeated retrieval during learning is the key to long-term retention. *Journal of Memory and Language, 57*, 151–162.

Karpicke, J. D., & Roediger, H. L. (2008). The critical importance of retrieval for learning. *Science, 319*, 966–968.

Kashy, D. A., & Kenny, D. A. (2000). The analysis of data from dyads and groups. In H. T. Reis & C. M. Judd (Eds.), *Handbook of research methods in social and personality psychology* (pp. 451–477). New York: Cambridge University Press.

Koppel, J., Wohl, D., Meksin, R., & Hirst, W. (2012). *The discrepant effects of expertise and mistrust on social contagion and socially-shared retrieval-induced forgetting: The pervasive influence of social factors*. Manuscript submitted for publication.

Lindsay, D. S., Hagen, L., Read, J. D., Kimberly, A., Garry, M. (2004). True photographs and false memories. *Psychological Science, 15*, 149–154.

Lippman, J. (2009). *Jury trial innovations in New York State: Enhancing the trial process for all parties. A practical guide for trial judges*. State of New York, United Court Systems. Retrieved from www.nyjuryinnovations.org/on September 1, 2011.

Loftus, E. F. (1996). *Eyewitness testimony*. Cambridge, MA: Harvard University Press.

Loftus, E. F. (2005). Planting misinformation in the human mind: A 30-year investigation of the malleability of memory. *Learning & Memory, 12*, 361–366.

Loftus, E. F., & Zanni, G. (1975). Eyewitness testimony: The influence of the wording of a question. *Bulletin of the Psychonomic Society, 5*, 86–88.

MacLeod, M. D., & Macrae, C. N. (2001). Gone but not forgotten: The transient nature of retrieval-induced forgetting. *Psychological Science, 12*, 148–152.

MacLeod, M. D., & Saunders, J. (2008). Retrieval inhibition and memory distortion: Negative consequences of an adaptive process. *Current Directions in Psychology Science, 17*, 26–30.

Marsh, E. J. (2007). Retelling is not the same as recalling: Implications for memory. *Current Directions in Psychological Science, 16*, 16–20.

Marsh, E. J., & Tversky, B. (2004). Spinning the stories of our lives. *Applied Cognitive Psychology, 18*, 491–503.

Meade, M. L., Nokes, T., & Morrow, D. G. (2009). Expertise promotes facilitation on a collaborative memory task. *Memory, 17*, 39–48.

Meade, M. L., & Roediger, H. L. (2002). Explorations in the social cognition of memory. *Memory & Cognition, 30*, 995–1009.

Meudell, P. R., Hitch, G. J., & Boyle, M. M. (1995). Collaboration in recall: Do pairs of people cross-cue each other to produce new memories? *The Quarterly Journal of Experiment Psychology A: Human Experimental Psychology, 48A*, 141–152.

Meudell, P. R., Hitch, G. J., & Kirby, P. (1992). Are two heads better than one? Experimental investigations of the social facilitation of memory. *Applied Cognitive Psychology, 6*, 525–543.

Migueles, M., & Garcia-Bajos, E. (2007). Selective retrieval and induced forgetting in eyewitness memory. *Applied Cognitive Psychology, 21*, 1157–1172.

Mize, G. E., Hannaford-Agor, P., & Waters, N. L. (2007). *The State-of-the-States Survey of Jury Improvement: A compendium report*. National Center for States Courts. Retrieved from http://.ncsconline.org/d_research/cjs/pdf/SOSCompendium Final.pdf on September 1, 2011.

Mulligan, N. W., & Lozito, J. P. (2004). Self-generation and memory. In B. H. Ross (Ed.), *The psychology of learning and motivation: Advances in research and theory* (Vol. 45, pp. 175–214). San Diego, CA: Academic Press.

Pasupathi, M. (2001). The social construction of the personal past and its implications for adult development. *Psychological Bulletin, 127*, 651–672.

Pennington, N., & Hastie, R. (1992). Explaining the evidence: Tests of the story model for juror decision making. *Journal of Social and Personality Psychology, 62*, 189–206.

Perfect, T. J., Stark, L.-J., Tree, J. J., Moulin, C. J. A., Ahmed, L., & Hutter, R. (2004). Transfer appropriate forgetting: The cue-dependent nature of retrieval-induced forgetting. *Journal of Memory and Language, 51*, 399–417.

Petroff, D. D. (1965). The practice of jury note taking—misconduct, right, or privilege? *Oklahoma Law Review, 18*, 125.

Pritchard, M. E., & Keenan, J. M. (1999). Memory monitoring in mock jurors. *Journal of Experimental Psychology: Applied, 5*, 152–168.

Pritchard, M. E., & Keenan, J. M. (2002). Does jury deliberation really improve jurors' memories? *Applied Cognitive Psychology, 16*, 589–601.

Rajaram, S., & Pereira-Pasarin, L. P. (2007). Collaboration can improve individual recognition memory: Evidence from immediate and delayed tests. *Psychonomic Bulletin & Review, 14,* 95–100.

Rajaram, S., & Pereira-Pasarin, L. P. (2010). Collaborative memory: Cognitive research and theory. *Perspectives on Psychological Science, 5,* 649–663.

Reysen, M. B., & Adair, S. A. (2008). Social processing improves recall performance. *Psychonomic Bulletin & Review, 15,* 197–201.

Roediger, H. L., Zaromb, F. M., & Butler, A. C. (2009). The role of repeated retrieval in shaping collective memory. In P. Boyer & J. V. Wertsch (Eds.), *Memory in mind and culture* (pp. 29–58). Cambridge, NY: Cambridge University Press.

Salerno, J. M., & Diamond, S. S. (2010). The promise of a cognitive perspective on jury deliberation. *Psychonomic Bulletin & Review, 17,* 174–180.

Slamecka, N. J., & Graf, P. (1978). The generation effect: Delineation of a phenomenon. *Journal of Experimental Psychology: Human Learning & Memory, 4,* 592–604.

Smith, V. L., & Ellsworth, P. C. (1987). The social psychology of eyewitness accuracy: Leading questions and communicator expertise. *Journal of Applied Psychology, 72,* 292–300.

Stasser, G., & Titus, W. (1987). Effects of information load and percentage of shared information on the dissemination of unshared information during group discussion. *Journal of Personality and Social Psychology, 53,* 81–93.

Stone, C. B., Barnier, A. J., Sutton, J., & Hirst, W. (2010a). Building social consensus about the past: Memorability, integration, and socially shared retrieval-induced forgetting. *Memory, 18,* 170–184.

Stone, C. B., Barnier, A. J., Sutton, J., & Hirst, W. (2010b). Forgetting our personal past: Socially shared retrieval-induced forgetting of autobiographical memories. Manuscript in preparation.

Stone, C. B., Coman, A., Brown, A. D., Koppel, J., & Hirst, W. (2011). *The sound—and mnemonic consequences—of silence.* Under review.

Storm, B. C., Bjork, E. L., & Bjork, R. A. (2005). Social metacognitive judgments: The role of retrieval-induced forgetting in person memory and impressions. *Journal of Memory and Language, 52,* 535–550.

Storm, B. C., Bjork, E. L., Bjork, R. A., & Nestojko, J. F. (2006). Is retrieval success a necessary condition for retrieval-induced forgetting? *Psychonomic Bulletin & Review, 13,* 1023–1027.

Tandoh, K., & Naka, M. (2007). Durability of retrieval-induced forgetting. *Japanese Journal of Psychology, 78,* 310–315.

Thorley, C., & Dewhurst, S. A. (2007). Collaborative false recall in the DRM procedure: Effects of group size and group pressure. *European Journal of Cognitive Psychology, 19,* 867–881.

Traynor, R. J. (1970). *The riddle of harmless error.* Athens: Ohio University Press.

Tschuggnall, K., & Welzer, H. (2002). Rewriting memories: Family recollections of the National Socialist past of Germany. *Culture & Psychology, 8,* 130–145.

U.S. v. Escotto, 121 F.3d 81, 85 (2nd Cir. 1997).

U.S. v. Montgomery, 150 F.3d 983, 999-1000 (9th Cir. 1998).

Warren, J., & Kuhn, D. (2010). How do jurors argue with one another? *Judgment and Decision Making, 5,* 64–71. Retrieved from http://sjdm.cybermango.org/10/10123/jdm10123.pdf on September 1, 2011.

Weber, E. U., & Johnson, E. J. (2009). Mindful judgments and decision making. *Annual Review of Psychology, 60*, 58–85.

Wegner, D. (1986). Transactive memory: A contemporary analysis of the group mind. In B. Mullen & G. Goethals (Eds.), *Theories of group behavior* (pp. 185–208). New York: Springer-Verlag.

Weldon, M. S. (2001). Remembering as a social process. In G. H. Bower (Ed.), *The psychology of learning and motivation* (Vol. 10, pp. 67–120). New York: Academic Press.

Weldon, M. S., & Bellinger, K. D. (1997). Collective memory: Collaborative and individual processes in remembering. *Journal of Experimental Psychology: Learning, Memory, and Cognition, 23*, 1160–1175.

Weldon, M. S., Blair, C., & Huebsch, D. (2000). Group remembering: Does social loafing underlie collaborative inhibition? *Journal of Experimental Psychology: Learning, Memory, and Cognition, 26*, 1568–1577.

Wells, G. L., Memon, A., & Penrod, S. D. (2006). Eyewitness evidence: Improving its probative value. *Psychological Science in the Public Interest, 7*, 45–75.

Wittenbaum, G. M., & Park, E. M. (2001) The collective preference for shared information. *Current Directions in Psychological Science, 10*, 70–73.

Wittenbaum, G. M., & Stasser, G. (1996). Management of information in small groups. In J. L. Nye & A. M. Brower (Eds.), *What is social about social cognition?* (pp. 3–28). Thousand Oaks, CA: Sage.

Wright, D. B., Self, G., & Justice, C. (2000). Memory conformity: Exploring misinformation effects when presented by another person. *British Journal of Psychology, 91*, 189–202.

8

Realizing the Potential of Instructions to Disregard

LINDA J. DEMAINE

INTRODUCTION

Rules of evidence govern what information may be presented to jurors during trials. By placing certain constraints on the facts, arguments, and opinions to which jurors are exposed and on which they may base their verdicts, the rules of evidence seek to promote fair and efficient trials (Fed. R. Evid. 102; Weinstein & Berger, 2007, pp. T-10 to T-15). Given these goals, the rules require that trial judges exclude—that is, declare inadmissible—evidence that would waste time, confuse or mislead jurors, or unfairly prejudice jurors against a litigant (Fed. R. Evid. 403; Weinstein & Berger, 2007, pp. T-30 to T-33).[1] Whereas some types of evidence that the rules declare inadmissible likely exert minimal influence on jurors (for example, evidence that is excluded because it is redundant with other evidence) unfairly prejudicial evidence has the potential to alter substantially jurors' judgments of the case.

The rules deem evidence to be unfairly prejudicial when it has an "undue tendency to suggest decision on an improper basis, commonly, though not necessarily, an emotional one" (Advisory Committee's Note to Fed. R. Evid 403). Federal and state courts have implemented this language in loosely similar ways, finding, for example, that unfairly prejudicial evidence "appeals to the jury's sympathies, arouses a sense of horror, provokes the instinct to punish, or otherwise may cause a jury to base its decision on something other than the established propositions in the case" (*Carter v. Hewitt*, p. 972). Such evidence, with its power to skew verdicts unjustly, is withheld from jurors despite the fact that it is legally relevant to the claims at issue (Fed. R. Evid. 401, 403; Weinstein & Berger, 2007, pp. T-30 to T-33).

Trial courts possess the authority to declare a mistrial in response to juror exposure to prejudicial inadmissible evidence. They use this drastic measure sparingly, however, due to competing concerns such as judicial economy, costs to litigants, and the loss or deterioration of evidence over time. Equally important is the realization that jurors see and hear inadmissible evidence so frequently that litigation would grind to a halt if courts were to grant mistrials liberally. Trial judges obviously lack the ability to erase all traces of inadmissible evidence from jurors' memories in order to ensure that verdicts are untainted. Even if they could accomplish this, moreover, such invasive manipulations of jurors' minds would raise thorny constitutional questions and might decrease citizens' already limited willingness to undertake jury duty. Social influence, in the form of instructions to disregard, is therefore the main tool at trial judges' disposal for curing the inappropriately damaging effects of prejudicial inadmissible evidence. Trial judges regularly sustain objections by counsel to particular evidence and admonish jurors to disregard that evidence.

Empirical studies paint a grim picture of the effectiveness of instructions to disregard. A meta-analysis of these instructions reveals that not only do they generally fail to eliminate the impact of inadmissible evidence on mock jurors' verdicts, but they often cause jurors to attribute greater importance to this evidence than they would absent an instruction to disregard (Steblay, Hosch, Culhane, & McWethy, 2006). Beneath the surface of these broad-stroke negative conclusions, however, are studies that provide clues to successful disregarding. In other words, while social science investigations often reveal that inadmissible evidence influences mock jurors despite an instruction to disregard, they also demonstrate that the instructions sometimes fulfill their purpose.

These contrary findings suggest that certain characteristics in the content and delivery of instructions to disregard can render them more or less effective in countering prejudicial inadmissible evidence. This chapter identifies these facilitating and impeding characteristics to answer a fundamental question about instructions to disregard: How can trial judges maximize the likelihood that jury verdicts will be uninfluenced by prejudicial inadmissible evidence? The first portion of the chapter articulates and critiques methods that legal scholars and psychology researchers have proposed to remedy juror exposure to prejudicial inadmissible evidence in lieu of, or supplemental to, the instructions to disregard traditionally issued by courts. While some of these proposals are inherently flawed in fundamental respects, others may substantially improve on courts' current practices. After discussing these proposals, the chapter identifies specific factors that are likely to increase the effectiveness of instructions to disregard regardless of whether trial judges continue to employ the traditional instructions or adopt some version of one of the viable proposals. Both parts of the chapter derive from the findings of empirical studies on persuasion and social cognition, as well as the inadmissible evidence literature.

PROPOSED METHODS FOR REMEDYING PREJUDICIAL INADMISSIBLE EVIDENCE

Explain to Jurors the Reasoning Behind the Inadmissible Ruling

Kassin and Studebaker (1998) proposed that trial judges provide jurors with an explanation for the inadmissible ruling. That they made this proposal is somewhat surprising, given the results of Kassin's own research. In an empirical investigation, Kassin and Sommers (1997) presented mock jurors with a murder trial. Some of the jurors were exposed to testimony by a police officer regarding a taped telephone conversation in which the defendant confessed to a friend that he committed the murder. Following an objection by defense counsel, some of these jurors were instructed that the testimony was admissible, others were instructed that the testimony was inadmissible on the ground that it was obtained without a proper warrant (a procedural explanation), and yet others were instructed that the testimony was inadmissible on the ground that the tape was not clearly audible (a validity explanation). Posttrial measures revealed that, when the court ruled the officer's testimony inadmissible on procedural grounds, the jurors were significantly more likely to render guilty verdicts than when the testimony was not presented. Jurors who were instructed that the evidence was ruled inadmissible on validity grounds, in contrast, rendered the same percentage of guilty verdicts as did jurors who were not exposed to the evidence.

Kassin and Studebaker (1998) conclude that jurors "cannot resist the temptation to use information they see as relevant—whether it satisfies the law's technical rules or not" (p. 424). The researchers distinguish between substantive and procedural reasons for declaring evidence inadmissible and assert that jurors are likely to follow instructions to disregard substantively flawed inadmissible evidence, whereas they are likely to reject instructions to disregard procedurally flawed inadmissible evidence (see also Kassin & Sommers, 1997; Sommers & Kassin, 2001). If this were true, Kassin and Studebaker's proposal that trial judges explain to jurors the reasoning underlying inadmissible rulings would provide a potentially effective means of countering objectively invalid inadmissible evidence but would fail to address instances in which evidence is ruled inadmissible despite being objectively valid. Even if the courts were to offer explanations only for inadmissible rulings concerning objectively invalid inadmissible evidence, which is the likely scenario under this method given that jurors are expected to ignore instructions to disregard that are based on procedural foundations, jurors might infer that rulings for which judges offer no explanation address objectively valid inadmissible evidence. That is, jurors might deduce that whenever a judge fails to justify the instruction to disregard, it is because the reason is unconvincing.

Kassin and Studebaker's (1998) conclusion that jurors are categorically unwilling to disregard objectively valid evidence is not necessarily correct, however, for two reasons. First, it is important to distinguish between the *actual* validity of the inadmissible evidence and jurors' *perceptions* of its validity. Jurors should be willing to disregard objectively valid inadmissible evidence as long as they perceive the evidence to be invalid. Second, research suggests that jurors can be persuaded to disregard evidence that is ruled inadmissible on purely procedural, or policy, grounds, even when they believe that the evidence is valid. For example, Diamond and Casper (1992) presented mock jurors with a civil antitrust price-fixing case. Some of the jurors were informed that their verdict would be trebled automatically—information that, according to the applicable law, they should not possess when arriving at a verdict. The jurors who were merely instructed to disregard this information ("The fact that the damage award will be tripled should in no way affect your decision.") rendered verdicts not significantly different from the jurors who were not instructed to disregard. In contrast, the jurors who were provided an explanation for the instruction to disregard ("If you reduce your damage award below what you believe to be the appropriate compensation amount in anticipation of its being tripled, you will be defeating Congress's purpose in providing for triple damages. Congress decided to have jury compensation awards tripled in order to provide for punishment of the defendants for their law violation and to deter them and others from future law violation.") rendered verdicts similar to those of jurors who were not informed that their verdict would be tripled. Thus, an instruction to disregard that included a policy explanation was effective, whereas an instruction to disregard without this explanation was not.

Given that the evidence in Diamond and Casper's (1992) study was ruled inadmissible despite being valid, the results contradict Kassin and Studebaker's (1998) conclusion that the deciding factor as to whether jurors will disregard inadmissible evidence is necessarily the validity of the evidence. The study provides some support, however, for their proposal that trial judges provide explanations for inadmissible rulings insofar as it suggests that a policy-based explanation for an inadmissible ruling can remove the effects of prejudicial inadmissible evidence.

It is imperative, of course, that the explanation be convincing. If jurors do not accept the rationale for the ruling, they may be more likely to base their verdict on the inadmissible evidence than if no explanation had been provided.[2] Indeed, courts' long-standing practice of not providing jurors with explanations for evidentiary rulings may be attributed in large part to such a concern, because explanations give jurors the tools with which to decide whether they agree or disagree with the rationales for the rulings.[3] Aside from uncertainty surrounding what makes for a convincing explanation in the opinions of jurors, an additional disadvantage of explaining the ruling's rationale is the need for trial judges to craft individualized instructions for each inadmissible ruling. A better approach would be to provide the same or a similar instruction to disregard for all inadmissible rulings in order to enhance clarity, consistency, and efficiency.

Forewarn Jurors of Inadmissible Evidence and Extract Their Commitment to Follow Instructions to Disregard

Tanford (1990) has suggested that trial judges (1) instruct jurors before trials begins that they must disregard evidence to which the judges sustain an objection; (2) "interrogate" jurors about this instruction (presumably to discern their understanding of it) and elicit promises that they will obey the inadmissible evidence rulings issued during the trials; and (3) merely sustain objections during trials rather than administer instructions to disregard. Tanford omits a discussion of the details surrounding what form the forewarning of inadmissible evidence might take, perhaps in part because it is difficult to predict whether or how a forewarning would alter jurors' reactions to this evidence (e.g., Quinn & Wood, 2004). Taken literally, the forewarning component of the proposal advocates that courts adopt a practice that is already long established. That is, courts have traditionally addressed the concept of inadmissible evidence in their preliminary instructions to jurors, thereby forewarning jurors that they may be exposed to inadmissible evidence during the trial (see note 3). Given that trial judges cannot foresee the precise inadmissible evidence to which jurors will be exposed, this would appear to be the best forewarning that they can administer.

Tanford (1990) specifically advocates that judges presiding over criminal cases instruct jurors that "any evidence of a defendant's criminal record may not be considered as evidence of guilt" (p. 108). Such an instruction, however, could unwisely suggest to jurors before trials begin that the defendant has a criminal record, whether or not this is true. Particularly if the defendant has no such criminal record, the instruction may unconstitutionally deny the defendant the right to a fair trial by falsely implying that such a record exists.

Evidence of prior criminal activity tends to be very persuasive with jurors, rendering them more likely to find defendants guilty of the charges at hand (e.g., Greene & Dodge, 1995). Perhaps this is why Tanford advocates that courts address the defendant's criminal record directly. To do so, though, may cause the very harm the forewarning was designed to avoid. A better strategy would be for trial judges to address this evidence if and when it is introduced.

Tanford's (1990) suggestion that trial judges ask jurors to commit publicly to disregarding inadmissible evidence is supported by empirical studies finding that people are more likely to behave in a certain manner if they have previously publicly committed to doing so (e.g., Deutsch & Gerard, 1955). These studies typically involve situations in which the committed-to behavior is readily visible to others—for example, quitting smoking or conserving natural resources. Jurors, in contrast, may be internally influenced by inadmissible evidence without conveying this change to the judge or other members of the jury. At least some jurors may nonetheless attempt to honor the public commitment, however. The main question raised by this aspect of Tanford's proposal is why the courts would extract a public commitment from jurors to follow instructions to disregard but not do so for other preliminary instructions. If this part of the proposal were implemented, jurors might conclude that it is not as important for them to follow the other instructions, because, if it were, trial judges would elicit a public commitment regarding those as well. Courts could, of course, elicit a commitment for each instruction, but this would be cumbersome. Rather, their established practice of administering to jurors a general oath to follow the instructions issued by the trial judge would appear to be the most feasible approach and may increase to some degree jurors' willingness to follow instructions to disregard (as well as other instructions).[4]

Trial judges implement a variant of the public commitment aspect of Tanford's (1990) proposal when they ask jurors if they are able to comply with a particular instruction to disregard. Judges most commonly make this inquiry following juror exposure that appears to most commonly follow juror exposure to inadmissible evidence that judges deem to be highly prejudicial. Because it is rare for jurors to respond negatively to these inquiries, their answers are in essence commitments to follow the instruction. Thus, while polling jurors in this manner likely produces minimal insight into whether they actuallys can disregard the inadmissible evidence (e.g., Nisbett & Wilson, 1977), it may increase their motivation to do so. Jurors would make a more direct commitment to follow instructions to disregard if trial judges asked them if they were willing to disregard the evidence. But this line of questioning simultaneously acknowledges that courts' presumption that jurors follow instructions to disregard may be unsound and underscores to jurors their right to decide cases in a manner contrary to judicial instructions, both of which courts are reluctant to do.

The final component of Tanford's (1990) proposal advocates that trial judges merely sustain objections to inadmissible evidence, rather than issue instructions to disregard, on the ground that instructions to disregard tend to exacerbate, rather than cure, the harm done by inadmissible evidence. Some courts have long taken this approach, seemingly to minimize the attention they pay to inadmissible evidence and thereby increase the likelihood that jurors will disregard it. Omitting instructions to disregard would appear to be unwise, however, as jurors may have difficulty keeping straight the meanings of *sustained* and *overruled*. Such confusion presents the possibility that jurors consider admissible evidence to be inadmissible or inadmissible evidence to be admissible. The better practice is to follow these terms with an instruction that clarifies whether the jurors should consider the evidence in question.

Kassin and Studebaker (1998) also have proposed that trial courts *inoculate* jurors to inadmissible evidence by warning them in pretrial instructions that some evidence offered during the trial may be ruled inadmissible. Unlike Tanford (1990), Kassin and Studebaker suggest that courts inform jurors that inadmissible evidence can alter their perceptions of admissible evidence. Again, courts already discuss inadmissible evidence in pretrial instructions, rendering the first part of Kassin and Studebaker's proposal moot.[5] The second part of the proposal, however, could increase jurors' understanding of, and vigilance about, the processes through which inadmissible evidence may unwittingly influence their conceptions of the case. While inadmissible evidence does not consistently taint admissible evidence in empirical studies, making jurors aware of the phenomenon may reduce its occurrence and is unlikely to have adverse consequences.

Induce Jurors to Be Suspicious of the Introducing Attorney's Motives

Tanford (1992) subsequently modified his proposal to suggest that trial judges forewarn jurors that attorneys and other trial participants may attempt to influence them improperly with inadmissible evidence. This proposal thus combines forewarning with the suggestion of manipulative (as opposed to merely persuasive) intent in order to induce psychological reactance within jurors. Generally speaking, people experience psychological reactance when a valued freedom is threatened, and this state induces them to restore the freedom (Brehm, 1966; Brehm & Brehm, 1981). Tanford anticipates that the suspicion-inducing warning would motivate jurors to defend their perceptions of the case from being influenced by the manipulative actions of trial participants who introduce inadmissible evidence.

As with his earlier articulation of the proposal, Tanford (1992) suggests that trial judges extract from jurors a public promise to resist being influenced by evidence to which the judge sustains an objection. However, he adds that this commitment to resistance should occur after the trial judge informs the jurors that the judge and other jurors expect them to resist the inadmissible evidence and that considering this evidence would undermine the fairness of the trial. Although Tanford does not explain why he proposed the expectation component, possibly he intended to apply the empirical literature on social norms, which reveals that persons take cues from others regarding what is appropriate conduct, particularly in unfamiliar situations (e.g., Asch, 1955; Milgram, 1974). According to Tanford, in posttrial instructions, trial judges would then remind jurors of the law governing inadmissible evidence and their previously expressed commitment to follow it. Given that courts traditionally have revisited jurors' duty to disregard inadmissible evidence in posttrial instructions,[6] the reminder component of the proposal suggests nothing new. However, mention of jurors' prior commitment would add a novel, and possibly helpful, dimension to posttrial instructions by making the prior commitment salient soon before the jurors arrive at a verdict. Tanford does not address the main concern likely to be raised in opposition to the reminder—namely, that it draws additional attention to the evidence that is to be disregarded. Moreover, the reminder would need to be carefully crafted so as to avoid inducing reactance in the jurors (e.g., Wolf & Montgomery, 1977).

Similar to the improper influence part of Tanford's (1992) proposal, Fein, McCloskey, and Tomlinson (1997) have proposed that trial courts instill in jurors suspicion of the trial attorney's ulterior motives in introducing prejudicial inadmissible evidence. The researchers suggest, though, that the courts induce this suspicion through instructions to disregard rather than pretrial instructions. Fein et al.'s proposal is based on an empirical study (1997, Study 2) in which they presented mock jurors with an aggravated assault case. The evidence of interest consisted of the following testimony of a prosecution witness: "Well, about a half-hour after the incident, one of the customers at my place told me that he heard [the defendant] fall and then he saw through the window that [the victim] had turned and started to walk toward the door when [the defendant] picked up a piece of glass and lunged at him." Some of the jurors read that the defense attorney objected to this evidence on hearsay grounds ("Your honor, this is a clear case of hearsay. I see no ambiguity here at all.") and the trial judge ruled the evidence inadmissible ("[S]ince the testimony came from an alleged witness who cannot be cross-examined, I must regard it as hearsay. The fact that [the witness] is here to give his testimony does not allow him to discuss the statements of someone who cannot be called to trial."). The judge then ordered the testimony struck from the record and instructed the jurors to disregard it. Other jurors were presented with a defense attorney's objection also based on hearsay but designed to arouse suspicion regarding why the prosecuting attorney introduced the testimony ("Your honor, the prosecution should be quite aware that this is a clear case of hearsay. There's no ambiguity here at all. The prosecution has deliberately asked a question that was designed to elicit a response that he knew would be inadmissible, your honor. Why else would he ask such a question?"). After striking the testimony from the record and instructing the jurors to disregard it, the judge added: "You should also keep in mind that sometimes inadmissible evidence is introduced into a trial in a deliberate attempt to manipulate the jury's thinking, and you should therefore try not to let this information affect your thinking about this case." The verdicts of the jurors who read the non-suspicion—inducing objection and instruction were influenced by the inadmissible evidence, whereas the verdicts of the jurors who read the suspicion-inducing objection and instruction were not—the suspicious jurors rendered verdicts comparable to those of jurors who were not exposed to the evidence.[7] Fein et al. conclude that suspicion of ulterior motives is an effective means of eradicating the effects of inadmissible evidence on jury decision making.

Granted that the suspicion instruction successfully addressed the damage done by the inadmissible evidence, it is important to consider how it operated in order to assess its viability in the court system. The suspicion instruction—whether given following jurors' exposure to inadmissible evidence, as Fein et al. (1997) suggest, or as a preliminary instruction, as Tanford (1992) proposes—clearly is an improper remedy for inadvertently introduced inadmissible evidence. It would be unfair—and likely unconstitutional[8]—for a trial judge to undermine the credibility of an attorney who unintentionally introduced inadmissible evidence by instructing the jurors that the attorney was attempting to manipulate them. One might also question whether the suspicion instruction to disregard is appropriate for intentionally introduced inadmissible evidence (assuming that the trial judge can make this determination) in that it introduces yet another nonevidentiary variable into jurors' decision-making processes. Rather than directly address the effects of the prejudicial inadmissible evidence in order to return the case to the state that it was in prior to the evidence's introduction, a suspicion-inducing instruction further alters the case by causing jurors to feel manipulated by the affiliated attorney (or other trial participants, given that a suspicion instruction could also be directed at a witness or litigant). Fein et al. do not report any measures that capture the effect of the suspicion instruction on jurors' perceptions of the prosecutor. Fein's previous work on the costs of suspicion (Fein & Hilton, 1994), however, indicates that when persons are induced to suspect another's motives, they view the other person more negatively (e.g., they like the other person less and view the other person as less tsrustworthy) than do persons who have not been made suspicious (see also DeCarlo, 2005). Fein et al.'s proposal thus could markedly diminish objectivity in a trial in order to counter a few isolated biasing incidents. More appropriately, the remedy for jurors' exposure to prejudicial inadmissible evidence would alter their perceptions of the inadmissible evidence without inducing negative impressions of the introducing attorney (and, by implication, other evidence and arguments presented by that attorney) or other trial participants.

Fein et al. (1997) did measure another potential means by which the suspicion-inducing instruction could affect jury verdicts—the degree to which the instruction undermined the inadmissible evidence itself, as opposed to the attorney who introduced it. Jurors who received the suspicion-inducing instruction viewed the inadmissible evidence as significantly less valid than did jurors given the non-suspicion-inducing instruction. Thus, although the suspicion instruction focused on alerting the jurors to the putatively underhanded motives of the prosecuting attorney, it significantly decreased jurors' perceptions of the validity of the inadmissible evidence. This may have caused the jurors to render verdicts uninfluenced by the inadmissible evidence, either by itself or in combination with the negatively altered perceptions of the introducing attorney. If it were possible to craft an instruction to disregard that undermined the validity of the inadmissible evidence without causing other defects, such as lowering the affiliated person's likability or credibility, the courts would possess an effective means to counter prejudicial inadmissible evidence. The next section discusses how this might be achieved.

Neutralize the Inadmissible Evidence

I have proposed that courts consider fundamentally changing their view of disregarding—from forgetting to neutralizing (Demaine, 2008). By abandoning their traditional view of disregarding as forgetting, which rests on the erroneous assumption that jurors can delete prejudicial inadmissible evidence from their minds on demand, the courts would be better positioned to consider more effective, and realistic, instructions to disregard. The neutralization view of disregarding, which focuses on negating the damaging effects of prejudicial inadmissible evidence on jurors' verdicts, provides the foundation for the precise forms these improved instructions to disregard might take. My investigation of one neutralizing instruction, a debiasing instruction, is discussed here, along with a previously unconsidered but potentially useful instruction that illustrates other ways the neutralization approach may be operationalized.

Debias Jurors' Verdicts

Instructions to disregard traditionally have taken one of two general forms. Trial judges instruct jurors to disregard the evidence either with a terse statement such as: "Sustained. And I'll instruct the jury to disregard that testimony"

(*United States v. Harris*, p. 871) or a more emphatic admonition such as "[T]he testimony... is being stricken in its entirety. It never happened. You never heard it. It plays no role in this case. It exists no longer and, therefore, is not part of this trial..." (*State v. McIntyre*, p. 396). These different admonitions apparently result from courts' conceptualization of disregarding as forgetting. Courts administer the terse admonition in order to avoid drawing additional attention to inadmissible evidence, because, the logic goes, when courts pay more attention to this evidence, jurors are less able to forget it. Courts issue the more emphatic instruction when they prioritize motivating jurors to disregard the inadmissible evidence, albeit at the expense of jurors' ability to forget the evidence. Conceptualizing disregarding as forgetting thus pits jurors' willingness to disregard in conflict with their ability to disregard, and places the courts in the inevitable quandary of choosing to foster one of these prerequisites of disregarding to the detriment of the other.

A debiasing neutralization instruction to disregard, in contrast, fosters disregarding by encouraging jurors to correct for the biasing influence of the prejudicial inadmissible evidence on their verdicts. The instruction contains four essential elements, derived from basic empirical research on how to eradicate the effects of bias from judgments (e.g., Wegener, Petty, & Dunn, 1998; Wilson & Brekke, 1994): (1) it alerts jurors that their views of the case may have been inappropriately influenced by the inadmissible evidence, (2) it restates the inadmissible evidence so that jurors understand what they are to disregard, (3) it offers an implicit explanation for the inadmissible ruling (i.e., the evidence is flawed in some important way), and (4) it suggests a method for disregarding (i.e., that jurors assess the degree to which the inadmissible evidence has biased their views of the case and adjust for that bias). In an empirical test (Demaine, 2008), the debiasing instruction eliminated the influence of highly prejudicial inadmissible evidence—the testimony of a police officer in a murder prosecution that he and a fellow officer found a hunting knife with the victim's blood on it in the defendant's apartment—on mock jurors' verdicts. The jurors were significantly more likely to find the defendant guilty when the evidence was ruled admissible than when it was absent from the case. The jurors given the debiasing instruction rendered a percentage of guilty verdicts significantly lower than jurors in the admissible condition and indistinguishable from jurors who had not been exposed to the inadmissible evidence. The debiasing instruction, worded as follows, thus negated the damaging influence of the inadmissible evidence on the jurors' verdicts:

> This testimony regarding the knife is inadmissible, a.nd the jury is instructed to disregard it. Now, I want to be very clear about something. It is important that you be aware that information sometimes biases our judgments even

though we believe we have disregarded it. There is thus a very real danger that [the officer's] testimony regarding the knife may lead you to the wrong verdict unless you account for its improper influence on your judgment of [the defendant] and adjust your verdict accordingly.

In the same experiment, I investigated the relative effectiveness of the two general types of instructions to disregard commonly used by trial judges. The emphatic admonition, which elaborately and explicitly orders jurors to forget the inadmissible evidence, consisted of the following language:

This testimony regarding the knife is inadmissible, and the jury is instructed to disregard it. You jurors must erase this evidence from your minds. Forget that you heard it. Put it out of your minds completely, and do not give it another thought. You must not even remember that it was presented.

Basic research on thought suppression has shown that instructions to avoid thinking about an item—for example, a white bear—invoke ironic processes of mental control that not only inhibit persons from intentionally ridding their minds of the item but actually cause an increase in item-related thoughts (e.g., Wegner, 1989). The foregoing emphatic admonition, however, also eliminated the damage done by the prejudicial inadmissible evidence. A potential explanation for this result appears to be that the majority of the jurors, regardless of the wording of the instruction to disregard, attempted to disregard the inadmissible evidence by debiasing their judgments, not by avoiding thoughts of the inadmissible evidence. Jurors could not fall prey to the ironic processes of mental control if they did not attempt to forget the inadmissible evidence. Moreover, one might question the degree to which findings from basic research on thought suppression generalize to the courtroom. The paradigmatic design for thought suppression studies entails providing participants with an isolated item and directing them not to think of it while in a socially sterile environment (e.g., Macrae, Bodenhausen, Milne, & Jetten, 1994; Wegner & Erber, 1992; Wegner, Schneider, Carter, & White, 1987). In contrast, in the courtroom, jurors are faced with the challenging task of comprehending, and forming a coherent story from, the voluminous evidence and arguments and deciphering and applying an array of legal instructions in order to render a verdict. This environment and these cognitive tasks may be less conducive to producing the ironic processes of mental control found in the basic thought control studies even when jurors try to forget inadmissible evidence.[9]

Unlike the debiasing and emphatic forget instructions, the terse admonition ("This testimony regarding the knife is inadmissible, and the jury is instructed to disregard it.") failed to cure the prejudice introduced by the inadmissible evidence. Rather, it resulted in a percentage of guilty verdicts midway between the admissible condition and the debiasing and emphatic forget conditions.

What underlying psychological mechanisms explain the effectiveness of the debiasing and emphatic forget instructions, and the ineffectiveness of the terse instruction? Jurors who received the terse instruction felt comparably obligated to disregard the inadmissible evidence as did jurors given the debiasing or emphatic forget instructions. However, jurors who received the debiasing or emphatic forget instructions were more likely to recall having been told to disregard the inadmissible evidence than were jurors given the terse instruction. It is thus unsurprising that jurors in the terse instruction condition were less likely to attempt to disregard the inadmissible evidence than were jurors in the debiasing and emphatic forget conditions. In addition, jurors in the terse instruction condition reported greater difficulty disregarding the inadmissible evidence than did jurors in the debiasing and emphatic forget conditions, perhaps because jurors who received the terse instruction tended to view the inadmissible evidence as more valid and more relevant to the case than did jurors given the debiasing or emphatic forget instructions.[10]

Path analyses reveal that the jurors disregarded through one of two general routes. The instructions to disregard caused some of the jurors to question the validity of the inadmissible evidence, which, in turn, made them less likely to find the defendant guilty. These jurors *discounted* the inadmissible evidence, because the instruction to disregard caused them to perceive that it lacked probative value. Other jurors were less likely to find the defendant guilty despite viewing the inadmissible evidence as valid. These jurors *corrected for the biasing influence* of the prejudicial inadmissible evidence on their verdicts. While the courts are less concerned with the route to disregarding than the end result, it is interesting to note that effective instructions to disregard cause jurors to engage in these processes, as this may provide clues for how best to handle more complex situations such as limited use evidence. Jurors know that limited use evidence is valid, because courts instruct them to consider it when making certain determinations that underlie the verdict. Consequently, limiting instructions should attempt to capitalize on the corrective route to disregarding. Effective methods for accomplishing this would be a fruitful subject for empirical study.

Given that the emphatic forget instruction performed comparably to the debiasing instruction, albeit in large part because the jurors ignored its suggestion regarding how to disregard and instead debiased their verdicts, some courts may be inclined to retain the forget approach to disregarding and merely discontinue using the terse instruction. Equating disregarding with forgetting is dysfunctional for a variety of reasons, however (Demaine, 2008). For example, when courts conceive of disregarding as forgetting, they often refrain from restating the inadmissible evidence in the instruction to disregard in order to avoid repeating to jurors the information that is to be forgotten. Yet omitting mention of the inadmissible evidence decreases the likelihood that jurors understand precisely what they are to disregard. Moreover, trial attorneys sometimes decide against requesting an instruction to disregard—and trial judges sometimes refuse to issue an instruction to disregard when one is requested—given the common knowledge that humans are incapable of forgetting on demand and the corresponding inference that instructing jurors to do so is therefore futile or counterproductive. For these and related reasons, such as the tension manifested in the two different traditional types of instructions to disregard described earlier, courts and litigants would be better served by the more realistic view of disregarding—one that accepts the fact that prejudicial inadmissible evidence remains in the minds of jurors but takes measures to prevent the evidence from influencing their verdicts. The neutralization view of disregarding presents the opportunity to consider multiple ways that courts could alter jurors' perceptions of unduly prejudicial inadmissible evidence through instructions to disregard, with the debiasing instruction being a prime illustration.

As is the case with all instructions to disregard, it is possible that neutralization instructions could cause jurors to overcorrect or undercorrect for the improper influence of the inadmissible evidence. When determining the appropriate amount of correction, jurors take cues from the instruction to disregard and their own theories about the degree to which the inadmissible evidence altered their views of the case. To avoid undercorrection, it is important that the instruction make jurors aware of the extent of the bias potentially introduced by the inadmissible evidence. The possibility of overcorrection may deter trial attorneys from intentionally introducing prejudicial inadmissible evidence because, ultimately, their own case is threatened. While this disincentive may not have a marked impact on accidental introductions of prejudicial evidence, it would seem just to place any resulting penalty on the introducing party. And, to reiterate, in my study, mock jurors accurately assessed and adjusted for the degree to which the inadmissible evidence had influenced their verdicts, suggesting that neutralization is not a "mental gymnastic" beyond the cognitive capabilities of jurors (*Nash v. United States*, p. 1007). On the contrary, humans naturally correct for bias in their daily lives, such that the debiasing instruction directs jurors to do something that is both possible (as opposed to erasing the inadmissible evidence from their minds) and frequently practiced.

CONSIDER THE OPPOSITE OF THE INADMISSIBLE EVIDENCE
Another method for neutralizing the effects of prejudicial inadmissible evidence may be found in the basic research literature on counterfactual thinking.

One particular form of counterfactual thinking, *considering the opposite*, has overcome powerful biases in human judgment by decreasing the accessibility of previously presented information (e.g., Lord, Lepper, & Preston, 1984; Mussweiler, Strack, & Pfeiffer, 2000). The concept rests on the premise that, other factors being equal, information has a greater influence on persons' judgments when they do not possess conflicting information to offset it. Applied to the courtroom, when jurors are exposed to prejudicial inadmissible evidence, the trial judge could instruct them to consider the opposite of that evidence in an effort to counter its biasing effects. Such an approach may also supply an implicit cue to the jurors that the evidence is invalid.

A consider-the-opposite instruction could take multiple forms, based on the manner in which it has been tested in basic research. For example, were a witness to testify that a defendant had confessed to the crime, the instruction to disregard might include something along the lines of the following: "It's important that each of you consider the possibility that the defendant did not confess to the crime" or "It's important that each of you consider that the defendant did not legally confess to the crime." Whichever consider-the-opposite instruction the court delivers would be accompanied by a further admonition that emphasizes to jurors the importance of following the instruction, for example: "You are instructed to disregard the statement that he did so. That statement should have no bearing on your verdict."

A benefit of the consider-the-opposite instruction is that, like the debiasing instruction, it directs jurors to engage in a cognitive task that they are capable of carrying out. A practical downside of the instruction at the present is that it remains empirically untested. A potential legal concern with some formulations of the instruction is that, by not merely addressing the inadmissible evidence, but rather introducing contrary evidence, the consider-the-opposite instruction could be viewed as improperly placing the trial judge in the role of advocate. However, given that the goal of the instruction is the same as that of other instructions to disregard—to negate inadmissible evidence—and that the instruction directly counters the content of the inadmissible evidence, it would appear to be appropriately neutral.

Interim Summary

Empirical studies demonstrating the general ineffectiveness of (mainly terse) traditional instructions to disregard have motivated legal scholars and psychologists to propose the alternatives described above. Rather than merely criticize the traditional instructions, these commentators have attempted to improve judicial methods for mitigating the effects of prejudicial inadmissible evidence on jurors. Some of these proposals fare better than others, however.

The foregoing critique clarifies the strengths and weaknesses of the proposals to provide courts and researchers with a more coherent picture of the expected effects of different types of instructions to disregard.

FOUNDATIONAL ELEMENTS OF EFFECTIVE INSTRUCTIONS TO DISREGARD

Whatever type of instruction to disregard the trial judge chooses—an emphatic forget instruction, a neutralization instruction, or some other—existing research indicates that it should incorporate certain key elements to facilitate juror disregarding of prejudicial inadmissible evidence. These elements, and their underlying psychological mechanisms, are discussed in this section.

Draw Jurors' Attention to the Inadmissible Evidence

Researchers, legal scholars, and courts assert that jurors are less likely to comply with instructions to disregard when the inadmissible evidence is salient (e.g., Lieberman, Arndt, & Vess, 2009). The dominant belief is that an attorney's objection to inadmissible evidence and the trial judge's instruction to disregard are counterproductive in that they cause jurors to pay more attention to the evidence and to view it as more important than they would absent these acts. The basic psychological literature, however, suggests that rendering inadmissible evidence salient to jurors is not harmful per se; on the contrary, salience is essential to the corrective process in which jurors must engage if they are to successfully disregard inadmissible evidence. When inadmissible evidence is salient, its biasing influence is more likely to be evident to jurors—a prerequisite for disregarding (e.g., Schul & Burnstein, 1985; Strack, Schwarz, Bless, & Kubler, 1993). Consistent with these findings, in my study (Demaine, 2008), jurors who received the terse admonition to disregard underestimated the degree to which the inadmissible evidence influenced their verdicts, whereas jurors who were given either the debiasing or emphatic forget instructions—both of which drew greater attention to the inadmissible evidence than did the terse instruction— accurately estimated the damaging effects of the inadmissible evidence on their perceptions of the case and countered them. Granted, under the courts' current conceptualization of disregarding as forgetting, the emphatic forget instruction draws jurors' attention to the inadmissible evidence while encouraging them to delete the evidence from their minds, an illogical request; it nonetheless performed well, apparently by enabling the jurors to discount the evidence or to correct for its biasing influence on their verdicts. Although the salience of the inadmissible evidence undergirds some of the other factors discussed below, it is sufficiently important and misunderstood to warrant this separate mention.

Restate the Inadmissible Evidence in the Instruction to Disregard

Many judges believe that restating inadmissible evidence in instructions to disregard increases the likelihood that the evidence will influence jurors' verdicts. In one case, for example, the appellate court viewed the fact that the trial judge had not repeated the inadmissible evidence as support for its conclusion that "the instruction was particularly well tailored to avert the prejudicial effect of the struck testimony" (*Commonwealth v. Adamides*, p. 1095 n.4). In another case, the appellate court considered the trial judge's restatement of the inadmissible evidence in the instruction to disregard as indicative that the instruction was flawed: "In giving his instruction to the jury, the judge reiterated the impermissible content of the testimony, again calling attention to [it]" (*United States v. Kallin*, p. 694). This view results from courts' conceptualization of disregarding as forgetting, under which restating the inadmissible evidence within the instruction to disregard hinders jurors' ability to eradicate thoughts of the evidence. If jurors fail to link the instruction to disregard with the inadmissible evidence, however, they are likely to use the evidence as though no instruction were given. Restating the inadmissible evidence within the instruction to disregard ensures that jurors understand precisely what information should not influence their verdicts.

Instruct Jurors to Disregard the Inadmissible Evidence, Not to Avoid Discussing It During Deliberations

Trial courts sometimes instruct jurors to avoid discussing inadmissible evidence during deliberations rather than to disregard the evidence. The reasons for this admonition seem, once again, to derive from courts' conception of disregarding as forgetting. First, if jurors have successfully forgotten the inadmissible evidence, they clearly should not be talking about it during deliberations. Second, this instruction directs jurors to take an action within their capabilities, as opposed to admonishing them to undertake the impossible task of erasing the inadmissible evidence from their minds. There is, however, an important distinction between disregarding inadmissible evidence and not discussing it during deliberations: Jurors may avoid mention of inadmissible evidence during deliberations yet still be strongly influenced by it. Moreover, although inadmissible evidence should not dominate jury deliberations, mention of it is unlikely to hinder jurors' ability to disregard. On the contrary, discussing inadmissible evidence may foster successful disregarding for the salience reasons previously discussed. A more productive course of action is for trial judges to actually instruct jurors to disregard the prejudicial inadmissible evidence so that they understand that this evidence should not influence their verdicts.

Include (Carefully Crafted) Emphatic Language in the Instruction to Disregard

Trial judges often use emphatic language in instructions to disregard in order to underscore to jurors the importance of disregarding. By the same token, appellate courts traditionally have considered emphatic language as an indication that instructions to disregard are effective: "To proceed properly we must weigh the forcefulness of the instruction and the conviction with which it was given against the degree of prejudice generated by the evidence" (*United States v. Johnson*, p. 62; see also *State v. Winter*). While instructions to disregard should be sufficiently forceful to motivate jurors to disregard, basic research on psychological reactance (introduced above in the context of the suspicion proposals) suggests that forceful instructions may induce jurors to give more weight to inadmissible evidence than if they received no instruction to disregard or a milder admonishment. If jurors view the instruction to disregard as an attempt on the part of the trial judge or the legal system to infringe on their freedom to render a fair verdict, they may consider the inadmissible evidence in an effort to assert control over the decision-making process.

Wolf and Montgomery (1977) demonstrated that a forceful instruction to disregard may induce reactance in jurors. In their study, depending on the condition, either the prosecution or the defense presented evidence that the judge ruled either admissible or inadmissible following an objection by opposing counsel. At the end of the case, the judge reminded the mock jurors of the admissibility ruling, and half of those who were reminded that the evidence was inadmissible were admonished as follows: "[The evidence] must play no role in [your] consideration of the case. You have no choice but to disregard it." The jurors who received this admonition were influenced by the inadmissible evidence, whereas those who were merely reminded that the evidence was inadmissible were not. The researchers' interpretation of these findings—that the jurors followed the instruction to disregard only when it was not perceived as a threat to their decision-making freedom—is supported by ancillary measures. Admonished jurors experienced a greater desire to consider the inadmissible evidence and placed less importance on disregarding it than did jurors who were merely given the inadmissible ruling.

The results of this study and those from the basic literature on psychological reactance suggest that forceful language in instructions to disregard may be counterproductive insofar as it decreases jurors' willingness to comply. This issue gains in importance when one considers that trial judges are particularly likely to use forceful language in instructions to disregard when they deem the inadmissible evidence to be highly prejudicial to a party's case.

A forceful instruction to disregard need not induce reactance in jurors, however. Mock jurors in my study (Demaine, 2008) who received the debiasing or emphatic forget instructions, for example, showed no signs of reactance, despite the fact that both instructions contained strong admonitions. These jurors were no more likely to report that the instruction limited their freedom to render a just verdict than were jurors given the terse instruction to disregard. The absence of reactance may be attributable to the forceful instructions having undermined the validity of the inadmissible evidence for some of the jurors. Jurors are unlikely to view an instruction to disregard as limiting their freedom to render a just verdict when they perceive the inadmissible evidence to be flawed, because the judge's strong admonition leads the jurors to a just verdict in this circumstance. As noted, however, some of the jurors in the experiment continued to view the evidence as valid following the instruction to disregard and nonetheless were willing and able to correct for its biasing influence on their verdicts. An additional potential explanation for the difference in findings between my study and that of Wolf and Montgomery (1977) is the latter's use of "you have no choice" language, which may be a trigger for reactance. It is also possible that Wolf and Montgomery's stern reminder at the end of the trial jolted the jurors, because until that time they had only been given a bare inadmissible ruling with no instruction to disregard. Finally, it is possible that the trial judge in my study had greater legitimacy with the mock jurors than did the trial judge in Wolf and Montgomery's study, such that my jurors were less likely to question his authority to make evidentiary rulings. Neither Wolf and Montgomery nor I measured this construct, so it is impossible to know if it contributed to the differential manifestation of reactance between the two studies, but future explorations of instructions to disregard might include measures of judicial and legal system legitimacy in order to discern their influence on jurors' willingness to comply. So long as jurors view instructions to disregard as legitimate attempts to guide their decision making, as opposed to illegitimate attacks on their freedom to render verdicts they believe to be just, the instructions are unlikely to be counterproductive despite being forceful.

Undermine the Perceived Validity of the Inadmissible Evidence

When jurors confront apparently valid prejudicial inadmissible evidence, they must choose between (1) contravening the instruction to disregard and rendering what they believe is the correct verdict and (2) following the instruction to disregard and rendering a verdict contrary to the information presented at trial. Some of the mock jurors in my study (Demaine, 2008) successfully disregarded the inadmissible evidence despite perceiving it as valid, which supports the idea that a subset of jurors resolves this conflict in favor of following the instruction to disregard. When jurors believe that inadmissible evidence is false or unreliable, however, this conflict disappears, because following the judge's instruction enhances the probability of arriving at a correct verdict in the case. Jurors are thus more likely to be motivated to disregard prejudicial inadmissible evidence when they perceive it as invalid.

Basic psychological research also offers an ability-based explanation for why jurors tend to follow instructions to disregard apparently invalid evidence and not to follow instructions to disregard apparently valid evidence. Evidence that is perceived to be useful in arriving at a correct decision is more likely to be attended to and elaborated on and, by definition, has a strong causal or inferential relationship with the judgment, all of which render it highly accessible in the jurors' minds (e.g., Schul & Burnstein, 1983). Consequently, jurors are likely to experience greater difficulty preventing apparently true evidence than apparently false evidence from influencing their judgments. As mentioned earlier, Fein and colleagues (1997) found that mock jurors who successfully disregarded the inadmissible evidence were more likely to question its validity, and some jurors in my study (Demaine, 2008) successfully disregarded the inadmissible evidence because the instruction to disregard led them to question its validity.

Again, the perceived validity, not the actual validity, of the inadmissible evidence is important. While an instruction that explains the basis for the inadmissible ruling, for example, can effectively underscore the flawed nature of objectively invalid inadmissible evidence, it will bolster the validity of objectively valid inadmissible evidence if there was any question in the jurors' minds. In contrast, an instruction to disregard that implicitly undermines the validity of the inadmissible evidence causes jurors to question both objectively valid and objectively invalid inadmissible evidence. In order to maximize the likelihood that instructions to disregard undermine the perceived validity of inadmissible evidence, it is, of course, important that attorneys phrase their objections in a way that does not bolster the validity of the evidence.

In my study (Demaine, 2008), the instructions to disregard did not directly decrease jurors' perceptions of the relevance of the inadmissible evidence to their verdicts; rather, some jurors perceived the inadmissible evidence as less relevant to their verdicts because they questioned its validity. This finding aligns with the reasoning of the rules of evidence insofar as prejudicial inadmissible evidence is prohibited in trials precisely because jurors are likely to view it as relevant to the case and be inappropriately swayed by it. It thus seems that, in the instruction to disregard, courts should concentrate on decreasing jurors' perceived validity of the inadmissible evidence—which will, in turn, decrease the degree to which they view the inadmissible evidence as relevant to their verdicts—rather than addressing the perceived relevance of the evidence directly (as explanation-based instructions do).

When the Instruction to Disregard Is Delayed, Address the Potential Subtle Influences of Inadmissible Evidence on Jurors' Verdicts

For various reasons, a trial judge may issue an instruction to disregard long after jurors have been exposed to inadmissible evidence. Courts frequently assert that instructions to disregard must follow close on the heels of inadmissible evidence if they are to cure the damage inflicted on the case. That an instruction is issued immediately argues for its effectiveness (e.g., *Profit Recovery Group v. Comm'r*), whereas a delayed instruction is faulty regardless of its content (e.g., *United States v. Kallin*). Empirical studies have focused on testing the effectiveness of instructions to disregard issued immediately following jurors' exposure to inadmissible evidence; consequently, they do not speak to the likely effectiveness of delayed instructions. Research outside of the inadmissible evidence context, however, is informative.

Jurors construct stories of the events underlying the case based on the evidence presented at trial and their personal knowledge (e.g., Pennington & Hastie, 1993).[11] The evidence that jurors incorporate into these stories exerts direct and indirect influences on their verdicts. That is, in addition to constituting an element of the story, evidence can alter jurors' interpretation and weighting of other evidence and arguments in the case (e.g., Lord, Ross, & Lepper, 1979). Moreover, jurors are likely to draw inferences from the inadmissible evidence that also become integral components of their stories. For example, Pennington and Hastie (1986) presented mock jurors with a criminal trial and then asked them to relate their story of the case; fully 45% of jurors' stories were inferences drawn from the evidence presented at trial rather than restatements of the actual evidence. Once jurors firmly integrate inadmissible evidence into their stories, as when an instruction to disregard is substantially delayed, they may be unable to discern the degree to which the inadmissible evidence directly and indirectly influenced the stories, at least without assistance from the instruction to disregard (e.g., Newman & Uleman, 1989).

Research on belief perseverance also suggests that jurors may experience greater difficulty complying with instructions to disregard administered long after inadmissible evidence is introduced (e.g., Anderson, Lepper, & Ross, 1980; Ross, Lepper, & Hubbard, 1975). Individuals tend to persist in their beliefs even when the information on which the beliefs were originally based is discredited. The phenomenon appears to be a function of two factors—biased assimilation of subsequently presented information and the generation of alternative explanations for the beliefs—that support the beliefs independently of the original foundation. New information can change beliefs, of course, but these cognitive processes tend to dampen its effect. Belief perseverance may be compounded by the general assumption that facts underlie assertions (e.g., Kassin, Williams, & Saunders, 1990; Swann, Giuliano, & Wegner, 1982) and the tendency to initially accept information as true (e.g., Gilbert, Krull, & Malone, 1990; Gilbert, Tafarodi, & Malone, 1993). These processes suggest that jurors generally assume that evidence is valid until they are told otherwise (particularly given the adversarial nature of trials) and that jurors would need to expend more effort rejecting initially unchallenged inadmissible evidence than continuing to accept it as part of their stories of the case.

Courts are appropriately wary of substantial lags between juror exposure to prejudicial inadmissible evidence and judicial instructions to disregard, given these basic research findings. Researchers could productively expand the existing science by investigating how biased assimilation, belief perseverance, and related psychological phenomena affect jurors' motivation and ability to disregard prejudicial inadmissible evidence when instructions to disregard are delayed. These studies could test whether jurors' verdicts are more likely to be untainted by inadmissible evidence when the instruction to disregard explicitly refers to the potential indirect and subtle influences of subsequently discredited information.

Remember That Jurors Possess Limited Cognitive Resources and Motivation to Comply with Instructions (to Disregard)

When formulating instructions to disregard, it is important that trial judges be aware of jurors' cognitive and motivational limitations. While the courts may presume that jurors follow all instructions to disregard, the degree to which the presumption aligns with reality depends in large part on the wording and delivery of the instructions. Equally important are characteristics of trials, which generally include multiple introductions of inadmissible evidence and corresponding instructions to disregard, as well as various other judicial instructions and large amounts of (often conflicting and difficult-to-understand) admissible evidence and arguments. In this complex environment, jurors may be taxed by listening to and processing the information and drawing conclusions from it, leaving minimal resources for the effortful process of disregarding inadmissible evidence (e.g., Martin, Seta, & Crelia, 1990). It is thus essential that instructions to disregard be clearly and concisely worded, and that they provide jurors with sufficient motivation and readily usable tools to disregard.

CONCLUSION

Courts face a challenging task in countering prejudicial inadmissible evidence, which doubtless remains in jurors' memories as they arrive at their verdicts. There surely will be instances in which jurors' conceptions of the case are irreversibly altered by this evidence, for which mistrials remain the most appropriate remedy. Research suggests, however, that the damaging effects of the vast majority of prejudicial inadmissible evidence can be mitigated by appropriately framed instructions to disregard, as the courts have long presumed but not actively investigated. It is simply essential to recognize the abilities, limitations, and propensities of the human mind and work within them. This chapter presents the current state of science regarding how this may be accomplished and identifies promising areas for future study, both of which should enable courts to more consistently produce jury verdicts untainted by prejudicial inadmissible evidence.

ACKNOWLEDGMENTS

The author thanks Aaron X. Fellmeth, Lynn Nadel, Steven Neuberg, Michael Saks, and Walter Sinnott-Armstrong for commenting on earlier versions of this chapter, and Beth DiFelice for research assistance.

NOTES

1. Technically, the courts define *evidence* narrowly. For example, in Arizona, jurors are informed in preliminary instructions that "evidence will consist of testimony of witnesses, any documents and other things received in evidence as exhibits, and any facts stipulated, or agreed to, by the parties or which you are instructed to accept" (State Bar of Ariz., 2005, Preliminary Civil No. 3). Given that other information jurors encounter in court—for example, attorneys' inquiries and remarks—may also sway their decisions, however, the concept is considered expansively in this chapter to include any information presented to jurors during trials.
2. Lieberman and Arndt (2000) have suggested that trial courts might increase jurors' willingness to comply with procedural-based instructions to disregard by reminding them of their own mortality. The authors invoke terror management theory, which posits that many aspects of human behavior are means of bolstering our cultural worldview to protect us from the anxiety that results from our knowledge that death is inevitable (e.g., Pyszczynski, Greenberg, & Solomon, 1997). There is evidence that mortality salience heightens concerns with procedural fairness (Van den Bos & Miedema, 2000). Yet there is also evidence that mortality salience causes persons to be more punitive in their judgments of others who have morally transgressed (Rosenblatt, Greenberg, Solomon, Pyszczynski, & Lyon, 1989). The consequences of courts administering a mortality salience manipulation to remedy the effects of inadmissible evidence thus may be difficult to predict, as it is unclear whether procedural fairness or punitive motivations would predominate in a given case. Aside from this, Lieberman and Arndt omit discussion of the policy implications of courts inducing mortality salience in jurors or how this highly unusual act would be incorporated into court procedure.

3. Courts routinely include provisions such as the following in their preliminary jury instructions: "Admission of evidence in court is governed by rules of law. I will apply those rules and resolve any issues that arise during the trial concerning the admission of evidence. If an objection to a question is sustained, you must disregard the question and you must not guess what the answer to the question might have been. If an exhibit is offered in evidence and an objection to it is sustained, you must not consider that exhibit as evidence. If testimony is ordered stricken from the record, you must not consider that testimony for any purpose. Do not concern yourselves with the reasons for my rulings on the admission of evidence" (State Bar of Ariz., 2005, Preliminary Civil No. 4).
4. In California, for example, courts administer the following oath: "Do you, and each of you, understand and agree that you will well and truly try the cause now pending before this court, and a true verdict render according only to the evidence presented to you and to the instructions of the court?" (Judicial Council of Cal., Step 1: Selection of a Jury).
5. Moreover, the term *inoculate* is inapt. Analogizing to the medical literature on disease prevention, inoculation is used in the persuasion literature to describe instances in which people are given a weak version of a persuasive appeal in order to bolster their defenses to a subsequent, stronger persuasive appeal on the same topic. In the courtroom, where the inadmissible evidence is generally unpredictable in content, trial judges cannot inoculate the jury against it.
6. Posttrial instructions generally include language such as the following: "You are to determine what the facts in the case are from the evidence produced in court. If the court sustained an objection to a lawyer's question, you must disregard it and any answer given. Any testimony stricken from the court record must not be considered" (State Bar of Ariz., 2008, Standard Criminal No. 4).
7. Fein et al. (1997) also included an "admissible" evidence condition. The results of this condition are minimized here, because the researchers introduced a confound to the study design by failing to include an objection and admissibility ruling in this condition. They align, however, with the conclusion that the suspicion instruction was effective, whereas the mere hearsay instruction was not. Jurors in this condition were significantly more likely to find the defendant guilty than were jurors who were not exposed to the evidence. Moreover, although the researchers do not report testing the difference between the admissible and suspicion conditions, the means suggest that jurors in the admissible condition were markedly, if not significantly, more likely to find the defendant guilty than were those in the suspicion condition.
8. The Fifth and Fourteenth Amendment guarantees of due process and the Sixth and Seventh Amendment rights to a fair trial may be implicated, depending upon whether the case is in federal or state court and whether it is criminal or civil (U.S. Const. amends. V, VI, VII, and XIV).
9. Lieberman and Arndt (2000) suggest that courts could overcome the ironic processes of mental control by training jurors in thought suppression and decreasing the overall cognitive demands experienced by jurors at the time they attempt to suppress inadmissible evidence. The ideas are based on Wegner's (1994) proposition that people may resist the ironic processes of mental control when they are

under minimal mental load or when thought suppression has become automatized through frequent practice. Lieberman and Arndt do not discuss the impracticality of courts implementing either component. It would appear, for example, that jury duty is inherently mentally taxing, such that efforts by the courts to decrease the mental load placed on jurors may have little effect on jurors' ability to engage in suppression of thoughts regarding inadmissible evidence. Likewise, courts are faced with many complex challenges in providing fair trials, such that they likely have little time available to run jurors through a tutorial on thought suppression. Elaborate measures to avoid the ironic processes of thought control also appear to be unnecessary. As mentioned, jurors seem unlikely to take thought suppression instructions literally, perhaps because they realize that they cannot forget information on demand and, moreover, because the cognitive demands placed on jurors may preclude efforts to suppress.

10. These findings suggest that the terse instruction may be sufficiently forceful to motivate jurors to disregard, contrary to the courts' concern. However, the instruction is easily missed or forgotten and does not provide jurors with a means by which to disregard effectively.
11. Although other models of juror decision making appear in the literature, the story model is the most comprehensive and detailed of the theoretical frameworks and has received the most empirical support.

REFERENCES

Advisory Committee's Note to Federal Rule of Evidence 403. Retrieved Feb. 29, 2012 from http://www.law.cornell.edu/rules/fre/ACRule403.htm

Anderson, C. A., Lepper, M. R., & Ross, L. (1980). Perseverance of social theories: The role of explanation in the persistence of discredited information. *Journal of Personality and Social Psychology, 39*, 1037–1049.

Asch, S. E. (1955). Opinions and social pressure. *Scientific American, 193*, 31–35.

Brehm, J. W. (1966). *A theory of psychological reactance.* New York: Academic Press.

Brehm, S. S., & Brehm, J. W. (1981). *Psychological reactance: A theory of freedom and control.* New York: Academic Press.

Carter v. Hewitt, 617 F.2d 961 (3d Cir. 1980).

Commonwealth v. Adamides, 639 N.E.2d 1092 (Mass. App. 1994).

DeCarlo, T. E. (2005). The effects of sales message and suspicion of ulterior motives on salesperson evaluation. *Journal of Consumer Psychology, 15*, 238–249.

Demaine, L. J. (2008). In search of an anti-elephant: Confronting the human inability to forget inadmissible evidence. *George Mason Law Review, 16*, 99–140.

Deutsch, M., & Gerard, H. B. (1955). A study of normative and informational social influences upon individual judgment. *Journal of Abnormal and Social Psychology, 51*, 629–636.

Diamond, S. S., & Casper, J. D. (1992). Blindfolding the jury to verdict consequences: Damages, experts, and the civil jury. *Law and Society Review, 26*, 513–563.

Federal rules of evidence. (2011). Washington, DC: U.S. Government Printing Office.

Fein, S., & Hilton, J. L. (1994). Judging others in the shadow of suspicion. *Motivation and Emotion, 18*, 167–198.

Fein, S., McCloskey, A. L., & Tomlinson, T. M. (1997). Can the jury disregard that information?: The use of suspicion to reduce the prejudicial effects of pretrial publicity and inadmissible testimony. *Personality and Social Psychology Bulletin, 23,* 1215–1226.

Gilbert, D. G., Krull, D. S., & Malone, P. S. (1990). Unbelieving the unbelievable: Some problems in the rejection of false information. *Journal of Personality and Social Psychology, 59,* 601–613.

Gilbert, D. G., Tafarodi, R. W., & Malone, P. S. (1993). You can't not believe everything you read. *Journal of Personality and Social Psychology, 65,* 221–233.

Greene, E., & Dodge, M. (1995). The influence of prior record evidence on juror decision making. *Law and Human Behavior, 19,* 67–78.

Judicial Council of California. *Learn about the trial process: Step 1: Selection of a jury.* Retrieved Feb. 29, 2012 from http://www.courts.ca.gov/2240.htm

Kassin, S. M., & Sommers, S. R. (1997). Inadmissible testimony, instructions to disregard, and the jury: Substantive versus procedural considerations. *Personality and Social Psychology Bulletin, 23,* 1046–1054.

Kassin, S. M., & Studebaker, C. A. (1998). Instructions to disregard and the jury: Curative and paradoxical effects. In J. M. Golding & C. M. MacLeod (Eds.), *Intentional forgetting: Interdisciplinary approaches* (pp. 413–434). Hillsdale, NJ: Lawrence Erlbaum.

Kassin, S. M., Williams, L. N., & Saunders, C. L. (1990). Dirty tricks of cross-examination: The influence of conjectural evidence on the jury. *Law and Human Behavior, 14,* 373–384.

Lieberman, J. D., & Arndt, J. (2000). Understanding the limits of limiting instructions: Social psychological explanations for the failures of instructions to disregard pretrial publicity and other inadmissible evidence. *Psychology, Public Policy, and Law, 6,* 677–711.

Lieberman, J. D., Arndt, J., & Vess, M. (2009). Inadmissible evidence and pretrial publicity: The effects (and ineffectiveness) of admonitions to disregard. In J. D. Lieberman & D. A. Krauss (Eds.), *Jury psychology: Social aspects of trial processes: Psychology in the courtroom* (Vol. 1, pp. 67–95). Surrey, UK: Ashgate.

Lord, C. G., Lepper, M. R., & Preston, E. (1984). Considering the opposite: A corrective strategy for social judgment. *Journal of Personality and Social Psychology, 47,* 1231–1243.

Lord, C. G., Ross, L., & Lepper, M. R. (1979). Biased assimilation and attitude polarization: The effects of prior theories on subsequently considered evidence. *Journal of Personality and Social Psychology, 37,* 2098–2109.

Macrae, C. N., Bodenhausen, G. V., Milne, A. B., & Jetten, J. (1994). Out of mind but back in sight: Stereotypes on the rebound. *Journal of Personality and Social Psychology, 67,* 808–817.

Martin, L. L., Seta, J. J., & Crelia, R. (1990). Assimilation and contrast as a function of people's willingness and ability to expend effort in forming an impression. *Journal of Personality and Social Psychology, 59,* 755–764.

Milgram, S. (1974). *Obedience to authority: An experimental view.* New York: Harper & Row.

Mussweiler, T., Strack, F., & Pfeiffer, T. (2000). Overcoming the inevitable anchoring effect: Considering the opposite compensates for selective accessibility. *Personality and Social Psychology Bulletin, 26*. 1142–1150.

Nash v. United States, 54 F.2d 1006 (2d Cir. 1932).

Newman, L. S., & Uleman, J. S. (1989). Spontaneous trait inference. In J. S. Uleman & J. A. Bargh (Eds.), *Unintended thought* (pp. 155–188). New York: Guilford Press.

Nisbett, R., & Wilson, T. D. (1977). Telling more than we know: Verbal reports on mental processes. *Psychological Review, 84*, 231–259.

Pennington, N., & Hastie, R. (1986). Evidence evaluation in complex decision making. *Journal of Personality and Social Psychology, 51*, 242–258.

Pennington, N., & Hastie, R. (1993). The story model of juror decision making. In R. Hastie (Ed.), *Inside the juror: The psychology of juror decision making* (pp. 192–221). New York: Cambridge University Press.

Profit Recovery Group, USA, Inc. v. Comm'r., Dep't. of Admin. & Fin. Servs., 871 A.2d 1237 (Me. 2005).

Pyszczynski, T., Greenberg, J., & Solomon, S. (1997). Why do we need what we need? A terror management perspective on the roots of human social motivation. *Psychological Inquiry, 8*, 1–20.

Quinn, J. M., & Wood, W. (2004). Forewarnings of influence appeals: Inducing resistance and acceptance. In E. S. Knowles & J. A. Linn (Eds.), *Resistance and persuasion* (pp. 193–213). Mahwah, NJ: Lawrence Erlbaum.

Rosenblatt, A., Greenberg, J., Solomon, S., Pyszczynski, T., & Lyon, D. (1989). Evidence for terror management theory I: The effects of mortality salience on reactions to those who violate or uphold cultural values. *Journal of Personality and Social Psychology, 57*, 681–690.

Ross, L., Lepper, M. R., & Hubbard, M. (1975). Perseverance in self-perception and social perception: Biased attribution processes in the debriefing paradigm. *Journal of Personality and Social Psychology, 32*, 880–892.

Schul, Y., & Burnstein, E. (1983). The informational basis of social judgments: Memory for informative and uninformative arguments. *Journal of Experimental Social Psychology, 19*, 422–433.

Schul, Y., & Burnstein, E. (1985). When discounting fails: Conditions under which individuals use discredited information in making a judgment. *Journal of Personality and Social Psychology, 49*, 894–903.

Sommers, S. R., & Kassin, S. M. (2001). On the many impacts of inadmissible testimony: Selective compliance, need for cognition, and the overcorrection bias. *Personality and Social Psychology Bulletin, 27*, 1368–1377.

State Bar of Arizona. (2005). *Revised Arizona jury instructions (civil) 4th, Preliminary Instructions*. Retrieved February 29, 2012, from http://www.azbar.org/media/58448/preliminary.pdf

State Bar of Arizona. (2008). *Revised Arizona jury instructions (criminal) 3rd, Standard Instructions*. Retrieved February 29, 2012, from http://www.azbar.org/media/58832/standard_criminal_instr.pdf

State v. McIntyre, 737 A.2d 392 (Conn. 1999).

State v. Winter, 477 A.2d 323 (N.J. 1984).

Steblay, N., Hosch, H. M., Culhane, S. E., & McWethy, A. (2006). The impact on juror verdicts of judicial instruction to disregard inadmissible evidence: A meta-analysis. *Law and Human Behavior, 30,* 469–492.

Strack, F., Schwarz, N., Bless, H., & Kubler, A. (1993). Awareness of the influence as a determinant of assimilation and contrast. *European Journal of Social Psychology, 23,* 53–62.

Swann, W. B., Giuliano, T., & Wegner, D. M. (1982). Where leading questions can lead: The power of conjecture in social interaction. *Journal of Personality and Social Psychology, 42,* 1025–1035.

Tanford, J. A. (1990). The law and psychology of jury instructions. *Nebraska Law Review, 69,* 71–111.

Tanford, J. A. (1992). Thinking about elephants: Admonitions, empirical research and legal policy. *UMKC Law Review, 60,* 645–664.

United States Constitution.

United States v. Harris, 325 F.3d 865 (7th Cir. 2003).

United States v. Johnson, 618 F.2d 60 (9th Cir. 1980).

United States v. Kallin, 50 F.3d 689 (9th Cir. 1995).

Van den Bos, K., & Miedema, J. (2000). Toward understanding why fairness matters: The influence of mortality salience on reactions to procedural fairness. *Journal of Personality and Social Psychology, 79,* 355–366.

Wegner, D. M. (1989). *White bears and other unwanted thoughts: Suppression, obsession, and the psychology of mental control.* New York: Guilford Press.

Wegner, D. M. (1994). Ironic processes of mental control. *Psychological Review, 101,* 34–52.

Wegner, D. M., & Erber, R. (1992). The hyperaccessibility of suppressed thoughts. *Journal of Personality and Social Psychology, 63,* 903–912.

Wegener, D. T., Petty, R. E., & Dunn, M. (1998). The metacognition of bias correction: Naive theories of bias and the flexible correction model. In V. Y. Yzerbyt, G. Lories, & B. Dardenne (Eds.), *Metacognition: Cognitive and social dimensions* (pp. 202–227). Thousand Oaks, CA: Sage.

Wegner, D. M., Schneider, D. J., Carter, S. R., & White, T. L. (1987). Paradoxical effects of thought suppression. *Journal of Personality and Social Psychology, 53,* 5–13.

Weinstein, J. B., & Berger, M. A. (2007). *Weinstein's federal evidence* (2nd ed.). J. M. McLaughlin (Ed.), Table of State and Military Adaptations of Federal Rules of Evidence. New York: Matthew Bender.

Wilson, T. D., & Brekke, N. (1994). Mental contamination and mental correction: Unwanted influences on judgments and evaluations. *Psychological Bulletin, 116,* 117–142.

Wolf, S., & Montgomery, D. A. (1977). Effects of inadmissible evidence and level of judicial admonishment to disregard on the judgments of mock jurors. *Journal of Applied Social Psychology, 7,* 205–219.

9

The Memory of Jurors

Enhancing Trial Performance

ANDERS SANDBERG, WALTER P. SINNOTT-ARMSTRONG,
AND JULIAN SAVULESCU

INTRODUCTION

In 1984, Ronald Cotton was sentenced to life plus 54 years for the brutal rape of Jennifer Thompson. Jennifer was intelligent and strong-willed. With his face pressed against hers, she was determined to remember every detail of the man who was destroying her life. Throughout her rape, she focused on remembering her attacker's face, voice, and mannerisms and on finding as much information as possible to one day bring him to justice. So, when police showed Jennifer a photo of Ronald Cotton, she was able to identify him easily. Cotton was jailed for the rape.

After serving 10½ years, Cotton was released, not because he had served his sentence, but because DNA evidence revealed that he was not the rapist Jennifer Thompson had so confidently and certainly identified. Her real attacker, Bobby Poole, was later jailed for the crime.

In fact, she had been introduced to Poole as a suspect before. Cotton had originally appealed his first conviction. Jennifer Thompson and a second rape victim of Poole's were both able to see Ronald Cotton and Bobby Poole together. They both testified that it was Ronald Cotton, not Bobby Poole, who was the perpetrator, despite later clear DNA evidence to the contrary. Thompson later said:

> He [Cotton] just looked exactly like the man who raped me. And not a lot of time had elapsed between the crime and me looking at the pictures, so

my memory was still very fresh. And then when I saw him in the physical lineup and I was actually able to see him as a person and his demeanor and his postures—it just further convinced me that Ronald Cotton was the man. He looked exactly like the man. He looked like the sketch that I had given to the police. His mannerisms, his voice, his height, his weight—it all just added up in my mind. And as the evidence started to come in, it was almost just conclusive to me that this had been the rapist. And so as time goes on, I think that my mind would always see Ronald Cotton. (PBS online, 2011)

Jennifer Thompson is now a campaigner for reforms in the use of eyewitness evidence. Jennifer was a highly intelligent, responsible and confident witness. There is no evidence that the police acted improperly, accidentally implanting false memories. Memory is simply highly fallible.

The limitations of eyewitness testimony are well known. However, almost nobody discusses the problem of the inadequacy of the memories of jurors and judges. It is reasonable to expect that this separate problem has serious implications for procedural justice, as we argue in the following section.

THE PROBLEM OF JUROR MEMORY

Human cognitive performance has crucial significance for legal trials, often making the difference between fair and unfair imprisonment. Lawyers, judges, and jurors need to follow long and complex arguments, extract crucial information, and draw inferences of their own. They need to understand technical language, interpret testimony by witnesses (sometimes including expert scientific witnesses), and see through attempts to obscure opposing points. They need to observe, understand, and remember what happens during the trial.

In particular, trials depend heavily on memory. Eyewitnesses must remember what they saw. Expert witnesses must remember their fields as well as their data and analyses in this particular case. Lawyers must remember which points they and the other side made and what each of their witnesses is supposed to say. Judges must remember intricate procedural rules as well as substantive laws and precedents.

The demands imposed on jurors' memory are especially sizable. Part of the problem is that most jurors are not used to listening to long arguments in technical language with cross-examination.[1] But even experienced and intelligent jurors face imposing challenges:

> The rules and procedures used to govern the conduct of jury trials reflect a great deal of faith in jurors' ability to understand and retain information

over long periods of time, often with much intervening information. Jurors are expected to operate as passive recipients of information presented by the parties, and generally are prohibited from taking notes, asking questions, or using other potentially memory-enhancing tools. In addition, little opportunity is provided for review or elaboration of the concepts presented. From this impoverished learning environment, jurors are expected to recall the evidence and testimony presented at trial, recall the judge's instructions about the law applicable to the case, and reach a rational conclusion regarding the proper verdict in the case. (Johnson 1993)

These memory demands likely affect real court cases. Johnson (1993) cites the experience of litigation consultants who test the comprehensibility and memorability of particular case presentations to surrogate jurors. These evaluations often find inaccurate recall of crucial information, especially in complex cases.

The legal process also assumes that jurors can accurately assess what they do and do not remember. *Metamemory* is memory or evaluation about what we remembered. Accurate metamemory is needed to guide the deliberation process. However, in mock jury trials there was no tight link between how confident jurors were about their memory and their actual accuracy: The most confident (and hence most likely to sway uncertain fellow jurors) were often not the most accurate. (See the chapters in this volume by Chua and by Roediger, Wixted, & DeSoto.) The same problem arose for individual estimates of memory for particular categories of evidence. Metamemory accuracy improved once the jurors answered questions about the evidence, suggesting that a proper jury deliberation procedure can partially compensate for some individual memory failure. Unfortunately, this solution requires a careful review of all evidence, which is hard to achieve in practice due to limitations on memory and communication (Pritchard & Keenan, 1999).

Jurors are often subjected to both tremendous decision complexity (because of intricate legal principles) and tremendous evidence complexity (because of high information load as well as low informational clarity and comprehensibility). Lawyers sometimes intentionally obscure their opponents' points, such as by introducing red herrings or continuously objecting in order to break the flow of testimony. When asked, jurors report that increasing the quantity of information they have to consider decreases their ability to understand the issues and the confidence in their verdict (Heuer & Penrod, 1989). Decisions of jurors in a simulated civil trial were affected by different levels of evidence complexity. In a high information-load situation, they attributed greater blameworthiness to the plaintiffs, contrary to the evidence, and were less able to distinguish between differently liable plaintiffs (Fosterlee & Horowitz, 1997).

In general, the psychology of decision making has found that decision quality decreases as information load increases (Hwang & Lin, 1999). To handle the information load, subjects typically use heuristics to rapidly weed out possibilities (Payne, 1976). This is a process that seems likely to introduce biases, such as ethnic stereotyping (Lam, Chiu, Lau, Chan, & Yim, 2006; Tamborini, Huang, Mastro, & Nabashi-Nakahara, 2007), clearly undesirable for a fair judicial process.

Learning and memory are strongly affected by other psychological factors, such as stress, alertness, attention, and emotion. The court environment is often stressful for jurors (The National Center for State Courts, 2002), and this stress will likely impair cognition. Equally, monotony and lack of stimulation and active participation can also produce inattention and sleepiness that interfere with learning. Gruesome evidence may also arouse emotion and thereby bias recall (Bradley, Greenwald, Petry, & Lang, 1992; Dolcos, Cabeza, & LaBar, 2005; Phelps, this volume).

For a trial to be fair, the jury needs to remember the details of the case, as well as their instructions from the judge, and to deliberate impartially until they reach a consensus based on this information. Cognitive limitations might preclude bringing accurate memories to the deliberation, might produce inaccurate pseudomemories, and might bias the deliberation. Unfairness can result if cognitive limitations systematically tend to favor particular outcomes for particular types of defendants or plaintiffs. In some cases, jurors are asked to disregard evidence, which requires an additional high degree of mental control. Overall, the expectations of juries are far higher than the actual performance (Arkes & Mellers, 2002).

Sleepiness in the courtroom is another cognitive problem. Judicial sleepiness is not uncommon (Grunstein & Banerjee, 2007). However, mistrials due to sleeping judges appear to be rare. In *United states v. White* (1979), the presiding judge fell asleep during the defense counsel's opening statement, but there was no mistrial because there was no evidence of prejudice to the defendant's case. Nonetheless, such somnolence is increasingly disparaged by the public and the profession.

> In many ways, the evidence from these cases suggests that judges are now held to a high standard similar to those in the trucking industry or hospital medical staff. While potential consequences of fall-asleep errors by truck drivers and hospital medical staff often involve death or serious injury, fall-asleep episodes by judges could possibly lead to serious consequences such as a wrong conviction or [an] incorrect sentence. (Grunstein & Banerjee, 2007)

Jurors are even more prone to sleep. In a survey of juror delinquency, 562 judges (69%) reported cases over the previous 3 years in which jurors had fallen asleep. This would correspond to 2,300 cases, approximately 5%–10% of all cases (King, 1996). There were probably many more cases in which jurors were sleepy, perhaps very sleepy, but did not actually fall asleep. However, the number of new trials actually granted due to juror misconduct (of any kind) was very low: 51 cases out of 26,000.

For all of these reasons, it is hard to be a good juror. Jurors need to observe long proceedings, determine which information is relevant, store crucial facts in memory, retrieve them during deliberation, reason impartially, and reach a fair verdict. Every step in this process is affected by the limitations and biases of human cognition.

A SOLUTION: COGNITIVE ENHANCEMENT

Some of these problems could be ameliorated if we could enhance the cognitive capacities, including attention and memory, of jurors as well as other players in trials. There are multiple ways to improve cognition, either by external tools or by biomedical interventions that act directly on the brain.

External Tools

Several kinds of external aids can enhance or extend our mental abilities (Clark & Chalmers, 1998; Dror & Harnad, 2009). Typical examples include counting on fingers or adding on calculators. There are many more possibilities for jurors.

Some external tools that enhance cognition are simple and obvious. Exercise (which is, strictly speaking, biomedical) can enhance attention and memory if it is not too intense (Tomporowski, 2003). One might suggest that courts allow jurors (as well as witnesses, etc.) to go for a run or brisk walk occasionally during trials when time permits. Requiring jurors to sit still for long periods can reduce memory and cognition in general.

Memory can also be enhanced by manipulating the environment. People tend to remember more, and more accurately, when they recall in the same circumstances as when they first experienced an event. Jurors then might recall more of the evidence in a long trial and might make fewer recall mistakes during their deliberations if they deliberate inside the courtroom where they heard the evidence.

Taking notes is an external memory enhancer that many people advocate:

> To the extent that trials are intended to be a search for the truth (of course, trials serve many other ends as well), it is not unreasonable for jurors to

expect that they will be permitted to use tools such as questions and notes that might aid them in getting to the truth. These are, of course, tools of inquiry and aids to decision making that are used every day by members of a literate society. (Penrod & Heuer, 1997)

However, note taking by jurors used to be forbidden in most U.S. jurisdictions, partly out of fear that jurors who took notes would gain inordinate dominance over illiterate jurors. Today, it is reportedly allowed in most but still not all jurisdictions. Note taking can enhance memory both by the process of recording notes and by providing memory cues for later recall. Even doodling might act as an indirect memory enhancer by reducing boredom (Andrade, 2010). Several studies have found that jurors taking notes recalled more trial events than non–note takers, and this might increase juror competence in some circumstances (Fosterlee & Horowitz, 1994, 1997; Rosenhan, Eisner, & Robinson, 1994). However, other field studies have questioned the improvement of recall of trial information (Heuer & Penrod, 1988, 1989), especially when the evidence was ambiguous (Fosterlee & Horowitz, 1997). Note taking may help the jury confront higher information loads: In an experiment with 6- and 12-member mock juries, note taking reduced the tendency for the smaller juries to give too high compensatory awards in high-complexity situations (Horowitz & Bordens, 2002).

Note takers, while showing better memory than those who did not take notes, performed even better in terms of decision making when given effective pretrial instructions (Fosterlee & Horowitz, 1997). Pretrial instructions and, more generally, preexisting knowledge tend to aid recall of related information by providing a framework for assimilating the new information. Careful pretrial instructions can then assist jurors' focus on relevant evidence as well as recall of it. This requires both understandable instructions (nontechnical language, simple grammar, good organization) and that the jurors receive the instructions before the evidence; otherwise, the jurors will not gain a mental framework helping them to focus (Elwork, Sales, & Alfini, 1977; Kassin & Wrightsman, 1979).

When memory fails, jurors can ask for access to transcripts and recordings. Courts could more strongly encourage jurors to refer to official records by making access easier. However, the ability to ask for transcripts is useful only if jurors remember enough to know which parts to ask for. These materials appear to be less effective than note taking for improving jury competence in complex trials (Horowitz & Forsterlee, 2001).

In these and other ways, courts could enhance jurors' memory and performance by the use of external tools. Each of these methods raises legal, moral, and practical issues that might preclude its use in actual trials. Still, the cost of refusing to use these tools will be decreased cognitive performance by jurors (and other legal actors).

Biomedical Enhancement

Like external tools, biomedical cognitive enhancers—typically drugs—could improve a wide variety of cognitive functions:

- **Wakefulness**: Caffeine, modafinil, stimulants in general
- **Attention**: Methylphenidate (Ritalin), nicotine
- **Memory encoding**: Glucose, cholinergic drugs (e.g., donepezil, nicotine, physiostigmine), levodopa, ampakines
- **Working memory**: Methylphenidate (Ritalin), modafinil, dopaminergic drugs
- **Stress reduction**: Beta blockers (propranolol)
- **Self-control**: Glucose
- **Executive inhibitory control**: Modafinil
- **Empathy/pro-social behavior**: Oxytocin

Some jurors already use some of these substances regularly. Glucose improves episodic memory and other cognitive abilities in middle-aged people, especially when the task is demanding (Riby, McLaughlin, Riby, & Graham, 2008). Many jurors also use caffeine and nicotine while serving on a jury. Some take stronger energy drinks, such as 5-Hour Energy™. Cognitive enhancer drugs are used deliberately by at least some professionals (Sahakian & Morein-Zamir, 2007).

Other biomedical cognitive enhancers are used less often but are still probably used by some jurors today. U.S. sales of methylphenidate (Ritalin) are growing so fast that many jury members probably already take it as a therapeutic medication. Levodopa, a precursor to dopamine used in the treatment of Parkinson's disease, improves learning (Knecht et al., 2004).

Much research has examined how to enhance the cognition of sleep-deprived healthy subjects. Stimulants (modafinil, caffeine, and dextroamphetamine) improved general alertness, reaction speed, and other cognitive abilities, including the ability to discriminate and label complex emotional blends in pictures of faces (Huck, McBride, Kendall, Grugle, & Killgore, 2008). This ability can be crucial for assessing witnesses. However, modafinil and caffeine appear more efficacious for improving executive function (Wesenstein, Killgore, & Balkin, 2005). Modafinil is able to restore humor appreciation (a complex cognitive ability), unlike the other stimulants (Killgore, McBride, Killgore, & Balkin, 2006). Modafinil also resulted in greater deliberation before making decisions than the use of amphetamines. Different stimulants are, thus, likely to have subtly different effects on cognitive subsystems (Killgore, Kahn-Greene, Grugle, Killgore, & Balkin, 2009). In a court setting, the basic stimulant effect would allow jurors to remain awake and vigilant while enhancing the higher cognitive abilities needed for making observations of subtle evidence (e.g., witness testimony), following lines of argument, and avoiding rash decisions during deliberation.

However, some biomedical cognitive enhancers have worrying side effects that could impair legal decision making. Propranolol, used for the treatment of hypertension, reduces anxiety in subjects forced to give a speech, so it might reduce anxiety and its distracting effects in witnesses and jurors. But it has also been found to impair recall of difficult words in anxious subjects (Hartley, Ungapen, Davie, & Spencer, 1983). Here the enhancement of calm might cause a selective disenhancement of memory (plus, as discussed below, potentially a biasing effect on how emotions are interpreted) that could be undesirable in jurors, for example by making them worse at recalling terminology or names. This illustrates an important point: Many jurors will be taking substances that affect, either positively or negatively, their memory and so their trial performance.

Some enhancers might improve memory performance among the worst performers but reduce it among the top performers, as was the case with injections of physiostigmine in healthy volunteers (Kukolja, Thiel, & Fink, 2009). The reason might be that there is an optimal level of activity in the relevant brain systems, and performance decreases above and below this level. This can be compared to the Yerkes-Dodson law, which states that task performance first improves and then deteriorates with increasing arousal for complex tasks (Diamond, Campbell, Park, Halonen, & Zoladz, 2007). Enhancer effects might, for example, be larger among older jurors, since they may be suffering from neuromodulatory deficits; but the same enhancers might have detrimental side effects on younger jurors who have closer to optimal levels of neuromodulators. Each biomedical enhancer must be tested separately and carefully for its costs as well as benefits to cognitive capacity, and these trade-offs can be different for different tasks.

Memory is also often state-dependent, that is, information that has been learned in one context is more available for recall in that context than in others. This also extends to caffeine: A study found that word recall was improved if participants were given the same beverage (placebo or one containing caffeine) during memory encoding and testing. However, it did not affect the metamemory (the certainty of recognition judgments; Kelemen & Creeley, 2003). Given that deliberations occur outside the courtroom, memory state dependence may play a role, and this effect might be increased by differences in caffeine availability.

Substance dependence may be a problem for users of cognition-enhancing substances who take them regularly: Interruptions in their use due to jury service may lead to cognitive impairments that reduce their ability as jurors. Nicotine abstinence is commonly found to impair memory, likely a factor among jurors unable to smoke except at breaks. One study found that while nicotine gum can improve smokers' performance in basic cognition, it does not eliminate the detrimental effects of abstinence on memory and metacognition (Kelemen & Fulton, 2008).

The possible roles of cognition-enhancing drugs in a jury might hence be to increase the ability to attend to the proceedings, reduce distractions, improve memory, and possibly boost perception and reasoning. In particular, enhancement of long-term memory encoding appears well supported by the findings of cognitive science: Memory traces laid down under the influence of enhancer drugs become easier to retrieve. The evidence for retrieval enhancers is weaker: It might be that it matters more for jurors' memory to be enhanced during the presentation of the evidence so that they can consider it later than for it to be enhanced during deliberation.

However, as discussed above, the use of enhancement drugs does not automatically produce improved performance. Even a substance taken with the intention to improve trial performance in one respect might be detrimental in other respects.

ETHICS OF COGNITIVE ENHANCEMENT IN COURT

Comparing Notes

Should cognitive enhancers be allowed, made readily available, provided for free, encouraged, or required for jurors or other participants in the legal process? These moral and legal issues can be illuminated by comparing biomedical enhancers with note taking. As we have said, note taking is allowed in most but not all jurisdictions. Where note taking is not allowed, various objections are raised, though not based on empirical research (Penrod & Heuer, 1997). Only some of these objections apply to the use of cognitive enhancers:

- Note taking is alleged to distract jurors.
  - No distraction occurs with the use of biomedical cognitive enhancers.
- Note taking is assumed to consume too much trial time.
  - No trial time is taken by biomedical cognitive enhancers.

- Jurors' notes are often not accurate records of the trial.
  - Enhanced memories might be more accurate than nonenhanced memories, but accuracy is not guaranteed by any method.
- Jurors' notes might favor one side or the other. For example, notes tend to trail off, so the side that goes first might get an unfair advantage if notes are allowed.
  - Biomedical cognitive enhancers give no such advantage to the side that starts, and might even reduce an unfair disadvantage to the side that goes last by counteracting detrimental effects of exhaustion, impatience, and boredom.
- Note takers might have undue influence over non–note takers.
  - Biomedically enhanced jurors might become overconfident, and jurors who are not biomedically enhanced might become overdeferential.

This brief comparison suggests that biomedical cognitive enhancers are no more questionable than note taking, unless they lead to excessive confidence by users and/or excessive deference by nonusers. Greater confidence of those who use biomedical cognitive enhancers might be justified by their greater cognitive abilities, but they might become even more confident than is warranted. In any case, these dangers should be taken seriously and tested empirically before policy decisions are made.

Since note taking is allowed, a principle of equal treatment and consistency suggests that at the very least, cognitive enhancers should be allowed. Whether they should be encouraged or even required must depend on the results of properly conducted "ecological experiments" of their effects on trial performance.

Enhancement-Induced Bias

There would be a strong reason to avoid the use of biomedical cognitive enhancers in courts if they biased judgment in some unfair way. Drugs can produce effects that are not strictly memory failures yet influence what is remembered and how deliberation is conducted.

Drugs can, for example, influence how easily jurors are swayed by persuasive communication. Caffeine appears to facilitate persuasion (Martin, Laing, Martin, & Mitchell, 2005; Mintz & Mills, 1971). In a double-blind test, moderate amounts of caffeine (3.5 mg/kg) led to greater agreement with a counterattitudinal message. The effect may be mediated by the increased arousal, attention, and information processing due to the drug, which facilitates systematic thinking about the message and hence being convinced by it. More persuasive arguments showed a stronger effect in the caffeine condition than in the noncaffeine condition, while less persuasive arguments had a similarly low effect (Martin et al., 2005). Contrary to common belief, alcohol appears to have the opposite effect (Bostrom & White, 1979). It is not clear, however, whether these effects carry over to conditions of lengthy cross-examination and opposing arguments, as in real trials.

The hormone oxytocin is often described as being a *pro-social* hormone that induces higher levels of trust and cooperation, and it is sometimes used as a putative cognition enhancer. However, one study found that it also strengthened in-group favoritism and out-group derogation in an ethnocentric manner (de Dreu, Greer, van Kleef, Shalvi, & Handgraaf, 2011). While the true interpretation of the study may be more complex (Chen, Kumsta, & Heinrichs, 2011), it is not implausible that oxytocin changes social cognition in ways that affect social biases. Oxytocin is released during breast feeding, but commonly employed drugs such as glucocorticoids for asthma and oral contraceptive pills increase its release.

Some drugs can also affect memory in ways that might bias trials. The ability to recall information is influenced by the emotional valence and strength of the information at the time of encoding. Drugs may affect this. Cahill and van Stegeren (2003) found a sex-related impairment of memory for emotional information by an adrenergic blockade. They gave test subjects the beta blocker propranolol and showed them slides of an emotionally arousing story, afterward asking central and peripheral questions. They found that in men the drug impaired memory for information central to the storyline but not peripheral details. Conversely, in women, the effect was opposite: They recalled more of the central storyline and fewer of the peripheral details. These effects on emotional memory might be relevant to trials: Trial testimony can have a strong emotional component, and recall of central and even peripheral details is relevant for making a correct decision.

Propranolol also affects facial expression recognition in healthy volunteers, slowing the reaction time to recognize sad facial expressions (Harmer, Perrett, Cowen, & Goodwin, 2001). It does not significantly reduce recognition accuracy, but even a slowing might be problematic in a situation such as watching witness testimony, where tiny details in a person's demeanor might reveal important aspects of trustworthiness and emotional state.

Propranolol likewise affects how some users deal with difficult memory tasks. In hypertensive patients given a memory task, treatment with propranolol gave them a more conservative bias—that is, an increased tendency to answer "no" when uncertain about whether they recognized an item (Halliday, Callaway, Perez-Stable, Coates, & Hauck, 1991). This effect appears similar to the conservative bias of depressed patients in a word-recognition task, while manics have the opposite bias (i.e., answering "yes" more often when uncertain; Corwin, Peselow, Feenan, Rotrosen, & Fieve, 1990). This effect might be mediated through noradrenergic mechanisms, making drugs that increase noradrenergic levels, such as amphetamine or atomoxetine, potential cognitive enhancers, have the positive biasing effect. Response bias effects may be relevant in juries, especially during deliberation. A conservative bias would generally favor the defense, whereas the opposite bias would favor the prosecution.

Drugs such as benzodiazepines, used among other things as treatment for anxiety and seizures (as well as misused recreationally), may impair memory in general (Stewart, 2005). While it is unlikely that jurors would believe their performance is actually enhanced by benzodiazepine medications, the drugs are commonly prescribed. Their amnestic effect can also include metamemory, the ability to judge how accurate one's memory is. In experiments, the drug lorazepam impaired the ability of test subjects to make accurate estimates of how well they recalled words or how well they were doing on a cognitive task (where their performance was impaired due to the drug; Mintzer & Griffiths, 2003, 2005).

In conclusion, some drugs, such as caffeine and propranolol, can bias judgment. Given that beta blockers are widely prescribed for cardiovascular disease and are used by many to relieve symptoms of stress (including reduction of stage fright among music performers; Slomka, 1992), it likely that some jurors are using these drugs and experience them as enhancing their abilities. These drugs can affect emotional memory and thereby trial outcomes, especially when trial testimony has a strong emotional component or when recall of central or peripheral details is relevant for making a correct decision. Benzodiazepines may undermine the ability of jurors to accurately recall evidence while making them overconfident about their faulty memories. These drugs may be used for valid medical or lifestyle reasons, but their potential biasing effects make them problematic in trials.

Comparison to Other Biases

It is unlikely, however, that the use of cognition-affecting drugs would result in a mistrial. Defendants have a right to a competent and fair jury, which has led to concerns about juror drunkenness. In the United States, 12 of the 562 judges surveyed (King, 1996) reported jurors under the influence of drugs or alcohol. Over time, the forms of juror drinking needed to grant a retrial have changed, from a strict view in the 1800s to an increasing view of it as a harmless form of misconduct, at least as long as it was the fault of the individual juror (King, 1996). After investigations into the excessive use of drugs by a jury, the Supreme Court ruled:

> The same policy considerations supported the Supreme Court's decision in *Tanner v. United States* upholding the trial judge's refusal to conduct an

investigation into broad allegations that a jury "was on one big party" and numerous claims alleging jurors' excessive use of alcohol and drugs. The Court rejected the defendant's contention that substance abuse constituted an improper external influence. According to the Court, "drugs or alcohol voluntarily ingested by a juror seems no more an 'outside influence' than a virus, poorly prepared food, or lack of sleep." As an internal matter, ingestion of drugs and alcohol was within the rule prohibiting juror testimony to upset a verdict. (Gershman, 2005, p. 340)

If drunkenness and excessive use of illegal drugs are not enough to justify a mistrial, then it seems unlikely that the use of caffeine or propranolol would be sufficient for a mistrial, even if such enhancers did have some biasing effect.

However, it should remain an open question whether such drugs should be banned. Allowing the use of such drugs does not serve justice well. Optimizing individual trial performance is but one goal. It is possible that exclusion of subperforming jurors would introduce bias in juror selection, having other, more negative effects on procedural justice. Nonetheless, there remains a prima facie case for attempting to maximize the performance, including recall, of every juror.

Jury deliberation *itself* can be a biasing factor. In many respects, juries may perform worse than individual jurors (Arkes & Mellers, 2002). Group deliberation tends to leave out facts known to few members and overemphasize facts known to many members (Sunstein, 2006). Forceful members can lead the discussion. Members with fixed opinions tend to sway less committed members (either because of persuasion or just exhaustion), possibly leading to a convergence to a verdict actually supported only by a few. Cognitive enhancement might help by reducing weak memories, allowing certain facts to be recalled by more members, but it will not correct the other deliberation biases. An enhancement or change of the jury deliberation process itself might be far more powerful than individual cognitive enhancement.

CONCLUSIONS

We have surveyed a range of beneficial and detrimental effects that external tools and biomedical substances can have on cognition. Some can adversely affect or bias deliberation, but their effects appear smaller than the biasing effects of jury selection and deliberation. Given the current low requirements for juror competence, it is not consistent with current legal practice to ban such substances. Similarly, given the low bar required for juror competence, coupled with rights to control what goes into one's body, courts could not legally require the consumption of even clearly safe cognition-enhancing drugs. Yet we must recognize that such practices do not appear to maximize trial performance or procedural justice.

Even if courts neither ban nor require biomedical cognitive enhancers in trials, other steps could be taken. An increasing number of agents that affect cognition are clearly entering use. Courts and jurors should be aware of the effects of these substances on cognition and how they may influence the trial. Better information about how to deliberate more effectively, including interventions and strategies, should be made available prior to the court process. Courts should also consider deployment of simple strategies, such as breaks and exercise, to improve juror performance.

As our range and knowledge of cognitive enhancers increases, some enhancers should be provided, as we now provide coffee, if they are safe and do not bias judgment. Substances like modafinil might well meet this criterion. In considering whether courts should provide cognitive enhancers to jurors, it is useful to ask what kind of jury one would want if one were innocent but accused of a crime. Innocent defendants want accurate verdicts, so they would prefer a jury with increased cognition, including improved attention and reasoning abilities as well as memory. If cognitive enhancers would not also introduce counterbalancing biases, then innocent defendants want and deserve jurors with the best cognition that enhancers can provide. They would also prefer a jury not using medications likely to bias their verdict. Given the stakes, we have a moral imperative to investigate ways to utilize these new technologies to improve cognitive performance in the courtroom. Innocent people's lives may well depend on them.

NOTE

1. In this chapter, we will not deal with the implications of inherent cognitive limitations of jurors due to low IQ or mental disorder.

REFERENCES

Alexander, J. K., Hillier, A., Smith, R. M., Tivarus, M. E., & Beversdorf, D. Q. (2007). Beta-adrenergic modulation of cognitive flexibility during stress. *Journal of Cognitive Neuroscience, 19*(3), 468–478.

Andrade, J. (2010). What does doodling do? *Applied Cognitive Psychology, 24*(1), 100–106.

Arkes, H. R., & Mellers, B. A. (2002). Can juries meet our expectations? *Law and Human Behavior, 26*, 625–639.

Bostrom, R., & White, N. (1979). Does drinking weaken resistance? *Journal of Communication, 29*(3), 73–80.

Bradley, M. M., Greenwald, M. K., Petry, M. C., & Lang, P. J. (1992). Remembering pictures—pleasure and arousal in memory. *Journal of Experimental Psychology:Learning, Memory and Cognition, 18*(2), 379–390.

Cahill, L., & van Stegeren, A. (2003). Sex-related impairment of memory for emotional events with beta-adrenergic blockade. *Neurobiology of Learning and Memory, 79*(1), 81–88.

Chen, F. S., Kumsta, R., & Heinrichs, M. (2011). Oxytocin and intergroup relations: Goodwill is not a fixed pie. *Proceedings of the National Academy of Sciences of the United States of America, 108*(13), E45.

Clark, A., & Chalmers, D. (1998). The extended mind (active externalism). *Analysis, 58*(1), 7–19.

Corwin, J., Peselow, E., Feenan, K., Rotrosen, J., & Fieve, R. (1990). Disorders of decision in affective disease: An effect of beta-adrenergic dysfunction? *Biological Psychiatry, 27*(8), 813–833.

de Dreu, C. K., Greer, L. L., van Kleef, G. A., Shalvi, S., & Handgraaf, M. J. (2011). Oxytocin promotes human ethnocentrism. *Proceedings of the National Academy of Sciences of the United States of America, 108*(4), 1262–1266.

Diamond, D. M., Campbell, A. M., Park, C. R., Halonen, J., & Zoladz, P. R. (2007). The temporal dynamics model of emotional memory processing: A synthesis on the neurobiological basis of stress-induced amnesia, flashbulb and traumatic memories, and the Yerkes-Dodson law. *Neural Plasticity, 2007*, 1–33.

Dolcos, F., Cabeza, R., & LaBar, K. S. (2005). Remembering one year later: Role of the amygdala and the medial temporal lobe memory system in retrieving emotional memories. *Proceedings of the National Academy of Sciences of the United States of America, 102*(7), 2626–2631.

Dror, I. E., & Harnad, S. (2009). Offloading cognition onto cognitive technology. In I. E. Dror & S. Harnad (Eds.), *Distributed cognition* (pp. 1–23). Amsterdam: John Benjamins.

Elwork, A., Sales, B. D., & Alfini, J. J. (1977). Juridic decisions: In ignorance of the law or in light of it. *Law and Human Behavior, 1*(2), 163–189.

Fosterlee, L., & Horowitz, I. A. (1994). Effects of notetaking on verdicts and evidence processing in a civil trial. *Law and Human Behavior, 18*(5), 567–578.

Fosterlee, L., & Horowitz, I. A. (1997). Enhancing juror competence in a complex trial. *Applied Cognitive Psychology, 11*(4), 305–319.

Gershman, B. L. (2005). *Contaminating the verdict: The problem of juror misconduct.* Pace Law Faculty Publications, Paper 123. http://digitalcommons.pace.edu/lawfaculty/123

Grunstein, R. R., & Banerjee, D. (2007). The case of "Judge Nodd" and other sleeping judges—media, society, and judicial sleepiness. *Sleep, 30*(5), 625–632.

Halliday, R., Callaway, E., Perez-Stable, E. J., Coates, T. J., & Hauck, W. W. (1991). Propranolol and response bias—an extension of findings eeported by Corwin et al. *Biological Psychiatry, 30*(7), 739–742.

Harmer, C. J., Perrett, D. I., Cowen, P. J., & Goodwin, G. M. (2001). Administration of the beta-adrenoceptor blocker propranolol impairs the processing of facial expressions of sadness. *Psychopharmacology, 154*(4), 383–389.

Hartley, L. R., Ungapen, S., Davie, I., & Spencer, D. (1983). The effect of beta-adrenergic blocking drugs on speakers' performance and memory. *British Journal of Psychiatry, 142*, 512–517.

Heuer, L., & Penrod, S. (1988). Increasing jurors' participation in trials—a field experiment with jury notetaking and question asking. *Law and Human Behavior, 12*(3), 231–261.

Heuer, L., & Penrod, S. (1989). Instructing jurors—a field experiment with written and preliminary instructions. *Law and Human Behavior, 13*(4), 403–430.

Horowitz, I. A., & Bordens, K. S. (2002). The effects of jury size, evidence complexity, and note taking on jury process and performance in a civil trial. *Journal of Applied Psychology, 87*(1), 121–130.

Horowitz, I., & Forsterlee, L. (2001). The effects of note-taking and trial transcript access on mock jury decisions in a complex civil trial. *Law and Human Behavior, 25*(4), 373–391.

Huck, N. O., McBride, S. A., Kendall, A. P., Grugle, N. L., & Killgore, W. D. (2008). The effects of modafinil, caffeine, and dextroamphetamine on judgments of simple versus complex emotional expressions following sleep deprivation. *International Journal of Neuroscience, 118*(4), 487–502.

Hwang, M. I., & Lin, J. W. (1999). Information dimension, information overload and decision quality. *Journal of Information Science, 25*(3), 213–218.

Johnson, M. T. (1993). Memory phenomena in the law. *Applied Cognitive Psychology, 7*(7), 603–618.

Kassin, S. M., & Wrightsman, L. S. (1979). Requirements of proof—timing of judicial instruction and mock juror verdicts. *Journal of Personality and Social Psychology, 37*(10), 1877–1887.

Kelemen, W. L., & Creeley, C. E. (2003). State-dependent memory effects using caffeine and placebo do not extend to metamemory. *The Journal of General Psychology, 130*(1), 70–86.

Kelemen, W., & Fulton, E. K. (2008). Cigarette abstinence impairs memory and metacognition despite administration of 2 mg nicotine gum. *Experimental and Clinical Psychopharmacology, 16*(6), 521–531.

Killgore, W. D., Kahn-Greene, E. T., Grugle, N. L., Killgore, D. B., & Balkin, T. J. (2009). Sustaining executive functions during sleep deprivation: A comparison of caffeine, dextroamphetamine, and modafinil. *Sleep, 32*(2), 205–216.

Killgore, W. D., McBride, S. A., Killgore, D. B., & Balkin, T. J. (2006). The effects of caffeine, dextroamphetamine, and modafinil on humor appreciation during sleep deprivation. *Sleep, 29*(6), 841–847.

King, N. J. (1996). Juror delinquency in criminal trials in America, 1796–1996. *Michigan Law Review, 94*(8), 2673–2751.

Knecht, S., Breienstein, C., Bushuven, S., Wailke, S., Kamping, S., Flöel, A., et al. (2004). Levodopa: Faster and better word learning in normal humans. *Annals of Neurology, 56*(1), 20–26.

Kukolja, J., Thiel, C. M., & Fink, G. R. (2009). Cholinergic stimulation enhances neural activity associated with encoding but reduces neural activity associated with retrieval in humans. *Journal of Neuroscience, 29*(25), 8119–8128.

Lam, S., Chiu, C., Lau, I., Chan, W., & Yim, P. (2006). Managing intergroup attitudes among Hong Kong adolescents: The effects of social category inclusiveness and time pressure. *Asian Journal of Social Psychology, 9*(1), 1–11.

Martin, P. Y., Laing, J., Martin, R., & Mitchell, M. (2005). Caffeine, cognition, and persuasion: Evidence for caffeine increasing the systematic processing of persuasive messages. *Journal of Applied Social Psychology, 35*(1), 160–182.

Mintz, P. M., & Mills, J. (1971). Effects of arousal and information about its source upon attitude change. *Journal of Experimental Social Psychology, 7*(6), 561–570.

Mintzer, M. Z., & Griffiths, R. R. (2003). Lorazepam and scopolamine: A single-dose comparison of effects on human memory and attentional processes. *Experimental and Clinical Psychopharmacology, 11*(1), 56–72.

Mintzer, M. Z., & Griffiths, R. R. (2005). Drugs, memory, and metamemory: A dose-effect study with lorazepam and scopolamine. *Experimental and Clinical Psychopharmacology, 13*(4), 336–347.

Payne, J. W. (1976). Task complexity and contingent processing in decision-making—information search and protocol analysis. *Organizational Behavior and Human Performance, 16*(2), 366–387.

PBS online. (2011). *Frontline: what Jennifer saw.* Retrieved August 30, 2011, from http://www.pbs.org/wgbh/pages/frontline/shows/dna/interviews/thompson.html

Penrod, S. D., & Heuer, L. (1997). Tweaking commonsense—assessing aids to jury decision making. *Psychology, Public Policy, and Law, 3*(2–3), 259–284.

Pritchard, M. E., & Keenan, J. M. (1999). Memory monitoring in mock jurors. *Journal of Experimental Psychology: Applied, 5*(2), 152–168.

Riby, L. M., McLaughlin, J., Riby, D. M., & Graham, C. (2008). Lifestyle, glucose regulation and the cognitive effects of glucose load in middle-aged adults. *British Journal of Nutrition, 100*(5), 1128–1134.

Rosenhan, D. L., Eisner, S. L., & Robinson, R. J. (1994). Notetaking can aid juror recall. *Law and Human Behavior, 18*(1), 53–61.

Sahakian, B., & Morein-Zamir, S. (2007). Professor's little helper. *Nature, 450*(7173), 1157–1159.

Slomka, J. (1992). Playing with propranolol. *Hastings Center Report, 22*(4), 13–17.

Stewart, S. A. (2005). The effects of benzodiazepines on cognition. *Journal of Clinical Psychiatry, 66,* 9–13.

Sunstein, C. R. (2006). *Infotopia: How many minds produce knowledge.* Oxford: Oxford University Press.

Tamborini, R., Huang, R.-H., Mastro, D., & Nabashi-Nakahara, R. (2007). The influence of race, heuristics, and information load on judgments of guilt and innocence. *Communication Studies, 58*(4), 341–358.

The National Center for State Courts. (2002). *Through the eyes of the juror: A manual for addressing juror stress.* Williamsburg, VA: Author.

Tomporowski, P. D. (2003). Effects of acute bouts of exercise on cognition. *Acta Psychologica, 112,* 297–324.

United States v. White. 589 F.2d 1283 1289 (5th Circuit, 1979).

Wesenstein, N. J., Killgore, W. D., & Balkin, T. J. (2005). Performance and alertness effects of caffeine, dextroamphetamine, and modafinil during sleep deprivation. *Journal of Sleep Research, 14*(3), 255–266.

PART FOUR

Neuroimaging Memories

10

Neuroimaging of True, False, and Imaginary Memories

Findings and Implications

DANIEL L. SCHACTER, JON CHAMBERLAIN,
BRENDAN GAESSER, AND KATHY D. GERLACH

In his 2004 book *Against All Enemies*, Richard A. Clarke—former counterterrorism chief in the Clinton and Bush administrations—shared his recollections of how administration officials responded to the events of September 11, 2001 (Clarke, 2004). He recalled, for example, that the Secret Service asked for fighter escorts to protect Air Force One, and that his national security colleague Franklin Miller urged Secretary of Defense Donald Rumsfeld to take a helicopter out of the Pentagon. Other administration officials challenged these recollections. Franklin Miller recollected that he himself had asked Condoleezza Rice about whether to call up fighter escorts, and further recalled that she told him to go ahead with their deployment. Miller also stated that he never spoke with Secretary Rumsfeld on September 11. Miller further opined that while Clarke's recollections would "make a great movie," they did not reflect the reality of what happened that day (Schacter, 2004).

Conflicting recollections of the same event are not uncommon in the courtroom. Consider, for example, the contrasting memories that emerged in testimony concerning the July 2005 death of Jean Charles de Menezes, an innocent man who was fatally shot by London police in a subway station. De Menezes was misidentified by police as one of several men who had carried out a failed bombing attempt the previous day:

> Firearms officers recalled running on to the Underground platform at Stockwell and challenging de Menezes by shouting "Armed Police," before shooting him seven times in the head. But 17 civilian witnesses could not remember such a thing being said. The police said that the electrician had stood up and walked "aggressively" towards them, but some witnesses do not remember him getting up from his seat. Everyone recalled a slightly different sequence of events, even when it came to such basic facts as the number of bullets fired or the clothes de Menezes was wearing. (O'Connell, 2008).

Such conflicting recollections could reflect willful distortion on the part of some or all parties, but they are more likely attributable to well-known imperfections of memory that render people vulnerable to various kinds of forgetting and distortion (Schacter, 2001, 2004; Schacter, Guerin, & St. Jacques, 2011). Memory errors are also highly relevant to eyewitness testimony: It is well known that eyewitnesses are prone to memory distortion, sometimes reporting highly confident but inaccurate memories that can have a large influence in the courtroom (e.g., Cutler & Penrod, 1995; Loftus, 1979; Semmler & Brewer, 2010; Wells & Olson, 2003). Indeed, faulty eyewitness testimony was a key factor in approximately 75% of the first 100 individuals who were exonerated by DNA evidence after being convicted of crimes they did not commit (Scheck, Neufeld, & Dwyer, 2000; Wells, Small, Penrod, Malpass, Fulero, & Brimacombe, 1998). These observations raise a question of great practical and theoretical interest: Is there any way to determine definitively whose recollection is accurate and whose is wrong?

The question of whether it is possible to distinguish between true and false memories has long been of interest to psychologists; it achieved special prominence and urgency during the 1990s in relation to the heated controversy concerning the accuracy of recovered memories of childhood sexual abuse (cf. Jacobs & Nadel, 1998; Loftus, 1993; Loftus & Davis 2006; McNally & Geraerts, 2009; Pendergrast, 1995; Schacter, 1996). Many cases of recovered memories that ended up in the courtroom involved conflicting recollections between accusing individuals who claimed to have recalled long-repressed memories of childhood abuse and accused individuals who denied that the abuse ever occurred, thereby posing a difficult challenge for the legal system (Loftus & Ketcham, 1994).

Psychologists have focused on attempting to distinguish between true and false memories based on their qualitative characteristics, asking such questions as whether true memories are more vivid or detailed than false memories (for review, see Bernstein & Loftus, 2009). During the past 15 years, however, another approach to the issue has emerged that focuses on measuring brain activity. Researchers taking this approach have relied on functional neuroimaging techniques that can accurately localize changes in brain activity associated with various aspects of memory, such as positron emission tomography (PET) and functional magnetic resonance imaging (fMRI), in an attempt to pinpoint specific brain regions that may be differentially associated with true versus false memories. In this chapter, we discuss this research that has attempted to distinguish brain activity associated with true and false memories using PET and fMRI (for review of related research using event-related potentials [ERPs], an electrophysiological technique that measures changes in voltage topography on the scalp over time, see Schacter and Slotnick, 2004; here, we will only note briefly ERP studies relevant to our key themes).

Some strong claims have already been made for the viability of using data generated by neuroimaging techniques to distinguish truth from fiction in settings such as the courtroom. For example, the company No Lie MRI offers the following claim on its website (http://www.noliemri.com):

NEW TRUTH VERIFICATION TECHNOLOGY

No Lie MRI, Inc. provides unbiased methods for the detection of deception and other information stored in the brain.

The technology used by No Lie MRI represents the first and only direct measure of truth verification and lie detection in human history!

This claim appears to be primarily focused on distinguishing truthful testimony from intentional deception, which is a related though distinct problem from distinguishing between true and false memories: Lies are generated with an intent to deceive, whereas people believe that they are telling the truth when they report false memories. Nonetheless, the claim is a strong one. In light of such claims, and with increasing interest in the possibility of applying neuroimaging techniques to courtroom settings, we believe that it is important to critically assess the state of our knowledge concerning both brain-based lie detection (for reviews, see Abe, 2009; Greely & Illes, 2007; Spence & Kaylor-Hughes, 2008) and brain-based attempts to distinguish true and false memories. We focus on the latter task here.

The chapter consists of three main sections. In the first section, we will discuss attempts to use PET and fMRI to distinguish between true and false memories under controlled laboratory conditions. We will discuss primarily work conducted in our own laboratory, but we will also attempt to relate our findings to those from other labs. In the second section, we will discuss a recent and related line of work that compares the neural underpinnings of actual memories of past experiences with imaginary experiences of events that might occur in the future, again focusing on work from our lab but also relating this work to research from other labs. Finally, in the third and concluding section, we will consider limitations of the research we have discussed along with its possible implications for the courtroom.

Neuroimaging of True and False Memories

Neuroimaging studies have attempted to distinguish between true and false memories either by measuring brain activity at the time of retrieval or by measuring brain activity during encoding and asking whether any aspects of encoding-related brain activity predict whether subsequent memories are accurate or distorted. In legal contexts, the potential use of neuroimaging techniques to distinguish between true and false memories would appear to be restricted primarily, if not entirely, to the time of retrieval. Therefore, we limit our discussion to studies that have measured brain activity during retrieval (for encoding-based studies, see Aminoff, Schacter, & Bar, 2008; Dennis, Kim, & Cabeza, 2007; Garoff, Slotnick, & Schacter, 2005; Gonsalves & Paller, 2000; Gonsalves, Reber, Gitelman, Parrish, Mesulam, & Paller, 2004; Kensinger & Schacter, 2005a; Kim & Cabeza, 2007a; Okado & Stark, 2005).

Most neuroimaging attempts to distinguish between true and false memories have been conducted in the context of what has been termed the *sensory reactivation hypothesis*: the idea that true memories are accompanied by retrieval of more sensory/perceptual details than false memories, which in turn reflect the reactivation of sensory/perceptual encoding processes that were engaged during the establishment of true but not false memories (for further discussion, see Schacter, Norman, & Koutstaal, 1998; Schacter & Slotnick, 2004). The hypothesis originated from behavioral studies that indeed revealed evidence for greater retrieval of sensory/perceptual details during true rather than false memory retrieval (e.g., Johnson, Foley, Suengas, & Raye 1988; Marche, Brainerd, & Reyna, 2010; Mather, Henkel, & Johnson 1997; Norman & Schacter, 1997; Schooler, Gerhard, & Loftus, 1986). This hypothesis naturally leads to the question of whether neural activity accompanying true recognition, compared with false recognition, shows signs of sensory reactivation.

Evidence for Sensory Reactivation in PET and fMRI Studies

Our laboratory initiated neuroimaging investigations of the relation between true and false memories in the mid-1990s. A necessary condition for conducting such investigations is the availability of an experimental paradigm that can induce robust, subjectively compelling false memories that participants believe to be true memories of past experience. Further, it is crucial in neuroimaging studies to obtain sufficient numbers of observations in order to generate a reliable signal that can be distinguished statistically from noise. Therefore, a suitable experimental paradigm must yield a large enough number of false memories to permit a meaningful statistical analysis.

We therefore turned to a then recently described paradigm by Roediger and McDermott (1995) that produces extremely high levels of a phenomenon known as *false recognition*, in which subjects incorrectly claim that a novel item has been encountered earlier in an experiment. False recognition is typically inferred when participants make "old" responses to novel items that are conceptually or perceptually related to previously studied items—that is, when the level of false alarms to related novel items is higher than the "baseline" level of false alarms to unrelated novel items. To produce robust false recognition, Roediger and McDermott modified a procedure developed earlier by Deese (1959) in which subjects hear lists of associated words (e.g., *candy, sour, sugar, bitter, good, taste, tooth*) that all converge on a nonpresented "theme word" or false target (e.g., *sweet*). Roediger and McDermott reported extremely high levels of false recognition (e.g., 80%) to the theme words across a variety of word associate lists. The level of false recognition responses to the false target was indistinguishable from the hit rate to studied items, and the false recognition responses were accompanied by very high confidence, comparable to the confidence associated with true recognition responses. These initial observations were confirmed and extended to numerous subsequent studies using the Deese-Roediger-McDermott (DRM) paradigm, which have delineated various cognitive properties of this potent false recognition effect (for a review, see Gallo, 2006, 2010).

In our first neuroimaging study of true and false recognition, PET scans were carried out while subjects performed a recognition test following study of various DRM associate lists (Schacter et al., 1996). After auditory presentation of lists containing 20 words that were associates of a nonpresented theme word, subjects were scanned during separate test blocks in which they responded separately to true targets (words that had been studied previously), false targets (nonstudied semantic associates of previously studied items), or target controls (nonpresented words that were unrelated to previously studied words). On balance, brain activity during true and false recognition was strikingly similar: Compared with a common baseline condition, both true and false recognition were associated with blood flow increases in various regions that prior studies had shown are commonly activated by memory retrieval tasks, including dorsolateral/anterior prefrontal, medial parietal, and medial temporal regions.

Nonetheless, there was also evidence that true and false recognition could be distinguished: Direct comparisons indicated greater activation during true than false recognition in a left temporoparietal region previously associated with auditory processing and memory. We interpreted this latter finding in light of the aforementioned sensory reactivation hypothesis: Because subjects had heard true targets—but not false targets—during the auditory study phase of the experiment, we reasoned that selective left temporoparietal activation for true recognition might be an auditory sensory signature that reflects memory for auditory/phonological aspects of previously studied words.

One methodological limitation of this early study concerns the fact that in PET imaging experiments, stimuli from different conditions are presented in separate blocks (e.g., all true targets are presented in one block, all false targets are presented in a separate block, and so forth), which is a departure from the typical practice in purely behavioral experiments of intermixing items from different conditions. Soon after we completed the initial PET study, however, *event-related* fMRI methods became available, which allow intermixing of items from different conditions. Schacter, Buckner, Koutstaal, Dale, and Rosen (1997) used event-related fMRI to investigate true and false recognition in a DRM paradigm in which true and false targets were randomly intermixed during the recognition test. While the results from this study replicated the PET findings showing that many of the same patterns of brain activity are observed during both true and false recognition, no regions showed greater activation for true than false recognition, including the left temporoparietal region observed by Schacter et al. (1996; for discussion of possible reason why blocked and event-related designs yielded different results, see Johnson, Nolde, Mather, Kounios, Schacter, & Curran, 1997; Schacter et al., 1997).

Our initial neuroimaging studies thus yielded inconclusive evidence regarding the question of whether brain regions involved in sensory/perceptual processing are differentially active during true and false recognition. In a subsequent study that also used event-related fMRI, our lab addressed the issue in a collaborative study with Roberto Cabeza's lab (Cabeza, Rao, Wagner, Mayer, & Schacter, 2001). The logic of this study emerged from previous findings that differences between true and false recognition can be increased when perceptual processing of target materials is increased during encoding (e.g., Schacter, Israel, & Racine, 1999), thereby providing a basis for subjects to differentiate true from false targets during a memory test. If increased perceptual encoding is reflected in patterns of brain activity during retrieval, then true-false differences in brain activity should show a greater contrast.

To produce increased perceptual encoding, prior to scanning Cabeza et al. (2001) instructed subjects both to remember lists of semantically associated words and, critically, to try also to remember the source (a man or a woman) that presented the word lists; during encoding, subjects viewed videotapes in which a male source spoke half of the words and a female source spoke the other half. The key hypothesis was that on the recognition test, previously studied words—but not semantically associated false targets—would activate regions initially involved in encoding perceptual information related to the sources. Consistent with this general idea, the experiment revealed that the parahippocampal gyrus, a region within the medial temporal lobe that has been linked with processing of contextual information (e.g., Bar & Aminoff, 2003; Bar, Aminoff, & Schacter, 2008), showed greater activation during true than false recognition, perhaps reflecting a lingering effect of contextual encoding processes that occurred for true but not false targets. Further, there was also greater activity during true as opposed to false recognition in the left parietal cortex (Brodmann's area [BA] 39/40), a region previously implicated in auditory word processing. These data are thus consistent with the early data reported by Schacter et al. (1996) suggesting reactivation of auditory word processing during true but not false recognition.

All of the previous studies used familiar words as target stimuli. In a subsequent study, Slotnick and Schacter (2004) used novel shapes as target stimuli in an attempt to engage more robustly visual processing regions and thereby provide a stronger test of the idea that brain activity associated with the recovery of sensory/perceptual information distinguishes true versus false recognition. All shapes presented in the study list were generated from, and physically related to, prototype shapes that were not presented during encoding. Later, subjects made old/new recognition decisions about previously studied shapes, nonstudied related shapes, and nonstudied unrelated shapes. Previous behavioral studies using such prototype paradigms have shown high levels of false recognition to nonstudied prototype shapes that are perceptually related to previously studied shapes (e.g., Koutstaal, Schacter, Verfaellie, Brenner, & Jackson, 1999; see also Posner & Keele, 1968). Further, neuroimaging studies of true recognition for pictures had already revealed reactivation during retrieval of some of the same visual processing regions that were active during encoding (Wheeler, Petersen, & Buckner, 2000), and similar sensory reactivation effects were observed during memory for sounds (Nyberg, Habib, McIntosh, & Tulving, 2000; Wheeler et al., 2000). Based on these observations and the sensory reactivation hypothesis discussed earlier, Slotnick and Schacter (2004) hypothesized that true recognition of previously studied shapes, as compared to false recognition of nonstudied related shapes, would be accompanied by a sensory signature involving increased activation of visual processing regions.

Behavioral data revealed that participants made significantly more old responses to studied shapes than to related nonstudied shapes (i.e., prototypes); they also made significantly more old responses to related nonstudied shapes than to unrelated nonstudied shapes, confirming the presence of a false recognition effect. Consistent with the sensory reactivation hypothesis, analysis of the fMRI data revealed significantly greater activity during true than false recognition in regions within primary visual cortex (e.g., BA 17, 18) that are concerned with processing such features of target stimuli as orientation and color. By contrast, higher-order visual areas in occipitotemporal cortex (e.g., BA 19, 37) showed comparable levels of activity during true and false recognition.

Slotnick and Schacter (2004) also attempted to delineate whether the observed true-false sensory reactivation effects were accompanied by conscious recollection of sensory features of studied shapes, since it is possible that sensory reactivation effects during true recognition reflect nonconscious or implicit priming (Schacter, 1987; Tulving & Schacter, 1990) rather than conscious recollection. Slotnick and Schacter attempted to determine whether activity in visual processing regions is specifically related to conscious memory, which would be indicated by greater activity during old than new responses to studied items. If, however, brain activity is similar during old and new responses to studied items, then such activity is likely associated with a nonconscious or implicit form of memory. To address the matter, Slotnick and Schacter compared activation associated with old responses to studied shapes (old-hits) and new responses to studied shapes (old-misses). This analysis revealed that both old-hits and old-misses were similarly associated with activity in early visual processing regions (BA 17, BA 18), suggesting that such activity reflects nonconscious memory. By contrast, the old-hits greater than old-misses contrast, which is assumed to index conscious memory, revealed activity in late visual processing regions (BA 19, BA 37), likely reflecting a form of conscious memory. Thus, activity in early visual processing areas may reflect specific memory for a particular shape, regardless of participants' conscious judgments of whether or not they had seen the item.

This conclusion is consistent with the possibility noted earlier that true and false recognition may be distinguished by nonconscious memory, such as perceptual priming effects that occur only for studied items. Although priming effects in neuroimaging studies are most commonly expressed by *reduced* activity in a particular region during a primed condition compared with an unprimed condition (for reviews, see Henson, 2003; Schacter & Buckner, 1998; Schacter, Wig, & Stevens, 2007; Wiggs & Martin, 1998), this conclusion is based primarily on studies in which familiar words or objects are used as experimental stimuli. In studies that have used unfamiliar materials more akin to the Slotnick and Schacter abstract shapes, such as faces (Henson, Shallice, & Dolan, 2000) or drawings of structurally possible and impossible objects (Schacter, Reiman, et al., 1995), priming-related increases have been observed.

To evaluate the priming hypothesis more directly, Slotnick and Schacter (2006) performed an additional experiment using the identical abstract shape stimuli as in the Slotnick and Schacter (2004) study. However, instead of testing memory with an old-new recognition test, as in the aforementioned experiment, Slotnick and Schacter (2006) assessed memory using a priming procedure. During the study phase, participants made line orientation judgments about each shape: They judged whether the lines within each shape were oriented upward or downward. Later, during the test phase, subjects made the same judgments about previously presented shapes, physically related shapes that had not been presented earlier, and novel, unrelated shapes. The key finding was that during the test phase, there was increased activity for old shapes compared with related new shapes in early visual areas (BA 17, 18) but not in late visual areas (BA 19, 37). These findings are consistent with the hypothesis that increased activity in early visual regions during true recognition compared with false recognition reflects a form of priming or nonconscious memory, at least in the visual shape paradigm used by Slotnick and Schacter.

Further evidence bearing on the sensory reactivation hypothesis comes from a study by Kensinger and Schacter (2006; see also Kensinger & Schacter, 2005a, 2005b) that used fMRI to examine brain activity during accurate and inaccurate retrieval of perceived and imagined items. Adapting a paradigm initially developed by Gonsalves and Paller (2000), prior to scanning participants viewed a series of concrete nouns and formed mental images of the named objects. A picture of the object followed half of the names. During the subsequent scan, participants saw the object names and tried to remember whether a corresponding picture had been studied. Kensinger and Schacter found that activity in two regions was associated with accurate assignment of an item to prior pictorial presentation compared with all other conditions: precuneus (BA 7) and left lateral parietal lobe (BA 7/40). Based on previous evidence, Kensinger and Schacter suggested that the precuneus activation could reflect retrieval of sensory details about the perceived picture, whereas the left lateral parietal lobe activation might reflect retrieval of contextual information.

In summary, the neuroimaging studies from our laboratory reviewed so far have provided a good deal of support for the sensory reactivation hypothesis, although the exact regions that have distinguished true from false recognition have varied from study to study. Our data are generally consistent with results reported in other laboratories. For example, using a variant of the DRM paradigm discussed earlier, Abe and colleagues (2008) reported greater activity during true than false recognition in the left temporoparietal regions initially reported by Schacter et al. (1996) and Cabeza et al. (2001). Abe and colleagues interpreted these findings as support for an auditory reactivation effect. In a study by Okado and Stark (2003), subjects studied verbal labels of common objects followed either by a picture of the object or instructions to imagine the object. They were subsequently given a "lie test" in which they were asked to indicate whether or not they had previously seen an actual picture of the object, and were strongly encouraged to tell a lie that they had seen a picture even when they had not. Subjects were then scanned during a standard memory test in which they indicated whether they had actually seen a picture of an object during the study phase. Results revealed that a number of regions showed greater activity during true than false recognition, including bilateral occipital cortices and right parahippocampal gyrus, which Okado and Stark suggested reflects greater recovery of sensory/perceptual information for true versus false memories. The findings concerning parahippocampal gyrus replicate and extend those reported previously by Cabeza et al. (2001).

Although our discussion of brain activity that distinguishes true from false recognition has emphasized the sensory reactivation hypothesis (for evidence from ERP studies that supports the sensory reactivation hypothesis, see Curran, Schacter, Johnson, & Spinks, 2001; Fabiani, Stadler, & Wessels, 2000; Nessler & Mecklinger, 2003; Nessler, Mecklinger, & Penney, 2001; Walla, Endl, Lindinger, Deecke, & Lang, 2000), not all neuroimaging studies of true versus false recognition have focused on this hypothesis. For example, using the DRM paradigm, Kim and Cabeza (2007b) reported that subjective confidence ratings associated with true recognition depend on recollective processes associated with the medial temporal lobe; by contrast, subjective confidence ratings associated with false recognition seem to reflect a familiarity-based process associated with activity in frontoparietal regions.

In a more recent study conducted in our laboratory, Giovanello, Kensinger, Wong, and Schacter (2010) used fMRI to examine brain activity during retrieval of true and false memories in a *memory conjunction error* paradigm. Memory conjunction errors occur when individuals falsely claim to recognize an item because components of the item were contained in previously presented items. For example, after studying compound words such as *blackmail, jailbird,* and *shoestring,* participants frequently claim to recognize *conjunction lures* such as *blackbird* in which both parts of the item had been studied previously, and less frequently claim to recognize *feature lures* such as *drawstring* in which one part is studied and one part is novel (e.g., Jones & Jacoby, 2005; Reinitz, Lammers, & Cochran, 1992). Using fMRI to compare brain activity in young and old adults, Giovanello et al. (2010) reported that activity in right anterior hippocampus distinguished between true recognition, on the one hand, and false alarms to conjunction and feature lures, on the other, in young but not old adults, likely reflecting a hippocampal contribution to binding and retrieval of components of target items. The older group, by contrast, showed increased activity in right inferior and middle prefrontal cortex during true versus false recognition, extending previous observations of a shift in processing from hippocampal to frontal mechanisms that has been observed in other fMRI studies of aging memory (e.g., Grady, McIntosh, & Craik, 2005; Gutchess, et al.,2005).

Is There a Neural Signature of False Memory Retrieval?

In the studies discussed thus far, we have considered brain activity that is preferentially associated with true memory retrieval, focusing in particular on neural evidence that bears on the sensory reactivation hypothesis. However, it is also important to ask whether there is neural activity that is preferentially associated with false memory retrieval. One point worth noting is that not all forms of false recognition depend on the same neural processes. Functional MRI evidence in support of this point comes from a study by Garoff-Eaton, Slotnick, and Schacter (2006) that used a variant of the shape prototype paradigm used previously by Slotnick and Schacter (2004). False recognition of new shapes that were perceptually related to previously studied items, like true recognition of the studied shapes, engaged prefrontal, parietal, and medial temporal regions, whereas false recognition of new shapes that were not perceptually related to previously studied shapes engaged distinct temporal regions associated with language processing (perhaps reflecting verbal coding strategies that gave rise to unrelated false recognition).

Although activity in a variety of brain regions has been associated with false memory retrieval in individual studies, attention has focused on regions within the prefrontal cortex that have been linked with retrieval monitoring—that is, evaluating the products of retrieval with respect to task goals. As noted earlier, it is well established that a variety of prefrontal regions show increased activation during standard recognition memory tests. Several of the previously reviewed PET and fMRI studies of false recognition using the DRM and related paradigms have also reported evidence for activation of several prefrontal regions during false recognition and, in some cases, greater activation during false than true recognition. Schacter et al. (1996) reported that a region in the dorsolateral/anterior prefrontal cortex, which has been associated with retrieval monitoring (e.g., Dobbins, Foley, Schacter, & Wagner, 2002; Dobbins, Rice, Wagner, & Schacter, 2003; Rugg, Fletcher, Frith, Frackowiak, & Dolan, 1996), showed greater activity during false than true recognition, perhaps reflecting the need for evaluation or monitoring of the strong sense of familiarity produced by false targets. Consistent with this suggestion, analyses of event-related time courses indicated a delayed onset for anterior prefrontal activity during both true and false recognition compared with other brain regions. Although various interpretations of this observation are possible (see Schacter et al., 1997), it is consistent with the idea that anterior prefrontal activity (especially on the right) reflects a late-occurring evaluation or monitoring of the products of retrieval. Cabeza et al. (2001) and Slotnick and Schacter (2004) provided additional evidence for greater activation of right prefrontal cortex during false than true recognition (see also Treyer, Buck, & Schnider, 2003; von Zerssen, Mecklinger, Opitz, & von Cramon, 2001; for converging evidence from ERP studies, see Curran et al., 2001, Fabiani et al., 2000, and Goldmann et al., 2003; but see Düzel, Yonelinas, Mangun, Heinze, & Tulving, 1997, Nessler et al., 2001, and Nessler & Mecklinger, 2003, for contrasting results).

Although much attention has focused on the possibility that increased frontal lobe activity during false versus true recognition is associated with retrieval monitoring operations, researchers have also considered other factors. One idea is that activity in certain frontal lobe regions reflects the influence of conceptual or semantic processing that contributes to false recognition. For example, Garoff-Eaton, Kensinger, and Schacter (2007) compared conceptual false recognition—false alarms that result from semantic or associative similarities between studied and tested items—with perceptual false recognition—false alarms that result from physical similarities between studied and tested items. Garoff-Eaton et al. found that multiple regions within the prefrontal cortex (BAs 6, 8, 9, 44, 45, 46, 47) showed increased activity during conceptual false recognition compared with true recognition, but not during perceptual false recognition compared with true recognition. Garoff-Eaton et al. considered it unlikely that these findings are attributable to postretrieval monitoring, because such monitoring should be required during both conceptual and perceptual false recognition when subjects attempt to evaluate the accuracy of retrieved information. Instead, Garoff-Eaton et al. noted that regions within the frontal cortex (especially left inferior frontal cortex) show increased activity in a variety of conditions that involved conceptual processing, including semantic elaboration (Demb, Desmond, Wagner, Vaidya, Glover, & Gabrieli, 1995; Kirchhoff, Schapiro, & Buckner, 2005), word generation (Petersen, Fox, Posner, Mintun, & Raichle, 1988), recovery of meaning/semantic retrieval (Wagner, Paré-Blagoev, Clark, & Poldrack, 2001), and semantic (versus perceptual) relational memory (Prince, Daselaar, & Cabeza, 2005). It therefore seems reasonable to hypothesize that the increased activity in left inferior and perhaps other frontal regions during conceptual versus perceptual false recognition reflects the retrieval of conceptual information about the meaning or gist of what was studied, which drives the false recognition response. Paz-Alonso, Ghetti, Donohue, Goodman, and Bunge (2008) offered a similar interpretation of left inferior frontal responses in a study that examined false recognition using the DRM paradigm.

Additional relevant evidence comes from work by Dennis, Kim, and Cabeza (2007, 2008) concerning age differences in true and false recognition, using an adapted version of the DRM semantic associates paradigm in which they used fMRI to measure brain activity during encoding (Dennis et al., 2007) or retrieval (Dennis et al., 2008). Both studies provided evidence for age-related increases in left middle temporal gyrus during processing of false memories. In light of previous evidence linking the left middle temporal region with processing of semantic information (e.g., Wise & Price, 2006), Dennis et al. (2007, 2008) suggest that their findings may reflect increased reliance on semantic gist information in older adults, an idea that is consistent with other behavioral evidence documenting age-related increases in gist-based processing (e.g., Koutstaal & Schacter, 1997; Norman & Schacter, 1997; Tun, Wingfield, Rosen, & Blanchard, 1998; see Paz-Alonso et al., 2008, for discussion of related issues in children and adolescents).

NEUROIMAGING OF TRUE AND IMAGINARY MEMORIES

Memory researchers have long been interested in the relationship between imagination and memory distortion, focusing mainly on the ways in which imagining events can contribute to the development of false memories for those events (e.g., Garry, Manning, Loftus, & Sherman, 1996; Gonsalves & Paller, 2000; Johnson & Raye, 1981; Goff & Roediger, 1998; Kensinger & Schacter, 2006; Loftus, 2003). During the past several years, however, there has been increasing interest in how memory contributes to imagination, as reflected in a recent outpouring of studies concerning the role of memory in imagining or simulating possible future events, also referred to as *episodic future thought* (for reviews, see Buckner & Carroll, 2007; Schacter, Addis, & Buckner, 2007, 2008; Szpunar, 2010). While some of the issues considered in the emerging literature concerning these "imaginary memories" focus on the nature of prospective cognition and thus are not directly relevant to the current discussion, a number of neuroimaging studies reported recently have examined the extent to which neural activity associated with remembering the past can be distinguished from that associated with imagining the future, and those studies will constitute the focus of our discussion (for an analysis of how cognitive characteristics of episodic future thought can help to distinguish between true and false intentions, see Granhag & Knieps, 2011).

In the first study from our laboratory to examine the issue, Addis, Wong, and Schacter (2007) scanned participants while they were either remembering a past experience or imagining an event that might occur in the future. Addis et al. divided each of these tasks into two phases. In the initial *construction* phase, participants generated a remembered or imagined event in response to a cue (e.g., *dress*) and made a button press when they had an event in mind, which typically required about 7 or 8 seconds. In the immediately following *elaboration* phase, participants generated as much detail as possible about the remembered or imagined event. The most striking finding was that brain activity was highly similar during remembering the past and imagining the future. This overlap was most apparent during the elaboration phase, when participants focused on generating details about the remembered or imagined event. A network of brain regions that had previously been implicated in the retrieval of episodic memories (Maguire, 2001) showed common activation during both remembering and imagining, including the hippocampus, parahippocampal and retrosplenial cortices, medial prefrontal and frontopolar cortices, and lateral parietal lobe.

The common activation observed in the hippocampus, a structure long known to be critically involved in aspects of memory, was especially intriguing, possibly reflecting the retrieval, integration, or encoding of event details into the remembered or imagined representation, and complementing evidence reported by Hassabis, Kumaran, Vann, and Maguire (2007) that amnesic patients with hippocampal damage, who have great difficulty remembering past events, are also impaired when they are asked to imagine novel scenes (see also Andelman, Hoofien, Goldberg, Aizenstein, & Neufeld, 2010, Kwan, Carson, Addis, & Rosenbaum, 2010, and Race, Keane, & Verfaellie, 2011, for similar observations; but see Maguire, Vargha-Khadem, & Hassabis, 2010, and Squire et al., 2010, for evidence that not all hippocampal amnesics have problems imagining future experiences or novel scenes).

The construction phase was also associated with common activity during remembering and imagining. Critically important for the present discussion, however, this phase also revealed some neural differences. Most interestingly, the right hippocampus was engaged to a greater extent when participants imagined future events than when they remembered past events. Because the hippocampus has been implicated in relational processing (i.e., linking together previously unrelated items; Eichenbaum & Cohen, 2001), Addis et al. (2007) suggested that this finding might reflect the additional relational processing required when one must recombine disparate details into an imagined future event (for further discussion, see Schacter & Addis, 2007, 2009).

A related observation was that in all regions that did exhibit significant differences, imagined events were associated with greater activity than remembered events, a finding that was also reported in similar studies by Okuda et al. (2003) and Szpunar, Watson, and McDermott (2007). Addis et al. (2007) suggested that this pattern reflects the more intensive constructive processes required by imagining future events relative to retrieving past events. Even though both the remembering and imagining tasks involve retrieval of information from memory and engage common memory networks, only the imagining task requires that details from various past events are flexibly recombined into a novel future event and that this imagined event is plausible given one's intentions for the future. Accordingly, additional regions supporting these processes are recruited by the future event task (for additional relevant findings and discussion, see Martin, Schacter, Corballis, & Addis, 2011).

Following up on the foregoing findings with respect to hippocampal activity, Addis and Schacter (2008) examined the relationship between brain activity and the amount of detail reported for remembered and imagined events during the elaboration phase. They observed that activity in the left *posterior* hippocampus was correlated with the amount of detail comprising both remembered and imagined events, whereas the left *anterior* hippocampus responded specifically to the amount of detail comprising imagined but not remembered events. In line with the previous discussion, Addis and Schacter suggested that this latter finding could reflect activity associated with the recombining of details into an imagined future event.

Further examining the possibility that hippocampal activity distinguishes remembering the past from imagining the future, Addis, Cheng, Roberts, and Schacter (2011) asked participants to remember specific past events or imagine specific future events, as in the aforementioned work, but in addition asked participants to remember general, routine events (e.g., having brunch after attending church) or to imagine general events that might occur in their personal futures (e.g., reading the newspaper each morning). The logic here is that a region that is responsive to the amount of detail recombined into a coherent imagined episode should show more activity when constructing specific future events relative to general future events (as well as specific and generic past events). Focusing on the increased right hippocampal activity previously associated with constructing imagined future events, Addis et al. (2011) found that this activity was evident only for specific imagined events; there was no evidence for right hippocampal activity during construction of generic imagined events. Thus, the results appear to provide evidence that right hippocampal activation constitutes a neural signature associated with the construction and encoding of specific imagined events. Addis et al. (2011) discuss several possible theoretical accounts of this finding.

An additional study from our laboratory has provided further information concerning neural activity that distinguished remembered from imagined experiences by using an *experimental recombination paradigm* (Addis, Pan, Vu, Laiser, & Schacter, 2009). Participants initially provided episodic memories of actual experiences that included details about a *person,* an *object,* and a *place* involved in that event. During a later scanning session, they were cued to recall some of the events that had actually occurred. Critically, for the conditions in which they imagined events, the experimenters randomly recombined details concerning person, object, and place from separate episodes that they had recalled previously. During scanning, participants were given cues for a person, object, and place taken from distinct episodes and were instructed to imagine a single novel episode that included the specified details. In some cases, participants were instructed to imagine possible future events, whereas in others, they were instructed to imagine events that might have occurred in the past. Brain activity during remembering and imagining recruited a network of regions similar to that observed in previous research, including medial temporal, parietal, and prefrontal structures as well as some posterior visual regions (lingual and fusiform gyri), thereby providing additional evidence for shared processes during remembering and imagining. However, Addis et al. (2009) also reported evidence that distinct subsystems of this common network were preferentially associated with imagining and remembering, respectively. The *imagining network* consisted of medial temporal lobe including anterior hippocampus, bilateral medial prefrontal cortex, inferior frontal gyrus, polar and posterior temporal cortex, and medial parietal cortex. The *remembering network* included posterior visual cortices such as fusiform, lingual and occipital gyri and cuneus, as well as parahippocampal gyrus and posterior hippocampus. Addis et al. (2009) interpreted the finding that visual cortices were preferentially associated with the remembering network in light of the sensory reactivation hypothesis we discussed earlier in relation to distinguishing between true and false memories, that is, that reactivation of sensory/perceptual and contextual details during retrieval recruits the neural regions involved in the original processing of the remembered information.

The foregoing studies, as well as related studies from other laboratories (e.g., Andrews- Hanna, Reidler, Sepulcre, Poulin, & Buckner, 2010; Botzung, Denkova, & Manning, 2008; Hassabis, Kumaran, & Maguire, 2007; Spreng & Grady, 2010; Szpunar, Chan, & McDermott, 2009; Weiler, Suchan, & Daum, 2010), converge with studies of true versus false memories in two ways. First, both sets of studies reveal extensive overlap in the brain activity that accompanies remembering of actual experiences compared with either imaginary or false memories. Second, both sets of studies show that despite the overlap, the neural activity associated with true memories can be distinguished from that associated with imaginary or false memories, with some evidence from both lines of work supporting the sensory reactivation hypothesis.

CONCLUDING COMMENTS

Our review indicates that research that has used neuroimaging methods to distinguish among true, false, and imaginary memories has progressed over the past decade. Some reliable findings have emerged, and several studies suggest that despite striking similarities in the brain activity that accompanies true, false, and imaginary memories, conditions exist in which neuroimaging techniques can distinguish patterns of brain activity associated with them. However, it is clear that this research is in a nascent stage, and that many obstacles need to be overcome before it will be possible to seriously consider applying neuroimaging technology to courtroom cases in which the veracity of memory is at stake. We will first consider several key limitations of the studies discussed in this chapter and then broaden the discussion to address concerns regarding potential applications to the courtroom.

Limitations of Current Research

One limitation of current research is that much of what we know about neuroimaging of true, false, and imaginary memories comes from studies on healthy young adults, primarily college students. Although we reviewed several fMRI studies of true versus false memories involving older adults (Dennis et al., 2007, 2008; Giovanello et al., 2010) and young children (Paz-Alonso et al., 2008), it seems fair to state that there has been a relative lack of subject diversity in published studies, thereby leaving unknown the effect of such variables as education, intelligence, socioeconomic status, psychiatric disorders, and medications on our ability to identify a memory's veracity (cf. Greely & Illes, 2007). Because diverse populations are encountered in the courtroom, it seems clear that future studies will need to examine more diverse populations.

A second important limitation concerns the kinds of materials that are typically used in neuroimaging studies. Many of the studies we reviewed examined memory for such simple materials as words, shapes, and faces. Using these kinds of simple materials allows researchers to exercise precise experimental control over what is encoded and recalled, which in turn facilitates attempts to specify the neural and cognitive processes that support memory. However, using such simple materials also constrains the generalizability of much laboratory research to the courtroom, where disputes concerning the veracity of memory often involve more complex and richer autobiographical memories. Underscoring the need for caution, there is evidence showing different patterns of activation for everyday autobiographical memories and memories based on information encoded in the laboratory (Cabeza et al., 2004; McDermott, Szpunar, & Christ, 2009).

Note, however, that the recent research that we reviewed concerning neural differences between remembering the past and imagining the future has relied on remembering and imagining of rich everyday experiences. But such an approach is not easy to apply to studies of true versus false memories: While it is relatively straightforward to ask participants to imagine experiences that might occur in their personal futures, it is more difficult to create subjectively compelling false memories for actual autobiographical events. Though there are empirical demonstrations that compelling false autobiographical memories can in fact be created (e.g., Hyman & Billings, 1998; Loftus & Pickrell, 1995; Mazzoni & Memon, 2003), such memories are often observed in only a minority of participants. Moreover, they typically involve only a single experience, whereas fMRI studies of true versus false memories have used experimental paradigms in which multiple items contribute to both kinds of memories.

This latter point highlights a third limitation of the studies reviewed here: Researchers have drawn conclusions about true, false, and imaginary memories by averaging across subjects and events (whether those events are words in a list or actual autobiographical experiences). Neuroimaging techniques have an inherently low signal-to-noise ratio, thereby hindering the ability to detect meaningful patterns of activation on any given trial. Accordingly, researchers have used statistical techniques that increase power by averaging effects across multiple trials and subjects. In the courtroom, where only a single event or possibly a few events are of interest, neuroimaging techniques currently lack the necessary power to be useful.

However, recent methodological advances show promise for detecting a participant's subjective experience of remembering during a single trial. For example, Rissman, Greely, and Wagner (2010) recently used a classification technique known as *multivoxel pattern analysis* to determine with a high degree of accuracy when individual participants did and did not *believe* that they were remembering a single event (see also Chadwick, Hassabis, Weiskopf, & Maguire, 2010). By contrast, they reported that the *objective status* of memory for single events could not be successfully decoded by the pattern classifier. Although classification of the subjective state of an individual is a significant achievement that has potential applications in the courtroom (e.g., in assessing perjury), ideally a classificatory technique should reliably establish the objective status of a memory as well, so that the technique could be applied to such issues as determining whether an individual was present at a crime scene. Further experiments are needed to determine whether this goal can be achieved. At the present time, we find ourselves in agreement with Bernstein and Loftus (2009), who concluded, based on their review of cognitive and neuroimaging studies of true versus false memories, that "it might be virtually impossible to tell reliably if a particular memory is true or false without independent corroboration" (p.373).

Even if each of the three preceding caveats could be overcome, a fourth limitation would have to be addressed: ensuring that individuals cannot be instructed to use strategies that allow them to "beat" a test that can reliably distinguish true from false or imaginary memories. For example, a recent behavioral experiment presented a new method of distinguishing true from false past autobiographical events using an autobiographical version of the Implicit Association Test (aIAT; Sartori, Agosta, Zogmaister, Ferrara, & Castiello, 2008). The standard IAT has been used in many studies to reveal potentially unconscious or hidden biases by asking participants to pair two concepts (e.g., *black/good*) under time pressure (e.g., Greenwald, Poehlman, Uhlmann, & Banaji, 2009; https://implicit.harvard.edu). The easier the pairing of two concepts in one's mind, the faster the response should be, thus reflecting the strength of association between the two concepts and revealing one's implicit attitude toward a concept. Sartori and colleagues (2008) made use of this method by presenting respondents with categorization trials pairing true autobiographical events with either true or false autobiographical events. Most of the autobiographical events were related to criminal activities, such as stealing a CD, using cocaine, or driving while drunk. The researchers found that associating true autobiographical events with other true autobiographical events sped up response times significantly compared to pairing true with false autobiographical events, thus providing a means to detect which autobiographical events were true and which were false. The authors claimed to be able to classify 91% of participants correctly as guilty or innocent using the aIAT, which suggested that the test could be a useful tool in forensic settings.

However, only a year later, Verschuere, Prati, and De Houwer (2009) reported ways in which respondents could cheat the aIAT to appear innocent when they were in fact guilty. Participants who were instructed to slow down their responses for those trials that paired a confessing statement (a true autobiographical event) with a true statement were classified as innocent and could not be identified as cheaters. Participants with prior experience with the aIAT were even better at beating the test, but prior experience was not necessary for successful undetectable faking. The aIAT can be cheated if a respondent is provided with simple instructions, lessening its potential use for distinguishing true and false autobiographical events in forensic settings unless measures can be developed that allow fakers to be detected reliably. Agosta, Ghirardi, Zogmaister, Castiello, and Sartori (2011) have recently provided evidence that they can detect faking on the aIAT, but further research is necessary before the technique can be applied to real-world settings. Strategies that allow participants to beat the test have also been reported for the polygraph (Ben-Shakhar & Elaad, 2003), and it has been suggested (Sartori et al., 2008) that fMRI-based lie detection relying on frontal lobe activity during deception might be thwarted by the use of conscious strategies that are known to activate relevant frontal structures (e.g., Cole & Schneider, 2007). Therefore, any neuroimaging-based method to distinguish between true and false or imaginary memories will have to address and overcome attempts to beat the test if that method is to be useful in everyday settings. Because we are unaware of any tests that meet this standard, these considerations reinforce our earlier point that current neuroimaging-based approaches to distinguishing among true, false, and imaginary memories are not yet ready for real-world application.

Applications to the Courtroom

During the last decade, there has been considerable debate over the legality of admitting neuroimaging results as evidence into the courtroom. While the courts have not yet specifically addressed research on true, false, and imaginary memories, related work on lie detection has received considerable attention. Because some of the issues that arise when discussing the possible use of neuroimaging to detect deception are similar to those that arise when attempting to detect the veracity of memories, the treatment of fMRI data for lie detection in the courts likely presages the challenges that neuroimaging of false memories will face.

There are several impediments to fMRI-based lie detection techniques gaining admissibility in the courts. The *Daubert* standard (*Daubert v. Merrell Dow Pharmaceuticals*, 2003), the benchmark test of the admissibility of scientific evidence in most federal courts, specifies four criteria that should be weighed when considering the admissibility of a scientific theory or technique: it should be empirically testable, subjected to peer review and publication, have a known and acceptably low error rate, and be generally accepted within the relevant scientific community.

Most of the criticism of fMRI-based lie detection's admissibility has centered on the latter two criteria, including attention to limitations such as those we just considered with respect to memory studies. In an analysis of the 28 peer-reviewed publications examining deception versus truth telling in neuroimaging studies, Wagner (2010, p. 22) concludes that "the published literature reveals no data that provides unambiguous evidence regarding the sensitivity and specificity of fMRI-based neuroscience methods in the detection of lies at the individual-subject or the individual-event levels." Additional objections to the courtroom admissibility of fMRI-based lie detection include lack of replication (Greely & Illes, 2007) and real-world applicability (Kanwisher, 2009), individual differences in brain function (Raichle, 2010), and inconsistencies in reported areas of brain activation (Alexander, 2007).

Even if in the future fMRI-based lie detection were to satisfy the guidelines outlined by the *Daubert* standard, judges could still deem it inadmissible if they determine that the probative value of the evidence is outweighed by its potential to confuse or mislead the jury. Additionally, critics have argued that it violates an individual's Fourth Amendment rights against unreasonable search and seizure (Luber, Fisher, Appelbaum, Ploesser, & Lisanby, 2009; New, 2008) and Fifth Amendment rights against self-incrimination (Holloway, 2008; Luber et. al., 2009; New, 2008).

In 2010, attorneys introduced fMRI-based lie detection in a U.S. federal court for the first time, prompting a precedent-setting *Daubert* hearing (Miller, 2010). Cephos, one of two companies specializing in fMRI-based lie detection, was hired to perform the testing, and scanned the defendant while he responded both truthfully and dishonestly to questions unrelated to the case in order to determine a baseline neural response for deceptive responses. The defendant was then scanned while being asked questions involving details of the case to compare neural activity across the two conditions. The judge decided that the evidence was inadmissible, finding that while fMRI-based lie detection is testable and has been subjected to peer review, it lacks established error rates and is not generally accepted by the scientific community. Additionally, he stated that the reported error rates came from controlled laboratory experiments and could not be directly applied to real-world scenarios.

Given this precedent, the current status of fMRI-based lie detection in the courts portends the need for considerable advancement and refinement in the basic science underlying neuroimaging of true, false, and imaginary memories before this research can have a place in the courtroom. While we hope that the field will make significant advances in the years to come, we believe that a cautionary stance is currently necessary in light of the present state of the art.

ACKNOWLEDGMENTS

Preparation of this chapter was supported by grants from NIMH and NIA. We thank Clifford Robbins for assistance with preparation of the manuscript and Nobuhito Abe for helpful comments on an earlier draft of the chapter.

REFERENCES

Abe, N. (2009). The neurobiology of deception: Evidence from neuroimaging and loss-of-function studies. *Current Opinion in Neurology, 22*, 594–600.

Abe, N., Okuda, J., Suzuki, M., Sasaki, H., Matauda, T., Mori, E., et al. (2008). Neural correlates of true memory, false memory, and deception. *Cerebral Cortex, 18*, 2811–2819.

Addis, D. R., Cheng, T., Roberts, R., & Schacter, D. L. (2011). Hippocampal contributions to the episodic simulation of specific and general future events. *Hippocampus, 21*, 1045–1052.

Addis, D. R., Pan, L., Vu, M. A., Laiser, N., & Schacter, D. L. (2009). Constructive episodic simulation of the future and the past: Distinct subsystems of a core brain network mediate imagining and remembering. *Neuropsychologia, 47,* 2222–2238.

Addis, D. R., & Schacter, D. L. (2008). Constructive episodic simulation: Temporal distance and detail of past and future events modulate hippocampal engagement. *Hippocampus, 18,* 227–237.

Addis, D. R., Wong, A. T., & Schacter, D. L. (2007). Remembering the past and imagining the future: Common and distinct neural substrates during event construction and elaboration. *Neuropsychologia, 45,* 1363–1377.

Agosta, S., Ghirardi, V., Zogmaister, C., Castiello, U., & Sartori, G. (2011). Detecting fakes of the *autobiographical* IAT. *Applied Cognitive Psychology, 25,* 299–306.

Alexander, A. (2007). Functional magnetic resonance imaging lie detection: Is a "brainstorm" heading toward the "gatekeeper?" *Houston Journal of Health Law and Policy, 7,* 1–56.

Aminoff, E., Schacter, D. L., & Bar, M. (2008). The cortical underpinnings of context-based memory distortion. *Journal of Cognitive Neuroscience, 20,* 2226–2237.

Andelman, F., Hoofien, D., Goldberg, I., Aizenstein, O., & Neufeld, M. F. (2010). Bilateral hippocampal lesion and a selective impairment of the ability for mental time travel. *Neurocase, 16,* 426–435.

Andrews-Hanna, J., Reidler, J., Sepulcre, J., Poulin, R., & Buckner, R. (2010). Functional-anatomic fractionation of the brain's default network. *Neuron, 65,* 550–562.

Bar, M., & Aminoff, E. (2003). Cortical analysis of visual context. *Neuron, 38,* 347–358.

Bar, M., Aminoff, E., & Schacter, D. L. (2008). Scenes unseen: The parahippocampal cortex intrinsically subserves contextual associations, not scenes or places per se. *Journal of Neuroscience, 28,* 8539–8544.

Ben-Shakhar, G., & Elaad, E. (2003). The validity of psychophysiological detection of information with the Guilty Knowledge Test: A meta-analytic review. *Journal of Applied Psychology, 88,* 131–151.

Bernstein, D. M., & Loftus, E. F. (2009). How to tell if a particular memory is true or false. *Perspectives on Psychological Science, 4,* 370–374.

Botzung, A., Denkova, E., & Manning, L. (2008). Experiencing past and future personal events: Functional neuroimaging evidence on the neural bases of mental time travel. *Brain and Cognition, 66,* 202–212.

Buckner, R. L., & Carroll, D. C. (2007). Self-projection and the brain. *Trends in Cognitive Sciences, 11,* 49–57.

Cabeza, R., Prince, S. E., Daselaar, S. M., Greenberg, D. L., Budde, M., Dolcos, F., et al. (2004). Brain activity during episodic retrieval of autobiographical and laboratory events: An fMRI study using a novel photo paradigm. *Journal of Cognitive Neuroscience, 16,* 1583–1594.

Cabeza, R., Rao, S., Wagner, A. D., Mayer, A., & Schacter, D. L. (2001). Can medial temporal lobe regions distinguish true from false? An event-related fMRI study of veridical and illusory recognition memory. *Proceedings of the National Academy of Sciences of the United States of America, 98,* 4805–4810.

Chadwick, M. J., Hassabis, D., Weiskopf, N., & Maguire, E. A. (2010). Decoding individual episodic memory traces in the human hippocampus. *Current Biology, 20,* 544–547.

Clarke, R. A. (2004). *Against all enemies: Inside America's war on terror.* New York: Free Press.
Cole, M. W., & Schneider, W. (2007). The cognitive control network: Integrated cortical regions with dissociable functions. *NeuroImage 37,* 343-360.
Curran, T., Schacter, D. L., Johnson, M. K., & Spinks, R. (2001). Brain potentials reflect behavioral differences in true and false recognition. *Journal of Cognitive Neuroscience, 13,* 201-216.
Cutler, B. L., & Penrod, S. D. (1995). *Mistaken identification: The eyewitness, psychology, and the law.* New York: Cambridge University Press.
Daubert v. Merrell Dow Pharmaceuticals. 509 U.S. (1993).
Deese, J. (1959). On the prediction of occurrence of particular verbal intrusions in immediate recall. *Journal of Experimental Psychology, 58,* 17-22.
Demb, J. B., Desmond, J. E., Wagner, A. D., Vaidya, C. J., Glover, G. H., & Gabrieli, J. D. (1995). Semantic encoding and retrieval in the left inferior prefrontal cortex: A functional MRI study of task difficulty and process specificity. *Journal of Neuroscience, 15,* 5870-5878.
Dennis, N. A., Kim, H., & Cabeza, R. (2007). Effects of aging on true and false memory formation: An fMRI study. *Neuropsychologia, 45,* 3157-3166.
Dennis, N. A., Kim, H., & Cabeza, R. (2008). Age-related differences in brain activity during true and false memory retrieval. *Journal of Cognitive Neuroscience, 20,* 1390-1402.
Dobbins, I. G., Foley, H., Schacter, D. L., & Wagner, A. D. (2002). Executive control during episodic retrieval: Multiple prefrontal processes subserve source memory. *Neuron, 35,* 989-996.
Dobbins, I. G., Rice, H. J., Wagner, A. D., & Schacter, D. L. (2003). Memory orientation and success: Separable neurocognitive components underlying episodic recognition. *Neuropsychologia, 41,* 318-333.
Düzel, E., Yonelinas, A. P., Mangun, G. R., Heinze, H. J., & Tulving, E. (1997). Event-related brain potential correlates of two states of conscious awareness in memory. *Proceedings of the National Academy of Sciences of the United States of America, 94,* 59731-59738.
Eichenbaum, H., & Cohen, N. J. (2001). *From conditioning to conscious recollection: Memory systems of the brain.* New York: Oxford University Press.
Fabiani, M., Stadler, M. A., & Wessels, P. M. (2000). True but not false memories produce a sensory signature in human lateralized brain potentials. *Journal of Cognitive Neuroscience, 12,* 941-949.
Gallo, D. A. (2006). *Associative illusions of memory.* New York: Psychology Press.
Gallo, D. A. (2010). False memories and fantastic beliefs: 15 years of the DRM illusion. *Memory and Cognition, 38,* 833-848
Garoff, R. J., Slotnick, S. D., & Schacter, D. L. (2005). The neural origins of specific and general memory: The role of the fusiform cortex. *Neuropsychologia, 43,* 847-859.
Garoff-Eaton, R. J., Kensinger, E. A., & Schacter, D. L. (2007). The neural correlates of conceptual and perceptual false recognition. *Learning and Memory, 14,* 684-692.
Garoff-Eaton, R. J., Slotnick, S. D., & Schacter, D. L. (2006). Not all false memories are created equal: The neural basis of false recognition. *Cerebral Cortex, 16,* 1645-1652.

Garry, M., Manning, C., Loftus, E. F., & Sherman, S. J. (1996). Imagination inflation: Imagining a childhood event inflates confidence that it occurred. *Psychonomic Bulletin and Review, 3*, 208–214.

Giovanello, K. S., Kensinger, E. A., Wong, A. T., & Schacter, D. L. (2010). Age-related neural changes during memory conjunction errors. *Journal of Cognitive Neuroscience, 22*, 1348–1361.

Goff, L. M., & Roediger, H. L. III (1998). Imagination inflation for action events: Repeated imaginings lead to illusory recollections. *Memory & Cognition, 26*, 20–33.

Goldmann, R. E., Sullivan, A. L., Droller, D. B. J., Rugg, M. D., Curran, T., Holcomb, P. J., et al. (2003). Late frontal brain potentials distinguish true and false recognition. *Neuroreport, 14*, 1717–1720.

Gonsalves, B., & Paller, K. A. (2000). Neural events that underlie remembering something that never happened. *Nature Neuroscience, 3*, 1316–1321.

Gonsalves, B., Reber, P. J., Gitelman, D. R., Parrish, T. B., Mesulam, M. M., & Paller, K. A. (2004). Neural evidence that vivid imagining can lead to false remembering. *Psychological Science, 15*, 655–660.

Grady, C., McIntosh, A. R., & Craik, F. I. M. (2005). Task-related activity in prefrontal cortex and its relation to recognition memory performance in young and old adults. *Neuropsychologia, 43*, 1466–1481.

Granhag, P. A., & Knieps, M. (2011). Episodic future thought: Illuminating the trademarks of forming true and false intentions. *Applied Cognitive Psychology, 25*, 274–280.

Greely, H. T., & Illes, J. (2007). Neuroscience-based lie detection: The urgent need for regulation. *American Journal of Law and Medicine, 33*, 377–431.

Greenwald, A. G., Poehlman, T. A., Uhlmann, E. L., & Banaji, M. R. (2009). Understanding and using the Implicit Association Test: III. Meta-analysis of predictive validity. *Journal of Personality and Social Psychology 97*, 17–41.

Gutchess, A., Welsh, R. C., Hedden, T., Bangert, A., Minear, M., Liu, L.L., et al. (2005). Aging and the neural correlates of successful picture encoding: Frontal activations compensate for decreased medial temporal lobe activity. *Journal of Cognitive Neuroscience, 17*, 84–96.

Hassabis, D., Kumaran, D., & Maguire, E. A. (2007). Using imagination to understand the neural basis of episodic memory. *Journal of Neuroscience, 27*, 14365–14374.

Hassabis, D., Kumaran, D., Vann, S. D., & Maguire, E. A. (2007). Patients with hippocampal amnesia cannot imagine new experiences. *Proceedings of the National Academy of Sciences of the United States of America, 104*, 1726–1731.

Henson, R. N. (2003). Neuroimaging studies of priming. *Progress in Neurobiology, 70*, 53–81.

Henson, R. N., Shallice, T., & Dolan, R. (2000). Neuroimaging evidence for dissociable forms of repetition priming. *Science, 287*, 1269–1272.

Holloway, M. B. (2008). One image, one thousand incriminating words: Images of brain activity and the privilege against self-incrimination. *Temple Journal of Science, Technology & Environmental Law, 27*, 141–175.

Hyman, I. E., & Billings, J. (1998). Individual differences and the creation of false childhood memories. *Memory, 6*, 1–20.

Jacobs, W. J., & Nadel, L. (1998). Neurobiology of reconstructed memory. *Psychology, Public Policy, and the Law, 4*, 1110–1134.

Johnson, M. K., Foley, M. A., Suengas, A. G., & Raye, C. L. (1988). Phenomenal characteristics of memories for perceived and imagined autobiographical events. *Journal of Experimental Psychology: General, 117*, 371–376.

Johnson, M. K., Nolde, S. F., Mather, M., Kounios, J., Schacter, D. L., & Curran, T. (1997). The similarity of brain activity associated with true and false recognition memory depends on test format. *Psychological Science, 8*, 250–257.

Johnson, M. K., & Raye, C. L. (1981). Reality monitoring. *Psychological Review, 88*, 67–85.

Jones, T. C., & Jacoby, L. L. (2005). Conjunction errors in recognition memory: Modality free-errors for older but not for younger adults. *Acta Psychologica, 120*, 55–73.

Kanwisher, N. (2009). The use of fMRI in lie detection: What has been shown and what has not. In E. Bizzi & S. E. Hyman (Eds.), *Using imaging to identify deceit: Scientific and ethical questions* (pp. 7–13). Cambridge, MA: American Academy of Arts and Sciences.

Kensinger, E. A., & Schacter, D. L. (2005a). Emotional content and reality monitoring ability: fMRI evidence for the influence of encoding processes. *Neuropsychologia, 43*, 1429–1443.

Kensinger, E. A., & Schacter, D. L. (2005b). Retrieving accurate and distorted memories: Neuroimaging evidence for the effects of emotion. *NeuroImage, 27*, 167–177.

Kensinger, E. A., & Schacter, D. L. (2006). Neural processes underlying memory attribution on a reality-monitoring task. *Cerebral Cortex, 16*, 1126–1133.

Kim, H., & Cabeza, R. (2007a). Differential contributions of prefrontal, medial temporal, and sensory-perceptual regions to true and false memory formation. *Cerebral Cortex, 17*, 2143–2150.

Kim, H., & Cabeza, R. (2007b). Trusting our memories: Dissociating the neural correlates of confidence in veridical vs. illusory memories. *Journal of Neuroscience, 27*, 12190–12197.

Kirchhoff, B. A., Schapiro, M. L., & Buckner, R. L. 2005. Orthographic distinctiveness and semantic elaboration provide separate contributions to memory. *Journal of Cognitive Neuroscience, 17*, 1841–1854.

Koutstaal, W., & Schacter, D. L. (1997). Gist-based false recognition of pictures in older and younger adults. *Journal of Memory and Language, 37*, 555–583.

Koutstaal, W., Schacter, D. L., Verfaellie, M., Brenner, C. J., & Jackson, E. M. (1999). Perceptually based false recognition of novel objects in amnesia: Effects of category size and similarity to category prototypes. *Cognitive Neuropsychology, 16*, 317–341.

Kwan, D., Carson, N., Addis, D. R., & Rosenbaum, R. S. (2010). Deficits in past remembering extend to future imagining in a case of developmental amnesia. *Neuropsychologia, 48*, 3179–3186.

Loftus, E. F. (1979). *Eyewitness testimony*. Cambridge, MA: Harvard University Press.

Loftus, E. F. (1993). The reality of repressed memories. *American Psychologist, 48*, 518–537.

Loftus, E. F. (2003). Make-believe memories. *American Psychologist, 58*, 867–873.

Loftus, E. F., & Davis, D. (2006). Recovered memories. *Annual Review of Clinical Psychology, 2*, 469–498.

Loftus, E. F., & Ketcham, K. (1994). *The myth of repressed memory*. New York: St. Martin's Press.

Loftus, E. F., & Pickrell, J. E. (1995). The formation of false memories. *Psychiatric Annals, 25,* 720–725.

Luber, B., Fisher, C., Appelbaum, P. S., Ploesser, M., & Lisanby, S. H. (2009). Non-invasive brain stimulation in the detection of deception: Scientific challenges and ethical consequences. *Behavioral Sciences and the Law, 27,* 191–208.

Maguire, E. A. (2001). Neuroimaging studies of autobiographical event memory. *Philosophical Transactions of the Royal Society of London B, 356,* 1441–1451.

Maguire, E. A., Vargha-Khadem, F., & Hassabis, D. (2010). Imagining fictitious and future experiences: Evidence from developmental amnesia. *Neuropsychologia, 48,* 3187–3192.

Marche, T. A., Brainerd, C. J., & Reyna, V. F. (2010). Distinguishing true from false memories in forensic contexts: Can phenomenology tell us what is real? *Applied Cognitive Psychology, 24,* 1168–1182.

Martin, V. C., Schacter, D. L., Corballis, M., & Addis, D. R. (2011). A role for the hippocampus in encoding simulations of future events. *Proceedings of the National Academy of Sciences of the United States of America,108,* 13858–13863.

Mather, M., Henkel, L. A., & Johnson, M. K. (1997). Evaluating characteristics of false memories: Remember/know judgments and memory characteristics questionnaire compared. *Memory and Cognition, 25,* 826–837.

Mazzoni, G., & Memon, A. (2003). Imagination can create false autobiographical memories. *Psychological Science, 14,* 186–188.

McDermott, K. B., Szpunar, K. K., & Christ, S. E. (2009). Laboratory-based and autobiographical retrieval tasks differ substantially in their neural substrates. *Neuropsychologia, 47,* 2290–2298.

McNally, R. J., & Geraerts, E. (2009). A new solution to the recovered memories debate. *Perspectives on Psychological Science, 4,* 126–134.

Miller, G. (2010). FMRI lie detection fails a legal test. *Science, 328,* 1336–1337.

Nessler, D., & Mecklinger, A. (2003). ERP correlates of true and false recognition after different retention delays: Stimulus- and response-related processes. *Psychophysiology, 40,* 146–159.

Nessler, D., Mecklinger, A., & Penney, T. B. (2001). Event related brain potentials and illusory memories: The effects of differential encoding. *Cognitive Brain Research, 10,* 283–301.

New, J. G. (2008). If you could read my mind: Implications of neurological evidence for twenty-first-century criminal jurisprudence. *The Journal of Legal Medicine, 29,* 179–198.

Norman, K. A., & Schacter, D. L. (1997). False recognition in young and older adults: Exploring the characteristics of illusory memories. *Memory and Cognition, 25,* 838–848.

Nyberg, L., Habib, R., McIntosh, A. R., & Tulving, E. (2000). Reactivation of encoding-related brain activity during memory retrieval. *Proceedings of the National Academy of Sciences of the United States of America, 97,* 11120–11124.

O'Connell, S. (2008). *The perils of relying on memory in court*. Retrieved June 30, 2010 from http://www.telegraph.co.uk/technology/3778272/The-perils-of-relying-on-memory-in-court.html

Okado, Y., & Stark, C. (2003). Neural processing associated with true and false memory retrieval. *Cognitive, Affective, and Behavioral Neuroscience, 3*, 323–334.

Okado, Y., & Stark, C. (2005). Neural activity during encoding predicts false memories created by misinformation. *Learning and Memory, 12*, 3–11.

Okuda, J., Fujii, T., Ohtake, H., Tsukiura, T., Tanji, K., Suzuki, K., et al. (2003). Thinking of the future and the past: The roles of the frontal pole and the medial temporal lobes. *NeuroImage, 19*, 1369–1380.

Paz-Alonso, P. M., Ghetti, S., Donohue, S. E., Goodman, G. S., & Bunge, S. A. (2008). Neurodevelopmental correlates of true and false recognition. *Cerebral Cortex, 18*, 2208–2216.

Pendergrast, M. (1995). *Victims of memory*. Hinesburg, VT: Upper Access.

Petersen, S. E., Fox, P. T., Posner, M. I., Mintun, M., & Raichle, M. E. 1988. Positron emission tomographic studies of the cortical anatomy of single-word processing. *Nature, 331*, 585–589.

Posner, M. I., & Keele, S. W. (1968). On the genesis of abstract ideas. *Journal of Experimental Psychology, 77*, 353–363.

Prince, S. E., Daselaar, S. M., & Cabeza, R. (2005). Neural correlates of relational memory: Successful encoding and retrieval of semantic and perceptual associations. *Journal of Neuroscience, 25*, 1203–1210.

Race, E., Keane, M. M., & Verfaellie, M. (2011). Medial temporal lobe damage causes deficits in episodic memory and episodic future thinking not attributable to deficits in narrative construction. *Journal of Neuroscience, 31*, 10262–10269.

Raichle, M. (2010). What is an fMRI? In M. S. Gazzaniga & J. S. Rakoff (Eds.), *A judge's guide to neuroscience: A concise introduction* (pp. 5–12). Santa Barbara: University of California, Santa Barbara.

Reinitz, M. T., Lammers, W. J., & Cochran, B. P. (1992). Memory-conjunction errors: Miscombinations of stored stimulus features can produce illusions of memory. *Memory & Cognition, 20*, 1–11.

Rissman, J., Greely, H. T., & Wagner, A. D. (2010). Detecting individual memories through the neural decoding of memory states and past experience. *Proceedings of the National Academy of Sciences of the United States of America, 107*, 9849–9854.

Roediger, H. L., III & McDermott, K. B. (1995). Creating false memories: Remembering words not presented in lists. *Journal of Experimental Psychology: Learning, Memory, and Cognition, 21*, 803–814.

Rugg, M. D., Fletcher, P. C., Frith, C. D., Frackowiak, R .S. J., & Dolan, R. J. (1996). Differential activation of the prefrontal cortex in successful and unsuccessful memory retrieval. *Brain, 119*, 2073–2083.

Sartori, G., Agosta, S., Zogmaister, C., Ferrara, S. D., & Castiello, U. (2008). How to accurately detect autobiographical events. *Psychological Science 19*, 772–780.

Schacter, D. L. (1987). Implicit memory: History and current status. *Journal of Experimental Psychology: Learning, Memory, and Cognition, 13*, 501–518.

Schacter, D. L. (1996). *Searching for memory: The brain, the mind, and the past*. New York: Basic Books.

Schacter, D. L. (2001). *The seven sins of memory: How the mind forgets and remembers*. New York and Boston: Houghton-Mifflin.

Schacter, D. L. (2004). The fog of war. *The New York Times*, April 5, A25.

Schacter, D. L., & Addis, D. R. (2007). The cognitive neuroscience of constructive memory: Remembering the past and imagining the future. *Philosophical Transaction of the Royal Society of London B, 362,* 773-786.

Schacter, D. L., & Addis, D. R. (2009). On the nature of medial temporal lobe contributions to the constructive simulation of future events. *Philosophical Transactions of the Royal Society of London B, 364,* 1245-1253.

Schacter, D. L., Addis, D. R., & Buckner, R. L. (2007). Remembering the past to imagine the future: The prospective brain. *Nature Reviews Neuroscience, 8,* 657-661.

Schacter, D. L., Addis, D. R., & Buckner, R. L. (2008). Episodic simulation of future events: Concepts, data, and applications. *The Year in Cognitive Neuroscience, Annals of the New York Academy of Sciences, 1124,* 39-60

Schacter, D. L., & Buckner, R. L. (1998). Priming and the brain. *Neuron, 20,* 185-195.

Schacter, D. L., Buckner, R. L., Koutstaal, W., Dale, A. M., & Rosen, B. R. (1997). Late onset of anterior prefrontal activity during true and false recognition: An event-related fMRI study. *NeuroImage, 6,* 259-269.

Schacter, D. L., Guerin, S. A., & St. Jacques, P. L. (2011). Memory distortion: An adaptive perspective. *Trends in Cognitive Sciences, 15,* 467-474.

Schacter, D. L., Israel, L., & Racine, C. A. (1999). Suppressing false recognition in younger and older adults: The distinctiveness heuristic. *Journal of Memory and Language, 40,* 1-24.

Schacter, D. L., Norman, K. A., & Koutstaal, W. (1998). The cognitive neuroscience of constructive memory. *Annual Review of Psychology, 49,* 289-318.

Schacter, D. L., Reiman, E., Curran, T., Yun, L. S., Bandy, D., McDermott, K. B., et al. (1996). Neuroanatomical correlates of veridical and illusory recognition memory: Evidence from positron emission tomography. *Neuron, 17,* 267-274.

Schacter, D. L., Reiman, E., Uecker, A., Polster, M. R., Yun, L. S., & Cooper, L. A. (1995). Brain regions associated with retrieval of structurally coherent visual information. *Nature, 376,* 587-590.

Schacter, D. L., & Slotnick, S. D. (2004). The cognitive neuroscience of memory distortion. *Neuron, 44,* 149-160.

Schacter, D. L., Wig, G. S., & Stevens, W. D. (2007). Reductions in cortical activity during priming. *Current Opinion in Neurobiology, 17,* 171-176.

Scheck, B., Neufeld, P., & Dwyer, J. (2000). *Actual innocence.* New York: Doubleday.

Schooler, J. W., Gerhard, D., & Loftus, E. F. (1986). Qualities of the unreal. *Journal of Experimental Psychology: Learning, Memory, & Cognition, 12,* 171-181.

Semmler, C., & Brewer, N. (2010). Eyewitness memory. In J. Brown & E. Campbell (Eds.), *The Cambridge handbook of forensic psychology* (pp. 49-57). Cambridge: Cambridge University Press.

Slotnick, S. D., & Schacter, D. L. (2004). A sensory signature that distinguishes true from false memories. *Nature Neuroscience, 7,* 664-672.

Slotnick, S. D., & Schacter, D. L. (2006). The nature of memory related activity in early visual areas. *Neuropsychologia, 44,* 2874-2886.

Spence, S. A., & Kaylor-Hughes, C. J. (2008). Looking for truth and finding lies: The prospects for a nascent neuroimaging of deception. *Neurocase, 14,* 68-81.

Spreng, R. N., & Grady, C. L. (2010). Patterns of brain activity supporting autobiographical memory, prospection, and theory of mind, and their relationship to the default mode network. *Journal of Cognitive Neuroscience, 22*, 1112–1123.

Squire, L. R., van der Horst, A. S., McDuff, S. G. R., Frascino, J. C., Hopkins, R. O., & Mauldin, K. N. (2010). Role of the hippocampus in remembering the past and imagining the future. *Proceedings of the National Academy of Sciences of the United States of America, 107,* 19044–19048.

Szpunar, K. K. (2010). Episodic future thought: An emerging concept. *Perspectives on Psychological Science, 5,* 142–162.

Szpunar, K. K., Chan, J. C. K., & McDemott, K. B. (2009). Contextual processing in episodic future thought. *Cerebral Cortex, 19,* 1539–1548.

Szpunar, K. K., Watson, J. M., & McDermott, K. B. (2007). Neural substrates of envisioning the future. *Proceedings of the National Academy of Sciences of the United States of America, 104,* 642–647.

Treyer, V., Buck, A., & Schnider, A. (2003). Subcortical loop activation during selection of currently relevant memories. *Journal of Cognitive Neuroscience, 15,* 610–618.

Tulving, E., & Schacter, D. L. (1990). Priming and human memory systems. *Science, 247,* 301–306.

Tun, P. A., Wingfield, A., Rosen, M. J., & Blanchard, L. (1998). Response latencies for false memories: Gist-based processes in normal aging. *Psychology and Aging, 13,* 230–241.

Verschuere, B., Prati, V., & De Houwer, J. (2009). Cheating the lie detector: Faking in the autobiographical implicit association test. *Psychological Science 20,* 410–413.

Von Zerssen, G. C., Mecklinger, A., Opitz, B., & von Cramon, D. Y (2001). Conscious recollection and illusory recognition: An event-related fMRI study. *European Journal of Neuroscience, 13,* 1–13.

Wagner, A. D. (2010). Can neuroscience identify lies? In M. S. Gazzaniga & J. S. Rakoff (Eds.), *A judge's guide to neuroscience: A concise introduction* (pp. 13–25). Santa Barbara: University of California, Santa Barbara.

Wagner, A. D., Paré-Blagoev, E. J., Clark, J., & Poldrack, R. A. 2001. Recovering meaning: Left prefrontal cortex guides controlled semantic retrieval. *Neuron, 31,* 329–338.

Walla, P., Endl, W., Lindinger, G., Deecke, L., & Lang, W. (2000). False recognition in a verbal memory task: An event-related potential study. *Cognitive Brain Research, 9,* 41–44.

Weiler, J. A., Suchan, B., & Daum, I. (2010). When the future becomes the past: Differences in brain activity patterns for episodic memory and episodic future thinking. *Behavioural Brain Research, 212,* 196–203.

Wells, G. L., & Olson, E. A. (2003). Eyewitness testimony. *Annual Review of Psychology, 54,* 277–295.

Wells, G. L., Small, M., Penrod, S., Malpass, R. S., Fulero, S. M., & Brimacombe, C. A. E. (1998). Eyewitness identification procedures: Recommendations for lineups and photospreads. *Law and Human Behavior, 22,* 603–647.

Wheeler, M. A., Petersen, S. E., & Buckner, R. L. (2000). Memory's echo: Vivid recollection activates modality-specific cortex. *Proceedings of the National Academy of Sciences of the United States of America, 97,* 11125–11129.

Wiggs, C. L., & Martin, A. (1998). Properties and mechanisms of perceptual priming. *Current Opinion in Neurobiology, 8,* 227–233.
Wise, R. J. S., & Price, C. J. (2006). Functional imaging of language. In R. Cabeza & A. Kingstone (Eds.), *Handbook of functional neuroimaging of cognition* (2nd ed., pp. 191–228). Cambridge, MA: MIT Press.

11

Detection of Concealed Stored Memories with Psychophysiological and Neuroimaging Methods

J. PETER ROSENFELD, GERSHON BEN-SHAKHAR, AND GIORGIO GANIS

INTRODUCTION

The idea of using physiological measures for detecting deception, and for discriminating between individuals involved in an illegal activity and innocent suspects, has been very appealing to law enforcement agencies (see Larson, 1932; Marston, 1917; 1938; Reid, 1947; Reid & Inbau, 1977). Indeed, several psychophysiological methods (popularly labeled *polygraph techniques*) have been developed since the beginning of the 20th century, and the study of psychophysiological detection of deception has attracted a great deal of interest among researchers as well as practitioners and has become an important area of applied psychology (e.g., Ben-Shakhar & Furedy, 1990; Lykken, 1998; National Research Council, 2003; Raskin, 1989; Reid & Inbau, 1977; Verschuere, Ben-Shakhar, & Meijer, 2011). These methods, which were mostly based on responses in the autonomic nervous system (ANS), can be broadly classified into two categories: (1) methods designed to detect deception, which rely on autonomic responses to direct questions (e.g., "Did you break into the jewelry store on Thursday night?") and (2) methods designed to detect concealed knowledge (e.g., "Was the stolen jewel a gold watch?," "Was it a diamond ring?"). This chapter is focused on the second category for two major reasons. First, psychophysiological tests of deception (called *comparison question tests*, formerly called *control question tests*) have been severely criticized and are now considered by most researchers to lack a scientific foundation (e.g., Ben-Shakhar, 2002; Iacono & Lykken, 2002; National Research Council, 2003). Second, as the topic of this book is memory and law, it seems that discussing methods for detecting concealed information stored in memory is much more appropriate than considering methods for detecting deception.

The method designed to detect concealed knowledge was traditionally labeled the Guilty Knowledge Test (GKT; see Lykken, 1959, 1960), but more recently it has been called the Concealed Information Test (CIT; see Verschuere et al., 2011). It utilizes a series of multiple-choice questions, each having one relevant alternative, also labeled a *probe* (e.g., a feature of the crime under investigation), and several neutral (control) alternatives, chosen so that an innocent suspect would not be able to distinguish them from the probe (Lykken, 1998). The relevant items are significant only for knowledgeable (guilty) individuals and there is ample evidence, mostly from psychophysiological research on orienting responses, indicating that significant stimuli elicit enhanced orienting responses (e.g., Gati & Ben-Shakhar, 1990; Siddle, 1991; Sokolov, 1963). Thus, if the suspect's physiological responses to the relevant alternative are consistently larger than to the neutral (or irrelevant) alternatives, knowledge about the event (e.g., the crime) is inferred. As long as information about the event has not leaked out to innocent subjects, the probability that an innocent suspect would produce consistently larger responses to the relevant alternative than to the neutral alternatives depends only on the number of questions and the number of alternative answers per question; hence, it can be controlled such that maximal protection for the innocent is provided. This feature of the CIT is particularly important if its outcomes are considered to be used as admissible evidence in criminal trials (Ben-Shakhar & Kremnitzer, 2011).

DETECTING CONCEALED INFORMATION WITH ANS MEASURES

Research on CIT can be traced back to the early 1940s and 1950s (e.g., Ellson, Burke, Davis, & Saltzman, 1952; Geldreich, 1941, 1942; van Buskirk & Marcuse, 1954), but two articles published by David Lykken (1959, 1960) were the first to make a real impact on the field and enhance interest in the CIT among various research groups. This early research relied on just a single physiological measure, the skin conductance response, and generally demonstrated an impressive ability to detect concealed information. Specifically, Lykken (1959) employed the mock-crime procedure in which some subjects committed one or two mock crimes (the "guilty" subjects), while others (the "innocents") did not. The results revealed that 88% of the guilty subjects were detected, while none of the innocent subjects were misclassified as guilty. Lykken's second study (1960) relied on a personal items paradigm and used 25 biographical details of 20 subjects, all of which were correctly detected.

Research interest in the CIT increased in the following decades and has expanded in several directions. First, the validity of additional autonomic measures in detecting concealed knowledge and discriminating knowledgeable from unknowledgeable subjects was examined (e.g., Cutrow, Parks, Lucas, & Thomas, 1972; Thackray & Orne, 1968). Second, attempts were made to shed light on the theoretical basis of the CIT effect—the enhanced autonomic responses elicited by the significant stimuli (e.g., Ben-Shakhar, 1977; Ben-Shakhar & Lieblich, 1982; Gustafson & Orne, 1963, 1965; Lieblich, Kugelmass, & Ben-Shakhar, 1970; Verschuere, Crombez, Declercq, & Koster, 2004; Verschuere, Crombez, Koster, Van Bockstaele, & De Clercq, 2007). Third, many studies examined the effects of various factors on the outcomes of the CIT (e.g., the effect of type of verbal responses to the CIT questions: Horneman & O'Gorman, 1985; Kugelmass, Lieblich, & Bergman, 1967; the effect of drugs: Iacono, Boisvenu, & Fleming, 1984; Verschuere, Crombez, Declercq, & Koster, 2005; Waid, Orne, Cook, & Orne, 1981). Finally, factors that may limit the applicability of the CIT have been examined (e.g., the vulnerability of the CIT to countermeasures: Ben-Shakhar & Dolev, 1996; Honts, Devitt, Winbush, & Kircher, 1996; the effect of leakage of critical CIT items to innocent suspects: Bradley & Warfield, 1984; Bradley & Rettinger, 1992). We shall briefly review each of these lines of research.

The Validity of Various Autonomic Measures in the CIT

As indicated above, the electrodermal measure has been most intensively studied in the context of the CIT. Indeed, the few studies that conducted systematic comparisons between measures often revealed an advantage for skin conductance responses over other autonomic measures, such as cardiovascular measures and changes in respiration (for a recent review, see Gamer, 2011). This was demonstrated by the two early studies that compared various autonomic measures (Cutrow et al., 1972; Thackray & Orne, 1968) and more recently by Gamer, Verschuere, Crombez, and Vossel (2008). In addition, because the electrodermal measure has been used in a relatively large number of CIT studies, it is the only measure that has been subjected to meta-analyses (see Ben-Shakhar & Elaad, 2003; MacLaren, 2001). The Ben-Shakhar and Elaad analysis was more extensive and covered 80 laboratory studies, which included 169 experimental conditions with a total of 5,198 participants tested under a variety of CIT paradigms (e.g., card test, mock crime). The overall average effect size (Cohen's d) was 1.55, and the corresponding average area under the receiver operating characteristic (or ROC) curve was 0.82. (The ROC curve is a function based on signal detection theory that in the present context expresses the test's efficiency in distinguishing guilty and innocent subjects. The area under the ROC curve varies from .5 to 1.0, with higher efficiencies associated with higher values; see Grier, 1971.) However, these figures depended on the specific paradigm used and also on several moderating factors. Ben-Shakhar and Elaad (2003) identified 10 experimental conditions with a total of 222 participants that, according to them, were conducted under optimal circumstances (mock crime studies with at least five CIT questions, with motivational instructions and a deceptive verbal response). The average effect size and ROC area based on these 10 studies were 3.12 and 0.95, respectively, which reflect very impressive validity estimates.

However, the advantage of electrodermal measures does not mean that other autonomic measures are ineffective. In particular, cardiovascular measures as well as changes in respiration, which are standard measures in commercial polygraphs, have been demonstrated to produce differential responses to the significant CIT items among knowledgeable subjects. Respiration is typically measured as changes in the volume of thorax and abdomen by attaching pneumatic transducers around the chest and the abdomen with belts or Velcro straps. Although the early studies reported by Thackray and Orne (1968) and by Podlesny and Raskin (1978) did not reveal consistently better than chance detection rates for either breathing amplitude or breathing cycle time, more recent studies that relied on the total respiration line length during the measurement period (typically 10–15 seconds) demonstrated that this measure has considerable validity for detecting concealed knowledge and differentiating between knowledgeable and unknowledgeable individuals. The respiration line length measure was initially proposed by Timm (1982, 1987), who showed a reduction in respiration line length when the significant CIT items were presented and demonstrated that this measure is no less valid than the skin conductance response. The respiration line length was subsequently adopted by other researchers, who corroborated Timm's initial findings (see Ben-Shakhar, Gronau, & Elaad, 1999; Bradley & Rettinger, 1992; Gamer, Rill, Vossel, & Gödert, 2006; Verschuere, Crombez, Koster, & De Clercq, 2007). In addition, Elaad, Ginton, and Jungman (1992) demonstrated that the respiration line length is a valid measure, along with the skin conductance response in a field setting.

Several cardiovascular measures have been examined in the CIT context. Heart rate deceleration following presentation of the significant item has received much research attention. Although the early studies reported disappointing results with this measure (see Balloun & Holmes, 1979; Podlesny & Raskin, 1978), more recent studies did demonstrate a differential heart rate deceleration elicited by the significant CIT items among knowledgeable participants (e.g., Ambach, Stark, Peper, & Vaitl, 2008a; Gamer et al., 2006; Verschuere, et al., 2005, Verschuere, Crombez, Koster, & De Clercq, 2007). Several researchers have noted that the heart rate changes following presentation of CIT items depend on whether or not examinees are required to give verbal responses to these items. Specifically, when verbal responses are made, heart rate initially accelerates followed by a subsequent deceleration, which is more pronounced for significant than for neutral items. However, when no verbal responses are required, the initial acceleration is often missing and the heart rate decelerates following stimulus onset (e.g., Gamer, Gödert, Keth, Rill, & Vossel, 2008; Verschuere, Crombez, Smolders, & De Clercq, 2009). It has been suggested (see the recent review by Gamer, 2011) that the initial acceleration represents the preparation for the verbal response, while the deceleration is an orienting response component reflecting the direction of attention to the item.

In addition to heart rate, several researchers examined plethysmographic measures, particularly changes in finger pulse. The early CIT studies that examined various autonomic measures reported that finger pulse volume and finger pulse amplitude, reflecting peripheral vasoconstriction, which is another orienting response component, were effective in the detection of concealed information (Cutrow et al., 1972; Podlesny & Raskin, 1978; Thackray & Orne, 1968). More recently, Elaad and Ben-Shakhar (2006, 2008) demonstrated that the overall length of the finger pulse signal (labeled *finger pulse waveform length*), which combines pulse amplitude and pulse rate, can differentiate knowledgeable and unknowledgeable individuals. Much like the respiration line length, a reduction in finger pulse waveform length is observed following the presentation of significant items. While Elaad and Ben-Shakhar (2006) reported that the finger pulse waveform length was a better indicator of concealed information than the skin conductance response, two subsequent studies (Ambach, Stark, Peper, & Vaitl, 2008b; Verschuere, Crombez, Smolders, & De Clercq, 2009) obtained validity estimates for this measure that were greater than chance but lower than the skin conductance response validity. However, a potential advantage of finger pulse waveform length over skin conductance response is its relative resistance to habituation (see Gamer, 2011).

Very few studies examined the validity of other autonomic measures in the CIT context. For example, pupil dilatation has been demonstrated to be sensitive to concealed information, such that larger dilatation is observed to critical compared with neutral items (Bradley & Janisse, 1981; Janisse & Bradley, 1980; Lubow & Fein, 1996). Thackray and Orne (1968) examined changes in the level of oxygen and found that they were effective in only some of their tests. Cutrow et al. (1972) demonstrated that eyeblink rate produced better than chance differentiation between critical and neutral items. More recently,

Pollina et al. (2006) examined whether concealed knowledge can be detected from subtle changes in facial skin surface temperature. They utilized thermography to measure infrared emission from the human face and found that examinees who committed a mock crime showed larger temperature increases on presentation of critical compared to neutral CIT items. Such differential responses could be examined briefly after stimulus onset and were absent in a group of uninformed examinees.

From a practical perspective, it is important to estimate not just the validity of individual measures, but also their incremental validity and whether and to what extent a combination of several measures can increase validity. A few studies examined this issue with the most frequently used measures (electrodermal, respiration and heart rate, or finger pulse waveform length). The validity of a combined measure derived from a simple averaging of the standard skin conductance response and respiration line length scores was examined by several studies (Ben-Shakhar & Dolev, 1996; Ben-Shakhar & Elaad, 2002; Ben-Shakhar et al.,1999). In four out of the five experimental conditions reported in these three studies, the ROC area, for discriminating knowledgeable from unknowledgeable subjects, produced by the combined measure exceeded the area produced by the single most valid measure. Elaad et al. (1992) obtained similar findings in one of the few published reports of field CIT validity studies. Several other studies (Elaad, 2009; Elaad & Ben-Shakhar, 2006, 2008; Verschuere, Crombez, Koster, & De Clercq, 2007) used a similar method to combine skin conductance response, respiration line length, and a cardiovascular measure (either finger pulse waveform length or heart rate). Again, in almost all experimental conditions reported in these studies, the simple combination of the three measures produced better detection efficiency than the best individual measure. The only exception is the prisoners' sample used by Verschuere, Crombez, Koster, & De Clercq (2007), where skin conductance response alone was more valid than the combined measure. A different approach was adopted by Gamer et al. (2006), who combined skin conductance response, respiration line length, and heart rate using a stepwise logistic regression that assigned relatively large weights to skin conductance response and respiration line length and a smaller weight to heart rate. Gamer, Verschuere, et al. (2008) cross-validated the regression function proposed by Gamer et al. (2006), using data from seven studies, and found that the weighted combination of the three measures significantly outperformed the best single measure.

The Theoretical Foundation of the CIT

A detailed review of the various theoretical approaches (including theories that highlighted emotional-motivational factors and those based on cognitive factors) proposed to account for the CIT effect (enhanced autonomic responses to the critical CIT items) was recently published by Verschuere and Ben-Shakhar (2011). In this chapter, we shall discuss only the main theoretical accounts. It is probably not surprising that the concept of the *orienting response* has been proposed to account for the CIT effect, because all the autonomic measures used in the CIT are components of the orienting response (see Lynn, 1966; Sokolov, 1963). Furthermore, Sokolov (1963) and his followers noted that stimuli that are significant for the individual ("signal-value stimuli," to use Sokolov's terminology) elicit enhanced orienting responses with slower habituation. The relationship between the CIT effect and the orienting response was highlighted by Lykken (1974), who wrote that "for the guilty subject only, the 'correct' alternative will have a special significance, an added 'signal value' which will tend to produce a stronger orienting reflex than that subject will show to other alternatives" (p. 728).

There is ample evidence supporting the orienting response account for the CIT effect. First, the physiological response pattern elicited by the relevant CIT items in knowledgeable individuals (e.g., increased skin conductance response [Lykken, 1959], heart rate deceleration [Verschuere et al., 2004], respiratory suppression [Timm, 1982], and increased pupil dilation [Lubow & Fein, 1996]) is typical of the orienting response. Second, several features characteristic of the orienting response have been demonstrated using the CIT paradigm. Specifically, response habituation has been observed in several CIT studies (e.g., Balloun & Holmes, 1979; Ben-Shakhar, Lieblich, & Kugelmass, 1975; Verschuere et al., 2005). Ben-Shakhar and Gati (1987) showed that the strength of the response to a stimulus was positively related to the degree to which it resembled the critical stimulus. On the other hand, research has failed to demonstrate dishabituation in the CIT (e.g., Ben-Shakhar, Gati, Ben-Bassat, & Sniper, 2000). Ben-Shakhar and colleagues argued, however, that dishabituation has not always been demonstrated in orienting response research either (see Siddle & Lipp, 1997). Third, the information processing view of orienting states that the orienting response serves to allow more elaborate processing of the orienting response-eliciting stimulus (Kahneman, 1973; Öhman, 1992; Wagner, 1978). Orienting response research that demonstrated positive correlations between orienting response and later recall of the stimulus material supports this view (e.g., Corteen, 1969). Indeed, several CIT studies found a positive association between recall and detection efficiency (e.g., Carmel, Dayan, Naveh, Raveh, & Ben-Shakhar, 2003; Iacono et al.,1984; Verschuere, Crombez, Koster, Van Bockstaele, & De Clercq, 2007; Waid, Orne, Cook, & Orne, 1978; Waid, Orne & Orne, 1981). In sum, orienting response theory can explain most of the research findings related to the CIT. Furthermore, it has also been successful in generating new predictions. For example, based upon orienting response theory, Elaad and Ben-Shakhar (2006) proposed and validated a new outcome measure (finger pulse line length) that combined two orienting response indicators—heart rate deceleration and peripheral vasoconstriction.

On the other hand, some research findings are hard to reconcile with the orienting response theory. Heart rate deceleration elicited by relevant CIT items is more extended than one would expect from orienting response theory. Heart rate typically decelerates 1–5 seconds after onset of the orienting response-eliciting stimulus and then returns to baseline (Richards & Casey, 1992). Yet, heart rate deceleration to relevant CIT items may last for 15 seconds. In addition, although orienting response theory predicts greater startle modulation to the relevant than to the irrelevant items, Verschuere, Crombez, Koster, Van Bockstaele, & De Clercq (2007) failed to support this prediction and proposed an alternative hypothesis, namely, response inhibition, to explain the startle data. Processes other than orienting may contribute to physiological responding in the CIT, and response inhibition seems a valuable candidate. This account is also supported by recent fMRI research (see Gamer, Bauermann, Stoeter, & Vossel, 2007).

Factors Affecting the Outcomes of the CIT

The effects of a large number of factors on the CIT's outcome have been examined during the past four or five decades. In this chapter, we shall focus on two major factors that attracted a relatively large number of researchers, probably because they may have not only practical but also theoretical implications. Martin Orne and his colleagues examined the role of motivation on the outcomes of the CIT in the 1960s. Specifically, Gustafson and Orne (1963) manipulated motivation to successfully avoid detection and demonstrated that motivational instructions were associated with increased detection efficiency. In a subsequent study, Gustafson and Orne (1965) used a more complex experimental design in which subjects were tested twice and received feedback after the first CIT. They demonstrated that motivational instructions interacted with the feedback, such that detection efficiency was higher when the feedback contradicted the subject's motivation (e.g., successful detection when motivated to avoid detection) than when it was in line with the subject's motivation. Subsequent studies produced inconsistent results (e.g., Davidson, 1968; Elaad & Ben-Shakhar, 1989; Furedy & Ben-Shakhar, 1991; Kugelmass & Lieblich, 1966; Lieblich, Naftali, Shmueli, & Kugelmass, 1974), but the results of a meta-analysis showed that motivation to avoid detection significantly improved detection efficiency (see Ben-Shakhar & Elaad, 2003, for more information about the magnitude of the motivation effect). On the other hand, this analysis also showed that successful detection was obtained under low-motivation conditions, implying that motivational instructions are not necessary for obtaining the CIT effect.

Another set of studies examined the role of verbal answers to the CIT items in detection efficiency. Specifically, most of these studies examined whether a deceptive verbal answer is associated with increased detection efficiency and whether deception is necessary for obtaining the CIT effect. This issue was examined by Kugelmass et al. (1967), who obtained nearly identical detection when participants deceived (answered "no" to all items, including the critical one) and when they answered truthfully (answered "yes"). However, as with the motivational manipulations, subsequent studies yielded inconsistent results (e.g., Elaad & Ben-Shakhar, 1989; Furedy & Ben-Shakhar, 1991; Horneman & O'Gorman, 1985; Verschuere, Crombez, Smolders, & De Clercq, 2009). The results of the meta-analysis revealed a tendency toward better differentiation with overt deception, but the effect failed to reach significance. Thus, it seems that overt denial can add to, but is not necessary for, a successful concealed information detection.

The findings regarding both the motivation and the deception factors may be interpreted as supporting orienting response theory, which postulates that recognition of the critical items is sufficient for producing enhanced orienting responses to these items. Factors like motivation and deception may increase the effect because they may enhance the significance of the concealed information.

Factors That May Limit the Applicability of the CIT

Finally, we shall discuss the external validity of CIT research and whether the results obtained in laboratory experiments can be generalized to the realistic criminal investigation context where the CIT might be applied. It should be noted that the majority of CIT studies were conducted in artificial laboratory settings where volunteering participants were requested to commit a mock crime, which had no consequences for their well-being. It is important, therefore, to examine the important factors that differentiate the experimental setting from real criminal investigations. As described in the Introduction, implementation of the CIT depends on successful concealment of the critical items. Typically, in mock-crime studies concealment is perfectly guaranteed. However, in real life this is not necessarily the case and critical items may leak to innocent suspects, either through the media or during the course of the police interrogation process. Several studies examined the effect of information leakage on CIT accuracy and particularly on false-positive outcomes. Most of these studies were conducted by Bradley and his colleagues (Bradley & Ainsworth, 1984; Bradley, MacLaren, & Carle, 1996; Bradley & Rettinger, 1992; Bradley & Warfield, 1984; see Bradley, Barefoot, & Arsenault, 2011, for a recent review of the leakage literature). Generally, these studies demonstrated that although informed innocent participants showed larger responses to the critical items compared with uninformed innocents, they could be differentiated from guilty participants. However, two recent studies demonstrated that informed innocents were not differentiated from guilty participants when the CIT was administered immediately after the mock crime (Gamer, Kosiol, & Vossel, 2010; Nahari & Ben-Shakhar, 2011). But when the test was delayed (as is usually the case in realistic criminal investigations), informed innocents showed smaller differential responses to the critical items compared with guilty participants. This was mediated in both studies by the fact that informed innocents forgot critical items more often than guilty participants. Several means to reduce the damaging effects of information leakage (in addition to improving police practices) were examined by some researchers. Ben-Shakhar et al. (1999) used target items to which participants had to respond in addition to the critical and control items. Under this procedure, the rates of false-positive outcomes among informed innocents were somewhat reduced. Bradley and Warfield (1984) proposed a modified version of the CIT, called the Guilty Action Test (GAT), in which the formulation of the questions emphasizes actions rather than knowledge (e.g., "Did you kill Mr. X with a gun?" "With a knife?" rather than "Was Mr. X killed with a gun?" "With a knife?"). Under the GAT, guilty suspects are lying when giving negative answers to these questions, whereas informed innocents are telling the truth. Bradley et al. (1996) directly compared the CIT and the GAT and showed that the GAT significantly reduced the false-positive rates, although these rates were still very high (50%). On the other hand, a more recent study by Gamer (2010) failed to find any differences between the two test formats: In both formats, informed innocents were undifferentiated from guilty participants.

While leakage of critical information may affect false-positive rates, other factors that can increase false-negative rates were also identified. Specifically, several studies demonstrated that the CIT is vulnerable to countermeasures, namely, deliberate techniques that might be used by suspects to alter their physiological reactions in order to avoid detection. Countermeasures can be employed in an attempt either to inhibit responses to the relevant items or to create excitation to the neutral-control items. Elaad and Ben Shakhar (1991) and Kubis (1962) examined countermeasures designed to distract the subjects' attention from the critical item (e.g., by instructing subjects to count sheep throughout the test) and thus inhibit responses to the critical items. This manipulation was mildly effective and reduced detection rates in some cases. Attempting to create or enhance responses to the neutral items turned out to be a much more powerful manipulation. This can be achieved either by physical means (subjects can bite their tongue to inflict pain when the control items are presented) or by mental countermeasures (subjects can recall exciting and emotional memories or perform mental activities during the presentation of control items). Two studies examined the effects of mental countermeasures on the outcomes of the CIT (Ben-Shakhar & Dolev, 1996; Honts et al., 1996). Both studies demonstrated a significant reduction in skin conductance response detection efficiency when the countermeasures were applied, but no countermeasure effect was detected with the respiration line length.

Clearly, both physical and mental countermeasures require some sophistication and certain knowledge. However, there is an extensive literature in which ANS-based polygraph procedures, including effective countermeasure techniques, are described in great detail. Thus, the danger that interested individuals might gain the necessary understanding to use countermeasures is real. For a more detailed review of the effects of countermeasures as well as means to reduce their effect, see Ben-Shakhar (2011).

A successful implementation of the CIT in the criminal investigation context depends on the identification of a sufficient number of salient features of the crime, features that are likely to be noticed by the perpetrator and stored in memory. Unfortunately, the bulk of CIT research has been conducted in artificial settings where it was guaranteed that participants would memorize the critical features of a mock crime. Furthermore, the CIT was typically administered immediately after participants committed the mock crime, whereas in the realistic criminal investigation polygraph tests are administered after a relatively long delay. Thus, it is questionable whether the results of mock-crime studies would be generalized. Recently, three studies examined the role of memory for critical items on the CIT's outcomes (Carmel et al., 2003; Gamer et al., 2010; Nahari & Ben-Shakhar, 2011). These studies revealed that when the CIT is administered 1 or 2 weeks after the mock crime, certain critical items are not recalled and consequently do not elicit differential responses. However, consistent with memory research (e.g., Kensinger, 2007), memory loss occurs mostly with peripheral items (features that are not directly related to the execution of the crime, such as a picture on the wall of the crime scene). Central features, such as the type of weapon used, are capable of eliciting large responses even when the test is delayed. This line of research has important practical implications for constructing proper CITs.

DETECTION OF CONCEALED KNOWLEDGE WITH EVENT-RELATED POTENTIALS

Background

An event-related potential is a series of peaks and troughs in the electroencephalogram (EEG; spontaneously occurring brain waves) elicited by a discrete stimulus or event. The eliciting event for the P300 event-related potential component can be any *rarely* presented stimulus having special meaning and that is therefore *salient* for the subject. The special stimuli are often called *oddballs* and the other, frequent stimuli are called *frequents*. The ongoing scalp-recorded EEG is noisy, and since P300 must ride on it, it is sometimes hard to see in single trial samples. One therefore averages event-related potential waveform responses to 30-40 presentations of oddballs and of each frequent item, all time-locked to the stimulus event onset. In CIT applications, the oddball is typically a meaningful word or picture (called a *probe*) related to some event, such as a crime of which the subject wants to conceal knowledge. It is presented randomly and rarely among a Bernoulli series of other, frequently occurring, nonmeaningful stimuli (frequent *irrelevants*) from the same category as the probe. For example, the name (or picture) of an actual murder weapon (e.g., a knife) used in a crime can be presented to a suspect in a series of other possible crime-irrelevant weapons (e.g., pistol, club, tire iron, rifle, rope, axe) in about 20% of the presentations. A guilty but not an innocent subject will recognize only the knife, and his or her brain will respond by showing the P300 sign of recognition in the knife-evoked probe wave but not in the irrelevant waves (see Figure 11.1 below). After obtaining averages of 30–40 presentations of probes and of each irrelevant, one then uses a statistical procedure to compare probe and irrelevant P300s. The *bootstrap* method, often used for this purpose and detailed in Rosenfeld (2011), gives the confidence (from 0 to 1.0) one has that in a given subject, the average probe P300 is larger than the average irrelevant P300. Typically, there must be at least a .9 level of confidence before one can conclude that a subject recognizes concealed information germane to a crime.

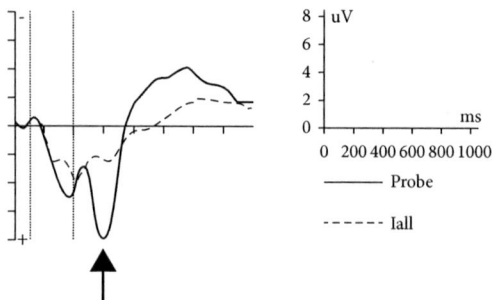

Figure 11.1 This figure shows an average probe P300 wave (arrow) of the brain's response (solid line) to a probe stimulus (a birth date) superimposed on an event-related potential without a P300 (dashed line) that was elicited by irrelevant dates. The dotted vertical lines show the onset and offset of the 300 millisecond long stimulus. These are recorded from the scalp.

The previous figure is an average probe P300 wave (arrow) of the brain's response (solid line) to a probe stimulus (a birth date) superimposed on an event-related potential without a P300 (dashed line) that was elicited by irrelevant dates. These are recorded from the scalp.

The idea of using P300 to detect concealed memories, as an indirect means of deception detection, came to the Rosenfeld lab from Emanuel Donchin's seminal work on the functional significance of P300. Karis, Fabiani, and Donchin (1984) demonstrated two important phenomena: (1) A list of words was learned, and then a subset of these words was presented among a larger set of other, novel words in a later test. It was found that the recalled, previously exposed, familiar words evoked larger P300s than novel words. (2) Some of the old words were initially presented in an unusual (oddball) font size, which made them more memorable. The P300s elicited during this initial presentation by the oddball words were larger than those elicited by words in ordinary font size, and they predicted correctly that the oddballs would be better recalled in subsequent tests. Karis and colleagues stated, "P300 is sensitive to the strength of a decaying memory representation" (p. 179). In a later study, these workers stated that "The elicitation of a P300 is associated with a change in the memory representation of a word" (Fabiani, Karis, & Donchin, 1986, p. 299). It was never implied that P300 represents a reading out from memory, but it is surely associated with recognition of memorable items. Moreover, the first phenomenon listed above suggested that P300 could be used as an index of "guilty knowledge" recognition in the CIT.

Older Protocols and Vulnerability to Countermeasures

The earliest P300-based CITs (e.g., Allen, Iacono, & Danielson, 1992; Farwell & Donchin, 1991; Rosenfeld et al., 1988, 1991) were called *three-stimulus protocols* since every trial in this CIT presented either a probe, irrelevant, or *target* stimulus. The target was simply another irrelevant, but one to which the subject had to make a unique button response different than the single button pressed either to the probe or the irrelevant, the idea being to force the subject to attend to whichever unpredictable stimulus was randomly presented on each trial. These older protocols appeared to be very accurate at first and were extensively reviewed in depth elsewhere (Rosenfeld, 2005, 2011), but they were not without limitations. A very serious problem with all three-stimulus protocols has been their vulnerability to countermeasures, which are anything a subject does to distort the results of deception test (Honts et al.,1996). In demonstrating the vulnerability of three-stimulus protocols to countermeasures, Rosenfeld, Soskins, Bosh, and Ryan (2004) and Rosenfeld et al. (2008) anticipated the ideal countermeasure: secret conversion by the subject of irrelevant items to target items requiring specific covert responses, behavioral or mental. (Mertens and Allen, 2008, also demonstrated similarly effective countermeasures to the three-stimulus protocol.) Rosenfeld et al. (2004) strongly suspected that this strategy would be effective, because in the ordinary uncountered three-stimulus protocol, the subject is instructed to make unique responses to explicitly assigned targets, and these responses are readily executed, typically resulting in large target P300s. It was reasoned that if the subject can follow an experimenter's instruction to respond uniquely to an experimenter-chosen irrelevant (an *explicit* target), then the subject could also define some irrelevants himself or herself (*covert* targets) to which to make unique (countermeasure) responses. These originally irrelevant stimuli but now secret targets would also elicit large P300s so that one could no longer depend on the probe P300 to exceed the irrelevant P300. The larger probe P300 is what, in the absence of countermeasures, would usually lead to the diagnosis of possession of concealed information.

We note here that the commercially available method called *brain fingerprinting* is one of the three-stimulus protocols, and as such, it is probably vulnerable to countermeasures, as are the other three-stimulus protocols for the same reasons reviewed above. We acknowledge that its developer claimed to the contrary (in a published meetings abstract [Farwell, 2008] not subjected to the usual peer review), but unfortunately, these claims were not supported by research published in peer-reviewed journals in psychology, neuroscience, or psychophysiology. The major difference between brain fingerprinting and the Farwell and Donchin (1991) paper noted above (and discussed in Rosenfeld, 2011) is that the former uses a purportedly novel EEG analysis technique called MERMER. This technique was deeply analyzed as well as it could be (based on limited information; see below) in Rosenfeld (2005), and it was shown there that although the method of combination of its elements has never been made explicit (not even in the patents covering the method), its key elements themselves were shown to be essentially various ways of measuring the previously well-known P300. Moreover, without a disclosure of these MERMER methods, to date it has been impossible for any independent researchers to attempt independent replication, as is usually required in science prior to general acceptance of a claimed novel finding or method. Indeed, there has never been a publication in any peer- reviewed journal in neuroscience, psychology, or psychophysiology in which MERMER is presented, not even by its developer. We have raised this issue since the editors of the current volume have encouraged us to discuss brain fingerprinting—and also another method called BEOS—since these putative concealed memory detectors have been recently much in the media, and thus are of possible interest to some readers of this volume. Indeed, BEOS was admitted to a court in India and strongly influenced the outcome of a murder case there, despite the fact that BEOS has never appeared in a peer-reviewed journal of any kind. As for brain fingerprinting, although its developer claims on the brain fingerprinting website (as of March 2011) that the method was admitted to an Iowa Supreme Court murder hearing and led to the convict's release from prison, in fact the convict (Harrington) was granted a new trial for reasons having nothing to do with brain fingerprinting, which the court decided not to consider in its decision since the other matters were dispositive. The details and relevant excerpts from the court proceedings are presented in Rosenfeld (2005), and the full case proceedings are also available (See *Harrington v. Iowa*, 2000. This is the final ruling by the Iowa Supreme Court. It contains references to the earlier proceedings.).

The Complex Trial Protocol: Theoretical Background, Early Examples, and RT as a Countermeasure Index

Rosenfeld et al. (2008) concluded that in the three-stimulus protocol, target and probe stimuli were competing for attention resources, a situation that tends to reduce P300 (Donchin, Kramer, & Wickens, 1986) and thus weaken the sensitivity of the three-stimulus protocol. That is, in each trial of the three-stimulus protocol, a dual task protocol is in effect in that subjects must be prepared to do an *explicit* target/nontarget discrimination task simultaneously with an *implicit* and involuntary probe recognition task, since on each trial, either targets, irrelevants, or probes could appear in the same trial-starting time position. To overcome this difficulty, Rosenfeld et al. (2008) developed a novel P300 protocol called the *complex trial protocol* that temporally separated (by about 1 second in each trial) the presentation of probe or irrelevant from target or nontarget. The trial begins with presentation of either a probe or an irrelevant (S1 for the first stimulus), to be immediately followed by a button press (R1, the "I saw it" response) signaling the operator that the stimulus was perceived. Then, after a randomly enduring delay of 1200 to 1600 milliseconds, the second stimulus (S2), either a target or nontarget is presented and the subject makes a second button press (R2) on either a target or nontarget button. As in the three-stimulus protocol, this S2/R2 sequence is meant to maintain attention throughout. To further enforce attention, the subject is warned that on occasion the protocol will be paused and the experimenter will ask the subject to recall the just presented S1. More than one error on these five or six unpredictable test trials will result in a report of noncooperation. The target used in our recent complex trial protocol studies is the number string "11111" among strings of other, nontarget numbers, "22222," "33333," and so on.

It was found in this first complex trial protocol that with a 4:1 ratio of irrelevant to probe items, each irrelevant requiring a unique, usually *physical* countermeasure, 90%–100% of all subjects were correctly classified into simple guilty (no countermeasures), guilty with countermeasures, and innocent conditions, yielding Grier (1971) A' test efficiencies varying from .91 to .98 (out of a maximum of 1.0) in two replications, each at two (.9 and .95) confidence levels for bootstrap tests. (A' is a nonparametric signal detection theoretical index of guilty vs. innocent discrimination efficiency by the test protocol. Related to the area under the receiver operating characteristic described above, it is a direct function of positive identification of guilty subjects and an inverse function of false-positive diagnosis of innocent subjects.) It was also found that reaction time (RT) to S1 indexed countermeasure use *within* the test block since countermeasure users' RTs to countered irrelevants were on average 160 milliseconds greater than probe RTs *within the same test block*. Thus, screening for countermeasure use was possible based on RTs. This screening involved comparing probe P300s only to averaged irrelevant P300s whose RTs were not significantly greater than the probe RT, since in simple guilty subjects not using countermeasures, the probe RT is usually significantly *greater* than the irrelevant RT (Rosenfeld et al., 2008; Seymour, Seifert, Mosman, & Shafto, 2000). The 2008 study used subjects' birth dates versus other irrelevant dates as probe stimuli, as one might do in cases of suspected malingering of memory disorders. Rosenfeld and Labkovsky (2010) extended this protocol in a situation where only two of four irrelevants were countered with purely *mental* countermeasures. (Countering fewer than all irrelevants is a more effective strategy from the perpetrator's point of view; see Meixner and Rosenfeld, 2010.) The critical summary observations in the Rosenfeld and Labkovsky study were that bootstrap tests comparing the probe P300 and average P300 for all irrelevants yielded 100% accuracy in both the simple guilty (without countermeasures) and guilty (with countermeasures) groups. With the low 8% false-positive values in the innocent control group, detection efficiency as measured by Grier's (1971) A' values remained high at .96 and .98 for countermeasure and simple guilty groups, respectively.

Winograd and Rosenfeld (2011) successfully extended the new P300-based complex trial protocol for use in mock crime situations for which three-stimulus protocols had been weak (Rosenfeld, Biroschak, & Furedy, 2006). The irrelevant/probe ratio was 6:1. Three groups of subjects were run as (1) *Innocent control* (IC), (2) *Simply guilty with no countermeasures* (SG), and (3) *Guilty with countermeasures* (CM) groups. Grier (1971) A' values based on diagnosis with P300 varied here from .93 to .98, with 100% correct detection in the CM group. It is additionally noted that all subjects were run in an innocent condition during a preliminary baseline (BASE) block, the aim being to obtain RTs to S1 in conditions in which no countermeasure motivation or instructions existed. Results for the three groups in baseline and experimental (EXP)

Table 11.1 RTs (ms) from the Winograd and Rosenfeld (2011) study

Group	BASE-P	B-IREL	EXP-P	EXP-IREL
SG	401.8	390.8	392.8	393.4
CM	483.9	460.3	806.5	1196.9
IC	469.1	442.2	393.7	397.3

blocks are presented in Table 11.1, showing probe (P) and irrelevant (IREL) RTs (in milliseconds).

There were no significant differences among the groups and stimuli in the baseline condition *prior to the mock crime commission* when all group members were identical as subjects guilty of concealing information about selected cards. In the experimental (*postcrime*) conditions, SG and IC RTs to probes and irrelevants were virtually identical and not significantly different than baseline RTs. However, in the countermeasure postcrime (experimental) condition, probe RTs were about double those of the other groups and irrelevant RTs were about three times as large. Thus, in this study, probe versus irrelevant RTs *within one test block* could be used to diagnose countermeasure use and to screen countermeasure users as described above. This is because, in this study and in Rosenfeld et al. (2008), subjects used countermeasure responses *before and separate from R1* ("I saw it") responses. The Rosenfeld group calls such countermeasure strategies *splitting* countermeasures. Six irrelevants were used, and subjects needed to pause on each trial to think (1) if a countermeasure was required and (2) if a countermeasure was required, which unique one should be used. The pauses probably caused increases in countermeasure users' RTs.

Sokolovsky, Rothenberg, Labkovsky, Meixner, and Rosenfeld (2011) studied a novel *lumping* countermeasure in which subjects are trained to execute the countermeasure and "I saw it" (R1) responses at the same time to half of the four irrelevants used. (The countermeasure and R1 responses are thus lumped rather than split.) This strategy does *not* affect the ability of the complex trial protocol to still detect more than 80% of the lumping countermeasure users based on probe versus irrelevant P300 size. However, it *does* destroy the ability of the S1 RT to index countermeasure use *within* the test block of a complex trial protocol with four irrelevants. Nor can this RT be used to screen irrelevant P300s based on elevated levels of RTs. Most recently, however, Hu et al. (2010) demonstrated that with the use of *eight* irrelevants, two, four, or six lumping countermeasures (performed by three independent groups) produce a systematically increasing effect on irrelevant RTs, and countermeasure use within the block can be detected to screen out irrelevant P300s associated with elevated levels of RTs. Thus, 84% of the lumping countermeasure users were detected (three group average) based on RT-screened P300. The Grier (1971)

A' indices of test efficiency were .96, .93, and .91, respectively across the two, four, and six countermeasure groups in this study. Also important was that while lumping countermeasures may threaten *within-block* identification of countered irrelevants via elevated levels of RTs in complex trial protocols with lower (e.g., 1:4) irrelevant/probe ratios, the data in Table 11.1 suggest that normative data might be obtained in situations in which the motivation to use countermeasures is lacking, so that one might diagnose even lumping countermeasure use by comparing normative and testing RTs, as Hu et al. (2010) did. Moreover, it should be recalled that even lumping countermeasures do not obviate P300-based detection of concealed guilty knowledge, particularly with higher ratios of irrelevant to probe (e.g., 10:1).

RT-Based Concealed Information Detectors

Perhaps another finding of broader relevance to the psychophysiology community is the demonstration in Sokolovsky et al. (2011) of a specific method for precise voluntary control of RT, a variable of broad general use in psychology. Others have suggested that RT is a poor variable to use in diagnostic situations such as deception detection because of its potential susceptibility to voluntary control (Farwell & Donchin, 1991; Gronau, Ben-Shakhar, & Cohen, 2005). Verschuere, Crombez, DeGrootte, and Roosseel (2010) argued in favor of RT as a good index of detection of concealed information, though he also (Verschuere, Prati, & De Houwer, 2009) demonstrated that in the context of the autobiographical Implicit Association Test (Sartori, Agosta, Zogmaister, Ferrara, & Castiello, 2008; see below), subjects may be trained to generally slow certain reaction times. Seymour et al. (2000) also showed that RT could be slowed if upper limits on response times were not imposed. However, until our first lumping countermeasure study (Sokolovsky et al., 2011), there has been no direct demonstration of a specific strategy for precisely (vs. slowing) controlling RT by timing a cognitive (e.g., a lumping countermeasure) response to coincide with a behavioral (e.g., "I saw it") response. This would appear to suggest a more general RT control technique that would allow one to generate RTs of specifically varying durations by timing the motor (button press) response to coincide with mentally recited words of systematically varying lengths. Thus, it should be possible to generate any target RT under all (e.g., upper-limit) conditions, thus rendering RT-based CITs of questionable value, as initially speculated by Farwell and Donchin (1991). It is emphasized that the ERP-based methods in the Rosenfeld group's complex trial protocol studies for detection of concealed information do *not* use RT as an index of recognition of guilty knowledge (the P300 serves that role), but use RT as an index of countermeasure use.

The findings of Sokolovsky et al. (2011) also pose a problem for a recent and extremely clever RT-based method for detecting concealed information known as the Implicit Association Test (IAT; Greenwald, McGhee, & Schwartz, 1998; Sartori et al., 2008). The website (https://implicit.harvard.edu/implicit/) that demonstrates and describes the method includes the following explanatory statement:

> The IAT asks you to pair two concepts (e.g., *young* and *good*, or *elderly* and *good*). The more closely associated the two concepts are, the easier it is to respond to them as a single unit. So, if *young* and *good* are strongly associated, it should be easier to respond faster when you are asked to give the same response [a common key press] to these two. If *elderly* and *good* are not so strongly associated, it should be harder to respond fast when they are paired. This gives a measure of how strongly associated the two types of concepts are. The more associated, the more rapidly you should be able to respond.

Sartori et al., (2008), extended this RT-based method to detect deception by observing that guilty versus innocent subjects respond differentially to linkages between true and innocent statements versus true and guilty statements. The results were most impressive, though as noted above, Verschuere, Prati et al. (2009) demonstrated that subjects can be trained to slow down RTs when needed to counter the test, though most recently, Agosta, Ghirardi, Zogmaister,Castiello, and Sartori (2011) have shown that it may be possible to detect such countermeasure use. As of this writing, the utility of the IAT in the detection of concealed information is controversial. In any case, the method of Sokolovsky et al. (2011) suggests the possibility of more precise control of RT than the general slowing used by Verschuere, Prati et al. (2009), and would appear to pose an even greater threat to the IAT, although this remains at present an empirical question.

Application of the Complex Trial Protocol for Antiterror Situations

A recent novel application of the complex trial protocol was in an antiterrorist situation. Since September 11, 2001, general interest in deception detection has increased, particularly in situations in which suspected terrorists might be captured and questioned prior to commission of a specific terrorist act. Such a situation poses new challenges for P300-based concealed information detection. For example, one may arrest a suspected terrorist, but one doesn't necessarily know where, when, or how he—or a coconspirator still at large—plans to strike. However, intelligence may provide a few ideas about reasonable and probable answers to these questions, so that one can construct lists of plausible item sets for each category of information in which one is interested—for example, a set of U.S. cities likely to be attacked. However, one is then faced with the issue of determining which probe item should be used in tests of whether or not it elicits the largest P300 among a set of such stimuli.

Meixner and Rosenfeld (2011) undertook to model this situation. A subject in a guilty (SG) group ($n = 12$) was given a briefing document explaining that he was to play the role of a terrorist agent and plan a mock terrorist attack on the United States. The document detailed several different possible options he could choose regarding how to carry out the attack. The subject then read detailed descriptions of five types of bombs that could be used, five locations in the city of Houston that could be attacked, and five dates in July when the attack could take place. The descriptions contained the pros and cons of each potential choice and instructed the subject to choose one type of bomb, one location in Houston, and one date on which to attack. After reading the briefing document, the subject was instructed to compose a letter describing the choices made to the fictitious superior in the terrorist organization. Subjects in the innocent (IN) group ($n = 12$) completed a similar task but planned a vacation instead of a terrorist attack. Then all subjects completed three separate blocks of the complex trial protocol task, with each block testing for a separate concealed information item relevant to the planned act of terror. So all (SG and IN) subjects were tested on the guilty scenario with potential (1) cities where the terrorist attack could occur, (2) weapon types that could be used, and (3) attack dates.

The data for each block were analyzed in three ways. In one way, the actually known guilty knowledge item was the probe, and its P300 was tested against the average P300 of all five other (irrelevant) items in each block for this study (the P vs. Iall test). The second analysis (P vs. Imax) tested the known probe P300 against the maximum irrelevant (without RT screening). Finally, as would be required in the field, an analysis was done *for antiterror situations in which ground truth was lacking*. It was simply assumed that if the subject was concealing information concerning one item of the six tested in each block, it would evoke the *largest* P300, so Meixner and Rosenfeld (2011) tested the largest P300 (the hypothesized probe P300) against the *next largest* P300 (the "blind" Imax test; they assumed this second largest P300 to be the largest evoked by an irrelevant item). They used 1000 bootstrapped iterations for each block, then combined data from three blocks and averaged across blocks to yield the results presented in Table 11.2.

The numbers under the guilty and innocent designations show the three-block average number (maximum = 1,000 = Bootstrap Confidence = 1.0) of bootstrap iterations in which the bootstrapped average probe or hypothetical

Table 11.2 From the Meixner and Rosenfeld (2011) Study

P vs Iall		P vs Imax		Blind Imax	
Guilty	Innocent	Guilty	Innocent	Guilty	Innocent
1000	648	985	287	985	603
1000	610	999	416	998	602
955	598	889	476	892	649
996	611	898	430	893	605
994	150	946	17	943	689
909	475	698	284	761	547
945	600	677	365	702	536
997	555	959	250	961	569
999	586	908	217	907	565
985	690	888	382	886	706
912	390	667	129	698	650
903	644	837	215	842	702
966	546	863	289	872	619
12/12	0/12	12/12	0/12	10/12	0/12
AUC = 1.0		AUC = 1.0		AUC = .979	

NOTES: The numbers under the guilty and innocent designations show the three-block average number (maximum = 1,000) of bootstrap iterations in which the bootstrapped average probe or hypothetical probe (for blind Imax) tested as greater than the average of other P300s as designated. Each of the 12 rows represents a subject in each column for guilty and innocent groups. Means are shown in the third row from the bottom. Guilty diagnostic fractions are shown in the second row from the bottom, and the respective areas under ROC curves (AUC) are shown in the bottom row.

SOURCE: From "A Mock Terrorism Application of the P300-Based Concealed Information Test," by J. B. Meixner and J. P. Rosenfeld, 2011, *Psychophysiology, 48*, 151. Copyright 2011 by *Society for Psychophysiological Research*. Reprinted with permission of the author.

probe (for blind Imax) tested as greater than the average of other P300s as designated. Each of the 12 rows represents a subject in each column for guilty and innocent groups. Means are shown in the third row from the bottom. Note that for comparisons of the first two columns, the investigators used the usual .90 confidence level (900 positive iterations) for guilt decisions, since the .90 level was developed for a P versus Iall comparison. However, for P versus Imax and blind Imax comparisons, .65 (650 positive iterations) and .75 (750 positive iterations), respectively, were the confidence levels used for guilty diagnoses since the innocent groups in those comparisons had counts not surprisingly (as explained in Meixner & Rosenfeld, 2011) well away from the 500 usually approximated in P versus Iall tests (e.g., 546 is the Probe vs. Iall mean in Table 11.2). Correct detection rates of both guilty and innocent persons are shown in the second row from the bottom. As these rates are based on classification rules that minimize false-positive rates in this sample, they should be treated cautiously. On the other hand, the respective areas under receiver operating characteristic curves (AUC; related to Grier's 1971 A' statistic) that are shown in the bottom row don't depend on these classification rules and are therefore more likely to be generalizable. It is apparent that Meixner and Rosenfeld (2011) obtained perfect guilty-innocent discrimination in P versus Iall and P versus Imax tests and excellent discrimination (AUC = .979) in the field-relevant blind tests.

A guilty decision in the above study was based on totals for three blocks of data. It is certainly also of interest to know how many (of three possible in each subject) details of the planned terrorist act could be discerned. For that datum, one needs to know how many *individual blocks* led to positive outcomes on bootstrap tests. Using a confidence interval of .9, with no a priori specification of the probe, Meixner and Rosenfeld (2011) were able to correctly identify 21 of 30 possible terrorist act details in the 10 of 12 guilty subjects correctly identified in blind Imax tests.

P300: Concluding Remarks

Certainly, questions remain to be answered about the complex trial protocol. For example, how many irrelevant items should be used? Rosenfeld and colleagues now believe that 8–10 should be used so as to increase probe rareness, which is directly related to P300 amplitude. For would-be countermeasure users, the use of multiple irrelevants increases the cognitive load, making it increasingly difficult to execute consistently correct countermeasures, each mapped to specific irrelevant items. An increased cognitive load enhances the ability of RT to index countermeasure use. It might be suggested that executing the same countermeasure response to multiple irrelevants might simplify things for the would-be countermeasure user. This would reduce irrelevant item RT. As noted above, Rosenfeld and colleagues have always hypothesized, however, that the important attribute of a target response (for P300 generation) is its uniqueness. They have completed but not yet published a study supporting this view by showing that executing the same single countermeasure for multiple irrelevant items does not enhance irrelevant P300 size as much as executing specific differing countermeasures for different irrelevant items, rendering this "one for all" countermeasure strategy ineffective.

There are probably many other questions and challenges for the complex trial protocol as a concealed information detector, so how close is the protocol to real field use? Its empirical track record in the laboratory to date suggests that the protocol might be tested in field situations now. As suggested in the previous discussion of ANS-based CITs, the field situation poses one well-known challenge that does not occur in a laboratory model: The consequences of test failure for a real subject in a deception detection situation are much higher than those for a lab volunteer. The attendant anxiety levels in the field could add noise to the P300 signal and thereby challenge accuracy. So, while research on increased tuning of the complex trial protocol should continue in the laboratory, now may be a good time to try it out in more realistic scenarios where a subject's state of mind is more similar to that of a real crime or terrorism suspect. It may be possible to do such tests in an experimental setting. It may also be time to consider careful studies of the complex trial protocol in the real world.

DETECTION OF CONCEALED STORED MEMORIES USING FUNCTIONAL MAGNETIC RESONANCE IMAGING

Introduction

During the last decade, brain imaging techniques such as functional magnetic resonance imaging (fMRI), positron emission tomography (PET), and near infrared spectroscopy (NIRS) have been used by researchers to monitor brain activity, under the hypothesis that brain measures with good spatial resolution may be better able to detect concealed memories than peripheral psychophysiological measures. Since almost all of the research has been conducted with fMRI, in this section we will focus on this technique.

Functional MRI works by measuring changes in regional cerebral blood flow produced by neural activity unfolding over the course of several seconds. As with event-related potentials, brain activation to specific classes of events is typically measured by time-locking the fMRI time series to the onset of the events of interest and by averaging at least tens of trials in order to achieve a sufficient signal-to-noise ratio. The actual computations carried out to analyze event-related fMRI time series are more complex than those used for event-related potentials because the fMRI signals are due to hemodynamic changes that are much slower than the neural changes measured by event-related potentials. Thus, there is substantial signal overlap between temporally adjacent trials that needs to be taken into account in the statistical models. The low temporal resolution of the hemodynamic signals makes it difficult to implement promising event-related potential paradigms such as the complex trial protocol discussed earlier. However, in contrast to the event-related potential technique, fMRI has outstanding spatial resolution, so it can determine the location of brain processes in space with exquisite precision (on the order of 1 cubic millimeter). Therefore, at first sight, this would suggest that fMRI should be the ideal tool to detect concealed memories directly, since such memories may be stored in spatially specific (most likely, distributed) locations in the brain. However, there are several reasons why this logic is not so straightforward, as discussed below.

Summary of MRI Studies of Concealed Information

To date, only a few studies using CIT paradigms have been conducted with fMRI (Davatzikos et al., 2005; Gamer et al., 2007; Gamer, Klimecki, Bauermann, Stoeter, & Vossel, 2009; Ganis, Rosenfeld, Meixner, Kievit, & Schendan, 2011; Langleben et al., 2002, 2005; Monteleone et al., 2009; Nose Murai, & Taira, 2009; Phan et al., 2005). Some of these studies will be reviewed briefly in this section. Note that a number of other (non-CIT) fMRI-based studies on deception have been carried out in the last few years (e.g., Abe et al., 2006, 2008; Abe, Suzuki, Mori, Itoh, & Fujii, 2007; Bhatt et al., 2009; Ganis, Kosslyn, Stose, Thompson, & Yurgelun-Todd, 2003; Ganis, Morris, & Kosslyn, 2009; Kozel et al., 2005, 2009; Kozel, Padgett, & George, 2004; Lee et al., 2002, 2005, 2008; Mohamed et al., 2006; Nunez, Casey, Egner, Hare, & Hirsch, 2005; Spence et al., 2001, 2004; Spence, Kaylor-Hughes, Farrow, & Wilkinson, 2008), but since they used paradigms not directly aimed at detecting concealed information (e.g., differentiation of deception or control question tests), they will not be reviewed here.

The first published fMRI work using a variant of the CIT was the study by Langleben and collaborators (2002). The stimuli used in the study were playing cards, of which there were four types. The first card type was always the 5 of clubs, the card each subject would find in the envelope given to him or her at the beginning of the study. Subjects were told to lie about whether they had this card, which therefore functioned as a probe card, by denying possession using the "No" button. The second and third card types were irrelevant cards (12 of them), requiring an honest "No" response. Finally, the fourth card type was a control card (10 of spades) to ensure that subjects paid attention rather than giving an indiscriminate "No" response on each trial. (This control card serves the same role as the target stimulus in the P300-based three-stimulus protocols discussed above.) Contrasting activation to denied probes and irrelevants resulted in activation in medial prefrontal cortex, including the anterior cingulate cortex, as well as various sensorimotor regions in the left hemisphere (including the left inferior parietal lobule). These results were interpreted in terms of response inhibition processes required during deceptive responses because some of these brain regions are also found in interference tasks that require monitoring and resolving conflict between potential responses but that are not deception-involving tasks.

A subsequent study by Phan and collaborators (2005) used an almost identical card paradigm but found a rather different pattern of results. In this study, stronger activation to probes than to irrelevants was found in dorsal medial prefrontal cortex (not including the anterior cingulate cortex), ventrolateral prefrontal cortex, right superior temporal sulcus, and left parietal cortex. The pattern of results was generally interpreted as reflecting increased engagement of executive processes during deception, but no explanation was provided for the discrepancy with the findings by Langleben and collaborators (2002). Small differences in the paradigms, such as the fact that 50 different cards were used as irrelevants in this study (as opposed to the 12 used by Langleben et al.), are likely to have played a role.

Two studies by Gamer and collaborators (2007, 2009) used three-stimulus CIT protocols with playing cards and bank notes. Four cards and four European Union (EU) bank notes served as irrelevants. In the first study, regions that were more engaged by probes than by irrelevants were the right insula and adjacent inferior frontal regions and the right middle cingulate gyrus. Another region showing more activation to probes than irrelevants, curiously mentioned only in the conjunction analysis of the second study (Gamer et al., 2009), was in the left inferior frontal cortex. No differences were found in the anterior cingulate cortex. This study also interpreted the right prefrontal activation as indexing response conflict monitoring and inhibition, but correctly pointed out an alternative episodic memory retrieval interpretation. This memory retrieval interpretation was tested in the second study, using the same stimuli employed in the first study but a different task in which subjects simply pressed one button to all items. Such a task was devised to minimize the role of interference and corresponding response monitoring and inhibition processes. Subjects were told not to reveal knowledge of the probe items until the end of the study. They were also told that they would be asked questions about the items after the study in order to ensure that they paid attention during the task. The contrast between probes and irrelevants showed differential activation in the same left and right inferior frontal cortical regions found in the previous study, as revealed by a conjunction analysis. Two other regions showed stronger activation to probes than to irrelevants: the right supplementary motor area and the right supramarginal gyrus. Given that response selection processes were minimized in this study, the differences between probes and irrelevants in lateral prefrontal cortex were attributed mostly to memory-related processes such as episodic retrieval. The study also found that the differences seen between probes and irrelevants in the right prefrontal focus were smaller than in the previous study, suggesting that response selection may be an amplifying factor.

A study by Nose and collaborators (2009) also used a three-stimulus CIT protocol based on playing cards, with the key inclusion of a group without concealed knowledge. Including such a group, or condition, is critical to ensure that the effects are not due to intrinsic differences among the items used in the test, especially when items are not counterbalanced across subjects. The task used here was simply to press one button upon seeing a target card (the 8 of diamonds) and another button upon seeing all other cards. Deception was mentioned only in the sense that the experiment was about seeing if it was possible to determine the identity of the probe card by using fMRI and that subjects should try not to disclose any information about the probe. The results showed stronger activation to probes than irrelevants in the concealed information group in ventrolateral prefrontal cortex, bilaterally (Broadman Area [BA] 47), in the left inferior frontal gyrus (BA 44), in the right middle frontal gyrus (BA 9), and in the right inferior parietal lobule (BA 40). No differential activation was found in the anterior cingulate cortex. No differences were found in the group without concealed knowledge. The region that showed the most robust difference was the right ventrolateral prefrontal cortex. The authors attributed differential activation in this region to the need to inhibit any external signs of recognition that may have revealed knowledge of the probe.

Finally, a study by Ganis and collaborators (2011) used a three-stimulus concealed information test with dates as stimuli. Subjects were instructed to lie about their date of birth (probe) and tell the truth about all other dates (four irrelevants and one target; this protocol was similar to the P300-based three-stimulus protocol used by Rosenfeld et al., 2004). A no-knowledge condition was included, within subjects, in which only irrelevant and target dates were presented. The results showed stronger activation in the concealed-knowledge (relative to the no-knowledge) condition for probes than irrelevants in numerous areas, including the ventrolateral prefrontal cortex bilaterally (BA 45, 47), the medial prefrontal cortex, including the anterior cingulate (BA 32, 33, and 6, among others), the middle cingulate gyrus (BA 23/24), and the inferior parietal lobule bilaterally (BA 40). The most robust differences were found in medial and ventrolateral prefrontal cortex. The interpretation put forward in this study focused on memory retrieval and novelty detection processes, emphasizing the high saliency of the probes.

Given the small number of fMRI-based CIT studies conducted so far, it is difficult to determine whether interstudy differences in results are due to noise or to systematic factors. The only meta-analysis conducted to date on fMRI studies of deception (Christ, Van Essen, Watson, Brubaker, & McDermott, 2009) has included mostly paradigms not aimed at detecting concealed knowledge. Nonetheless, it is interesting that this meta-analysis found some of the same regions reported by the concealed information studies described above, including the lateral prefrontal and insular cortex, bilaterally (BA 6, 44, 45), the anterior cingulate (BA 24/32), and the inferior parietal lobule bilaterally (BA 7, 39, 40). Many of these regions overlap with those found in meta-analyses of executive processes such as working memory, inhibitory control, and task switching, all processes that are likely to be involved to some extent in concealed information tasks. What can be said so far is that lateral and medial prefrontal cortices are engaged by a nontrivial combination of memory- and response-selection- related processes unfolding during performance of a concealed information task.

Accuracy of fMRI Methods

One critical issue for any potential real-life applications of brain imaging is whether the methods are sufficiently accurate for detecting concealed memories in single cases. Although most studies have examined only group data, some have also estimated the accuracy of the methods in single subjects (Davatzikos et al., 2005; Ganis et al., 2011; Langleben et al., 2005; Monteleone et al., 2009; Nose et al., 2009). Davatzikos and collaborators used high-dimensional nonlinear pattern classification methods (support vector machines) in a group of 22 individuals to discriminate patterns of brain activation associated with producing deceptive and truthful responses in a simple CIT paradigm. This procedure uses information from the entire brain at the same time. One analysis modeled single trials for all subjects together, training a classifier on 99% of the trials and testing its performance on the remaining 1%. Results showed an accuracy at testing of 87.9% (90% sensitivity and 85.8% specificity). An additional cross-validation analysis trained a classifier on the average data for 21 subjects (each subject providing two datasets, one for deceptive and one for honest responses) and tested it on the left-out subject. The results indicated that predictive accuracy at testing was 88.6% (90.9% sensitivity, 86.4% specificity).

Using a related multidimensional classification method, Rissman, Greely, and Wagner (2010) employed multivoxel pattern analyses to determine if it was possible to classify whether a face was perceived as old or new, as well as whether a face was actually old or new. Note that this paradigm is different from that used in other CIT tests since each face was presented only once at test and there were no instructions to deceive. Results indicated that hits and correct rejections could be correctly distinguished with 85% accuracy on average. In contrast, classification of faces that were objectively old or new (maintaining subjective recognition status constant) was very poor.

Monteleone and collaborators (2009) performed one-out single subject analyses on the data collected by Phan and colleagues (2005) and found that the region that best discriminated between deceptive and honest cases was the medial prefrontal cortex, which could identify 71% of subjects as lying without false alarms.

Nose and collaborators (2009) used a one-out cross-validation analysis using activation in the right ventrolateral prefrontal region. With this analysis, they could discriminate individuals with and without concealed knowledge with 84.2% accuracy (the rate was identical for specificity and sensitivity).

The study by Ganis and collaborators (2011) used a one-out approach and linear support vector machines applied to activation in three regions found in the main contrast between probes and irrelevants: left and right ventrolateral prefrontal cortex and medial prefrontal cortex. The results showed that these three regions could be used to discriminate concealed knowledge and no-concealed-knowledge cases with 100% accuracy.

Based on these few studies using different analytic methods, the average sensitivity is about 86% and the average specificity is about 92%.

Replicability of fMRI Methods

A second key issue that has received insufficient attention is the replicability of fMRI studies. A direct comparison of brain imaging methods with others, such as ANS and event-related potential methods, is not trivial because of the different temporal and spatial resolutions and signal-to-noise levels associated with each technique. Nonetheless, one can ask whether the key results important for detecting concealed knowledge using whatever variable is appropriate for each technique replicate across studies and laboratories. The only published replication of a study using exactly the same methods, procedures, and equipment is the one by Ganis and collaborators (2011). In this study, a second group of subjects (region of interest, ROI group) performed the same tasks as the main group for the purpose of defining ROIs to be used in the main analysis in order to avoid circularity (Kriegeskorte, Simmons, Bellgowan, & Baker, 2009). Seven out of 14 activation foci, the largest ones, overlapped between the two groups with an extent of more than 40 voxels. Some of these regions were summarized earlier. The fact that it was possible to classify subjects with 100% accuracy in the main group using ROIs defined in the second group suggests that fMRI replicability may not be an issue, provided that the same stimuli, tasks, and equipment are used.

However, the seemingly large differences in results found even by the same group when using paradigms that appear to differ only slightly is potentially problematic. For example, Langleben and collaborators (2005) tried to replicate their own original work, with small changes to the paradigm. However, the pattern of results was very different. On the one hand, the anterior cingulate and inferior parietal activations found originally were not replicated. On the other hand, the parietal lobes showed greater activation during honest compared to deceptive responses, the opposite of what was found in the first study (Langleben et al., 2002).

The dependence of brain imaging results on small changes in paradigms is not necessarily a problem, since it may simply reflect the sensitivity of the technique. However, currently there is no clear understanding of how subtle changes in concealed information paradigms affect the precise pattern of brain activation, a potential issue for application of the methods to complex real-life situations.

Generalizability of fMRI Methods

A third set of issues is related to generalizability, that is, the extent to which the laboratory results can be generalized to field situations. First, fMRI methods have to deal with the same problems already discussed for the ANS and event-related potential techniques: that our memories are not perfectly reliable and that memory is a constructive process. So far, no fMRI study has studied false memories in the context of a concealed information paradigm to determine whether they can be distinguished from true memories in single subjects.

Second, in addition to the important issue of the reliability of memory, in field situations potential suspects are likely to use countermeasures, methods used to confound deception detection procedures. A classic countermeasure is to increase arousal intentionally and thereby confuse the polygraphic methods—such as by biting one's tongue right after comparison questions. Although these types of physical countermeasures would not work with neuroimaging techniques (other than in the easily detectable way of overtly disrupting fMRI data recording with head motion), mental countermeasures that rely on inducing specific changes in brain activation to irrelevants can be highly problematic. Earlier, it was noted that simple countermeasures in which subjects generate covert responses to some irrelevant stimuli in concealed information paradigms (effectively transforming these stimuli into targets) disrupt deception detection procedures in event-related potential-based three-stimulus protocols. Critically, similar effects of countermeasures previously shown to be effective with event-related potentials (Rosenfeld et al., 2004) have been found recently in an fMRI study with a concealed knowledge information test using dates of birth as probe stimuli (Ganis et al., 2011). In this study, deception detection rates were 100% without countermeasures, but only 4 out of 12 (33%) participants with concealed knowledge but also using countermeasures were classified correctly (Ganis et al., 2011). The effect of these countermeasures is likely to be even stronger when less salient probes are used (Rosenfeld et al., 2006). This result indicates that although fMRI methods use brain activation to detect deception, they are not intrinsically immune to countermeasures.

Given that this is a rather young field, (the first fMRI study of deception was published by Spence et al., 2001), there is no strong reason to believe that accuracy rates, reliability, and robustness against countermeasures cannot be improved in the future with more advanced paradigms and analyses and with progress in brain imaging techniques. However, it is clear from the evidence just summarized that much more research is needed before these methods can begin to compete with more traditional techniques and show potential for forensic applications.

CONCLUSIONS

The extensive research reviewed in this chapter reveals that both ANS and brain-related measures can be used effectively in the CIT to detect concealed information in single individuals, who may then be classified as having or lacking knowledge about criminal acts. In this concluding section, we wish to discuss the applicability of the CIT for law enforcement and its possible use as admissible evidence in criminal courts. In spite of the impressive validity demonstrated by CIT research (e.g., Ben-Shakhar & Elaad, 2003; Rosenfeld, 2011), this method has rarely been applied by law enforcement agencies. In fact, it is being applied routinely only in Japan (see, Osugi, 2011, for a review). Numerous reasons for this rather strange situation have been proposed (e.g., Iacono, 2011; Krapohl, 2011), but we believe it mainly reflects the difficulty of modifying police investigation practices, such that critical features of crimes will be identified and concealed from the general public and from suspects. However, the Japanese experience with the CIT over five decades proves that with some effort, conditions that allow for CIT usage can be created. We recommend that law enforcement agencies seriously consider the application of the CIT instead of the questionable detection of deception methods (comparison or control question tests) that are presently favored by many enforcement agencies but that are unsupported by scientific theory and research and do not supply sufficient protection for innocent suspects.

The question of whether the CIT results can be used as admissible evidence is a bit more complex. Ben-Shakhar, Bar Hillel, and Kremnitzer (2002) and, more recently, Ben-Shakhar and Kremnitzer (2011) argued that the CIT has the potential of meeting the *Daubert* criteria for admissibility (*Daubert v. Merrell Daw Pharmaceuticals, Inc.*, 1993). The main obstacle is the lack of field studies designed to estimate the validity of the CIT when real persons suspected of committing crimes are interrogated. As indicated above, many factors differentiate artificial laboratory conditions from realistic criminal investigations. Consequently, our current knowledge does not allow for a proper estimation of the CIT's validity in the applied setting.

Two possible solutions can be offered to overcome this obstacle. First, proper field validity studies should be conducted. The few field studies conducted so far (Elaad, 1990; Elaad, Ginton, & Jungman, 1992; Hira & Furumitsu, 2002) suffer from methodological problems (see Ben-Shakhar, Verschuere & Meijer, 2011). Thus, in future field studies, ground truth should be established independently of the CIT or other polygraph test outcomes, and the CIT should be administered as early as possible, and separately from any other test. Second, controlled experiments should be designed that better approximate realistic conditions. The first steps in this direction were made by Carmel et al. (2003), Gamer et al. (2010), and Nahari and Ben-Shakhar (2011). But these efforts should be expanded and in particular, future studies should try to manipulate the level of emotional arousal both while executing the mock crime and during the administration of the CIT. We believe that adopting these recommendations would lead to enhanced implementation of the CIT and possibly also to its use as admissible evidence in criminal courts.

REFERENCES

Abe, N., Okuda, J., Suzuki, M., Sasaki, H., Matsuda, T., Mori, E., et al. (2008). Neural correlates of true memory, false memory, and deception. *Cerebral Cortex, 18*(12), 2811–2819.

Abe, N., Suzuki, M., Mori, E., Itoh, M., & Fujii, T. (2007). Deceiving others: Distinct neural responses of the prefrontal cortex and amygdala in simple fabrication and deception with social interactions. *Journal of Cognitive Neuroscience, 19*(2), 287–295.

Abe, N., Suzuki, M., Tsukiura, T., Mori, E., Yamaguchi, K., Itoh, M., et al. (2006). Dissociable roles of prefrontal and anterior cingulate cortices in deception. *Cerebral Cortex, 16*(2), 192–199.

Agosta, S., Ghirardi, V., Zogmaister, C., Castiello, U., & Sartori, G. (2011). Detecting fakers of the autobiographical IAT. *Applied Cognitive Psychology, 25*, 299–306.

Allen, J. J. B., Iacono, W. G., & Danielson, K. D. (1992). The identification of concealed memories using the event-related potential and implicit behavioral measures: A methodology for prediction in the face of individual differences. *Psychophysiology, 29*, 504–522.

Ambach, W., Stark, R., Peper, M., & Vaitl, D. (2008a). Separating deceptive and orienting components in a concealed information test. *International Journal of Psychophysiology, 70*, 95–104.

Ambach, W., Stark, R., Peper, M., & Vaitl, D. (2008b). An interfering go/no-go task does not affect accuracy in a Concealed Information Test. *International Journal of Psychophysiology, 68*, 6–16.

Balloun, K. D., & Holmes, D. S. (1979). Effects of repeated examinations on the ability to detect guilt with a polygraph examination: A laboratory experiment with a real crime. *Journal of Applied Psychology, 64*, 316–322.

Ben-Shakhar, G. (1977). A further study of the dichotomization theory in detection of information. *Psychophysiology, 14*, 408–413.

Ben-Shakhar, G. (2002). A critical review of the Control Questions Test (CQT). In M. Kleiner (Ed.), *Handbook of polygraph testing* (pp. 103–126). San Diego, CA: Academic Press.

Ben-Shakhar, (2011). Countermeasures. In B. Verschuere, G. Ben-Shakhar, & E. Meijer (Eds.), E. *Memory detection: Theory and application of the Concealed Information Test* (pp. 200–214). Cambridge: Cambridge University Press.

Ben-Shakhar, G., Bar-Hillel, M., & Kremnitzer, M. (2002). Trial by polygraph: Reconsidering the use of the GKT in court. *Law and Human Behavior, 26*, 527–541.

Ben-Shakhar, G., & Dolev, K. (1996). Psychophysiological detection through the guilty knowledge technique: Effects of mental countermeasures. *Journal of Applied Psychology, 81*, 273–281.

Ben-Shakhar, G., & Elaad, E. (2002). Effects of questions' repetition and variation on the efficiency of the guilty knowledge test: A reexamination. *Journal of Applied Psychology, 87*, 972–977.

Ben-Shakhar, G., & Elaad, E. (2003). The validity of psychophysiological detection of deception with the Guilty Knowledge Test: A meta-analytic review. *Journal of Applied Psychology, 88*, 131–151.

Ben-Shakhar, G., & Furedy, J. J. (1990). *Theories and applications in the detection of deception: A psychophysiological and international perspective*. New York, Springer-Verlag.

Ben-Shakhar, G., & Gati, I. (1987). Common and distinctive features of verbal and pictorial stimuli as determinants of psychophysiological responsivity. *Journal of Experimental Psychology: General, 116*, 91–105.

Ben-Shakhar, G., Gati I., Ben-Bassat, N., & Sniper, G. (2000). Orienting response reinstatement and dishabituation: The effects of substituting, adding and deleting components of nonsignificant stimuli. *Psychophysiology, 37*, 102–110.

Ben-Shakhar, G., Gronau, N., & Elaad, E. (1999). Leakage of relevant information to innocent examinees in the GKT: An attempt to reduce false-positive outcomes by introducing target stimuli. *Journal of Applied Psychology, 84*, 651–660.

Ben-Shakhar, G., & Kremnitzer, M. (2011). The CIT in the courtroom: Legal aspects. In B. Verschuere, G. Ben-Shakhar, & E. Meijer (Eds.), *Memory detection: Theory and application of the Concealed Information Test* (pp. 276–290). Cambridge: Cambridge University Press.

Ben-Shakhar, G., & Lieblich, I. (1982). The dichotomization theory for differential autonomic responsivity reconsidered. *Psychophysiology, 19*, 277–281.

Ben-Shakhar, G., Lieblich., I. & Kugelmass, S. (1975). Detection of information and GSR habituation: An attempt to derive detection efficiency from two habituation curves. *Psychophysiology, 12*, 283–288.

Ben-Shakhar, G., Verschuere, B., & Meijer, E. (2011). Epilogue: Current status and future developments in CIT research and practice. In B. Verschuere, G. Ben-Shakhar, & E. Meijer (Eds.), *Memory detection: Theory and application of the Concealed Information Test* (pp. 303–309). Cambridge: Cambridge University Press,

Bhatt, S., Mbwana, J., Adeyemo, A., Sawyer, A., Hailu, A., & Vanmeter, J. (2009). Lying about facial recognition: An fMRI study. *Brain Cognition, 69*, 382–390.

Bradley, M. T., & Ainsworth, D. (1984). Alcohol and the psychophysiological detection of deception. *Psychophysiology, 21*, 63–71.

Bradley, M. T., Barefoot, C. A., & Arsenault, A. M. (2011). Leakage of information to innocent suspects. In B. Verschuere, G. Ben-Shakhar, & E. Meijer (Eds.), *Memory detection: Theory and application of the Concealed Information Test* (pp. 187–199). Cambridge: Cambridge University Press.

Bradley, M. T., & Janisse, M. P. (1981). Accuracy demonstration, threat, and the detection of deception: Cardiovascular, electrodermal, and pupillary measures. *Psychophysiology, 18*, 307–315.

Bradley, M. T., MacLaren, V. V., & Carle, S. B. (1996). Deception and nondeception in guilty knowledge and guilty action polygraph tests. *Journal of Applied Psychology, 81*, 153–160.

Bradley, M. T., & Rettinger, J. (1992). Awareness of crime-relevant information and the guilty knowledge test. *Journal of Applied Psychology, 77*, 55–59.

Bradley, M. T., & Warfield, J. F. (1984). Innocence, information, and the guilty knowledge test in the detection of deception. *Psychophysiology, 21*, 683–689.

Carmel, D., Dayan, E., Naveh, A., Raveh, O., & Ben-Shakhar, G. (2003). Estimating the validity of the guilty knowledge test from simulated experiments: The external validity of mock crime studies. *Journal of Experimental Psychology: Applied, 9*, 261–269.

Christ, S. E., Van Essen, D. C., Watson, J. M., Brubaker, L. E., & McDermott, K. B. (2009). The contributions of prefrontal cortex and executive control to deception: Evidence from activation likelihood estimate meta-analyses. *Cerebral Cortex, 19*(7), 1557–1566.

Corteen, R. S. (1969). Skin conductance changes and word recall. *British Journal of Psychology, 60*, 81–84.

Cutrow, R. J., Parks, A., Lucas, N., & Thomas, K. (1972). The objective use of multiple physiological indices in the detection of deception. *Psychophysiology, 9*, 578–587.

Daubert v. Merrell Dow Pharmaceuticals, Inc., 113 S. Ct. Supp. 2786 (1993).

Davatzikos, C., Ruparel, K., Fan, Y., Shen, D. G., Acharyya, M., Loughead, J. W., et al. (2005). Classifying spatial patterns of brain activity with machine learning methods: Application to lie detection. *Neuroimage, 28*(3), 663–668.

Davidson, P. O. (1968). Validity of the guilty knowledge technique: The effect of motivation. *Journal of Applied Psychology, 52*, 62–65.

Donchin, E., Kramer, A., & Wickens, C. (1986). Applications of brain event related potentials to problems in engineering psychology. In M. Coles, S. Porges, & E. Donchin (Eds.), *Psychophysiology: Systems, processes and applications* (pp. 702–710). New York: Guilford Press.

Elaad, E. (1990). Detection of guilty knowledge in real-life criminal investigations. *Journal of Applied Psychology, 75*, 521–529.

Elaad, E. (2009). Effects of context and state of guilt on the detection of concealed crime information. *International Journal of Psychophysiology, 71*, 225–234.

Elaad, E., & Ben-Shakhar, G. (1989). Effects of motivation level and verbal response type on psychophysiological detection in the guilty knowledge test. *Psychophysiology, 26*, 442–451.

Elaad, E., & Ben-Shakhar, G. (1991). Effects of mental countermeasures on psychophysiological detection in the guilty knowledge test. *International Journal of Psychophysiology, 11,* 99–108.

Elaad, E., & Ben-Shakhar, G. (2006). Finger pulse waveform length in the detection of concealed information. *International Journal of Psychophysiology, 61,* 226–234.

Elaad, E., & Ben-Shakhar, G. (2008). Covert respiration measures for the detection of concealed information. *Biological Psychology, 77,* 284–291.

Elaad, E., Ginton, A., & Jungman, N. (1992). Detection measures in real-life criminal guilty knowledge tests. *Journal of Applied Psychology, 77,* 757–767.

Ellson, D. C., Burke, C. G., Davis, R. C., & Saltzman, I. J. (1952). *A report of research on detection of deception.* Contract NG onr-18011, Office of Naval Research. Bloomington, IN: Indiana University.

Fabiani, M., Karis, D., & Donchin, E. (1986). P300 and recall in an incidental memory paradigm., *Psychophysiology, 23,* 298–308

Farwell, L. A. (2008) Brain fingerprinting detects real crimes in the field despite one-hundred-thousand dollar reward for beating it [Abstract]. *Psychophysiology, 45*(Suppl 1), S104.

Farwell, L. A., & Donchin, E. (1991). The truth will out: Interrogative polygraphy ("lie detection") with event-related potentials. *Psychophysiology, 28,* 531–547.

Furedy, J. J., & Ben-Shakhar, G. (1991). The role of deception, intention to deceive, and motivation to avoid detection in the psychophysiological detection of guilty knowledge. *Psychophysiology, 28,* 163–171.

Gamer, M. (2010). Does the Guilty Actions Test allow for differentiating guilty subjects from informed innocents? A re-examination. *International Journal of Psychophysiology, 76,* 19–24.

Gamer, M. (2011). Detecting concealed information using autonomic measures. In B. Verschuere, G. Ben-Shakhar, & E. Meijer (Eds.), *Memory detection: Theory and application of the Concealed Information Test.* (pp. 27–45). Cambridge: Cambridge University Press.

Gamer, M., Bauermann, T., Stoeter, P., & Vossel, G. (2007). Covariations among fMRI, skin conductance and behavioral data during processing of concealed information. *Human Brain Mapping, 28,* 1287–1301.

Gamer, M., Gödert, H. W., Keth, A., Rill, H.-G., & Vossel, G. (2008) Electrodermal and phasic heart rate responses in the Guilty Actions Test: Comparing guilty examinees to informed and uninformed innocents. *International Journal of Psychophysiology, 69,* 61–68.

Gamer, M., Klimecki, O., Bauermann, T., Stoeter, P., & Vossel, G. (2009). fMRI-activation patterns in the detection of concealed information rely on memory-related effects. *Social Cognitive and Affective Neuroscience* [Epub ahead of print].

Gamer, M., Kosiol, D., & Vossel, G. (2010). Strength of memory encoding affects physiological responses in the Guilty Action Test. *Biological Psychology, 83,* 101–107.

Gamer, M., Rill, H. G., Vossel, G., & Gödert, H. W. (2006). Psychophysiological and vocal measures in the detection of guilty knowledge. *International Journal of Psychophysiology, 60,* 76–87.

Gamer, M., Verschuere, B., Crombez, G., & Vossel, G. (2008) Combining physiological measures in the detection of concealed information. *Physiology & Behavior, 95,* 333–340.

Ganis, G., Kosslyn, S. M., Stose, S., Thompson, W. L., & Yurgelun-Todd, D. A. (2003). Neural correlates of different types of deception: An fMRI investigation. *Cerebral Cortex, 13*(8), 830–836.

Ganis, G., Morris, R., & Kosslyn, S. M. (2009). Neural processes underlying self- and other-related lies: An individual difference approach using fMRI. *Social Neuroscience, 4*(6), 539–553.

Ganis, G., Rosenfeld, J. P., Meixner, J., Kievit, R. A., & Schendan, H. E. (2011). Lying in the scanner: Covert countermeasures disrupt deception detection by functional magnetic resonance imaging. *Neuroimage, 55*(1), 312–319.

Gati, I., & Ben-Shakhar, G. (1990). Novelty and significance in orientation and habituation: A feature-matching approach. *Journal of Experimental Psychology: General, 119,* 251–263.

Geldreich, E. W. (1941). Studies of the use of the galvanic skin response as a deception indicator. *Transactions of the Kansas Academy of Science, 44,* 346–351.

Geldreich, E. W. (1942). Further studies of the use of the galvanic skin response as a deception indicator. *Transactions of the Kansas Academy of Science, 45,* 279–284.

Greenwald, A. G., McGhee, D. E., & Schwartz, J. L. K. (1998). Measuring individual differences in implicit cognition: The implicit association test. *Journal of Personality and Social Psychology, 74,* 1464–1480.

Grier, J. B. (1971) Non-parametric indexes for sensitivity and bias: Computing formulas. *Psychology Bulletin, 75,* 424–429.

Gronau, N., Ben-Shakhar, G., & Cohen, A. (2005). Behavioral and physiological measures in the detection of concealed information. *Journal of Applied Psychology, 90*(1), 147–158.

Gustafson, L. A., & Orne, M. T. (1963). Effects of heightened motivation on the detection of deception. *Journal of Applied Psychology, 47,* 408–411.

Gustafson, L. A., & Orne, M. T. (1965). Effects of perceived role and role success on the detection of deception. *Journal of Applied Psychology, 49,* 412–417.

Harrington, Terry J. v. State of Iowa, November 14–15, 2000.No. PCCV073247.

Hira, S., & Furumitsu, I. (2002). Polygraphic examinations in Japan: Application of the guilty knowledge test in forensic investigations. *International Journal of Police Science and Management, 4*(1), 16–27.

Honts, C. R., Devitt, M. K., Winbush, M., & Kircher, J. C. (1996). Mental and physical countermeasures reduce the accuracy of the concealed knowledge test. *Psychophysiology, 33,* 84–92.

Horneman, C. J., & O'Gorman, J. G. (1985). Detectability in the card test as a function of the subject's verbal response. *Psychophysiology, 22,* 330–333.

Hu, X., Hegeman, D., Landry, E., Rosenfeld, J. P., Winograd, M., Sokolovsky, A., et al. (2010). Counter countermeasures: The Complex Trial Protocol (CTP) in deception detection using P300: Increasing the number of irrelevants increases its resistance to countermeasures [Abstract]. *Psychophysiology, 47,* S65.

Iacono, W. G. (2011). Encouraging the use of the Guilty Knowledge Test (GKT): What the GKT has to offer to law enforcement. In B. Verschuere, G. Ben Shakhar, & E. Meijer (Eds.), *Memory detection: Theory and application of the Concealed Information Test* (pp. 12–23). Cambridge: Cambridge University Press.

Iacono, W. G., Boisvenu, G. A., & Fleming J. A. (1984). Effects of diazepam and methylphenidate on the electrodermal detection of guilty knowledge. *Journal of Applied Psychology, 69*, 289–299.

Iacono, W. G., & Lykken, D. T. (2002). The scientific status of research on polygraph techniques: The case against polygraph tests. In D. L. Faigman, D. H. Kaye, M. J. Saks, & J. Sanders (Eds.), *Modern scientific evidence: The law and science of expert testimony* (Vol. 2, pp. 483–538). St. Paul, Minn: West Publishing.

Janisse, M. P., & Bradley, M. T. (1980). Deception, information and the pupillary response. *Perceptual and Motor Skills, 50*, 748–750.

Kahneman, D. (1973). *Attention and effort*. Englewood Cliffs, NJ: Prentice Hall.

Karis, D., Fabiani, M., & Donchin, E. (1984). P300 and memory: Individual differences in the von Restorff effect. *Cognitive Psychology, 16*, 177–216.

Kozel, F. A., Johnson, K. A., Grenesko, E. L., Laken, S. J., Kose, S., Lu, X., et al. (2009). Functional MRI detection of deception after committing a mock sabotage crime. *Journal of Forensic Science, 54*(1), 220–231.

Kozel, F. A., Johnson, K. A., Mu, Q., Grenesko, E. L., Laken, S. J., & George, M. S. (2005). Detecting deception using functional magnetic resonance imaging. *Biological Psychiatry, 58*(8), 605–613.

Kozel, F. A., Padgett, T. M., & George, M. S. (2004). A replication study of the neural correlates of deception. *Behavioral Neuroscience, 118*(4), 852–856.

Krapohl, D. J. (2011). Limitations of the Concealed Information Test in criminal cases. In B. Verschuere, G. Ben Shakhar, & E. Meijer (Eds.), *Memory detection: Theory and application of the Concealed Information Test* (pp. 151–170). Cambridge: Cambridge University Press.

Kensinger, E.A. (2007). Negative emotion enhances memory accuracy. *Current Directions in Psychological Science, 16*, 213–218.

Kriegeskorte, N., Simmons, W. K., Bellgowan, P. S., & Baker, C. I. (2009). Circular analysis in systems neuroscience: The dangers of double dipping. *Nature Neuroscience, 12*(5), 535–540.

Kubis, J. F. (1962). *Studies in lie detection: Computer feasibility considerations*. Technical Report #62-205. Prepared for the Air Force Systems Command. Contract No. AF 30 (602) -2270, project No. 5534, Fordham University.

Kugelmass, S., & Lieblich, I. (1966). Effects of realistic stress and procedural interference in experimental lie detection. *Journal of Applied Psychology, 50*, 211–216.

Kugelmass, S., Lieblich, I., & Bergman, Z. (1967). The role of "lying" in psychophysiological detection. *Psychophysiology, 3*, 312–315.

Langleben, D. D., Loughead, J. W., Bilker, W. B., Ruparel, K., Childress, A. R., Busch, S. I., et al. (2005). Telling truth from lie in individual subjects with fast event-related fMRI. *Human Brain Mapping, 26*(4), 262–272.

Langleben, D. D., Schroeder, L., Maldjian, J. A., Gur, R. C., McDonald, S., Ragland, J. D., et al. (2002). Brain activity during simulated deception: An event-related functional magnetic resonance study. *Neuroimage, 15*(3), 727–732.

Larson, J. A. (1932). *Lying and its detection: A study of deception and deception tests.* Chicago: University of Chicago Press.

Lee, T. M. C., Au, R. K., Liu, H. L., Ting, K. H., Huang, C. M., & Chan, C. C. (2008). Are errors differentiable from deceptive responses when feigning memory impairment? An fMRI study. *Brain Cognition, 69*(2), 406–412.

Lee, T. M. C., Liu, H. L., Chan, C. C., Ng, Y. B., Fox, P. T., & Gao, J. H. (2005). Neural correlates of feigned memory impairment. *Neuroimage, 28*(2), 305–313

Lee, T. M. C., Liu, H.-L., Tan, L.-H., Chan, C. C. H., Mahankali, S., Feng, C.-M., et al. (2002). Lie detection by functional magnetic resonance imaging. *Human Brain Mapping, 15*, 157–164.

Lieblich, I., Kugelmass, S., & Ben Shakhar, G. (1970). Efficiency of GSR detection of information as a function of stimulus set size. *Psychophysiology, 6*, 601–608.

Lieblich, I., Naftali, G., Shmueli, J., & Kugelmass, S. (1974). Efficiency of GSR detection of information with repeated presentation of series of stimuli in two motivational states. *Journal of Applied Psychology, 59*, 113–115.

Lubow, R. E., & Fein, O. (1996). Pupillary size in response to a visual guilty knowledge test: New technique for the detection of deception. *Journal of Experimental Psychology: Applied, 2*, 164–177.

Lykken, D. T. (1959). The GSR in the detection of guilt. *Journal of Applied Psychology, 43*, 385–388.

Lykken, D. T. (1960). The validity of the guilty knowledge technique: The effects of faking. *Journal of Applied Psychology, 44*, 258–262.

Lykken, D. T. (1974). Psychology and the lie detector industry. *American Psychologist, 29*, 725–739.

Lykken, D. T. (1998). *A tremor in the blood: Uses and abuses of the lie detector.* New York: Plenum Trade.

Lynn, R. (1966). *Attention, arousal and the orienting reaction.* New York: Pergamon.

MacLaren, V. V. (2001). A quantitative review of the guilty knowledge test. *Journal of Applied Psychology, 86*, 674–683.

Marston, W. M. (1917). Systolic blood pressure changes in deception. *Journal of Experimental Psychology, 2*, 143–163.

Marston, W. M. (1938). *The lie detector test.* New York: Smith.

Meixner, J. B., & Rosenfeld, J. P. (2010). Countermeasure mechanisms in a P300-based concealed information test. *Psychophysiology, 47*, 57–65.

Meixner, J. B., & Rosenfeld, J. P. (2011). A mock terrorism application of the P300-based concealed information test, *Psychophysiology, 48*, 149–154

Mertens, R., & Allen, J. J. (2008). The role of psychophysiology in forensic assessments: Deception detection, event-related potentials, and virtual reality mock crime scenarios. *Psychophysiology, 45*, 286–298.

Mohamed, F. B., Faro, S. H., Gordon, N. J., Platek, S. M., Ahmad, H., & Williams, J. M. (2006). Brain mapping of deception and truth telling about an ecologically valid situation: Functional MR imaging and polygraph investigation—initial experience. *Radiology, 238*(2), 679–688.

Monteleone, G. T., Phan, K. L., Nusbaum, H. C., Fitzgerald, D., Irick, J. S., Fienberg, S. E., et al. (2009). Detection of deception using fMRI: Better than chance, but well below perfection. *Social Neuroscience, 4*(6), 528–538.

Nahari, G., & Ben-Shakhar, G. (2011). Psychophysiological and behavioral measures for detecting concealed information: The role of memory for crime details. *Psychophysiology, 48*(6):733–744.

National Research Council. (2003). *The polygraph and lie detection.* Washington, DC: National Academies Press.

Nose, I., Murai, J., & Taira, M. (2009). Disclosing concealed information on the basis of cortical activations. *Neuroimage, 44*(4), 1380–1386.

Nunez, J. M., Casey, B. J., Egner, T., Hare, T., & Hirsch, J. (2005). Intentional false responding shares neural substrates with response conflict and cognitive control. *Neuroimage, 25*(1), 267–277.

Öhman, A. (1992). Orienting and attention: Preferred preattentive processing of potentially phobic stimuli. In B. A. Campbell, H. Hayne, & R. Richardson (Eds.), *Attention and information processing in infants and adults* (pp. 263–295). Hillsdale, NJ: Erlbaum.

Osugi, A. (2011). Daily application of the Concealed Information Test: Japan. In B. Verschuere, G. Ben Shakhar, & E. Meijer (Eds.) *Memory detection: Theory and application of the Concealed Information Test* (pp. 253–275). Cambridge: Cambridge University Press.

Phan, K. L., Magalhaes, A., Ziemlewicz, T. J., Fitzgerald, D. A., Green, C., & Smith, W. (2005). Neural correlates of telling lies: A functional magnetic resonance imaging study at 4 Tesla. *Academic Radiology, 12*(2), 164–172.

Podlesny, J. A., & Raskin, D. C. (1978). Effectiveness of techniques and physiological measures in the detection of deception. *Psychophysiology, 15*, 344–359.

Pollina, D. A., Dollins, A. B., Senter, S. M., Brown, T. E., Pavlidis, I., Levine, J. A., et al. (2006). Facial skin surface temperature changes during a "concealed information" test. *Annals of Biomedical Engineering, 34*, 1182–1189.

Raskin, D. C. (1989). Polygraph techniques for the detection of deception. In D. C. Raskin (Ed.), *Psychological methods in criminal investigation and evidence* (pp. 247–296). New York: Springer.

Reid, J. E. (1947). A revised questioning technique in lie-detection tests. *Journal of Criminal Law and Criminology, 37*, 542–547.

Reid, J. E., & Inbau, F. E. (1977). *Truth and deception: The polygraph ("lie detector") technique* (2nd ed.). Baltimore: Williams & Wilkins.

Richards, J. E., & Casey, B. J. (1992). Development of sustained visual attention in the human infant. In B. A. Campbell, H. Hayne, & R. Richardson (Eds.), *Attention and information processing in infants and adults: Perspectives from human and animal research* (pp. 30–60). Hillsdale, NJ: Erlbaum.

Rissman, J., Greely, H. T., & Wagner, A. D. (2010). Detecting individual memories through the neural decoding of memory states and past experience. *Proceedings of the National Academy of Sciences of the United States of America, 107*(21), 9849–9854.

Rosenfeld, J. P. (2005). "Brain fingerprinting": A critical analysis. *Scientific Review of Mental Health Practice, 4*, 20–37.

Rosenfeld, J. P. (2011). P300 in detecting concealed information. In B. Verschuere, G. Ben Shakhar, & E. Meijer (Eds.) *Memory detection: Theory and application of* the *Concealed Information Test* (pp. 63–89). Cambridge: Cambridge University Press.

Rosenfeld, J. P., Angell, A., Johnson, M., & Qian, J. (1991). An ERP-based, control-question lie detector analog: Algorithms for discriminating effects within individuals' average waveforms. *Psychophysiology, 38*, 319–335.

Rosenfeld, J. P., Biroschak, J. R., & Furedy, J. J. (2006). P300-based detection of concealed autobiographical versus incidentally acquired information in target and non-target paradigms. *International Journal of Psychophysiology, 60*(3), 251–259.

Rosenfeld, J. P., Cantwell, G., Nasman, V. T., Wojdac, V., Ivanov, S., & Mazzeri, L. (1988). A modified, event-related potential-based guilty knowledge test. *International Journal of Neuroscience, 24*, 157–161.

Rosenfeld, J. P., & Labkovsky, E. (2010). New P300-based protocol to detect concealed information: Resistance to mental countermeasures against only half the irrelevant stimuli and a possible ERP indicator of countermeasures. *Psychophysiology, 47*, 1002–1010.

Rosenfeld, J. P., Labkovsky, E., Winograd, M., Lui, M. A., Vandenboom, C., & Chedid, E. (2008), The Complex Trial Protocol (CTP): A new, countermeasure-resistant, accurate P300-based method for detection of concealed information. *Psychophysiology, 45*, 906–919

Rosenfeld, J. P., Soskins, M., Bosh, G., & Ryan, A. (2004). Simple, effective countermeasures to P300-based tests of detection of concealed information. *Psychophysiology, 41*(2), 205–219.

Sartori, G., Agosta, S., Zogmaister, C., Ferrara, S. D., & Castiello, U. (2008). How to accurately assess autobiographical events. *Psychological Science, 19*, 772–780.

Seymour, T. L., Seifert, C. M., Mosmann, A. M., & Shafto, M. G.(2000). Using response time measures to assess "guilty" knowledge. *Journal of Applied Psychology, 85*, 30–37.

Siddle, D. A. T. (1991). Orienting, habituation, and resource allocation: An associative analysis. *Psychophysiology, 28*, 245–259.

Siddle, D. A. T., & Lipp, O. V. (1997). Orienting, habituation, and information processing: The effects of omission, the role of expectancy, and the problem of dishabituation. In P. J. Lang, R. F. Simons, & M. T. Balaban (Eds.), *Attention and orienting: Sensory and motivational processes* (pp. 23–40). Mahwah, NJ: Erlbaum.

Sokolov, E. N. (1963). *Perception and the conditioned reflex*. New York: Macmillan.

Sokolovsky, A, Rothenberg, J., Labkovsky, E., Meixner, J., & Rosenfeld, J. P. (2011) A novel countermeasure against the reaction time (RT) index of countermeasure (CM) use in the P300-based complex trial protocol for detection of concealed information. *International Journal of Psychophysiology, 81*, 60–63.

Spence, S. A., Farrow, T. F., Herford, A. E., Wilkinson, I. D., Zheng, Y., & Woodruff, P. W. (2001). Behavioural and functional anatomical correlates of deception in humans. *Neuroreport, 12*(13), 2849–2853.

Spence, S. A., Hunter, M. D., Farrow, T. F., Green, R. D., Leung, D. H., Hughes, C. J., et al. (2004). A cognitive neurobiological account of deception: Evidence from functional neuroimaging. *Philosophical Transactions of the Royal Society of London B, Biological Science, 359*(1451), 1755–1762.

Spence, S. A., Kaylor-Hughes, C., Farrow, T. F., & Wilkinson, I. D. (2008). Speaking of secrets and lies: The contribution of ventrolateral prefrontal cortex to vocal deception. *Neuroimage, 40*(3), 1411–1418.

Thackray, R. I., & Orne, M. T. (1968). A comparison of physiological indices in detection of deception. *Psychophysiology, 4*, 329–339.

Timm, H. W. (1982). Effect of altered outcome expectancies stemming from placebo and feedback treatments on the validity of the guilty knowledge technique. *Journal of Applied Psychology, 67*, 391–400.

Timm, H. W. (1987). Effect of biofeedback on the detection of deception. *Journal of Forensic Sciences, 32*, 736–746.

Van Buskirk, D., & Marcuse, F. L. (1954). The nature of errors in experimental lie detection. *Journal of Experimental Psychology, 47*, 187–190.

Verschuere, B., & Ben-Shakhar, G. (2011). Memory detection: Theory of the concealed information test. In B. Verschuere, G. Ben-Shakhar, & E. Meijer (Eds.), *Memory detection: Theory and application of the Concealed Information Test* (pp. 128–148). Cambridge: Cambridge University Press.

Verschuere, B., Ben-Shakhar, G., & Meijer, E. (Eds.). (2011). *Memory detection: Theory and application of the Concealed Information Test.* Cambridge: Cambridge University Press.

Verschuere, B., Crombez, G., Declercq, A., & Koster, E. (2004). Autonomic and behavioral responding to concealed information: Differentiating defensive and orienting responses. *Psychophysiology, 41*, 461–466.

Verschuere, B., Crombez, G., De Clercq, A., & Koster, E. (2005). Psychopathic traits and autonomic responding to concealed information in a prison sample. *Psychophysiology, 42*, 239–245.

Verschuere, B., Crombez, G., DeGrootte, T., & Rosseel, Y. (2010). Detecting concealed information with reaction times: Validity and comparison with the polygraph. *Applied Cognitive Psychology, 24*, 991–1002

Verschuere, B., Crombez, G., Koster, E. H. W., & De Clercq, A. (2007). Antisociality, underarousal and the validity of the concealed information polygraph test. *Biological Psychology, 74*, 309–318.

Verschuere, B., Crombez, G., Koster, E., Van Bockstaele, B., & De Clercq, A. (2007). Startling secrets: Startle eye blink modification by concealed crime information. *Biological Psychology, 76*, 52–60.

Verschuere, B., Crombez, G., Smolders, L., & De Clercq, A. (2009). Differentiating defensive and orienting responses to concealed information: The role of verbalisation. *Applied Psychophysiology & Biofeedback, 34*, 237–244.

Verschuere, B., Prati, V., & De Houer, J. (2009). Cheating the lie detector. *Psychological Science, 20*, 410–413.

Wagner, A. R. (1978). Expectancies and the priming of STM. In S. H. Hulse, H. Fowler, & W. K. Honig (Eds.), *Cognitive processes in animal behavior* (pp. 177–209). Hillsdale, NJ: Erlbaum.

Waid, W. M., Orne, E. C., Cook, M. R., & Orne, M. T. (1978). Effects of attention, as indexed by subsequent memory, on electrodermal detection of information. *Journal of Applied Psychology, 63*, 728–733.

Waid, W. M., Orne, E. C., Cook, M. R., & Orne, M. T. (1981). Meprobamate reduces accuracy of physiological detection of deception. *Science, 212*, 71–73.

Waid, W. M., Orne, E. C., & Orne, M. T. (1981). Selective memory for social information, alertness, and physiological arousal in the detection of deception. *Journal of Applied Psychology, 66*, 224–232

Winograd, M. R., & Rosenfeld, J. P. (2011) Mock crime application of the complex trial protocol P300 based concealed information test. *Psychophysiology.* 48, 155–161.

PART FIVE

Legislative Issues

12

Criminalizing Cognitive Enhancement at the Blackjack Table

ADAM J. KOLBER

INTRODUCTION

Blackjack players who "count cards" keep track of cards that have already been played and use this knowledge to turn the probability of winning in their favor. Though casinos try to eject card counters or otherwise make their task more difficult, card counting is perfectly legal. So long as card counters rely on their own memory and computational skills, they have violated no laws and can make sizable profits.

By contrast, if players use a device to count cards, like a calculator or smartphone, they have committed a serious crime. Use of a device turns an otherwise legal activity into a felony. For example, there is an iPhone application that helps players count cards and even has a "stealth mode" that lets users enter data and receive feedback while the device appears to be off. In response, the Nevada Gaming Control Board issued an open letter reminding the public that the use of such an application violates the state's antidevice statute (2009). Other states with legalized gambling have similar prohibitions (see, for example, Miss. Code Ann. §75-76-303, 2011; Cal. Penal Code §337v, 2011).

So, though there is no criminal prohibition on counting cards, if you use a device to help you count cards (or even if you merely possess such a device with the intent to use it) at a Nevada casino, you can be imprisoned for as long as 6 years for a first offense (Nev. Rev. Stat. §465.088, 2010). Somehow using a device to augment our abilities to remember and to calculate turns a perfectly legal activity into an offense with a very serious penalty.

The fact that we do not criminalize natural, unassisted card counting raises interesting questions of criminal law: Should we criminalize natural card counting? Could we criminalize natural card counting without violating fundamental principles that protect thought privacy?[1]

Here, however, I focus on a puzzle about technological enhancement. Namely, can we justify criminalizing device-assisted card counting but not unassisted card counting? The importance of the question extends far beyond the world of blackjack and casino gaming. The question is important because it appears, at least superficially, that antidevice statutes criminalize a kind of technological enhancement.

Some ethicists distinguish *therapies* that seek to return us to normal, healthy functioning from *enhancements* that promise to give us extraordinary abilities. So, while some neuroscientists seek to develop therapies to treat Alzheimer's disease, others try to help healthy people think and remember even better than normal. They are searching for new drugs and devices that will enhance our abilities to concentrate and recall information beyond what we can do with our natural capacities.

Though most ethicists favor creation of new therapies, some are quite pessimistic about the societal implications of enhancements. Because we prohibit device-assisted card counting while permitting natural card counting, we criminalize a perfectly safe enhancement technology. The challenge, then, is to determine what, if anything, justifies our criminalization of a safe enhancement technology.

If we can justify criminalizing an enhancement technology at the blackjack table, perhaps we can justify criminalizing many other forms of cognitive enhancement. On the other hand, if we cannot justify criminalizing cognitive enhancement, perhaps we are entitled to the cognitive liberty to enhance our minds without the threat of criminal sanction. Perhaps it is inappropriate to use the most coercive forms of government control—namely, criminal penalties—to prohibit the use of perfectly safe cognitive enhancements. Prohibitions on device-assisted card counting put such a view to the test because we do, in fact, criminalize perfectly safe cognitive enhancements at the blackjack table.

As a historical matter, casinos lobbied for antidevice statutes in the 1980s to protect their revenue as computers were becoming more popular and accessible (Rose, 1998, pp. 82–83). Whatever the historical explanation, however, we can ask a deeper question: Is there any *justification* for permitting an activity, like card counting, when it uses only our natural cognitive abilities but severely punishing the activity when it is technologically enhanced?

In this brief chapter, I will propose two possible justifications for the differential treatment of ordinary and device-assisted card counting. I will argue that neither justification is very convincing, at least absent much more elaboration.

Criminalizing Cognitive Enhancement   309

While these attempted justifications are not hopeless, I describe some of the challenges they must overcome in order to successfully justify criminal prohibition of device-assisted card counting.

BACKGROUND

At most U.S. casinos, blackjack players receive two cards face up at the beginning of play. They are then permitted, among other options, to request additional cards (one at a time) or to stick with the cards they have. The central goal of blackjack is to hold cards that total more than the sum of the dealer's cards. Hands above 21, however, are "busted" and lose immediately. The best hand, called *blackjack*, consists of any hand containing only an ace (valued at 11 in such instances) and a *10 card* (meaning the 10 card itself or any picture card). Much of the strategy of blackjack consists of knowing when to take additional cards and when to stop so as to maximize the probability that one's hand is closer to 21 than the dealer's without going over 21.

The dealer also starts with two cards (one of which is face down while players are betting) and may receive additional cards after players have decided how to play their hands. When dealers play their hands, however, they have no discretion. They must follow strict rules that govern their play for every possible hand. Most importantly, casinos usually require dealers to take additional cards until their hands total 17 or higher.

Since players compete against a dealer rather than each other, most casinos allow players to see each other's hands. By seeing which cards have already been played, clever players can adjust their betting decisions based on the publicly available information as to which cards remain to be played. For example, when few 10 cards have been played, they are more likely to arise in subsequent hands. Generally speaking, when upcoming hands are heavily loaded with 10 cards, players can gain a slight advantage over the house. They are more likely to have blackjack (which typically pays out at 150% of a player's investment), and they can more easily take advantage of the dealer's obligation to take additional cards even when the dealer has a relatively high hand of 16 (Cabot & Hannum, 2005; Julian, 2005).

Using knowledge of previously dealt hands to benefit one's odds at blackjack is called *card counting*. Card counters have various systems to help them keep track of played cards so that they can dramatically ramp up the amounts they bet when the odds are in their favor. Counting cards is exceptionally difficult because cards are dealt quickly, and players must engage in several cognitive tasks at once. They must use nearly flawless strategy to play the hands that they are dealt, which requires them to memorize a fairly complicated table of basic blackjack strategy. At the same time, they must monitor all of the other face-up cards dealt to the table. Under many card-counting systems, players convert each face-up card into a number that they add to a running total. The running total informs how they play their hands. The task of counting cards has been made even more difficult in recent decades because casinos now play with multiple decks of cards at the same time and frequently shuffle the cards.

Nevertheless, players with good memory and computational skills can develop an edge over the house. When playing the best possible strategy *without counting cards*, players can reduce the house advantage below 0.5%, but the house nevertheless still has an advantage. By playing the best possible strategy *and counting cards*, players can actually gain an advantage over the house of about 0.5% to 1.5% (Millman, 1983).

Given that skilled card counters have a positive expected cash flow when playing blackjack, it is no surprise that casinos seek to exclude card counters from their casinos. Nevertheless, though many casinos are permitted to eject suspected card counters, no U.S. jurisdiction criminalizes ordinary card counting.[2] By contrast, players can be charged with a crime if they use a device to help them count cards. Since Nevada is the gambling capital of the United States, its laws are often illustrative of the laws of other jurisdictions that permit gambling. Nevada Revised Statutes §465.075 (2010), entitled "Use of device for calculating probabilities," provides as follows:

> It is unlawful for any person at a licensed gaming establishment to use, or possess with the intent to use, any device to assist:
> 1. In projecting the outcome of the game;
> 2. In keeping track of the cards played;
> 3. In analyzing the probability of the occurrence of an event relating to the game; or
> 4. In analyzing the strategy for playing or betting to be used in the game, except as permitted by the Commission.

The antidevice statute is quite broad. In fact, the term *device* is never defined. Presumably, one's brain is not a device; otherwise, all card counting would be criminalized. Using a computer to count cards, however, is clearly prohibited by the statute, probably under all four prongs. In a case from the 1980s, for example, a defendant was convicted of violating the statute for wearing "computer shoes" at the blackjack table (*Clark County v. Anderson*, 1987). He used his toes to press switches in his shoes that were wired to a computer strapped to his calf. The computer sent signals to an athletic supporter that would vibrate to indicate how he should play his hands.

Other prohibited devices are less obvious. In Colorado, two players were prosecuted for allegedly using casino chips to signal the card count to each other (Loeb, 1998, p. 86). And some law enforcement authorities in Canada sought to punish the use of beads that were allegedly used to keep track of blackjack hands (Loeb, 1998, p. 86). It is not clear, however, whether courts would agree with the interpretation of these law enforcement officials, as courts have said little on the matter so far. Though the statute does a poor job of describing precisely what conduct it prohibits, it may nevertheless pass constitutional muster. The defendant convicted of wearing computer shoes argued that the antidevice statute was unconstitutionally vague, but he was unsuccessful (*Clark County v. Anderson*, 1987).[3]

The breadth of the statute can also be seen in the way it prohibits seemingly innocuous uses of what are clearly devices. When players decide how to play their hands, they always add up the cards right in front of them to see how close they are to 21. This mathematical task, which I'll call *elementary school card counting*, is relatively easy for most people. But it is a task that has to be done under pressure, and it is common for dealers to speed the game along by telling players the value of their hands. Some people might find it helpful to have a calculator to help with the task. Using a calculator in this fashion, however, would presumably violate the antidevice statute, since players would be using the information provided by the device to help "analyz[e] the strategy for playing or betting to be used in the game" (Nevada Revised Statutes §465.075, 2010).

The last part of the antidevice statute allows the state gaming commission to make exceptions to the law. So, for example, the commission could permit certain uses of calculators at the blackjack table. While the commission has permitted devices (actually, certain "handwritten records") in baccarat, roulette, and faro, there are no exceptions listed for blackjack (Regulations of the Nevada Gaming Commission and State Gaming Control Board, 5.150, 1987).[4]

POSSIBLE JUSTIFICATIONS OF ANTIDEVICE LEGISLATION

We now have a sense of what card counting is and how casinos prohibit the use of devices that assist card counters. Given that all casinos seek to prohibit card counting (either by ejecting suspected card counters or by using countermeasures to make card counting difficult), it is fair to say that they do not consider card counting part of an appropriate blackjack strategy.

Yet we do not criminalize all kinds of card counting. We only criminalize card counting when it is device-assisted. The fact that criminalization turns on the use of a device presents something of a puzzle. Perhaps, one might think, we should prohibit all forms of card counting because they make blackjack less profitable for casinos. Or, one might think, we should permit all forms of card counting because they rely only on public information and prohibiting them would infringe on rights to use our own minds. But why permit ordinary card counting and prohibit device-assisted counting?

As a preliminary suggestion, one might think it too difficult to detect card counting absent the use of a device. In fact, however, purely mental card counting is easier to identify than one might expect. The betting pattern of a card counter is so statistically anomalous that, after enough time, it would be almost impossible to explain without assuming that the bettor is counting cards. These betting patterns can be disguised by working in teams: One person can make small bets and signal to others when they should sit at a table and place large bets. But such coordinated activity may be just as easy to spot as the use of small devices, maybe even easier. So, it's not at all clear that evidentiary concerns can justify the very different ways we treat ordinary and device-assisted card counting.

I will now consider in more detail two other attempts to justify our current practices.

The Enhancement Justification

As noted in the Introduction, some ethicists distinguish between things we do to make our bodies normal or healthy (like curing a disease) and things we do to enhance our bodies (like having facelifts to hide wrinkles and using binoculars to see farther than we ordinarily could). At least superficially, antidevice laws seem to punish a kind of technological enhancement because card counting is legal in the absence of a device that improves our abilities. If enhancement is sufficiently bad for us, we arguably have a justification for laws that prohibit enhancement at the blackjack table. Before discussing whether the antidevice statute can be justified as a ban on enhancement, I will first briefly describe some emerging enhancement techniques that might be appealing to card counters.

Emerging Neurotechnological Forms of Enhancement

A number of quite common substances are known to enhance our cognitive abilities. Caffeine, for example, can boost alertness and attention (Adan & Serra-Grabulosa, 2010). Even glucose has memory-enhancing properties (Adan & Serra-Grabulosa, 2010). Neuroethicists have focused attention on Food and Drug Administration (FDA)-approved pharmaceuticals that may have even more powerful cognitive enhancement properties. For example, many college students use stimulants like Ritalin and Adderall to boost academic performance by improving their memory and attention (Greely et al., 2008). There is also some evidence that people use modafinil (a drug intended to treat narcolepsy) and donepezil (a drug intended to treat Alzheimer's disease) to improve cognitive performance (Greely et al., 2008).

The antidevice law bans the use of devices to help count cards but does not define the term *device*. Though there is little or no law in this particular context, substances like caffeine or glucose, we can safely assume, do not fall under the ban on devices. Similarly, antidevice statutes probably do not criminalize the use of emerging and futuristic pharmaceuticals that are supposed to boost memory, attention, or concentration above our ordinary abilities, even though such drugs could be a boon to card counters. In the more distant future, we can imagine nanotechnologies that blur the distinction between pharmacological enhancements and device-based enhancements. The statute provides no help in determining whether such futuristic enhancements will be prohibited.

Vague as the antidevice statute is, however, it may already make it a crime to use certain other neurotechnological enhancement techniques that are already showing promise in research contexts. Perhaps the most important such technology for current purposes, given its relative safety and portability, is transcranial direct current stimulation (tDCS). Using a safe, small device that can be powered by a 9-volt battery, electrical current is applied to particular regions of the scalp. Precisely how the current affects brain activity is unknown, but it is believed to create an electric field that affects the likelihood that neurons in a particular region of the brain will fire (Clark et al., 2010).

Researchers have reported using tDCS to improve subjects' ability to learn. Those who received 2 milliamps of electrical current to the scalp had almost twice as much improvement in playing a military training video game as those who received a much weaker amount of current (Clark et al., 2010; Fox, 2011). Researchers have also used tDCS to improve subjects' visual memory (Chi, Fregni, & Snyder, 2010), as well as their ability to process and remember symbols (Cohen Kadosh, Soskic, Iuculano, Kanai, & Walsh, 2010). In other words, tDCS could potentially enhance many of the skills important for card counting.

While it seems unlikely that a court would deem pharmaceutical enhancement to be a prohibited device, use of tDCS in a casino (or possessing a tDCS device with intent to use it) *might* be deemed to violate the statute. This is certainly an open question. It's also an important question, because it is possible that a tDCS device could be hidden under a gambler's hat. Moreover, even if tDCS does not actually improve card-counting skills, if persons possess or use such a device intending to enhance their card-counting ability, they might have criminal liability under the statute even if the device fails to actually improve their ability.

In some tDCS studies, the cognitive-enhancing effect of the technique extended well past the period in which the current was applied. If so, one might use tDCS *prior* to entering a casino. Because the antidevice statute only prohibits the use or possession of a device in casinos, the statute does not criminalize preparatory uses of the technology. By contrast, the statute would presumably prohibit the use of brain-computer interfaces in the casino like those recently shown to improve the memory of rodents (Berger et al., 2011).

The Enhancement Ban Is Both Over- and Underinclusive

As the previous discussion shows, if the antidevice statute can be justified as a ban on a form of enhancement, the law is very underinclusive. It likely does not prohibit any form of pharmacological enhancement and does not prohibit the use of cognitive-enhancing devices that are used prior to entering the casino. So antidevice laws are, at best, only partial implementations of a moral prohibition on enhancement.

Interestingly, antidevice laws also do not prohibit card counting based on the advice of other players who may themselves be exceptionally good natural card counters. In the movie *Rain Man*, the character played by Dustin Hoffman uses his extraordinary powers of recall and computation to signal his brother when the card count favors casino patrons. The two make quite a bit of money in a short time, and there are indeed real-life teams of card counters who are able to disguise their efforts by working in teams (Mezrich, 2008). If one considers such human-assisted card counting to be a kind of enhancement, then this is another form of enhancement not addressed by the antidevice statute.

At the same time, if the antidevice statute is read as a ban on enhancement, it is also overinclusive. Some people may have memory disorders or difficulty with basic arithmetic. They might seek to use devices simply to give them normal memory and mathematical abilities. Nevertheless, at least according to the letter of the law, those who use devices violate the law, even if the devices merely serve a therapeutic role to help people obtain ordinary, average abilities.[5]

Of course, there is little we can conclude about the statute simply because its enhancement prohibition is under- and overinclusive. When the statute was passed in 1987, legislators probably did not anticipate new and emerging pharmaceuticals and devices that may enhance card-counting ability. Even if legislators considered the issue today, they might decide that such new technologies are still too weak to substantially contribute to card-counting ability. If we had good methods of pharmaceutical enhancement, we might still criminalize only device-based enhancements because it is administratively easier to discover and prosecute the use of devices *in* the casino than the use of pharmaceuticals at any time or the use of devices that take effect before entering. Moreover, legislators might not have considered the possibility that the statute would be used against people with below-normal memory and computational skill.

My interest, however, is not in the motivations of the actual legislators who enacted antidevice laws. Rather, I seek to determine if antidevice laws can be justified on the ground that they prohibit a noxious form of human enhancement. On that score, some of the examples I give may actually support common antienhancement intuitions. Many people likely think that it is an inappropriate kind of cheating to use a device to boost one's skills at blackjack above ordinary levels but have no problem with the use of a device by people with learning disabilities who simply want help adding up the cards on the table. Many people, I suspect, believe it is only cheating at blackjack when one enhances abilities above those of neurotypicals, while the use of devices as therapy—to help one function at the level of a neurotypical—will be viewed as completely harmless.

Arguments against enhancement tend to focus on two concerns. One is that enhancements are bad because they are unnatural or make our lives inauthentic. The other is that they are bad because they increase inequality and are therefore unfair to certain people or groups of people. I will examine these claims in order.

The Claim That Enhancements Are Unnatural

The President's Council on Bioethics, under President George W. Bush, repeatedly urged caution over the use of enhancement technologies. In 2002 and 2003, for example, the Council held a series of hearings about the use of pharmaceuticals to alter our moods and memories. They examined, for example, the use of drugs to dampen the emotional intensity of recent traumatic memories. If such drugs work, they would enhance our memories in the sense that they would enable us to do things to our memories—voluntarily alter their character—in a way that we could not otherwise do with just our natural abilities.

The Council was especially concerned that memory-dampening drugs would worsen our lives in various ways:

> Acknowledging the giftedness of life means recognizing that our talents and powers are not wholly our own doing, nor even fully ours, despite the efforts we expend to develop and to exercise them. It also means recognizing that not everything in the world is open to any use we may desire or devise. Such an appreciation of the giftedness of life would constrain the Promethean project and conduce to a much-needed humility. (Kass, 2003, p. 288)[6]

If one shares these concerns about enhancement, one might argue that those who seek to profit from card counting should do it the old-fashioned way: with excellent memory and computational skills. Enhanced card counting is a shortcut that sidesteps the more difficult but arguably more rewarding approach to card counting in which one actually keeps track of cards without the assistance of modern technology. On this view, blackjack is supposed to pit our *natural* human abilities against the luck of the cards.

I suspect, however, that few will find this argument compelling as a justification for a criminal prohibition. We regularly use all sorts of devices and technologies to enhance our life spans and the quality of our lives. Surely, automobiles and telephones enhance our natural abilities to travel and communicate, yet few oppose such technologies in general, let alone seek to criminalize their use. For some reason, arguments against enhancement usually only garner support when they involve new or futuristic technologies.

Moreover, we do not generally seek to prohibit people from enhancing when they play games. Hopscotch, for example, is played on streets and driveways around the world, but we would hardly seek a criminal prohibition on devices that enhance players' balance. And we surely do not enforce antidevice legislation when people play blackjack at home for no stakes. While legal authorities have sought to prosecute the use of steroids in baseball, they have done so on the grounds that the steroids were prescribed or administered illegally or players lied about their use under oath, not because players were cheating at baseball. We would not, for example, expect the government to enforce the prohibition of spit balls in Major League Baseball. Thus, we are not so opposed to enhancement devices either in general or in the context of games and athletic competitions that we can justify antidevice laws on the grounds that they promote what is natural and authentic.

The Claim That Enhancement Is Cheating Fails

Perhaps, then, concerns about enhancement justify antidevice laws when they focus on unfairness and inequality. Ethicists have argued that those with greater financial resources will generally have better access to cognitive enhancements. They claim that better access to enhancement tools will then further perpetuate resource inequality. So, perhaps we should prohibit devices in the casino because such enhancements will allow those who can afford computers to more easily profit at the casino and thereby perpetuate inequality.

But given how inexpensive it has become to buy a card-counting device, concerns about perpetuating inequality *among players* seem rather weak. The more plausible concern focuses on unfairness and inequality in the relationship between casinos and players. One might think that using computers is a form of high-stakes cheating. If blackjack is supposed to test our unenhanced cognitive abilities, then perhaps we should prohibit enhancement devices, just as we prohibit students taking an arithmetic test from using calculators. Card counting with a device creates a kind of inequality by giving players an unfair advantage relative to the house in an environment where millions of dollars change hands every day. Indeed, at least one commentator has defended such a view:

> There is something about using a computer that smacks of cheating. Perhaps it is that by taking the human element out of the game, by forcing the human casino dealer to play against the unbeatable machine, we see ourselves in the unequal fight. Beating a dealer by skill is a challenge, beating a dealer by the use of a machine is somehow not fair. (Rose, 1998, p. 81)

There are two problems, however, with the unfairness justification for antidevice laws. The first is that it depends on the debatable view that using devices when playing blackjack is cheating. Since neither the criminal law nor the traditional rules of blackjack prohibit natural card counting, it is far from obvious why using a device to count cards should be understood as a form of cheating.

What really underlies the cheating concern is that, absent antidevice legislation, casinos would lose a lot of revenue. Not many people have the skill to profitably count cards without a device, while many more people have the skill to use technology to count cards. In fact, it's quite possible that casinos generate a good bit of revenue from people who try to count cards naturally and simply fail to do so properly. Technology, however, opens up card counting to a much wider range of people who need not train very hard to count cards and can increase their profit per unit time invested. So, the prohibition on technologically assisted counting may simply reflect a view about fair profit for casinos.

To really spell out this idea, however, we should be told something about what casino profits *should* be. After all, the game of blackjack is not structured as a fair fight. Absent card counting, the house has a built-in advantage. It would be ironic to think that using a device is cheating because it gives players an edge when the entire game of blackjack is structured to give casinos an edge over those who do not count cards.

The second and more serious problem with a cheating-based justification is that, even if one has a vision of the game of blackjack in which device assistance should be deemed cheating, it is hardly clear why the power of the state—especially its power to deprive people of their liberty by incarceration—is being called upon to enforce the rule.

After all, we could surely imagine ways that casinos could allow devices and still be profitable. For example, they could change certain aspects of game play to regain a house advantage or could require players to pay for the privilege of playing. More dramatically, we could play blackjack by switching the traditional role of dealer and player. Players would be required to play hands in the same way that dealers currently do, while dealers would have the choices now available to players. Dealers would use devices to count cards, and the advantage they would have would enable the casino to make a profit. While some may have a preference for the traditional precomputer days of playing blackjack, if the antidevice law merely amounts to an aesthetic preference, it is not obvious why this preference should be formalized in the criminal law.

Similarly, casinos could virtually eliminate the advantage from both assisted and unassisted forms of card counting simply by shuffling decks more frequently and limiting the number of players with face-up cards at the table (*Uston v. Resorts International Hotel*, 1982). Doing so might slow games down a bit and reduce profitability per table. But, again, that hardly seems like a strong rationale for regulating player behavior with a criminal statute.

We could also imagine a world in which, just as Nevada casinos eject natural card counters, they also eject those they suspect of counting cards with device assistance. The ejection option would not require the force of the state to back a criminal prohibition. Casinos also have other options, aside from ejection. They could establish clearer contractual relations with players. Contracts could prohibit players from using device assistance on pain of owing back proceeds they make along with, perhaps, certain reasonable penalties. The best casinos could say is that such contractual remedies are too onerous or will not do enough to deter device users, absent serious penalties like incarceration.

So, it seems, rather than having some high-minded justification for antidevice laws, we are left to view the legislation as a method of bolstering casino profits at a traditional casino game. That's not an especially strong justification for a criminal prohibition. If the prohibition can be justified at all, it can probably only be justified as part of some more general theory about casino gambling and why the state should be using the *criminal law* to support the industry.

The Freedom of Mind Justification

An alternative justification for antidevice legislation requires us first to consider why we *do not* prohibit natural card counting. Perhaps a prohibition on natural card counting would infringe our rights to mental privacy. In *Lawrence v. Texas*, the U.S. Supreme Court stated that "[l]iberty presumes an autonomy of self that includes freedom of thought, belief, expression, and certain intimate conduct" (2003, p. 562). A prohibition on natural card counting may implicate such freedoms because the only difference between a card counter and an ordinary bettor is that the card counter is using superior memory and computational skills to process publicly available information. It may seem unfair to punish card counters for using these skills, skills that we ordinarily encourage people to develop. Thus, perhaps we permit ordinary card counting because a prohibition would interfere with important cognitive liberties, including what I have called our "freedom of memory" (Kolber, 2006, pp. 1622–1625; Kolber, 2011).

So, a possible justification of antidevice statutes goes as follows: All card counting is a kind of cheating. But prohibiting ordinary card counting would infringe too deeply on the privacy of our minds. Antidevice laws, by contrast, only prohibit the memory and computational tasks that are done by machines or other devices, not by us. Thus, the concern about mental privacy that applies to ordinary counting does not apply to device-assisted card counting. We are, therefore, justified in prohibiting device-assisted card counting but not the ordinary variety.

The Claim That Only Natural Card Counting Invades Cognitive Liberty

To examine this view in more detail, I will first consider the claim that a prohibition on natural card counting invades important cognitive liberties. I will then consider the claim that the antidevice statute invades cognitive liberty to a lesser extent.

Proponents of the view that a natural card-counting prohibition would interfere with our mental privacy could argue that card counting, unlike, say, insider trading in financial securities, relies only on public information. What makes the card counter different from an ordinary player who happens to pay attention to the other cards on the table is the way that the card counter stores and manipulates data about past hands. By performing certain calculations and then acting on what he views as the best strategy, the counter uses public information in a particularly advantageous way. Criminalizing the card counter's wagering, one might argue, would be like criminalizing his thoughts.

Not only might card counting seem like the criminalization of thought, it criminalizes a kind of thinking that we ordinarily encourage. Anyone who plays blackjack is rewarded for the ability to engage in certain kinds of mathematical manipulations: For example, players should be able to engage in what I called elementary school card counting by adding up the value of their cards and those of the dealers and then using some basic strategy to play their hands. A criminal prohibition on natural card counting would still permit elementary school card counting. So, such a rule would only prohibit betting based on certain kinds of mental mathematical calculations. Prohibiting these more complicated calculations would be puzzling because we ordinarily seek to reward clever thinking, especially in games that involve strategic choices.

Moreover, one might argue, even if the particular thoughts associated with card counting are not especially valuable, the freedom to think and remember without state interference might be so important that we protect freedom of thought generally without attempting to assess the value of particular thoughts. Just as we protect the rights of Nazis to march in a Jewish neighborhood to engage in *offensive* expression (*Village of Skokie v. National Socialist Party*, 1978), we might protect the thoughts and memories that underlie card counting simply because they are instances of thoughts and memories, and some mental processes should be protected from the government's prying eyes (Blitz, 2010). So, the argument goes, if a card-counting prohibition criminalizes thoughts and memories and if a prohibition on device-assisted card counting does not, then we might be able to justify the prohibition of one and not the other.

This proposed justification has two major problems, however. First, whether a criminal prohibition on card counting should actually be characterized as criminalizing thought is hardly so simple. No one, it seems, is interested in prohibiting card counting when it is a purely mental exercise. That is, no one would stop you from merely standing by the blackjack tables counting cards, so long as you do not wager or help others to wager. Rather than merely implicating our thoughts, the kind of card counting we are considering presumably involves an action, namely, betting in such a way as to profit from card counting.[7]

Moreover, we punish people for acting on knowledge they gain from mathematical manipulation in other contexts as well. For example, suppose three National Aeronautics and Space Administration (NASA) scientists develop a particular component for a manned spacecraft. The night before a team of astronauts is slated to launch into space, one of the scientists makes an ingenious discovery. Based solely on his mental manipulation of publicly available data like the component's construction and the weather forecast, he recognizes that the shuttle will explode soon after liftoff. His discovery is so original and important that it would be worthy of a Nobel Prize. Nevertheless, if he fails to alert his supervisors to the danger (which he no doubt has a duty to do), then he could be charged with murder. His fellow scientists, however, will have no liability whatsoever, given that even reasonable scientists would not have had the insight to recognize the danger of the launch. Both the ingenious scientist and the card counter manipulate public information and then take action based on the mental manipulation. There is no obvious reason why we could not punish them both.

In the NASA example, the brilliant scientist could be found guilty of murder despite his *failure to act* on his superior knowledge. But we could just as easily imagine circumstances in which his powers of mental manipulation make him guilty for an action. Suppose the brilliant scientist proposed a design modification to the space shuttle that he knew his colleagues would find quite appealing but that only he secretly knew—given his exceptional cognitive abilities—would ultimately lead to the destruction of the shuttle and its crew. In that case, we would have no difficulty convicting the scientist for his action based on the knowledge he derived from his superior cognitive abilities.

The second major problem with the proposed thought privacy justification is that even if a card-counting prohibition would infringe cognitive liberty, a prohibition on device-assisted card counting would seem to infringe the same interests. If we want to encourage thought, then perhaps we ought to encourage machine-assisted thought as well. After all, our rights to freedom of expression also include rights to use the printing press, public address systems, the Internet, and many other forms of technology-assisted communication.

In fact, some have argued that we cannot limit what is part of our "minds" in any principled way to the confines of our brains or bodies. Andy Clark and David Chalmers illustrate the point using the videogame Tetris (Clark & Chalmers, 1998; Levy, 2007). To play Tetris, one must move and rotate two-dimensional geometrical figures as they gradually drop to the bottom of the screen so that the figures land in a particular orientation. When deciding how to rotate the figures, one can mentally manipulate them oneself or use a feature of the software to rotate the image on screen. (Before the figure is ultimately placed, it will have to be manipulated using the software.) The point is that the particular cognitive task of rotating the figure can be done largely in one's own head or less so by "offloading" the task to the computer. It's not clear why only one of these should be deemed a mental manipulation.

Similarly, we can store to-do lists in our long-term memories or offload them to a pad of paper or a portable electronic device. What Clark and Chalmers (1998) argue is that we cannot give an account of the mental (and related concepts) that draws a principled distinction between activities in our brains and bodies and activities in the rest of the world. Therefore, even if there are special moral grounds for protecting the mental lives of human beings, if Clark and Chalmers are right, the mental lives of human beings extend to the physical world, including certain devices.

None of this is to say that Clark and Chalmers (1998) have an airtight thesis but rather that quite a lot of argumentation is needed to prove the point that there is something importantly different about mental processes associated with our nervous system and similar processes that occur elsewhere. The mental processes associated with our own brains may well be more personal or unique than the mental processes that we offload to the rest of the world, but we cannot simply make that assumption. And even if the mental processes associated with brains are more personal and unique, it is not obvious why such qualities warrant special protection.

CONCLUSION

I considered two possible justifications for the fact that we criminalize device-assisted card counting but not ordinary card counting. The first was that, unlike natural card counting, device-assisted card counting requires technological enhancement. It makes card counting less natural and is unfair to casinos and should therefore be prohibited.

The first proposed justification fails because concerns about the unnaturalness of card counting, if they have any merit at all, are too weak to justify a criminal prohibition. Concerns about the unfairness of card counting to casinos are also unpersuasive absent evidence of what the casino's advantage should be, especially because casinos could modify the game of blackjack to maintain a statistical advantage over players.

The second proposed justification was that card counting is a kind of cheating that warrants punishment. We do not criminalize natural card counting on this view because such laws would interfere with our thought privacy. Since concerns about thought privacy are less applicable to device-assisted counting, we can prohibit device-assisted counting without violating our rights to freedom of memory and mind.

The second proposed justification faces two major obstacles. First, it must show that we really should not punish natural card counting. Second, it must show that there is significantly greater value in protecting the privacy of thoughts that are more closely associated with the brain than in protecting the privacy of thoughts that are less closely associated with the brain (because they are partly encoded in smartphones and other devices that are external to our bodies). Both of these obstacles are substantial. While I do not purport to have proven that these two proposed justifications fail, I have presented some of the obstacles that must be addressed before they can be deemed successful.

ACKNOWLEDGMENTS

For helpful comments, I thank Larry Alexander, Margo Kaplan, Larry Solan, and especially, Walter Sinnott-Armstrong. I also thank participants at conferences and workshops at Georgetown Law School, the University of Arizona, and the University of Pennsylvania Law School. This project was generously supported by the Brooklyn Law School Summer Stipend Program and by a visiting fellowship at NYU Law School's Center for Research in Crime and Justice.

NOTES

1. Contact the author to request a manuscript addressing such questions.
2. In New Jersey, however, state gaming statutes have been interpreted to prohibit casinos from ejecting players merely because they count cards (*Uston v. Resorts International Hotel*, 1982).
3. Subsequent case law, however, leaves it unclear whether the holding of the case is still valid (*Las Vegas v. Eighth Judicial Dist. Court ex rel. County of Clark*, 2002).
4. The regulation does describe a procedure whereby the chairman of the state gaming control board can provide exceptions to the law upon the request of certain casinos. One imagines, however, that casinos rarely seek to make it easier for patrons to use devices to improve their odds.
5. Some patients with Alzheimer's disease have started wearing special cameras around their necks that help them remember events of the day. The use of such memory aids at the blackjack table may technically violate antidevice statutes. Enforcing the statutes in such contexts, however, may run afoul of laws against disability discrimination.
6. I have challenged the view of the President's Council elsewhere (Kolber, 2006, 2011).
7. Importantly, however, one might *refrain* from placing a large bet on the basis of the card count. That kind of card counting would be especially difficult to criminalize.

REFERENCES

Adan, A., & Serra-Grabulosa, J. M. (2010). Effects of caffeine and glucose, alone and combined, on cognitive performance. *Human Psychopharmacology: Clinical and Experimental, 25*(4), 310–317.

Berger, T. W., Hampson, R. E., Song, D., Goonawardena, A., Marmarelis, V. Z., & Deadwyler, S. A. (2011). A cortical neural prosthesis for restoring and enhancing memory. *Journal of Neural Engineering, 8*(4), 1–11.

Blitz, M. J. (2010). Freedom of thought for the extended mind: Cognitive enhancement and the Constitution. *Wisconsin Law Review, 2010*, 1049–1117.

Cabot, A., & Hannum, R. (2005). Advantage play and commercial casinos. *Mississippi Law Journal, 74*, 681–778.

Chi, R. P., Fregni, F., & Snyder, A. W. (2010). Visual memory improved by non-invasive brain stimulation. *Brain Research, 1353*, 168–175.

Clark, A., & Chalmers, D. J. (1998). The extended mind. *Analysis, 58*, 7–19.

Clark County v. Anderson, 103 Nev. 560, 746 P.2d 643 (1987).

Clark, V. P., Coffman B. A., Mayer. A. R., Weisen M. P., Lane T. D. R., Calhoun, V. D., et al. (2010). TDCS guided using fMRI significantly accelerates learning to identify concealed objects. *Neuroimage, 59*, 117–128.

Cohen Kadosh, R., Soskic, S., Iuculano, T., Kanai, R., & Walsh, V. (2010). Modulating neuronal activity produces specific and long-lasting changes in numerical competence. *Current Biology, 20*, 2016–2020.

Fox, D. (2011). Brain buzz. *Nature, 472*(7342), 156–159.

Greely, H., Sahakian, B., Harris, J., Kessler, R. C., Gazzaniga, M., Campbell, P., & Farah, M. J. (2008). Towards responsible use of cognitive-enhancing drugs by the healthy. *Nature, 456*(7223), 702–705.

Julian, T. (2005). Exclusions and countermeasures: Do card counters have a right to play? *Gaming Law Review, 9*(2), 165–171.

Kass, L. (2003). *Beyond therapy: Biotechnology and the pursuit of happiness*. Washington, DC: President's Council on Bioethics.

Kolber, A. J. (2006). Therapeutic forgetting: The legal and ethical implications of memory dampening. *Vanderbilt Law Review, 59*, 1561–1626.

Kolber, A. (2011). Give memory-altering drugs a chance. *Nature, 476*, 275–276.

Las Vegas v. Eighth Judicial Dist. Court ex rel. County of Clark, 118 Nev. 859 (2002).

Lawrence v. Texas, 539 U.S. 558 (2003).

Letter from State of Nevada Gaming Control Board [Letter to All Nonrestricted Licensees and Interested Parties]. (2009, February 5).

Levy, N. (2007). *Neuroethics: Challenges for the 21st century* (pp. 26–68). Cambridge: Cambridge University Press.

Loeb, R. A. (1998). Computers and devices. In I. N. Rose & R. A. Loeb, *Blackjack and the law* (pp. 84–89). Oakland, CA: RGE Publishers.

Mezrich, B. (2008). *Bringing down the house*. London: Arrow.

Millman, M. H. (1983). A statistical analysis of casino blackjack. *American Mathematical Monthly, 90*, 431–436.

Mississippi Gaming Control Act, Miss. Code Ann. §75-76-303 (2011).

Penalties for violation of NRS §§ 465.070 to 465.085, inclusive, Nev. Rev. Stat. §465.088 (2010).

Prohibited devices, Cal. Penal Code §337v (2011).

Regulations of the Nevada Gaming Commission and State Gaming Control Board 5.150, "Devices prohibited under NRS 465.075; exceptions" (1987).

Rose, I. N. (1998). Card counting devices made criminal. In I. N. Rose & R. A. Loeb, *Blackjack and the law* (pp. 80–83). Oakland, CA: RGE Publishers.

Uston v. Resorts International Hotel, 445 A.2d 370 (N.J. 1982).

Village of Skokie v. National Socialist Party, 69 Ill.2d 605 (1978).

13

Monetizing Memory Science
Neuroscience and the Future of PTSD Litigation

FRANCIS X. SHEN

> Battles and wars leave deep wounds and scars
> And deep wounds are long in the mending
> While reflecting upon all that is gone
> Life rushes on to its ending
> Thou the joy and the pain in our memory remain
> And by memories lifetimes are measured
> — SEAN MONE, *"Lovers and Friends"*

"By memories lifetimes are measured" sings the Scottish songwriter Sean Mone. This sentiment—that memories matter and that we should use them as a benchmark for evaluating the quality of life—lies at the heart of one of the most challenging tasks confronted by the American tort law system: translating the psychological and neurological scars from traumatic events into dollar amounts for victim recovery.

This chapter examines the monetization of memory science in the civil justice system at a moment when "the study of traumatic memory is currently benefiting from an unprecedented collaboration between neuroscientists, experimental psychologists, and clinicians, with contributions from numerous disciplines such as neuroanatomy, electrophysiology, cognitive psychology, clinical neuropsychology, and phenomenology" (Brewin, 2005, p. 145).

The central argument of the chapter is that trial lawyers, both plaintiff and defense, may improve their representation of clients by learning from this unprecedented collaboration.

Law, memory, and the brain sciences have a long-standing, if at times contentious, relationship in civil litigation. This chapter focuses on one aspect of that relationship—cases involving posttraumatic stress disorder (PTSD)—and draws on evidence from an original survey experiment to address the question: What, if anything, might cognitive neuroscience mean for litigation involving a party whose claim for damages rests on a diagnosis of PTSD? Put another way, will advances in neuroscience mean more money, less money, or no change in compensation for PTSD harms?

The chapter argues that cognitive neuroscience, by mobilizing public and legislative sentiment to revisit and redefine legal conceptions of *mental injury* and *bodily injury*, may change the dynamics of personal injury litigation involving mental duress. While, for a neuroscientist, there is typically no such hard distinction between *mental* and *bodily*—because all mental states are understood to be instantiated physically—the law (for better or for worse) employs a different conceptual framework. Whether it is statutory law generated by legislatures, common law interpreted by courts, or insurance contracts agreed to between private parties, the law in many instances carves out purely *mental* (or *emotional*) injury and then treats those mental injuries as distinct from bodily injuries. The goal of this chapter is to explore how cognitive neuroscience research may affect public opinion and legal decision making on where to draw this mental/bodily line (or whether to abolish the line altogether).

Whether revised line-drawing will ultimately be a victory for the plaintiff or the defense bar remains to be seen. On the one hand, the view that *mental* injuries are never purely mental, but also bodily, could open up new "deep pockets" for trial lawyers to pursue. On the other hand, however, it may be the case that upon cross-examination and the introduction of expert witnesses, juries are no more likely to favor plaintiffs who claim that their PTSD should be considered a bodily injury. Moreover, legislatures and insurance companies may simply rewrite their statutes and policies using more precise language to avoid such claims. What *is* clear is that both the plaintiff and defense bars have a vested interest in exploring state legislative agendas drawing on neuroscience findings and preparing for the increasing introduction of neuroscientific evidence in PTSD litigation. Being the first mover in framing novel neuroscientific issues may generate benefits both in enactment of legislative policy and in improved representation for clients.

The chapter consists of five sections. The first section provides context from the emerging law and neuroscience literature, and presents a brief background discussion of the scientific controversies surrounding PTSD and its legal applications. The second section begins to explore whether neuroscience will change legal conceptualizations of *bodily* and *mental* injuries—through discussion of the illustrative case *Allen v. Bloomfield Hills*. The third section reviews the methods currently used for monetary valuation of PTSD and explores the possibilities that neuroscience offers for improving those valuation methods. The fourth section then describes the experimental design and data used. The fifth section presents the results of the analysis and concludes with a discussion of policy and legal implications.

BACKGROUND

Neurolaw Scholarship: Beyond Criminal Cases and Common Law

Since its official recognition in 1980 by the American Psychiatric Association (APA) in the *Diagnostic and Statistical Manual of Mental Disorders-III* (DSM-III), diagnosing a client with PTSD has become part of many types of personal injury litigation, and has spawned a cottage industry of lawyers and scientists working at this intersection (Sparr & Pitman, 2007). Plaintiffs' lawyers often do not limit their PTSD practice to major traumatic events but also remind potential clients that garden variety personal injuries may also give rise to PTSD.[1] Expert witnesses too have jumped into the fray. New York psychologist Joseph Hammer, for instance, announces on his website that he looks "forward to assisting you or your clients who have posttraumatic stress disorders resulting from motor vehicle or work-related accidents."[2]

The growth of PTSD civil litigation has raised a number of challenges, including whether PTSD exists to begin with, what a valid PTSD diagnosis is, the causal link to the traumatic event, and how to tell if an individual is malingering (Young, Kane, & Nicholson 2006a, 2006b). These are just a few of the many concerns that skeptics raise about PTSD (Brewin, 2003; Rosen, Lilienfeld, Frueh, McHugh, & Spitzer, 2010). Indeed, some have suggested that PTSD is actually prolonged by the litigation process, arguing that "ongoing litigation acts as an artificial reinforcing factor for unpleasant memories and their accompanying affect" (Field, 1999, p. 36).[3] Moreover, there is vigorous debate over how the fifth edition of the *Diagnostic and Statistical Manual of Mental Disorders* will define PTSD (McNally 2009; Rosen et al. 2010). How this debate is resolved will have a significant impact on future PTSD litigation.

Yet, despite its uncertain future and the many valid scientific concerns voiced since its initial inclusion in the DSM, PTSD has to date been of increasing practical legal importance. From 1950 to 2007, per capita, inflation-adjusted tort costs in the United States rose by a factor of 8 and as of 2007 were estimated to be over $250 billion (Towers & Perrin, 2008, Table 3). The PTSD slice of this tort pie is not insubstantial. Clearly, pain and suffering damages, particularly PTSD claims, are a lucrative legal business. Indeed, it has been suggested that by at least one commentator that "no diagnosis in the history of American psychiatry has had a more dramatic and pervasive impact on law and social justice than PTSD."[4]

But while it does not take long on Google to discover that PTSD is big business for some lawyers, one does have to look harder within legal scholarship generally, and neurolaw scholarship in particular, to find scholarly analyses that keep up with the realities of legal practice.[5] Legal scholarship at the intersection of law and neuroscience, with a few notable exceptions (e.g. Grey, 2011; Kolber, 2007, 2011; Viens, 2007), has focused primarily on the criminal justice system (Goodenough & Tucker, 2010; Shen, 2010). This chapter, by focusing on the intersection of neuroscience and PTSD litigation, shifts scholarly focus to the civil side.[6]

In addition to focusing almost exclusively on criminal law, most existing neurolaw research has narrowed its analysis to doctrinal issues, failing to recognize the political and legislative links that will surely shape the future of neuropolicy. It is widely acknowledged that we live in an "age of legislation" and that most new law is statutory law (Garrett, 1999). Recognizing this, and recognizing too that tort law is most commonly state law, million-dollar lobbying efforts by groups interested in tort issues are not uncommon. One of the stated missions of the U.S. Chamber Institute for Legal Reform (ILR), for instance, is to "neutralize plaintiff trial lawyers' excessive influence over the legal and political systems."[7] In addition to influencing the outcomes of elections and swaying legislators, the plaintiff and defense bars also spar in the court of public opinion. In 2006, for instance, the Association of Trial Lawyers of America renamed itself the American Association for Justice (AAJ) in an effort to improve the public image of trial lawyers (Carter, 2007). This move was seen by observers as an effort "to turn back what the other side has done in lobbying the public mind for decades" (Carter, 2007, p. 39).

Those who follow memory and law issues will be familiar with the importance of state legislative action and lobbying through the political and legislative activity surrounding the issues of false memory and childhood sexual abuse. The legal dynamics of these two issues changed when state legislatures began to tinker with the applicable legal rules—for example, modifying the statute of limitations for claims. It remains too early to know exactly how new findings from neuroscience research labs will influence state legislatures, but it is not too early to begin investigating the pathways of influence. The statehouse, as well as the courthouse, deserves our scholarly attention.

Neuroscience and Value-Added for Lawyers

Stress-related mental injuries, especially those accrued due to exposure to military combat, have long been scrutinized, though PTSD was officially recognized by the APA for the first time in 1980 in DSM-III (American Psychiatric Association, 1980). Due in large part to concerns about veterans' mental health upon their return from the battlefield, since the 1980s PTSD has been and continues to be well studied (Friedman, Keane, & Resick, 2007). The National Center for PTSD, established in 1989 within the Department of Veterans Affairs, has, for instance, invested tens of millions of dollars to improve PTSD research, clinical practice, and awareness.[8]

As the research base on PTSD has grown, so too have criticisms (Brewin, 2003). The controversies include debates about whether PTSD is a legitimate diagnosis, PTSD's failure to account for cross-cultural variation, its litigious nature, and concerns about the reliability of verbal reports and traumatic memories (Rosen, 2004; Rosen et al., 2010). While acknowledging these critiques and returning to several of them later in the chapter, the purpose of this section is simply to elucidate for lawyers a basic understanding of what we know (and do not know) about PTSD, with an emphasis, given the subject of this volume, on PTSD and the neuroscience of memory.[9]

Many plaintiff and defense lawyers who litigate personal injury cases are familiar with clients and claimants, respectively, complaining of PTSD symptoms. PTSD is "a favored diagnosis in tort law because it is incident specific, easy to understand, and tends to rule out other factors potentially involved in causation" (Sparr & Pitman, 2007, p. 449). PTSD is also, at present, defined and diagnosed exclusively through behavioral measures. The diagnostic criteria for PTSD (American Psychiatric Association, 2000) make no explicit mention of the brain. Compensation is tied to deficits in behavioral outcomes (caused by the specific event at issue), both for personal injury cases and for veterans' PTSD claims. It is not enough for a client's brain to change due to a traumatic event; if those brain changes do not lead to the behavioral outcomes specified in the diagnostic criteria, then PTSD is not diagnosed and no successful claim can be filed.

If behavior is front and center in PTSD litigation, what does neuroscience research add to the legal landscape? In gaining purchase on this question, it is helpful for illustrative purposes to take the view of a plaintiff's attorney who is considering accepting a case for which PTSD is the potential client's major injury.[10] In order for a PTSD case to be economically viable, at least three important prerequisites must be met. First, there must be both a legal avenue for recovery and a defendant with deep enough pockets to pay for the recovery.[11] Second, it must be possible to establish both the existence of PTSD in the client and specific causation between the defendant's actions and the plaintiff's PTSD injury.[12] Third, the damage suffered by the plaintiff must be monetized to a sufficient size to warrant the lawyer's investment in litigating the claim. If any of these links in the chain does not hold, it is unlikely that an attorney will take on the case.

While experts have produced volumes on the role of neuroscience research in the second link of this chain—establishing the PTSD diagnosis and what caused it (Young et al., 2006a, 2006b)—this chapter turns its attention to the first and third components. Specifically, neuroscience evidence may play a critical role in determining whether PTSD is understood as a *mental* or a *bodily* injury. Because of the way that many insurance policies and government immunity statutes are written, the mental/bodily distinction serves a gateway function. Plaintiffs can only potentially recover from certain deep pockets (i.e., insurance policies and governmental bodies) if their PTSD is deemed bodily (Grey, 2011). Cognitive neuroscience evidence is likely to be mustered in support of such efforts, as it was in the *Allen* case to be discussed later in this chapter.

In addition to finding new deep pockets, neuroscientific evidence may also help the plaintiff's bar increase recovery amounts for clients. This is due in part to what has been called the "seductive allure" of brain imaging data (Weisberg et al., 2008). The success of tort recovery often relies on the packaging of the client's injuries. It has long been recognized that "the variety of witnesses who can 'dress up' the damages is limited only by the imagination of the advocate" (Agoglia & Beckett, 1983, p. 140). Lawyers writing three decades ago did not know that part of the dressing up would someday involve functional magnetic resonance imaging (fMRI) scans, but they had a premonition, when they spoke of X-rays: "the drama of their impact upon the jury cannot be overestimated as the room is darkened while the shadowbox displaying the X-rays is lighted up" (ibid., p. 153). Although the empirical evidence, focusing primarily on the impact of neuroscience data on criminal outcomes, remains mixed (see Schweitzer et al., 2011), an important question is whether, and how, neuroscience data on PTSD will affect damage verdicts and settlements. This chapter takes a first step in answering that question.

PTSD and the Brain

As noted earlier, from the perspective of neuroscience, what the law labels as purely *mental* is not distinct from the *bodily* (or *physical*). To see why, and before turning to the law's view later in the chapter, this section provides a very basic introduction to the neuroscience of PTSD. As will be emphasized here and throughout, PTSD has been and continues to be a contested diagnosis. Brain science will only add to the complexity, and this complexity, the chapter argues, presents both opportunities and challenges for practicing trial attorneys.

Although "many questions remain unanswered" about PTSD (Shin, Rauch, & Pitmaan, 2005, p. 75), and although translating neuroimaging research into legally relevant evidence remains a tricky business, lawyers doing intake interviews with potential clients can think of PTSD as an inability to properly regulate one's fear response. The three brain regions of most interest for understanding PTSD are the amygdala, prefrontal cortex, and hippocampus (Shin et al., 2005). Each of these structures has been discussed previously in this volume. Setting aside for the moment myriad complexities and individual differences, the basic story emerging from neuroimaging research on PTSD is one of "exaggerated responsivity in the amygdala, diminished responsivity in medial prefrontal cortex, and an inverse relationship between these two brain regions" along with "diminished volumes, neuronal integrity, and functional integrity of the hippocampus" (Shin et al., 2005, p. 74).

Activity in these areas of the brain, as with all areas of the brain, is primarily mediated by neurotransmitters that carry signals from one neuron to the next. These biochemical processes underlie our mental activity and behavior, and are fundamentally no different from the various processes underlying the functioning of other organs in the body. From a neuroscientific perspective, mental activity can be readily labeled as *bodily* or *physical* in the same way that the function of any other organ in the body, such the beating of a heart, would be considered physical.

Clients diagnosed with PTSD typically exhibit either hyperactive or dissociative fear reactions.[13] A small, almond-shaped brain region called the *amygdala* plays a central role in fear response, signaling when we should genuinely be frightened, and behave accordingly, and when the coast is clear. In the case of a client with PTSD, these complex systems function abnormally, and the abnormal functioning of the brain's biochemistry results in the client's inability to live life as he or she normally would—for example, experiencing fear at moments when (but for the traumatic event) this would normally not occur.

Because of a client's preexisting vulnerabilities, the nature of the traumatic event, and subsequent events, the client's brain has been rewired (through changing neuronal connections and firing patterns). PTSD involves dysregulation of several neurotransmitter/neurohormone systems: the noradrenergic system, the serotonergic system, and the hypothalamic-pituitary-adrenal (HPA) axis (Southwick et al., 2007). Increased levels of catecholamine and cortisol "enhance the functioning of the amygdala, promoting fear conditioning and the consolidation of emotionally relevant memories" (ibid., p. 30). At the same time, the release of these hormones can "*impair* the cognitive functioning of the PFC" (ibid., p. 31; italics in the original). In short, the neurochemical environment during a stressful moment sets the stage for the memory encoding that may eventually lead to observed PTSD behavioral outcomes.

The relationship between memory and trauma, which has been touched upon at other points in this volume, plays an important role in PTSD as well.[14] Experimental research on memory for trauma-relevant and -irrelevant words, as well as tests of autobiographical memory, have found that PTSD may involve both "unwanted recall of the traumatic event" and "mild impairments in recall of newly acquired information" (Constans, 2005, p. 116).

To understand why some memories evoke this fear response while others do not, we must review the important role of the hippocampus, a part of the brain critically involved in memory (Nadel, 2008). Relevant to this chapter's discussion of PTSD, "the hippocampus is essential for the acquisition of episode memories with spatiotemporal content" (Nadel & Jacobs, 1996, p. 457). To illustrate the role of the hippocampus, consider, for example, the *episode* of a car crash and how a client's memory of that crash may be affected by stress.

Imagine that a client walks through the door and states that he was involved in an automobile accident a year ago while on vacation, when a truck ran a stop sign and slammed into his car. The client suffered a shoulder strain, which is no longer painful, but the client reports that he is still having trouble resuming normal activities because when he pulls up to stop signs he often recalls the crash and panics. What can explain the client's reexperiencing of the crash? If his brain's memory systems were functioning normally, the episode of the car crash would have been stored as a memory with a specific spatial content (i.e., not the stop signs he sees when driving to work in the morning) and a specific temporal content (i.e., this happened a year ago). But because the memory was formed in the midst of a stressful traumatic event, his brain's memory systems were *not* functioning normally. More specifically:

> When memories are formed under intense stress, a critical component of normal memory formation—the hippocampus—is disabled, and memories without spatiotemporal content are created. At the same time, another component of normal memory function—the amygdala—can be potentiated, leading to stronger-than-usual memory for highly charged emotional events. When a person retrieves a traumatic event memory, the retrieved information is bereft of spatiotemporal context. Instead of being bound firmly to the past, this "disembodied" event memory is conflated with the ongoing spatio/temporal frame.... The memory takes on a quality of the here and now so strongly that the individual may literally *re-experience the event*. (Nadel & Jacobs, 1996, p. 459)

Those who experience PTSD are less able to successfully engage in *context discrimination*—discriminating between a new context that is not threatening and the old context that was. This, in turn, may lead to an inability to resume the normal life course, such as driving, working, or engaging in relationships. By uncovering the neural mechanisms that cause these behavioral outcomes, memory science allows lawyers to speak of mental injuries in the brain-based terminology of the hippocampus, the amygdala, and the biochemical processes by which the two structures function with each other and with the rest of the brain.

Much debate remains over the reliability of the memory of those who have experienced severe trauma (Brown, Hammond & Scheflin, 1998). An illustrative example, discussed at length by Sparr and Bremner (2005), is the 1998 trial of a Bosnian-Croatian soldier for interrogation and abuse of a female prisoner. Expert witnesses for the defense argued that the woman's memories were inaccurate due her traumatic experiences, while prosecution experts suggested precisely the opposite. Both sides relied, in part, on neuroscientific evidence to support their arguments.

This last example reminds us that questions surrounding PTSD and memory are "subtle and complex" (Brewin, 2007, p. 129). Any neuroscience expert used at trial is very likely to be fiercely cross-examined and challenged by an opposing expert who is also likely to invoke neuroscience research. Just to name a few of the issues, PTSD can be challenged by questioning: the causal relationship between the traumatic event and the claimed PTSD symptoms; the quality of the victim's memory for the relevant facts at issue; comorbidity (how we identify PTSD vis-à-vis other anxiety disorders such as depression; Kessler, Sonnega, Bromet, Hughes, & Nelson, 1995); making individualized assessments from group-based neuroscience data, accounting for individual differences in PTSD incidence rates; and the reliability of the PTSD diagnosis (i.e. is the client malingering?; Young et al., 2006a, 2006b). For these and other reasons, establishing a PTSD diagnosis that will hold up in court, and convincing a jury that it was caused by the defendant's actions, is not an easy task.

PTSD, NEUROSCIENCE, AND THE CONCEPTUALIZATION OF INJURY IN TORT LAW

A plaintiff's lawyer is hired, in part, to creatively search for legal avenues of recovery. And civil defense lawyers, in turn, attempt to counteract those searches and limit liability and exposure for their clients. At the policy level, the plaintiff's bar actively works to lobby for expansion of liability, and the defense bar contests such efforts. PTSD compensation questions arise primarily in five contexts (Sparr & Pitman, 2007): (1) Social Security disability,

(2) private disability and health insurance, (3) veterans' disability benefits, (4) workers' compensation, and (5) personal injury.

One possible new avenue for recovery would be to open up liability that had previously been restricted solely for what the law deems *bodily*, as distinct from *mental*, injuries. As discussed earlier, this distinction persists in law but is not employed in neuroscience.[15] In modern U.S. tort law, the distinction between bodily and mental injury plays an important role in delineating the contours of governmental immunity and insurance coverage (Grey, 2011). This section discusses how courts handle the distinction through several illustrative cases.

The Case of *Allen v. Bloomfield Hills*

Although it ended up settling out of court, in 2010 the Michigan Supreme Court had before it a case that would have dealt with precisely the question of whether PTSD constitutes a *bodily* injury (*Allen v. Bloomfield Hills School District*, 2008). The case was brought by plaintiff Charles Allen, who was conducting a train when he hit a school bus (with only a driver inside) that had moved around the railroad barriers and onto the train tracks. Allen's train hit the bus at a speed of 65 miles per hour, and the bus driver was seriously injured. Allen brought his suit against the owner of the school bus, the Bloomfield Hills School District.

By making the school district the target of the suit, Allen was aiming to take advantage of Michigan's motor vehicle exception to government immunity. Michigan law (MCL 691.1405) states that "governmental agencies shall be liable for bodily injury and property damage resulting from the negligent operation by any officer, agent, or employee of the governmental agency, of a motor vehicle of which the governmental agency is owner." The operative words, and the reason this case is of great interest for the chapter, are "liable for bodily injury." Since Allen's damages claim arose primarily from PTSD, and not more traditional *bodily* injury, his recovery would be barred by statute unless he could convince the court that in fact the Michigan legislature, when enacting the statute, intended to include PTSD as a *bodily* injury.

An affidavit was presented on Allen's behalf by Dr. Joseph C. Wu, who found that a positron emission tomography (PET) scan of Allen "depicted 'decreases in frontal and subcortical activity consistent with depression and post traumatic stress disorder'...[and] that the abnormalities in Mr. Allen's brain as depicted on the September 8, 2006, PET scan are quite pronounced and are clearly different in brain pattern from any of the normal controls. They are also consistent with an injury to Mr. Allen's brain" (pp. 57–58). Allen also submitted a report by Dr. Gerald A. Shiener noting to the court that PTSD "causes significant changes in brain chemistry, brain function, and brain structure" (ibid., p. 57).

The trial court sided with the defense (which argued that proper statutory interpretation did not warrant inclusion of PTSD as a bodily injury), but an appeal was made and the appellate court ruled in favor of Allen. The appellate court found that

> [t]he brain is a part of the human body, so "harm or damage done or sustained" is injury to the brain and within the common meaning of "bodily injury" in MCL 691.1405, as elucidated in *Wesche*. The question on appeal then becomes, for purposes of reviewing the trial court's grant of summary disposition to defendant, whether plaintiff produced sufficient evidence to create a material question of fact that he suffered a "bodily injury" as so defined. In doing so, we must still adhere to the court rules and follow the law. We must review any evidence of a claimed "bodily injury" in a light most favorable to the nonmoving party. Also, we must conduct our review with common sense, and with cognizance of modern medical science and the human body. Here, plaintiff presented objective medical evidence that a mental or emotional trauma can indeed result in physical changes to the brain.
>
> Although the brain is the organ responsible for our thoughts and emotions, it is also the organ that controls all our physical functions. The fact that it serves more than one function hardly detracts from the fact that it is one of our major organs. It can be injured. It can be injured directly and indirectly. It can be injured by direct and indirect trauma. What matters for a legal analysis is the existence of a manifest, objectively measured injury to the brain. Consequently, to survive a motion for summary disposition, we must determine whether plaintiff produced sufficient evidence that Allen suffered from an objectively manifested physical injury to his brain. (p. 58)

This ruling led to a further appeal, this time by the school district, to the Michigan Supreme Court, where again both sides made their case through briefs. The briefs submitted to the Michigan Supreme Court sparred over the proper statutory interpretation of the phrase "bodily injury." Allen's legal team cited multiple scientific sources, including the U.S. Surgeon General's *Report on Mental Health* (1999, p. 6), which stated that "people continue to see mental and physical as separate functions, when, in fact, mental functions (e.g. memory) are physical as well."

The defense did not so much counter the science as point to legislative intent and past case law. On legislative intent, the defense argued in its brief that "Nothing in the statutory language of the motor vehicle exception reflects intent by the Legislature to apply the motor vehicle exception to mental, emotional, or psychiatric disorders, even if the secondary effect of such disorders is a change in the brain or any other part of the body" (Cox, Restuccia, & Sherman, 2009, p. 7). Relying on an earlier case (*Wesche v. Mecosta Co Rd Comm.*, 2008), the defense argued in several ways that "damages of a spiritual or mental nature are not encompassed within the plain language of the motor vehicle exception" (ibid., p. 7). The defense also made a slippery-slope policy argument, warning that swinging open the doors of bodily injury in this case would ultimately force the school district to allocate less money to students.

The Michigan Supreme Court received amicus briefs from the Michigan Association for Justice, the Michigan Defense Trial Counsel, Inc., the Insurance Institute of Michigan, and the Brain Injury Association of Michigan. That so many third parties took a large interest in the case speaks to the potential magnitude of the decision for tort recovery. And while we do not know how the Michigan Supreme Court would have ruled (since the case settled), we can use experimental methods to study the court of public opinion. The fourth section of this chapter lays out the methodology for doing just that.

Insurance and Bodily Injury

The *Allen* case is not the only case law dealing with the issue of bodily injury. A small but not insubstantial set of cases have litigated the question in the context of insurance coverage. Nationally, insurance "liability policies also typically afford coverage for bodily injury caused by an occurrence. Some policies expressly define bodily injury to include emotional distress. Most do not" (Windt, 2010, § 11:2). Many courts have distinguished between purely emotional injuries and emotional injuries that include physical manifestations (ibid., § 11:2).

In *Bader v. United States Automobile Association* (2009), for instance, the plaintiff sought recovery for both physical and emotional injuries emanating from an accident. The defendant insurance company moved for summary judgment, "claiming that all of the plaintiff's injuries are emotional in nature" and therefore "that there is no genuine issue of fact as to whether the plaintiff's damages constitute a 'bodily injury' as that term is defined in the plaintiff's insurance policy" (p. 1). Thus, in parallel to the statutory interpretation conducted in *Allen*, the court in *Bader* had to interpret the language of the insurance policy.

In this case, and in hundreds of cases where questions about *bodily injury* have been litigated, it seems that the neuronal argument (i.e., that emotions, and thus emotional injury, are *physical* and *bodily*) has yet to be fully pressed, let alone accepted, as it was (at least by the appeals court) in *Allen*.

An opportunity thus awaits for the right combination of science and creative litigators. The analysis in this chapter gives those litigators data which may help to assess lay response to such arguments.

VALUATION OF PTSD INJURIES

American tort law attempts to accomplish a complicated mix of compensation, insurance, and deterrence objectives (Fried & Rosenberg, 2003). In the background for all of these functions is the issue of valuation: How much, in dollars, should be paid to compensate for harms experienced? Similar questions are asked by administrative agencies such as the Veterans Administration (VA) when faced with injury compensation issues. This section reviews current methods used for answering these questions and then explores the ways in which neuroscientific evidence may affect the valuation process.

Monetizing PTSD: Current Options

As established in multiple disciplines, placing a dollar value on injuries is often perceived as a taboo trade-off (Shen, in press). Nevertheless, such trade-offs are important for optimal allocation of scarce resources within both the criminal and civil systems. In the criminal justice system, it has been observed that

> [i]gnoring the nonmonetary benefits of crime reduction can lead to a misallocation of resources. For example, suppose that an additional year of incarceration for a rape offender would prevent one additional rape incident. Considering only tangible, out-of-pocket costs, the average rape (or attempted rape) costs $5,100—less than the $15,000–$20,000 annual cost of a prison cell. The bulk of these expenses are medical and mental health care costs to victims. However, if rape's effect on the victim's quality of life is quantified, the average rape costs $87,000—many times greater than the cost of prison. (Miller, Cohen, & Wiersema 1996, p. 1)

In the case of PTSD, the VA addresses the problem of valuation by utilizing a statutorily defined rating scale to evaluate disability compensation levels (38 C.F.R. §4.1). The VA has spent considerable time and money both compensating veterans for PTSD and learning how to better operate their compensation system. These efforts were driven in part by a great rise in PTSD claims. From 1999 to 2004, there was nearly an 80% increase in PTSD cases, and payments reached over $4 billion (DVA, 2005). Those numbers have continued to expand (National Research Council, 2007). Although the language of the statute points only to compensation for lost income, in practice it is established that compensation also accounts for reductions in the claimant's quality of life generally (DVA, 2004).[16] Similar to the need to establish causation in the civil context, to qualify for compensation a veteran must show a service connection to the PTSD symptoms.[17] A specialized segment of the bar works to help veterans meet this requirement (Roche, 2007).

In the civil litigation context, there is now an extensive economics literature on estimating money damages for injuries and death called *forensic economics* (Kaufman, Rodgers, & Martin, 2005). These scholars often provide expert testimony and counsel lawyers on how much to seek in certain cases. A method developed extensively by economist Kip Viscusi is the Value of a Statistical Life (VSL) approach, used, for example, by federal agencies weighing the costs and benefits of particular policies. The VSL approach, which is not without its critics (see, e.g., Cameron, 2010), uses willingness-to-pay estimates (e.g., how much would you be willing to pay to reduce the risk of some injury?) in order to arrive at an estimated benefit from reducing (to zero) the risk of dying. These methods produce estimates for the price of life at roughly between $1 and $2.5 million (Mrozek & Taylor, 2002).

Most relevant to the discussion in this chapter are what are termed *hedonic damages*, which "refer to the dollar value of the loss of enjoyment of life in wrongful death and non-fatal injury cases" (Kaufman et al., 2005, p. xxvii). Arising in the 1980s and now a fixture in personal injury law (Palfin & Danninger, 1990), the hedonic damages approach is, in its simplest form, a theoretically straightforward (if difficult to implement) three-step process. First, estimate the value of a given life. Second, estimate the reduction in percentage terms of lost ability to enjoy life. Then, multiply #2 by #1 and you arrive at a valuation; for example, losing 50% enjoyment of a life worth $2M results in a valuation of the personal injury of $1M.

Even with hedonics, putting a price on emotional harms remains quite difficult. While many possible reforms have been proposed by legal scholars (e.g., Avraham, 2006; Geistfeld, 1995), it is fair to say that jurors still have little guidance about how best to evaluate such harms. In a review of the relevant literature, Samra and Koch (2002, p. 308) write that "a glaring hole in the literature pertaining to the economics of psychological injuries is the absence of literature speaking to the pain and suffering costs of psychological injuries and tortuous events." In practice, jurors are typically given an instruction such as "No fixed standard exists for deciding the amount of these damages. You must use your judgment to decide a reasonable amount based on the evidence and your common sense."[18]

Over and above these general complications in estimating damages for emotional harms, PTSD is difficult to valuate, in present dollar terms, because although it is often chronic, the life course of the symptoms varies

(Shalev, 2002). An accurate monetary valuation of PTSD must account for the number of bad days over the course of a lifetime, not just how a client is feeling during the time of litigation. Some have argued that, in general, we tend to overestimate future pain and suffering because we fail to account for hedonic adaptation (Sunstein, 2008; though see Swedloff & Huang, 2010).

Given this state of affairs—where it is not an overstatement to say that valuation of psychological damages remains just as muddy as it was decades ago—one inevitably wonders if cognitive neuroscience can provide even mild additional clarity.

Monetizing PTSD: Neuroscientific Possibilities

The first, though very unrealistic in the foreseeable future, way that neuroscientific evidence could affect monetization of PTSD is through the construction of an accurate and reliable brain-based index of PTSD injury. Such an index, ideally, would generate an accurate measure of pain comparable across individuals. But the likelihood of a PTSD injury index, at least in the immediate future, is not high.[19] While the possibilities are tantalizing, and recent work from the lab of Apostolos Georgopoulos et al. (2010) suggests that a PTSD biomarker is possible, such methods have not reached the courtroom, and attempts to "relate neurobiological alterations to symptoms or diagnoses" remain "both challenging and risky" (Southwick et al., 2007, p. 182).

Even in the midst of ongoing scientific debate, however, brain data may still be used by lawyers in efforts to alter jurors' decision making. Legal applications of scientific materials need not wait, and historically often have not waited, for scientists to arrive at a consensus. Adopting the perspective of lawyers who are hired to fully litigate their clients' interests, we can understand why this is the case. So long as it does not violate professional ethics standards, lawyers can make good faith judgments about when, in the interests of achieving justice for their client, particular scientific evidence is appropriate to use. Lawyers are not hired to conduct peer-review of the scientific literature. Rather, in strategizing for a case, they answer the question "Is the science *useful for achieving a better outcome for my client in this case*?" In the tort context, this can be crudely translated as "Will it enhance (for plaintiffs) or reduce (for defense) the likelihood of reciving greater money damages?" To clinicians and memory researchers, this legal perspective may seem quite foreign. But the question of monetization is an important one in legal practice.

It should be recognized that there are many instances in which brain science and trial law already intersect. For instance, lawyers routinely draw on neuroscience experts when their clients have suffered brain injuries.[17] Today, lawyers litigating brain injury claims look not only to traditional PET and MRI scans, but also to newer forms of brain imaging (Weaver & Stern, 2011). The reasons offered for using such imagery are practical. One practice manual, for instance, advises that advanced techniques such as quantitative electroencephalography (qEEG) will provide "illustrative charts clearly showing the damaged areas of the brain. This is important, because this can be shown to a jury for purposes of establishing a clear visual demonstrative aid.... Now, the injuries are real. Now, you are more likely to obtain compensation" (Weaver & Stern, 2011, § 53:5). The defense bar, of course, can also use images (or the plaintiff's failure to proffer them) to critique a plaintiff's case. Thus, it remains an open question whether neuroscience in the context of PTSD will be of greater payoff to the plaintiff or defense bar. The survey experiment presented in the next section begins to answer one aspect of this question.

DATA AND METHODS

The potential of cognitive neuroscience to either expand or contract the PTSD personal injury litigation market rests in part, this chapter has thus far argued, on (1) whether or not neuroscience information will make individuals more likely to view PTSD as a bodily injury and (2) whether neuroscience information will affect the valuation of PTSD claims. These two questions are informed, but cannot be adequately answered, by the literature on empirical studies of juror decision making (Devine, Clayton, Dunford, Seying, & Pryce, 2001; Hans & Albertson, 2003) and by the emerging literature on neuroscientific evidence in the courtroom (Schweitzer et. al., 2011). Thus, this chapter presents results from two new survey experiments designed to provide data with which to gain some leverage on where neuroscience may take PTSD claims in the future.

Experimental Design

A historical distinction between psychologists and political scientists is the former's emphasis on lab-based experiments and the latter's preference for fieldwork and large-N survey work (McDermott, 2002). Threading the needle between the two, external validity concerns are addressed in the present study through the use of a large-N web-based sample that, while not truly nationally representative, is nonetheless drawn from across the country. Across the two experiments reported in this chapter, subjects came from 46 different states (only the small states—North Dakota, South Dakota, Vermont, and Wyoming—were not represented). The drawback in pursuing this strategy is, of course, the limitations it places on what the experimenter can ask the subject to do. Thus, instead of a mock juror research design or a design that exposed subjects to significant case material, each of the two experiments asked subjects to read and evaluate one short vignette.

Subjects in Experiment 1, the bodily/mental experiment, were randomly assigned to read one of three case summaries. Each summary was based on the *Allen* case described in the second section (see Figure 13.1). Group 1, the Baseline group, was exposed to only the summary, which made no mention of neuroscience. Group 2, the Plaintiff group, was exposed to only the plaintiff's expert providing a neuroscience explanation to support the plaintiff's case that PTSD is a bodily injury. Group 3, the Both group, was exposed to both a plaintiff and a defendant expert's testimony.

After reading the vignette, subjects were then asked: "Imagine for a moment that you were deciding this case, and you had to rule one way or the other. How would you rule?" Subjects were offered two choices: (1) John's experience of PTSD *is* a bodily injury, and he should be able to collect on his insurance policy; (2) John's experience of PTSD is *not* a bodily injury, and he should *not*

John was operating a train near an intersection in the city of Sunset Hills when he observed a Sunset Hills School District school bus enter the railroad-grade crossing by recklessly maneuvering around the lowered gate. The train, which was traveling at a speed of approximately 65 miles an hour, was unable to stop and collided with the school bus. After stopping the train and running approximately one-half mile back to the accident scene, John was informed that there were no children on the bus at the time of the accident, but that the bus driver was severely injured. John was subsequently diagnosed with post traumatic stress disorder (PTSD) stemming from the accident.

John had insurance to cover accidents at work, but when he filed a claim, he was told that the policy only covered "bodily injury". The insurance company determined that since John's only injury was his PTSD, this was mental or psychological injury and did not constitute a "bodily injury".

John took his case to court to challenge the insurance company's interpretation of the term "bodily injury" in his policy.

<*"Plaintiff" and "Both" Groups exposed to this information*: During the court's hearings, Dr. David McCarthy, a board-certified neuropsychologist and neurologist testified about the scientific consensus that PTSD is the result of a neurobiological and neurocognitive change in the brain. He talked specifically about the brain regions known to be affected by PTSD (prefrontal cortex, amygdala, and hippocampus). Since the brain is part of the human body, and bodily functions such as chemical reactions and electrical signaling in the brain are involved in PTSD, John made the case that his PTSD was just as "bodily" as a broken arm. Just because it was hard to see inside his brain, John said, didn't mean it was any less real.>

<*Only "Both" Group exposed to this information*: Experts and lawyers for the insurance company countered that the term "bodily" in the insurance policy must be interpreted by its plain language meaning. They pointed out that if John's definition was accepted by the court, then every "mental" disability would have to be regarded as a "physical" disability, with no way to distinguish between the two. Such a position, they suggested, was not in keeping with ordinary understanding of the words mental, physical, and bodily. Moreover, they argued that if we began to consider every mental injury a "bodily" injury, we would produce sky-rocketing insurance premiums.>

Figure 13.1 PTSD vignettes utilized in Experiment 1. See text for detailed description of the experiment.

be able to collect on his insurance policy. The experiment did not, nor did it intend to, present subjects with a realistic trial experience. Moreover, it should be emphasized that the *Allen* case concerned a distinct legal question (related to a motion for summary judgment to be decided by a judge and not a jury). These and other shortcomings aside, the experiments reported here do provide us with initial insights into the dynamics of public support for legislative policymaking in this arena.

Subjects in Experiment 2 were also randomly assigned to a Baseline, Plaintiff, or Both group and were asked to read a short case summary (see Figure 13.2). The case summary in Experiment 2 was based on an actual reported PTSD civil litigation case, *Sapirman v. Walmart* (2009). The case was chosen because it is a relatively straightforward case of premises liability and because we know

---

On Nov. 30, 2006, plaintiff David Williams, a 32-year-old nursing home administrator, was attacked and beaten by several men at 9:10 p.m. in a big public parking lot in North Miami Beach. The attacker then stole David's car and he was nearly run over. He claimed a shoulder injury.

David sued the security provider for the parking lot, National Security, alleging that the security was inadequate in the parking lot. The security guards were not adequately trained, and the lot was not adequately lit, claimed plaintiff's counsel.

Although defense counsel contended that security could not have prevented the attack, the Court found that the security provider was liable.

Thus, the only question remaining was how much recovery David should receive for his injuries.

In a hearing on the injuries, David stated that he suffers from post-traumatic stress disorder. He has sought counseling and reports a heightened level of anxiousness in busy areas and in parking lots. David sought $6,000 in medical costs, plus the costs of living with the bad memories brought on by the PTSD.

The security company agreed to cover the $6,000 in medical costs, but argued that the plaintiff is not suffering from PTSD, noting that he was able to gain a promotion at work and had a child with his wife.

Plaintiffs' counsel countered that David still suffers from PTSD even though he was able to get a promotion.

<*"Plaintiff" and "Both" Groups exposed to this information*: At the trial, Dr. George Poulos, a clinical neuropsychologist and neurologist, testified that his research team had taken magnetoencephalographic (MEG) recordings of David's brain, and based on comparisons with control subjects, had determined that David's brain activity was abnormal and suggestive of PTSD.>

<*Only "Both" Group exposed to this information*: Upon cross-examination, however, Dr. Poulous admitted that since he had not scanned David before the parking lot incident, his methods could not determine whether the parking lot incident itself, as opposed to another traumatic event previously, was the cause of David's differential brain activity. Dr. Poulous also noted that there are many individual differences in how one responds to trauma, and thus it was not possible for his brain scan research to quantify the level of PTSD David might be experiencing.>

Figure 13.2 PTSD vignettes utilized in Experiment 2. See text for detailed description of the experiment.

(from official reported records) the actual settlement amount: $207,500.[21] The facts of the case were these: The plaintiff was attacked in a Walmart parking lot one night in 2006, and he then sued Walmart to seek damages both for a shoulder injury and for PTSD. The plaintiff reported that he "sought counseling and report[ed] a heightened level of anxiousness in busy areas and in parking lots." He sought only $6,000 in medical costs, leaving the rest—roughly $200,000—for pain and suffering from PTSD. The defense argued that the plaintiff was "not suffering from PTSD, noting that he was able to gain a promotion at work and had a child with his wife."

The neuroscience information provided on behalf of the plaintiff was inspired by the magnetoencephalography (MEG) research being conducted in the Georgopoulos lab and mentioned earlier in the chapter. In the experiment (not in the real case), the plaintiff's expert witness testified that he could confirm the plaintiff's PTSD via MEG. The Both group, however, learned that upon cross-examination of the plaintiff's expert, the case for biomarking PTSD was not as strong. In this way, the vignette allows us to glimpse how individuals might respond both to the unchecked promise and to the more realistic complexity of neuroscientific research on PTSD biomarkers.

All three groups in Experiment 2 were asked after reading the vignette: "Imagine for a moment that you were deciding this case, and you had to award some damage amount to David [the plaintiff]. How much would you award for the bad memories from PTSD?" Subjects used a slider bar to choose an amount ranging from $0 to $1 million.

Subjects

Subjects were recruited, separately for Experiment 1 and Experiment 2, via modest payments made available through Amazon Mechanical Turk's (MTurk) payment service. Studies assessing the quality of MTurk subjects have found them to be engaged in the online experimental stimuli, and to be significantly more representative than the convenience samples that would otherwise be used (Berinsky, Huber, & Lenz, forthcoming; Buhrmester, Kwang, & Gosling, 2011; Horton, Rand, & Zeckhauser, 2010). While certainly not as good as truly nationally representative samples, MTurk nonetheless provides high-quality, low-cost subjects.

Concerns about subjects' compliance with task instructions are especially important to address with online experiments because subjects cannot be monitored while engaged in the experimental tasks.[22] To address this issue, experimental psychologists have developed *attention filters* designed to ascertain whether subjects are in fact paying attention to the material being presented to them online (Oppenheimer, Meyvis, & Davidenk, 2009). The present study employed a modified version of the filter developed by Oppenheimer et al. The design of the attention filter question was such that users who did not read carefully would only read the large-font headline stating "Background Questions on Sources for News" and the large boldface question "From which of these sources have you received information in the past month?" Had they been paying attention and read the detailed instructions, presented in smaller type just below the headline, they would have known that the boldface question was misleading. A series of check-box options was provided (e.g., local newspaper, local TV news), but subjects reading the instructions carefully learned that they were *not* to check any of the boxes. Instead, they were instructed to type the numbers 123 into the text box provided.

Across the two subject pools, 1,265 subjects completed the experiment, and of these, 977 (77%) successfully answered the attention filter question. This filter rate is consistent with that obtained in other work using similar protocols (Kriner & Shen, 2010). These 977 subjects, 491 in Experiment 1 and 486 in Experiment 2, provide the responses that are analyzed in this fourth section.

Experiments were run via the Qualtrics platform. Qualtrics is an online provider of survey tools.[23] It is well established that legal decision making is the product of many situational and individual factors (Devine et al., 2001). Thus, subjects were asked a short set of demographic questions after completing the experimental tasks. Data were collected in August and September 2010.

Analytic Methods

Separate regression models were utilized for each of the two outcome variables of interest: (1) whether or not PTSD in vignette 1 is viewed as bodily injury and (2) what level of damages should be awarded for the PTSD injury in vignette 2. Because the first outcome variable is discrete, taking on values of 0 or 1, while the second is continuous, different statistical procedures are required for each. For Experiment 1, the fully specified logit regression model used was

$$BODILY_i = \beta_0 + \beta_1 PLAINTIFF_i + \beta_2 BOTH_i + \beta_3 EDUCATION_i + \beta_4 AGE_i$$
$$+ \beta_5 MALE_i + \beta_6 NONWHITE_i + \beta_7 CONSERVATIVE_i$$
$$+ \beta_8 LAWKNOWLEDGE_i + \beta_9 NEUROKNOWLEDGE_i + \varepsilon_i$$

where *BODILY* is a dichotomous variable (1 = yes, 0 = no) measuring subject *i*'s evaluation of PTSD as a bodily injury; *PLAINTIFF* is a dichotomous variable indicating whether or not subject *i* was exposed to the plaintiff-only expert information; *BOTH* is a dichotomous variable indicating whether or not subject *i* was exposed to both plaintiff and defendant expert information; *EDUCATION* is a categorical variable (ranging from 1 to 6) measuring each subject's highest level of educational attainment; *AGE* is subject age; *MALE* and *NONWHITE* are dichotomous variables indicating whether the subject is male and nonwhite, respectively; *CONSERVATIVE* is a 7-point measure of ideology (with higher values indicating more conservative ideology); and *LAWKNOWLEDGE* and *NEUROKNOWLEDGE* are each 7-point measures of subject self-reported knowledge on law and on neuroscience, respectively.

The dependent variable in the second regression model is the dollar value assigned by the subject to the PTSD injury. A robust regression model, utilizing the same set of explanatory variables, was used for estimating the effect of exposure to neuroscientific information on the valuation of a PTSD injury. Because ordinary least squares (OLS) regression is quite sensitive to outliers in the data, and because the data were skewed to the right (with a small number of subjects awarding the plaintiff very large amounts), robust regression methods were required (Western, 1995).[24]

RESULTS AND DISCUSSION

Results

Looking first at the simple bivariate statistics (Figure 13.3), the data pattern suggests (1) that at baseline, a strong majority of subjects (72%) believe that PTSD constitutes a bodily injury; (2) that if subjects are exposed only to neuroscientific information that is favorable to the plaintiff, they are more likely (88%) to feel this way; but (3) that if subjects are exposed both to the plaintiff's scientific expert and to a critique from a defense expert, support for the bodily claim drops (to 62%).

Further statistical analysis confirms that these differences are significant. Because the outcome variable of interest here is dichotomous (1 = PTSD is bodily; 0 = PTSD is not bodily), a logit regression model was employed, including dichotomous variables for (1) exposure to just the expert testimony for the plaintiff and (2) exposure to both the plaintiff and defense expert testimony. Postestimation chi-square tests confirm that there is a statistically significant difference in the responses of subjects exposed to the two treatment conditions compared to the baseline. Relative to the baseline, subjects exposed to just the plaintiff expert neuroscience testimony are more likely to consider PTSD a bodily injury (chi2(1) = 10.04, $p < .01$), while subjects exposed to both the plaintiff and the defense neuroscience testimony are less likely to see PTSD as a bodily injury (chi2(1) = 3.09, $p < .10$).

Running the full model, with the results presented in Table 13.1, we see that both of the independent variables of interest remain statistically significant: Exposure to just the plaintiff expert information produces greater support

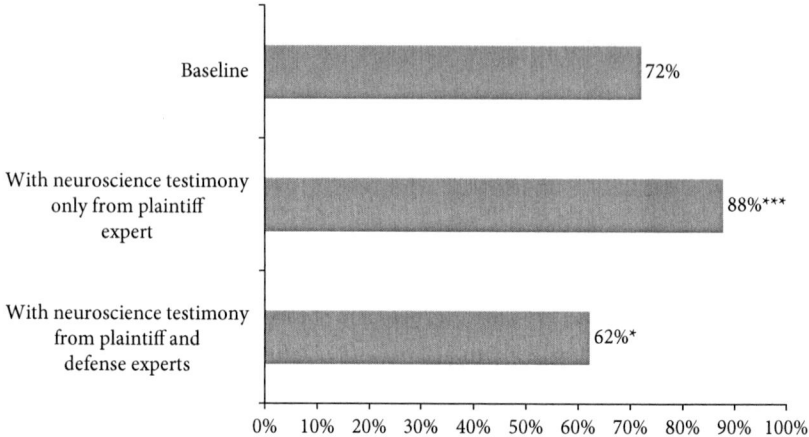

Figure 13.3 Effect of neuroscience evidence on subject evaluation of PTSD as a "bodily" injury for the purposes of collecting on his insurance policy. Statistical significance denoted as * $p < .10$; ** $p < .05$; *** $p < .01$. See text for description of the experiment and statistical analyses.

for the bodily injury claim, and exposure to both experts produces a drop in support.[25] Turning to the question of valuation of PTSD injury, the results show that (1) there is an average baseline valuation of the injury depicted in the scenario of roughly $150,000, with a median injury level of $35,000 (Table 13.2); (2) exposure to just the plaintiff's expert has a significant positive effect on the size of the award (Table 13.1, column 2); but (3) there is no significant effect when subjects are exposed to both plaintiff and defendant expert information (Table 13.1, column 2).

In addition to affecting average outcomes, it is possible that neuroscience, by providing extra information and allowing for Bayesian updating, will enable individuals to reduce uncertainty in their legal decision making. To gain a bit of traction on this question, in addition to asking subjects to place a dollar value on John's PTSD injury, subjects were asked to rate the confidence of their choice. Subjects could choose one of four choices: very certain, pretty sure, not sure, or just guessed.[26] Statistical analysis found that there was no statistically significant relationship between exposure to the neuroscience information and reduction in uncertainty surrounding the valuation choice. Nor did it reduce uncertainty in evaluation of the bodily injury question. While it is difficult to draw robust inferences from the survey experiment—given that it provided only a small amount of neuroscience and did so in a way quite different from an actual legal setting—this is nonetheless some evidence that valuation of emotional injuries remains muddled even with the addition of brain evidence.

Table 13.1 REGRESSION ANALYSIS OF EFFECT OF NEUROSCIENCE INFORMATION ON PTSD EVALUATION AND DAMAGE VALUATION

	DEP VAR: IS PTSD A BODILY INJURY?	DEP VAR: $$ AWARD FOR PTSD INJURY
	Logit Regression (odds ratios presented)	*Robust Regression*
Plaintiff Neuro Only	2.50***	26,014.78***
	(0.73)	(8,199.37)
Both Plaintiff + Defense Neuro	0.58**	3,178.98
	(0.14)	(8,283.68)
Education	0.93	−3,174.70
	(0.08)	(2,671.52)
Age	1.01	299.39
	(0.01)	(290.93)
Male	0.49***	−4,670.20
	(0.11)	(7,267.48)
Nonwhite	0.90	1,269.34
	(0.26)	(8,860.33)
Conservative	0.83***	−6,547.57***
	(0.05)	(2,175.89)
Law Knowledge	0.97	523.04
	(0.08)	(2,806.34)
Neuroscience Knowledge	1.19**	1,998.31
	(0.10)	(2,440.10)
Constant	4.45**	60,303.10***
	(2.73)	(18,841.05)
Observations	493	488
R-squared	0.084	0.051

NOTES: Statistical significance denoted as $*p < .10$; $**p < .05$; $***p < .01$. Standard errors reported in parentheses. Pseudo R-squared is reported for the logit model.

Discussion

To be sure, there are many limitations of the present experiments. More sophisticated and lengthy experimental designs are needed to better compare the addition of neuroscience information vis-à-vis the addition of other scientific and expert evidence; variations in types of neuroscience evidence proffered; and more exposure to lawyer-witness interaction. And, of course, a glaring omission from the present experiment is the visual element of brain images. Nevertheless, the experiments are the first of their kind on this important

Table 13.2 SUMMARY OF SUBJECT VALUATION ON PTSD INJURY

	MEAN	MEDIAN	STD. DEV.
Baseline	$153,183	$34,869	$227,196
With neuro testimony only from plaintiff expert	$165,786	$79,796	$214,170
With neuro testimony from plaintiff and defense experts	$163,947	$51,195	$226,817

issue, and they provide us with useful information about the possible reactions of jurors and the public to these types of arguments.

Taken together, the experiments take some of the wind out of the neurolaw sails in the PTSD civil litigation context. In terms of putting a price on PTSD damages, it seems that neuroscientific evidence, so long as it is contested (as it surely will be), is not likely to persuade individuals to change their valuation strategy. The traditional factors that make for a "good case"—a sympathetic plaintiff, a deep-pockets defendant, and so forth—seem likely to outweigh the neuroscientific evidence. Even if a PTSD biomarker were to survive scrutiny by the scientific community, it might not survive a good cross-examination. To conduct a good cross-examination, of course, as well as to develop a strong initial case, will require both the plaintiff and the defense bar to remain up-to-date on the fast-moving memory and neuroscience fields. While the science remains premature today, that could change quickly. And increasingly, scientific literacy, and more developed partnerships between law and science, may pay off for clients.

The experimental results also suggest that the plaintiff's bar may find it advantageous to engage in legislative lobbying related to definitions of bodily injury. The defense bar will, in turn, have an interest in countering such lobbying activity. How policy and statutory revision progresses will depend, in part, on public sentiment and at least under the (admittedly oversimplified) fact pattern presented in Experiment 1, a majority of subjects, even when presented with some information on both sides, are supportive of a definition of bodily injury that includes PTSD. In the real world of policymaking, of course, much more information (and misinformation) will be presented by both sides. The definition of PTSD in DSM-V is also likely to change, and with uncertain effects on the legal system. Thus, we do not know for sure who the public will side with, and further litigating these issues could prove profitable or costly, depending on one's clients.

For researchers, the experiments reported in this chapter are the first step in what can develop into a rich and very practical line of scholarship. As with the criminal law, the courtship of neuroscience and tort law involves many possible couplings. This chapter has focused solely on the question of determination of damages, but attention should also be paid to issues such as causation. Future research might investigate *imbalances* in expert testimony when someone is clearly incompetent at explaining the science. More work is also to be done in the area of neuro-mitigation. Pharmacological mitigation for emotional injuries is rarely litigated, and courts have been historically hesitant to embrace it (Noah, 2009).[27] But this situation may change (Kolber, 2006). Empirical research can provide lawyers some benchmarks for how jurors and judges might react to such proposals.

For the neurolaw scholarly community in particular, it is time to strengthen connections with practitioners. While the criminal implications of brain research are only beginning to be explored in scholarship, brain scientists and trial lawyers have been collaborating for decades on the civil side. The term *neurolaw* was in use by the plaintiff's well before it became in vogue in the legal academy (Taylor, 1998).[28] And in October 2010 the North American Brain Injury Society held its 23rd annual Conference on Legal Issues in Brain Injury. The trial lawyers' organization, the American Association for Justice, in partnership with their Traumatic Brain Injury Litigation Group, regularly hosts seminars on brain injury cases, and groups such as the Brain Injury Association of America (BIAA) have been active in supporting brain-related litigation by connecting clients to legal representation and lobbying for legal changes. Not all of this brain-related activity is specifically about memory, but certainly an important portion of it, like the PTSD litigation reviewed in this chapter, is.

We stand at a moment when PTSD and the many lines of PTSD research are firmly established in our lexicon and legal system. But we also stand at a moment when virtually every aspect of PTSD, from its very existence to its treatment, remains debated. With the financial stakes so high and the science still so fluid, battles will continue to be fought both in the courtroom and in legislative chambers. Neuroscience research, if utilized by both sides, may have a net neutral effect on PTSD litigation. But if one side, or even one litigator, can move (however briefly) ahead of the curve, there may be significant gains to be realized from monetizing memory science.

ACKNOWLEDGMENTS

Preparation of this chapter was supported in part by the John D. and Catherine T. MacArthur Foundation (Grant # 07-89249-000 HCD), The Regents of the University of California, Tulane University and Vanderbilt University. Valuable comments were received from Lynn Nadel, Walter Sinnott-Armstrong, Sophia Beal, and participants in the Memory and Law Conference. Jonathan Ord and Lauren Ramos provided valuable research assistance.

NOTES

1. For example, on the website http://www.caraccidentattorneys.com the introduction to PTSD reads: "When most people think of post-traumatic stress disorder (PTSD) they usually think of soldiers returning from a war and having bad memories of their experiences. However, post-traumatic stress disorder can occur in all areas in which the person is unable to cope after a traumatic event in his or her life. Thus it is possible to have PTSD after experiencing a car accident, even if the person had only minor injuries."
2. See http://www.hammer-ps.com/html/ptsd.html. The target of Dr. Hammer's advertisement, focusing on motor vehicle and work-related accidents, speaks to the power of legal and social institutions in establishing and shaping the contours of the legal marketplace. The United States has developed, over time, a legal regime in which auto insurance is mandatory and compensation for certain injuries experienced on the job can be recovered. Thus, experts such as Dr. Hammer interact with the law in these arenas.
3. However, see the National Academy Study (2007, p. 9) on veterans' compensation for PTSD, which concluded that "compensation does not in general serve as a disincentive to seeking treatment."
4. Stone, A. A. (1993). Posttraumatic stress disorder and the law: Critical review of the new frontier. *Bulletin of the American Academy of Psychiatry and the Law, 21*, 23–36 (at p. 23).
5. To be sure, the disjunction between scholarship and legal practice is well-worn territory (see, e.g., Edwards 1992). Civil recovery in particular is especially maligned. It has been called "unloved" in the academy (Goldberg, 2002, p. 1501) and as one commentator observes: "no other doctrinal area is both central to the curriculum and widely disdained" (Ripstein, 2007, p. 1).
6. There are, of course, many additional civil applications beyond tort law. See Tovino (2007).
7. "About ILR": http://www.instituteforlegalreform.com/about-ilr.html
8. See http://www.ptsd.va.gov/index.asp
9. Grey (2011, p. 17) has provided a more comprehensive introduction for legal audiences, synthesizing neuroscience research and showing how "the physiological changes that occur in the brain after an individual experiences or witnesses a traumatic event can result in a dysfunction of the neural networks that regulate memory and fear."
10. This thought experiment is, of course, an oversimplification, but it serves the purpose of emphasizing the importance of deep pockets and monetizing injuries.
11. The lack of deep-pocket defendants is why, in part, civil cases after sexual assault are so rare (Shen, 2011).
12. For more on causation and the science of PTSD in the literature on PTSD expert testimony, see, for example, Smith (2010) and Young, Kane, and Nicholson (2006).
13. For those individuals experiencing hyperarousal, one interpretation is that reduced activity in the prefrontal cortex—a part of the brain responsible for much executive function—can be interpreted as a failure "to inhibit subcortical limbic,

especially amygdala, reactivity" (Hopper, Frewen, van der Kolk, & Lanius, 2007, p. 714). Hopper et al. (2007), Lanius et al. (2006), and others note that activation patterns differ for those whose PTSD manifests itself in dissociation rather than hyperarousal.

14. As discussed elsewhere, moderate and extreme stressors may have different effects on memory systems affecting PTSD. The relationship between arousal and performance takes on an inverted-U shape that psychologists have long recognized in a number of performance areas.
15. I do not discuss here a broader inquiry into the mind-body problem, about which questions were raised long ago by Descartes and are debated to this day by philosophers (Robinson, 2003).
16. The statute reads: "The percentage ratings represent as far as can practicably be determined the average impairment in earning capacity resulting from such diseases and injuries and their residual conditions in civil occupations" (38 C.F.R. §4.1).
17. A *service connection* means "that the facts, shown by evidence, establish that a particular injury or disease resulting in disability was incurred coincident with service in the Armed Forces, or if preexisting such service, was aggravated therein" (38 C.F.R. §3.303).
18. CA Jury instruction: 3905A. Physical Pain, Mental Suffering, and Emotional Distress.
19. Georgopoulos and colleagues (2010, p. 7), using bootstrapping statistical techniques and magnetoencephalographic (MEG) recording methods, concluded that "the excellent results obtained offer major promise for the usefulness of the SNI test for differential diagnosis." The researchers used a fixation task on a sample of veterans in Minnesota and Wisconsin—a useful sample because clinical PTSD data had already been coded. The researchers used novel statistical techniques to develop a classification method. The classifications predicted by the researchers' algorithms could be compared to the externally validated data.
20. As just two of many examples: The Brain Law firm (http://www.BrainLaw.com) specializes in recovery for brain trauma. Nevada personal injury lawyer Timothy R. Titolo writes that for clients who have suffered a traumatic brain injury, a "bankruptcy lawyer is typically not proficient to offer such advise [sic] and should refer the person, immediately, to his trial lawyer or, if one is not retained a trial lawyer who practices neurolaw." Retrieved from http://www.titololawoffice.com/docs/Bankruptcy-and-Traumatic-Brain-Injury.pdf. Michigan personal injury lawyers Buckfire & Buckfire explain to their clients: "Based on the results of the neurological exam and the diagnostic tests (EEG, EMG, CT, MRI), a neurologist may refer a patient with head injury to a neuropsychologist for an understanding of which brain functions are impaired and which remain intact. A neuropsychological evaluation will be able to tell how the injury specifically affected thinking and behavior." Retrieved February 2011 from http://www.buckfirelaw.com/library/the-role-of-the-neueurologist.cfm.
21. As reported, the amount was reached via mediation with mediator Cindy Hanna.
22. A filter employed after data collection allowed for the experiment to exclude from the dataset subjects with duplicate IP addresses.

23. See http://www.qualtrics.com.
24. A number of options are available for robust regression (Verardi & Croux, 2009). The analysis in this chapter relies on Stata's "rreg" command.
25. Although not the focus of this study, the models also uncover an additional, inverse relationship between male and more conservative subjects and evaluation of PTSD as a bodily injury. Subjects who self-reported a greater knowledge of neuroscience were significantly more likely to view PTSD as a bodily injury, providing some support to the Greene and Cohen (2004) argument that as knowledge about the brain permeates society, we will see different decision making manifest in the legal arena.
26. The precise wording of the choices was: (a) I am very certain of my decision, (b) I am pretty sure of my decision, but I'd like more information, (c) I am not very sure of my decision, and I really need a lot more information, and (d) I just guessed. I really have no idea.
27. As one example, the Court in *In re Air Crash Disaster at Charlotte* (1997, p. 1111) reasoned that the plaintiff's "choice not to take antidepressant medications is not a wholly unreasonable choice. He has, instead, made major efforts in other ways and obviously declined the reliance on medication based on the same attitude of self-reliance and determination that have brought him this far in his recovery."
28. As just one of many examples of neurolaw on the civil side, consider The Brain Law firm (http://www.BrainLaw.com), specializing in recovery for brain trauma.

REFERENCES

Agoglia, E. J., & Beckett, K. M. (1983). Personal injury. In N. J. Itzkoff (Ed.), *Dealing with damages* (pp. 137–154). New York: Practicing Law Institute.

Allen v. Bloomfield Hills School District (2008). 281 Mich. App. 49.

American Psychiatric Association. (1980). *Diagnostic and statistical manual of mental disorders* (3rd ed.). Washington, DC: Author.

American Psychiatric Association. (2000). *Diagnostic and statistical manual of mental disorders* (rev. 4th ed.). Washington, DC: Author.

Avraham, R. (2006). Putting a price on pain and suffering damages: A critique of the current approaches and a preliminary proposal for change. *Northwestern University Law Review, 100,* 87–119.

Bader v. United States Automobile Association. (2009). WL 4852644 (Con.Super).

Berinsky, A. J., Huber, G. A., & Lenz, G. S. (forthcoming). Using Mechanical Turk as a subject recruitment tool for experimental research. *Political Analysis.*

Brewin, C. R. (2003). *Posttraumatic stress disorder: Malady or myth?* New Haven, CT: Yale University Press.

Brewin, C. R. (2005). Encoding and retrieval of traumatic memories. In J. J. Vasterling & C. R. Brewin (eds.), *Neuropsychology of PTSD: Biological, cognitive, and clinical perspectives* (pp. 131–150). New York: Guilford Press.

Brewin, C. R. (2007). Remembering and forgetting. In M. J. Friedman, T. M. Keane, & P. A. Resick (Eds.), *Handbook of PTSD: Science and practice* (pp. 116–134). New York: Guilford Press.

Brown, D., Hammond, D. C, & Scheflin, A. W. (1998). *Memory, trauma treatment, and the Law.* New York: Norton.

Buhrmester, M. D., Kwang, T., & Gosling, S. D. (2011). Amazon's Mechanical Turk: A new source of inexpensive, yet high-quality, data? *Perspectives on Psychological Science, 6*, 3–5.

Cameron, T. A. (2010). Euthanizing the value of a statistical life. *Review of Environmental Economics and Policy, 4*, 161–178.

Carter, T. (2007). New name, new strategies. *ABA Journal, 93*, 39–43, 60.

National Research Council (2007). *PTSD Compensation and Military Service.* Washington, DC: The National Academies Press.

Constans, J. I. 2005. Information-processing biases in PTSD. In J. J. Vasterling & C. R. Brewin (Eds.), *Neuropsychology of PTSD: Biological, cognitive, and clinical perspectives* (pp. 105–130). New York: Guilford Press.

Cox, M. A., Restuccia, B. E., & Sherman, A. M. (2009). Allen v. Bloomfield Hills School District (2008). Brief of Amicus Curiae Attorney General in Support of Defendant-Appellee Bloomfield Hills School District's Application for Leave to Appeal. Supreme Court of Michigan.

Devine, D. J., Clayton, L. D., Dunford, B. D., Seying, R., & Pryce, J. (2001). Jury decision making: 45 years of empirical research on deliberating groups. *Psychology, Public Policy, & Law, 7*, 622–727.

DVA (Department of Veterans Affairs). (2004). *VA disability compensation program: Legislative history.* Washington, DC: VA Office of Policy, Planning and, Preparedness.

DVA (Department of Veterans Affairs). (2005). *Review of state variances in VA disability compensation payments.* Report No. 05-00765-137. Washington, DC: Veterans Administration Office of the Inspector General.

Edwards, H. T. (1992). The growing disjunction between legal education and the legal profession. *Michigan Law Review, 91*, 34–78.

Field, L. H. (1999). Post-traumatic stress disorder: A reappraisal. *Journal of the Royal Society of Medicine, 92*, 35–37.

Fried, C., & Rosenberg, D. (2003). *Making tort law: What should be done and who should do it.* Washington, DC: American Enterprise Institute.

Friedman, M. J., Keane, T. M., & Resick, P. A. (2007). PSTD: Twenty-five years of progress and challenges. In M. J. Friedman, T. M. Keane, & P. A. Resick (Eds.), *Handbook of PTSD: Science and practice.* (pp. 3–25). New York: Guilford Press.

Garrett, E. (1999). Legal scholarship in the age of legislation. *Tulsa Law Journal, 34*, 679–698.

Geistfeld, M. (1995). Placing a price on pain and suffering: A method for helping juries determine tort damages for nonmonetary injuries. *California Law Review, 83*, 773–852.

Georgopoulos, A. P., Tan, H.-R. M, Lewis, S. M., Leuthold, A. C., Winskowski, A. M., Lynch, J. K., & Engdahl, B. (2010). The synchronous neural interactions test as a functional neuromarker for post-traumatic stress disorder (PTSD): A robust classification method based on the bootstrap. *Journal of Neural Engineering, 7*, 1–7.

Goldberg, J. C. P. (2002). Unloved: Tort in the modern legal academy. *Vanderbilt Law Review, 55*, 1501–1519.

Goodenough, O. R., & Tucker, M. (2010). Law and cognitive neuroscience. *Annual Review of Law and Social Science, 6*, 28.1–28.32.

Greene, J., & Cohen, J. (2004). For the law, neuroscience changes nothing and everything. *Philosophical Transactions of the Royal Society of London B, 359*, 1775–1785.

Grey, B. J. (2011). Neuroscience and emotional harm in tort law: Rethinking the American approach to freestanding emotional distress claims. In M. Freeman (Ed.), *Law and neuroscience: Current legal issues* (pp. 203–230). Oxford: Oxford University Press.

Hans, V. P., & Albertson, S. (2003). Empirical research and civil jury reform. *Notre Dame Law Review, 78*, 1497–1523.

Hopper, J. W., Frewen, P. A., van der Kolk, B. A., & Lanius, R. A. (2007). Neural correlates of reexperiencing, avoidance, and dissociation in ptsd: symptom dimensions and emotion dysregulation in responses to script-driven trauma imagery. *Journal of Traumatic Stress, 20*, 713–725.

Horton, J. J., Rand, D. G., & Zeckhauser, R. J. (2010). The online laboratory: Conducting experiments in a real labor market. Retrieved February 2011 from http://ssrn.com/abstract=1591202

In Re Air Crash Disaster At Charlotte, North Carolina On July 2, 1994 (1997). 982 F.Supp. 1101.

Institute of Medicine. (2007). *PTSD compensation and military service.* Washington, DC: National Academies Press.

Kane, A. W. (2006). Psychology, causality, and court. In G. Young, A. W. Kane, & K. Nicholson (Eds.), *Psychological knowledge in court: PTSD, pain, and TBI* (pp. 13–51). New York: Springer.

Kaufman, R. T., Rodgers, J. D., & Martin, G. D. (2005). *Economic foundations of injury and death damages.* Cheltenham, UK: Elgar Refrence.

Kessler, R. C., Sonnega, A., Bromet, E., Hughes, M., & Nelson, C. B. (1995). Posttraumatic stress disorder in the National Comorbidity Survey. *Archives of General Psychiatry, 52*, 1048–1060.

Kolber, A. J. (2006). Therapeutic forgetting: The legal and ethical implications of memory dampening. *Vanderbilt Law Review, 59*, 1561–1626.

Kolber, A. J. (2007). Pain detection and the privacy of subjective experience. *American Journal of Law and Medicine, 33*, 433–456.

Kolber, A. J. (2011). The experiential future of the law. *Emory Journal of Law, 60*, 585–652.

Kriner, D. L. & Shen, F. X. (2010). *The casualties hypothesis and non-fatal casualties: A pilot investigation.* Paper presented at the annual meeting of the Midwest Political Science Association, Chicago.

Lanius, R.A., Bluhm, R., Lanius, U., & Pain, C. (2006). A review of neuroimaging studies in PTSD: Heterogeneity of response to symptom provocation. *Journal of Psychiatric Research, 40*, 709–729.

McDermott, R. (2002). Experimental methods in political science. *Annual Review of Political Science, 5*, 31–61.

McNally, R. J. (2009). Can we fix PTSD in DSM-V? *Depression and Anxiety, 26*, 597–600.

Miller, T. R., Cohen, M. A., & Wiersema, B. (1996). *Victim costs and consequences: A new look.* A Final Summary Report presented to the National Institute of Justice. Washington, DC: U.S. Department of Justice.

Mrozek, J. R., & Taylor, L. (2002). What determines the value of life? A meta-analysis. *Journal of Policy Analysis and Management, 21,* 253–70.

Nadel, L. (2008). Multiple memory systems: A new view. In H. L. Roediger III (Ed.), *Cognitive psychology of memory.* (pp. 41–52). Volume 4 of *Learning and memory: A comprehensive reference,* J. Byren (Ed.). Oxford: Elsevier.

Nadel, L., & Jacobs, W. J. (1996). The role of the hippocampus in PTSD, panic, and Phobia. In N. Kato (Ed.), *The hippocampus: Functions and clinical relevance* (pp. 455–463). Amsterdam: Elsevier.

Noah, L. (2009). Comfortably numb: Medicalizing (and mitigating) pain-and-suffering damages. *University of Michigan Journal of Law Reform, 42,* 431–480.

Oppenheimer, D. M., Meyvis, T., & Davidenko, N. (2009). Instructional manipulation checks: Detecting satisficing to increase statistical power. *Journal of Experimental Social Psychology, 45,* 867–872.

Palfin, R. A.. & Danninger. B. B. (1990). *Hedonic Damages: Proving damages for lost enjoyment of living.* Charlottesville, VA: Michie Company.

Ripstein, A. (2007). Tort law in a liberal state. *Journal of Tort Law, 1,* 1–41.

Robinson, H. (2003). Dualism. In S. Stich & T. Warfield (Eds.), *The Blackwell guide to philosophy of mind* (pp. 85–101). Oxford: Blackwell.

Roche, J. D. (2007). *The veteran's PTSD handbook: How to file and collect on claims for post-traumatic stress disorder.* Washington, DC: Potomac Books.

Rosen, G. M. (2004). *Posttraumatic stress disorder: Issues and controversies.* Chichester, UK: Wiley.

Rosen, G. M., Lilienfeld, S. O., Frueh, B. C., McHugh, P. R., & Spitzer, R. L. (2010). Reflections on PTSD's future in DSM-V. *British Journal of Psychiatry, 197,* 343–344

Samra, J., & Koch, W. J. (2002). The monetary worth of psychological injury: What are litigants suing for? In J. R. P. Ogloff (Ed.), *Taking psychology and law into the twenty-first century* (pp. 286–324). New York: Kluwer Academic.

Sapirman v. Walmart. (2009). WESTLAW 4731140 (Fla.Cir.Ct).

Schweitzer, N. J., Saks, M. J., Murphy, E., Roskies, A., Sinnott-Armstrong, W., & Gulley, L. (2011). Neuroimages as evidence in a mens rea defense: No impact. *Psychology, Public Policy, and Law, 17,* 357–393.

Shalev, A. Y. (2002). Post-traumatic stress disorder: Diagnosis, history, and life course. In D. Nutt, J. R. T. Davidson, & J. Zohar (Eds.), *Post-traumatic stress disorder: Diagnosis, management, and treatment* (pp. 1–15). London: Martin Dunitz.

Shen, F. X. (2010). The law and neuroscience bibliography: Navigating the emerging field of neurolaw. *International Journal of Legal Information, 38,* 352–399.

Shen, F. X. (2011). How we still fail rape victims: Reflecting on responsibility and legal reform. *Columiba Journal of Gender and Law, 22,* 1–80.

Shen, F. X. (in press). Rape, money, and the psychology of taboo. *Journal of Applied Social Psychology.*

Shin, L. M., Rauch, S. L., & Pitmaan, R. K. (2005). Structural and functional anatomy of PTSD: Findings from neuroimaging research. In J. J. Vasterling & C. R. Brewin (Eds.), *Neuropsychology of PTSD: Biological, cognitive, and clinical perspectives* (pp. 59–82). New York: Guilford Press.

Smith, D. M. (2010). The disordered and discredited plaintiff: Psychiatric evidence in civil litigation. *Cardozo Law Review, 31,* 749–822.

Southwick, S. M., Davis, L L., Aikins, D. E., Rasmusson, A., Barron, J., & Morgan, C. A., III. 2007. Neurobiological Alterations Associated with PTSD. In M. J. Friedman, T. M. Keane, & P. A. Resick (Eds.), *Handbook of PTSD: Science and practice* (pp. 166–189). New York: Guilford Press.

Sparr, L. F., & Bremner, J. D. (2005). Post-traumatic stress disorder and memory: prescient medicolegal testimony at the International War Crimes Tribunal? *Journal of the American Academy of Psychiatry and the Law, 33*, 71–78.

Sparr, L. F., & Pitman, R. K. (2007). PTSD and the law. In M. J. Friedman, T. M. Keane, & P. A. Resick (Eds.), *Handbook of PTSD: Science and practice* (pp. 449–468). New York: Guilford Press.

Sunstein, C. R. (2008). Cass R. Illusory losses. *Journal of Legal Studies, 37*, S157–S191.

Swedloff, R., & Huang, P. H. (2010).Tort damages and the new science of happiness. *Indiana Law Journal, 85*, 553–595.

Taylor, S. (1998). *Neurolaw: Brain and spinal cord injuries,* Washington, DC: ATLA Press.

Tillinghast-Towers, P. (2008). *Update on U.S. tort cost trends.* Retrieved February 2011 from http://www.towersperrin.com/tp/getwebcachedoc?webc=USA/2008/200811/2008_tort_costs_trends.pdf

Tovino, S. (2007). Functional neuroimaging and the law: Trends and directions for future scholarship. *American Journal of Bioethics, 7*, 44–56.

U.S. Department of Health and Human Services. (1999). *Mental health: A report of the surgeon general.* Rockville, MD: U.S. Department of Health and Human Services, Substance Abuse and Mental Health Services Administration, Center for Mental Health Services, National Institutes of Health, National Institute of Mental Health.

Verardi, V., & Croux, C. (2009). Robust egression in Stata. *The Stata Journal, 9*, 439–453.

Viens, A. M. (2007). The use of functional neuroimaging technology in the assessment of loss and damages in tort law. *American Journal of Bioethics: Neuroscience, 7*, 63–65.

Weaver, D. J., & Stern, B. H. (2011). Brain injuries. In R. B. Conlin & G. S. Cusimano (Eds.), *Litigating tort cases* (§ 53). Washington, DC: AAJ Press.

Weisberg, D. S., Keil, F. C., Goodstein, J., Rawson, E., & Gray, J. R. (2008).The seductive allure of neuroscience explanations. *Journal of Cognitive Neuroscience, 20*, 470–477.

Wesche v. Mecosta County Road Commission, (2008). 480 Mich. 75.

Western, B. (1995). Concepts and suggestions for robust regression analysis. *American Journal of Political Science, 39*, 786–817.

Windt, A. D. (2010). Interpretation of important policy provisions. *Insurance Claims and Disputes, 3*, 5th §11:2.

Young, G., Kane, A. W., & Nicholson, K. (Eds.). (2006a). *Psychological knowledge in court: PTSD, pain, and TBI.* New York: Springer-Verlag.

Young, G., Kane, A. W., & Nicholson, K. (Eds.). (2006b). *Causality: Psychological knowledge in court: PTSD, pain, and TBI.* New York: Springer-Verlag.

PART SIX

CODA

14

Ten Things the Law and Others Should Know about Human Memory

MARTIN A. CONWAY

When I became an expert witness about 8 years ago, two things struck me profoundly. The first was how the law, at various levels, was riddled with ill-informed opinion about memory, opinions that were misleading and, more often than not, plain wrong. The second was that virtually anyone was prepared to give a court a supposedly "expert" opinion on memory (usually individuals with a medical background, but not always; there were others too). Later, as I progressed in my expert witness baptism by fire (try being cross-examined for 3 hours by appeal court judges!), I was struck by how remarkably resistant the law, and especially (appeal court) judges, are to expert opinion—and not just memory expert opinion, virtually any expert opinion. Finally, I encountered something I had never expected to encounter: colleagues who, acting for the other side, would utterly oppose one's own scientific, rational, carefully thought out, and obviously utterly correct expert opinion. My surprise was with hindsight a reflection of my own naivety when entering this area. I had unrealistic ideals—a chance, I thought, after decades of researching autobiographical memory, to make a contribution to society based on our (new) understanding of autobiographical memory and memory more generally; actually, I still think that, but now my belief is somewhat tempered by experience.

Partly to deal with the above issues, all of which I will comment on shortly, I persuaded the Research Board of the British Psychological Society to convene a working party on Memory & the Law[1] and produce a report summarizing the relevant scientific findings and legal considerations in a way that would be accessible to all those who had to deal with memories as evidence in their professional practices, from lawyers, to insurance brokers, to accident assessors, and beyond. The Memory & the Law (M&L) report (British Psychological Society, Research Board, 2008) had a number of contributors and international advisors (fully listed in the report) and made 10 key points that I will elaborate on below. However, the ultimate aim of the M&L report was to produce something of a "bible" of what the scientific data told us about the nature of human memory, a bible that could be consulted by practitioners and guide them in their approach, assessment, and treatment of issues in which memory was key evidence; interestingly, it nearly always is used, which makes the law's indifference to what the science of memory has to tell it even more surprising. The M&L report fell short of being the bible I had envisaged and is currently undergoing a major revision. Nonetheless, it has, I think, proved to be a useful start, and I hope it will continue as a "live" document, regularly updated until one day it is the bible of memory for practitioners we originally hoped it might become. Before turning to the 10 points of the M&L report, I will briefly elaborate on some of the issues that I raised above.

ON BEING AN EXPERT WITNESS

In the United Kingdom—and I am not sufficiently familiar with the legal systems of other countries to extrapolate, but I imagine the situation in these countries is probably much the same—the view is that because jurors have their own memories upon which they can reflect, there is no need for expert advice. The jurors in effect have sufficient self-knowledge about memory to be able to make sound and safe judgments. In my experience, the public has little understanding of the nature, functions, and mechanisms of memory; indeed, why should they? Nor do they have much awareness of just how constructive and error-prone human memory is or how relatively simple it is to create false memories. When I give talks to groups of lawyers and judges, I always include the simple and elegant demonstration of Roediger and McDermott (1995), the so-called Deese, Roediger, and McDermott (DRM) procedure, and induce a false memory of having seen the word "sleep" in a list of words referring to sleep but not including the word itself. I usually also get them to tell me who "really" *remembers* seeing this word in the original list; that is, they have an image of it, recall something they thought about it when they saw it, and so on. Typically, more than 90% falsely recall the word and remember it too. Reactions range from outrage at such a "cheap trick" to wry amusement, but none miss the point (they are, after all, lawyers) and that is: they all now have a false memory themselves. Interestingly, another impression I have from these exercises with professionals is a certain degree of resistance. They are interested in the science and have a lot of testing questions and good insights into the implications, but at base they resist the view of memory that the DRM and other procedures so powerfully imply. And, indeed, the view of memory we have come to from the broader study of autobiographical memory, neuropsychology of memory, neuroscience of memory, and malfunctioning memory in psychological illness (all of which, incidentally, I tell the professionals about in the 50 minutes between list presentation and recognition test in the talk). The law and many other areas are highly resistant to the notion that memory is complex.

AN EXAMPLE MEMORY FROM A CASE OF SEXUAL ABUSE

Consider the jurors and, indeed, the public in general for that matter. A very common belief is that the more specific a memory is, the more likely it is to be correct, whereas memory research tells us that the more specific and detailed an account of a memory, the more likely there are to be errors. This in fact is the reverse of what courts believe. By way of illustration here is a memory in an extract of a transcript of a police video interview that I have created from the many of cases of *historic sexual abuse*[2] in which I have given an expert opinion. Reflect upon how this transcript triggers your own implicit everyday beliefs about memory. Note that, typically in these cases, an adult complainant (C) describes one or more memories dating to childhood, often to early childhood. Also note that the police officer's (PO) questions reflect what I have come to believe is an obsession on the part of the police, in Britain at least, with remembering clothes, rooms, furniture, weather, time, duration, spoken utterances, feelings, and thoughts. They too suffer from the erroneous belief that remembering many specific details is a sign of accuracy.

PO: You're here to see us today about something that happened when you were little—a long time ago, right?
C: (Nods)
PO: You're 37 now; is that correct?
C: (Nods)
PO: Sorry C, I meant, meant to say that well, really, you need to you know er speak up, say "yes" or "no" or whatever. Can you do that?
C: (Nods)—yeh, sorry
PO: Its ok, so can you, uhm, tell me then about this first incident as best as you can and don't worry if you say things, you know you wouldn't say, difficult things, y'know in this room I have heard a lot. I know it's difficult but that's why we're here...and it doesn't matter if you can't remember everything; just tell me what you remember and if there's something you don't remember well just say "Don't remember" and that's fine.
C: Mum was about to go out, I don't know, to the chippie I think...I wanted to go but she wouldn't take me, I just was sort of not feeling comfortable

	with 'im, didn't know why, just a feeling…you know…on me own and all…
PO:	And who was he, C? Did you know his name?
C:	Well he was called Johnno…but his full name was John McWilliam and he was Mum's boyfriend…just for a few months I think.
PO:	Why do think that?
C:	I remember that this was just before I went to school. I had my fourth birthday in August and was going early…late birthday you see but had got my uniform, hanging up on the front of the cupboard in my room, grey skirt and white shirt I was really made up about it…
C:	But at Christmas I remember Frank was with us, and he became my step-dad until Mum left him. He was nasty too, beat her up, never done nuthin' to me 'tho, just like Johnno, both bastards…
PO:	Take us back to your Mum going out to the chip shop; what exactly was happening?
C:	I was watching TV, Tellie Tubbies I think, can't really remember but sort of can see you know that green grassy place they use to have, like a park or sumit', and sort of tunnels—holes in the ground like, or sumit' they lived in…Johnno's sitting on the couch next to me and he starts sort of tickling me…(pauses)…
C:	…then he says "Come and sit on my knee C." I was just a girl y'know, I didn't know about it…well about anything like that, he was a sort of Dad, anyway I did…(stops)
PO:	C I know it is difficult…would you like a break? Maybe have a cig outside and I'll get us some coffee?
C:	(Shakes head) No…let me try…it's hard (starts to cry)
PO:	Here have some of these (hands tissues)…
C:	(Takes deep breaths)…he starts to stroke my legs, I had a skirt on…and I could feel y'know, feel him underneath me, anyway he says "Let's go in your bedroom" and picks me up…
C:	We lived in Chiselwick Street Flats then, knocked 'em down now, just down the bottom off Borough Road they used to be, on the right there, just a car park now…me mum had a flat from the council, it were just two bedrooms, living room and this really small bathroom and then the kitchen. My small bedroom was off the living room and Mum's was next to it…bigger.
PO:	When he picked you up, how did he do that, can you remember?
C:	He just put one arm under my legs, sort of behind my knees and other round my back and just stood up and carried me in, he was laughing, like it was something funny he—we—were doing some sort of game…and he put me on the bed and pulled my knickers down until they were off…I was just little I didn't get it, what he was doing…(cries)
PO:	And when Johnno laid you on the bed, what position was that in?

C: Oh, on me back with me head towards the headboard and then he stood up but I wasn't really looking then but I can remember the sound of him unzipping his pants... and then when I looked, sort of turned me head, he had nothing on, below...
PO: So, he'd taken his trousers and underpants, completely off?
C: Yeh.
PO: But kept his top on?
C: Yeh
PO: Can you remember what his top was like?
C: Used to wear these black t-shirts all the time and, oh I dunno, but I think I remember it was black...
PO: A black t-shirt
C: Yeh...
PO: ...and what did he look like?
C: I dunno, didn't know what to make of it, do now, his thing was sticking out and he got my hand and put it on it and moved it sort up and down and said "You do it" and I did, but dunno, I think I was just sort of baffled or something, didn't know what to make of it, I was just lying there looking up at me new school uniform on the cupboard, thinking about that, about going to school...(cries)...

Is it possible to remember in such detail an event that took place 33 years earlier? Adult recall of childhood rarely contains much detail, even for negative events. An assumption often made is that the event was so traumatic that it would be remembered in detail; it would be "burnt into the brain." But the scientific evidence is that traumatic memories are fragmentary, disordered, disjointed, and often contain details that do not derive from experience. Furthermore, this line of reasoning assumes that the event would have been traumatic for the 4-year-old C, but would it? In order for an event to be traumatic, it must surely be understood at least at some level, but would a 4-year-old have the conceptual knowledge to understand such an event? The evidence indicates that a child of that age probably would not. On the other hand, consider how convinced you are by this made-up extract—very convinced, I would guess. It plays on our implicit everyday beliefs or assumptions about memory. It confirms those assumptions and makes us feel that our everyday understanding of memory must be correct. If C can remember the school uniform hanging up in her room, surely she can remember everything else. Surely it all must be true.

MEMORIES FOR RAPE IN CHILDHOOD AND ADULTHOOD

Memory for childhood sexual abuse (CSA) is an emotive issue. In the scientific arena, findings are hotly contested and entrenched positions abound. Nobody contests the idea that CSA occurs or that it can be damaging. All that the M&L report suggests, and that I suggest here, is simply that judgments and appraisals of accounts purportedly of memories should be much more informed by our scientific understanding of the nature of human memory. Perhaps C was abused in the manner described but retains only a few fragmentary memories of what occurred. During the long retention interval of 33 years, while thinking about these fragments, she has gradually built up a narrative in which even she cannot now distinguish what has been added from what is remembered. This probably happens all the time in human memory—something our legal system should be aware of.

A further implication of the modern view of human memory is that had C presented with a fragmentary mixed-up memory full of amnesic gaps, with distorted and incomprehensible details, that would have been almost completely acceptable to a memory researcher. It is what we would expect on the basis of all we now know about memory. In contrast, legal agencies would have found such an account extremely worrying, and almost certainly it would never have reached a court because of the present system of ill-informed and erroneous beliefs about memory. Such memories are typical of adult women who have been raped, and because of their nature, that is, fragmentary, containing amnesic gaps, and with details inconsistently recalled, they do not go to court since their evidence can be easily made to look unreliable. The defense lawyer only has to say, "So, you are telling the court that you cannot remember what he looked like, the time of day, how long this supposed assault lasted, anything he said, or indeed what he was wearing—yes?" and the credibility of the witness's evidence is seriously compromised, particularly when followed up with the aggressive question "So, Ms. C, how do we know you can remember anything at all about this rape?" It is a tragic irony that the erroneous beliefs about human memory that permeate our legal agencies lead to prosecution on the basis of fluent, highly detailed narratives of events that took place in childhood (for which there usually is no other evidence), but a fragmentary, jumbled account, with gaps, of an assault that took place on the weekend is not accepted because it is viewed as too easy to discredit in court. The point is that the very features of reports that make them more likely to be accurate are taken by courts as evidence of unreliability, whereas features of reports that make them more likely to be filled with errors are taken as evidence that they are accurate. This, of course, is only possible because everyday beliefs about human memory, ones that are largely implicit, powerfully influence how we respond to accounts of "memories." The modern view of memory shows us, however, that people should *not* remember everything or even very much; when they do, that's where the problems lie. It is this modern view of the complexity of human memory that the law finds so troubling.

NONEXPERTS, EXPERTS, VIVID MEMORIES AND TRAUMA

What of the individual who is prepared to give an expert opinion when he or she is not an expert, and what, too, of the courts that are prepared to so naively accept such opinions? Actually, the nonexpert "experts," the courts, and jurors are all similar in that they hold everyday beliefs about memories. One belief is that the more *vivid*, the more "burnt in" a memory is, the more likely it is to be accurate. The evidence in fact shows that there are plenty of documented, highly vivid memories that are in fact wrong, and occasionally even wholly false. Here is one of my favorites, given to me by a barrister who realized it was false during a talk I was giving to his bar association:

> A middle-aged man recalled his father distracting him when he was a young boy (about 4 years old) by asking him who was the first man on the moon. He had been intensely interested in the moon landings when he was a young boy, and this incident occurred while his father was talking on the telephone to his mother, who had just given birth to his younger brother. My informant had a vivid and fond memory of his father placating him in this way; he was highly agitated by the birth, and in his memory he could see his father on the telephone and almost hear his voice. It was only decades later that he realized that his brother had been born in 1968, 1 year before the first moon landing.

Another common belief is that a traumatic event will lead to memories that will have an enduring effect on a person's life. It seems that sometimes they do, sometimes they do not, and for quite a lot of people, the majority in fact, they seem to have no enduring effect at all. An important question here is: what is traumatic? What is traumatic for one person may not be so for another. Furthermore, what we think is traumatic for children, on an (implicit) assumption that it would be traumatic for an adult, may not be so at all. These are complicated matters on which there is much and often conflicting research, and an expert is required to present the scientific view to a court.

Interestingly, it often is the case that all a scientist such as a memory researcher can do is say, "There is no scientific evidence bearing on this matter" or "The evidence is too weak to make any strong recommendation." I think that too is useful for a court because the court has sought expert advice in good faith and has been reassured that there is none; it can then get on with the business of administering justice. The nonexpert is usually not in a position to make such definitive statements. When I became an expert witness, one of the first cases in which my advice was sought was one in which a very young preverbal infant had been sexually assaulted. At the trial, a professional medical expert witness was asked for his view, based on his expert knowledge, of how likely it was that the infant, a girl, would be affected by the abuse later in life. His view was that she certainly would be affected, but he wanted to consult before giving a definitive answer. Later he reported to the court that he had consulted a senior medical colleague, who also considered that she was unlikely to have a normal sex life because of the enduring effects of the memory of the abuse event, which might possibly influence her, even unconsciously, for the rest of her life. This was also the view of the medical expert. One still occasionally encounters such nonexpert "expert" views, especially about memory, in our courts. My own statement was that there was no body of scientific evidence either way. We simply did not know whether the girl would be adversely affected, and if so how, or whether there would be an effect or no effect. The so-called expert opinions were based on belief and not on any (scientific) evidence.[3] Toward the close of the next section, I consider what expertise a memory expert should ideally have. Here we might note that someone who has read the M&L report is *not* a memory expert. Nor, in my view, is someone who has taken a course, or several courses, on memory or read textbooks, journals, or other specialist materials. It seems to me that a memory expert is someone who has contributed scientifically to the study of human memory and that contribution has been recognized by his or her peers. As we will see, however, this is not a popular view among other (nonmemory) expert witnesses who are often asked to comment on specific memories.

TEN THINGS THE LAW AND OTHERS SHOULD KNOW ABOUT HUMAN MEMORY

The M&L report was an idealistic attempt to show the complexity of human memory (to a broad nonexpert audience), to rule out erroneous everyday beliefs (such as those evoked in you when you read the fictitious case of C above), but most of all to produce a statement that *all* memory researchers could accept and say to the courts and other professionals "At a minimum this is what we know, this is what we suspect, this is what we are uncertain about, and this is what we do not know" and to back it up with full references to review articles and the relevant bodies of scientific evidence. The aim was to place a document in the public arena that memory experts could point to as support for the points they make in specific cases. It has to some extent been successful in doing that and, hopefully, the revised version will be even more authoritative. In court there is a problem when time is limited, and typically one cannot go through the evidence supporting any single point in detail and sometimes not even at all. This can give rise to the selective use of findings by others to undermine the expert view. Indeed, the selective use of evidence to undermine or refute another expert's evidence is one of the most common tactics encountered in our courts. Having an agreed-on and comprehensive document that one can point to and say "Here is the scientific evidence upon which my expert advice is based" will surely help. This is especially true when that document is balanced and lists points of relevance in a way a court can understand, and those points are in turn backed up by full reference to the evidence from which they originate.

The main advice in the M&L report is contained in a series of key points/guidelines that are reproduced in Table 14.1: the 10 things the law and other professional bodies should know about memory. The report also contains extended sections describing the research supporting the guidelines; for that reason, I do not describe the research here. The reader is referred to the report itself, which is available at the Internet address given in note 1 below. The M&L report provides accessible recommended reading, and for those who wish to study further, there is a full technical reference section. For ease of comprehension, the guidelines are presented in a jargon-free, nontechnical manner. They give a view of human memory that accurately captures its complexity, as well as the great difficulties in determining what "accuracy" might mean here and how it could ever be determined. Indeed, the bottom line is that accuracy cannot be established without corroborating evidence that, as far as possible, is independent of the rememberer. However, because we now have a much better understanding of the nature of memories, there are informed judgments that can be made about, for example, how closely an account that is claimed to be of a memory actually corresponds to what we know of memories. In other words, the guidelines in Table 14.1 can be used to gauge how memory-like an account is. This will be useful in evaluating accounts of memories that, when there is no other evidence, may well be all that a proceeding hinges on.

The guidelines are also something of an antidote to commonly held largely incorrect beliefs about human memory. Consider, for example, the belief that if there are gaps in a memory, then that memory is unreliable and, ultimately, so is the witness who reports it. Guidelines i and iv in Table 14.1 address this incorrect belief. Memories for experienced events are time compressed, contain only short time slices of experience, and are never complete. In other words, exactly the opposite is true: *a valid memory must contain omissions, gaps, and forgotten details.* Another common belief is that when a specific detail or set of details is recalled, the account is probably of a memory and, moreover, that account is more likely to be accurate than an account of a memory containing no specific details. Guidelines v and vi in Table 14.1 speak directly to this belief. In fact, recalling highly specific, often incidental details such as exact times and dates, spoken utterances verbatim, feelings, thoughts, weather, clothes worn during childhood experiences, and so on is comparatively rare. Also, it has been found that such highly specific details can be wrong and, indeed, even

Table 14-1 GUIDELINES ON MEMORY

Key Points

i. *Memories are records of people's experiences of events and are not a record of the events themselves.* In this respect, they are unlike other recording media such as videos or audio recordings, to which they should not be compared.
ii. *Memory is not only of experienced events but it is also of the knowledge of a person's life,* i.e. schools, occupations, holidays, friends, homes, achievements, failures, etc. As a general rule memory is more likely to be accurate when it is of the knowledge of a person's life than when it is of specific experienced events.
iii. *Remembering is a constructive process.* Memories are mental constructions that bring together different types of knowledge in an act of remembering. As a consequence, memory is prone to error and is easily influenced by the recall environment, including police interviews and cross-examination in court.
iv. *Memories for experienced events are always incomplete.* Memories are time-compressed fragmentary records of experience. Any account of a memory will feature forgotten details and gaps, and this must not be taken as any sort of indicator of accuracy. Accounts of memories that do not feature forgetting and gaps are highly unusual.
v. *Memories typically contain only a few highly specific details.* Detailed recollection of the specific time and date of experiences is normally poor, as is highly specific information such as the precise recall of spoken conversations. As a general rule, a high degree of very specific detail in a long-term memory is unusual.
vi. *Recall of a single or several highly specific details does not guarantee that a memory is accurate or even that it actually occurred.* In general, the only way to establish the truth of a memory is with independent corroborating evidence.
vii. *The content of memories arises from an individual's comprehension of an experience, both conscious and non-conscious.* This content can be further modified and changed by subsequent recall.
viii. *People can remember events that they have not in reality experienced.* This does not necessarily entail deliberate deception. For example, an event that was imagined, was a blend of a number of different events, or that makes personal sense for some other reason, can come to be genuinely experienced as a memory (these are often referred to as "confabulations").
ix. *Memories for traumatic experiences, childhood events, interview and identification practices, memory in younger children and older adults and other vulnerable groups all have special features.* These are features that are unlikely to be commonly known by a non-expert, but about which an appropriate memory expert will be able to advise a court.
x. *A memory expert is a person who is recognised by the memory research community to be a memory researcher.* It is recommended that, in addition to current requirements, those acting as memory expert witnesses be required to submit their full curriculum vitae to the court as evidence of their expertise.

SOURCE: From *Guidelines on Memory and the Law: Recommendations from the Scientific Study of Human Memory* (p. 3) by the British Psychological Society, 2008. Leicester: British Psychological Society, 2008. Copyright 2008 by the British Psychological Society. Reprinted with permission.

wholly false. *Specificity does not guarantee correctness.* Indeed, very specific incidental details might serve the purpose of what is known as "trivial persuasion." The scientific evidence shows that accounts of memories that contain incidental and/or idiosyncratic, highly specific details are *believed* by the public to be more accurate. These types of (trivial) details act to persuade an audience that an account really is a memory of an experienced event, even though it may be incorrect or even not a memory of an experienced event at all.

In closing, let's apply the guidelines to some evidence. Imagine that an adult complainant in a case of historical sexual abuse recalls the following memories when making a witness statement:

I have two very early memories, funnily enough both about bath time, but I now think this is because that's how it started out—that's when he first started doing things. The first is standing shivering without any clothes on in our bathroom, having just got out of the bath, and I remember looking at the paint peeling on the wall round a mirror the bottom part of which had a funny sort of brown stain on it. The house needed decorating, but my father didn't do things like that, probably too drunk or out at the pub. Anyway this was when I would have been about four, maybe three. The second is my father taking me up to the bedroom after bath time. My mother was still bathing my older sister, and he was going to read me a bedtime book. I had my pink Barbie nightie on, and I remember him next to me when I was lying down. He was holding the book in his right hand and he sort of slipped his other hand under the sheet and up my nightie and started touching the tops of my legs. I mustn't have had any knickers on because I remember his fingers stroking my vagina. I just lay really still; I think I must have been shocked. Suddenly he closed the book, stood up, said, "Mum's coming; go to sleep now." My sister was seven then, so I would have been four.

There is no other evidence, and the defendant strongly denies this and the other allegations of sexual abuse contained in the statement. (Note that these statements are an amalgam of memories drawn from several recent cases.) Given that these accounts of memories, and of course other accounts from persons of later ages, are all the evidence there is, what can be made of them? Guideline ix in Table 14.1 is important here, and its elaboration in the report focuses in part on the concept of childhood amnesia. The term "childhood amnesia" refers to the well-established finding that people have few memories dating to 7 years of age and younger, and even fewer dating to 5 years of age and younger, and it is most unusual to find any memories at all dating to about 2.5 years and below. Thus, these two memories dating to 3 and 4 years of age, although not outside the normal range, are very early and well within the period of childhood amnesia. Memories from this period are often rather idiosyncratic in that a rememberer often does not know why they are remembered or what they might mean. Often there is considerable doubt about whether they are memories or not (maybe they come from a family story, derive from a photograph, etc.), and often they are not experienced as full memories. The two memories in our example do not appear to have these features, making them unusual for very early memories. It does not follow from this comparison that they are erroneous or wholly false. Nonetheless, given their unusual nature, there are grounds for at least some concern.

Guideline vii makes the very important point that memory is strongly influenced by the individual's comprehension of an event when that event is experienced. In other words, the person's understanding of an experience influences not only whether it is remembered at all but also, given that it is remembered, *what* is remembered, that is, the content of the memory. The second memory in the previous example essentially shows an adult comprehension of the alleged event with an adult reaction. Moreover, both memories contain implausible details (see guideline v). The peeling paint and stained mirror are very unusual details to recall in a memory dating to 3 years of age. Remembering which hand was used to do what is also implausible given that children of age 4 do not have the concept of "handedness." In addition, the concept of a "vagina" is most unlikely to be held by a 4-year-old. Such adult knowledge could only have been added later, perhaps during periods of thinking and/or talking about the events. It may be the case that the witness can no longer distinguish between what has been added and actual memory fragments. In other words, the witness makes a permanent source monitoring error. Thus, the guidelines indicate that these memories, if that is what they are, are highly unusual and permeated with adult concepts. This information would, of course, be useful to a court.

Guideline x, surprisingly, turned out to be the most contentious guideline, at least for other expert witnesses. The original M&L report recommended that a "memory expert" should be someone with an acknowledged publication record in the area of memory research. In other words, the expert should be, or have been, an active memory researcher and one recognized by the community of memory researchers. This is a view that I still hold, although an expert who has made a scholarly contribution to the field rather than an empirical one would also have the appropriate degree of expertise. Additionally, it would be important for a court to be assured that the memory expert had the relevant expertise in the area of memory. These suggestions, however, led to something of a howl of outrage by other psychologists, some with professional and/or clinical qualifications, some of whom had long acted as expert witnesses but none of whom would be recognized by the memory research community as memory researchers. In the end, we were forced to drop this requirement and instead used the rather weaker recommendation that a memory expert must submit his or her curriculum vitae as part of the evidence; then a court could at least make an informed judgment of the witness's expertise. This is a recommendation that I believe courts should routinely adopt.

Much more could be said about the above example memories, and the guidelines would help develop our understanding of them further. Importantly, however, the guidelines are not intended to *replace* decision making but rather to help *inform* the decision-making process. Also, they are not intended to be used to evaluate accuracy or truth. Their aim is rather more limited. It is simply to allow people who are not experts in the study of memory to gain some understanding of the extent to which accounts that claim be of memories actually correspond to what we know about memories. Also, and in many ways of equal importance, the guidelines provide a basis for challenging (spurious) claims of expertise and for identifying the selective use of evidence.

NOTES

1. http://www.bps.org.uk/sites/default/files/documents/guidelines_on_memory_and_the_law_recommendations_from_the_scientific_study_of_human_memory.pdf
2. The phrase "historic sexual abuse" is used in British courts to refer to adults remembering and reporting sexual abuse from childhood.
3. The court accepted this but made it clear that it was not especially helpful. Experts are not much liked by courts, and experts who disagree with other experts are not liked at all!

REFERENCES

British Psychological Society, Research Board. (2008). *Guidelines on memory and the law: Recommendations from the Scientific Study of Human Memory.* Leicester: British Psychological Society.

Roediger, H. L., & McDermott, K. B. (1995). Creating false memories: Remembering words not presented in lists. *Journal of Experimental Psychology: Learning, Memory, and Cognition, 21,* 803–814.

Name Index

Abe, N., 235, 241, 286
Adair, S. A., 167
Adan, A., 312
Addis, D. R., 245–248
Adolphs, R., 10, 19
Agoglia, E. J., 330
Agosta, S., 251, 281
Ainsworth, D., 271
Aizenstein, O., 246
Akbudak, E., 124
Albertson, S., 340
Alexander, A., 252
Alfini, J. J., 218
Allan, K., 166
Allen, J. J. B., 275
Allwood, C. M., 99
Althoff, R. R., 129, 132
Ambach, W., 267
Ambinder, M. S., 60
Aminoff, E., 236, 239
Andelman, F., 246
Andersen, S. M., 5
Anderson, A. K., 12
Anderson, C. A., 205
Anderson, M. C., 170–171
Andersson, J., 164–165
Andrade, J., 218
Andrews-Hanna, J., 248
Appelbaum, P. S., 253
Appio, L., 121
Ariss, L., 123
Arkes, H. R., 216, 225

Arnal, J. D., 65
Arndt, J., 200, 207–208
Aron, A., 168
Arsenault, A. M., 271
Asch, S. E., 149, 192
Ask, K., 144, 152
Augath, M., 129
Avraham, R., 338

Bacon, E., 123, 128
Bailey, P. J., 32, 53–54
Baker, C. I., 290
Balkin, T. J., 219
Balloun, K. D., 266, 269
Banaji, M. R., 251
Bandy, D., 237
Banerjee, D., 216
Bangert, A., 243
Bar, M., 236, 239
Bar-Hillel, M., 292
Barber, S., 168
Barefoot, C. A., 271
Barnier, A. J., 170–172
Baron, R. S., 149
Bartlett, F. C., 4, 89–90
Basden, B. H., 165
Basden, D. R., 165
Batchelder, W. H., 71
Bauermann, T., 270, 286
Beckett, K. M., 330
Behrman, B. W., 76
Bekerian, D. A., 146

Bell, B., 44
Bellgowan, P. S., 290
Bellinger, K., 73, 168
Ben-Bassat, N., 269
Ben-Shakhar, G., 251, 263–273, 292–293
Berger, T. W., 314
Bergman, Z., 265
Berinsky, A. J., 343
Bernstein, D. M., 175, 235, 250
Bhatt, S., 286
Billings, J., 250
Biroschak, J. R., 278
Bjork, E. L., 170
Bjork, R. A., 170
Blackstone, W., 67
Blair, C., 165
Blanchard, L., 245
Blank, H., 122–123
Bless, H., 120, 200
Blitz, M. J., 320
Blumen, H. M., 168
Bodenhausen, G. V., 196
Boisvenu, G. A., 265
Bordens, K. S., 218
Bornstein, B. H., 33, 60, 69
Bosh, G., 291
Bostrom, R., 223
Botzung, A., 248
Bowers, J. N., 146
Boyle, M. M., 164
Bradfield, A. L., 65, 99, 119, 146–147
Bradley, M. M., 216, 267, 271
Bradley, M. T., 265–266, 272
Bradshaw, J. T., 174
Brainerd, C. J., 37, 85, 236
Braus, D. F., 125
Brehm, J. W., 191
Brehm, S. S., 191
Brekke, N., 195
Bremner, J. D., 23
Brenner, C. J., 239
Brewer, N., 35, 73, 96, 120, 122–123, 148, 234
Brewer, W. F., 92, 102–103, 105
Brewin, C. R., 325, 327, 329, 333
Brigham, J. C., 60, 102

Brimacombe, C. A. E., 234
Brown, A., 174
Brown, D. P., 333
Brown, R., 8, 167
Brubaker, L. E., 288
Bruce, V., 33, 34, 50
Bruck, M., 107
Brunsman, B., 149
Bryner, S., 165
Buchel, C., 125
Buck, A., 244
Buckhout, R., 85
Buckner, R., 238,–240, 244–245, 248
Buhrmester, M. D., 343
Bunge, S. A., 244
Burke, A., 21
Burke, C. G., 264
Burke, T. M., 152
Burnstein, E., 200, 204
Burton, A. M., 32–33
Busey, T. A., 93, 97
Butler, A. C., 173
Buttaccio, D. R., 75

Cabeza, R., 125–126, 134, 216, 236, 238, 241–242, 244, 249
Cabot, A., 309
Cahill, L., 223
Callaway, E., 223
Camerer, C. F., 132
Cameron, T. A., 338
Campbell, A. M., 220
Carle, S. B., 271
Carlson, C. A., 67–69, 105
Carlucci, M., 143
Carmel, D., 269, 273, 293
Carroll, D. C., 245
Carson, M. M., 135
Carson, N., 246
Carter, S. R., 186, 196
Carter, T., 328
Casey, B. J., 270, 286
Caspar, J. D., 174
Casper, J. D., 188
Castel, A. D., 128–129
Castiello, U., 251

Ceci, S. J., 107
Chadwick, M. J., 250
Chalmers, D., 217, 321–322
Chamberlain, J., 6
Chan, J. C. K., 169, 172, 248
Chan, W., 216
Charman, S. D., 119, 143
Chen, F. S., 223
Cheng, T., 247
Chi, R. P., 313
Chiu, C., 216
Christ, S. E., 249, 288
Christiaansen, R. E., 146
Christianson, S. A., 10, 19, 21
Chua, E. F., 6, 124–127, 129–134, 215
Ciranni, M. A., 170
Clancy, S., 37
Clark, A., 217, 321–322
Clark, J., 244
Clark, S., 122
Clark, S. D., 68, 76, 105
Clark, S. E., 59, 61–64, 67–68, 70
Clark, V. P., 313
Clarke, A. C., 233
Coates, T. J., 223
Cochran, B. P., 242
Cohen Kadosh, R., 313
Cohen, A., 246
Cohen, J. D., 132
Cohen, M. A., 337
Cohen, N. J., 126, 129, 132
Cole, M. W., 251
Cole, S. A., 153
Coman, A., 6, 167, 172, 174–178
Coman, D., 175
Constans, J. I., 332
Conway, M. A., 6, 170–171
Cook, M. B., 38
Cook, M. R., 265, 269
Corballis, M., 247
Corkin, S., 135
Corteen, R. S., 269
Corwin, J., 223
Craik, F. I. M., 88, 243
Creeley, C. E., 220
Crelia, R., 206

Crombez, G., 265–266, 268
Cuc, A., 166–168, 171–173
Culhane, S. E., 186
Curran, T., 237–238, 242, 244
Cutler, B. L., 45–47, 52, 60, 63, 65, 119–120, 234
Cutrow, R. J., 265, 267

D'Argembeau, A., 19
Dailey, S. B., 67
Dale, A. M., 238
Danninger, B. B., 338
Darling, S., 61
Daselaar, S. M., 244
Daum, I., 248
Davachi, L., 19, 126
Davatzikos, C., 286, 289
Davey, S. L., 59, 76, 122
Davidson, M. L., 135
Davidson, P. O., 270
Davie, I., 220
Davis, D., 37, 44–45, 49
Davis, M., 14, 34–35
Davis, R. C., 234, 264
Dawes, R. M., 46
Dayan, E., 269
De Clercq, A., 265–266
de Dreu, C. K., 223
De Houer, J., 251
De Jong, M., 35
DeCarlo, T. E., 193
Deecke, L., 242
Deese, J., 237
Deffenbacher, K. A., 33, 60
Delgado, M. R., 135
Demaine, L. J., 6, 194–195, 200
Demb, J. B., 244
Denkova, E., 248
Dennis, I., 69, 75, 236, 245
Dennis, N. A., 249
Desmarais, S. L., 43, 45, 53
Desmond, J. E., 244
DeSoto, K. A., 6, 92–93, 103, 105, 215
Deutsch, M., 190
Devenport, J. L., 46, 48, 52
Devine, D. J., 174, 340, 344

Devine, P. G., 62
Devitt, M. K., 265, 275
Dewhurst, S. A., 165, 167
DeWitt-Rickards, T. S., 71
Dexter, H. R., 45–46, 65
Dhami, M. K., 53
Diamond, D. M., 22, 220
Diamond, S. S., 174, 188
Diana, R. A., 126
Dillon, J. M., 72
Dobbins, I. G., 243
Dodd, D. H., 174
Dodge, M., 190
Dodson, C. S., 118
Dolan, R. J., 126, 150, 240, 243
Dolcos, F., 216
Dolev, K., 265, 268, 273
Donchin, E., 275–277, 280
Donohue, S. E., 244
Douglass, A. B., 65, 122, 146, 148, 154
Driest, J., 149
Dror, I. E., 152, 217
Dudai, Y., 150
Dunlosky, J., 91, 107
Dunn, M., 195
Dunning, D., 73
Dupuis, P., 74
Düzel, E., 244
Dwyer, J., 234
Dysart, J. E., 67, 74, 122

Easterbrook, J. A., 13
Ebbesen, E. B., 32, 42, 99
Echterhoff, G., 164–165, 167, 170, 172
Edelson, M., 150
Egner, T., 286
Eichenbaum, H., 126, 246
Eisenstadt, D., 45
Eisner, S. L., 218
Elaad, E., 251, 265–268, 270–271, 292–293
Eldridge, L. L., 16
Ellson, D. C., 264
Ellsworth, P. C., 91, 118, 154, 174
Elwork, A., 218
Endl, W., 242
Engle, R. W., 60

Epstein, J., 53
Erber, R., 196
Esgate, A., 67
Ezzyat, Y., 19

Fabiani, M., 242, 244, 275
Farmer, J. J., 153
Farrow, T. F., 286
Farwell, L. A., 275–276, 280
Feenan, K., 223
Fein, S., 192–194, 204, 267, 269
Ferguson, T. J., 45–46, 65
Field, L. H., 327
Fieve, R., 223
Findlay, K. A., 143
Fink, G. R., 220
Finklea, K., 32, 42
Finklea, M., 32, 42
Fisher, C., 253
Fleming, J. A., 265
Fletcher, P. C., 243
Flowe, H. D., 32, 42
Foley, H., 236, 243
Follette, W. C., 34–35, 44–45
Fosterlee, L., 215, 218
Fox, D., 313
Fox, E., 14, 23
Fox, P. T., 244
Fox, S. G., 65
Frackowiak, R. S. J., 243
Frascino, J. C., 246
Fraser-Mackenzie, P. A., 152
Fried, C., 337
Friedman, M. J., 329
Frith, C. D., 243
Fujii, T., 241, 286
Fulero, S., 67, 122, 234
Fulford, J. A., 69, 71
Fulton, E. K., 221
Furedy, J. J., 263, 270–271, 278
Furumitsu, I., 293

Gabbert, F., 149, 166–167
Gabrieli, J. D., 244
Gaesser, B., 6
Gallo, D. A., 85, 237

Gamer, M., 265–268, 270, 272–273, 286–287, 293
Ganis, G., 6, 286, 288–291
Garcia-Bajos, E., 171
Garcia-Dubus, E., 142
Garoff, R. J., 236
Garoff-Eaton, R. J., 243–244
Garrett, B. F., 47–48, 86
Garrett, E., 328
Garry, M., 168, 245
Gati, I., 264, 269
Geistfeld, M., 338
Geldreich, E. W., 264
George, M. S., 286
Georgopoulous, A. P., 339
Geraerts, E., 234
Gerard, H. B., 190
Gerhard, D., 236
Gerlach, K. D., 6
Gershman, B. L., 225
Ghetti, S., 244
Ghirardi, V., 251
Gigerenzer, G., 112
Gilbert, D. G., 206
Ginton, A., 266, 293
Giovanello, K. S., 242, 249
Gitelman, D. R., 236
Giuliano, T., 206
Glascher, J., 125
Glover, G. H., 244
Gödert, H. W., 266
Godfrey, R. D., 61–62, 67
Goense, J., 129
Goff, L. M., 245
Goldberg, I., 246
Goldmann, R. E., 244
Goldstein, E. B., 67
Gomez-Ariza, C. J., 175
Gonsalves, B., 236, 241, 245
Goodenough, O. R., 328
Goodman, G. S., 244
Goodsell, C. A., 5, 67–69, 71, 75
Goodstein, J., 128
Gosling, S. D., 343
Grady, C., 243, 248
Graf, P., 168

Graham, C., 219
Granhag, P. A., 144, 245
Gray, J. R., 128
Greathouse, S. M., 64
Greely, H. T., 235, 249–250, 252, 289, 312
Greenberg, J., 207
Greene, E., 152, 190
Greenwald, A. G., 281
Greenwald, A. G.., 251
Greenwald, M. K., 216
Greer, L. L., 223
Gregory, A. M., 143
Grey, B. J., 328, 330, 334
Grier, J. B., 266, 278–279
Griffiths, R. R., 224
Groll, S., 167
Gronau, N., 266, 268, 280
Gronlund, S. D., 5, 67–69, 72, 75–76, 105, 153
Groome, D., 67
Gross, J. J., 23
Grugle, N. L., 219
Grunstein, R. R., 216
Guerin, S. A., 234
Gusnard, D. A., 124
Gustafson, L. A., 265, 270
Gutchess, A., 243

Habib, R., 239
Hafstad, G. S., 65
Hall, C. C., 123
Halliday, R., 223
Halonen, J., 220
Hammond, C., 333
Hancock, P. J. B., 33
Handgraaf, M. J., 223
Hannaford-Agor, P. L., 162, 174
Hannula, D. E., 129
Hannum, R., 309
Hans, V. P., 174, 340
Hare, T., 286
Harley, E. M., 35
Harnad, S., 217
Harris, C. B., 165
Harsch, N., 8
Hartley, L. R., 220

Hasel, L. E., 6, 143, 149, 151–152
Hashtroudi, S., 167
Hassabis, D., 246, 248, 250
Hastie, R. K., 46, 166, 168, 175, 205
Hauck, W. W., 223
Hedden, T., 243
Heinrichs, M., 223
Henderson, Z., 33
Henkel, L. A., 236
Henson, R. N., 126, 240
Herndon, F., 120
Hertwig, R., 112
Heubsch, D., 165
Heuer, F., 10, 215, 218, 221
Higgins, E. T., 165
Hilton, J. L., 193
Hira, S., 293
Hirsch, J., 286
Hirst, W., 6, 8, 19, 164, 166–167, 170–172, 174–178
Hitch, G. J., 164
Hoffman, D. D., 38
Hoffman, M. B., 142
Hollins, T. S., 106, 119
Holloway, M. B., 253
Holmes, D. S., 266, 269
Honts, C. R., 265, 273, 275
Hoofien, D., 246
Hopkins, R. O., 133, 246
Horneman, C. J., 265, 271
Horowitz, I. A., 53, 215, 218
Horton, J. J., 343
Hosch, H. M., 118, 186
Howell, R. T., 59
Hu, X., 279
Huang, R. H., 216, 339
Hubbard, M., 205
Huber, G. A., 343
Huck, N. O., 219
Hung, L., 170–171
Hunt, A. L., 106
Hunt, C., 119
Hussy, W., 167
Hwang, M. I., 216
Hwe, V., 98
Hyman, I. E., 250

Iacono, W. G., 264–265, 269, 292
Iglesias-Parro, S., 175
Illes, J., 235, 249, 252
Imrich, J., 154
Inbau, F. E., 263
Israel, L., 238
Itoh, M., 286
Iverson, G., 68

Jackson, E. M., 239
Jacobs, W. J., 234, 332
Jacoby, J. D., 85, 121
Jacoby, L. L., 242
Janisse, M. P., 267
Jetten, J., 196
Johansson, M., 99
Johansson, N. O., 165
Johnson, E. J., 175
Johnson, J. T., 105, 120
Johnson, M. K., 167, 236, 238, 242, 245
Johnson, M. T., 215
Jones, T. C., 242
Jonsson, P., 67
Joselson, R., 143
Josephs, O., 126
Julian, T., 309
Jungman, N., 266, 293
Juslin, P., 91, 96, 109
Justice, C., 166

Kahn-Greene, E. T., 220
Kahneman, D., 269
Kane, A. W., 327, 333
Kane, M. J., 60
Kanwisher, N., 252
Kapardis, A., 161
Kaplan, S., 14
Karis, D., 275
Karpicke, J. D., 168
Kass, L., 315
Kassin, S. M., 91, 118, 151–152, 187, 191, 206, 218
Kaszniak, A. W., 127–128
Kaufman, R. T., 338
Kaylor-Hughes, C. J., 235, 286
Keane, M. M., 246

Keane, T. M., 329
Keast, A., 120, 123
Keele, S. W., 61, 239
Keenan, J. M., 166, 168, 174–175, 215
Keil, F. C., 128
Kelemen, W. L., 220
Kelley, C. M., 120, 130–131
Kemp, R., 33
Kemp, R. I., 165
Kendall, A. P., 219
Kensinger, E. A., 22, 135, 236, 241–242, 244–245, 273
Kessler, R. C., 333
Ketcham, K., 60, 234
Keth, A., 267
Kievit, R. A., 286
Killgore, D. B., 219
Killgore, W. D., 219
Kim, H., 125–126, 134, 236, 242, 245
Kimbrough, C. D., 46, 52
King, J. F., 88
King, N. J., 217, 224
Kirby, P., 164
Kircher, J. C., 265, 275
Kirchhoff, B. A., 244
Kleinsmith, L. J., 14
Klimecki, O., 286
Kline, P. B., 44
Knecht, S., 219
Kneller, W., 71, 122
Knieps, M., 245
Knutsson, J. J., 99
Koch, W. J., 338
Kohler, S., 16
Kolber, A. J., 6, 319, 328, 349
Koppel, J., 171–172, 174
Koriat, A., 120–121, 124, 131
Kosiol, D., 272
Kosslyn, S. M., 286
Koster, E., 265, 266
Kounios, J., 238
Koutstaal, W., 118, 236, 238–239, 245
Kovera, M. B., 63
Kozel, F. A., 286
Kramer, A., 277
Krapohl, D. J., 292

Krapohl, D. j., 292
Kremnitzer, M., 264, 292
Kriegeskorte, N., 290
Kriner, D. L., 344
Krull, D. S., 206
Kubis, J. F., 272
Kubler, A., 200
Kucharski, L. T., 142
Kugelmass, S., 265, 269–270
Kuhn, D., 161
Kukolja, J., 220
Kulik, J., 8
Kumaran, D., 246, 248
Kumsta, R., 223
Kvavilashvili, L., 8
Kwak, J. Y., 38
Kwan, D., 246
Kwang, T., 343

LaBar, K. S., 15, 216
Labkovsky, E., 278
Laing, J., 222
Laiser, N., 247
Lam, S., 216
Lammers, W. J., 242
Lampinen, J. M., 65
Lane, S. M., 69
Lang, P. J., 216
Lang, W., 242
Langleben, D. D., 286–287, 289–290
Lanius, R. A., 331
Larson, J. A., 263
Lau, I., 216
Lea, J. A., 69, 71
Leding, J. K., 65
Lee, T. M. C., 286
Leippe, M.R., 45–46
Lenz, G. S., 343
Lepper, M. R., 199, 205
Levett, L. M., 149
Levi, A. M., 72
Levine, J. M., 165
Levy, B. J., 170
Levy, N., 321
Lewis, H. L., 74
Lieberman, J. D., 154, 200, 207–208

Lieblich, I., 265, 269–270
Lin, J. W., 216
Lindinger, G., 242
Lindsay, D. S., 119–120, 130–131, 167
Lindsay, R. (2001), 67, 122
Lindsay, R. C. L., 34–35, 37–38, 42, 45–46, 62, 64–67, 69, 71–74, 121–122, 168
Lindsey, S., 112
Lipp, O. V., 269
Lippman, J., 162
Lisanby, S. H., 253
Lisuzzo, M. C., 143
Liu, L. L., 243
Lockhart, R. S., 88
Loeb, R. A., 311
Loftus, E. F., 10, 19, 21, 35, 37–38, 49, 60, 85, 93, 145, 152, 161, 167–168, 175, 234,–236, 245, 250
Loftus, G. R., 42, 93
Logie, R., 65
Logothetis, N. K., 129
Lord, C. G., 199, 205
Lozito, J. P., 168
Luber, B., 253
Lubow, R. E., 267, 269
Lucas, N., 265
Luus, C. A., 121–122
Lykken, D. T., 264, 269
Lynn, R., 269
Lyon, D., 207

Macdonald, C. J., 19
MacLaren, V. V., 265
MacLeod, M. D., 170
Macrae, C. N., 74, 171, 196
Maguire, E. A., 246, 248, 250
Malone, P. S., 206
Malpass, R. S., 61–62, 66–67, 234
Manier, D., 166, 172
Manning, L., 245, 248
Marche, T. A., 236
Marcuse, F. L., 264
Markoswitch, H. J., 19
Marsh, E. J., 165
Marshall, T. E., 64
Marston, W. M., 263

Martens, T. K., 60
Martin, A., 240
Martin, D., 143
Martin, G. D., 338
Martin, L. L., 206
Martin, P. Y., 222
Martin, R., 222
Martin, V. C., 247
Mastro, D., 216
Mather, M., 10, 19, 21–22, 236, 238
Matsuda, T., 241
Mauldin, K. N., 246
Mayer, A., 238
Mazzoni, G., 123, 250
McAllister, H. A., 72
McAuliff, B. D., 63
McBride, S. A., 219
McCabe, D. P., 128–129
McCloskey, M., 146, 192
McClure, K. A., 99, 111
McDaniel, M. A., 107
McDermott, K. B., 85, 103, 121, 125, 169, 237, 246, 248–249, 288, 360
McDermott, R., 340
McDuff, S. G. R., 246
McEwan, B. S., 22
McGaugh, J. L., 11, 15
McGorty, E. K., 33, 60
McIntosh, A. R., 239, 243
McKinnon, A. C., 73
McLaughlin, J., 219
McNally, R. J., 234
McQuillan, P. J., 143
McQuiston, D. E., 66
McQuiston-Surrett, D., 61, 66–67
McWethy, A., 186
Meade, M. L., 167, 174
Mecklenburg, S. H., 32, 53–54
Mecklinger, A., 242, 244
Megreya, A. M., 32–33
Meijer, E., 263
Meissner, C. A., 60, 69, 102
Meixner, J. B., 278, 282–284, 286
Meksin, R., 172, 174
Melara, R. D., 71
Mellers, B. A., 216, 225

Memon, A., 54, 61, 65, 71, 112, 118, 122, 149, 161, 166, 250
Mertens, R., 276
Mesulam, M. M., 236
Metcalfe, J., 91, 107
Meudell, P. R., 164
Mezrich, B., 314
Mickes, L., 89, 91, 98, 100
Miedema, J., 207
Migueles, M., 171
Milgram, S., 192
Miller, G., 253
Miller, P., 33
Miller, T. R., 337
Millman, M. H., 310
Mills, J., 222
Milne, A. B., 196
Minear, M., 243
Mintun, M., 244
Mintz, P. M., 222
Mintzer, M. Z., 224
Mitchell, J. P., 121, 126
Mitchell, M., 222
Mize, G. E., 162
Mnookin, J. L., 113
Mohamed, F. B., 286
Monteleone, G. T., 286, 289
Montgomery, D. A., 192, 202–203
Morein-Zamir, S., 219
Morey, R. D., 68
Mori, E., 241, 286
Moritz, S., 125–126, 134
Morris, R., 286
Morrow, D. G., 174
Most, S. B., 13
Mott, N. L., 174
Mrozek, J. R., 338
Mulligan, N. W., 168
Munsterberg, H., 41, 85
Munsterman, G. T., 174
Murai, J., 286
Murphy, W. L., 143
Murray, D. M., 91
Musch, J., 122–123
Mussweiler, T., 199

Nabashi-Nakahara, R., 216
Nadel, L., 5, 19, 234, 332
Naftali, G., 270
Nagel, R., 132
Nahari, G., 272–273, 293
Nairne, J. S., 74
Naka, M., 171
National Research Council, 263–264
Naveh, A., 269
Navon, D., 61
Neisser, U., 8
Nelson, T. O., 127
Nesmith, K., 19
Nessler, D., 242, 244
Nestojko, J. F., 171
Neufeld, P., 86, 234, 246
Neuschatz, J. S., 65, 147–148, 154
New, J. G., 253
Newman, L. S., 205
Nicholson, K., 327, 333
Nickerson, R. S., 152
Nisbett, R., 190
Noah, L., 349
Nokes, T., 174
Nolde, S. F., 238
Norman, K. A., 118, 236, 245
Nose, I., 286, 288–289, 290
Nunez, J. M., 286
Nussinson, R., 120
Nyberg, L., 239
Nystrom, L. E., 132

O'Brien, T. P., 71
O'Connell, S., 234
O'Connor, F. J., 46
O'Gorman, J. G., 265, 271
O'Rourke, T. E., 63
Ochalek, K., 146
Ochsner, K. N., 10, 16, 22
Odinot, G., 91, 99, 107
Oeltermann, A., 129
Öhman, A., 269
Okado, Y., 236, 241
Okuda, J., 241, 246
Olson, E. A., 60, 73, 76, 118–119, 148, 234
Olsson, N., 91

Opitz, B., 244
Oppenheimer, D. M., 343
Orne, E. C., 265, 269
Orne, M. T., 265–267, 269–270
Osugi, A., 292
Otten, L. J., 123
Ozuru, Y., 166

Padgett, T. M., 286
Palfin, R. A., 338
Paller, K. A., 236, 241, 245
Palmer, J. C., 60, 85, 145
Palmer, M. A., 73
Pan, L., 247
Pannu, J. K., 127–128
Paré-Blagoev, E. J., 244
Park, C. R., 220
Park, D. C., 243
Park, E. M., 175
Parks, A., 165, 265
Parrish, T. B., 236
Pasupathi, M., 165
Paterson, H. M., 165
Pauls, J., 129
Payne, D. G., 90
Payne, J. W.G., 216
Paz-Alonso, P. M., 244–245, 249
Pearlstone, Z., 90
Pendergrast, M., 234
Penney, T. B., 242
Pennington, N., 166, 168, 175, 205
Penrod, S. D., 33, 45–46, 54, 60, 63, 65, 76, 112, 119–120, 161, 215, 218, 221, 234
Peper, M., 267
Pereira-Pasarin, L. P., 165, 168
Perez-Stable, E. J., 223
Perfect, T. J., 18, 69, 73–74, 106, 119, 170
Perretta, S., 73
Peselow, E., 223
Petersen, S. E., 239, 244
Petroff, D. D., 162
Petry, M. C., 216
Petty, R. E., 195
Pfeiffer, T., 199
Phan, K. L., 286–287, 289
Phelps, E. A., 5, 12, 15, 135

Phillips, M. R., 63
Pickrell, J. E., 250
Pike, G., 33
Pitman, R. K., 327, 329, 331, 333
Ploesser, M., 253
Pochon, J. B., 132
Podlesny, J. A., 266, 267
Poehlman, T. A., 251
Pohl, R. F., 122–123
Poldrack, R. A., 126, 244
Pollina, D. A., 268
Pontoski, K., 121
Posner, M. I., 61, 239, 244
Poulin, R., 248
Pourtois, G., 14
Pozzulo, J. D., 72
Prati, V., 251
Pratt, D., 65
Preston, E., 199
Price, C. J., 245
Prince, S. E., 244
Pritchard, M. E., 166–168, 174–175, 215
Pryke, S., 74
Pyszczynski, T., 207

Quinlivan, D. S., 30, 38, 45, 47, 49–51, 54, 65, 147–148
Quinn, J. M., 189

Race, E., 246
Racine, C. A., 238
Raichle, M. E., 124, 244, 252
Rajaram, S., 165, 168, 172
Rand, D. G., 343
Rand-Giovannetti, E., 124
Ranganath, C., 123, 126, 129, 130
Rangel, A., 132
Rao, S., 238
Raskin, D. C., 263, 266–267
Rauch, S. L., 331
Raveh, O., 269
Rawson, E., 128
Raye, C. L., 236, 245
Raymond, J. E., 12
Read, J. D., 34–35, 43, 45, 53, 119–120, 168
Rebellius, A., 144

Reber, P. J., 236
Reid, J. E., 263
Reidler, J., 248
Reifman, A., 154
Reiman, E., 237, 240
Reinitz, M. T., 242
Reisberg, D., 10, 67
Reno, J., 153
Resick, P. A., 329
Rettinger, J., 265–266, 271
Reutskaja, E., 132
Reyna, V. F., 37, 85, 236
Reysen, M. B., 167
Riby, D. M., 219
Riby, L. M., 219
Rice, H. J., 243
Richards, J. E., 270
Rienick, C. B., 99
Riis, J., 132
Rill, H. G., 266
Rimmele, U., 10–11, 18–19
Rishworth, A., 120
Risinger, D. M., 152
Rissman, J., 250, 289
Roberts, R., 247
Robertson, D. A., 120
Robinson, M. D., 105, 120, 130
Robinson, R. J., 218
Robinson-Riegler, B., 67
Robinson-Riegler, G., 67
Roche, J. D., 338
Rodgers, J. D., 338
Roediger, H. L. III, 6, 18, 84–85, 88, 90, 92–93, 103, 105, 107, 121, 125, 167–169, 173, 215, 237, 245, 360
Rönnberg, J., 164–165
Rose, I. N., 308, 317
Rosen, B. R., 238, 245
Rosen, G. M., 327, 329
Rosenbaum, R. S., 246
Rosenberg, D., 337
Rosenblatt, A., 207
Rosenfeld, J. P., 6, 274–279, 282–286, 288, 291–292
Rosenhan, D. L., 218
Rosenthal, R., 64, 152

Ross, D. F., 34–35
Ross, L., 205
Rotrosen, J., 223
Rouder, J. N., 68
Rubin, D. C., 9, 90
Rugg, M. D., 123, 126, 243
Ryan, A., 291
Ryan, J. D., 129, 132, 133
Rydell, S. M., 61

Sahakian, B., 219
Saks, M. J., 152
Salerno, J. M., 174
Sales, B., 154
Sales, B. D., 218
Saltzman, I. J., 264
Sampaio, C., 92, 102–103, 105
Samra, J., 338
Sandberg, A., 6
Sanfey, A. G., 132
Sanna, L. J., 123
Sartori, G., 251, 251, 280–281
Sasaki, H., 241
Sauer, J. D., 73, 96
Saunders, J., 170, 206
Savulescu, J., 6
Schacter, D. L., 6, 18, 21, 60, 118, 124–125, 135, 150, 233–248
Scheck, B., 86, 234
Scheflin, A. W., 333
Schendan, H. E., 286
Scherer, K. R., 22
Schmidt, K., 19
Schmolck, H., 8
Schneider, D. J., 196, 251
Schnider, A., 244
Schooler, J. W., 236
Schul, Y., 200, 204
Schwartz, B. L., 123, 128
Schwarz, N., 200
Schweitzer, N. J., 330, 340
Scott, J., 65
Scott, M. S., 143
Seelau, E. P., 61, 121–122
Self, G., 166
Semmler, C., 35, 122–123, 148, 234

Sepulcre, J., 248
Serra-Grabulosa, J. M., 312
Seta, J. J., 206
Seymour, T. L., 278, 280
Shaked, N., 120
Shakhar, G. B., 6
Shalev, A. Y., 339
Shallice, T., 126, 240
Shalvi, S., 223
Shapiro, M. L., 244
Sharma, K., 119
Sharot, T., 15, 17, 135, 150
Shaughnessy, J. J., 88
Shaw, J. S. III, 99–111, 121–123
Shen, F. X., 6, 328, 337, 344
Sherif, M., 149
Sherman, S. J., 245
Shimamura, A. P., 170
Shin, L. M., 331
Shmueli, J., 270
Shulman, G. L., 124
Siddle, D. A. T., 264, 269
Simmons, W. K., 290
Simons, D. J., 60
Sinnott-Armstrong, W. P., 5–6
Skagerberg, E. M., 65, 146–149
Slamencka, N. J., 168
Slomka, J., 224
Slotnick, S. D., 235–236, 239–241, 243–244
Small, M., 234
Smith, A., 151–152
Smith, C. N., 132–134
Smith, J. B., 71
Smith, V. L., 91, 109, 118, 174
Smolders, L., 267
Snell, A., 69, 75
Sniper, G., 269
Snyder, L. C., 143
Sokolov, E. N., 264, 269
Sokolovsky, A., 279–280
Solomon, S., 207
Sommer, T., 125
Sommers, S. R., 187
Soskins, M., 291
Southwick, S. M., 331, 339

Sparr, L. F., 327, 329, 333
Speckman, P. L., 68
Spence, S. A., 235, 286, 292
Spencer, D., 220
Sperling, R. A., 124–125
Spinks, R., 242
Sporer, S. L., 119–120, 122–123
Spreng, R. N., 248
Squire, L. R., 132–134, 246
St. Jacques, P. L., 234
Stadler, M. A., 242
Stark, C., 236, 241
Stark, R., 267
Stasser, G., 165, 168
Steblay, N., 60, 63, 65, 67–68, 122, 146, 186
Stern, B. H., 340
Stern, L. B., 73
Stevenage, S., 71, 122
Stevens, S. S., 44
Stevens, W. D., 240
Stinson, B., 46
Stoeter, P., 270, 286
Stone, C. B., 6, 172–173
Storm, B. C., 171
Stose, S., 286
Strack, F., 199, 200
Stretch, V., 119
Studebaker, C. A., 187, 191
Stuve, T. E., 63, 119
Suchan, B., 248
Suengas, A. G., 236
Sun, D., 68
Sunstein, C. R., 225
Sutherland, M., 21–22
Sutton, J., 172
Suzuki, M., 241, 286
Swann, W. B., 206
Szpunar, K. K., 245–246, 248–249

Tafarodi, R. W., 206
Taira, M., 286
Talarico, J. M., 9
Tamborini, R., 216
Tandoh, K., 171
Tanford, J. A., 189, 191
Taylor, L., 338, 349

Thackray, R. I., 265–267
Thiel, C. M., 220
Thomas, K., 265
Thomas, R. L., 165
Thompson, W. C., 152
Thompson, W. L., 286
Thorley, C., 165, 167
Timm, H. W., 266, 269
Titus, W., 168
Todorov, A., 123
Toglia, M. P., 34–35, 37–38, 42
Tollenaar, M. S., 22
Tomlinson, T. M., 192
Tomporowski, P. D., 217
Tousignant, J. P., 46
Towell, N., 33
Tranel, D., 129
Traynor, R. J., 162
Tredoux, C. G., 61, 66–67
Treyer, V., 244
Trinath, T., 129
Tschuggnall, K., 167
Tsukada, M., 241
Tubb, V., 118
Tucker, M., 328
Tuholski, S. W., 60
Tulving, E., 4, 19, 88–90, 97, 104, 150, 239–240
Tun, P. A., 245
Tunnicliff, J. L., 61, 93
Turtle, J. W., 152
Tversky, B., 165

Uhlmann, E. L., 251
Uleman, J. S., 205
Ungapen, S., 220

Vaidya, C. J., 244
Vaitl, D., 267, 267
Valentine, T., 61, 67
Van Bockstaele, B., 265
Van Bruskirk, D., 264
Van den Bos, K., 207
van der Horst, A. S., 246
van der Shrier, J. H., 35
Van Essen, D. C., 288

Van Hollen, J. B., 153
van Kleef, G. A., 223
van Koppen, P. J., 91
van Stegeren, A., 223
Vandello, J. A., 149
Vann, S. D., 246
Vannucci, M., 123
Vargha-Khadem, F., 246
Veins, A. M., 328
Verfaellie, M., 239, 246
Vernon, L. L., 72
Verschuere, B., 251, 263–271, 280–281, 293
Verstijnen, I. M., 35
Vess, M., 200
Villate, C., 130
von Cramon, D. Y., 244
Von Zerssen, G. C., 244
Vossel, G., 265, 266, 268, 270, 272, 286
Vu, M. A., 247
Vuilleumier, P., 13–14

Wagenaar, W. A., 35, 42
Wagner, A. D., 126, 238, 243–244, 250, 252, 289
Wagner, A. R., 269
Wagstaff, G. F., 106
Waid, W. M., 265, 269
Wais, P. E., 98
Walla, P., 242
Wallace, W. T., 90
Walters, H. A., 65
Warfield, J. F., 265, 271–272
Warren, J., 161
Waters, N. L., 162
Watson, E. L., 106
Watson, J. M., 246, 288
Weaver, D. J., 340
Weber, E. U., 175
Weber, N., 35, 73, 96, 123
Wechsler, H., 142
Wegener, D. T., 195
Wegner, D. M., 164, 174, 196, 206, 208
Weiler, J. A., 248
Weinstein, J. B., 185
Weisberg, D. S., 128–129, 330

Weiskopf, N., 250
Weldon, M. S., 165, 168
Wells, G. L., 30, 33, 38, 45–47, 49–51, 54, 60–62, 64–67, 70–71, 73, 75–76, 91, 99, 112, 118–119, 121–123, 135, 146–147, 149, 161, 234
Welsh, R. C., 243
Welzer, H., 167
Wesenstein, N. J., 219
Wessels, P. M., 242
Western, B., 345
Weston, N., 75
Wetmore, S. A., 148
Wetzels, R., 68
Whalen, P. J., 14
Wheeler, M. A., 239
White, N., 223
White, T. L., 196
Whitlow, S., 129
Wickens, C., 277
Wiersma, B., 337
Wiest, W. M., 44
Wig, G. S., 240
Wiggs, C. L., 240
Wigmore, J. H., 48
Wilkinson, I. D., 286
Wilkinson, M., 154
Williams, L. N., 206
Wilson, T. D., 190, 195
Winbush, M., 265, 275
Windt, A. D., 336
Wingfield, A., 245
Winman, A., 91

Winograd, M., 278
Wise, R. J. S., 245
Witmer, B. G., 44
Wittenbaum, G. M., 165, 168
Wixted, J. H., 6, 215
Wixted, J. T., 89, 91, 98, 119
Wogalter, M. S., 66
Wohl, D., 172, 174
Wolf, S., 192, 202–203
Wolters, G., 35, 91
Wong, A. T., 242, 245
Wood, W., 189
Wright, D. B., 65, 146–149, 166–167
Wrightsman, L. S., 218

Yim, P., 216
Yokoyama, O., 128
Yonelinas, A. P., 119–120, 123, 126, 130
Young, G., 327, 330, 333
Yun, L. S., 237
Yurgelun-Todd, D. A., 286

Zaller, J., 348
Zanni, G., 167
Zaragoza, M. S., 121, 146
Zaromb, F. M., 173
Zechmeister, E. B., 88
Zeckhauser, R. J., 343
Zerr, T., 121
Zogmaister, C., 251
Zoladz, P. R., 22, 220
Zweck, T., 96

Subject Index

Against All Enemies (Clarke), 233
Allen v. Bloomfield Hills (2010, Michigan Supreme Court), 334–336. *See also* neuroscience and the future of PTSD litigation
American Association for Justice (AAJ), 328
amygdala
   memory formation role, 12–13, 15, 16, 19, 332
   neurotransmitter mediation of, 331
Association of Trial Lawyers of America, 328
attentional blink task, 12, 13–14
autobiographical Implicit Association Test (aIAT), 251, 280
autobiographical memory, 4, 19, 151, 332, 359
autonomic nervous system (ANS) measures. *See* Concealed Information Test

Bader v. United States (2009, Connecticut Supreme Court), 336
Bayes factor (BF) methodology, use in lineup research, 69
behavioral influences in lineups, 63–66
bias/biases
   biased vs. unbiased foils (study of judges' rulings), 47
   biomedical enhancement-induced, 222–224
   corrections/adjustments for controlling, 153–154
   debiasing juror's verdicts, 194–198
   filler face choice and, 61
   hindsight bias, 123–124
   in identification procedures, 38–39, 48, 54
   information sampling bias, 165
   in instructions given in lineups, 63, 65
   non-biasing identification procedures, 45, 54
   in police procedures, 51, 54, 65
   studies
      mock crime lineup, 64
      staged theft, 62–63
biomedical (drugs) cognitive enhancements, for jurors during trials, 219–224
blackjack table (card counting), criminalizing cognitive enhancement at, 307–322
   allowable exceptions, 311
   anti-device statute lobbying by casinos, 308
   blackjack basics, strategies, 309
   "card counting" (defined), 309
   card counting methods, 307, 309–310
   Colorado/Canada, penalties for counting, 310–311
   Enhancement Justification (for anti-device legislation)

blackjack table (card counting), (Cont.)
  claims that enhancements are unnatural, 315–316
  claims that enhancements is cheating fails, 316–318
  enhancement ban as over-/underinclusive, 314–315
  neurotechnological forms of enhancement, 312–313
  ethicist's opinions, 308
  Freedom of Mind Justification (for anti-device legislation), 318–322
  Nevada anti-device statute, 307–322
  players vs. the house, 309
  President's Council on Bioethics warning, 315
  selective criminalization of card counting, 311–312
  technological advancements iPhone application, 307
bodily injury case law, 334, 336–337, 341
bombing of train investigation (Madrid, 2004), 145–146
brain/brain studies. *See also* fMRI brain studies; neuroimaging of true, false and imaginary memories; neuroimaging studies of memory confidence and accuracy; PET (positive emission tomography) studies
  amygdala
    mediation by neurotransmitters, 331
    memory formation role, 12–13, 15–16, 19, 332
  circuitry involved with memory formation, 16
  eye movement measurements and, 130
  fMRI confidence studies, 125–129
  hippocampus, memory formation role, 4, 15, 19, 246–247
  imagining network, 248
  MRI/emotional, neutral scene study, 15–16
  multiple representational systems in, 4
  9/11 attack/autobiographical memory study, 17

  posterior parahippocampus, memory formation role, 16–17
  and posttraumatic stress disorder, 330–333

Challenger space shuttle explosion, 8
co-witnesses
  influence of memories of, 150–151
  influence on confidence, 123–124
  informational influences of, 150–151
cognitive biases during investigations, 142–143
cognitive enhancement, criminalization of. *See* blackjack table (card counting), criminalizing cognitive enhancement at
cognitive enhancements, for juror memory
  biomedical (drugs), 219–221
  ethics of, in court
    comparing notes, 221–222
    comparison to other biases, 224–225
  external tools, 217–219
collaborative facilitation, 164
collaborative remembering. *See also* socially shared retrieval-induced forgetting; within-individual retrieval-induced forgetting
  effect on remembering during collaboration, 164–166
    collaborative facilitation, 164
    collaborative inhibition, 165
    information sampling bias, 165
  effect on subsequent memory, 166–174
    cueing/retrieval-induced facilitation, 169
    moderating factor of SS-RIF, 173–174
    rehearsal, 168–169, 173
    retrieval-induced forgetting, 169–173
    social contagion, 166–168, 173
    SS-RIF and collective forgetting, 172–173
  group size influence, 165
  self-corrective nature of groups, 167–168

Complex Trial Protocol (P300 protocol), 277–280
  anti-terror application, 281–284
  development/description of, 277
  Lumping countermeasure study, 279–280
  subject groups, 278–279
Concealed Information Test (CIT), 264–273
  Event-Related Potentials applications, 274–275
  historical background, 264–265
  mock-crime procedure, 264–265, 272–273
  orienting responses, 264, 267, 269–271
  outcomes, factors affecting, 270–271, 273
  potential limiting applicability of, 271–273
  successful implementation factors, 273
  theoretical foundation of, 268–270
  validity of autonomic measures in, 265–268
    Breathing Amplitude/Breathing Cycle Time, 266
    cardiovascular measures, 266–267, 270
    Receiver Operating Characteristic curve, 265–266, 268
    skin conductance response/ respiration line length scores, 268
concealed stored memory detection, with psychophysiological/ neuroimaging methods, 263–293
  comparison question tests, 263–264
  Complex Trial Protocol, 277–280
  Concealed Information Test, 264–273
  fMRI detection methods, 285–292
  Guilty Action Test (GAT), 272
  Guilty Knowledge Test (GKT), 264
  P300 Event-Related Potentials, 273–285
  RT-based concealed information detectors, 280–281
confessions
  DNA evidence vs., 144
  false/coerced confessions, 87, 143–144
  DNA evidence vs., 144–145
  investigator-supplied information and, 152
  power of confession evidence, 152
confidence and accuracy, in reports from memory, 84–115.
  See also eyewitness testimony
  calibration experiments, 97
  cognitive psychology research, 92
  conflicting claims of psychologists, 92–94
  conviction of innocent defendants, 85–88, 119
  DNA evidence/testing and, 69, 87–88, 119
  errors made with high eyewitness confidence, 86–88
  faces in eyewitness situations (research), 92
  factors in making confidence judgments, 120–124
    confidence malleability, 123–124
    experience-based judgments, 121
    hindsight bias, 123–124
    illusion of knowledge, 124
    inflated confidence from information-based judgments, 123
    information-based judgments, 121–122
    markers/assessment variables, 124
    sequential vs. *simultaneous* lineups, 122–123
    system variables, 122
  factors tainting testimony, 86
  five analyses of, 94–112
    between-events correlations, 94–95, 103–106
    between-subjects correlations, 95, 106–108
    manipulation of independent variables, 94, 97–102
    summary of, 110–112
    within/between hybrid analysis, 95, 109–110
    within-subjects correlations, 95, 108–109

confidence and accuracy, (*Cont.*)
   Ingrado-Goldberg-Silverio case, 119–120, 123
   measurement computation variability, 93
   practical implications for legal system, 112–113
   social/applied psychology research, 92
   trace theories of remembering, 88–91
   use of language issues, 84
Convicting the Innocent (Garrett), 87
conviction of innocent defendants, 85–88
covert remembering, 169
criminal investigators, 144–145
   confession vs. DNA evidence (case study), 144
   malleability of opinions of, 145
   tunnel vision of, 144–145

death of Princess Diana, 8
Deese-Roediger-McDermott (DRM) paradigm, 126, 237, 238, 242–243, 245
Diagnostic and Statistical Manual of Mental Disorders-III (DSM-III)
   recognition of PTSD, 327, 329
disregarding instructions.
   See instructions to disregard
DNA evidence. *See also* Innocence Project
   confession vs. DNA evidence (case study), 144
   exoneration of cases, 69, 119, 149
      Deskovic case, 144
      Dotson and Vasques case, 142–143
      Evans case, 149
      Thompson/Cotton rape case, 213
      wrongful conviction factors, 143
   Ohio/Innocence Protection Act, 77–78
   origin of use of, 87

emotion's impact on memory, 3, 7–23
   accuracy for contextual details of spatial location, temporal order, 19–20
   alterations of memory arousal manipulations, 15
   attentional blink task, 12–14
   distortion/resilience over time and circumstance, 37–39
   enhancement of attention and perception, 12–13, 19
   impairment/"narrowing of attention," 13–14
   modulation of memory consolidation, 15
   MRI brain systems study, 15–16
   role of amygdala, 12–13, 15
   stages, 11–17
   components of emotion, 22–23
   enhanced confidence in accuracy vs. actual accuracy, 8–11
   studies/explanatory findings, 17–20
   flashbulb memories, details comparisons, 8–11
   future research directions, legal system implications, 20–23
   individuals, factors related to, 23
   laboratory study limitations, 10
   shocking events (examples), 8
enhancement justification (for anti-device legislation), 312–318
   claims enhancements are cheating fails, 316–318
   claims enhancements are unnatural, 315–316
   emerging neurotechnological forms of enhancement, 312–313
   enhancement ban as over-/underinclusive, 314–315
episodic memory
   glucose intake for improvement of, 219
   semantic memory vs., 151
erroneous information, in eyewitness testimony, 86
Event-Related Potentials. *See* P300 Event-Related Potentials
evidence-/decision-based complexity for jurors, 215
evidence collection and interpretation, 142–155
   cognitive biases during investigations, 142–143

criminal investigators, 144–145
eyewitnesses
    information from a co-witness, 150–151
    information from an investigator, 151–153
    misinformation effect, 146–147
    post-identification feedback effect, 147–149
    forensic scientists, 145–146
evidence interactions by eyewitnesses, 149–153
    information from a co-witness, 150–151
    information from an investigator, 151–153
experience-based retrospective confidence judgments, 121
experimental recombination paradigm, 247
expert witnesses
    confidence reliability and, 112
    example of advertising by, 327
    identification accuracy opinion, 54
    memory-based reports from, 29
    memory requirements of, 214
eye movement monitoring studies, 129–135
    brain activity measured, 130
    cue familiarity/cue utilization measures, 132
    distinguishing correct from incorrect guesses, 134
    face-scene paradigm, 134
    fMRI compared with, 130
    limitations of, 135–136
    manipulated vs. repeated scenes comparison, 134–135
    relative *evidence assessment* effects on confidence judgments, 132–133
    relative evidence factors, 132
    target recognition experience measures, 131–132
    viewing behavior during scene cueing period, 133
    viewing novel and repeated scenes, 133–134

eyewitness identification, 5–6, 27–55. *See also* jurors, memory of/enhancing trial performance; lineup procedures in eyewitness identification
    conviction of innocent defendants, 85–88, 119
    description of Kevin Keith's trial, 59–60
    distorting influences on memory, 37–39
    eyewitness performance, laws and expressed beliefs about, 49–53
    judges, assessment study, 46–47
    jurors
        adequacy of instructions to, 51–52
        assessment study, 46
        knowledge needed by, 48
        memory distortions, 151
    move to adopt standardized procedures, 154
    policy recommendations, 53–55
    safeguards against inaccurate convictions, 47, 49–50
        failures of safeguards (examples), 48
    suggestiveness augmentation effect, 51
    two-pronged test for identification exclusion, 30
    unintentional conveyance of information to, 143
    U.S. law, 30–31, 36–37, 47–48
    witness accuracy judgement criteria
        determination of necessary relevant information, 40–41
        necessary relevant information for observers, 41–44
        observer application of knowledge consideration, 45–49
        scientific and lay knowledge, 44–45
        witness self-reports, 44–45
    witness considerations
        differences in exposure and test targets, 33–34
        limits under ideal conditions, 31–33
        perceptual difficulties/inconsistencies, 34–44

eyewitness memory paradigm, 100
eyewitness testimony
  contrasting memories of same events, 233–234
  corroborating evidence recommendation, 53
  DNA evidence/testing and, 69, 87–88, 119, 143
  errors made with high eyewitness confidence, 86–88
  evidence interactions, 149–153
    information from a co-witness, 150–151
    information from an investigator, 151–153
  factors tainting testimony, 86
  importance of, minus physical evidence, 85–86
  influence of witness confidence, 65
  misinformation effect, 146–147
  post-identification feedback effect, 147–149
  remembering, trace theories of, 88–91
  rulings on motions to exclude (study), 46
  specific criteria for evaluation of, 49–53
Eyewitness Testimony (Loftus), 86

face matching studies, 33–34, 39
face-scene paradigm, 134
false recognition studies.
    See neuroimaging of true, false and imaginary memories
filler faces (for lineups) choice strategies, 61–62
fingerprint examination mistakes, 145–146
First Amendment (U.S. Constitution), protections of thought privacy, 308
flashbulb memories, 8–11
  accuracy issues, 9–11
  influence of time on details, 8
  9/11 details comparison, 8–9
fMRI (functional magnetic resonance imaging) brain studies
  concealed stored memory detection studies, 285–292
    accuracy of methods, 289–290
    generalizability of methods, 291–292
    replicability of methods, 290–291
  confidence studies, 125–129
    absolute/relative measures of metacognitive accuracy, 128–129
    elicitation of false recognition, 126–127
    excess influence from fMRI images, 129
    eye movement measures compared with, 130
    face-name relational memory task, 127–128
    limitations/possible uses for future testing, 127
    memory distortion study, 151
    questions about accuracy/use of, 129
    use of DRM paradigm, 126, 237
  hippocampus studies, 242
  sensory reactivation studies, 236–243
  true vs. false memory studies, 250
  use in legal matters, 330
forensic sciences/scientists
  mistakes made by, 145–146
  National Academy of Sciences recommendations, 154
  unintentional conveyance of information to, 143
freedom of mind justification (for anti-device legislation), 318–322

Guilty Knowledge Test (GKT), 264

hippocampus
  fMRI studies, 242
  future/past memory activity, 247
  and high confidence decisions, 126–127
  as imagining network component, 248
  impact of lasting stress on, 22
  influence of damage to, 130
  memory formation role, 4, 15, 19, 151, 246–247
  posterior parahippocampus, 16–17

Subject Index

and PTSD, 331–333

imaginary and true memories, 245–248
implanted memories, 147, 168, 175
Implicit Association Test (IAT), 281
inadmissible evidence, methods for remedying
    explanations given to jurors, 187–189
    forewarning jurors, commitments to disregard, 189–191
    inducing juror suspicions of attorney's motives, 191–194
    mock jurors and trials, 186–188, 192–193, 198, 202
        inadmissible evidence studies, 205
    neutralizing inadmissible evidence, 194–199
        consider the opposite of inadmissible evidence, 198–199
        debiasing juror's verdicts, 194–198
    reflection on the proposals, 199–200
information-based confidence judgments, 121–122
information sampling bias, 165
informational influences of co-witnesses, 150–151
Innocence Project, 87–88, 119, 142–143
Innocence Protection Act (2010, Ohio), 77–78
innocent defendants, conviction of, 85–88
instructions for witnesses for lineups, 62–63. *See also* inadmissible evidence, methods for remedying
instructions to disregard, 185–209
    effective instructions, foundational elements
        delayed disregard/addressing subtle influences on juror's verdicts, 205–206
        drawing jurors' attention to inadmissible evidence, 200
        juror disregarding evidence vs. not avoiding discussions, 201
        limited juror cognitive resources, motivation to comply, 206
        restating inadmissible evidence, 201
        undermining perceived validity of inadmissible evidence, 203–204
        use of empathic language, 202–203
    effectiveness of (meta-analysis), 185–186
    rules of evidence
        description/purpose of, 185
        trial courts/mistrials and, 186
        unfairly prejudicial evidence (description), 185–186

judges. *See* trial judges
jurors. *See also* jurors, deliberation and memory; jurors, judge's instructions to disregard given to; jurors, memory of/enhancing trial performance; mock jurors and trials
    adequacy of instructions to, 51–52
    delinquency data, 217
    knowledge needed by, 48
    memory of jurors/enhancing trial performance, 213–226
    note-taking permissibility variation, 218
    study related to eyewitness testimony, 46
jurors, deliberation and memory (collaborative memory), 161–179. *See also* collaborative remembering
    collective memory and decision-making, 174–175
    goals during deliberations, 173–174
    induced forgetting and, 172
    PERSON-PRO/alteration of memories study, 176–178
    practice effects and RIF, further investigations, 175–178
    psychological literature/mnemonic consequences, 164
    relevant court rulings, 162–164
jurors, judge's instructions to disregard given to
    debiasing verdicts of jurors, 194–198
    disregarding vs. avoiding discussions of inadmissible evidence, 201

drawing attention to inadmissible evidence, 200
forewarnings
  disregarding of inadmissible evidence, 189–191, 194–198, 201
  suspicion of introducing attorney's motives, 191–194
  gaining commitment to follow instructions, 189–191
  inducing suspicions of attorney's motives, 191–194
  judge explanation of inadmissible ruling, 187–189
  restating inadmissible evidence, 201
jurors, memory of/enhancing trial performance, 213–226
  cognitive enhancements
    biomedical (drugs), 219–221
    external tools, 217–219
  ethics of cognitive enhancement in court
    comparing notes, 221–222
    comparison to other biases, 224–225
    enhancement-induced bias, 222–224
  problems of juror memory, 214–217
    cognitive limitations, 216
    demands imposed on memory, 214–215
    evidence/decision complexity, 215
    metamemory accuracy issues, 215
    psychological factors, 216
    sleepiness in the courtroom, 216–217
  Thompson/Cotton rape case (example), 213–214

Lawrence v. Texas (2003), 318
legal system
  assumptions about memory, v
  goals of, 21
  life events relevant to, 7
  need for corroborating information, 21
  U.S. eyewitness evidence law, 30–31, 38
  ways in which dependent on memory, 3
lineup procedures in eyewitness identification, 59–78

Bayes factor methodology, use in lineup research, 69
co-witnesses
  influence of memories of, 150–151
  informational influences of, 150–151
content of lineups, 61–62
  filler face choice strategies, 61–62
  perpetrator present vs. perpetrator absent, 61
description of Kevin Keith's trial, 59–60
identification enhancement methods, 74–75
identification studies, 32
instructions given at lineups, 62–63
lineup administrators/double-blind administration, 64–65
memory encoding, retrieval, maintenance phases, 60
post-identification feedback effect, 65
presentation methods
  alternative approaches, 73–76
  mock crime study, 67–68
  simultaneous and sequential lineups, 66–70, 77
  theory, contributions of, 70–73
state lineup legislation, 66–67
WITNESS model, 71–73
Loma Prieta earthquake, 8

Manson v. Braithwaite (1977), 30, 49, 50–51, 119
memory (human memory). *See also* confidence and accuracy, in reports from memory; emotion's impact on memory; eye movement monitoring studies; flashbulb memories; neuroimaging of true, false and imaginary memories; neuroimaging studies of memory confidence and accuracy
  autobiographical vs. semantic, 4, 151
  basic assumption/popular beliefs about, 4
  collective memory and decision-making, 174–175

conflicting recollections of same
events, 233–234
distorting influences on, 37–39
encoding, retrieval, maintenance
phases, 60
episodic vs. semantic, 151
face matching studies, 33–34, 39
false vs. true, 3
implanted memories, 147, 168, 175
instability of, 5–6
lineup identification studies, 32
misinformation effect, 146–147
modification of memory for original
events, 60
multiplexity of, 5
trace theories of remembering, 88–91
true vs. false memories, distinguishing
between, 234–235
"Memory & The Law Report," on
complexities of the human
memory, 366–371
memory conjunction error paradigm, 242
metamemory accuracy issues, for jurors,
215
misinformation effect, on eyewitnesses,
146–147
Missouri v. Hutching (1966), 147
mock-crime procedure, 264–265,
272–273, 278–279
mock jurors and trials
assessment of eyewitness reports, 46
inadmissible evidence studies, 186–188,
192–193, 198, 202, 205
monetization of posttraumatic stress
disorder (PTSD)
current options, 337–339
neuroscientific possibilities, 339–340

National Center for PTSD (Department
of Veterans Affairs), 329
neuroimaging. *See* concealed
stored memory detection,
with psychophysiological/
neuroimaging methods;
neuroimaging of true, false
and imaginary memories;

neuroimaging studies of memory
confidence and accuracy
neuroimaging of true, false and
imaginary memories, 233–253
conflicting recollections of same
events, 233–234
conjunction lures, feature lures, 242
courtroom applications, 252–253
memory conjunction error paradigm,
242
multivoxel pattern analysis, 250
neural signature of false memory
retrieval, 243–245
No Lie MRI, Inc. technology, 235
PET scan/fMRI studies, 236–243
priming hypothesis, 240–241
sensory reactivation hypothesis, 236,
238–239, 241
shape prototype paradigm, 243
true and imaginary memories, 245–248
current research limitations,
249–252
experimental recombination
paradigm, 247
true vs. false memories, distinguishing
between, 234–235
neuroimaging studies of memory
confidence and accuracy, 6,
124–136. *See also* eye movement
monitoring studies
fMRI confidence studies, 125–129
absolute/relative measures of
metacognitive accuracy, 128–129
elicitation of false recognition,
126–127
excess influence from fMRI images,
129
face-name relational memory task,
127–128
limitations/possible uses for future
testing, 127
questions about accuracy/use of,
129
limitations of, 135–136
methods (three) of examining
metacognition, 124–125

neurolaw scholarship, 327–328
neuroscience and the future of PTSD
    litigation, 325–349
  background information, 327–333
    the brain and PTSD, 330–333
    neurolaw scholarship, 327–328
    neuroscience and value-added for
      lawyers, 329–330
  conceptualization of injury in tort law,
    333–337
    Allen v. Bloomfield Hills case,
      334–336
    insurance and bodily injury, 336–337
  data and methods, 340–345
    analytic methods, 344–345
    experimental design, 340–343
    subjects, 343–344
  results and discussion, 345–349
    discussion, 347–349
    results, 345–346
  valuation of PTSD injuries, 337–340
    current monetization options,
      337–339
    current options, 337–339
    neuroscientific possibilities, 339–340
Nevada Gaming Control Board. *See*
    blackjack table (card counting),
    criminalizing cognitive
    enhancement at
Niel v. Biggers (1972), 49
9/11 terrorist attacks
  autobiographical memory study, 17
  flashbulb memory, details
    comparisons, 8–9, 20
No Lie MRI, Inc. neuroimaging
  technology, 235
note-taking by jurors, 218, 221–222

On the Witness Stand (Münsterberg),
  92–94
orienting response research/theory, 264,
  267, 269–271

P300 Event-Related Potentials
  bootstrap method, 274, 278
  CIT applications, 274–275
  Complex Trial Protocol, 277–280
    anti-terror application, 281–284
    development/description of, 277
    Lumping countermeasure study,
      279–280
    subject groups, 278–279
  described, 273–275
  eliciting events (oddballs, frequents),
    274
  "guilty knowledge" detection origin,
    275
  older protocols/vulnerability to
    countermeasures, 275–277
    BEOS method, 276–277
    "Brain Fingerprinting" (3-stimulus
      protocol), 276
    "MERMER" EEG analysis
      technique, 276
    3-stimulus protocols, 275–277
  RT-based concealed information
    detectors, 280–281
People v. Wright (1987), 52
perpetrator present with guilty suspect
  vs. perpetrator absent lineups, 61
PET (positive emission tomography)
  studies
  Allen vs. Bloomfield Hills case, 334
  true vs. false memories, 235, 238
  use in brain injury claims, 339
post-identification feedback effect
  (in lineups), 65, 147–149
  mechanisms in altering memories,
    148
  negative vs. positive feedback, 148–149
posttraumatic stress disorder (PTSD)
  litigation, 325–349
  background information, 327–333
    the brain and PTSD, 330–333
    neurolaw scholarship, 327–328
    neuroscience and value-added for
      lawyers, 329–330
  conceptualization of injury in tort law,
    333–337
    Allen v. Bloomfield Hills case,
      334–336
    insurance and bodily injury, 336–337

Subject Index

data and methods, 340–345
  analytic methods, 344–345
  experimental design, 340–343
  subjects, 343–344
growth of related civil litigation, 327–328
results and discussion, 345–349
  discussion, 347–349
  results, 345–346
valuation of PTSD injuries, 337–340
  current monetization options, 337–339
  current options, 337–339
  neuroscientific possibilities, 339–340
President's Council on Bioethics, 315
psychophysiological methods of concealed stored memory detection. *See* concealed stored memory detection, with psychophysiological/neuroimaging methods

Receiver Operating Characteristic (ROC) curve, 265–266
relevant information
  confidence judgment and, 120
  lay understanding of, 43
  scientific understanding of, 41–43
Remembering (Bartlett), 90
retrieval-induced forgetting (RIF) paradigm, 170, 175–178. *See also* socially shared retrieval-induced forgetting; within-individual retrieval-induced forgetting
rules of evidence
  description/purpose of, 185
  instructions to disregard and, 204
  trial courts/mistrials and, 186
  unfairly prejudicial evidence (description), 185–186

Sapirman v. Walmart (2009, Florida Circuit Court), 342
semantic memory, 4
  episodic memory vs., 151

sensory reactivation hypothesis, 236, 238–239, 241. *See also* neuroimaging of true, false and imaginary memories
sequential lineups, 77
  criticism of, 68
  false identification rate issue, 69
  mock crime study, 67–68
  presentation of lineup members, 66
  sequential advantage
    defined, 67
    empirical study of robustness of, 68–69
  states conducting, 66–67
  20-person/multiple selections, 73–74
shape prototype paradigm, 243
Signal Detection Theory, 265–266
simultaneous lineups
  mock crime study, 67–68
  presentation of lineup members, 66
  relative judgments included in, 66
sleepiness in the courtroom issues, for jurors, 216–217
social contagion, 166–168, 173
socially shared retrieval-induced forgetting (SS-RIF)
  cause of, 171
  collective forgetting and, 172–173
  defined, 170
  free-flowing conversation studies, 171
  moderating factors, 173–174
  sources of, 171–172
stress
  harmfulness to memory encoding, 60
  influence on memory, 3
  negative effects on memory performance, 22
suggestiveness augmentation effect, 51
Supreme Court decisions
  Lawrence v. Texas, 318
  Manson v. Braithwaite, 30, 49–51, 119
  Missouri v. Hutching, 147
  Niel v. Biggers, 49, 52
  People v. Wright, 52
  United States v. Telfaire, 52, 119

target-absent lineups
  post-identification feedback paradigm and, 147–148
  vs. target-present (meta-analysis), 33
thought privacy, First Amendment protections of, 308
tort law. *See* neuroscience and the future of PTSD litigation
trace theories of remembering
  absence of retrieval process in, 90–91
  common sense relation to, 89–90
  historical origins, 88–89
  wrongness of, 90
transactive memory systems, 164
transcranial direct current stimulation (tDCS), 313–314
trial judges
  explaining inadmissible ruling to jurors, 187–189
  forewarning to jurors
    disregarding of inadmissible evidence, 189–191, 194–198, 201
    suspicion of introducing attorney's motives, 191–194
  instructions to disregard, foundational elements, 200–206
  role of, 186
  sleepiness experiences, 216
  study related to eyewitness testimony, 46–47
true and false recognition. *See* neuroimaging of true, false and imaginary memories

United States v. Telfaire (1972), 52, 119
Utah Model Jury Instruction (CR404), 52

within-individual retrieval-induced forgetting (WI-RIF)
  defined, 170, 171
  sources of, 170–172
WITNESS model, for eyewitness identification, 71–73
witnesses, considerations in eyewitness testimony. *See also* lineup procedures in eyewitness identification
  accuracy judgement criteria
    determination of necessary relevant information, 40–41
    necessary relevant information for observers, 41–44
    observer application of knowledge consideration, 45–49
    relevance of information, 40–41
    scientific and lay knowledge, 44–45
    witness self-reports, 44–45
  differences in exposure and test targets, 33–34
  distorting influences on memory, 37–39
  limits under ideal conditions, 31–33
    face matching studies, 33–34, 39
    lineup identification studies, 32
    target-present vs. target-absent lineups (meta-analysis), 33
    perceptual difficulties/inconsistencies, 34–36, 44
  questioning by investigators/courtroom testimony, 5
  U.S. law, 30–31, 36–37, 47–48
wrongful conviction factors, 143